W9-BKE-488

EAST
TO THE
DAWN

EAST
TO THE
DAWN

The Life of Amelia Earhart

SUSAN BUTLER

ADDISON-WESLEY

Reading, Massachusetts

Many of the designations used by manufacturers and sellers to distinguish their products are claimed as trademarks. Where those designations appear in this book and Addison-Wesley was aware of a trademark claim, the designations have been printed in initial capital letters.

Library of Congress Cataloging-in-Publication Data
Butler, Susan.
    East to the dawn : the life of Amelia Earhart / Susan Butler.
      p.   cm.
    Includes bibliographical references and index.
    ISBN 0-201-31144-5
    1. Earhart, Amelia, 1897–1937.   2. Women air pilots—United
States—Biography.   I. Title.
    TL540.E3B88   1997
    629.13′092—dc21
    [B]   97-19123
                                                  CIP

Addison-Wesley is an imprint of Addison Wesley Longman, Inc.

Jacket design by Suzanne Heiser
Text design by Karen Savary
Set in 11.5-point Bembo by Pagesetters

1 2 3 4 5 6 7 8 9—MA—0100999897
First printing, September 1997

Find us on the World Wide Web at
http://www.aw.com/gb/

To my mother, Grace Liebman Breslauer

Contents

PART THREE

Preface

• • • • Like many young girls looking for a role model, I became interested in Amelia Earhart at an early age. After all, she was so appealing: she was courageous, glamorous, and mysterious. She was that rare bird—an American woman who had achieved fame and fortune by virtue of her own natural talents.

She appealed to me for an additional personal reason as well. My mother was a pilot in the 1930s, when most people were still afraid to get into an airplane, much less fly one. Her parents bought an airplane and hired a pilot to fly them around. The pilot had a lot of downtime, and my mother, Grace Liebman, in her early twenties, wanted to fly. So he taught her. Before long she was a pilot, had her own plane—an open-cockpit Waco biplane, dark green with white trim—and was a member of the Ninety-Nines, the women's flying organization of which Amelia Earhart was the most illustrious member. Flying out of the airport, in Red Bank, New Jersey, my mother had a wonderful time doing what the early pilots did in those days—buzzing friends, flying under the bridges that link Manhattan with the rest of the world, and landing in cornfields, hay fields, and on beaches.

Those were the days when there was something magical about

flying. There was the incredible thrill of being in the air, the heady sense of accomplishing something people had been dreaming about at least since Icarus.

To women, though, flying was something more. Still hemmed in by all sorts of restrictions, still valued for looks and decorative skills, still steered toward passive accomplishments, for women it was the ultimate escape: total freedom, total mastery—no interference. Total liberation. Women who became pilots won something additional along the way: respect.

Amelia Earhart was the looming, absent genius of our household. When her name came up, it usually caused a reflective pause in the conversation—she was obviously so special. My mother had known her only slightly. I always wanted to know what kind of a person she was, why she was so famous, what kind of a life she really lived. I read Amelia's books, and the books about her. They didn't satisfy my curiosity. They just whetted my appetite. I decided to research her life, and I found out that not only was Amelia an amazing flier, easily the greatest female pilot of her time, but that she was a person of judgment and integrity with a strong sense of mission—that she had started out as a social worker and had gradually become as single-mindedly dedicated to improving the status of women as Elizabeth Cady Stanton and Margaret Sanger.

Appearances are deceiving. Her contemporaries knew Amelia Earhart in all her permutations: as fashion plate, as lecturer, as educator, and of course as flier. But the passage of time has winnowed away everything except "pilot," so that what comes down to us across the years is the image of a tousle-haired androgynous flier clad in shirt, silk scarf, leather jacket, and goggles. Those alive when she was saw much more—the famous Steichen photo that appeared in *Vanity Fair* showing a chic, slender, contemplative woman; the news photos of her as she testified before congressional committees; and clips of her on the lecture circuit, where she spent the greater part of her time. Although it was her piloting skills that made her famous, Amelia was much more than just a pilot—that was why she was so much missed.

So I started on her trail. I spent days at the Schlesinger Library, where the Earhart papers are. I interviewed Fay Gillis Wells, one of the original members of the Ninety-Nines. I pored through the old newspapers she gave me. In one of them I found a reference to Amelia's beloved cousin, Kathryn (Katch) Challiss. It gave Katch's married name, and through that I tracked her down. I interviewed her for the first time ever, and when she died, her daughter Pat Antich gave me her diaries and the diaries of her sister Lucy, who lived with Amelia for several years. In the diaries were endless entries mentioning Amelia. Another cousin gave me the personal history of Amelia's mother's family, which had been gathered into a book and never unearthed. I tracked down another branch of the family with the help of Amy Kleppner, whose mother Muriel, Amelia's sister, is still alive. The cousin that chase led me to was Nancy Balis Morse, who gave me the gut-wrenching correspondence between Amelia's mother, uncle, and brother: through those letters I learned how desperately poor the Earharts were in Amelia's growing-up years.

Gore Vidal, whose father was one of Amelia's closest friends, told me of an unpublished biography written by a journalist friend of Amelia's. He knew only that it had been submitted to Putnam's and been turned down. I pestered Putnam's for the names of old-timers. I went through Boston and suburban Boston telephone directories, for Janet Mabie wrote for *The Christian Science Monitor,* and I queried the newspaper as well. And then one day, as I was leaving the Schlesinger Library, in the information rack just inside the front door, Janet Mabie's name popped out at me—and I saw that the Schlesinger now had her papers. In the papers was Mabie's unpublished biography. It is full of gems.

Those were the big finds—there were many smaller ones. Flipping through the A's in one of the big black books that contain the New York Public Library's older, non-computerized holdings, I came upon a publication called *The Ace, The Aviation Magazine of the West.* I pulled it out and found it was a monthly covering Los Angeles in the early 1920s—and that Amelia flitted in and out of the pages. I found, in Boston newspapers, articles on her flying and on her feminist activities before her flight in the *Friendship.* I interviewed pilots who had known her. I went up to Newfoundland to see for myself what Trepassey was like, and to walk on that famous field in Harbor Grace built especially for the first transatlantic flights. I heard of someone who heard of a woman Amelia's navigator Fred Noonan wrote letters to while they were flying around the world; I tracked Helen Day Bible down.

I started wearing brown clothes, because Amelia did.

Peeling away the layers, the cobwebs the years had laid on her, I found a capable, caring, energetic woman who had succeeded in life beyond her wildest dreams. Yet she never lost sight of her beginnings, and took it as her mission in life to show other women how to climb the ladder as she had, rung by rung, so that they could have a piece of the good life, too. That didn't mean rejecting men, far from it. She was married to a bright, successful entrepreneur who adored her and gave up his career to manage hers. She wanted women to develop themselves to their fullest potential, as she had. Her fame came from her flying exploits, but she was one of the most successful businesswomen of her day. She made her living on the lecture circuit, was one of the four founding stockholders and vice-president of the airline that became Northeast Airlines, was involved in various air-related businesses, was the author of two books and countless magazine articles, was under contract to the *New York Herald Tribune,* and was on the staff of Purdue University as consultant in careers for women. She gave her students positive reasons to succeed:

> I advise them all to identify themselves with some form of economic activity. I believe that a girl should not do what she thinks she should do, but should find out through experience what she wants to do. For that reason I ask the girls to measure themselves against others who are earning their living. I endeavor to find out why girls select particular subjects for study, what other interests they have, and to let them see what other women are doing in these various fields.
>
> I try to help them understand that it is just as important to give work to women as men, for they have an equal need for mental stimulus and feeling of accomplishment and economic independence.

She was a feminist who appealed to men as well as women because she used her position to promote not women's causes but women's self esteem.

At the same time she was a bit of a romantic, a bit of a dreamer. And she loved taking chances. There is an old English saying: all things are sweetened by risk. That was the way she felt.

EAST
TO THE
DAWN

PART ONE

1
Colonial Heritage

•••• Atchison, Kansas, situated on the banks of the Missouri River at the farthest point of a great lazy western bend in the river, was a small town with a population of some 15,000 in 1897. The earliest settlers, those who had arrived during the 1850s and 1860s, who had the taste and the means, had built their houses on the bluff overlooking the river, on a street then known as First Street, later as North Terrace.

It was in one of these houses, a fine Gothic structure that pioneer settler Alfred Gideon Otis had built for his bride, Amelia Harres Otis, that their daughter Amy Earhart waited to give birth on July 24, 1897, in the midst of a heat wave that had kept the temperature hovering near a hundred degrees for days. Amy had come from Kansas City, Kansas, where she and Edwin Earhart made their home, and now was installed in her childhood bedroom on the second floor, watched over and cared for by her parents and the servants, the cook Mary Brashay, and the old coachman-gardener Charlie Parks, both of whom had worked for the Otises since before Amy was born. Next door was Amy's aunt, Amelia Otis's older sister, Mary Ann Challiss, dubbed the "Queen" by her husband William for her imperious ways, who was so different from retiring Amelia.

Amy, a reed of a woman with wonderful thick chestnut hair, looked frail but was not: before her marriage she had been a fine rider and the first woman to reach the summit of Pikes Peak. Her mother, a plain-looking stout lady who claimed never to have done anything in her life more strenuous than rolling a hoop, was by contrast timid. But there were plenty of people around to help her see her daughter through the ordeal.

Nearby lived Mary Ann's and William's numerous progeny—Amy's first cousin and childhood friend James Challiss and his wife Rilla; and half a block away James' elder sister Ida Challiss Martin, stolid, competent widowed wife of the governor, with her seven children. Other relatives—cousins, nephews, nieces, relatives by marriage—were spotted about the town. There was a doctor in attendance. Amy's younger sister Margaret, who had cared for their recently deceased great-grandmother Maria so well and carefully, was also home. It was as nurturing an environment and as safe a situation in which to give birth as nineteenth-century America could provide.

For those who believe in omens, the signs were propitious for the birth, for one of the sharpest electric storms in a long while hit the town that afternoon and cracked the heat wave. "The sky turned the color of tin, the air stood stock still," Rilla Challiss recalled, and there was no twilight, for a violent rainstorm began as night fell. By late evening the storm was over, the stars were out, the air clear and cool. The break in the weather made it easier for everyone. At eleven thirty P.M. on that last July Saturday, Amy gave birth to a strapping, healthy infant, nine pounds—a lot for a girl.

The baby was baptized Monday, October 10, twelve weeks later, also in Atchison rather than in Kansas City, and for that event, too, there was a memorable weather change. This time it was rain, breaking a six-week dry spell that had threatened the harvest. "The blessed rain," proclaimed the headline in *The Atchison Globe*. It would have put everyone in a good mood. The site was the Otises' place of worship, Trinity Episcopal Church at Fifth and Utah Street, a handsome Gothic church faced with irregular limestone blocks with great arched doorways and soaring stained-glass windows designed by Richard Upjohn. A twin of Upjohn's Trinity Church at the foot of Wall Street in Manhattan, it still made an imposing statement as the century was drawing to a close. It was the handiwork of Amy's father; he had been the prime mover as well as the largest contributor in the parish, and Amy and her brothers and sister had all been baptized there. The gray light that filtered through the stained-glass panes of the church barely illuminated the black walnut beams and pews fashioned from trees that grew in the Missouri River valley; no one cared.

It was a small, intimate gathering that was assembled, as was the custom among nice Atchison families. The baby was dressed in the same lace christening dress her mother had been baptized in twenty-eight years before. When the Episcopal minister, the Reverend John Henry Molineux, pronounced the chosen names, Amelia Mary, then intoned, "I baptize thee in the name of the Father, and of the Son, and of the Holy Ghost" and sprinkled the infant with holy water, placing her in the Episcopal Church, the Otises must have been pleased but relieved as well, for they had managed to symbolically erase all vestiges of the Lutheran religion in which Edwin Earhart had been raised and all influence of *his* father, the Reverend David Earhart, who was one of the most revered Lutherans in Kansas. If Alfred's aim had been to make it look as if the Earhart heritage didn't exist, he succeeded.

As Amy had been baptized Amelia (but always called Amy) after her mother, now her daughter, too, was baptized Amelia. Edwin was recognized in one detail only, his daughter's middle name: Mary was for Edwin's mother.

It was perhaps inevitable that in all these early choices, it was Amy's family rather than Edwin's that prevailed. Hers was a powerful family. Along with their relatives the Martins and the Challisses, they were the powers in the town. Her austere father, "the Judge," as he was called, one of the first Atchison settlers, had had a hand in organizing and running just about every institution in the town, including the banks, the rail lines, and the gas company. Now, at seventy, he was still a force.

Undoubtedly the thoughts of many, as the christening ceremony progressed in the muted light, would have turned to another of Amy's family—her grandmother Maria Grace Harres, extraordinary both for her vigor and her intelligence, who had lived with the Otises at North Terrace and died just months before. This baby was the first of Maria's issue to be born after her death. Maria had set her stamp on her amazingly numerous progeny, providing a network of sisters and brothers, aunts and uncles and cousins—four generations of descendants centered in Atchison, radiating across Kansas, reaching all the way to the governor's mansion, the governor's wife being her granddaughter Ida. It was through Maria that the Otises were related to all the people that mattered, most of them the off-spring of Amelia Otis's sister Mary Ann. Maria had lived to see the birth of twenty grandchildren, thirty great-grandchildren, and two great-great-grandchildren. Over the years the generations had gotten into a chrono-logical muddle; Amelia Earhart, born less than a year after Maria died, was merely a great-grandchild.

Amy, sweet, compliant, pretty, even though in love with Edwin, was totally preoccupied with her own family. Now, that preoccupation showed in the way she entered the presents Amelia received in the baby book. She listed the gifts: three silver spoons, three gold pins, an entire wardrobe, a gold ring, a bracelet, a silver comb and brush, a pillow. And then, tellingly, "Best of all her grandmother's undying "love and devotion." And then the very last entry, her own gift, the crib quilts her grandmother Maria had made for *her* when she had been born. There is no mention—no mention at all—of any Earhart gift. And yet one must presume that the Reverend Earhart would have given something, and certainly that Edwin would at the very least have given *his* "love and devotion"'—he was a very affectionate and demonstrative father, but Amy didn't think it worthwhile to mention.

Amy did think it important to write down the old truism regarding the day of the week a baby is born. What she inscribed is such an accurate description of her daughter's future life that one must speculate upon the possibility that an early family myth, strongly reinforced, can influence the subsequent personality development of a child. Amelia was a Saturday child. Amy, who never worked a day in her life, daughter of Amelia who never worked, and of Amelia's mother Maria, who never worked, carefully wrote down, "But Saturday's bairn must work for a living."

• • • •

Maria Grace Harres was born in Germantown, Pennsylvania, in 1796; she died in Atchison September 17, 1896. Her parents, the Graces, shipowners, were English Quakers who came to America with William Penn. Maria attended the dame school; legend has it that she was chosen to throw flowers in General Lafayette's path when he visited Philadelphia. She had married a Prussian, Gebhard Harres, who fled to America to avoid being pressed into the army. Gebhard, six foot four, with curly hair, was a toolmaker, designer of steam-powered pistons, and such a good craftsman that, according to family legend, he had impressed Robert Fulton. There is no photograph of Maria as a young woman, but a photo of her in later years shows her distinctive high forehead, which her daughters and their issue inherited, and piercing eyes. Gebhard must have been quickly drawn to her; she certainly was to him. Amy Earhart wrote, "He thought Grandmother the most beautiful woman in Philadelphia and I judge she must have been very good-looking, as he was. Mother said people used to turn and look at him often, as he walked along the street.

But Gebhard was a Lutheran. "Marrying out of meeting," they called it when someone married someone of another faith, and by Quaker law such an action caused the person's name and record to be erased from Quaker records and the person shunned. It was not a step for a weak-willed woman to take. One can only speculate upon the misery this caused—being ostracized by the dominant religious group in a city so preoccupied by religion that it stunned the visiting Englishwoman Frances Trollope, into writing, "The religious severity of Philadelphian manners is in nothing more conspicuous than in the number of chains thrown across the streets on a Sunday to prevent horses and carriages from passing. . . . Spain, in its most catholic days, could not exceed it."

Nonetheless Maria and Gebhard made the decision to remain in Philadelphia, and although Maria was separated from her Quaker heritage, she never separated from the basic tenets of the Quaker faith—the idea of service was part and parcel of her being.

Gebhard became a successful cabinetmaker and before long was able to move his growing family into a large three-story house on the corner of Northwest Tenth and Catherine Street. It was one of the handsomer Philadelphia houses of the day, boasting front steps of white marble, a silver door knocker, and a rarer touch of opulence, a white marble frame around the front door. Seven servants helped Maria keep up the establishment and care for her family. Their five children, Mary Ann, Amelia, John, Charles, and Theodore, grew up in ever-increasing luxury, the children of privileged parents in America's most cosmopolitan city. But amassing wealth did not turn Maria into a frivolous woman; she started the family vocation of caregiving. She was a gifted and courageous healer, "a natural born nurse," who nursed stricken friends back to health during the 1832 cholera epidemic that killed a thousand people as it swept through Philadelphia. She also cared for victims of smallpox (against which she had been vaccinated) and because of her superb health gradually acquired the reputation of being immune to all infections. And indeed no one—not one of her children or grandchildren or great-grandchildren or nephews or nieces—could ever remember seeing Maria ill.

The upper-class young ladies of Philadelphia were singled out by Frances Trollope, who was notably unimpressed by most of what she saw in America, for the "delicacy and good taste" they exhibited in their dress.

Two of those cosseted young women, Mary Ann Harres, the eldest, and her younger sister Amelia, would as young brides move out west to Atchison, Kansas—to the very edge of civilization. It was a wrenching change. Mary Ann, married, the mother of two children, moved first. At some point Amelia Harres went west to visit her, and there she met Alfred Otis. On April 22, 1862, in Philadelphia, Amelia and Alfred were married. The wedding announcement in *The Philadelphia Enquirer* was days late and incomplete, mute testimony to a nation in the midst of the Civil War and absorbed by the great battle being fought at Shiloh in Tennessee. Alfred and his bride traveled by steamer up the Missouri to Atchison, making way against the river swollen by the rains and melting snows of spring. Amelia would have seen the ragged islands in the wide muddy river and the still mostly forest-covered shores that Francis Parkman had seen and written about just ten years earlier.

. . . .

Alfred was an interesting, bright, complex, difficult man, also of a distinguished lineage. At the time he was born, in Little York, New York, in 1827, his family had already been in the New World for generations. John and Margaret Otis, Puritans, emigrated from Hingham, England, to Hingham, Massachusetts in 1631. Their descendants, Alfred's forebears, were among the first trained doctors in colonial America, early graduates of Harvard and Yale. But as Alfred well knew, there were other Otises, distant cousins also descended from John and Margaret, who were much more famous and much more distinguished: James, the famous patriot who in 1761 so eloquently proclaimed the basic colonial principle that "taxation without representation is tyranny" in the Council Chambers of the Old State House in Boston, and James's nephew, Harrison Gray Otis, the Federalist senator whose elegant red brick house would become one of Boston's enduring landmarks. Alfred falsely claimed them as his forebears. So enamored was Alfred of this idea (he named his firstborn son, who died in infancy, Harrison Gray) that he implanted in his children the belief that they were descendants of James.

Alfred had a difficult childhood. He was the first child of Isaac and Caroline Curtiss Otis, who had left him, as a little boy, with his grandparents in Little York while they picked up stakes and, taking his baby brother George with them, joined the great westward migration to Michigan, where 200,000 homesteaders claimed land in the first part of the century. They settled in Prairieville in Barry County, cleared land, and put up a log cabin and later a proper house. It would be six long years before Caroline returned for him and he was rejoined with George and met his new brothers and sisters. It made him a loner.

Alfred, having studied in the evenings after farm chores, entered the University of Michigan at Ann Arbor as a sophomore, graduated as a classics major three years later, and attended law school in Louisville, Kentucky. After a brief stint in Louisville, he settled in Atchison, Kansas. His brother George also became a lawyer, set up his law practice in St. Paul, Minnesota, and one by one three of the younger brothers who also became lawyers joined George there. None would follow with Alfred.

Alfred was intensely ambitious, obsessed with the idea of becoming rich, and channeled all his energy into his career. He never changed. "As to my course after graduation," he informed George, "money is the first object. I can be admitted at the bar in three months. Money I say first, money money and then Glory—Is this putting first last. " He never lost sight of his goal.

As the American frontier continued to roll west, new choices appeared for the ambitious in Alfred's generation, just as for his parents. Never again in history would there be such a plethora of open, arable land free for the taking as then, as the land became territories and the territories became states. The choices were almost limitless. Alfred chose Kansas, still grazed by buffalo herds and home to Indian tribes. And in Kansas he chose Atchison, one of the new settlements. It was a brave choice. Not only was Kansas on the brink of war, but Alfred was an abolitionist, and he was settling in a pro-slavery town.

• • • •

On May 30, 1854, President Franklin Pierce signed into law the Kansas-Nebraska bill. It accorded Kansas territorial status, which meant people could legally take title to land, but at the same time it repealed the Missouri Compromise, which had excluded slavery—forever—from all Louisiana territory north of 36 degrees 30 minutes latitude. Passage of the law stunned the free-soilers who had thought that Kansas territory, by virtue of geography, was safe forever from the "peculiar institution." The Kansas-Nebraska law reopened the question—it returned the choice to the people living in the territory. It also set Kansas up to be the first battleground of the Civil War.

By leaving it to the settlers to decide by vote whether Kansas would be admitted to the Union slave or free, the pro-slavery forces had won a great victory. As Senator William H. Seward put it so eloquently for the North just before the territory was opened for settlement and the opposing forces poured in, it would be a fight to the bitter end: "Come on then, gentlemen of the slave States, since there is no escaping your challenge. I accept it on behalf of freedom. We will engage in competition for the virgin soil of Kansas, and God give the victory to the side that is stronger in numbers, as it is in right." It was the militant Missouri senator David Rice Atchison who controlled the fledgling town in the beginning. He planned to make the settlement on the western bank of the Missouri a showcase for the pro-slavery forces. Three months after Pierce signed the Kansas-Nebraska bill

into law, on the September day the town lots were put up for sale, Senator Atchison, a charismatic orator, was on site making a widely publicized
speech, and as the result of the well-orchestrated effort, southerners came
in droves to stake their claims to land. The first newspaper in Atchison was
The Squatter Sovereign, and emotions ran so high that one committed
southerner on the staff swore "to kill a baby if he knew it would grow up
an abolitionist."

Alfred settled in Atchison largely because of Eli Thayer of Worces-
ter, Massachusetts, who had founded the New England Emigrant Aid
Company and turned the antislavery sentiment in the North into a free-
soil crusade to save Kansas. Though never large in terms of numbers,
the Emigrant Aid Company drew to Kansas solid, committed northerners who believed they could do right and at the same time pursue the American dream of success. Senator Green, speaking in 1861,
said that, "but for the hotbed plants that have been planted in Kansas
through the instrumentality of the Emigrant Aid Society, Kansas would
have been with Missouri this day." One such, Samuel Clarke Pomeroy,
from Massachusetts, a financial agent of the Emigrant Aid Company,
accompanied the second party of settlers to Kansas in '54; he would
become the first mayor of Atchison and a U.S. senator when Kansas
achieved statehood.

The eloquent, impassioned Thayer fashioned his crusade in a typically "New England" practical way—by appealing to the enlightened self-
interest of his audience. Before the ink on the Kansas-Nebraska bill was
dry, he was buying up land in the territory and forming free-soil colonies. By the time Kansas was opened for settlement, hundreds of Kansas leagues and Kansas committees were in formation. Word was passed
that the antislavery colonies would be receiving steam engines, saw-
mills, gristmills, and other machinery; that newspapers, churches, and
schools would be established. As Thayer noted, "From these facts emigrants inferred readily enough that in these incipient cities, with organized emigration flowing in rapidly, there would be an excellent prospect
for making money by the rise of property." It was just such a sentiment
as would appeal to courageous, ambitious young men. Eli Thayer
described his "ideal" settlers: "The men who say little or nothing. They
show the greatest impatience, and even disgust, when they hear a ranting
resolution-maker berating slavery. They seem to think that every Northern man understands the evils of slavery without being informed of
them."

Just such men as Alfred Gideon Otis and others who, their feet firmly
set in the new, bustling frontier town, believed the risks were more than

outweighed by the prospects of success. John Greenleaf Whittier, the popular abolitionist poet, picked up the idealistic mood of the country in his "Emigrants' Song."

> We cross the prairies as of old
> Our fathers crossed the sea;
> To make the West, as they the East,
> The homestead of the free.

The attraction of Atchison was that it was so strategically situated. The Missouri River makes a great bend to the west as it divides the northern regions of Missouri and Kansas between St. Joseph to the north and Fort Leavenworth to the south. Atchison lies at the westernmost point in this bend, on the western side of the river. Being those twelve miles farther west than the established settlements at St. Joseph and Leavenworth meant two days saved for early settlers heading west in ox-drawn wagons. It meant that at the moment of its founding, Atchison assumed importance as the eastern terminus of the overland stagecoach lines. There was money to be made caring for and feeding the travelers, repairing their wagons, buying and selling them livestock. Rapidly, in growing numbers, came young, idealistic, enterprising northerners bent on establishing themselves and keeping the territory free; they started to tip the balance early on. What drew them was the prospect of good land, of course, and the opportunity to be in on the beginning, to have a hand in the formation of a new government and a new society, but there was something else; those conditions, those opportunities existed elsewhere, where there was no chance of blood being spilled over the slavery question. Kansas was not for the fainthearted. The free-soil men who settled Atchison had to possess an extra quality—a large dose of physical courage had to be part of their makeup—for they were settling a town just being formed in a territory about to be torn asunder.

There was no question, given his free-soil stand, that Alfred would establish himself quietly and circumspectly: at just about the time he arrived that fall, a southern mob tarred and feathered and set adrift on a raft the Reverend Pardee Butler, who had trumpeted his abolitionist views after being warned not to. Incidents escalated into violence with ever-increasing frequency.

In May 1856 Senator Atchison, at the head of an armed mob, sacked the free-soil settlement of Lawrence, forty miles to the south of Atchison. Nor was the violence just in Kansas—the day following the sack of Lawrence, the prominent and persuasive abolitionist Senator Charles Sumner was beaten unconscious on the floor of the United States Senate. That act was followed within days by a singularly ugly abolitionist act: John

Brown dragged from their beds and murdered five pro-slavery settlers on the Pottawatomie Creek, to the west of Atchison. The violence in Kansas territory—unrestricted, devastating, widespread—was finally curbed by Governor John Geary, who called in federal troops to stop the Missouri pro-slavery forces, the border ruffians, the Free State marauders, and the thieves who followed in their tracks. Even David Rice Atchison was forced to disband his army. Alfred described the situation to his brother: "The grand jury indicted on an average every other man in the territory all over it—pro-slavery and free soilers all have to catch it. Almost all our citizens are indicted for something or other. I took but little active part in last row and am thus out of the scrape. During the war every man did as he pleased—pressed horses, took provisions, cattle, wagons, teams, etc. and raised the devil generally. Many did it in good faith believing it was all right; others did it for plunder."

1857 was the watershed year for the territory, the year the settlers, in a resounding vote, rejected being admitted to the Union as a slave state. In the face of the defeat of their cause, most of the southerners gave up. John Martin, twenty years old, arrived from Pennsylvania, bought *The Squatter Sovereign,* renamed it *Freedom's Champion,* and ran it for the free-soil cause; Samuel Pomeroy, former agent of the New England Emigrant Aid Company, became Atchison's first mayor.

Alfred had arrived in October 1855 with little more than the clothes on his back, yet he was so capable and such a hard worker that even against this backdrop of violence and mayhem, he had managed to prosper. "His capital stock was a copy of Blackstone, a genial temperament and an abundance of brains," a contemporary wrote of him later. So well did he do, primarily in land litigation, that by 1862 he had enough money to buy his land and build his house and marry.

Mary Ann arranged Amelia's marriage. She and William Challis had moved out to Atchison from New Jersey in 1857. William was a doctor who gave up his practice to join his entrepreneur brothers George and Luther in buying land and starting businesses in the fledgling town. William's first task—bringing the first ferry up the Missouri to Atchison and running the ferry franchise that connected Kansas with Missouri—was the first of many he would creditably perform. They started out in a log cabin, but within a short time William and Mary Ann lived in a "handsome" big brick house, at 203 North Terrace on the bluff overlooking the Missouri.

There is a photograph of Amelia Otis that shows timid, lashless, apprehensive eyes, brunette hair curled carefully, limply, flatly, and very unflatteringly on her head, attired in an ill-fitting dress; she is devoid of brooch, lace, or any adornment. Mary Ann, with whom she had in common the high forehead and chiseled features of their mother Maria, in contrast, was a handsome woman: there was a vibrancy and assuredness and warmth about Mary Ann entirely lacking in her sister. It is hard to overstate the difference in expression and outlook in these two women so strikingly similar in feature. Mary Ann was vivacious, pretty, outgoing, and a good organizer. Amelia, lacking in confidence, single in her twenties, was clearly in danger of spinsterhood—not just because of her retiring nature but because time was pressing—at her age in those years, most young women were long married. To avoid spinsterhood, she would need the help of her family. And there, as if by Providence, Mary Ann produced her family's new Atchison friend, Alfred Otis. Alfred was an obvious choice of husband: upstanding staunch churchgoer, already a lawyer of note and wealthy, and most important, never married. Alfred was a thin man with a strikingly broad skull, a spade beard, thick brows, and heavy-lidded eyes. He didn't have the gentle sense of humor or the friendly mien of his brother-in-law William, but he was honest, upstanding, and a very hard worker. He was thirty-five; it was time for him to settle down and raise a family—he would have been looking for a wife. Amelia came out for a visit.

Cold and remote are the words family members use to describe him. He was respected but not loved. Still, he certainly evinced the normal interest in girls as he wrote to his brother. (The part of going to church he liked best when he was an impecunious law school student in Kentucky, he had written George, had been shaking hands with the "many pretty young sisters whom of course none should slight.") Now he had amassed sufficient fortune to marry. Alfred knew that for a wife, he couldn't do better than shy, well-brought-up, well-connected Amelia. His new bride would even look up to him—being ten years his junior, she would consider him a man of the world.

It was in the spring of 1862 that Amelia Otis took up life on the shores of the Missouri River. Atchison was still a raw, ugly frontier town. "It presents a very fine appearance from the river, having a thrifty, flourishing look, rising gradually from the levee to the grassy horizon. Nearness dissipates the illusion, and entry destroys it," observed John Ingalls, another transplanted easterner who put down roots in the first years and became one of the Otises' best friends as well as one of Atchison's most illustrious citizens.

There was a railroad line, the first in Kansas, but it only went upriver as far as St. Joseph, Missouri; and a telegraph office, also the first in Kansas. But instead of the beautiful Philadelphia stalls where food was carefully displayed on snow-white napkins, Amelia shopped at Atchison's general store, owned by the Challisses, shelves stocked with a hodge-podge—everything from gunpowder to coal oil, white sugar, soda crackers, St. Louis nails, oolong tea, grain, dried buffalo meat, and more often than not fresh antelope, turkey, quail, and prairie chickens. Next door on Commercial Street was the coffee-roasting plant.

The streets were dismal, a far cry from the paved streets and brick sidewalks of Philadelphia. They were dirt—dusty until it rained, muddy afterward, so muddy that after a really heavy rain, pigs would sometimes rout in the middle. Nor were there sidewalks where walkers could take refuge. "In winter time the mud was very deep. I am sure if all the rubber overshoes that were lost in those tramps up the hill could be recovered, it would be easy to break the rubber trust," wrote a friend of Amelia Otis's of their Sunday trudges to church services on North Fifth. Still, Amelia had it easier than any other young bride arriving in Atchison to live. Alfred had chosen as his land the widest and choicest part of the bluff overlooking the Missouri, and there, finished and waiting for Amelia, stood the large white clapboard two-story house Alfred had commissioned. Although not as big as Mary Ann's house, it was a gracious design in the manner of the popular architect Andrew Jackson Downing, with such details as Gothic fretwork, a triple-paned Gothic window centered over the front door, and a wide veranda that stretched across the front of the house. From the windows could be seen all of the river. Her elder sister Mary Ann Challiss and Bill were right next door to welcome and help her. There, side by side, Amelia and Mary Ann would live out their lives.

Amelia had the misfortune to arrive during the darkest period in Atchison history. Many of the town's able-bodied men had left to join the army. The streets were periodically thronged with soldiers on their way to the front, some of whom pillaged as they passed through. A few months after she arrived, Atchison passed a law prohibiting the carrying of concealed weapons, but the measure did not stop the looting: many businesses closed; law-abiding citizens locked their doors and stayed inside.

As the war spread, Atchison was fair game for both sides. Just the year before she arrived, the last thirty southern families had fled, hastily rising from their midday meals too flee aboard the Challiss ferry the *Ida* to Missouri and safety, as a rider galloped through the town warning that Free State ruffians and thieves were riding in to hang every pro-slavery man. Those empty houses bore mute witness to the violence of the times. Now the fear was that the Bushwackers—Missouri pro-slave bands—would storm the town and torch it as they had other Free State border settlements.

The southerners had been the backbone of the Episcopal community, and when they left, the parish was reduced to just a few hardy souls, so that each new parishioner was embraced with open arms. Amelia Otis's arrival was noted with joy in church records but, undoubtedly because of her retiring nature, she took little active part in church activities. The early records are very complete; they list those who arrived on Sundays to sweep, build the fire, dust the chairs, and get everything in readiness for the service, as well as the members of the sewing society, those who organized the Sunday school, and those who sang in the choir; Amelia Otis's name is nowhere to be found. There was a lull in the fighting Amelia's first Christmas season that made it more bearable; families felt secure enough to open their houses and make and receive calls.

Amelia became pregnant soon after her marriage, and Maria and Gebhard, accompanied by their youngest child Theodore, braved the vicissitudes of war and traveled out to Atchison to be with her when she gave birth to her first child in the spring of 1863. Theodore, liking what he saw of the town, decided to stay and open a hardware store on Commercial Street, advertising in *Freedom's Champion* that in his store there would be a "Glorious victory over high prices in hardware." A short while later Gebhard had a stroke and died; from then on, except for a brief trip back to Philadelphia to dispose of their house, Maria made her home with the Otises.

She was given the northeast bedroom, with its window looking out over the river. Maria was a godsend to the retiring and fearful Amelia, particularly just then, for Alfred was a Union soldier, serving in the Eighth Kansas Infantry Volunteers commanded by John Martin. She fit right into the rhythm of the house and the town. A constant comfort to Amelia as well to Mary Ann, she became a valued and financially generous member of Trinity Episcopal Church, which was such an important part of the Otises' social life. When the war was over, her place was happily assured. Alfred was consumed by work; furthermore, it was his custom to return to his office after dinner, often remaining there until the early hours of the morning. Maria remained useful, companionable, and helpful for Amelia. Even Alfred appreciated how much she helped.

Alfred was mustered out in 1865 and returned to Atchison April 14, the day Lincoln was shot. By that time Amelia Otis, with Maria at her side, had given birth to another child, William, born February 2.

After the war ended and the dangers were past, the town turned again toward commerce and peaceful pursuits. The great stage companies returned. The wagon trains began gathering, provisioning while they waited, marking time before they started across the prairies to Pikes Peak, Salt Lake, to California, Colorado, and Montana. Now Amelia and her mother could see Atchison plain as it had been before the war, and take in the lack of amenities, and the great swings in the climate that alternately turned the town to mud or—worse—to dust. Because the prairies had not yet been planted with crops, because the trees planted around the houses were still too small to protect them and there was "nothing to be seen but the grass and sky," the wind swept through—constant, strong, and unending—and brought the dust. One of the first of Atchison's preachers, a "scrupulously neat" man, returned east because he couldn't stand it. The winds "were the trial of his life. . . . The dust would powder his clothes, and the wind carry beaver and wig away so far that it was tiresome to recover them without the assistance of friends." A young woman described life in the early years: "When we first came to Kansas, the climate was nothing like it is today. The winds then were not hot as they are now, but they blew incessantly and so powerfully that one could scarcely walk against them. It was worse in the daytime than at night. It seldom rained in the daytime, and the night showers were nearly always local and sometimes covered very small areas. After five or six years, all this began to change. Planting trees and tilling the soil made a difference."

• • • •

Amelia bore eight children in her gracious house, six of whom would reach adulthood. Amy, Amelia Earhart's mother, born in 1869, was the eldest girl.

Amy was slender and pretty and popular. She had a delicate face and the high Harres forehead; her most arresting feature was her mass of chestnut hair, which as a child she wore in thick braids that were long enough to sit on. With her brothers and sisters she attended the Latin School, a private school organized by the Martins, the Ingallses, and her parents. She grew up cared for by her grandmother Maria as well as by her mother, with all the comforts that Alfred's wealth could command. She loved to ride, first on her own Indian pony, a hand-me-down from a brother, and later on increasingly powerful mounts, and was watched over by a succession of upstairs maids and the Otises' two faithful servants, Mary Brashay and Charlie Parks, both of whom would be there still to care for Amelia Earhart. Amy's best friend and schoolmate was Constance, the daughter of their neighbor, Senator John Ingalls. When the senator was in town, he and the two girls would go out for rides every morning, the girls, like proper young eastern women, decorously riding sidesaddle.

As the 1860s drew to a close, Kansas effectively put its violent heritage behind; change accelerated by leaps and bounds. First the Indians disappeared, dispossessed of their deeded lands and resettled in the so-called Indian territories. Next, the great herds of buffalo dwindled, then disappeared, as they were slaughtered for their hides.

Kansas was a famous state in Amy's youth, and Atchison a famous town. *The Atchison Globe* was well known and quoted clear across America. Mark Twain wrote about two of its colorful characters: Slade, superintendent of the Ben Holliday stage line, who chased stolen horses, mules, and thieves until he himself was hung by a vigilance committee; and Samuel Pomeroy, the Emigrant Aid agent who became Atchison's first mayor and U.S. senator. Famous people such as Horace Greeley and Artemus Ward, and even Oscar Wilde, who "drifted" in to lecture, were "frequently" seen on its streets.

Following the Civil War came the period of rapid railroad development that changed the face of Kansas forever. By 1875 Atchison could boast of a railroad bridge spanning the Missouri, a mechanical marvel that turned in order to open. Senator Ingalls predicted that all the nearby towns, including Leavenworth, St. Joseph, and Kansas City, would start declining in importance and that the population of Atchison would zoom to 25,000 in a year. Ed Howe, the famous publisher of *The Atchison Globe* (known as the Sage of the Potato Patch), writing in 1877, trumpeted to the world that Atchison had "aspirations and prospects." Everything seemed to point that way. Within a few years the Atchison, Topeka and the Santa Fe reached Atchison. The energy emanating was such that it seemed as if the eyes of the nation were turned on the state. Soon, across America, everyone was singing about "The Atchison, Topeka and the Santa Fe." By the mid-1880s Atchison had gas and electricity, a hospital, a good library, and an opera house. Not only was it booming commercially, but Atchison citizens, those young men who had settled Atchison in the 1850s, were the engine driving Kansas and making their mark on the national scene. The first Kansas senators were Atchison men. The first was Samuel Pomeroy, the second was John Ingalls, who served three terms; for the years from 1861 to 1893 there was an Atchison man in the U.S. Senate. Two Atchison men served as governers as well—George Glick, followed by John A. Martin, who served two terms. Considering that it was a town of only some 14,000 people, its vitality—the political and commercial clout it wielded both locally and nationally—was truly astounding. Alfred Otis was at the center of everything. John Ingalls was his best friend, George Glick was his law partner, and John Martin was not only his old friend and the colonel of his regiment in the Civil War but his nephew, by virtue of his marriage to Mary Ann Challiss's eldest daughter Ida.

Alfred Otis and George Glick, partners in Otis and Glick since 1858, were the preeminent lawyers in that part of Kansas, having snared the biggest fish of all as a client—the Central Branch of the Union Pacific Railroad. The two influential men helped found the Atchison Savings Bank, the Atchison Gas Company, and the Atchison and Nebraska Railroad. And always, along the way, Alfred bought land.

In 1876 Alfred was elected judge of the Second Judicial District. He served his term with honor and declined renomination. He never went back to the law, instead taking over active management of the Atchison Savings Bank and the Atchison Gas Company.

• • • •

Even as Atchison was the center of power in Kansas, and her family at the center of Atchison, so in her own way was Amy, the eldest daughter, the star in her own world. In later years she loved to tell her own children about her triumphs—how she and her best friend Constance Ingalls "were the undisputed leaders of the young social set, going to balls at Fort Leavenworth and cotillions at St. Joseph, often by specially chartered steamer." But the stories she told to amuse her daughters were too glowing—Amelia Earhart at least would later detect the fairy-tale quality in them, writing, "Among the best stories my mother told were those of her own girlhood. My sister [Muriel] and I always spoke of that mysterious and far away period as 'thousands of years ago when Mother was little.' " Amy glossed over the bad times. She survived two life-threatening diseases. At sixteen she was stricken with typhoid fever, which took her a long time to get over. Her practical grandmother, Maria, who was taking care of her, decided that her long hair was absorbing her strength, and so it was cut off. "Sheep shearing," her kid brother Carl, four years old at the time, called it. Four years later a diphtheria epidemic hit Atchison, and Amy contracted the dreaded, highly contagious disease then without cure that would in later years kill two of her brothers. Maria, then ninety-one, saved her life. The usual cause of death was asphyxiation caused by the growth of a false membrane that slowly but inexorably closed off the throat, making breathing impossible. Maria brought Amy into her own bedroom, isolated her from the rest of the family, nursed her night and day, and recognized the moment when Amy was reaching the characteristic breathing climax caused by the growth of the false membrane. She had the presence of mind and the knowledge to have a doctor present at that moment; he inserted a tube into Amy's throat and sucked out the material clogging the passage. The crisis past, Amy slowly, with her grandmother's continuing care, beat back the disease.

Amy couldn't face unpleasantness. In her well-meaning way, she always put the best face on everything, whether it was true or not. She told her children that she would have gone to Vassar the fall of 1889 if she hadn't been recovering from diphtheria. That was the reason she gave for leading the traditional life of the unmarried upper-class young woman of her day. She was convalescing those years in Atchison, she said, keeping herself busy by organizing a Dickens Club, presenting "literary tableaux," teaching Sunday school, and helping her father by copying his legal opinions. But it wasn't true.

The real reason was that as far as Alfred was concerned, it was out of the question to send either of his daughters to college. Her younger sister Margaret, a born healer like Maria and a more serious candidate for college, wasn't allowed to go either. As a teenager, Margaret with Amy's help tried to adopt a tubercular child; she wasn't allowed to, but she did contribute part of her allowance and persuaded her parents to make a serious enough commitment to fund the child's stay in a sanitarium. When Margaret finished school, she spent her days poring over medical books in their doctor's office—preparing herself to be a medical student at Cornell—but the Judge put his foot down and "that was the end of it," she told her daughter, Nancy Balis Morse. "My mother had wanted to be a doctor so badly that she bribed the Otis family doctor until he allowed her to sit in his office and read his medical books but she told me her father wouldn't hear of it. He [Alfred] didn't believe in education for women. As for Aunt Amy, I doubt she ever applied."

Amy embroidered the history of the family as well. Alone of the Harres descendants' accounts in the *Family Tree,* she claimed that the ancestral Harres home in Philadelphia was on Chestnut Street when it was actually on prosperous but less elegant Northwest Tenth and Catherine.

She even fibbed about her slight deafness, claiming it was the result of her bout with typhoid fever, but typhoid fever is an infectious disease that causes inflammation and ulceration of the intestines, and as serious as it was in the nineteenth century, it would be stretching the imagination to blame it for a hearing impairment.

The truth was that deafness ran in the family. Maria Harres was slightly deaf, and Margaret was even more so. Margaret's problem would later be diagnosed as otosclerosis, a hereditary condition in which one of the three small bones in the middle ear thickens so that it does not vibrate, causing deafness; Margaret became one of the early users of a hearing aid. Amy, in contrast, simply endured her bad hearing.

Tradition as established by Alfred simply did not admit the existence of flaws. Amy's denial mirrors Amelia and Alfred's denial that one of their children, Theodore, was retarded.

The summer of 1890 was an eventful and happy time for Amy because it was the summer of her coming-out party, a tale she told well and evidently often—Amelia and Muriel loved to hear her talk about it. The ball, "the way she told it," according to Muriel, was a very grand party, held on an evening in mid-June when "everything would be lovely and yet it would not be too hot." Seven musicians imported from St. Joseph sat on the front porch playing the popular waltzes and reels of the day. A wooden dance floor had been laid out on the lawn around a big wrought-iron stag, too heavy to move, that Amy had garlanded with scarlet roses. As the dancers whirled around the dance floor, they whirled around the stag. At nine o'clock, just as the last light of day faded, Charlie Parks lit the candles inside the Japanese lanterns that were strung every ten feet throughout the garden and up to the porch. The almost-still night air on the bluff smelled of syringa and heliotrope. And that night Amy and Edwin Earhart met, for Amy's brother Mark in time-honored fashion had brought his eligible college friend home for his sister's coming-out party. Amy told her children about it this way: "I was standing by the porch steps with Grandmother and Grandfather greeting all our guests when up came your Uncle Mark bringing a young man with him. He said: 'This is Edwin Earhart, the law student who has pulled me through this year's examinations!' "

Edwin was mesmerized by the slender, plucky, pretty girl with the beautiful thick chestnut hair whirling skillfully around the dance floor. She seemed like a princess to him, not just for her social graces but for her social standing and wealth. Most of the important families in the state would have been there; it was the grandest party Edwin had ever attended—and Amy was the center of it all.

Amy, in turn, was fascinated by the tall, handsome young man. He was so obviously intelligent; so charmingly articulate; so incredibly well read. And best of all, he was studying to be a lawyer, just like her father.

They fell in love, and Edwin proposed.

Alfred was less than pleased.

• • • •

Edwin Earhart's ancestors were God-fearing, German-speaking Lutheran farmers who had also come to America when it was still a colony. The progenitor was Johann Earhardt, a Prussian who had served in the guard of Frederick the Great and emigrated to York County, Pennsylvania, sometime before the Revolution. Joining the Tenth Pennsylvania Regiment of the Line, he fought with his regiment at Brandywine, Germantown, and Bull's Ferry, and in the Christmas Eve attack at Trenton; he wintered with George Washington at Valley Forge.

The chronicle of his descendants is a chronicle of bare subsistence, of God-fearing clannish farmers fiercely protecting their Lutheran heritage and German customs, wresting farms out of the virgin forests of western Pennsylvania for several generations, intermarrying with other like-minded, German-speaking Lutheran families, working hard yet barely having enough to clothe and feed themselves. David, Amelia's grandfather, one of twelve children of Catherine Altman Earhart and David Earhart, grew up working with his siblings at the backbreaking chores involved in turning the raw, timbered land of western Pennsylvania into productive farmland. He was born February 28, 1818, on a farm located between Johnstown and Pittsburgh on the Conemaugh River. Besides doing his share of farm chores, young David helped his father run his boat, the *Liberty*, between the two towns.

In 1838 David's father sold the farm at a great profit and bought timbered land ten miles north in Indiana County, and all the children, including two older brothers who had moved away, returned to help the family move and settle and then clear the property. At one point in David's generation, too, food became short, and there was only cornmeal mush and milk to eat, but the bad time passed. After six years David's father sold this farm too, which had been conquered from the wilderness at such great cost, again at a profit, built a raft upon which he loaded family, possessions, and furniture, and joining the many other ambitious, restless souls of his day, moved farther west. He floated down the Conemaugh and the Allegheny, then on down the Ohio to the Mississippi, ending up in Davenport, Iowa, where he commenced farming again. By the time he died, he was farming two hundred acres, owned extensive livestock, and was rich enough to leave Catherine and all their children adequately provided for; David's share would be $150.

David stayed east, however, attended an academy in Indiana where he studied "some English branches," Latin, Greek, and mathematics, and became a Lutheran minister. He married Mary Wells Patton of nearby Somerset, Pennsylvania, who was a descendant of Colonel James Wells, of English extraction and Revolutionary War fame, granddaughter of an Irishman from Londonderry who edited a weekly newspaper and operated a bookbindery in Somerset. Mary would have twelve children, nine of whom grew to maturity. The youngest, Edwin, would be Amelia Earhart's father.

David settled with Mary in Pennsylvania near where he had been raised. He was a grim man, consumed with a sense of mission and possessed of an enormous amount of energy. Taking note of his proselytizing nature, his zeal, determination, and willingness to travel, the Lutheran Synod sent him out to organize the Kansas Territory. He arrived in June 1857, traveling up the Mississippi a few months after Mary Ann and William Challiss, bound for Sumner, three miles to the south of Atchison. There he succeeded in building the second Lutheran church in Kansas. He toiled there with only a small degree of success in attracting worshippers, but he must have thought the future of Lutheranism in eastern Kansas looked at least promising because he returned east to fetch Mary and their three girls and four boys, returning in the spring of 1860.

He picked a disastrous year. A severe drought caused most of the crops to fail, then winds reaching hurricane force destroyed what was left. The situation became so desperate and life threatening that, even with the Civil War pressing in upon them, the neighboring states sent in aid—in all, eight million pounds of provisions, seeds, and clothes—to the starving Kansans. Sumner became a ghost town; his parish failed. In the ensuing years the county was ravaged by plagues of grasshoppers.

Nor was that all. In those years the country around the beleaguered minister was in turmoil—because of the border war between Kansas and Missouri, which would claim 27,000 civilian lives by the end of the Civil War. To this man of God, however, this grimly determined preacher, such outside maelstroms were of interest only to the extent they got in his way. He doggedly pressed on, undeterred that more of his ministries failed than flourished, encouraged by the fact that he was highly regarded by his parishioners and was considered important enough to be appointed a regent of the State Agricultural College, in which capacity he served for many years. The unstinting nature of the Reverend Earhart's labors on behalf of the Church (he thought nothing of traveling fifty miles by horse and carriage to conduct a service) would become legendary. But legendary also would be the meager results, as would be described by the Kansas Evangelical Lutheran Synod: "None labored so long as he in this pioneer work, and none endured such trials, hardships and privations, none sacrificed as freely in time and physical labor, and none left such permanent results in the Kansas Territory of his labors as he—yet it was eleven years before there were enough congregations to effect the organization of the Kansas Synod in 1868."

For his family it was a life of hardship and sacrifice. They survived only with help—$100 from a Lutheran minister in 1860 and $150 in 1861 and 1862 from the Home Missionary Society.

On March 28, 1867, the last child, Edwin Stanton Earhart, was born. In these early years of Edwin's childhood, nothing had changed for the better; the Earharts were as usual utterly destitute. A family anecdote gives us a glimpse of the Reverend's single-minded vision and his youngest child's first efforts to enjoy life. On a Sunday when Edwin was six and there was nothing in the larder except johnnycake (a form of cornbread) and turnips, the hungry boy sneaked off to go fishing. He brought home six fish, but fishing on Sunday was a desecration, and it was only after the anguished Mary Earhart pleaded that her children were hungry that their father allowed the fish to be eaten. Later that year Reverend Earhart finally gave up on Kansas and, with his wife and the five youngest children, settled again in western Pennsylvania, having secured a pastorate in Somerset County.

Edwin was so bright that he entered Thiel College, a Lutheran institution in Greenville, Pennsylvania, that gave scholarships to the children of Lutheran ministers and teachers, at the unusually young age of fourteen. There the religious instruction started by his father, who for all the lean years had been his schoolteacher, continued. Since it was one of Thiel's goals to make sure that this American-born generation knew the Lutheran catechisms and creeds in German, Edwin was also force-fed the German language. He received his degree at eighteen, the youngest graduate in Thiel history. Edwin's oldest sister, Harriet Earhart Monroe, twenty-five years his senior, was the success in the family. A formidable lady, she had founded the Atchison Institute, a private school for young ladies and gentlemen in Atchison. When the Lutheran Synods were looking for a site for a college west of the Mississippi, they bought the Institute buildings and opened Midland College of the General Synod of the Evangelical Lutheran Church.

Upon his graduation from Thiel, Edwin became the first head of the Preparatory Department at Midland. He was twenty years old, tall and good-looking, with straight dark hair, a great deal of self-possession, and a disarming manner. He had been hired to teach at Midland at least partially because of his family connections, but he was well qualified for the work: he was an extremely literate young man with an extensive vocabulary, well grounded in the classics. A copy of the college catalogue lists the seven faculty members, presumably in their order of importance. Of the seven, Edwin is fourth: "Edwin S. Earhart, A.M., Instructor of Preparatory Classes." Edwin taught those students who lacked academic credentials "all the studies of a thorough English education"—which included Latin, Greek, German, algebra, geometry, and outlines of history. Edwin taught at Midland for a year, then he went off to study law at Kansas State at Lawrence. He worked his way through law school, according to his father, by "assisting the professors in Belletres and in tutoring slower but more affluent students."

One's religion was a serious matter in those years in that part of the world, and Lutherans didn't rate at all high in the social pecking order in Atchison. They were nowhere near "the top of the pole" with the Episcopalians, the Presbyterians, the Baptists, and the Methodists. Socially they were down somewhere with the Catholics. One of Ida Challiss Martin's daughters married a German-speaking Lutheran, Paul Tonsing, about this time, much to the annoyance of the rest of the family. Of course the older generation (after all, Maria was alive and Gebhard had been a Lutheran) would have been kind to this couple, but kindness wasn't enough—others in the Challiss family would permanently look down on this branch because it stayed so persistently German.

Alfred, a man concerned with social and class distinctions, a man who had worked hard to achieve financial success and social standing for himself and his family, was not at all happy with Amy's choice of Edwin for a husband; in his eyes it wasn't enough that Edwin's father David Earhart was one of the most respected Lutherans in the state—Lutheranism was the wrong religion. Nor did Edwin's sister Harriet count for much in Alfred's eyes, even though she was important enough for the local paper to chronicle her comings and goings. ("Mrs. Monroe will not leave the city before the middle of July" ran a typical social note in *The Atchison Globe*.) Alfred's wife and daughters were as he wanted them to be—cultured (finished, that is, but not educated as in college-educated), and idle. "Energetic" and "useful," the two adjectives *The Atchison Globe* used to describe Harriet, were not admirable from the Judge's point of view. The desired role of the upper-middle-class woman at the turn of the century was not the woman who worked—rich women were supposed to be literate, well read, and genteel, and idle—only poor women worked. It was for exactly this reason that Alfred made Amy give up all thoughts of Vassar and made Margaret, who had plotted so industriously with her doctor to prepare herself, give up notions of medical school.

Furthermore, any conceivable status that Harriet might have conferred upon the Earharts was decidedly offset by the lack of status of Edwin's brothers, three of whom listed themselves in the Atchison Directory as roofpainters for all to see and hire. It was not Alfred's kind of family.

When, later in the summer, Alfred went west in search of a new minister for the church, in the classic manner he took Amy with him, hoping that the western air would clear her head. Amy had a marvelous time; it was on this trip that she became the first woman to reach the top of Pikes Peak (much to the chagrin and embarrassment of several men in the climbing party who were forced to turn back because of altitude sickness) and returned to Atchison more determined than ever not to give Edwin up. There followed for Amy several years at home when she kept herself busy helping her father and cultivating her "literary" tastes. All the while she and Edwin were courting.

There may have been something else at work. Family accounts that come down to us suggest that Alfred simply didn't trust the tall, dark-haired young man. Whether it was Edwin's religion that was the sticking point and, rather than admit it, Amy's family made up other compelling reasons why the marriage was unwise cannot be known. But others besides Alfred were against the marriage. Rilla Challiss, married to Amelia Otis's nephew James, also thought it a mistake. Edwin was long on charm but short on substance, was the feeling; he told tales a bit too deftly. This minister's son was very different from his stern father; he had fallen, Rilla thought, too far from the tree.

Alfred wanted Amy to marry someone in their own social circle, as their eldest, William, had done. William had married Grace Hetherington, who was not only of impeccable Yankee stock but the daughter of his good friend William Hetherington, the wealthy founder and chairman of the Exchange Bank of Atchison.

But finally, in the face of Amy's persistence, Alfred agreed to the marriage if and when Edwin proved himself—specifically, when he achieved an income of at least fifty dollars a month. It was not an unreasonable sum—it was less than Alfred had earned when he had first hung out his shingle in Louisville, Kentucky, where he had briefly practiced after graduating from law school.

Edwin started practicing law not in Atchison but in Kansas City, Kansas, setting himself up with an office on Minnesota Avenue with a partner, Mr. J. E. Barker. In 1895 his income reached the level stipulated by Alfred, and the young couple made plans to marry. By that time Amy was twenty-six.

The wedding was held in Trinity Episcopal Church in Atchison on Wednesday, October 16, 1895, at eleven A.M.. Although there were two ministers—the Reverend John Henry Hopkins, the popular minister who had left just that summer and came back especially to marry Amy, and Reverend John E. Sulger, who replaced him—and the altar was bedecked with palms and white roses, the wedding was a very restrained affair. Amy and Edwin entered the church unaccompanied; the church was mostly empty; only relatives and "their most intimate friends" were present. Edwin's father, Reverend Earhart, probably wasn't there, not just because following the death of his wife Mary he had returned to Pennsylvania, but because as a devout Lutheran minister, he would have been bound by Church doctrine to disapprove of a marriage where the Lutheran religion did not prevail.

There was no reception after the ceremony. The bride and groom went from the church to the station and were on the noon train for Kansas City, Kansas, where they would make their home. Their destination in Kansas City was a rather ordinary white frame house on a small lot only twenty feet wide, but the house was new, it was furnished, and it was all theirs—for the Otises had given it to them as a wedding present. They sent out proper engraved announcements that they would be "At Home after November First" at 1021 Ann Street.

There is a wedding photo of the bride and groom. Amy looks happy and confident, her chestnut hair piled elegantly on her head, a curl accentuating her high Harres forehead, her large eyes under her arched eyebrows staring off into the distance as she smiles ever so slightly. Edwin, dressed impeccably, his dark hair neatly parted, stares straight into the camera with a look that is at once self-conscious, guilty, and pleased, rather like the cat that has swallowed the canary.

By the time Amelia Earhart was born, her parents were living in an undistinguished house in the undistinguished suburb of a large town. She never witnessed the legendary days of her parents and grandparents and later regretted it—she would miss the excitement, the "woolliness" as she called it, that had vanished. She heard about the Indians in Atchison that Amelia Otis had found so frightening, that "lifted the lid of her basket and peered within, and felt the fabric of her dress, until she was quite terrified."

When she was a child, Amy Otis had seen the last vestige of the Old West—the stacks of buffalo bones by the sides of the railroad tracks. Once, picking berries near a tree, she looked up and saw a bear picking berries on the other side. She was thirteen when Jesse James, the last of the famous gunslingers who roamed Kansas, was shot and killed in St. Joseph, just twenty miles away.

There were no Indians for Amelia to see; the old rotting robe made from buffalo hides that she found in her grandparent's barn was the only trace left. She would remember as an adult of thirty-five how as a little girl in Kansas she had kept her eye out for Indians—had "hoped for many a day some would turn up." *She* would never have been terrified, as her grandmother told her she had been.

2
Kansas Girl

• • • • As Amelia Earhart recounted it in later years in *The Fun of It,* she had been sent off to live with her grandmother in Atchison because Amelia Otis was "very lonesome." "I . . . was lent her for company during the winter months," as Amelia put it, ". . . until the eighth grade." There is a certain charm about it—the little girl named after her grandmother sent to live with her, even acquiring the same nickname. It didn't even seem that unusual an arrangement, for as everyone concerned knew, her grandfather had lived with his grandparents for a number of years.

But Amelia was bundled off at the age of three to North Terrace because her grandmother needed companionship and distraction to cope with the trauma of the deaths, in three years, of her mother, her eldest son William, and William's wife. First Maria, for the first time ever, took to her bed on a summer day; eight weeks later she died. Then Grace Otis, William's wife, died of unknown causes in Colorado Springs, where she and William and their daughter Annie Maria had gone to live. The following summer William died of diphtheria.

And then Margaret, Amelia Otis's younger daughter, upon whom not just she but everyone else in the family relied, left taking with her Annie, Amelia's first grandchild. That was just as great an immediate emotional loss. Not only Amelia but everyone in the family relied on Margaret. It was she who had cared for Maria and then, on a visit to her brother in Colorado Springs, had nursed first Grace and then William. Margaret had then returned to North Terrace bringing with her Annie, who had become her ward. But Margaret had no intention of staying—she was twenty-eight and engaged to Clarence Balis, a Philadelphia businessman who had been patiently waiting for years for her to set the date. Now, having done all she could for her family, there was no further reason to postpone the wedding. The thought of losing their kind daughter, their ray of sunshine, and in addition the orphaned granddaughter who would go wherever Margaret went (including her honeymoon, Margaret's own children always suspected) was more than Amelia Otis could stand. Even Alfred was dismayed.

As the years passed, he had become increasingly withdrawn. "Dignified and of aristocratic bearing" was the way a reporter for *The Atchison Globe* delicately described Alfred, but to his children and grandchildren he was cold, remote, and impatient at best. At sixty-four he had suffered a complete mental breakdown. Mental illness was little understood at the time; *softening of the brain* and *neurasthenia* were the usual words used to describe the condition. Hospitalized in Kenosha, Wisconsin, in 1892, fully expecting to die, he went so far as to make a will, but within two years he had recovered and was managing his own affairs. But from then on he suffered recurrent bouts of depression. "He realizes fully, to use his own language, that he has passed the three score and ten and that the autumn leaves are thick about him. He seems to have no bodily ailments like so many old folks have, but there is nothing I wouldn't give or do to give him 'a quiet mind and a contented spirit,' " wrote a younger brother sorrowfully after spending time with him.

Now Margaret's departure weighed heavily even on Alfred, who confided his anguish to another brother, Charles: "It grieves me to tell you but it is a fact all the same that if nothing unforeseen happens she will be married in the late spring or early summer to a Philadelphia man. . . . He has been here and gotten our consent as we believe him to be noteworthy and everything a gentleman ought to be but I feel pretty badly about it though I do not mean to be selfish at all."

Margaret married Clarence Balis on June 5, 1900, and moved to Philadelphia. Alfred became increasingly morose, and Amelia Otis increasingly lonely. Amy was relatively nearby, only fifty miles distant in Kansas City, but she was again pregnant and so could not help; on December 29 Muriel was born. With her new infant to care for and Amelia just three, Amy had more than she could handle. The solution was at hand to lighten Amy's chores in Kansas City and Amelia Otis's spiritual burden in Atchison—to send Amelia, her namesake grandchild. Again young laughter would fill the house. And so at three Amelia Earhart was bundled off to Atchison. There, as her mother had, she puttered around in the kitchen mindful of Mary Brashay, the Irish cook, grown fatter as well as older over the years, and prowled the grounds under the watchful eye of the gardener Charlie Parks, who had strung the lanterns for her mother's coming-out party. She learned to stay away from her crusty grandfather. It worked beautifully for everyone concerned.

Millie Otis, whom her Millie Earhart called "Grandma," grown stouter with the years, was now in her sixties. Her great interests in life were her children, her grandchildren, her gardens, and the church. When she moved out west, she had carried with her three volumes filled with the dance tunes and sentimental songs popular in Philadelphia at that time. She kept those volumes—those remnants of her eastern society life—with her always. She finally gave them not to any of her own children but to Millie Earhart, who, understanding their importance, as an adult would number them among the possessions she treasured most. Millie Otis appears never to have tried to absorb the culture and the ways that she found on the banks of the Missouri—the new world of the Indians and the farmers and those other pioneers who traveled west. She carried with her the values of the eastern seaboard, sought to perpetuate them, and succeeded. The literature she fed her children and grandchildren—the books Amelia Earhart found in the library and grew up on—were the tales of Beatrix Potter, the writings of Thackeray, Dickens, Swinburne—almost all English except for a few Americans like Cooper and Poe—the same literature that was being read in Philadelphia and Boston and New York. It was not surprising that both Amelia Otis's daughters and *their* sons and daughters, having been taught to value the cultural icons of the East from the time they were born, would eventually return east, from whence that culture came. Even Amelia Otis's lovely flower gardens—that Amelia raced around and through—were fashioned after those she had left behind in Philadelphia—the hollyhocks, phlox, gladioli, the heliotrope, the rows of roses in the beds separated by strips of lawn in the sunken garden, the wonderful orchard full of apple and peach trees she had planted, and the vineyard between her house and her sister's where she grew malaga and concord grapes. So Amelia, although brought up in Kansas, absorbed the eastern establishment culture her family had imported west.

Amelia was given the northeast bedroom for her own, the room her great-grandmother Maria Harres had lived in for thirty-three years, with its huge window that gave such a spectacular view of the river below. She felt Maria's presence. On long winter evenings Amelia would hear about Maria firsthand from her grandmother—how Maria had saved Amy's life, how extraordinarily vigorous she had been, how she had lived to see two great-great-grandchildren born and had almost lived to see her—as well as hearing stories about the early years of the town.

For Amelia it was a happy experience. There was no abdication of parental responsibility on her mother's part; Kansas City was only fifty miles away—not halfway across the continent, as had been the case with Alfred and his parents—and Amelia went home in the summers. Furthermore her mother took every opportunity to visit and was around often, bringing Muriel, two and a half years younger, with her. The main drawback was that Edwin rarely visited North Terrace. His separation from his daughter was a wrench for Edwin, acknowledged by him or not, because when Amelia had been very little, he had spent so much time with her and they were so fond of each other that Amelia's first word was *Papa,* not *Mama.* Now he had to be content with seeing a great deal less of her.

Amy kept a baby book titled *Queer Doings and Quaint Sayings of Baby Earhart.* The entries detail the progress of a likable, slightly precocious baby with a strong self-sufficient streak. "She sleeps all the time," wrote Amy, once for the amazing duration of nine hours. She never sucked her thumb. At twelve weeks she "laughed and talked to herself in the looking glass." On March 4 she caught hold of the end of her buggy and twice pulled herself to her feet. By May she was creeping. On August 27 she took her first step. "After she was two years old," her mother writes, "she went to bed by herself, often singing herself to sleep . . . invariably taking a rag doll with her." Her imagination "was largely developed. . . . Will amuse herself for hours with imaginary people and playthings." The concluding entry is the most charming and the most revealing: "I overheard her talking to herself and on her discovering me in the room she said, 'If you are not here to talk to I just whisper in my own ears.' "

Her health was a hallmark of her personality. In this she was unlike her mother, who though fit, had been stricken with so many assaults on her health. It was as if Maria's genes had jumped the generations inbetween. Even Amelia's teeth were unusually strong; her first tooth came in at four months, on the early side, and she never had a cavity until she was twenty. She managed to avoid most of the childhood contagious diseases; in those prevaccine days the only illness she succumbed to was measles, for which she had an early and healthy respect. When her thirty-one-year-old cousin Ruth Martin came to visit, Amelia, even though only seven, ignoring the ordinary rules of conduct, warned the family, "Don't go near Cousin Ruth. She's got measles at her house." And she stood across the room until Ruth left. In her instinctive awareness of health precautions that should be taken and her personal fitness, Amelia was such a throwback to her great-grandmother Maria that one imagines Amelia Otis would have noted it and been comforted.

She learned to read at five and after that spent hours in the Otises' library devouring the back issues of *Harper's Magazine for Young People,* or reading the novels of Scott, Dickens, George Eliot, and Thackeray. Hawthorne, too, she read, but she thought him too given to description. ("Why doesn't he *say* Judge Pyncheon's dead in that chair," she fumed.) She could also at least get glimpses of the world beyond Atchison in the New York and Chicago newspapers and in *Harper's Weekly,* which also came to the house.

She was thin—so thin her friends sometimes called her Skinny—and growing up was always on the tall side for her age. She had freckles, level gray eyes, a round nose, and straight dark blond hair parted in the middle. Photos of her show her hair drawn smoothly back in pigtails and tied with the enormous ribbon bows fashionable at the time.

There in Atchison Amelia grew up secure of her place, secure of her family's position, nurtured by tradition, and surrounded by friends. Every one of the friends she would mention in later life were the ones she made then, in Atchison, and all would remain her best friends for as long as she lived.

Yet if she was raised in a family that had achieved local, state, and national recognition, still its day, like Atchison's, was past; in Amelia's growing-up years, Atchison was subsiding into a sleepy town. Gone was the vibrancy of the years when Amy was growing up. In its 1880s exuberance—its certainty that it was about to become the gateway to the West—a sign had been put up at the railroad station that read, "Atchison Kansas population 30,000," strategically placed so that passengers in the trains approaching from the south could see it before they turned west to go out across the Kansas plains. In Amelia's day the sign was still there, but now it served only as a reminder of past dreams. The population was scarcely half that. The famous of the world no longer strolled through town as they had when her mother was a child. The most exciting thing going on in town was to watch Deefie Bowler—the deaf and dumb bricklayer with the powerful shoulders and crippled stumps for legs, famous throughout Kansas for being able to lay more bricks than anyone else in America—finish paving the outlying roads.

It must have seemed to Amelia as if the whole world were connected either by blood or by marriage—all bound together by the intertwined linkage that grew out of fifty years of common history. When she was three, she would have been present when the far-flung Challiss clan gathered in the Challiss house next door for Mary Ann and William's golden wedding anniversary, when they were remarried by the Baptist minister Dr. Comes with all ten children in attendance. She would get to know her august great-aunt Ida Challiss Martin, now widowed, who spent her life doing good works and keeping an eye on the John A. Martin Memorial Library at the Soldier's Orphan's Home on the outskirts of town, which had been started after Governor Martin's death. She played with her Challiss cousins, who lived next door. There were four Challiss children in Amelia's generation: Jack, just Amelia's age; Lucy (Toot), with the big brown eyes and brown hair and bangs, two years younger than she; Kathryn (Katch), five years younger, with mischievous green-blue eyes and light brown hair; and Peggy, the baby of the family. Lucy and Katch became her best friends. Then there was her second cousin Orpha Tonsing, Ida Martin's granddaughter, who lived half a block away, whom Amelia Otis would invite over to play and for dinner. Although they were not close, Amelia and Orpha would play together with the toys stashed under the stairs—the stone blocks, the Jack Straws, and the big bisque doll in its carriage.

Amelia's closest friend besides Katch and Toot was Virginia Park, nicknamed Ginger, whose grandfather had provisioned the wagon trains going west back in the pioneer days and been a friend of Alfred Otis and William Challiss. Virginia and her younger sister Ann lived two blocks away on North Third Street and also were great friends of the Challisses. Although Amelia and Ginger went to the College Preparatory School and the Episcopal Sunday school and the Challisses went to public school and the Baptist Sunday school, they all got along so well and lived so near each other, they were all practically inseparable. The younger sisters Katch and Ann adored Amelia, but then so did most younger girls, because even when she was young, Amelia enjoyed teaching skills to those who wanted to learn. She taught all the younger sisters how to ride a bicycle. It was not Toot but Amelia who taught Katch to ride, not Ginger but Amelia who taught Ann. Katch never forgot how Amelia steadied her, running alongside her as she pedaled her bike down Second Street. "Such a kind, thoughtful person," she recalled, a smile playing about her lips, as she remembered the event more than fifty years later. Ann, too, recalled the fun of Amelia, "getting me up there—giving me a shove, telling me to hang on, don't fall off." They were just two of her pupils.

Amelia's grandmother was not only timid, she was a worrier, and she treated Amelia far differently from her own children. Her own mother Maria and her sister Mary Ann had been able to stiffen her spine and give her courage all those years before, when her own children were growing up. Now she was older and nervous and alone—her mother dead, her sister recently moved away to live with one of their children, Alfred withdrawn; there was no one left to stop her from saying no, to shake her out of her natural timidity and fears. So the ordinary everyday things that children did became scary in her eyes. Although Amy had possessed her own Indian pony at the age she was now, Amelia Otis wouldn't permit Amelia to ride. Amelia Earhart solved the problem her grandmother presented by keeping her own counsel. She didn't argue. "Amelia was much too kind to bother her grandmother, even when she was unhappy about something," observed her wise cousin Katch. She was also instinctively wise enough and gutsy enough to know she could do anything she wanted as long as it didn't make waves. Instead, she found a way to ride by becoming friends with the daughters of the butcher, who made deliveries in his horse-drawn wagon. When business was slow, the butcher allowed his girls and Amelia to unhitch the two horses from the traces and ride. Of the two animals, Amelia liked the sorrel who bucked, best: "this horse opened vistas of pleasure," she bragged. She also explored the sandstone caves that dotted the bluff as it dropped down to the Missouri, which were off limits because at the water's edge were the tracks of the Burlington roundhouse, where the trains turned, and the tramps who rode the rails occasionally dropped off there. And indeed once Amelia came upon three men huddled in one of the caves. She found that she enjoyed exploring and kept going back, even putting up "beware" signs to keep others away from her favorite caves. She found the river itself "exciting," with the "large and dangerous looking whirlpools to be seen in its yellow depths, and the banks . . . forever washing away."

In small ways she had to be careful, and she found it was more difficult to hide her everyday tomboy habits from her grandmother than her larger escapades. Her grandmother observed her vaulting the fence surrounding the house, as she habitually did on her way home from school or going to or from the Challisses', and objected with such force that in later years Amelia never forgot that her grandmother had made her feel "extremely unladylike." She went around by the gate — "for several days in succession." Her grandmother, in her own defense, claimed understanding from her granddaughter. "You don't realize that when I was a small girl I did nothing more strenuous than roll my hoop in the public square." "I think," Amelia Earhart would write of Amelia Otis, "inside she never quite got used to the West for now and then something came popping out which made me feel Philadelphia must be quite superior to Atchison."

Nor did Amelia Otis have a sense of humor. Her family said of her that they had to diagram all the jokes for her, which also seemed not to bother her granddaughter. Sometimes, in fact, Amelia would tease her grandmother—but gently. If Cousin Annie Otis, in Atchison for a visit, was late for a meal, Amelia would say, "Cousin Annie is just coming down the waterpipe, she will be in to lunch just as soon as she gets the peacock feather put in her hair." Her grandmother didn't seem to mind, even if she couldn't follow, for her granddaughter's sense of fantasy and love of nonsense often left her completely bewildered. Amelia Otis did forbid Amelia to go on the snake hunt into the hills organized by Virginia Park's stepfather Dr. Beitzel, respected doctor and family friend. The expedition had great luck, and came back with various specimens. Although Amelia went through a stage when she wouldn't even kill a fly—she would catch houseflies, take them outdoors, and set them free—she particularly wanted to hunt snakes, viewing them as a threat to horses, and was so bothered by her grandmother's interdiction that she made a rare exception and complained about it to her mother. When next the good doctor organized a hunt, Amelia went along, but on this trip only one snake was found.

Amelia usually did get her way, one way or another. When she was seven, Edwin took the family to the St. Louis World's Fair. For Amelia a high point of the trip was riding with her father on the Ferris wheel; the lowest point was having her mother forbid a ride on the roller coaster. Even at that age Amelia liked heights.

She also liked working with her hands and building things. So, once home, she decided to build her own roller coaster and capture the sensation—the rushing dropping-down-out-of-control speed trip she had been denied. She found some wooden two-by-fours, propped them at an angle against the toolshed roof to make the track, and made a cab out of a wooden packing box, to which she attached roller-skate wheels. Various willing hands, including her school friend Balie Waggener joined in the project. Giving her advice was her mother's youngest brother, Uncle Carl. The first ride, naturally, was hers. She started from the ridge pole, slid down the steep incline—and somersaulted head over heels as the cab hit ground. Undaunted, she added more track to make the incline less steep and the ending less abrupt. Amelia tried again, and this time the roller coaster worked. Balie Waggener, fifty years later, recalled that "a ride down that thing was a thrill."

Amelia Otis's views on proper ladylike behavior for young girls was by no means unusual—she was merely reflecting the existing mores of the day. Amelia wasn't the only little girl in Atchison who felt the unfairness of the limitations of being born female; Lucy and Katch Challiss also chafed at the restrictions imposed upon them. Fretting over things they were not allowed to do, envying the freedom they didn't have, they would vent their frustration by pretending they were boys, for therein, they were certain, lay freedom. "We thought being a boy was much better than being a girl," recalled Katch. And when the opportunity presented itself, they jumped at the chance to rough-house with their boy friends—including Balie Waggener and his friends Jared and Ed Jackson. The girls gave as good as they got, according to Balie; they were tough for girls, but of the three, Amelia was the toughest: "She could get as rough as we did." A bit later, grown out of their tomboy phase, they would discuss how when they were grown, they would be different from their mothers, how they would control their own lives, not let the men do it.

She used her conciliatory skills to get along with her remote grandfather, who provided so little company for her grandmother. Amelia's response to her unresponsive grandfather was to relegate him to oblivion—in her eyes, he was nowhere near as important as her grandmother. If she knew of his accomplishments, and she must have, she never mentioned it. He impinged on her consciousness so little, in fact, that she would write, describing her childhood, "Until the eighth grade I stayed the school year with my grandmother in Atchison, Kansas"; she would even describe the Atchison barn as "my grandmother's barn." Muriel, younger by three years and only a visitor in the house, didn't notice her grandfather's moods. She would associate the creaking of his heavy black square-toed shoes as he walked about, or as he stood rocking in front of the fire, with a sense of well-being, speaking of the Atchison home as "our home, creaking with plenty." She would also remember him sawing wood for exercise. But the only time Amelia ever referred to her grandfather in her writings, it was merely to describe what he did—a very different treatment from what she accorded the other members of her family, all of whom she described in some detail and with obvious affection. Nevertheless in Amelia's genes was the grit that had carried him through.

Often when Amelia was alone she would while away the time reading tales she knew by heart, then after a time she would put her book down and dream. She wrote a poem about one dream.

> I watch the birds flying all day long
> And I want to fly too.
> Don't they look down sometimes, I wonder,
> And wish they were me
> When I'm going to the circus with my daddy?

Often she constructed her own tale. One path her imagination took her on—preoccupied as she would be for hours with fantasies of traveling into the past, into the future, and always out of Atchison—eventually turned into a game called Bogie. Present in the game is Amelia's sense of adventure, the thrill of embarking on a long dangerous voyage; demonstrated is her inherent personal magnetism.

Bogie was played in the barn on the bluff above the river which—once full of horses and carriages—now contained just one carriage, complete with carriage lamps. Amelia, with her vivid imagination, turned this vehicle into a magic chariot in which she, accompanied most often by Katch and Lucy and Muriel, traveled the world. They placed sawhorses in front of the carriage in place of real horses, equipped themselves with wooden pistols, and then settled down in the carriage and went on an adventure. Katch's favorite voyage was a trip to a town called Pearyville, so full of exciting and dangerous happenings, so encrusted with tradition, that Katch drew a detailed map of the journey, complete with distances. In this make-believe world they all (naturally) took the roles of boys. According to Katch, it was Amelia who saved them when, along the way to Pearyville, the carriage was attacked by hairy men. They shouted, "Oh hairy men hairy men," at the same time pointing the pistols and yelling "bangbang," but if Amelia hadn't remembered that the hairy men "were afraid of red" and produced a red gumdrop, they would have been carried away forever, according to Katch. There were all sorts of other dangers, too, along the way to Pearyville—night riders, giant spiders, and snakes, as well as witches, a Man of the Woods, ghosts, and corpses. There was a Bridge of Skeletons to pass over, the Old Gallows to pass, the Cave of Sighs, the Witches Cave, the Red Lion, the Robber Bridge—so many things, in fact, that although it was clearly drawn on the map, they never ever reached Pearyville. And that was part of the game, too.

In the more sophisticated version of the game, it becomes apparent that Amelia's later fascination with long-distance flying is just the adult, real-life version of Bogie. In youthful Bogie they would be in a carriage "dashing wildly across country to London, Paris, and Berlin" or careening down the post road to Vienna. "A knight in armor came galloping swiftly toward us. 'Dispatches, Sir Knight!' I shouted." Amelia, with maps "that fell into our clutches," embarked on "imaginary journeys full of fabulous perils. . . . The map of Africa was a favorite." The carriage became an elephant or a camel, as the need arose. "We weighed the advantage of the River Niger and the Nile, the comparative ferociousness of the Tauregs and Swahili. No Livingstone, Stanley or Rhodes explored with more enthusiasm than we," Amelia would write as she waited for her Lockheed Electra to be repaired in 1937 on her round-the-world flight.

She loved poetry, but that didn't stop her from appreciating the comics. They were words, too, and she was above all a wordsmith, as virtually all the letters she wrote to friends throughout her life demonstrate.

Her favorite comic was "The Katzenjammer Kids." This strip, featuring words phonetically spelled to capture the German accent ("I tell der kink uf Sveden! . . . I got a liddle bizness vot iss important! . . . Lets take a ride in der airyplaner!" are representative sentences) amused Amelia so much that she appropriated the idea of phonetic spelling and for the rest of her life would weave deliberate phonetic bloopers into her letters. In 1932, when she gave Katch a copy of her book *The Fun of It,* she wrote on the flyleaf, "To mine angel cousin Katch from her darlink cousin Mill." And Amelia, who had written her first poem when she was four (dedicating it "especially" to her mother), opened that world also to her playmates. She recited from memory passages from *Alice in Wonderland,* or Lear's "Owl and the Pussycat," or "Horatius at the Bridge," and a bit later verses from Browning.

But her favorite poem was "Atalanta in Calydon" by the popular English poet Algernon Charles Swinburne and so, inevitably, Swinburne became Katch's favorite poet and that poem became her favorite, too. Amelia always memorized great chunks of her favorites, so before long Katch, too, memorized the poem. It made such a deep impression upon Katch that seventy years later, she could still recite passages from it.

It is a fascinating tale. The poem is a rarity in English literature—an epic poem about a warrior maiden. Its images are beautiful, but its message had a special appeal to Amelia. Atalanta was a role model Amelia could relate to. She had no patience with the passive princesses of mythology; Those heroines she read about in the fairy tales who could have had everything but managed only to get themselves into distress bored her. Like Ariadne marking her way in the labyrinth, Atalanta found a path to Amelia's soul.

Atalanta is a virgin huntress—fleet of foot, deadly with bow and arrow, and very courageous. She joins the Greek warriors hunting a boar that the gods have sent down to menace the kingdom. Meleager, leader of the hunt, adores Atalanta; he is "beyond measure enamoured of her" and calls her to his side:

> "Come with bows bent and with emptying of quivers
> Maiden most perfect, lady of light."

All the great warriors of Greece are hunting the boar, but it is Atalanta whose arrow first finds the beast, and Meleager who deals it a mortal blow. When Meleager awards her the slain boar as spoils, the warriors become furious. Meleager slays his uncles, who are in the forefront of those who would destroy Atalanta. In the ensuing struggle, Meleager dies.

The poem is both a celebration of Atalanta and a warning of the dangers to such females who compete in the male world. Swinburne makes plain that men and women feel equally threatened by her. Thus Meleager's mother:

"A woman armed makes war upon herself."

And Meleager's father:

"Not fire nor iron and the widemouthed wars
Are deadlier than her lips or braided hair."

And Meleager's uncle, who rails that it is against the natural order of things,

"and the bride overbear the groom."

Atalanta tries to blunt the censorious attitude, telling of her sacrifice, that she has given up so much. That too is an integral message of the poem—that she shall have

"no man's love
Forever, and no face of children born
nor being dead shall kings my sons
Mourn me and bury,
and tears on daughters' cheeks burn."

She asks them to understand her.

"yet in my body is throned
As great a heart, and in my spirit, O men,
I have not less of godlike."

In the end Atalanta is shunned by all except the dying Meleager. No literary work could more eloquently or plainly spell out the dangers that exist for the woman who competes in male pursuits.

• • • •

From first grade on Amelia attended the private College Preparatory School along with Ginger and Ann Parks; the Fox sisters, Marjorie and Virginia; Mary Campbell, a neighbor whose mother had been a friend of Amelia's mother; and Balie Waggener, whom she had known forever—her grandfather had given Balie's father his first job. The coeducational school was just a short walk for all of them. It had been founded by Helen Schofield in 1896, in what had been a stable. Sarah Walton, the headmistress, a gifted educator and an active member of Trinity Church, assisted by Yale graduate Charlie Gaylord prepared "her" children so well that most went on to top colleges.

The College Preparatory School was tiny, having between thirty and forty students spread out in the twelve grades. The stable had become two large rooms, one upstairs and one down. The lower forms—through the eighth grade—studied upstairs, grades nine through twelve studied downstairs. Classes in the various subjects for the diverse grades were taught in one corner of each floor, while the children studied in the other part. It worked because the grades were so small—Annie Park remembers days when she was the only one in her class.

It was comfortable and intimate and friendly. The desks were the kind with chairs attached, so that as the children slid in and out, there was a minimum of disruption. When their class was over, students would take their belongings off to a corner to read and study, and the next class would slide into place. At the end of the day Amelia and Ginger and the others packed their belongings into their string bags and walked or biked home.

Amelia was a good student, but bright as she was, her strong streak of independence did not go unremarked. In seventh grade she missed the arithmetic honors that were hers for the taking because, according to Headmistress Sarah Walton, "Amelia's mind is brilliant, but she refuses to do the plodding necessary to win honor prizes. She deduces the correct answers to complex arithmetic problems, but hates to put down the steps by which she arrived at the results." Sarah Walton also noted that prizes were not of great interest to Amelia—not the carrot they were for many children: that she listened to a different drummer. She did manage to receive one prize from the headmistress, though—a beautiful copy of Macaulay's *Lays of Ancient Rome.*

In the time-honored fashion of the day, girls didn't play team sports. Their role was to cheer on the boys at the school basketball and baseball games by yelling the school chant:

Rickety X
Co Ex
Co Ex
Bully for you
CPS

It wasn't enough for Amelia; she wanted more. She wanted to play basketball too, although being a realist, she probably didn't expect to play at school, only on her own with her girl friends. To play, she needed to know the rules. If she had been a timid child, she would probably have asked her friend Balie Waggener. But no; she went to the top of the school world—to team captain Frank Baker, who was older and whom she barely knew. One day during basketball practice, she approached him. They had never talked because she was so much younger and because boys hung out with boys and girls with girls; in approaching him, she was breaking custom. "We girls would like to play," she threw out, which startled him, but he agreed to teach her how to hold a ball and shoot for the basket. Amelia thereupon taught Ginger Park and Lucy. This game, too, they played across the road in Charlie's Park, where there was a single basketball hoop on the side of a barn—all their game required. (The boys at the school also played with just one hoop.) Under Amelia's guidance, they also played a form of baseball they called One-O-Cat that required only three people—pitcher, catcher, and batter—each out for themselves—another game the boys played.

Her activist nature is perfectly caught in two photos in Lucy's 1911 photograph album. In one picture Amelia and three friends—Katherine Dolan (referred to as Dolan), Lucy (Toot), Virginia Park (Ging) are lying on their stomachs, their chins cupped in their hands, staring at the camera either before or after a basketball game; it is Amelia who is holding the ball. In another photo Amelia is standing with her Challiss cousins—but the photo is being taken from too far away, she notices: Amelia's arm is stretched out toward the camera; she is beckoning the photographer to come closer.

On cold winter days, when ice floes ten inches thick bubbled on the river and the land was covered with snow, the children—cousins, school friends—would meet at the top of the North Second Street hill with their sleds and coast down to the bottom in waves, the boys lying face-down on their models, the girl sitting upright on theirs. Amelia had a boys' sled, one of her prize possessions, a gift from her father, and she was the only girl who could lie down while coasting down the hill. She credited it with saving her life, recounting that once, zipping down an icy hill, she found herself heading straight for a junkman's cart and horse. The junkman didn't hear her yells so, unable to stop, she aimed for the space between the horse's front and back legs. Head down, she made it. Other winter days, they all went ice skating on the pond at Jackson Park.

When Muriel was in Atchison, she played with Ann and Katch. She had a bit of a difficult time, not only because she was only an occasional participant but also because Amelia was so dramatic, so clever, and so inventive that both Katch and Annie infinitely preferred her over "Moonie," as they called her. "I didn't care for her as much as Millie," Ann would recall. Katch would say, "I always seemed to get stuck with Muriel."

Clearly Amelia was a hard act to follow. She was the glamorous, daring one—Muriel was the younger, timid, plump, solemn younger sister. Amelia was always dreaming up new activities and yet, a natural teacher, always managed to be kind and patient to the younger girls. Naturally they all wanted to be with her—so did Muriel. So deep an impression did Amelia make on Ann Park, one of the younger sisters, that seventy years later Ann, over eighty years old, still remembered clearly that "Millie was always the instigator. . . . She would dare anything; we would all follow along." Katch said, "I just adored her. . . . She was not only fun . . . she could do *everything*."

Amelia had a passionate interest in animals, which manifested itself, more often than not, in those preautomobile times, on that most ubiquitous animal in North America—the horse. Anna Sewall's *Black Beauty* had made a great impression on her, and the result was that Amelia believed she had a personal mission to intercede on behalf of any horse she saw being mistreated. This inevitably led to confrontations with delivery men, when they found she had loosened the taut check reins of their horses, which kept them from being able to relax their necks, and once to a fight with her mother, when she refused to be polite to a neighbor in Kansas City who was cruel to his horse Nellie. Nor did she change as she grew older; her love for animals never left her. She never forgot Nellie, who died as a result of mistreatment. In the 1930s she would read Vachel Lindsay's poem "The Broncho That Would Not Be Broken of Dancing" to her husband, and he would know she was thinking of Nellie. Blanche Noyes, friend and fellow pilot, driving out west with Amelia many years later, remembered, "If there was an animal hit along the road, no matter whether she had an appointment or not, she'd stop and either take the animal to the next town, or we'd find someone to take care of the animal . . . or we'd check to see if it was dead."

Amelia remained close to her parents and her sister through the summers spent in Kansas City. Amy seems to have done a superb job of making each of her children content with their disparate lives, for both sisters seemed perfectly happy with the arrangement. Amelia in Atchison had Virginia Park, Toot, and Katch, a school she "loved," her own very special room, and her grandmother Millie, whom she could wind around her finger; Muriel had her mother and father and her own room in Kansas City. Amy would make frequent short visits to her family on North Terrace, always bringing Muriel.

Muriel enjoyed Atchison, but she wasn't as comfortable there as she was at home. For her there was "no comparison" between Atchison and Kansas City. "My family was in Kansas City; I liked Kansas City better," she would recall. One reason Muriel felt strange in Atchison was that she had to be on her best behavior for her grandparents. But another more important reason was her status as a visitor, which was underscored by the sleeping arrangements: Muriel slept with her mother in her mother's old bedroom. Muriel, recalling that sleeping arrangement, seventy years after the fact, still had a tinge of resentment in her voice as she continued, "Amelia had her *own* room." The special room—Maria's.

• • • •

Summertime life in Kansas City was simpler, less structured than it was in Atchison. Because Amelia had no network of school friends and cousins as in Atchison, she was thrown back on the company of her family—her sister, her mother, and particularly her father, who rarely, if ever, visited Atchison. There was more freedom in the Earhart house; Edwin particularly believed in letting young girls do what they wanted, whether it was proper or not. Amelia seems to have adjusted and benefited from the change. In particular, it gave her a chance to be with her father, whom she adored. Amy read Amelia and Muriel to sleep at night with selections from Dickens and Sir Walter Scott, but it was Edwin's knowledge that impressed Amelia. "I thought that my father must have read everything and, of course, therefore, knew everything. He could define the hardest words as well as the dictionary, and we used to try to trip him and he to bewilder us. I still have a letter he wrote me beginning, 'Dear parallelepipedon,' which sent me scurrying for a definition," she wrote.

Both in Atchison and in Kansas City from the time they were tots, Amelia and Muriel were taught by example and by lesson that it was the obligation of the rich to help out the poor. Well into the 1900s there were black shantytowns outside of Leavenworth, Atchison, and Kansas City. The blacks had come in huge numbers in the 1870s because the railroads, in an effort to encourage travel by rail, had distributed circulars promising good land and plenty of work in the state. It was a cruel joke, one that had left many impoverished blacks stranded. By the first decade of the 1900s the names of the white families whom they could turn to were being passed along among the desperately poor. Amy's name was on that list. "We watched, wide-eyed, the pathetic procession of decrepit Negroes, often crippled and scarred from their days of slavery, who stopped to beg. . . . Mother always gave them a few pennies or some bread and bacon, and this sent them on their way blessing her and perhaps a little strengthened in hope and faith."

On the outskirts of Atchison was the large red brick Soldiers' Orphans' Home that had been built after the Civil War for the indigent and orphaned offspring of Kansas veterans. The Home, by Amelia's day, was open to all dependent children in Kansas, including those who were physically disabled; it was one of the causes that civic-minded Atchison took to its heart, providing free tickets when the circus came to town, presents at Christmas, and various other contributions to make the orphans' lives happier. The Home was special to the Harres family; the library had been named the John A. Martin Memorial Library, in honor of Ida Challiss Martin's husband, and Ida maintained a particular interest in its well-being. As a matter of course, Amy invited children from the Home over to play. The favorite of these visitors was a girl named Lily who had a badly scarred hand. Amelia befriended her, treating her as she did her other friends, introducing her to all her friends—imaginary as well as real—involving her in whatever endeavor she was pursuing, with such effect that Lily lost all trace of self-consciousness about her status or her hand. In Kansas City, too, poor children were invited over to play with Amelia and Muriel and to dine with the family. Amy took particular care to set her table with nice china and glass at such times, to expose them to an environment they would not ordinarily see. Occasionally she gave each child a small purse containing a few coins and sent them off with Amelia and Muriel to shop at Emery, Bird & Thayer, the big Kansas department store. Once one of the little boys became totally unreasonable and demanded that he be allowed to buy one of the elevators. Amelia told him that it was almost impossible to buy an elevator. The little boy jumped up and down with rage, saying that he had been told he could buy what he wanted, and what he wanted was the elevator.

Amelia's cleverness and her imagination and her sure touch with people enabled her to come up with a solution.

"This particular elevator isn't for sale," she said. "But," she continued, looking secretive and mysterious, "I know how we can rent it for the afternoon."

"You do? Sure?" the little boy asked.

"I do. Dead sure. Shall we rent?"

"Sure. Let's," said the boy.

They spent the afternoon in the elevator, and except that the elevator operator was a little stunned, everything went off very well.

Amelia suffered through the self-conscious phase as most preadolescents do. Bloomers were much easier to move in than the ruffled pinafores over long full-skirted dresses that they usually wore, as Amy's sister Margaret had proved as a young girl, when she had secretly had a pair of bloomers made and gone bike riding. Amy had not joined Margaret's bloomer escapade, but it had made a deep impression on her; now she had dark blue flannel bloomers made for Amelia and Muriel to wear while pursuing their more strenuous activities. But the dress code in Atchison was still rigid—so rigid, a girl at school a few years older than Amelia was branded as "fast" because three or four inches of calf above her ankle became exposed when she crossed her legs. So Amelia's bloomers, being unusual, even though a generation later than her aunt's, still drew comment. Amelia observed that "though we felt terribly 'free and athletic,' we also felt somewhat as outcasts among the little girls who fluttered about us in their skirts."

Edwin gave the girls baseballs and bats and, in response to Amelia's request one Christmas, a football. Another of his Christmas presents was a .22 rifle. The girls already possessed a BB gun, with which they popped bottles off the back fence; the .22 was to shoot rats in the barn. There were a lot of rats, for according to the faithful Charlie Parks, the grain bins and side walls of the harness room got to look "pretty much like a sieve" by the time they were through.

Amelia was a collector. She had a special trunk in which she kept a collection of bones, including a cow's skull that Amy wanted her to throw out, and spiders. A particular species of spiders—trap spiders—were the ones she particularly cherished, for they had hinged backs. "That," Amelia pointed out to her mother, referring to the hinged backs, "is efficiency." She collected various moths, including a luna, a regal, and a cecropia, as well as katydids, toads, and a praying mantis. Sometimes with Muriel's aid she held worm races. For this novel activity Amelia would make a harness of a blade of grass, a sulky out of a small leaf, and mark out a course that she tried to make the worms follow.

Another occupation to which Amelia applied her penchant for the unusual and the inventive was cooking. Because there was no outdoor cooking facility at her grandparents' house, on nice days she and Katch and Lucy made their Saturday lunches outdoors "on a brick oven of our own construction." Most of what they cooked was basic: "Fried eggs were the principal dish, as I remember," Amelia admitted. But she also tried to make manna, after hearing in the Trinity Church Sunday school how it dropped down from Heaven on the children of Israel. She decided it "should be small, white, round muffins, a cross between a popover and angel food cake," and she "expended a good deal of energy and flour and sugar in trying to reproduce it," but it never did come out anything close to what she wanted.

A few years later in Des Moines, Amelia was drawn to food experiments of a different kind. She loved radishes and, on the premise that if small ones were good, big ones might be even better, she decided to experiment. The result of her labor was radishes that were, when harvested, the size of potatoes—slightly pink, with porous centers. She ate a morsel of one of the firmer specimens and "concluded then that overgrown radishes were inedible." A while later she persuaded her mother to cook a quart of peas in their pods. The cooked peas were also a failure, forcing even Amelia to agree that it would probably be better to shell them first. "I had hoped," Amelia recalled of her attempts to find new foods, "to create original and palatable dishes." Whether Amelia named the radishes Eardishes and the peas Earpods or the family hung those names on them is not known. It was not for years, not until Amelia was living at Denison House and working with Chinese children and ate her first Chinese pea pods, that she felt vindicated.

Whether it was cooking or collecting or shooting, each activity was shaped by Amelia's creativity. Just as when she was a baby and "talked into her own ears" for hours on end to amuse herself if her mother wasn't around, the older child, left to her own devices, created imaginary playmates Laura and Ringa, who "came frequently to call; there were long, earnest conversations." She introduced Muriel to Laura and Ringa, and then the four of them would decide what games to play. She also invented some small black creatures, a cross between the Krazy Kat comic strip figures and a miniature jabberwocky whom she called deejays, who "took the last piece of candy, lost clothes, and talked out of turn." She doodled pictures of these creatures in her books—exotic knights fiercely mounted on what look like cats. (In later years, if she was being interviewed by someone whom she believed to be unduly prying about the personal side of her earlier life, she would make a quick and confusing allusion to "my little girl Ringa" to throw them off course.)

Her lively imagination led her to do interesting things. At least once she turned herself, running around her grandmother's garden in Atchison, into a galloping horse—not just any old horse, naturally, but a complicated horse she named Saladin after a favorite character in a Walter Scott novel who liked to assume disguises. She transformed the twin maple trees in the front yard of their Kansas City home into Philemon and Baucis, the couple in Ovid's *Metamorphoses* whom Jupiter, after having promised to keep them together after their death, turned into an oak and a linden tree, with their top branches intertwined. Her moody cat she named Von Sol, after a grouchy German officer in a story she happened to be reading at the time. She called the level area near the barn where they sometimes played croquet Charlie's Park—a play on Charlie Parks's name.

Her friends adored her. Katherine Dolan observed, "We always waited for her to decide what we were going to do." Lucy Challiss would recall, "All I knew was that Amelia was more fun to play with than anyone else—I admired her ability, stood in awe of her information and intelligence, adored her imagination, and loved her for herself—and it held true always."

3
The End of Childhood

•••• To a midwesterner, the laying of the rails across the United States and the formation of the companies that controlled them was the most compelling spectacle of the latter part of the nineteenth century. For a midwestern lawyer to be associated with one of those companies—the Atchison, Topeka and the Santa Fe, the Union Pacific, the Rock Island—was to have achieved success—always on the assumption, however, that the association was at the management level. The best lawyers of the day inevitably became involved with the railroads. So it was with Judge Otis: he and his brothers and his associates were intimately part of this powerful new corporate world. Alfred's brother Charles had set the railroad rates for the state of Minnesota, while his partner George Glick was a director of the Union Pacific.

Edwin Earhart was a railroad lawyer, but his job was too inconsequential to count—he was a claims agent, the lowest rung on the ladder. Even Edwin's brother-in-law Clarence Balis, Margaret's husband, whom everyone agreed was an unusually gentle, tolerant man, rarely judgmental, referred to Edwin as "a claims chaser" and did so in such a cutting tone that his children never forgot it because the way he said it made it "the worst thing Clarence Balis was ever heard to say about any man."

Casting Edwin's situation in an even worse light, the two Atchison men of his age, close friends of Amy's since childhood, Mary Ann's son James Challiss, Katch and Lucy's father, and Senator Ingalls's son, Sheffield, brother of Amy's friend Constance, both lawyers, were partners in an Atchison firm and shared a good, solid practice. Edwin had started out at about the same time as they, and if he had been of a different mettle, he might have — should have — been their law partner, for a bright, steady son-in-law of Alfred Otis would have been a perfect addition to the firm; in glaring contrast there Edwin was, struggling in Kansas City.

Not that Edwin didn't get along with James and Sheffield; he *did* have a relationship with the two men, but it was a social and drinking relationship. Sheffield and James enjoyed his convivial nature, his storytelling ability, and most particularly his appetite for alcohol. When Edwin visited Atchison, the three men would retire to the Challisses' basement, drink bathtub gin, and trade tall tales. Edwin was at his best at those times, the Challiss women remembered ruefully.

All of which made him less and less popular with Rilla Challiss, James's wife, who from the beginning had taken a dim view of him. She conceded he was handsome, she was aware he was bright and had done well at school, she even understood how Amy had fallen in love with him — but from the first moment she had known about it, she had thought the marriage unwise. For her, and for everyone except Alfred, it was a matter of character. The swings in his moods were too much even for the children. "I didn't like him," Katch recalled.

And though he was charming even at the best of times, there was a dark side to his character. After all, what manner of man would use as a nickname for a severely pigeon-toed daughter "Pidge," as he did Muriel? And force her not only to accept but to like it.

A generous, creative, impulsive man, bright enough to go through Thiel College on scholarship, industrious enough to tutor his fellow law students while still a student himself, he was temperamentally unsuited for the law, and once out of school, he never really applied himself.

Even worse, he was extravagant — money ran through his hands like water. In spite of the fact that the Otises had given Amy the house on Ann Street free and clear, that they were paying for Amelia's education at College Preparatory School, leaving Edwin only the expense of Amy and Muriel (whom Amy was tutoring at home) — in spite of the fact that her parents continually gave Amy pocket money, still Edwin couldn't make ends meet. By 1903 his law practice was going so badly, he literally ran out money. If his heart had been in the law, he would have redoubled his efforts to succeed at it. Instead, clever with his hands and imaginative, he threw his energies into being an inventor, and dreamer that he was, he was already counting on the money he would make as he worked at his invention.

Significantly, it was not Edwin bent over law books spread out on the dining-room table but Edwin intently bent over wires and wood and pieces of metal that Muriel would remember—and even more significantly, she would remember with such clarity across the years those times he was tinkering because when so occupied, he was always in a wonderful mood—which made them for her "the happiest of times."

Edwin eventually designed a flag holder to hold the signal flags that always flew from the last car, the caboose, of a railroad train. He planned to patent the flag holder and then sell it, and he was so sure he would make a fortune that he poured every cent he could lay his hands on into the project—and still he needed more money, so he sold the valuable law books Alfred had given him. Then he dipped into the money Amy had given him to pay the property taxes due on their house (undoubtedly given her by her parents).

He finally went to Washington, D.C., in May 1903 with the completed models of the flag—only to discover that such a device had been patented two years previously. He was devastated, as he wrote Amy from Washington. "This news is a terrible blow, because I had been counting on receiving several hundred dollars from the railroad for my flag holder. However, spilled milk and out-dated patents are two things equally useless, so I shall catch the late train tomorrow. Give love to our small daughters, and much to your own sweet self."

The letter, which he signed, "Ever thine Edwin," was charming, but when the tax collector came to the house with a delinquent tax notice, secure, innocent Amy was stunned. Then, because in a small professional community it is natural for gossip to get about, Alfred found out that Edwin had sold the law books he had given to him. And so now not just Amy but her parents and anyone else who was interested knew how bad a provider he was.

• • • •

The next summer, 1904, was the St. Louis World's Fair. It was the miracle of its time, a magnificent spectacle that provided a glimpse of the future by showcasing the possibilities of steam power and electric light. Edwin, in spite of his precarious financial situation, was one of the thousands who couldn't stay away. He had received a hundred dollars for legal work; he used it to take Muriel, Amelia, and Amy to St. Louis, a trip they would never forget. He had a wonderful time. He rode on an elephant and on the Ferris wheel, taking only Amelia with him. Since Edwin apparently could do no wrong in her eyes, Amy, not only the first woman to ascend Pikes Peak but a fearless horsewoman, stood, seemingly contented, and watched, with four-year-old Muriel at her side. It was at the fair that Amelia, seven, became so mesmerized by the roller-coaster ride that she later constructed her own.

To escape the worst heat of the summer, it was the pattern for midwestern families that could afford it to escape to the cooler lake areas to the north. The Earharts managed to do this for the years 1907 to 1911. They went to a vacation spot in Worthington, in southwestern Minnesota, a small farming community on the shores of Lake Okabena. There, periodically joined by various Challiss and Park children, and by Amy's brother Carl Otis and his wife, they took rooms at a farm home on the lake belonging to Clinton Mann and took their meals at Mrs. Twitchell's boarding house nearby. Amelia and Muriel became friends with the Mann daughters; at both places they were made to feel part of a great extended family. They loved it.

Amelia had always been wild about horses, even to the point, as she admitted later, of being "obsessed" with the idea of riding. But the only riding she had succeeded in doing had been in Atchison on the back of the butcher's draft horses.

In Worthington, for the first time, Amelia could ride to her fill on Prince, a twelve-year-old Indian pony owned by the Manns, who although small made up in spirit what he lacked in size. She and Muriel rode bareback because there was no saddle, and "half the time my sister's and my riding consisted of walking home," recalled Amelia—just the kind of challenge she thrived on. "He could be bribed by cookies to do almost anything," wrote Amelia. According to Lucy Challiss, the cookies were very special, one might almost say Amelia-special creations; Lucy called them horse pies. The bottom layer was composed of "the tenderest of grass," covered by a layer of Mrs. Twitchell's sugar cookies, covered by a layer of clover leaves, on top of which reposed Prince's name spelled out in mulberries.

The girls helped out on the Mann farm with the haying, and milked the cows, and on some tennis court in Worthington—whose is unknown—Amelia learned to play tennis. And they swam out to the raft in the lake. Nearby there was a pasture in which lay the bleached bones of three cows that had died in a blizzard. Amelia, fascinated, spent hours trying to sort out the bones to form one complete skeleton—so many hours that the locals took to calling her Dr. Bones. It was there in Worthington that Amelia also had her first ride in a car. The occasion was a picnic, and the twenty-mile ride to the picnic site in the Mann car, a Reo, with the Mann daughters, took almost two hours.

Edwin joined the family when he could, and then his favorite pursuit was to take Amelia and Muriel lake fishing for bass, pickerel, and sunfish. It was a seemingly happy time for Edwin, too, who kept writing letters as he traveled about the country. One letter to Muriel, dated August 1909 on "official" Rock Island Line stationery, possibly written while in his private railroad car, certainly written when he was in an expansive frame of mind, survives. "Dear Madam: I have your claim for $5.00 for having been bitten by a mosquito on our train. Before we can pay the same, we would, at least, like to know how big a bite the mosquito took and we would like to see the mosquito."

• • • •

In 1908 Edwin was offered and accepted a job as a claims agent with the Chicago, Rock Island and Pacific Line (commonly known as the Rock Island), where Amy's brother Carl also worked, but it was contingent on moving to Des Moines, Iowa. Moving would mean changes for all of them, particularly Amelia because for her it would be the end of living with her grandparents, the end of living in a town where she knew everybody and everybody knew her, the end of College Preparatory School, and separation from her friends.

It was difficult for Amelia Otis as well. She missed her "Millie" and began to fill in the lonely hours with visits from her other relations; Orpha Tonsing, particularly, noticed that after "Millie" Earhart left, invitations to dine with Millie Otis in the state dining room came with greater frequency.

That last Christmas at North Terrace with her grandparents was ringed with sweet nostalgia for Amelia. All the wonderful presents and the excitement and the sense of place that comes with being part of a close, loving circle of friends and relatives would all be gone within a few years. From a childhood spent with caring parents and grandparents, in comfort, surrounded by friends, all wants fulfilled, they would be plunged into the dismal ranks of broken homes and poverty. Des Moines marked the beginning of the end of Amelia's childhood.

The first house they lived in, in Des Moines turned out to be just the first of many; Amy, steady mother that she was, blunted the blows, but the fact was that in the four years they were in Des Moines, they lived in four houses. They started out at 1443 Eighth Street in 1909, then moved down the street to 1530 Eighth Street in 1910, to 4201 University Avenue in 1911, and finally to fashionable Cottage Grove in 1912. Each was nicer than the last—they moved up as Edwin's financial situation improved—but the constant movement was unsettling.

Edwin in those first years in Des Moines was still, when he was around, a wonderful father. On Saturday afternoons he would organize the neighborhood children into a game of cowboys and Indians, with himself as Chief Indian. Amelia loved those games and would never forget how once her father had become so excited that he had even bruised himself. "He bore on his nose the marks of one raid, after some chasee, during the heat of the battle, had tried to push shut the sliding door to the hayloft just as the Chief Indian had poked his head through the opening."

Other times Edwin took his girls fishing, as he had in Worthington, only now they caught perch and catfish in the Des Moines River.

Within a year Edwin was in charge of the Rock Island claims department, and as a result there came "an end to the pinchpenny days of waiting for small legal fees to be paid."

Because of the nature of Edwin's work, traveling by railroad had always been a free perk for the Earhart family. As a result, as Amelia remembered fondly, she never paid for a train ticket until she was sixteen and looked forward to "the joyful interruptions" when Edwin "used to pack the family off when he made a trip of any consequence"—at least once taking them as far as California. For now that he was more important, Edwin rated the use of a private railway car equipped with its own kitchen, dining facilities, and Tokimo, a "superb" Japanese majordomo. It was truly a mark of privilege. "Bring the girls and Sadie [the maid] and meet me at . . . ," he would wire Amy. The Ozarks were one part of the country they saw in such luxury. Since Edwin was so genuinely fond of Amelia and Muriel and wanted them to be happy, on some trips, Amelia remembered, they were even allowed to invite friends to travel and dine with them.

Once the private car and Tokimo were put solely at the disposition of Amy, Amelia, and Muriel. They traveled in it to Atchison, picked up Katch and Lucy Challiss and Ginger and Ann Park, whisked them back up north to Des Moines for a visit of a few days, and then Amy and the three sets of sisters in the private car continued north all the way to Worthington, Minnesota. Each leg involved an overnight in berths made up by Tokimo and meals he cooked. It was a grand adventure for the girls.

After his years of snubs at the hands of the Otises, Edwin had the exquisite pleasure of showing off his new status by taking Amy and his girls to visit his in-laws in Atchison in the private car. During their stay he invited the Judge and Mrs. Otis to dine with them, and Tokimo cooked and served a sumptuous dinner that included lamb chops and charlotte russe. Muriel was so proud and so impressed, she never forgot it.

Edwin's new affluence enabled Amy to hire a cook as well as a maid. In a move that matched his father-in-law, Edwin became a warden of his church. Their final move in Des Moines was into an impressively large classic American "foursquare" house—a style fashionable at the time—one block from Drake University, at 3002 Cottage Grove Avenue. It was a definite step up. The Cottage Grove area was "the" place to live. It was an enclave of stimulating people, active in their community, and successful in their professions, including bank presidents, judges, lawyers, doctors, newspaper editors, businessmen, and various educators associated with Drake University. The same year the Earharts moved to Cottage Grove, the governor of Iowa, Beryll Carroll, whose term had just ended, also moved into the neighborhood.

One of the house moves in Des Moines precipitated the first recorded instance of Amelia's penchant for climbing. In the midst of a move Von Sol, Amelia's moody gray-and-white cat, wandered off just as they were taking the last load; they departed without him. Later, under cover of darkness, Amelia, equipped with a gunny sack, and accompanied by Muriel, sneaked back to their old house. They found Von Sol, but when they tried to stuff him into the sack, he jumped up into a birch tree near the house. Amelia shinnied up the porch post, climbed onto the roof of the house, crawled to the edge and into the tree, finally got Von Sol into the sack, and hauled the cat home.

Both Edwin and Amelia had considerable musical talent, and at some point they had acquired a piano, which both enjoyed playing. Now the Earharts could afford season subscriptions to the concert series sponsored by the Drake Conservatory of Music, which regularly attracted such luminaries as Fritz Kreisler, Madame Ernestine Schumann-Heink, and Alma Gluck. The concerts, held in the evening, were a big family event. Amelia and Muriel in the wintertime went dressed up in high-necked silk party dresses and gaiters, and in summertime in white dotted Swiss with pink or blue sashes and shoes that had to be buttoned with a button hook. Amy wore formal silk dresses with a "sweep" of skirt, long white kid gloves that were buttoned with a silver glove hook, a sealskin coat, and her grandmother Maria Harres's round fur muff. Edwin too got all dressed up for the concerts; he wore a white shirt with a stiff white collar, Prince Albert coat, and gray pants. Amelia had developed quite sophisticated tastes in music—she liked the German composers, particularly Wagner, and "certain" of the Italian operas (although sometimes she was put off because the words were "so silly"). Now, after the concerts, she and Edwin would sit at the piano, playing by ear what they had heard.

It was a time of pleasant social contacts, and living so near Drake, many of their new friends were associated with the university. The Earharts were included in a group of seven neighborhood families that pooled magazine subscriptions, so their horizons broadened as they kept up with the world and their neighbors reading *Scribner's, The Atlantic Monthly,* and *The Century.* Amy took Amelia and Muriel to art exhibits at the college. With it all, Amelia kept up with happenings in Atchison through her correspondence with Virginia Park and Lucy and Katch, all of whom came for visits.

And then suddenly the wonderful, protected world of childhood that had enwrapped Amelia and Muriel like a cocoon was gone. Edwin changed—and the change broke their world apart.

Edwin had never had the discipline to see the world as it was, only as he wanted it to be. Now, so close to real success, he still could not. His spendthrift carelessness had simply moved to a higher level. He had the tastelessness to give Amy an expensive set of Kipling's works, upon which he had paid only the first installment—expecting her, as she found out only later, to pay for the subsequent installments, which were considerable. Amy tried to make light of it to Amelia and Muriel, who inevitably found out. Eventually Amy forgave Edwin, as she always forgave him no matter what he did.

But in 1911, their last summer at the lake, things started to go seriously wrong between Edwin and Amy. Undoubtedly for Edwin it had been building for a long time, but because he spent so much time traveling, the extent of his unhappy relationship with Amy didn't show. What was becoming evident was that he was drinking heavily. He decided the time had come to leave Amy. He gathered his belongings and left for good.

Muriel, eleven, never even realized what had happened. Amy could easily explain his absence as another long business trip—a not-unusual occurrence, in fact the norm for Edwin. Amelia undoubtedly knew—being fourteen at the time, it would have been exceedingly hard for Amy to have fooled her, particularly since Amelia was such an aware child and Amy was so devastated. She "wrote him the most hysterical appeals to return," according to her brother Mark, to whom Edwin sent one of her letters, probably because he was worried about Amy and wanted Mark to make sure she was all right. Totally distraught, Amy told her parents.

Finally Edwin changed his mind and returned—undoubtedly under duress—but when he did, he was still drinking heavily. It unnerved Amy, and inevitably, she again confided in her parents.

Now the Otises' worst nightmares had come true—they were faced with a son-in-law who, they were sure, did not love their daughter, who drank. In their eyes a reconciliation was to be avoided at all costs. They went so far as to dangle financial incentives in front of Amy if she would agree to a separation, according to Mark, but "although Mother offered to make suitable provision for her and the children, she would have none of it."

Amy could have divorced Edwin. Under Iowa law at the time, women had unusually strong rights: a married woman controlled her property as if she were single; neither husband nor wife were liable for what were clearly the debts of the other—and even more to the point, habitual drunkenness was considered sufficient grounds to terminate a marriage. She could easily have fulfilled the residence requirement, which was just one year, and she would have had no problem proving Edwin's drunkenness.

But from Amy's point of view, divorce was not an option; she wanted above all to keep the family together, and the mores of the time reinforced her. Divorce was so seriously frowned upon in the genteel Atchison society where Amy had grown up that, as *Atchison Globe* publisher Ed Howe succinctly put it, "It is a great deal more satisfactory and respectable to bury a husband than to get a divorce from one." Her parents, on the other hand, were beyond caring about such niceties—they were more concerned with what would happen to Amy after they died. Their apprehensions took an obvious turn—they changed their wills.

When they had first made their wills years before, Amelia and Alfred Otis had divided everything equally among their children, although they had put Theodore's share in trust. Now, on October 14, 1911, with their servants Charlie Parks and Mary Brashay as witnesses, Amelia Otis, seventy-four years old, having heart spells from which she would die in a few months, and Alfred, eighty-four, each in identical language, added a codicil that demoted Amy to the status of her retarded brother Theodore—Theodore, whom Mary Brashay cared for—Theodore, who sat all day in Atchison next to his derelict old horse and spring wagon that had "Lightning Express" painted on the side. Mark and Margaret would receive their inheritance outright, but Theodore's share, and now Amy's, were put in trust for fifteen years. For those fifteen years, the wills gave the designated trustee absolute control, and the trustee was Mark. If Mark failed to qualify as trustee, Margaret was designated to take his place.

It is doubtful that Mark or Amy or Margaret had any idea of what was in store for them.

• • • •

As 1911 drew to a close, Amelia Otis lay dying; Amy and Margaret were in attendance. On December 23, too weak to write, she dictated a letter to Alfred's younger brother Charles telling him how she had treasured his help following Alfred's breakdown. "What you have been to me all these years all of the sad years especially no one will ever know—both friend and brother. And I want you to know before I go away just how much I think of you. Ever since you came into my life when you were only a boy. We have been together but little in person, but in heart, I am sure we have been much with each other. May you and yours always be blessed as you deserve is the prayer of Your loving sister Millie."

Shortly after Amelia Otis's death, the terms of her will became known to the family, and because she was such an illustrious citizen of Atchison, on February 24, the same day the will was filed, it became common knowledge all over town—*The Atchison Globe* printed the terms in great detail on the front page, so everyone got to read that "the deceased bequeathed to her children share and share alike her interest in the Otis Real Estate Co. The children are Mark E. Otis, Margaret Balis, Amy O. Earhart and Theodore H. Otis. The shares of the last two named children shall be held in trust for them for fifteen years after the death of Amelia Otis and Mark Otis was named as trustee."

The account wasn't totally accurate, but it was close enough: Amelia left half to her children—she left the other half to Alfred. The estate consisted of real estate in Atchison, Kansas City, Kansas, and Philadelphia valued at $65,730; stocks and bonds totaling $55,880; and over $50,000 in mortgage loans. It was a great deal of money in those days, and in the form she left it, most of it actually consisted of shares of the Otis Real Estate Company.

Mark, a year younger than Amy, had worked most of his life for his father as secretary-treasurer of the Dayton-Otis Grain Company, then as secretary-treasurer of the Chicago office of the Otis Real Estate Company; Alfred was always president. Alfred had finally put Mark in control, but only because he had to—William was dead, Carl was dead, Mark was the last one left. Certainly if Alfred had trusted Mark's judgment, he would have turned over the reins of his businesses to him years before, but he avoided it until, at eighty-four, he had no other choice.

Amy liked Mark, although as she would later make plain, she didn't respect his business sense any more than Alfred did, and she certainly didn't think he was competent to be trustee of her money. Treading carefully, she enlisted Margaret on her side (who, shocked, had refused to qualify as her sister's trustee) and, with her uncle Ephraim Otis advising her, within thirty days forced Mark's resignation as trustee in favor of the Northern Trust Company, a well-known, well-respected Chicago investment firm that specialized in trust estates. Ephraim even agreed to witness the legal document drawn up between his nephew and niece that effected the change.

In spite of the furor the codicil caused, life went on much as before. Amy and Margaret and Mark weighed possible alternatives for their increasingly infirm father and finally decided that he should remain exactly where he was, in familiar surroundings, cared for by the faithful Charlie Parks and Mary Brashay, who had been caring for him for years. Alfred's nephew James Challiss and his wife Rilla, who lived next door, could also keep an eye on him there.

Alfred at eighty-four was still alert, but his will to live had weakened. There was no shattering decline. One day at the beginning of May, he felt well enough to go into town, accompanied by Charlie Parks, to have a shave at the barber shop and then to inspect a portion of riverbank the town was fixing up. On the first Sunday in May, he attended services at Trinity Church, walking the six blocks to and fro. On Monday evening, according to the *Globe,* "he sat on the porch of his home and talked to Mrs. J.M. [Rilla] Challiss." The next morning he was found dead in his bed.

The *Globe* estimated his fortune at more than $200,000 and noted the buildings he owned on the main town thoroughfare, Commercial Street.

The funeral, at Trinity Episcopal Church, was notable for the family members who attended and for those who did not. Alfred's brother Charles came from St. Paul; Mark, with his wife Isabel, came from Chicago; Carl's widow Anna arrived from Kansas City; Amy arrived from Des Moines. Margaret, delayed by a sick child, came from Philadelphia. But not surprisingly, Edwin stayed away.

On May 11, Alfred's will was filed for probate. In spite of the bitter protestations Amy must have made to her father regarding the codicil in Amelia's will, in spite of the fact that Alfred knew Mark had been replaced as trustee because he also had signed the document appointing the Northern Trust Company trustee in Mark's place, the identical wording that his wife had put in her will was also in his will. Alfred had taken his feelings about Edwin with him to the grave.

Again the public read all about the humiliating blow, for again *The Atchison Globe* published the terms for everyone to read and ponder: "The entire estate was bequeathed to the four children, share and share alike. The children are Mark E. Otis, Amy O. Earhart, Theodore H. Otis, and Margaret Balis. The will provides that Mark E. Otis act as executor of the estate, also as trustee of the shares bequeathed to Amy O. Earhart and Theodore Otis for a period of fifteen years after the death of Judge Otis."

Amy wasted no time. That same day a lengthy document was filed on her behalf in the Atchison County courthouse, in which Margaret and Mark again declined to act as Amy's trustee and again the Northern Trust Company was designated in their place. By the end of June, the Northern Trust Company was trustee of this inheritance also. But there was a price that Amy had to pay—she had to agree to make Mark no further trouble "And the said Amy O. Earhart agrees that she will make no objection contest or controversy whatsoever over the provisions of said will or the execution thereof."

The terms of the wills dealt the Earharts a stunning blow. There was no doubt that the change was directed at and had been caused by Edwin, no doubt that it publicly branded Edwin a ne'er-do-well, no doubt that it was a clear vote of no confidence in Amy. No matter what Edwin did, no matter what Amy did, there was no way for them to escape from this humiliating public condemnation of their character.

Up until now, Edwin had been able to hold himself together and hide his drinking from most people. Now the last vestiges of self-control went; he became a bitter, angry, sullen drunk, too far gone to have any regard for the proprieties. Not only did he drink in private, now he stumbled his way home for all the world to see.

The Prohibitionist sentiment erupting throughout the United States would culminate, in 1919, in the passage of the Volstead Act, the eighteenth amendment to the Constitution. Iowa was historically a strongly Prohibitionist state; since the 1880s laws had been on the books banning the manufacture and sale of alcoholic beverages. Unfortunately for Edwin, Cottage Grove was the center of the state's Prohibitionist activity; many of Cottage Grove's most prominent residents—university officials, church leaders, politicians "of all stripes"—were actively involved in the movement. It made Edwin's drinking particularly unforgivable. Muriel, many years later, would write, "All the old bitterness toward Mother's family was accentuated, as Dad alternately brooded and raged. . . . He seemed to drink now with a distorted idea of punishing Mother because of Grandmother's canny intuition, which made her regard the establishing of a trust fund for Mother as a safeguard, while he looked on it as an insult."

The scene of Amelia's great pleasure, the Saturday cowboy-and-Indians game, provided the denouement. It was a spectacular fall from grace that took them all down—a major public humiliation. Assembled were Amelia and Muriel and a group of their friends from the neighborhood. All were waiting on a Saturday afternoon for the beginning of the game, all were gathered in front of the house, killing time till Edwin came home. And then they saw him getting off the streetcar and raced to meet him. And saw that he was walking slowly, placing one foot carefully in front of the other, as if to keep from stumbling. He told them he couldn't play because he didn't feel well, walked past them, lurched up the steps. Amy opened the door with a smiling face. "Your Indian clothes are upstairs, Edwin," she said, then looking at him, her face changed, her smile froze. She helped him over the threshold, then firmly shut the door. Ten children plus two daughters—Amelia and Muriel stood exposed to the shock and horror in public, in front of their peers, each of whom, knowing the ugly truth, would relay it back to their families.

Edwin did public penance, appearing, for a change, in church the next day. Privately he promised it wouldn't happen again. And because they wanted to so much, at first they believed him. But his drinking grew worse. His work became so erratic that a supervisor came from Chicago, caught Edwin drinking in his office, replaced him (temporarily, he said), and sent him to a hospital that specialized in alcoholism. He stayed a month, and when he came home he was, they all hoped, cured.

As a welcome when he came back from the hospital, Amy bought him a carpenter's bench and a set of tools for metal and woodworking. (She, as well as Muriel, must have been impressed with Edwin's energy and happy state of mind when he had been working on his invention all those years before.) Amelia and Muriel, with three dollars they had earned picking cherries, purchased a jointed fishing rod with a reel on the handle. The homecoming scene, as remembered by Muriel, was poignant: "It was our 'old' Dad, bright-eyed and buoyant, who came up the porch steps two by two at a time to seize Mother around the waist and waltz her joyously a few steps down the front hall while Amelia and I laughed and applauded until we came in for our share of hugging."

It didn't last. No business would hire him, and given his history, it was not surprising. Indeed, one of his job-seeking letters reveals just how close he was to his next drink, for he saw his alcoholism as a function of his surroundings rather than of his own mind, and thus he wrote, rather ingenuously, to one possible employer (italics mine): "I am now safe in saying that I am free from this unfortunate habit, not unqualifiedly or absolutely, but I have been burned and suffered so much from it that I am safe in saying that I am safely and surely beyond any future danger. *Of course environment and associates have and did have everything to do with my difficulties, but in Omaha I would have a clean slate.* I make you the promise that there will be absolutely no offence or reproach as to my ever taking a drink while in your service. If upon any reliable authority you should hear of it, I will leave your office without delay, feeling myself wholly disgraced. This will enable me to walk the straight and narrow path and do a good job for you and the railroad."

Before long, according to Muriel, Edwin was again "drinking a little at a time."

In spite of the document Amy had signed agreeing not to contest the wills, she inevitably became embroiled in a fight with Mark, for upon going over the list of properties of the Otis Real Estate Company that he had given to the Northern Trust Company, she found what she was sure were serious discrepancies. She wanted an independent inventory.

Amy was a decent, moral person herself, and she believed her brother was "cut from the same cloth" as she was. She thought of him in terms of having poor business judgment (she and her mother had been of the same mind about that) and of keeping sloppy records—and she feared she was being shortchanged through his incompetence. She didn't actually suspect Mark of deliberate wrongdoing.

To challenge the company records, Amy needed help. She turned first to Margaret, but Margaret and Mark were still close. Margaret had named one of her sons after Mark, and he had more than once appeared at the Balis home in Germantown, Pennsylvania, and swept her three boys off for a weekend in Atlantic City—which the boys adored and in which the two girls hungered to be included. To Margaret, who believed that Mark was carefully preserving her inheritance—*her* 249 shares in the Otis Real Estate Company—Amy's demanding an inventory seemed like an act of war. The sisters became estranged.

Next, Amy turned to her Uncle Charles, whom she had met for the first time when he came to Atchison for Alfred's funeral. As happens sometimes at funerals, there had been a reestablishment of family ties. Charles had been terribly moved by Amelia Otis's deathbed letter to him, which she had dictated to Margaret.

Amy, particularly, had felt she had lost a father but gained an uncle; her feelings were reciprocated by Charles. Scarcely was he back in St. Paul after the funeral when he had written to Amy, "We did have such a delightful visit together in Atchison and I hope we will continue to keep in touch with each other as we have not properly done in the past."

So now Amy decided to write Charles to see if he would help her. In her letter she laid out the sorry state of her affairs—how the enmity between her husband and her brother was making it impossible for her to get an inventory of her inheritance.

> I cannot depend on my husband's opinions in this matter as the
> feeling between Mark and himself is so bitter that an unbiased
> opinion would be impossible while when I ventured to ask Mark
> for explanations of certain things, he immediately felt that I had
> been incited to ask by my husband, and has been suspicious and
> angry ever since.

She assured Charles that she had no intention of breaking her mother's will. She also explained that although Mark blamed her for an atmosphere of "seeming distrust" of his business abilities, that opinion existed in Atchison independent of her. The letter was long and well thought out, and her request was eminently reasonable. She was, after all, asking that "discrepancies" in Mark's listings be investigated. Whether or not Charles thought she had a case, he was a good uncle and a careful corporate lawyer, and he would have seen an inventory as an eminently reasonable request—one that, once carried out, might settle the troubled waters in the family.

But Amy made what turned out to be a mistake of incredible consequence: she had Edwin deliver the letter personally to Charles in St. Paul. Apparently Edwin fortified himself with drink for the encounter and threatened Charles with the specter of a lawsuit, for in her next letter Amy had to apologize for her husband, writing that she would never go into court, "preferring rather to lose every penny than to bring such dishonor upon the family. Mr. Earhart conveyed a very wrong impression if he gave you think otherwise." Again she requested that he simply have someone go over the books with Mark for her.

This letter seems to have done the trick as far as restoring Amy to her uncle's good graces. He unbent to the extent of inviting her to visit and to meet his children, Maribel and Jim, and by March the inventory was done. Amy wrote him a long letter, full of appreciation and love:

> I know truly all you have done for me you have done for father's
> and her dear sake. Thank you very much for your kind offer to
> have your door open to me wherever you are, and I can think of
> no place now where I would more gladly go for advice comfort
> or anything else.

"Plain, modest, and self assuming" were contemporary descriptions of Charles. It was also written of him, "His pure and innate integrity dominates his conduct, both in public and private life." Charles had at various times been a member of the St. Paul common council, the school board, and the city library board, as well as district judge and president of the Minnesota Bar Association. He was widely respected for his work as special master in chancery in the Minnesota Railroad Rate cases in 1910. When he returned to private practice, he had taken in his son James as his partner. He was a careful man, and his word was law. He was undoubtedly gratified when the inventory revealed that all Mark's accounts were in order. Amy accepted the result unquestioningly, and she wrote that she was happy that Mark was proving to be equal to the trust placed in him.

But following the law of unintended consequences, the immediate result of Amy's request for an inventory was that Mark became closer to his uncle—for after the inventory Mark was vetted, so to speak, and for the foreseeable future, Charles would rely on his nephew for information and family news and accept as fact whatever Mark told him.

In March 1913, life in the Earhart household went on as before. Amy could still complain about "the combination of a sick maid and company" that made her life difficult. But Edwin hadn't worked since the previous fall—her money was starting to run out. Again she began casting around for help.

Mark, in a preemptive strike, went on the attack to discredit her with Charles. He explained that Amy shouldn't be having money problems, that she had received $3,000 from the sale of her house, that she was receiving the interest on $14,750 "in addition to her first of dividend of $500 which was paid her direct" (the interest on the $14,750 was paid by the Northern Trust Company), and further, that he was about to declare a dividend that would give her more. But given Mark's propensity to lie about financial affairs, it is doubtful that Amy was getting even half the amount he said. Certainly it wasn't true that she had sold the house on Ann Street; it remained hers at least through 1916, as is evident in the papers she filed in the Kansas court that year. The fact was that by summertime Amy was absolutely broke, but Charles, viewing her situation through the lens provided by Mark, saw what appeared to be merely a silly, improvident woman.

Mark couldn't afford to have Charles think ill of him—he needed to shore up his business reputation with his illustrious uncle. He sent Charles a glowing letter from his "good" sister, Margaret. "I have just received and answered the enclosed letter from Margaret," he wrote Charles. "While the same is on the order of an 'unsolicited testimonial' as we refer to it in the fountain business, still I want you to see it as it shows her attitude regarding the Otis Realty Company and my management of it." Mark couldn't bear the fact that as a result of Amy's demand for an inventory—combined with the fact that the Northern Trust Company was keeping tabs from that moment forward—she had put the money her property represented beyond his reach. He wanted it to spend, as he was spending Margaret's funds.

Mark had always had very grand, expensive tastes. Amelia referred to him as "The Magnificent." Since he had married in 1910, his tastes had become even grander. He had led everyone to believe that his wife Isabel was "very wealthy" and the source of much of his opulent lifestyle, which was on a scale far beyond the rest of the family—its most visible sign the chauffeured Rolls-Royce he always appeared in for his visits. It was Amy who correctly assessed her brother, although not even she plumbed the depths of his duplicity. As Margaret would learn to her grief when Mark died, of all the Otis holdings their father had built up with such care, nothing was left—in five years Mark had dissipated it all—all, that is, except Amy's portion, which had been watched over by the Northern Trust Company. Mark had spent on himself or lost on unwise investments Margaret's whole inheritance; she would remember his Rolls with bitterness.

But that was still four years in the future. In the meantime, in 1913, foiled by Amy in his attempt to get his hands on all the family funds and forced to defend his business reputation with his uncle because of her actions, he struck back at her. He proceeded to destroy her reputation and her relationship with Charles. Diligently he did everything he could to cast Amy in a bad light, always at the same time painting himself as the generous, tolerant brother. It wasn't that hard: she *was* married to an alcoholic, Edwin *did* squander her money, and she wasn't, to begin with, a very good manager.

That summer Edwin was offered a job as a clerk with the Great Northern Railway in St. Paul, Minnesota. It wasn't a great offer, but he was in no position to turn it down, and St. Paul seemed the perfect place to start over, because Charles lived there and Amy was sure he would help her, and because Amy knew from her family history that the Otis name was, if anything, more highly regarded there than in Atchison.

There had been an Otis law firm in existence in St. Paul since 1857. The first to move there had been George, the closest in age to her father, in his day the most respected railroad lawyer in Minnesota, who had been a member of the state legislature, the Democratic candidate for governor, and mayor of St. Paul. Then there was his brother Ephraim (Amy's Uncle Eph), his law partner until the Civil War. George next had taken in brother Charles, who had moved to St. Paul to study law under him. When George died, Charles, following the tradition established by George, had taken in his youngest brother, Arthur, as partner. Ephraim was in Chicago and Arthur had left for Grand Rapids, but Charles, Amy's helpful and affectionate Uncle Charles, the most important uncle of all, was in St. Paul and still practicing law—a pillar of his church, a pillar of society and, she hoped, a helping hand for her.

And so suddenly Edwin and Amy and Amelia and Muriel moved to St. Paul. It was only a menial job—clerk in the railway office—but Edwin hadn't worked for almost a year. In the fall of 1913 they moved.

Their journey was most inauspicious; it was more of a flight than a move and was undoubtedly so disorganized because of Amy's distraught frame of mind. Instead of informing her "Dear Uncle Charlie" that they were even thinking of moving to St. Paul, much less consulting him as to where to live, she simply literally arrived on his doorstep. He learned of her move to St. Paul only when she asked him to endorse the check to the movers.

Amy wrote Mark to tell him about their move, and unaware of his true character, told him how desperate their situation was.

September 3 1913

Dear Mark;

You will be surprised perhaps to hear from me at the above address and still more so perhaps to know unless Uncle Charlie to whom I had to go to endorse a check in connection with the moving expenses has written you that I have moved here. Something however had to be done as I was nearing the end of my resources and had to get somewhere where I might partly support the girls and myself.

I have tried to rent rooms as I had all my furniture which I did not want to give away, but have been unsuccessful so far as I dare not try to board people, fearing both the expense and the strength required to cook for boarders so today I have inserted an ad to take charge of two or three girls during the school year or longer promising careful motherly care, and hope I may be able to get an answer as I feel sure I can bring up and care for children properly though my own girls, owing to the great strain and anxiety of the last year are not so well and strong as they used to be, and Muriel frightened me somewhat a couple of weeks ago by fainting dead away and in falling struck her head against a table, which gave her such a headache she had to stay in bed for a couple of days. They are both in the High School, taking the teachers course and Millie hopes to finish next year.

Mark promptly sent this heartbreaking letter on to their Uncle Charles, at the same time cleverly blunting its impact by enclosing an explanatory letter of his own, in which he listed the funds Amy had so far received and informed his uncle "this will be supplemented by at least $2000 more between this [September 9] and October 1st"—funds that Amy undoubtedly never received. That letter, however, was merely a warm-up for his next letter to Charles. A week later, feeling on firmer ground, evidently emboldened by a letter he had received from his uncle, he carefully, nastily, and with surgical skill cut the ground out from under his sister:

> Now, about Amy, pray dismiss any qualms you may have about your
> inattention to her; the mere fact of her taking up her residence
> in St. Paul imposes no social obligation upon you or Maribel and
> Amy has long since shown a marked preference to associating with
> E. and his ilk to any of her own family.
>
> As a matter of fact Amy is less deserving of my assistance than
> most anyone I know; however, she is my sister and as you say, must
> be treated as a child. Now, what I am willing to do is to advance
> her $100.00 per month for a time (a little more or less as you may
> discover conditions warrant) either from me personally or from The
> Otis Real Estate Co. (the latter preferred) if it can be satisfactorily
> and safely arranged; but from whatever source, it must be simply
> an advance to temporarily tide her over her difficulties.

The next day Mark received a letter from Amy. It frightened him, for in it she took him to task for the hostility he had shown toward her, Amelia, and Muriel. He couldn't send this letter on to Charles as he had done with her others, because of her accusations that he had conducted himself callously and unfeelingly. But if he denied getting the letter, he would undoubtedly eventually be caught out, since he had positioned himself in the role of long-suffering brother in constant correspondence with his sister. He resolved the dilemma by telling Charles that Amy seemed to be in desperate straits and that he had "immediately wired her to see you, as you have full power to act for me."

He took another day to write to his sister, assuring her there was no bitterness in his heart toward her or her children, and that she should go to their Uncle Charles, give him a true statement of all her debts, and figure out how much money she needed to tide her over—which sums would be in the nature of a secured loan.

• • • •

Mark's advice to his uncle not to worry about any "social obligation" to his sister bore bitter, bitter fruit. The result, if he was ever apprised of it, would have warmed Mark's heart. For Charles, a socially retiring person to begin with who had been a widower for fifteen years; for his son, James, ten years younger than Amy, a hard-working young lawyer becoming involved in municipal government, married, with three young children on his hands; and for his daughter Maribel, unmarried, who presided over Charles's house, Mark's advice relieved them of what would have been at best a difficult and probably unhappy situation. If they didn't take the Earharts up, then they wouldn't have to deal with an alcoholic who had brought his family to the verge of destitution. The barest of financial help was the full extent of Charles's aid.

During the long cold Minnesota winters, skating and the sport of curling (a game played on ice between two teams of four players) were the major social pastimes among the nice families in St. Paul. They were carried out at private clubs, but Amy didn't have the money for Amelia and Muriel to join the curling club on Selby Avenue, which under ordinary circumstances they would have joined—the one founded by Charles's father-in-law. No offer of financial help, no kind invitations to join them in club activities were forthcoming from Charles. So Amy, who had thought that as an Otis she would be welcomed in the city where her Uncle George had been mayor and where her "Dear Uncle Charlie" and his children lived, saw her dream shattered. No invitations for Amelia and Muriel to meet St. Paul children were extended by Charles or James or Maribel, no Otis friends called her up. The door that Charles had promised to keep open to Amy "wherever" he was, remained closed, except for the barest crack.

• • • •

Amy and Edwin had chosen for their residence in St. Paul a house at 825 Fairmont Avenue. It was a bad choice—it was so big that heating it required an inordinate amount of coal that they could ill afford, with the result that in winter much of the house was uninhabitable. Since nothing ever came of Amy's ad offering "to take charge of two or three girls during the school year," they rattled around in the large, cold house. To save pennies, Amelia and Muriel shopped for food miles away from their house, sometimes walking to save the bus fare.

Edwin worked fitfully at his menial job of freight clerk, continuing to disappoint his family. His drinking grew worse. At Christmastime Edwin was due home to perform his fatherly duty of escorting Amelia and Muriel to the Christmas party at St. Clement's, the neighborhood Episcopal church that provided the major part of their social life. Both girls very much wanted to go. They each had a date waiting for them at the party, and they had made quite elaborate preparations, both in terms of clothes and in decorating the house, for they expected that the boys would walk them home when the party was over. But Edwin came home hours late, and dead drunk. They missed the party. Forty years later Muriel would still remember the night with bitterness.

Blocked from every other social outlet, the church provided Amelia with friends and activities: she joined the Altar Guild, was a member of the Junior Auxiliary, and sang in the choir. Each Sunday she and Marion Blodgett, a student a year ahead of her at high school who lived a block away on Osceola Avenue, walked to St. Clements together. As members of the Altar Guild, they ran errands, learned how to set the altar for services, and helped wherever they were needed. They polished the silver chalice that held the wine, the paten, upon which the wafers rested, and before Christmas and Easter services, they scrubbed the marble floor between the altar rail and the altar. However, appreciative as Amelia was of the companionship and activity—something she had taken for granted in earlier years—her heart was no more in cleaning up at church than in cleaning up at home. Marion would remember the times when what Amelia had done had to be redone by someone else. Marion would also remember how much Amelia loved singing in the choir, and that the two of them sometimes giggled so loudly they drew a reprimand. It didn't bother either one of them. Marion thought her "lots of fun."

In those areas of her life where she functioned on her own—at school and at church—Amelia's concentration and enthusiasm carried her through. At the St. Paul Central High School she took advantage of the extensive range of courses offered. She took physics, maintaining an 85 grade point average for the year, and she did even better in Latin, achieving an 88 grade point average. She started German, which should have made her father happy, and she did quite well in this course too, in fact achieving her best mark for the year, a grade of 91. She played basketball, making the basketball team, which she enjoyed, writing her Atchison school chum Virginia Park, "You miss much by not having Gym." The letter to Virginia, written in the spring of 1914, as usual replete with arch phrases and spellings, is remarkable for its high spirits and feeling of normalcy:

Blessings on thee, Little Ginger—

How goes everything mit Innen (mit governs the dative). . . .
Of course I am going to B.M. [Bryn Mawr] if I have to drive a

grocery wagon to accumulate the cash. You see I'm practicing growing boy language because if I use up all my money going to grand "Hopery" why—Ill be minus later that's all. I wish you were up her because Parsifal and I don't know what are coming here. I suppose they will be in K.C. I'm all thrills. Did you hear Paderewski. . . . I wonder if he played Chopin Funeral March down at St. Joe as he did here. . . .

All the girls are so nice it's a joy to be with them don't you know. I am doing my best to get some of them to go to B.M. with Ginger and Millie.

Your letter was scrummy. So long and joysome. I'll send you the translation of your Cicero. I'm a shark. That Maulian law is the hardest old mess I've had in ages. Your letter was very funny. I lawffed ex'cessively.

Speaking of funny things, my dear freshman of a sister spoke very importantly of "forum" in their class meeting (All those lambs attend their meeting religiously) completely mystifying the family until mother had the happy thot she meant quorum. . . .

It's so hot today I am just baked. I want this reading matter to go off on the next mail so I'll cease.

Love, Mill.

I'll write you a sensible letter someday. You needn't ans. this communication unless you have nothing else to do. All contributions, however, are thankfully received at this end.

Still, in spite of the brave front, the anguish of her home life made it increasingly hard for Amelia to concentrate, and her marks inched down as the school year progressed. Her 91 grade point average in the first term slipped to an 85 in the second.

4
Teenage Years

• • • • They left St. Paul as they had come, in disarray. Edwin thought he had found a job in the claims office of the Burlington Railroad in Springfield, Missouri, so they packed up and boarded the train to Springfield *en famille.* Upon arrival Edwin went into the Burlington claims office at the station, to find there had been a terrible mistake; there was no job. They spent that night at a cheap railway boarding house hard by the tracks.

For Amy this was the last straw. The stress of the year in St. Paul had been enormous; she was so exhausted and nervous that the slightest noise made her jump, and several times she had shivering fits during which her legs stopped working. Amelia, on whose shoulders Amy's care had fallen, was so worried, she went to discuss Amy's symptoms with their doctor, who told her that Amy was on the verge of a nervous breakdown and needed rest and quiet. Old friends, the Shedds, had previously offered to take them in until Edwin could get back on his feet. Before, it hadn't seemed like a reasonable idea because it meant splitting up the family, the thing Amy and Amelia and Muriel dreaded above all else, but now even her daughters could see that Amy needed a change—a respite—so it was agreed: Amy and Amelia and Muriel would go to Chicago to live with the Shedds and then possibly find a modest place of their own; Edwin, alone, would return to the house on Fairmont Street in St. Paul. It was a painful time.

When, as an adult, Amelia spoke of her youth; she drew a curtain around these years so cleverly that in her lifetime no one knew of the trials of the Earharts. She made it sound artless:

> The family rolled around a good deal during my father's railroad years, Kansas City, Des Moines, St. Paul, Chicago—forward and back. What we missed in continuous contacts over a long period, we gained by becoming adapted to new surroundings quickly. I have never lived more than four years in any one place and always have to ask "Which one?" when a stranger greets me by saying "I'm from your home town."

Upon their arrival in Chicago that summer of 1914, they were dutifully taken in hand by the Shedds. But before they really settled in, Amelia, alone, went to visit her cousins, the Challisses, in Atchison. She arrived at the train station, with trunk, on August 6. Returned to home territory, she sank back into Atchison to do as she had done all her life before—returned to her old haunts, picked up with her old friends, fell into her old pastimes. She told no tales of woe, expressed no fear about the future, shed no tears, asked for no sympathy, and none was given. She acted as she always had, played as she always had, gossiped as she always had, and fitted in as before.

Seamlessly she wove herself into the Challiss family. She was treated like a sister by Jack, Tootie, Katch, and the baby, Peggy, and like a daughter by James and Rilla, all of whom immediately involved her in whatever they were doing.

It is from Katch's diary that a record exists of Amelia's visit. It details the lazy relaxed summertime pursuits in the small town. For Katch it was just like old times—the only difference she could see in "Mill," now that she had moved away, was that she seemed "awfully grown up." If there had been any conversation or worries about Amelia's lack of clothes, or clothes that looked threadbare, Katch would have remarked on it. If there had been any "serious" conversations between Rilla and "Millie," as the Challisses called Amelia, Katch would have noticed it. But there was apparently *nothing* out of the ordinary: Amelia just seemed normal to this observant, interested record-keeper who let no change of dress, no change of plans, no expedition go unnoticed.

Rilla and Katch met her at the railroad station, took her home, and installed her in the old nanny's room, and she settled in. As soon as she unpacked her trunk, she went over to see Ginger Park, who being Katch and Lucy's friend also already knew that she was there. Another friend of her cousins and an old friend of hers, Katherine Dolan (known to one and all as Dolan) gave an afternoon whist party in honor of Amelia, gathering together enough girls for eight tables.

Katch spent a lot of time those first days just "fooling around" with Amelia, taking advantage of the fact that Toot was out of town. When Rilla took Katch to Kansas City for the day, to buy handerkerchiefs, a panama hat, and yellow ribbons, she took Amelia, too. On Sunday morning Amelia went to Sunday school with Katch. She stayed for the service and sat in the old Otis pew (and went back the following Sunday). With Katch in tow she went next door into her grandparents' house, now silent and empty, looked around, and brought out, "some books and stuff"—an act Katch thought quite daring. "The little devil," Katch wrote after the escapade. One moonlit evening, following a walk with Rilla, Amelia and Katch wandered in the garden in their nightgowns, drinking in the beauty.

Toot came back, and she and Amelia picked up their friendship. "Toot" gave a card party too; it was the thing to do in spite of the summer heat. Hers had two tables of teenage girls, and "auction" and rummy were the favorite games. Katch, too young, was at the Park house playing jacks with Ginger's younger sister Annie. Pineapple sandwiches, jelly sandwiches, ripe olives, and lemonade were served. The one afternoon Toot was busy, Katch snatched Amelia back: "Mill and Peggy and I went over to Ginger P's." One morning Toot didn't want to go in swimming so, entered Katch in her diary on August 28, "Mill and I went—had packs of fun."

Amelia slept late, spent long mornings reading, or swimming, or playing tennis with Toot, or making fudge, and whiled away many peaceful evenings with the family sitting on the porch listening to James Challiss playing the guitar or competing in games of cribbage or hearts or parcheesi. Many days she and Toot just "fussed"—Katch's word for hanging out.

Occasionally they went to parties, or dated. A young man named Charles came to see Toot, and a boy named Dutch came for Millie. (Katch's reaction was "ugh.") Sometimes they all played cards. One of the last nights, Amelia begged off going to a party and stayed home, so Toot stayed home too. They sat on the porch after dinner and talked.

The last week, Amelia got out her camera and took pictures of all the Challisses, and then at her request they took pictures of her with them. She left on Monday, September 7. By that time Toot and Amelia, now woven together by the strong threads of adolescence, made Katch, so much younger, feel left out. Adolescence was a world she could not yet enter. This alert child, who had written when her younger sister Peggy was born, "I lost my place as the youngest child," now observed, in her diary entry for Monday, September 7, "Mill left this morning at 10:00 and I'm sorry to say that I wasn't very sorry to see her go. Toot and I cleaned the house up wonderfully."

She had her sister back.

. . . .

The plan had been for Amy and Amelia and Muriel to live somewhere in the Morgan Park district of Chicago near the Shedds and for Amelia and Muriel to go to the Morgan Park high school with the Shedd daughter. When Amelia, however, saw the school, she was appalled by its low standards (she likened the chemistry lab to a kitchen sink) and refused to enroll.

The Chicago public school system operated on the "neighborhood" concept—one went to the high school in the district where one lived. So when Amelia chose Hyde Park High School, in the Hyde Park district, it meant they had to find lodgings there.

Amy had never been a match for Amelia. Even when Amelia was young, she had been able to bend her mother to her will. As a tot, she had succeeded in dawdling for over an hour over a glass of milk to keep Amy reading *Ivanhoe* because her mother had promised to read until the milk was finished. Now no more than before could Amy stand up to her, even though she wanted to live near her friends and Muriel had her heart set on going to the same school the Shedd daughter attended.

Hyde Park was the best public high school in Chicago. Located near the University of Chicago, challenged by the infusion of the bright, motivated children of University of Chicago faculty, Hyde Park excelled in all disciplines and offered extensive extracurricular activities. Its student body was notable for the high percentage who went on to attend top colleges, as well as for the extraordinary number of alumni and alumnae who would become distinguished musicians, artists, scientists, and athletes—among them, in later generations, TV personality Steve Allen, jazz vocalist Mel Torme, economist Paul Samuelson, and Olympic medalist Jim Fuchs.

But Amelia made no friends and participated in no activities. She was seventeen when school opened that fall of 1914. She never made the slightest effort to fit in. In contrast to the exuberance she had exhibited the previous spring, enabling her to rise above her disastrous home life and take part in the various activities in St. Paul, Amelia participated in none of the organized student activities at Hyde Park. She arrived that fall the outsider in the senior class, and she remained the outsider. Each day when classes were over, she left and went home and cared for Amy.

Hyde Park was a school way ahead of its time. The sports facilities

were not only superb but were available to girls as well as boys. The glorious
sports she had worked so enthusiastically to master and to teach her friends
to play when she had been at College Preparatory School—basketball and
baseball—were played with full teams and official rules by girls as well as
boys. There was even a girls' indoor baseball team. Here was an incredible
cornucopia of riches—and Amelia took no part. She played on no team
at all.

Nor was that the extent of her nonparticipation in school activities.
Hyde Park had dozens of extracurricular student clubs covering every possible activity. Amelia was among the few who belonged to none—not the
Dramatic Club, the Discussion Club, the Civics Club, the Choral Society,
the Camera Club, Honor Society, Pythagorean Club, or the Glee Club, to
single out a few.

In *The Aitchpe,* the senior class yearbook, there is a very odd description
of Amelia, as well as a very odd picture. The description reads, "Meek loveliness is 'round thee spread." It is so far off the mark that it indicates beyond
question that she had remained an unknown quantity to her classmates
who produced the book. The square space next to her photo—which for
other students contains a list of achievements, hopes, and interests—is a
blank. For the first and last time in her life, Amelia was too preoccupied
to interact with her peers. There is a picture of her in the yearbook: her
hair is attractively piled on her head, and she is wearing a ribbon choker.
She looks collected, and composed—serious and very mature—but old
for her years as she stares off into the distance. And different. There is a
hint of primness, a sense of tenseness—she is unlike her usual self. The
painfully neat clothes bear witness that, depressed as she was, she allowed
no chink in her armor. Among the many things her classmates did not
know about Amelia was that her family was so poor, she and her mother
and sister were living in rooms in an apartment belonging to two spinster
sisters who made their life miserable. And she went home to those rooms
every day after school to be with Amy.

The Aitchpe also listed college choices, and Amelia's choice was Bryn
Mawr; she was at least still holding on to her dream of going there with
Ginger, as they had planned together for so many years.

She kept so much to herself that her Hyde Park classmates used the
words "boy shy" and "reticent" and "diffident" to describe her. They
would also remember that she did not attend graduation or bother to pick
up her diploma and that she was the only one in her class who "dared to
break the school tradition by refusing to attend the senior class banquet."

Even though Amelia participated so little in school activities, she
harbored no ill feelings toward Hyde Park. In 1928, within weeks of

her return to the United States after the *Friendship* flight, she visited the school, in the process enthralling everyone with whom she came in contact. (She laughingly remarked that what she remembered most vividly was her German teacher always asking *"Was meint das Fräulein?"* because the teacher couldn't understand her German.) And her picture was taken while she stepping onto a piano on her way down from the auditorium stage.

• • • •

Edwin, meanwhile, after the disaster in Springfield, attempted to resurrect his law practice in St. Paul. When the lease on the house ran out, he moved to Kansas City, Missouri, to live with his elderly widowed sister Mary Woodworth, at seventy-two almost a generation older than he. Sometime in the fall of 1915, Amy and Amelia and Muriel left Chicago and moved there too, into a small house at 3621 Charlotte Avenue. Edwin joined them. It looked terribly good after all they had been through. But there was still no money, and Amelia wanted to finish her education in a proper manner at a private school or college. It was a difficult time for her. Her own plans had to be put on hold. Mitigating that state of affairs, however, was the positive change in her father: Edwin had pulled himself together and was again functioning.

Amy had never given up trying to get control of her inheritance. Now, with Edwin drawing on his knowledge of the law, his anger redirected into positive channels, husband and wife joined forces to fight Mark. Edwin began probing into the dealings of the Otis Real Estate Company, looking for evidence of financial mismanagement. At every turn Mark rebuffed him, and as he did so, Mark's enmity toward Amy became more and more apparent. As Edwin pressed him, he and Amy became surer of their ground. In September 1915 Amy filed suit. Edwin's brief sought an accounting from Mark, challenged the legality of the Otis Real Estate Company to function as a company in the state of Illinois, and demonstrated that Mark hadn't had the courtesy to be civil to his brother-in-law: ". . . and he refused to show said books and records of said corporation, and said agent then wrote a letter to Mark E. Otis, demanding an inspection of said books, which letter was refused by said Mark E. Otis, and returned to the writer unopened."

Things began to move, although at a glacial pace, in Amy's favor. On February 17, 1917, the Atchison County District Court granted the petition. "Except for the funds in the hands of the Northern Trust Company," the *Journal* entry stated, Mark had to turn over to his sister all the real estate legally hers—forthwith, upon presentation of her shares of stock, and "the Otis Real Estate Company upon receipt of said stock, [shall] deed to the plaintiff all the said property within two days thereafter." The property involved "certain real estate described as follows"—listing more than thirty pieces of property in Kansas City, Kansas, and several in Kansas City, Missouri.

And then, finally, the long agony came to an end. On April 16, Amy was notified, her brother had died in Chicago.

That summer Amy sought control over the funds still managed by the Northern Trust Company, and with Mark dead, she encountered no opposition. On August 21, 1917, Amy's inheritance was finally, totally, irrevocably hers.

It would take a while for Mark's financial records to be unraveled, but when they were, Margaret Balis and Theodore Otis would find out that of the extensive holdings their father had so carefully built up, virtually nothing was left. Mark had wasted and spent it all—all except Amy's portion. Margaret would be forced to recognize that Amy had been correct in her assessment of their brother and that she had been wrong. The sisters, reunited, would pick up the closeness they had once enjoyed, and their children would once again become friends.

• • • •

In the fall of 1916 Ginger Park, but not Amelia Earhart, became a freshman at Bryn Mawr. Amelia became a student at one of the most exclusive finishing schools in the country, a school called Ogontz. A mix of factors were at work. Money was certainly a major consideration, as were location and academic background.

Ogontz had the attribute of being located in a suburb of Philadelphia, near both Bryn Mawr and Margaret Balis, who would be able to look after her niece. Amelia must have considered it temporary—assuming that in another year she would be at Bryn Mawr—and in the meantime she would be nearby, and near the Balis family, with whom she got along well.

But Ogontz was a particularly social school—so social that virtually everyone, including the Challiss family, thought it a great mistake for Amelia to go there. Rilla Challiss thought Ogontz "a very silly place for Amy to have sent her"—it was that dreaded thing, Rilla thought, "rather *too* stylish." Lucy Challiss was going to Wheaton and would have liked her to go there; Edwin favored Kansas State. Nor did Ogontz appeal to Margaret Balis, who was strongly bound to the Quaker tradition of their great-grandmother Maria. She would send her daughters, a few years younger than Amelia, to Germantown Friends for their final years and then to Bryn Mawr.

Amy had always had social pretensions. She alone, of all her aunts and uncles and cousins, in her description in the family history book of the large ancestral Harres home in Philadelphia, where her mother and Mary Ann Challiss had grown up—she alone claimed the house was on Chestnut Street, the most fashionable street in the city, when in fact it had been on more modest South Third Street, by no means as fine. Her yearning for gentility, her insistence on patrician ancestry would impress Muriel (but not Amelia, who never made any such claims). When Muriel wrote her biography of her sister, she made much of their supposed grand lineage, claiming that they were descended from a niece of a king of France through Edwin, as well as being direct descendants of the Revolutionary War hero James Otis.

The years of being snubbed, of being so poor in Chicago that rooms in a dismal apartment were the best she could do, had taken their toll on Amy. After what she had endured in St. Paul, social standing became not just one interest among many but a serious goal in life. While in earlier years her efforts had been directed at maintaining the family position, now she felt they had slipped, and she and her daughters had to regain their place. With such a goal, an ultrasocial finishing school would help—it would add a certain cachet to her daughter's social standing.

Margaret and Clarence Balis lived a few miles away from Ogontz, at 137 East Johnson Street, in a big house with their five children—fifteen-year-old Otis, eleven-year-old Mark Edwin, ten-year-old Clarence, and the twins, Nancy and Jane, six—plus niece Annie, by then grown and about to be married. The Balises were a happy, normal family, something Amelia, except during her brief visit with the Challisses, had not been around in years. It would have been comforting for Amelia to be near her first cousins and her aunt, always the family caregiver, now devoted to taking young relatives under her wing. (A few years later Margaret would even gather into her fold Charles Otis's son James, and James's children, whom Amy had so desperately tried to become friendly with in St. Paul.) Margaret managed to accomplish so much even though she was almost totally deaf—something her own children were made aware of only when they started school and their classmates asked them, "Why are you shouting?"

Margaret was undertaking the education of her twin daughters Nancy and Jane at home, but unlike Amy's feeble attempt, which had so quickly ended in failure, Margaret, in the forefront of educational change, was deep into the new Montessori method and a highly successful teacher. "I can still remember the big boxes from Italy, and the big colored letters," Nancy, one of the twins, would say many years later. Keeping an eye on another niece was for Margaret the most natural thing in the world. As a matter of course, particularly since money was still short, Amelia spent vacations with her aunt.

What Margaret had not expected, however, were the jams Amelia got into—especially those caused by her penchant for climbing. Margaret as parent-in-place was held accountable and telephoned by school authorities whenever there was a problem. Several times she had to deal with the school when Amelia was caught climbing on the roofs of the school buildings, "I remember Mother wearing a gray dress and a very snappy hat," Nancy would recall, "I remember Mother putting on the hat, her mouth full of hat pins [holding the hat pins in her mouth] and saying, 'I have to go out to Ogontz to see about Amelia. She has been climbing on the roof in her nightie again.' " But at the beginning of the term the Balis house was off limits to Amelia, because, as her cousin Annie Otis was deputed to call and tell her, Jane was sick and the house in quarantine until mid-November—necessitating even Clarence Balis's enforced absence.

• • • •

Ogontz was a school with a strong conservative tradition. It had begun life in 1850 as the Chestnut Street Female Seminary in Philadelphia. By Amelia's day, it was a finishing school located on the Jay Cooke estate outside of Philadelphia and had a new name: Ogontz, the name of an Indian chief after whom Cooke had named the house. The headmistress, Abby Sutherland, originally from Cape Breton Island, Nova Scotia, fluent in French and German, a cum laude graduate of Radcliffe, began her career at Ogontz in 1902 teaching English. In 1913 she became head of the school, which under her stewardship grew rapidly and shed some of its more austere traditions. It was, however, still the goal of the school to seek out and educate what the headmistress proudly described as "the *jeunesse dorée*," by which she meant, as she put it, those from "the best social stratum." However, if Ogontz was consciously filled with the children of families of the "best" American lineage and culture, it did at least seek geographical diversity; almost every class included students from all over the United States and usually from foreign countries as well. And if it had no black students, it did have at least a few Jewish ones. As Abby Sutherland delicately put it, "In 1903 the then head of the school, Miss Eastman, with conscientious Christian scruples, decided to accept a few individuals of the Jewish race and fit them into the group, thus solving the problem empirically."

Abby Sutherland was less interested in spoiling her young charges than in inculcating sound values; less interested in shielding them from the world than in instilling healthy habits. During her years as headmistress, "the training in neatness and thriftiness; the beautiful surroundings, and above all the Christian atmosphere" would overwhelmingly impress the girls.

Under Miss Sutherland's stewardship, Ogontz paid good salaries and provided excellent housing, with the result that the teachers were of a very high caliber; many were college graduates or had unusually varied backgrounds. Abby Sutherland, herself rather worldly, insisted on the constant interaction of faculty and students with what was going on in the world. During the summers teachers were expected to travel abroad and otherwise keep in touch, and guest lecturers were constantly sought out and brought to the school. Throughout the year the girls made trips to art centers in New York, Washington, and Chicago.

The result of all this was that Ogontz did a very good job of educating its *jeunesse dorée*—more than half of its students went on to institutions of higher learning, and many of those institutions gave college credit for Ogontz courses. Ogontz students became singers at the Metropolitan Opera, heads of civic organizations, doctors, lawyers, State Department officials, teachers, and artists. But being a wife and mother came first; it was a rare Ogontz girl who did not marry.

The physical well-being of the girls was considered to be just as important as their mental health, and therefore vigorous exercise was an integral part of the school day. Fencing was taught by a fencing instructor from the Drexel Institute, field hockey by an English lady who coached at Bryn Mawr, and dancing by (among others) Martha Graham; the horseback riding program ended with a horse show each June. There were also tennis and basketball. For the "unathletic" who, according to the diligent Abby Sutherland, "were always with us . . . the required hours of exercise . . . could include a walk, not a stroll, in the open country." During military drill, obligatory at many of the girls' schools of the period, the girls marched in uniform, complete with wooden guns, to the orders of the headmaster of Bordentown Military Institute. Miss Sutherland attributed the fine carriage and walking manner "characteristic of all alumnae" to the marching, and it was evidently very popular with the girls, although not with Amelia, who informed her mother, "Drill is awful," in her first letter.

Amelia took to Ogontz quickly. Putting distance between herself and Amy was like a tonic. Able at last to put down the burden of caring for her mother, Amelia became once again the teenager, the child, the student—she could act her age and enjoy life. She threw herself into everything.

As she wrote her mother:

I don't have a minute for anything because I want to get all possible. Weekdays this is the program.

7:00 Get up to a cow bell.

7:30 Prayers and afterward setting up exercises.

8:00 Breakfast and morning walk till school begins at nine. Classes until two. One fifteen in my case. Then, Hockey, b. ball or drill in turn with an hour or two for tennis.

4 to 5:30 Study hall

5:30—6:30 Dress for dinner.

6:00 Dinner and prayers immediately after. Then spelling. Then every evening we have something to do. Thursday and Tuesday conversation classes in French German etc. Wednesday a lecture or something like that (Joseph Hoffman this Wednesday) and Friday always something else. Saturday and Monday are our free nights. Sunday prayers and a lecture take up the time till luncheon. Then everybody takes two hours of exercise out-doors. Then Study at four as usual. You see every minute is accounted for and you have to go by schedule.

Amelia immediately excelled in field hockey, informing her mother, "I played hockey yesterday and made two goals, the only ones made. I am continuing this letter Monday evening. I played Hockey again to-day and made a goal thru my legs." As a result of her prowess, she was invited to become a member of one of the secret societies, Alpha Phi, the athletic sorority. She also did well in her studies and was pleased to be placed in French III her first term. ("Did I tell you that I have a reputation for brains?" she writes her mother.) By Christmas she had dropped the chemistry lab she had started.

In all her classes in the year and a half Amelia spent at Ogontz, her marks varied within a very narrow range from G (good) to G+ to E (excellent), even in drill and punctuality, subjects on which the girls were also meticulously marked (although she did get two fairs in Bible). In light of Amelia's habit of deliberately misspelling and otherwise fooling around with words for her own amusement, it is interesting and informative to note that after two semesters of spelling class, in both of which she received a grade of excellent, she was exempted from spelling for the rest of her time at Ogontz. In her literature class that first year, among other authors she read Wordsworth, Byron, Burns, and Shakespeare; in Latin she read Horace; in her French class, George Sand. Even so, she found time to devour books on her own—so many, it came to the notice of Abby Sutherland, who wrote, "Amelia was always pushing into unknown seas in her reading."

There were still worries about money, though. Compared with the other girls, Amelia was poor. She tried to reassure Amy and not complain. "I can wear an old suit with a little alteration so it will be more reasonable. I hate to spend money for things I never will need nor want." She bought a pair of used high-heeled pumps from a friend for five dollars. At the end of a letter to her mother in the spring, she wrote: "Dearie, I don't need any spring clothes so don't worry about sending me money. I have a few dollars still in the bank and I know you all need things more than I." The next fall she is apologizing to her mother for needing twenty-seven dollars for senior caps and gowns, an obligatory expense and the alternative was that she must borrow from Miss Sutherland "if it is not convenient to send me some cash soon as is the custom." Abby Sutherland thought she handled the situation with aplomb. "Her style of dressing was always simple and becoming. At that period her purse as well as her innate taste required the fewest and simplest clothes. But she helped very much to impress the overindulged girls with the beauty and comfort of simple dressing."

• • • •

Carefully supervised, Ogontz girls were encouraged to go on cultural expeditions into Philadelphia. In the fall Amelia went to a concert performance of the Philadelphia Symphony. In the spring she went on excursions to hear Ian Hay, to visit the Victor Talking Machine Company, and to see theatrical productions of *Treasure Island* and *Joan the Woman*. Then there were the cultural events brought to Ogontz, such as the Orpheus Club, a phenomenon she described to her mother as "a musical organization of Philadelphia, composed of about twenty men aged from twenty-five to eighty." They "came out to dinner here and gave us a concert. There were some magnificent voices caged in very unprepossessing exteriors and one German Baron looked as tho he would burst his earthly shell when he sang, but his voice was a wonderfully clear barytone. He sung from Faure and Die Walkyrie (I know how to spell it.)"

Her horizons were broadening: she was beginning to think of the future and what she would do with her life. She started to look for and clip newspaper and magazine articles about women who had careers, and she quickly had enough to paste into a scrapbook that she called "Activities of Women." Among the women thus singled out: a League of Women Voters activist who was the mother of five; Mrs. Paul Beard, a fire lookout in the Federal Forestry Service, whose post was on Harney Peak in South Dakota, in a glass house lashed to a rock; a budding film producer; a county medical society that "breaking all precedents . . . last night elected a woman as president"; a police commissioner in Fargo, North Dakota;

Miss R. E. Barrett who was city manager of Warrenton, Oregon, the first Indian woman admitted to the Bombay Bar; Queen Victoria's goddaughter, Victoria Drummond, the first Englishwoman to win an engineer's certificate, who wanted to skipper an ocean liner; and four women in the Belgian Union of the League of Nations. One of the few pictures in the scrapbook shows an enormous open touring car with the top down, in which sit Lillian Gilbreth, identified as an industrial psychologist, her husband, and their twelve children. Interestingly, there is no clipping of any woman who was famous as a result of battling for women's suffrage, which was just on the brink of becoming law. (Women would vote for the first time in the presidential election of 1920.) Amelia's focus was narrow—she was only interested in women achievers.

That summer Amelia, having been invited to vacation with her new school friends, stayed as far from home as she could. She spent several weeks vacationing at a camp on Lake Michigan with a girl named Sarah. She had acquired a boyfriend, Ken, and as she wrote her mother, "The boys have been lovely and Kenneth has done so much for me. He is very nice and sensitive and almost brilliant. We four [her friend Sarah and Sarah's friend Harry] have just ideal times together and have gone on innumerable canoe trips, walking jaunts etc. together." The foursome were going to stop off together at Chicago on their way home, but disappointingly Amelia's hostess became sick, she informed Amy. "Harry and Ken were going to take us to everything in Chicago this week as I had been urged to visit, at Miss Tredwell's. Grand opera, baseball, sand dunes, anything we would go to. They are such nice boys and we had had a wonderful time with them."

Amelia had left for summer vacation with serious reservations about returning to Ogontz, viewing herself as too grown up, but she returned in the fall of 1917 because Abby Sutherland was promising to change Ogontz from a finishing school to a combined school and junior college. In her first letter home to Amy that fall, she sought to assure her she had not made a mistake. "The general age of the school is older perhaps because the young girls are over at another house, but whatever it is, I am much more satisfied."

Over the summer Abby Sutherland had moved the school to greatly enlarged facilities in Abington Township, in the Rydal hills near Philadelphia. So Amelia returned to a different campus and a changed institution: the girls were split up into a lower and upper school, and all the rules had been changed. The junior college was in the works but not yet in place. The swimming pool was still an empty hole, the hockey field unfinished. The first few weeks were slow and painful.

Amelia wrote approvingly about the cultural revolution that had

taken place, particularly the abolition of the secret societies. "It is a sweeping blow and only one who has seen them in action knows how tremendous
it is. She [Miss Sutherland] has instituted in the same breathless iconoclas-
tic measure the honor system which will I imagine stop all surreptitious
student activities." In her effort to raise the level of the student body, Abby
Sutherland also changed the student mix, adding seventy-six new girls to
the thirty-nine returning students.

The abolition of the sororities evidently did not take place without
a great deal of resistance. Standing up for what she believed in, fighting in
the thick of things, Amelia blossomed. Her natural tendency, which she
had honed to a fine art during her years with her grandmother, to suppress
knowledge of any possible problems she might be encountering, was now
applied to Amy. "I was a little worried when I wrote you last and want
now to correct any impression of unhappiness I may have given you." Her
leadership qualities had come to the fore: some of the girls tried to go back
on their promise to Abby Sutherland to dissolve their societies, a course of
action Amelia viewed as unethical, so she "landed into some of them for
their conduct." Her own society, Alpha Phi, was evidently the only one
that kept its word to dissolve. It made her momentarily very unpopular,
but she stuck to her guns even though, as she admitted in a letter to her
mother, "very few people understand what I mean when I go at length
into the subtleties of moral codes."

As a result of her actions, Amelia became even more popular and
within a short time was practically running Ogontz. She was one of five
students elected to the new student honor board, in which capacity she
had the temerity to stand up against the headmistress's demand for faculty
representation. She was elected vice-president of her class, and in a nod
to her musical talent, she was chosen to write the senior song. Then she
became secretary and treasurer of something called Christian Endeavor,
commenting to her mother, "It has been rather an institution of torture
heretofore, and not well liked but we are trying to put something into it
that will make it stand for something."

In a close-up picture of Amelia, wearing her cap and gown, her level
gray eyes stare composedly out; one curl of her blond hair shows. There
is a glint in her eye. The tall beanpole had become an attractive young
woman.

5

A Life of Purpose and Action

•••• In April 1917 the United States entered World War I. In mid-June the first U.S. troops landed on European soil. Ogontz, like the rest of the United States, was drawn into the war effort. Scarcely had school started than Amelia's roommate Eleanor was elected chairman and Amelia secretary of the Ogontz Red Cross. The student body resolved to set aside one class period of forty-five minutes each day for the purpose of knitting sweaters for Allied troops, and to eliminate an article of food from each meal, the money thus saved to be donated to the Red Cross.

Although Amelia stayed at Ogontz for Thanksgiving, for Christmas it was arranged that she would travel to Toronto, as would Amy, to rendezvous with Muriel, who had become a student at St. Margaret's there in the fall.

The war was much closer to the Canadians than to the Americans. Canadians had won the reputation of being the finest soldiers on the Western Front, but they had paid dearly in casualties. Now, as the year drew to a close, Canadian soldiers, many of them wounded, filled the streets of Toronto. Amelia—fresh from the States, fresh from the sequestered existence of a school where the burning issues of the day were secret sororities, the outer limits of student government, and knitting sweaters—was stunned by the sight of so many wounded soldiers—men without arms, without legs, some blind, some on crutches. "Returning to school was impossible, if there was work that I could do."

The work she had in mind was nursing.

Amy, happy to be reunited with her girls for Christmas vacation, suddenly found herself faced with Amelia's decision to withdraw from school. Clearly, given the devotion to nursing shown by Amy's grandmother Maria Harres and by her sister Margaret's lifelong interest in medicine, Amy could not object to Amelia's choice of career. As for the timing, there was very little she could do about that either. In fact, there was very little she had been able to do with Amelia for years.

It must be noted that Amelia's decision was audacious as well as sudden—very few American girls volunteered for the Canadian war effort. Amelia wrote Abby Sutherland of her decision and asked her to send on her things. She and Muriel moved into a small apartment hotel at the St. Regis, a hotel that catered to gentlewomen.

Amelia promptly enrolled in the first aid course given by the Voluntary Aid Detachment of the St. John Ambulance Brigade, at the end of which, certified to administer first aid, she became a VAD, as the graduates were called. Between the nurses' course and her newfound freedom to date boys, she was so busy she almost forgot to look after Muriel, she admitted in a letter to her mother. She was thoroughly enjoying herself, she assured Amy, and had a very full social life. She had a beau named Reg who had asked her to go to the most exciting professional hockey game of the season. She had friends with whom she went to concerts. She had plenty to read, having procured a library card. She was making new friends, she assured her mother, and that very night she was meeting an American girl whose primary attraction was a good-looking brother, a Cornell graduate who was in the coast guard. She was carrying on a voluminous correspondence with her friends, male and female, fretting if they didn't write back promptly. She passed along photos and letters from family and friends for Amy to read. "Muriel and I sent Miss Macdonald a box of violets and she was very pleased, Muriel said. She said it was just like you which is the greatest compliment she can give—and we can receive. . . . I am sending you a funny letter from Ginny Park. Its nice to feel there are more deluded people who have confidence in one." The letter, written over several days, concludes, "Oh, and I *did* hear from Ken," and is signed, " 'Zever (as Harry says) Amelia."

A short while later Amelia enrolled in the home nursing course given by the St. John Ambulance Brigade and was quite pleased with all her activities:

I *am* a busy person. I entered into a class of home nursing . . .
and am going on with the class altho they are half thru. . . . Mrs.
Holland's physician asked me to come to his clinic, where he diag-
noses and prescribes to poor people and asks the class to diagnose
before he tells what really is the matter. That is not compulsory of
course but I am getting everything I can. Also all lectures possible.
I am going to see an operation if I can wheedle anybody into
letting me.

Clothed in a white cap and the gray and white VAD uniform, Amelia
went to work as a nurse's aid in the children's wing at Victoria Memorial
Hospital. There she watched her first tonsillectomy, fearful she would be
put off by the sight of what was then a bloody operation. Instead she found
it "interesting."

Shortly thereafter she transferred to Spadina Military Hospital, where
on her first day, while she was in the shell-shock ward, someone turned
on the fire alarm, traumatizing the sick patients. Unfazed, she helped put
the patients back to bed. Most of the days, however, were more humdrum:
she made beds, carried trays, and tried to bring a little "merry sunshine"
to the wounded men. Among her jobs were "backs to be rubbed—some
lovely ones!" as she noted, not letting the monotony of the work dull her
appreciation for the male body. But it was a strenuous regimen; the day
began at seven and ended at seven, with two hours off in the afternoon.

After a while she began working in the laboratory at the hospital,
staining germs and doing other tests. Her days there began at nine and continued until about four forty-five, after which she went to the diet kitchen
and helped with the evening meal.

When Amelia had spare time, she headed for the stables, and it was
through her riding that she got her first exposure to airplanes. She was
riding a horse named Dynamite, whom she had "gentled" with a combination of horsemanship and apples, when she was joined by three air
force officers. They were so impressed by how well she controlled her
mount—famous for bucking off a colonel—that they asked her to go out
to Armour Heights, an airfield at the edge of the city, to watch how they
controlled their planes.

Amelia had seen planes before. She saw her first at a fair in Des
Moines when she was ten, but "it was a thing of rusty wire and wood and
looked not at all interesting." The chances are, it was the same first plane
that Clarence Chamberlin, who also grew up to be a crack pilot, saw in
his home town of Denison, Iowa, at about the same time—an old-style
pusher, with the pilot sitting out front "on a sort of birdcage seat," and the

propeller and engine in the rear. He too had been "frankly unimpressed
. . . quite willing to let anyone take such fool chances who would."

But ten years had passed. These planes were a different generation;
now they were beautiful: "They were full sized birds that slid on the hard-
packed snow and rose into the air with an extra roar that echoed from the
evergreens that banked the edge of the field." She stood close to them—so
close that the propellers threw snow in her face, and "I felt a first urge to
fly." She tried to get permission to go up, but failed—"not even a general's
wife could do so—apparently the only thing she couldn't do." So she did
"the next best thing" and got to know the fliers.

One day she had a chance to test her faith in planes, not by flying
but by standing in the path of one. It was at a Toronto fair, and the pilots,
war aces, were giving exhibitions of stunt flying. She and a girlfriend
were standing in the middle of a clearing off by themselves in order to see
better. The pilot began diving at the crowd. She would never forget what
happened next.

"He was bored. He had looped and rolled and spun and finished his
little bag of tricks, and there was nothing left to do but watch the people
on the ground running as he swooped close to them." Then he started
diving at the two girls off in the clearing. "I remember the mingled fear
and pleasure which surged over me as I watched that small plane at the top
of its earthward swoop. Commonsense told me if something went wrong
with the mechanism, or if the pilot lost control, he, the airplane and I
would be rolled up in a ball together. I did not understand it at the time
but I believe that little red airplane said something to me as it swished by."
Her friend ran off. Amelia didn't; she was fascinated.

That summer a deadly influenza epidemic hit North America,
brought from Europe by the troops returning home after the war was over.
The first shipload of infected soldiers reached Canada in June. The spread
of the disease was so quick that young men who had seemed perfectly well
at night, who had even been on guard duty, would be found dead in the
morning. The contagious disease spread quickly, fanning out from the soldiers to their families and to the health workers caring for them, then into
the general population. By fall the disease, first thought a minor illness,
was an epidemic. Many of those who survived the flu were felled by the
pneumonia that often followed. Before it had run its course in Canada, it
would kill somewhere between 30,000 and 50,000 people, almost as many
Canadians as had died fighting.

All over Canada, hospitals, already shorthanded because of the war,
were overwhelmed as the numbers of patients mounted. In Toronto, which
was enduring the coldest, wettest September in a century, the death toll

mounted, and by October the flu was killing seventeen people a day. Masked figures could be seen making their way through the deserted Toronto streets; black crepe sashes hung from the doorways.

As the epidemic continued, many of the hospitals became even more shorthanded as their staff members fell ill. Amelia, as an American, could have done the prudent thing and left—but she didn't. She stayed. She went on the night shift in the pneumonia ward, where she helped dispense care and medicine. But the medicines were not effective against flu and pneumonia. Sulfa drugs, penicillin and other antibiotics had not yet been discovered. It must have been then that Amelia first thought of becoming a doctor herself.

Amelia was tough, but finally she too, fell ill. She was hit with a pneumonococcal bacterial infection in her frontal antrum, where the pressure so builds up in the sinuses that severe, chronic pain results. Without antibiotics, the only treatment was to surgically open the cavity, drain the infection, and keep it open and draining until all traces of the infection completely disappeared. Amelia was operated upon. It was a long, debilitating course of treatment, lasting months, and it so seriously weakened Amelia that it took the rest of the winter for her to recover her strength. Even then it turned out that the infection had not been totally eradicated; it would remain a serious problem for years.

She spent her convalescence in Northampton, Massachusetts, where Amy had taken an apartment in order to be with Muriel, who was now studying at Miss Capen's School so she would do well on the College Board examinations required for entrance to Smith College. There Amelia rested. As she regained her strength, the sisters "walked over the lovely country roads . . . climbed Mt. Tom . . . explored the byways of Northampton." Muriel thought it idyllic, but Amelia was bored. As she had instinctively, from childhood on, masked her feelings, she put on a good face for her sister and mother; but the better she felt, the more restless she became, exploding in a letter to one of her boyfriends, still abroad, "If only I were over there instead of gravitating in enforced idleness in the confines of this bally little New England Village."

She bought a banjo; she also enrolled in a class for ambulance drivers that Smith College was sponsoring, run by John Charlesbois, owner of the Auto Infirmary, a local garage. The ten-week course was designed to teach female ambulance drivers serving abroad how to repair their own vehicles in the field. Charlesbois taught the girls how to overhaul engines, change piston rings, work on ignition systems, and understand carburetors and camshafts. Amelia began to feel better—the essay she wrote on car mechanics, a course requirement, won first prize. The class would later serve Amelia in good stead, giving her her first practical knowledge of how engines worked.

In the spring Amy informed her daughters that Edwin, cured of drinking, wanted to move from Kansas City to Los Angeles, and wanted them to join him in the fall after he was settled. The Otis family house in Atchison had finally been sold that February, so Amy could afford to splurge a little. She, Amelia, and Muriel would summer in New England. Amelia did some investigating and settled on Lake George, one of the most beautiful lakes in New York, as a pleasant place for them to spend the summer. She found a cottage to rent in the Hamlet, a collection of vacation cottages near Hulett's Landing, at the waist of the lake. Once they were settled in, Amelia read poetry, played, swam, boated, and thought about what to do with her life.

Margaret Balis had arrived for a visit—and Margaret, whose desire to become a doctor had been thwarted when she had been Amelia's age, apparently now reinforced Amelia's desire to study medicine. "The life of the mind, combined with a life of purpose and action" was how Amelia, at about this time, described the kind of life she wanted to fashion for herself. She'd been a nurse; she'd learned a lot; she felt she had an aptitude for medicine. Her next logical step would be to begin studying when the summer was over.

And Margaret brought her twins Nancy and Jane, eight; Clarence, thirteen; Mark, fourteen; and Otis, eighteen. Amelia had come to the conclusion that she would be like a doctor. Undoubtedly Margaret helped strengthen her resolve.

In the meantime, it was Amelia who ruled the family roost. Marian Stabler, vacationing in the same community, was amused to watch Amelia installing her sister and various combinations of her young cousins—Margaret's five children—in a canoe, putting the cousins in the bow and the stern to do all the paddling and allowing Muriel to lounge with her at ease amidships.

Marian, tall, slender, well spoken, and bright, a graduate of Vassar the previous year, was spending the summer studying to become an artist at the New York School of Fine Arts (later the Parsons School of Design). Before she arrived at Lake George, Marian had been the recipient of endless letters from her parents, Walter and Clara Stabler and her brother Frank, about life there. She especially kept hearing about the interesting new family that was renting the cottage just across the road, and especially about one member.

When Marian finally arrived in August, she too was drawn to Amelia, whom she found "very poetic," with "serious, aesthetic ideas." Frank, who had served in the navy during the war, and was about to be a senior at Williams College in Massachusetts, was equally taken. Playing a game of Truth with her brother, Marian realized that he had a crush on Amelia. The four of them—Amelia, Marian, Frank, and Muriel—spent a lot of time together reading, canoeing, playing hide and seek, dancing to phonograph records on the porch, and toasting marshmallows around a campfire—usually trying to evade the young male Balis cousins who loved spying on Amelia.

All the Stablers were impressed with Amelia's looks and temperament. Marian was amazed at her limber body. She could, according to Marian, balance on her hands with her knees drawn up close to her chest. She could also curl within the area of one cushion on a three-cushion couch "with nothing hanging over," and take a nap of indefinite length, in no apparent discomfort. Another favorite position of Amelia's was sitting on one foot.

• • • •

Unlike Margaret, whose desire to be a doctor had been thwarted all those years before, no one who could block Amelia's plan to become one now. Indeed, Margaret had undoubtedly urged her on. And so, the summer over, Amelia registered at Columbia University in the University Extension Program, which was designed for men and women like her, with practical as well as educational backgrounds. The Columbia program was enjoying enormous popularity because it offered the widest possible latitude both in studies and in its entrance requirements.

It was an exciting time to be at Columbia. The Extension had been founded in 1915 "to afford extraordinary educational opportunities . . . and to serve the University by introducing and testing new educational schemes and plans." Out of the Extension would grow the university's Graduate School of Arts and Sciences, the Business School, the School of Journalism, and the School of General Studies.

In the fall of 1919, swelled by the great postwar rush, the Extension was in a state of flux—its 12,873 students were by far the largest student unit at the university, completely dwarfing the undergraduate Columbia College enrollment of 1,001, the Barnard enrollment of 755 girls, and the 6,548 students enrolled in the existing graduate and professional schools.

The Extension teaching staff ranged from the pedestrian to the extraordinary. Among the famous professors in the program were Rexford Tugwell, who was teaching economics; Raymond Moley, government; Franz Boas, anthropology; and Thomas Merton, author (in 1948) of *The Seven Storey Mountain,* English. The science department boasted a Nobel

Prize winner; the philosopher John Dewey and the journalist Heywood Broun were also on the staff.

Female students under twenty-one were required to live in dormitories or approved residences. Amelia, twenty-two (admitting to twenty-one), was therefore free to live where she pleased. After checking out Whittier Hall ("some dump," she thought it) she rented "a fairly well furnished room" in a large apartment at 106 Morningside Drive, a nine-story stone-and-brick structure on the south corner of 121st Street and Morningside Park. She then signed up for the maximum allowable course load of sixteen points, taking EA, an elementary biology and zoology course, and EB, Vertebrate zoology and evolution, both taught by Dr. James McGregor and H. J. Muller; French 3, Psychology 1, and Chemistry 3, all in the Extension Program. For spring term she got special permission to add Chemistry 42a at Barnard to her schedule, which meant she was carrying an unusually heavy course load of twenty-two points.

There were only two blond coeds in the elementary biology and zoology classes, Amelia and Louise de Schweinitz, and they were assigned desks next to each other. Louise, three weeks younger than Amelia, a graduate of Smith College, tall and blondish, was taking courses at Columbia to fulfill the requirements necessary for entrance to the Johns Hopkins School of Medicine, from which she would take a degree in 1924. The two of them immediately became fast friends. They were great favorites of Professor McGregor, managing to get two of the four A's he gave out among the sixty-four students in that elementary biology and zoology class. McGregor thought Amelia was particularly suited by temperament for scientific work because she had such a lively interest. This interest, he recalled, was especially noticeable during the ten-minute breather he allowed his students during the course of the long Saturday-afternoon lab session. During those breaks tea was brewed over Bunsen burners, and he sat back and answered questions. Louise and Amelia were also both enrolled in an inorganic chemistry course at Columbia and an organic chemistry course at Barnard.

When they were together, according to Louise—who thought Amelia "so capable she could have done anything"—Amelia was always the leader and she the follower; Amelia was the "keen, electric one," while she herself was "the steady plodding worker." Amelia, who "wanted everyone to be treated fairly," involved Louise in an effort to get a promotion for a professor whom she believed had been wrongfully passed over.

From the time she was a little girl, Amelia had been a climber—climbing up and out and into things. She was geographically curious, one might say. Above the earth, below the earth, on the earth, like Alice, curiouser and curiouser. Now she did a very curious thing: she explored all the subterranean passages connecting the Columbia buildings. Louise came with her. Another time, on a mild May afternoon, Amelia was taken with the idea of sitting in the lap of the Alma Mater, the famous gilded statue by Daniel Chester French that guards the front steps of Low Library. It was not a difficult climb, but was certainly an unusual thing to do. Louise recalled that they sat on the statue's lap eating cherries out of a paper bag and taking turns reading Browning's "Pippa Passes," which Amelia had in her pocket—at the same time trying to look nonchalant as people walked by staring.

Low Library was also the scene of Amelia's most famous Columbia exploit—climbing to the top of the dome, the highest point on the campus. No one else would have even considered it. The route to the dome is an interior spiral stairway behind a locked metal door—but Amelia appears to have had no problem securing the key. The dome is paved with what look like descending overlapping fish scales, designed to make snow and ice and everything else slip downward. Amelia talked Louise into accompanying her on this escapade too, and they took photos of each other, with Louise's Brownie, lying and standing on the dome. The photo shows plainly their hats and long skirts; it doesn't show their shoes—low-heeled, with slippery leather soles. Some students saw them that spring afternoon and clapped. Then they had to slither their way down—no mean feat. But all their exploits and explorations suddenly came to an abrupt end.

At the end of spring term, having maintained a B+ average for the year and earned thirty-eight course credits, of which eighteen were in chemistry, Amelia quit. It was very sudden. She had changed her goals, she later maintained; she was now leaning more to a life of laboratory research rather than pure medicine. She gave a number of reasons for her change of plans: "after a year of study I convinced myself that some of my abilities did not measure up to the requirements which I felt a physician should have." She also wrote: "It took me only a few months to discover that I probably should not make the ideal physician" because she was bothered, "among other possibilities of sitting at the bedside of a hypochondriac and handing out innocuous sugar pellets to a patient with an imaginary illness."

None of these explanations ring true—particularly after the heroic courseload she had just so creditably shouldered. In fact it was her parents who suddenly derailed her. Amelia was on the receiving end of what she described as "pleadings" from her mother and father to come live with them in Los Angeles. It was not a free choice. In the 1920s young unmarried women still did what their parents wanted. Amelia felt obligated and went, albeit unwillingly.

She still intended to pursue a career in medical research and planned to enroll in college in the fall, but Los Angeles during summer vacation was a whole new world. Came September, she never signed up, because "aviation caught me."

6
California

• • • • For early fliers, belonging to the Caterpillar Club was the ultimate badge of honor—proof that they were brave and seasoned, serious and lucky at the same time, for only fliers who had parachuted out
of their planes and lived to tell about it were eligible for membership.
As one of the founders explained, the club took the name Caterpillar because it seemed so appropriate "for several reasons: The parachute
main sail and lines were woven from the finest silk. The lowly worm
spins a cocoon [out of silk,] crawls out and flies away from certain
death."

Lieutenant Harold R. Harris of the U.S. Signal Corps was the first
person to parachute out of a crippled plane and live to tell about it—and
the first member of the club. His jump, on October 20, 1922, made
front-page headlines across the nation because it seemed unbelievable that
someone could leap free from a doomed plane and live.

Flying a plane was not at all a safe proposition in the early
1920s—things always went wrong. The Curtiss Jenny and the Canuck
were among the safest planes flying, which was the reason the United States
and Canada had extensively used them as training planes during the recent
war. But they were far from safe; the Curtiss handbook that accompanied

each new plane worriedly advised fliers to "never forget that the engine may stop, and at all times keep this in mind."

That summer of 1920, when Amelia moved to Los Angeles, Laura Bromwell, the most famous American female pilot, the "foremost American aviatrix" as the newspapers styled her, holder of the women's speed record, got into her plane for the last time. A few weeks earlier, she had enthralled the crowd of ten thousand assembled for the opening of Curtiss field on Long Island by completing an incredible record-breaking 199 loop-the-loops. Now, on a June day, as she was halfway through a loop, she fell to her death. The plane, upside down with Laura still in it, fluttered downward "like a falling leaf," crushing her under the wreckage. Her body was badly mutilated, the newspapers reported. She was exactly Amelia's age. A few weeks later, Owen Locklear, "greatest of all daredevil fliers," the first pilot to do aerial stunts for the movies, while working on a film sequence, put his plane into a tailspin he never came out of, and crashed within the environs of Hollywood.

Of the first forty pilots hired by the post office to deliver the aerial mail, as it was called in those days—all highly trained, the best of their day—all but nine died. In the one year, 1920—the year Amelia fell in love with flying—fifteen aerial mail pilots died.

No doubt it was a deadly pastime in those years. George Dade, growing up near Curtiss field, became a pilot even though he knew the dark side of aviation in the 1920s. He kept a diary of those killed: "I stopped counting when the list reached one hundred."

"In those days the motor was not what it is today. It would drop out, for example, without warning and with a great rattle like the crash of crockery," wrote the novelist and aviator Antoine de Saint Exupéry, "and one would simply throw in one's hand: there was no hope of refuge." Clarence Chamberlin, one of the best pilots, was in ten plane crashes, due either to faulty engines or to poor landing fields; he walked away from them all.

But the risk was part of the magic of those early years—the fact that every pilot had narrow escapes, near misses, that Chamberlin's experience was the norm. There were no walking wounded, no agonized hospital stays, no maimed pilots to mar the scene. Suffering was not part of the picture—there was only excitement and daring to balance against sudden, clean death.

When Amelia learned to fly in 1921, Lieutenant Harris's parachute jump was still almost two years in the future. There was no Caterpillar Club yet, no way out of a doomed plane.

The danger was part of the fascination.

It was not surprising that Amelia went to an air meet soon after she arrived. California was preoccupied with flying, and new airfields were opening virtually every week. It was the promised land for this newest outdoor sport: the temperature was balmy, the climate dry, the land flat and open. The movie moguls were taking it up. Stars, directors, writers, and studio heads, including Will Rogers and Cecil B. DeMille, bought planes and hired pilots to teach them how to fly. DeMille went on to buy his own field, and thereafter countless stars began flying or posing in flying clothes to get noticed. Colleen Moore, a starlet as wise in the ways of the world as she was pretty, put it best: "It's the fashion and I cannot afford to be out of fashion."

When Amelia evinced a desire to go to an air meet, whatever her father's private reservations, he had to admit it was just about the most popular outdoor activity around. There were twenty fields in the Los Angeles area alone, and each weekend something was going on at at least one of them. The most famous airfield, the one with the biggest runway—500 feet wide and 4,000 feet long—and the busiest, was Earl Daugherty's airfield, just west of Los Angeles. It was there that Amelia saw her first California air meet.

The meet featured a hundred-mile free-for-all and shorter handicap races, most of which were won by army and navy pilots. As a matter of course, it included the standard heart-stoppers that drew the crowds: plane-changing and wing-walking, which looked and sometimes was incredibly dangerous. And because the lighter-than-air machines were still in the running as rivals for the heavier-than-air airplanes, there were also dirigible races, and rides were available in a blimp.

Amelia went to every air meet she could. By December, she had talked Edwin into making inquiries about instruction. The first step was to get someone to take her aloft.

Earl Daugherty, thirty-three, had been flying since 1911 and was the acknowledged dean of flying in the United States. He had rolled up more hours in the air than any other pilot. Undoubtedly Edwin would, given the chance, have preferred that Amelia make her first flight with him. "Experience is insurance" was Earl's motto. Instead, she took her trial hop a few days later at Rogers airport, run by Emery Rogers, a personable, young, handsome ex-army flier. Emery, whose field lay across from DeMille's Mercury field at the intersection of Fairfax Road and Wilshire Boulevard, had new Pacific Standards, two Curtiss Jennys, and a Curtiss Oriole, which seated three. The day was "characteristically fair," as Amelia remembered, when she and her father arrived at the field. It fell to Frank Hawks, also a young ex-army officer, short and stocky, good looking, with curly hair, to take Amelia up for her first ride. Frank, who had learned to fly at the army's Brooks field in San Antonio, Texas, would later become famous for setting all kinds of speed records, but at that moment in his life he was still merely a "local air thrill maker" whom Rogers paid fifty dollars a week to fly wing-walkers, teach flying, and occasionally give rides to passengers.

Amelia loved her trial hop. Nothing could spoil it for her, not even that Frank had another pilot aboard because he was afraid that, being female, she might jump out. It was instant infatuation—she "knew" she had to learn. But not with Frank, whose attitude bothered her. His boss, Emery Rogers, was at the time teaching at least one other woman how to fly—Cornelia McLoughlin would get her license that June. Nevertheless, Amelia went to another field where there was a female instructor, Neta Snook, because she felt that she would learn more quickly and easily from a woman.

Neta, twenty-four, who owned a Canadian Canuck, had left Iowa for California the year before so she could fly in the winter as well as the summer. That fall she had leased commercial rights to Kinner airport and immediately became notorious as the only female flier in southern California who was in the business of carrying passengers and giving lessons.

A thin young woman with a mop of curly red hair, when she was flying she dressed in the universal fashion that pilots had adopted—which is to say in variations on the uniform of the cavalry: high boots and jodhpurs and a leather coat. But she spent a great deal of time working on her plane, which she serviced herself, so more often than not, she was in grimy overalls.

Neta would never forget her first glimpse of Amelia. On a hot December day in 1920, as she was about to climb into her Canuck to give a lesson, she saw a tall, slender young woman approach, accompanied by an elderly man.

> She was wearing a brown suit, plain but a good cut. Her hair was braided and neatly coiled around her head; there was a light scarf around her neck and she carried gloves. She would have stood out in any crowd and she reminded me of the well-groomed and cultured young ladies at the Frances Shimer Academy back in Mount Carroll, Illinois, my childhood home.
>
> The gentleman with her was slightly gray at the temples and wore a blue serge business suit.
>
> "I'm Amelia Earhart and this is my father. I see you are busy, but could I have a few words with you?"

She stated her objective, which Neta remembered because she put it so succinctly: "I want to fly. Will you teach me?" The meeting was mutually agreeable, and the first lesson was scheduled. There was a problem—Amelia's lack of funds—but it was solved when Neta agreed to take payments when Amelia found the money, "so in a few days I began hopping about on credit with her."

Neta and Amelia had much in common. They were both from the Midwest, had both attended college (Neta had gone to Iowa State University), and were near the same age (Neta was a year older). Of even more significance, both were elder daughters in families that consisted of two girls only, and both had fathers who approved of and fostered their early childhood activist ways.

It seemed like a perfect pairing, and for a while it was, but they were miles apart in terms of character and personality. Neta was much more single-minded about flying than Amelia. In the middle of her sophomore year at the university, she had suddenly quit to enroll in a flying school nearby. When the school abruptly folded, she was broke, but instead of throwing in the towel and returning home, she walked, hitchhiked, and hopped freight trains across the country to Newport News, Virginia, where the famous Curtiss School of Aviation was located, and talked her way into the all-male program. The United States entered World War I, and Curtiss was forced to shut down before Neta had a chance to solo. After the armistice, Neta bought an old wrecked plane, the Canadian version of the Curtiss JN4 called a Canuck. She brought it to her home in Ames, Iowa, and using the knowledge of plane construction she had gained in the flying schools, where students had first had to build the planes they would fly, she rebuilt it in the backyard. She had never soloed, but when she finished, she took the Canuck up for a trial spin. She wasn't worried about herself, only about her plane because, as she explained, "I knew I could fly."

Kinner Airport was a large tract of weeds and grass rimmed by truck gardens in what was then farm country south of Los Angeles. It was reasonably accessible from the city—an electric streetcar ran partway out, leaving only the last few miles, to the intersection of Tweedy Road and Long Beach Boulevard, to be covered on foot or by car. It was a sleepy place, as laid back as a flying field could be. There was only one building—a hangar big enough to hold three planes. A wind sock flew from the roof.

Neta had been at Kinner field for several months by the time Amelia arrived on the scene. The owner was Bert Kinner, a tall, slightly stooped forty-year-old with friendly black eyes and a mop of ragged black hair who spent all his time in the hangar working on a revolutionary new sport plane. Neta did aerial advertising (at one point she had "Wilshire Gasoline" painted in big letters on the bottom of the Canuck's lower wings), gave lessons, and conducted aerial tours of the neighboring towns of Santa Ana, Corona, Riverside, San Bernardino, and Pasadena, which she grandly publicized as "The Orange Empire Air Voyage."

On the day of her lesson Amelia arrived at Kinner field dressed in brown jodhpurs, laced boots reaching to midcalf, and jacket. She hadn't bought it recently, as Neta would learn; it was her riding outfit. The date was January 3, 1921. Amelia, ever the student, ever the library ferret, arrived on that day with a book on aerodynamics tucked under her arm. That book and the many others that followed became the basis for endless discussions between the two women.

Amelia had a splendid time with Neta. In these early golden moments, before anyone she knew was killed, nothing went wrong. There was just the experience of mastery of a new element, the glorious sense of power, and the freedom.

· · · ·

Amelia's flying outfit was either jodhpurs or slacks, for since planes of the day had no doors, access was via the top—the flier climbed up the side, swung a leg over, and then dropped into the open cockpit. To get into Neta's Canadian Jenny—every plane, including the one Amelia would shortly buy—meant doing a giant leg stretch, bracing the lower leg against an indented toehold and swinging the upper leg into the cockpit. Since male pilots the world over wore the uniform of the cavalry—breeches and high boots—women adopted it too, rather than simple slacks. Those few who wore dresses did so at their peril.

Amelia had always been acutely aware of her own attributes—and self-conscious about her drawbacks. She was rather vain of her hands, which were beautiful, with long tapering fingers. She didn't mind her blond hair, except that it was straight and needed constant curling. But she knew she had a problem—she had been aware of it at a very young age: her legs. They were long but far from shapely. The problem specifically was her fat ankles. Her observant cousin Katch Challiss thought she showed great objectivity, that she was quite right not to like her legs, that because of her thick ankles her legs "seemed to be the same all the way down." Piano legs, they are sometimes called.

Pants were a godsend. With her long legs, she looked superb in pants, and she knew it. In pants she walked unselfconsciously with a graceful, loose-jointed stride, and as a pilot, she had a legitimate reason to wear them. So she seized the chance to wear first the breeks, as breeches were called, and boots and then, as flying styles evolved and "piloting clothes" changed, ordinary trousers, until pants—beautifully tailored—became her signature outfit.

She also knew she would look well in the new shingle haircut suddenly all the rage, but she was afraid the combination of short hair and pants would take her over the edge and that, like Neta, she might look—the word she used—"eccentric."

She didn't want Waldo Waterman, pilot and airplane designer on the local scene whom she liked, or any of his friends, to class her with Neta, whom they thought looked just awful. "We were not quite sure as to whether 'Snooky' was a man or woman, as few of us ever saw her except in a pair of dirty coveralls, her reddish hair closely cropped, and her freckled face usually made up with the assistance of airport dust and a dash of grease," Waldo observed. Amelia took a great deal of pride in her appearance, and indeed even Neta thought her friend dressed much better than she, writing that the jacket and breeches she wore made "a beautifully tailored outfit." Amelia was very hesitant about bobbing her hair. It wasn't until after a little girl said to her that she didn't look like an aviatrix because her hair was too long that she finally, irrevocably, cut it short. After that, she would carefully curl her tousled blond "bob," which looked so natural, no one thought she ever touched it. And she managed to gain even Waldo Waterman's approval. In contrast to Neta, he wrote approvingly, when Amelia was dressed for flying in riding breeches and boots, she still "looked thoroughly feminine."

• • • •

The Canuck had two open cockpits. In each was a duplicate set of controls, consisting of a rudder bar and a stick. Neta, as the instructor, sat in the rear cockpit, and whatever she did in the way of steering was duplicated in the forward seat, where Amelia sat. The rudder bar, manipulated by the feet, turned the plane in the same direction in which it was depressed, and the stick, a lever that rose from the floor, made the plane dive when pushed forward, climb when pulled back, and depress the wing when pushed to the side.

As she began her lessons, what always stuck in Amelia's mind was how hard it was to make the plane fly level. It was a problem encountered by many student pilots no matter what sort of plane they flew, but it was worse in the Canuck, which had a peculiar tendency—a marked tendency, admitted the Curtiss company—"to nose down on a right-hand turn and to climb on a left one."

The Canuck was a biplane (two sets of wings) with a maximum speed of seventy-five miles per hour and a landing speed of about forty-five. Although it was slightly lighter and faster than the Curtiss Jenny that was the standard-issue plane Glenn Curtiss had developed for the U.S. Army—and had a more rounded rudder and double ailerons—it was basically the same plane. Neta's had the engine standard to both, the 90-horsepower, eight-cylinder, water-cooled OX-5. The skin of the plane was linen panels that were sewn together, stretched, and tacked onto the frame, then painted with cellulose dope that shrank the fabric to a drumlike tension and made it waterproof. The plane had no gas gauge, no brakes, and no rear wheel. A tail sked, in place of a rear wheel, dragged on the ground and eventually slowed the plane to a stop. Like all Canucks, Neta's was notoriously slow to climb and, underpowered, couldn't go very high.

It rained mightily at the beginning of 1921: seven inches fell the first six weeks, more than usually fell on Los Angeles in the whole year, and as a result, many of Amelia's lessons had to be canceled. By the end of February she had managed to log only four hours in the Canuck. It was enough time for her to realize she didn't like it.

Amelia had her eye on the little plane Bert Kinner was still tinkering with in the hangar. Bert was a mechanical and aeronautical engineer who had honed his skills building custom bodies for Model T Fords before getting bitten by the flying bug. In 1919 he formed the Kinner Airplane and Motor Corporation, bought a 230-acre field on Long Beach Boulevard near Lynwood at Tweedy Road, and taught himself how to fly. He planned to build a line of sport planes—light, maneuverable, small enough to fit in a garage, and financially within everyone's reach. The first prototype, built with the help of his wife Cora, who ran the office and had charge of the sewing, was ready in May 1920, in time to be included in the Industrial Parade in Los Angeles—although it was pulled through the streets on a flatbed truck rather than proceeding under its own power, as most of the other planes did. By June he had worked out the serious bugs and was in business, giving lessons and demonstrations.

The Aero Club of Southern California had scheduled and publicized a "free for all" at the Beverly Hills Speedway for Sunday, February 27, 1921. "Speed kings of the board bowl will vie with pilots of dashing airplanes in endeavoring to throw a few extra thrills into the pop-eyed populace," ran the teaser in the newspaper. The Washington's Birthday extravaganza of racing cars and racing planes drew thousands to see the exciting events. A 250-mile nonstop race from Los Angeles to San Diego and back—canceled at the last minute because of fog—and three sprints where the planes circled the grandstand drew the then-unprecedented number of thirty-two civilian entries. The civilian fliers felt they had finally come of age; it was the first time since the war that a large air-racing event had not been dominated by the military fliers.

Bert Kinner entered and flew the Airster, as he called his new plane, in one of the thirty-six mile sprints, racing against the pros—Emery Rogers, Frank Hawks, and Earl Daugherty, the latter of whom won, with an average speed of 104 miles an hour. Bert dropped out after the fifth lap, presumably because of engine trouble, but the Airster performed creditably, and he had the satisfaction of having the air world know that Kinner was a name to contend with. Amelia was impressed. She had been absorbedly watching the plane even as she "cut her aviation teeth" at Kinner field. It hadn't taken her long to see that it took off more quickly, climbed more steeply, and was faster and easier to handle than planes with greater wing spread and more powerful engines. Now she had seen it hold its own even when matched against the best. She wanted it desperately.

In the summer of 1921, for her twenty-fourth birthday, Amelia managed to buy the little plane, with help from her parents, going against the advice of Neta and other experienced pilots. She was more than pleased with her purchase—she was thrilled. The plane responded so perfectly that she bonded to it like a pet, as her mother noticed. "It was like a favorite pony. We said goodnight to it and patted its nose and almost fed it apples."

It must be taken as a mark of Amy and Edwin's high regard for Amelia and of their respect for her decisions that they were so supportive of her desire to fly and of her choice of the Airster—for flying was a very expensive sport, and the Kinner Airster a very expensive plane. Following World War I, such a large pool of surplus planes had been dumped on the market that a plane in reasonable condition—a JN4-D (Jenny) or a Canuck—could be bought for less than $1,000. In comparison, Amelia's Airster cost $2,000. So when she talked her parents into helping her finance flying, it was perilously close to an impecunious young man falling in love with polo and getting his family to help him purchase a string of the best polo ponies.

As her contribution, Amelia took the first paying job of her life, becoming a back-office mail and file clerk with the telephone company, a job she kept for several years. A clerk's salary didn't begin to cover the expenses she was incurring, but the small dent it made was enough to win Amy to her daughter's side. Convinced of the soundness of Amelia's motives and her seriousness, she agreed to pay for the Airster: "It . . . affected mother to the extent that she finally wiped out my indebtedness, on condition I resign and stay home a little," Amelia later wrote.

• • • •

The Kinner Airster was a biplane, as was the Canuck, but it was smaller, with a wingspan of 27 feet, as opposed to the Canuck's 44; it was 19 feet long, as compared with the Canuck's 27; and in spite of the fact that it had a sturdier exterior than the Canuck, with a fuselage of three-ply mahogany instead of fabric, it weighed only 600 pounds, as compared with the Canuck's 1,430. The Airster was, in fact, so light and so well balanced that Amelia could pick it up by its tail and easily move it anywhere she wanted. As for performance, the Canuck didn't even come close. The Airster with two passengers had a range of 200 miles compared with the Canuck's 100 miles, and a top speed of 90 mph as compared with 75; and it could fly as high as 13,000 feet, where the Canuck topped out at 10,000. It was a swallow compared with a turkey.

The main reason the Airster was so light was that it was driven by an air-cooled engine, one of the first developed in the United States. Amelia, who loved beautiful things (horses, cars, or airplanes) loved the simplicity, the elegance, the very conception of the air-cooled motor, which, substituting for the water-cooling system, made the craft pounds lighter, enabling Bert Kinner to realize his dream of a small light plane.

The designer of the engine was Charles Lawrance, a brilliant aircraft engineer who had graduated from the Ecole des Beaux Arts and Yale and was one of the first to see the possibilities of using air instead of water as the engine coolant. He founded the Lawrance Aero Engineering Corporation in a modest Manhattan factory and began to build small air-cooled motors. When World War I started, he enlisted in the navy, where he did further aeronautical engine research, and following the armistice, he began turning out the light, efficient two- and three-cylinder engines that would shortly make him famous. One of his first air-cooled models, revolutionary but still, with a solid six years of experimentation behind it, not untried—a 60-horsepower, three-cylinder engine weighing a mere 149 pounds—was the model Bert Kinner ended up buying to power his first plane.

Lawrance would go on developing and refining increasingly powerful air-cooled engines and within a few years would be acknowledged as the foremost designer of aircraft motors in the country. In 1923 he would fold Lawrance Aero Engineering into the Wright Aeronautical Corporation, of which he would become president, and would shortly be turning out the big air-cooled Wright Whirlwind engines that would power Commander Byrd's plane to the north pole in 1926 and Charles Lindbergh's *Spirit of St. Louis* across the Atlantic in 1927, as well as all the famous Fokkers, including the *Friendship*, that would catapult Amelia to fame. In 1928 he would win the Collier trophy, and in 1929 a Wright Whirlwind engine would power the plane with which William Brock and Edward Schlee set the world's endurance record of 150 hours in the air.

But in the winter of 1920–21 an air-cooled engine was such a startlingly radical concept that Neta and others tried to persuade Amelia not to buy it. Neta thought Amelia had had her head turned, having been beguiled because the plane was, as Neta grudgingly admitted, "the prettiest plane we had ever seen." Neither she nor many of the other pilots had the vision to realize they were looking at the future. Neta was supposed to have been Kinner's test pilot, but when the moment came for her to fly her first Kinner, she was scared. "I remember thinking, 'The field is long. I can set it down again if I don't feel it's airworthy.' " She never lost her feeling of unease. In fact, by her own admission, she flew the Airster only "a few times." She didn't like the way it handled; she thought her Canuck, the training ship for a generation of fighters, was dangerous enough. Among other things, she complained, the third cylinder "periodically became clogged." The real reason was that the Airster was tougher to land than the Canuck because it came in at a faster speed, and was easier to ground-loop because it had a wheel tread of only five feet; it couldn't be banked as easily, and all in all, complained Neta, "it didn't have the stability." So scary did Neta find the plane that when she reconstructed those days in her autobiography, she retroactively and totally inaccurately shrank the Airster's wingspread from twenty-seven feet to seventeen.

• • • •

Will Rogers's definition of an airfield was "a tract of land completely surrounded by high tension wires and high chimneys, adjacent to a cemetery." The Kinner field almost qualified; it had two sets of high-tension wires on its eastern perimeter. Since the landing field had to be approached from the east because of the prevailing winds, the wires inevitably had to be crossed. Amelia liked to come in high in the little Airster, then drop down and fly between the two sets of wires; she did it quite often. The two wires were close—to Neta's mind's eye there was about eight feet between them. It drove Neta crazy with fear. Amelia gave her some soothing explanation about daydreaming and said she wouldn't do it anymore; Neta accepted the explanation at face value.

Neta was unable to comprehend Amelia's attitude toward what she considered a very dangerous pastime, and she didn't realize that Amelia was dealing in mental gymnastics to keep her as a friend. All she saw was that Amelia *seemed* to exhibit a callous disregard for danger (flying the Airster at all, much less buying it, and flying between high-tension wires), yet in the one major area, soloing, Amelia was obdurate: under Neta's supervision she wouldn't do it. It drove Neta to the edge of distraction. Amelia simply would not agree to solo. "By this time she had had four hours and 45 minutes in the Canuck and four hours in the Airster, and I told her I felt she was capable of flying alone. . . . She'd look at me with her winsome half smile, but she never committed herself."

· · · ·

From the beginning Neta felt threatened by Amelia's intellect and probing mind. Neta was a Seventh Day Adventist and a fundamentalist who believed in the imminent end of the world; Amelia was an inquiring agnostic and an insatiable searcher for knowledge. Between them was a gulf that grew wider as they got to know each other better.

Before the first summer was upon them, Amelia had changed instructors. What undoubtedly strengthened Amelia's resolve to drop Neta were the two crashes they had. Once as they were taking off from nearby Goodyear field, a malfunctioning cylinder made the Airster's rate of climb too slow to clear the grove of eucalyptus trees at the far end of the runway. Amelia, in the rear seat, instinctively put the nose up and went into a stall—the only thing to do. "I would have done the same," Neta admitted. The result was a mild crash; as they hit the ground, the propeller broke and the landing gear gave way. Before Neta had a chance to say anything, indeed before she had thought to turn off the engine—necessary to prevent a fire—novice Amelia, with great presence of mind, cut the switch. By the time Neta had pulled herself together and turned around, Amelia was collectedly powdering her nose because, as she said, "We have to look nice when the reporters come." The other crash came about because the plane ran out of gas. Amelia did not, at the time, accuse Neta of negligence, but later she did, publicly, for all the world to read about, in her first book, *20 Hrs. 40 Min.* writing, "Crashes were frequent enough in these earlier days. I had one myself, during my instruction period. Owing to carelessness in not refuelling, the motor cut out on the take-off, when the plane was about 40 or 50 feet in the air. Neta Snook was with me, but she couldn't help depositing us in a cabbage patch nearby. The propeller and landing gear suffered and I bit my tongue."

Neta undoubtedly brooded over this enigmatic passage, because in *her* book fifty-two years later, she tried to get even; she wrote about a time when the two of them were setting out, at Amelia's instigation, on a longer trip than usual. Soon Neta made Amelia abort the trip because she hadn't personally checked the gas tank. She found out upon landing back at Kinner field that they had only half a tank of gas. "I was almost angry at her. Perhaps I had misjudged her abilities," Neta primly wrote.

Amelia, whose loyalty to friends was legendary, who made it a point to stay close to all the people she cared for from childhood, would never lay eyes on Neta again after she left California in 1924. The significance of that fact, in terms of Amelia's personality, is enormous. Amelia would stay rooted in Neta's memory, looming ever larger, but the closest Neta ever got to Amelia after 1924 would be corresponding with her sister. When, fifty years later, Neta wrote her autobiography, she called it *I Taught Amelia How to Fly*. In it she goes on for pages about her beloved old friend. She deals in her own way with the fact that she was merely Amelia's first instructor, that Amelia abandoned her, and that Amelia wouldn't solo with her because she didn't believe Neta knew enough to teach her competently.

The friendship, so important to Neta, actually would wither on the vine; she was too intrinsically different from Amelia for the relationship to continue. Even in their attitudes toward men they were at opposite ends of the pole. Neta loved going out on dates with any reasonable young man, it seemed, but Amelia didn't. As Neta could not help but observe, the boys were certainly interested in Amelia. Tall at five foot eight but not too tall, and willowy, with her new short blond bobbed hair, nose freckled from the California sun, she was quick to smile at the boys that hung around her at the field, and just as quick to turn them down. Unless she was really interested, Amelia thought dating a waste of time; her preference was to spend her evenings at the library, reading up on something she considered interesting, such as California history. Amelia's mindset at the time can be seen from the following, which she copied down in her small notebook: "Sowing wild oats is putting cracks in the vase of our souls—which can never be obliterated or sealed—even by love. As G. B. S. [George Bernard Shaw] says, 'Virtue does not consist in abstaining from vice but in not desiring it.' "

The gulf grew wider as they got to know each other better. Amelia must have been amused by Neta, although she would not have shown it. Neta was remarkable in that she was one of the first fliers in the world and had an enormous amount of courage, but the singleness of purpose that had enabled her to achieve goals against outstanding odds carried with it a penalty: once set on a path, she never swerved. Just as for her the only book was the Bible, the Canuck for her was the only plane—and one did not experiment with either. If Neta had not been as closed-minded about planes as she was about the Bible, the relationship between the two might have continued, but as it was, Amelia gently disengaged from her friend.

For Amelia, the flying that Neta taught was merely phase one; phase two—learning to get into trouble and learning to get out of it, in the next-generation plane—was the next step. Just as walking a school horse in a ring will not teach a person how to control a spirited horse at a gallop, so taking off, flying level, and then landing would not teach mastery of the Airster. If Amelia were going to fly the Airster, she wanted to learn how to take it through *all* its paces. And that meant what was called stunting. Amelia never explained any of it to Neta; later, from a distance, she explained it to the world.

> I refused to fly alone until I knew some stunting. It seemed foolhardy to try to go up alone without the ability to recognize and recover quickly from any position the plane might assume, a reaction only possible through practice. In short, to become thoroughly at home in the air, stunting is as necessary as, and comparable to, the ability to drive an automobile in traffic.

It was natural that Amelia chose an ex-army pilot to teach her stunting—they were the best. Her choice was John Montijo who, like many ex-army pilots, had been knocking about the country trying to make a living out of flying and was another recent arrival on the Los Angeles scene. He was a superb pilot and liked and had full confidence in the Airster. As Neta faded out of the picture, he faded in. Within a short time he knew the Airster like the back of his hand and had taken over demonstrating and racing it. Before many months elapsed, he had as well become financially involved in Bert Kinner's enterprise.

Short and stocky, always well dressed to the point of wearing a shirt and tie with his jodhpurs, he exuded competence. Monte, as everyone called him, and his wife Alta became Amelia's friends.

Amelia learned stunting under his watchful eye, to become competent in the air no matter what the conditions. Under John's instruction, she learned how to sideslip the Airster, do forty-five-degree banked turns, vertical banked turns, dives, tailspins, loops, and barrel rolls, "and their relatives and friends"—not so useful, she had to admit, but she learned them "mostly for fun." She practiced until it became second nature, likening stunting to the necessity of learning how to drive a car in traffic when the right reactions are vital.

Within a few months she would solo, in a flight that was a bit of an anticlimax. As she was taking off, one of the Airster's shock absorbers broke, causing the left wing to sag, and she had to abort the flight. After the damage was repaired, she took off again, climbed to about five thousand feet, fooled around, and returned to the field. The flight ended with a "thoroughly rotten landing."

Before the year was out, it was not Neta Snook but Amelia with the calm gray eyes and freckled nose who was the celebrity aviatrix at Kinner field, whose exploits were being written about in *The Ace.*

> On November 3, Miss Earhart with a 175 pound passenger and a full tank of gas climbed to 10,200 feet in one hour and twenty eight minutes and during the course of the flight was 3000 feet directly over Mt. Wilson.

She was not only participating in air meets but was featured as a drawing card to boost attendance: "The Pacific Coast Ladies Derby will bring out two of our best lady pilots Miss Amelia Earhart and . . . Miss Aloysia McLintic."

• • • •

On November 12, at Daugherty field, Bert entered the Airster in the first air rodeo. The air rodeos, dreamed up by the Commercial Aircraft Association of Southern California and run by the Aero Club of Southern California, were designed to attract people and money into the aviation world while simultaneously offering the pilots fun and exposure. Those behind the rodeos were emphatically of the camp that approved of stunting for a very pragmatic reason—for most people, the novelty of just seeing an airplane fly by had worn thin. To draw crowds now, there had to be more of everything—more thrills, and more and new stunts.

It was at this first rodeo that the first aerial refueling was carried out. Wing-walker genius Wesley May strapped a five-gallon can of gasoline onto his back, walked out onto the wing of the Jenny that Earl Daugherty was maneuvering through the air as Frank Hawks flew perilously close, jumped onto the wing of Frank's Standard, walked to his gas tank, poured in the gasoline, and finally walked back into the Standard's cockpit. The Airster performed in three events—stunt flying, landing over an obstacle, and a tug-of-war that was dramatically advertised as a test between the plane and a one-ton truck but in fact ended up as a contest between the plane and a large seven-passenger automobile loaded to capacity; it ended in a draw. Undoubtedly the Airster used was Amelia's, for her name is included in the list of those whom the Commercial Aircraft Association thanked for their assistance in making the Long Beach Air Rodeo a success, putting her name on a short list with such luminaries of the air world as Earl Daugherty, Frank Clarke, Frank Hawks, Wesley May, and Waldo Waterman.

On Sunday, November 27, Emery Rogers, racing against a French Nieuport in his C1 Monoplane, banked on a turn above his field from which he never came out. In reporting the fatal accident, the press made sure, as they always did in those days, to point out that it wasn't because flying was inherently dangerous that the plane had crashed but because the pilot had made an incredible error. In this case, the error was not only that Rogers had not yet recovered from a "severe" case of the flu but that he "had been given strict orders by his doctor not to fly as he was subject to dizzy spells. . . . There can be but one answer. Emery Rogers became dizzy from the speed and strain of the race, perhaps only for a fraction of a second, but the ship was but forty-five feet from the ground and the speed was 140 miles per hour."

Overlooked was that Emery Rogers had been a pilot of such talent that he had graduated two weeks ahead of all the others in his army training class at Souther Field, that he was a man of such leadership qualities that the army shortly thereafter put him in charge of Souther field, and a man of such judgment that while he ran Souther field not one officer, not one cadet, had ever been seriously hurt.

His death didn't change Amelia's plans, or those of anyone else in the flying fraternity. On December 17, Amelia and silent screen star Aloysia McLintic were a featured attraction of the second air rodeo at the Sierra airdrome in Pasadena, a by-invitation-only air show. The rodeo consisted of twelve events—everything from the usual tug-of-war between a plane and a truck, to aerial tumbling, landing contests, aerial transfers, wing-walking, a mail-bag-dropping accuracy contest, a three-lap relay race, a parachute jump (which did not take place), and a radio hookup from a plane to a waiting General Pershing in Washington, D.C., which also failed to come off. Amelia and Aloysia's event was number ten on the program: "Pacific Coast Ladies Derby," consisting of Amelia in her Kinner Airster and Alyosia in her Laird Swallow. The two women doing stunts flew similar planes—light sport model biplanes, although the Swallow, at close to six thousand dollars was much more expensive.

During the afternoon before and between events, many of the seven thousand spectators who had paid to attend were free to wander about the field and examine the planes up close—a necessary inducement to lure nonpaying customers, parked on the perimeter of the field, out of their cars and through the gates onto the field. The curious, who circled, questioned, or merely gawked at her elegant little Airster, gave the twenty-four-year-old Amelia her first taste of dealing with crowds.

Amelia had turned up even though something was the matter with the Lawrance engine—actually, it was out of the Airster, being repaired.

At that stage in the development of planes, parts were constantly being interchanged: land planes would have their wheels taken off, replaced with pontoons and become seaplanes; wings would be replaced with other wings; engines would be exchanged with other engines. Nor was it unusual for engines to be put to use in vehicles other than the kind they had been designed for. Motorcycle engines, being small and light were pressed into service to power planes; amateur automobile builders put powerful but inexpensive plane engines into cars.

Reflecting this practice, aviation magazines ran as many ads for pieces of planes as for whole ones. Jenny wings "new and covered" went for $20; an OX-5 motor somewhere between $150 to $275; a new Lawrance engine "complete," probably a two-cylinder, could be bought for $85.

Replacing one engine that was temporarily down with another was done all the time. If it hadn't been, pilots would have been grounded for unsuitably long stretches. It was just another one of the risks one had to accept. So Amelia didn't let the fact that her Lawrance engine was on the bench stop her—she simply hunted up another to put in its place. Her substitute came from a somewhat unusual source, however: the Goodyear pony blimp, a midget dirigible that usually ran at a speed of only thirty-nine miles per hour and carried three people. Such usage made far lower demands on the engine than the Airster, and as a result, as Amelia was fly-ing, one of the three spark plugs blew out and the engine quit, luckily just as she arrived over the Pasadena airdrome. She made a dead stick landing over the field, which must have been excellent because it went totally unnoticed: "the chatterers never knew they came near having something actually to talk about." After a new extralong spark plug was inserted, Amelia decided to participate anyway.

As 1921 drew to a close everything was falling into place for Amelia. She had won her wings, had her own plane, had earned the respect of her fellow pilots for her flying prowess, and had been accepted as an equal by the California flying fraternity. She was full of plans and high hopes—looking forward to buying the newest model Kinner Airster that Bert was designing, turning over in her mind the possibilities of flying it to New York in the spring to compete in the 1922 flying season there and, once there, re-enrolling at Columbia.

Amelia had a wonderful time piloting her pet. Sometime that win-ter she (momentarily) established a new altitude record, which found its way into the papers. In an unusual departure from her usual modesty, she included the clipping in her first book. The newsclip reported that "Miss Amelia Earhart, local aviatrix, established a new altitude record for women yesterday under the auspices of the Aero Club of Southern California. Flying her own Kinner Airster, containing a 60 horse power motor, she ascended more than 14,000 feet." She was becoming so well known that beginning in April, Bert Kinner used her in the full-page ads he regularly took out in *The Ace* to advertise his plane—and of course the exposure made her even better known. "A Lady's Plane as well as a Man's," ran the headline of his advertisements.

On August 8, 1922, the *Los Angeles Examiner* ran a story on the probable departure of the famous local aviatrix Amelia Earhart. It was a puff piece ("Vassar College is primed for its thrill of thrills. Some sunny day next fall a large and dusty airplane is due to pull a near-tailspin over its exclusive campus and, descending, to disgorge Miss Amelia Earhart, Los Angeles society girl-student aviatrix.") and it featured a half-page photo of Amelia in flying togs in front of an Airster. But she didn't go. "I lingered on in California, another sunkist victim of inertia—or was it the siren song of the realtors," she wrote, glossing as usual over problems.

Amy and Edwin were still struggling with their lives. That first summer when Edwin had moved out to Los Angeles alone, he had been taken in hand by members of the Christian Science Church, and it was as a result of the efforts of the Church that he no longer drank and had returned to his old self. By the time Amelia and Amy moved out, he was part of a law firm, Earhart and Maine, located in the Fay Building in Los Angeles, was full of plans for the future, and was exploring the possibility of running for the state legislature. To support his political plans, he had old friends write references. A former mayor of Kansas City obligingly wrote, "I am sure that he would make a safe, active and intelligent member of the Legislature, and one in whom the District he represents can place absolute confidence."

In 1921 they had moved from the modest home on West Twenty-third Street, where they had been living, into a larger, more comfortable house on West Fourth. The move, however, was based more on optimism about Edwin's prospects than anything else. They were, as usual, just getting by.

Having, by reason of their history, scant faith in their own business judgment, Amy and Edwin had begun to rely on Amelia's. On her suggestion, they decided to make an investment in a gypsum mine in Nevada that Peter Barnes, a friend of Amelia's, had purchased the fall of 1921. In spite of the fact that it was Amy's money, her role appears to have been totally passive. Amelia and Edwin went out to Moapa, Nevada, to see Peter and the mine. They arrived on site after a heavy rain, were almost engulfed in a flash flood, and watched Peter die as the rushing water caught and overturned his truck loaded with gypsum. Amelia wrote to her sister back east at Smith, "Peter is drowned, the mine seems irreparably flooded, and all of mother's investment is gone. We are still reeling from the blow."

They had to resort to extreme measures just to get by. Amy decided to do what she had set out to do in St. Paul—take in boarders—and this time she followed through. One of them was Sam Chapman, twenty-nine years old, from Marblehead, Massachusetts, who had recently graduated from Tufts. Tall and thin, with dark brown hair, and blue eyes, he was an engineer. He appeared to share Amelia's appetite for knowledge and her admiration for whatever was new. There is no record of his flying with Amelia, but they played tennis and discussed books and philosophy. They discovered they were both idealists and shared a common concern for the inequalities of society; they went to at least one Industrial Workers of the World meeting together.

Sam loved Amelia's spirit, her daring, her independence. For her part, Amelia found herself seriously interested in him. He was kind and considerate, and there was something else that appealed to her—theirs was a relationship of two equal people. Sam would never dominate her the way Edwin did Amy. Amelia began dropping his name into the letters she wrote Muriel at Smith. She began thinking about marriage, not right away, but sometime in the future.

• • • •

That June, following the mine disaster, Amelia sold her plane to a former flying instructor named Maynard Morley and began casting about for a fulfilling career that paid well.

Becoming a flying instructor herself would apparently have solved all Amelia's money problems, but teaching, in spite of the example of Neta, was a chancy occupation in those years. The particular risk in teaching was due to the fact that all the training planes of the period were, without exception, locked into dual control mode—so that if a student sitting alone in his cockpit froze at the stick, he could send the craft crashing to earth. The number of students who had killed themselves and their instructors was a constant source of anxiety. It had been brought forcefully to Amelia's attention almost the first moment she arrived in Los Angeles and fell in love with flying: Clifford Prodger, an internationally known test pilot with an awesome six thousand flying hours to his credit, had been killed on an August day that summer of 1920 up at Redwood City when one of his students had lost his head, frozen at the stick, and sent the plane diving into the earth. When the wreckage was examined, it was found that Clifford had bent his steel stick with his hands in a desperate and futile effort to break the student's hold over the plane. The only way to deal with the problem, according to Amelia, was for the instructor to keep a belaying pin of sorts about, with which to knock the student unconscious. Teaching was therefore never an option for her, averse as she was to ceding control of her life in *any* circumstance to someone else.

In her search for a paying occupation that would leave her time for flying, Amelia had been investigating photography studios and had actually been offered a part-time job in one studio. Although she had not taken it, she decided it was a promising way to make money and decided to study photography. Thorough as usual, she worked to become good at her new trade, photographing ordinary objects to get unusual effects. For a while her favorite subject was garbage cans. She photographed the garbage can on the cellar steps, the empty garbage can alone on the curb—"I can't name all the moods of which a garbage can is capable." She went into business with a fellow student, Jean Brandreth, making "home portraits," but their subjects demanded so many sittings, they didn't make any money. She became adept at filming with a motion picture camera as well as still camera. Once she had the great good fortune to be driving by just as an oil well started gushing, and she sold the resultant film to a local real estate promoter. In June 1923 she went to work for an established commercial photographer and there learned how to develop color film. But the studio ran into financial problems and "nearly became bankrupt." She left in October, disillusioned with the moneymaking potential of the profession.

Amelia's next foray was so unusual, in the 1920s for an educated young woman, as to be almost strange. She began driving a sand and gravel truck. Noting that a building boom was turning outlying airfields into housing subdivisions, she decided money could be made hauling paving and building materials for the burgeoning market. Lloyd Royer, a young midwesterner, a top-notch mechanic looking to get into his own business, was her partner in the enterprise. They bought a truck and proceeded to drum up business. The truck, a Moreland, was, since Amelia always bought the latest thing, state of the art. The Moreland Company, located in Burbank, was famous for producing the first trucks that ran on low-grade fuel and used more than a three-speed transmission; it gave a one-year guarantee. Amelia's friends were less than impressed. Several, in fact, dropped her. Whether or not she was "ostracized by the more right-thinking girls," as she claimed years later, there is no doubt that she was made to feel distinctly uncomfortable.

In the meantime Edwin was coming to the conclusion that the time had come to terminate his marriage. His interests hadn't included Amy for a long time. His friends were now the members of the Church who had supported and encouraged him; his spiritual life was intertwined with them. But in spite of the fact that he had grown so far apart from her, in spite of his obvious indifference to her needs, in spite of the fact that he paid so little attention to her, Amy still clung to him. She still loved him and wouldn't let him go. She would have gone on clinging to him forever, always hoping that he would change and that the marriage would get better. Finally he came to realize that if he were to separate his life from hers, he would have to make it happen. And he did; he forced the issue. Amy, Amelia, and Muriel moved out to 5314 Sunset Boulevard, then an area of small shops and modest houses on the east side of Hollywood.

In spite of the family troubles, Amelia was carefully and methodically putting money aside for a new plane — and not just any plane, but another Kinner.

Bert Kinner was now developing his own engines, had just put into production his own design, a 60-horsepower three-cylinder radial air-cooled motor weighing, at 150 pounds, just one pound more than the Lawrance. He finished the first engine in the spring of 1922; by September the motor was in production and the following year it was standard on the Airster.

The prototype engine, only 50 horsepower, was bought by David R. Davis, a wealthy entrepreneur who was an early backer of the engineer and industrialist Donald Douglas. (The Douglas Company was first called the Davis-Douglas Company; the first Cloudster turned out was called the Davis-Douglas Cloudster.) David Davis had intended to install the Kinner motor in the one-passenger monoplane he was designing, which he planned to fly between Los Angeles and his Imperial Valley ranch, but his plans changed, the plane was not built, and he had no immediate use for the finished engine.

Amelia, her finances considerably reduced, saw an opportunity and set about getting her Kinner. The method she resorted to was novel, not so much for the times but for her. Presumably at a reduced price, she bought Davis's engine and somehow, undoubtedly with Bert Kinner's help, "collected" an Airster to put it in. The engine, Amelia found, had a few flaws.

> The greatest pleasure I found in my experience with Kinner's
> motor was that of perhaps having a small part in its development.
> Its many little ailments had to be diagnosed and cured later. It
> smoked and spattered oil. Adjustment of a proper propeller was
> difficult. One of its eccentricities was an excessive vibration which
> tickled the soles of the feet when they rested on the rudder bar,
> putting a new meaning into joy ride.

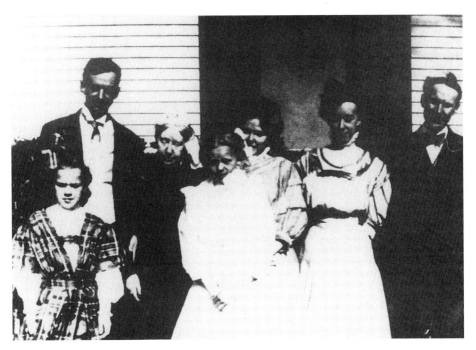

Three generations. In front, left to right: Amelia's sister Muriel and Amelia. In rear: Amelia's uncle, Carl Otis; her grandmother, Amelia Harres Otis; Carl's wife, Anna; Amelia's parents, Amy Otis Earhart and Edwin Earhart.

Courtesy of Muriel Earhart Morrissey.

On Prince, the 12-year-old Indian pony that Amelia rode during the summers in

Amelia as a young girl.

Worthington, Minnesota.

Courtesy of Corbis-Bettmann.

Courtesy of Kenneth Clapp.

Amy and Edwin's wedding photo. They were married at Trinity Church on October 16, 1895. After the ceremony, they went directly to the train station and were on the noon train to Kansas City.

Courtesy of the Schlesinger Library, Radcliffe College, and Muriel Earhart Morrissey.

Amelia "Millie" Otis with Amelia "Millie" Earhart. Amelia spent most of her childhood with her grandmother.

Courtesy of Corbis-Bettmann.

Graduation photo of Amelia that appeared in **The Aitchpe,** *The Hyde Park School yearbook, 1915. She looks very prim and proper, not like her usual self, and the caption reads, "Meek loveliness is round thee spread."*

Courtesy of Hyde Park High School.

Amelia with her cousins, Katch Challiss (far left) and John Challiss (far right). Amelia is beckoning the photographer (her cousin Lucy) to come closer.

Courtesy of Patricia Antich.

Katch's map of her favorite version of Bogie, the game Amelia dreamed up, always played in her grandparents' barn in Atchison. Amelia, Katch, Lucy, and Muriel would sit in the old carriage in the barn and embark on dangerous and exotic voyages.

Courtesy of Patricia Antich.

After graduating from Hyde Park High School, Amelia went to Ogontz, a finishing school outside of Philadelphia. The headmistress had a number of unusual ideas, among them that the girls should dress in their graduation gowns for Halloween. Here is Amelia in hers, October 1917.

Courtesy of Corbis-Bettmann.

Amelia went to Toronto for Christmas vacation to be with her mother and sister, and never returned to Ogontz. Instead, stunned by the sight of so many wounded soldiers, she decided to stay in Toronto and become a nurse. She lived with Muriel at the St. Regis Hotel, where this photograph was taken. Courtesy of Kenneth Clapp.

Both Louise de Schweinitz and Amelia were pre-med students at Columbia. Amelia involved Louise in a number of escapades, including this one—climbing onto the dome of the Low Library, the focal point of the Columbia campus. Louise brought her Brownie camera. Courtesy of Louise de Schweinitz Darrow.

Amelia was engaged to Sam Chapman for several years. She broke off the engagement in 1928 after the **Friendship** flight. He never married, never got over her.

Courtesy of Corbis-Bettmann.

This is a self-portrait, taken by Amelia after she returned east from California, winter 1925–26.

Courtesy of Kenneth Clapp.

Amelia and Neta Snook, her first flight instructor, on the day of Amelia's first lesson, January 3, 1921. Amelia is wearing her riding clothes, which Neta thought "a beautifully tailored outfit."

Courtesy of Oklahoma Air and Space Museum, and the grandchildren of Neta Snook Southern.

One of the publicity photos for Denison House, where Amelia was a social worker, that appeared in Boston newspapers. Amelia flew over Boston and Cambridge dropping passes for a fund-raising carnival for the settlement house. May 25, 1927. Courtesy of Corbis-Bettmann.

Being greeted in Southampton, England. Amelia was only a passenger on the transatlantic flight of the **Friendship** *in June 1928, but she was the first woman to make the crossing, and the world went wild. From the left: Amy Guest, who financed the flight; Louis Gordon (pilot), Amelia, Bill Stultz (mechanic), and Mrs. Foster Welch, the mayor of Southampton.* Courtesy of Corbis-Bettmann.

After Amelia finished her speech at the Hyde Park High School, from which she graduated, she exited the stage by way of the piano so she could mingle with the students. July 1928. Courtesy of Corbis-Bettmann.

Amelia and George Palmer Putnam, shortly after their marriage, February, 1931. On the morning of the wedding, she handed George a letter listing conditions he must meet if he wanted to marry her. It didn't seem to faze him a bit.
Courtesy of AP Wide World Photos.

On May 21, 1932, exactly five years after Charles Lindbergh's flight, Amelia became the second person to fly the North Atlantic solo. She was not only the first woman to make the flight, but the first person to fly the Atlantic twice. She landed in a pasture in Londonderry, Ireland.

Townspeople of Londonderry greeting Amelia.

By 1923 the Kinner field, the old Mercury field, and the Rogers field had been sold for subdivisions, for houses for the droves of people moving to Los Angeles who would that year make it the fifth largest city in the country. In February Bert Kinner moved his operation to a new field in nearby Glendale, which became upon completion the nearest airfield to downtown Los Angeles. It too was none too safe; its short twelve-hundred-foot runway was bracketed on one end by power lines and on the other by a peach orchard. Nevertheless, within a short time the Aero Club of Southern California and most of the local fliers, including Amelia, were flying out of Glendale, less than fifteen minutes from her new home on Sunset Boulevard, and it became the favorite site for most of the aviation segments filmed by the studios.

By now the Kinner Airster was the accepted, popular sport plane of the day, and Bert Kinner was in the happy predicament of being hard put to turn out a sufficient number to keep up with demand. Amelia's prescience in selecting the avant-garde Airster two years earlier was vindicated everywhere she turned. As *The Ace* somewhat pompously put it, even Jenny owners—and Jenny was understood to include its Canadian sister ship the Canuck as well—"could now see the necessity of developing a smaller plane with a greater performance range to eventually supercede the 'old faithful' which is so prevalent at most of the flying fields today." (On September 1, 1927, the U.S. Army would ground the Jenny forever, stating "Today they are obsolete.")

The opening of the Glendale airport on Saturday, March 17, 1923, was marked by an air rodeo held under the auspices of the Aero Club of Southern California, the Commercial Aircraft Association, and the city of Glendale. All the usual local fliers were invited to perform, including Amelia, who was paired with the movie attraction of the moment, Andrée Peyre, a sloe-eyed film star just featured by *The Ace* on its cover attired in high boots, jodhpurs, leather jacket, helmet, and goggles. Brave as well as beautiful, Andrée, who came to Los Angeles in 1919 as an actress under contract to United Studios, had learned to fly from French ace Captain Étienne Poulet following the deaths of her three aviator air ace brothers in the war. When she arrived in Hollywood, she had taken further instruction from Earl Daugherty, who taught her stunting. She had just taken delivery on a new French-made Sport Farman, the hot plane of the hour.

Earl Daugherty led off the stunting in a Canuck; Amelia and Andrée were the second featured event. Although they shared equal billing, it is noteworthy, in that land of touchy egos where such things matter, that Amelia's name ran first: "The Ladies Sportplane Special. Miss Amelia Earhart flying Kinner Airster, Miss Andrée Peyre flying Sport Farman." It was particularly noteworthy since not only was Andrée more famous than Amelia, but her plane was better known. The Farman, also a 2-seater biplane, smaller than the Airster with a 23-foot wingspan and 150 pounds lighter at 450, was a marvelous machine that held the world's record for range in speed—from a low of 15⅝ mph to a high of 87. And it came from a famous maker: another Farman, a Goliath, had held the endurance record in 1921.

The two women performed barrel rolls, loops, tailspins, and other stunts. They were followed by an accurate landing contest, balloon strafing by Frank Clarke (simulating the air battles of World War I), a parachute jump from the wing of a plane by Miss Gladys Roy, a skywriting exhibition—"Lucky Strike" would float across the sky, the work of a "master aerial penman"—and a Jenny Scramble (actually a five-mile race) among other events. There was an added event to the program: "If weather conditions are suitable, Miss Amelia Earhart, flying her Kinner Airster, will attempt to break the altitude record of 13,200 feet for plane equipped with 50 H.P. motor," which for some reason, presumably the weather, didn't occur. (Her previous record of 14,000 feet had been made in her first plane, which had a 60-horsepower engine.) In May Andrée would briefly take the altitude record for women away from Amelia when she recorded 15,700 feet, then would lose it in July to Bertha Horchem of Ransom, Kansas, who would establish a record of 16,300 feet. But none of them took their records seriously—Lieutenant John Macready, in a Lepere biplane with a 400-horsepower Liberty motor, had gone up an astounding 34,509 feet.

On May 16 Amelia took and passed the test to get her pilot's license. The test, under the aegis of the Aero Club of America, consisted of two parts. The first part, Test A, in those days where engines were always cutting out, was to check out a pilot's ability to make a dead stick landing. Amelia had to cut the engine off at 4,921 feet (1,500 meters) above the ground, then glide and land within 492 feet (150 meters) of a predetermined point without restarting the engine. For the second part, Test B, Amelia was required to make an uninterrupted series of five figure eights around posts not more than 1,640 feet (500 meters) apart, at an altitude of not more than 656 (200 meters) above the ground. She also had to, upon landing, stop the aircraft within a distance of 164 feet (50 meters) from a point fixed beforehand.

In June Amelia would be admitted to membership in the Aeronautical Hall of Fame, the worldwide honor roll of men and women "influential in advancing aeronautics." In July she would get public recognition of her unique flying status—it would be duly noted by Daisy Elizabeth Ball in the prestigious *Aeronautical Digest,* the magazine of the Aero Club of America, that "Miss Earhart, who resides in Los Angeles, is the only woman licensed by the N.A.A. since its organization last October." As Daisy Ball, herself a member of the Women's Press Club of New York, would note, the new association, the National Aeronautic Association (NAA) "has declared its intention of including women in its membership." It was one of the few professional organizations in the United States that would.

Amelia, at the age of twenty-five, had already become one of those early mythical heroes of the sky whom people came to see at air meets and dreamed of emulating. She was one of those exotic beings whom popular songs commemorated, the subject of flying having become a favorite in the early 1920s:

> Tis a wonderful thing to be a King
> Not a monarch of Royal Birth
> But a sovereign of Air in a realm so fair
> That Covers the wide, wide Earth

By 1924 Bert Kinner was so successful that he was floating another issue of stock in his expanded company and, spending all his time at Glendale, had become field manager of the airport, which was averaging almost a thousand flights a month. Amelia continued to fly out of Glendale in the Airster, which Bert now advertised as so well designed that it was still "essentially the same sport plane, with the exception of a few minor details, that was designed by this company more than five years ago." When her old friend and fellow pilot Aloysia McLintic Huzar came back from China after a year-long honeymoon, the two women would go flying in Amelia's Airster, an event notable enough to be worthy of mention in flying circles and written up in the press.

By this time Amelia had been dating Sam Chapman for two years. They appear to have settled into a comfortable if not exciting relationship largely controlled by Amelia. Sam was patiently waiting for her to give up her career plans, deeply in love with her. Amelia had no intention of giving up her career plans, but she was certainly fond of him, and before the year was out she had agreed to be engaged.

1
Breaking Through

• • • • Once Amy and Edwin's divorce was final, once it was clear that family life as they knew it was over, Amelia was free to lead her own life. She decided to return east and resume her studies at Columbia—to pick up her life where she had left off. One by one, those around her also decided to go back east. Sam Chapman returned to Marblehead, the seaport town north of Boston where he came from, and went to work for the Edison Electric Company in Boston. Muriel, still intent on getting her undergraduate degree, enrolled in Harvard summer school and set off by train for Boston; the plan was that she would find a place to live for herself and Amy. Edwin was the only one in the family who felt at home in Los Angeles and remained there.

Amelia was laid low by a return of the infection in her antrum, the result of the strain of packing up all the Earhart possessions, trying to sell her truck, tying up the loose ends of four suddenly dislocated lives, and again taking care of her mother. The main problem was Amy, who was so devastated by the ordeal of divorce, so obviously miserable, that Amelia was sure that once they left, her mother would never set foot in California again.

An operation was called for to drain the pneumonococcal infection. The procedure cost five hundred dollars, which Amelia left unpaid.

She could have scraped together the money, particularly since she now proceeded to sell her plane, but she had other plans for her slim resources; she bought a rakish yellow touring car made by the Kissell Company. Her action made her fair game for nasty letters from a collection agency, to whom the debt had been turned over; undeterred, she went about her business.

Amelia had always planned that, when she returned east, she would fly there in her own plane; the maps and data for such a flight had long been ready. But that idea had been superseded by Amy's needs. The Kissell was so that she and Amy could drive across the country, stopping to see the famous national parks of the West on the way—an adventure of a different sort on the unpaved roads of the 1920s. "Which way are we going?" asked Amy as they left Hollywood that first morning. "I am going to surprise you," replied Amelia and headed north. They visited Sequoia, then continued north to Yosemite, farther north into Oregon to Crater Lake, then north into Canada to Banff and Lake Louise, after which, turning southeast, they began heading back, stopping on the way to see Yellowstone Park in Wyoming. It was a long, leisurely trip, and by the time they reached Boston, they had covered more than seven thousand miles. The last part of it was a labor of love for Amelia, for the operation had not completely drained out the infection, and there was pressure and pain in her sinus.

Three days after their arrival in Boston, Amelia checked into Massachusetts General Hospital, where yet again doctors opened up her sinus and drained the infection. This time her recovery was excruciatingly slow. She spent the months in Medford, a suburb of Boston where Muriel had found a teaching job and a house nearby for herself and her mother to live in.

Sometime in the late fall, Amelia felt well enough to go to New York. By that time, however, the combination of the move east and Amelia's medical expenses had eaten such a hole in the Earhart finances that Amelia departed for New York in her Kissell with hardly any money in her pocket.

Amelia had a terrible time that winter. It was not until the spring term, which started in February, that she enrolled at Columbia, and even then she entered after the term had started. Before that, she stayed for weeks at a stretch with her old friend Marian Stabler out in Great Neck, Long Island. Marian observed that Amelia was so severely debilitated that the least strain or exertion exhausted her. Her convalescence was as unduly slow as before, and for the same reason—there were still no potent drugs with which to fight the infection.

But she was still game. Ailing as Amelia was, Marian remembered, she still went on at least one winter picnic. Nor had she lost her nerve, as evidenced by her conduct one night when Marian heard a strange noise. Marian's impulse was to run for the bedroom and lock the door until the servants came home. Amelia refused, insisting upon searching the house until she had allayed Marian's fears.

Marian realized years later that, as close as they were, Amelia never really confided in her. By Marian's admission, it becomes apparent that Amelia's habit of concealment extended even to her closest friends, for Marian would remember that although they talked for hours on end for days and nights on end "about everything under the sun," Amelia never mentioned her parents' problems. Even when she divulged their divorce, it was in such a manner that she gave away no real information. "It seems odd that a family could be broken up by geography but my mother hates the west and my father hates the east," Marian remembered her saying. And that was all Amelia ever said on the subject. She never admitted that Edwin was an alcoholic, never talked about the pain and suffering his drinking had caused the family. When, years later, Marian finally learned about Edwin's drinking, it was from another source.

Nor did Amelia complain about her lack of money. And yet Marian couldn't help but notice it—Amelia was virtually penniless. The only thing she spent money on was her car, remembered Marian; in order to maintain it, she "went without everything but essentials."

By January of 1925 Amelia felt better, and on January 25 she climbed the dome of Low Library to watch the eclipse of the sun, bringing with her a "known biologist," as she wrote in her second book—undoubtedly her old professor, Dr. James McGregor, whom she couldn't name without bringing the wrath of the university down upon his head.

Five years before, Amelia had carried five courses one term and six the other. Now Amelia enrolled in only two, an intermediate course in algebra, Mathematics eX6, and an elementary course in general physics, Physics eA4. Two courses were probably all she could afford. And she had difficulty scraping together the fifty-six dollars due for these two courses, for she couldn't register without paying, and so she didn't register until February 10, six days after the term started. She rented a room in an apartment at 50 Morningside Drive.

But having taken those crucial steps, almost immediately she felt her prospects brighten and a science degree to be within her reach. She had registered as a nonmatriculated student, but in March she reregistered in the University Undergraduate Matriculated Program. In the interim, having been exposed to the engineering profession through Sam Chapman, her focus had changed; she was now planning, she wrote on the form, to take a degree in engineering.

Then, on April 20, she withdrew from Columbia. One month after she had gone to the trouble of changing her status from a nondegree to a degree candidate, more than a month before the term was over, she was gone.

The problem was again money. Sometime in March she had received a letter from her old partner Lloyd Royer, in which he informed her he had finally sold the Moreland truck she had entrusted to his care and put the money into her bank account. But it was evidently nowhere near as much as Amelia expected. And strapped as she was, she knew he was equally strapped, having netted only a hundred dollars after building a plane in partnership with John Montijo. He had just gone into the aircraft repair business and owed money for the space he had leased. Amelia insisted he keep part of the money. She wrote him back: "Please hold out something for yourself; I want you to. Heaven knows you've had enough trouble with the thing. Please." She closed with the sentence, "Write me when you have time," giving as her return address 50 Morningside Drive. She mailed her letter on March 22; doing it with flair in spite of her straitened circumstances, she sent it airmail, setting her back twenty-six cents. To Lloyd no more than to Marian would she reveal distress.

• • • •

In spite of her precipitous withdrawal and missed classes, she received a B in physics, which may be taken as an indication of unusual industry and talent. (Later she could joke about her brief stint, noting that when she couldn't think of the answer to the weekly physics quiz, "I inserted a little French poetry.") But she almost failed the intermediate algebra course—"planned especially for students who have had a course in elementary algebra to quadratics"—which would certainly have challenged her even if she hadn't missed so many classes, since she hadn't had a math course since high school. She received a C— which meant, in addition to not receiving credit, that her standing as a matriculated student was in jeopardy, for her acceptance as a degree candidate had been granted "conditional on Intermediate Algebra."

If ever she needed money, it was then. If ever her independence was threatened, it was then. The Stabler family, comfortably well off with their big house and servants, could have helped her if she had asked. She didn't ask. She was too tough and too proud. Instead, she drove to Boston and settled into the small, neat, decidedly modest two-story wood-frame house at 76 Brooks Street in West Medford, where Amy and Muriel lived.

Grimly determined to erase the blot on her academic record, she enrolled at Harvard summer school—but only for one course, Math

S-1, a trigonometry course that assumed a grounding in algebra "through Quadratics and Plane Geometry." It was exactly the material she had covered so badly at Columbia. Yet if she wanted to pursue her goal of a degree in engineering, she had to remove the blot and pass with flying colors. With nothing to distract her, she performed with her usual thoroughness, earning three credits and an A.

Taking just the one course left Amelia with plenty of time to learn about her new academic institution. Harvard summer school would have been a tantalizing experience for her. Assiduous tracker of achieving women that she still was, she must have taken comfort in the fact that for the first time there was a woman on a Harvard faculty, Dr. Alice Hamilton, assistant professor of industrial medicine, the pioneer investigator of industrial pollution in the United States, author of the just-published *Industrial Poisons in the United States,* which would shortly prompt the surgeon general to initiate a study of the dangers in tetraethyl lead.

But the inclusion of Alice Hamilton on the Harvard faculty in those years was an anomaly. Nowhere at that time was there an institution that gave out a more conflicting set of messages for the aspiring female than Harvard. In winter Harvard was exclusively a male domain. Only during the six-week summer school were women permitted to enroll, although even then they were excluded from courses in architecture, engineering, and geology. They were welcomed in the library (in the summer), but not in the recreation areas, or the dormitories. In the winter women went to Radcliffe, where Harvard professors taught them in special classes. During this time the libraries were restricted to men. And not even Professor Hamilton was immune to slights—she was barred from marching in commencement exercises, barred from the Harvard Club, and not permitted to claim the usual professorial quota of football tickets. For Amelia, the conditional status of females would have ruled out Radcliffe.

And so, in pursuit of a scientific career, Amelia applied to the Massachusetts Institute of Technology for the fall term. MIT, in contrast to its rival institution across the Charles, accepted women as well as men without reservation. What made it especially attractive to Amelia was that it was in the process of forming a department of aeronautical engineering.

But being short of funds, she needed a scholarship to go, and in spite of her Columbia and Harvard credits, she was turned down. It put an end to her dream of earning an engineering degree in the Boston area—and because her mother's funds were so slender, and because living with her mother and sister in West Medford, where Muriel was teaching in a junior high school, was rent free, Boston, however depressing, was Amelia's only choice.

In later years she would claim that she had never tried to get a degree in engineering, categorically stating, "During my collegiate experience I never sought a degree." Failure was not allowed to intrude upon the seamless past Amelia presented to the world.

• • • •

It was truly a terrible time. Amelia was twenty-eight and farther from a career than she had been at twenty-one. None of her plans had jelled. What was worse, she had nothing to build on. Her state of mind that fall was desperate; she was on the verge of despair, as she admitted to Marian Stabler. "Thanks for your as usual delightful letter(s). I am ashamed I have tried to write but every time I didn't finish. . . . No, I did not get into M.I.T. as planned, owing to financial difficulties. No, I can not come to New York, much, ah much as I should like owing to when I leave Boston I think I'll never come back."

She, who had always effortlessly helped her friends, who was the rock everyone leaned on, now had to admit that she was useless. She couldn't even promote Marian's woodcuts for Christmas cards, she admitted to Marian. "Do you want your samples back? I haven't decided yet and may not be able to send anybody anything. Isn't that sad?"

She couldn't get out of the habit of giving advice, however, admonishing Marian to read Sherwood Anderson's *Winesburg, Ohio*. But even her choice of this book indicated a negative frame of mind. For if Anderson's brilliantly realistic writing managed to capture the atmosphere of middle America and lay bare the midwestern soul, what he uncovered was a very bleak landscape indeed. He wrote of the shy, the lonely, the defeated, the dreamers: a boy who never grew up, a doctor who dared not practice, an artist who gave up painting, a mother who drove away her son, a young woman resigning herself to spinsterhood, a man who finds himself robbed even of his dreams.

There was one remotely positive note: never one to be idle, Amelia had begun teaching, she confided to Marian. "I am tutoring blind guys in Trig. Did I tell you before?"

The problems of the unassimilated immigrant, particularly the non-English-speaking immigrant, were very much on the minds of Boston's educators and politicians. Massachusetts had begun a crash program to teach English to foreign-born adults working throughout the state, setting up for the purpose a program in the University Extension Department of the State Board of Education. Harvard summer school offered classes specifically tailored to this specialized need, a program that almost immediately was broadened to include classes in citizenship, classes for the blind, and classes in English for the children of the foreign-born.

When Amelia began teaching, 27,759 foreigners were enrolled in the state program in 104 cities and towns throughout the state, 2,987 of whom were blind. The evening classes were usually held in the schools, while day classes were held in homes or in factories during lunch hour and after work. An average class met three times a week for twenty weeks. She would have been teaching in Lynn, Lawrence, Quincy, Salem, and even farther afield, driving to outlying immigrant enclaves in her Kissell. But the pay was low, most of the classes met in the evening, and the traveling allowance was minuscule. She decided to take a break and try and do it on her own.

By now it was spring. Building on her experience, Amelia persuaded the Biddle and Smart Company in Amesbury, Massachusetts, which employed a great many foreigners, of the wisdom and the practical advantage of letting her run "an office class in the Miller Course of Correct English." The course ran for fifteen weeks, from March 16 through June 22. Although Biddle and Smart were pleased with her ("She has a pleasant and pleasing personality and handled her work and the class well"), before many weeks were out she quit. She didn't find teaching English to foreigners challenging or stimulating.

Lucy Challiss passed through Boston one Saturday that June. Lucy lunched with a friend and shopped; she was readying herself for the European cruise she was about to take. She had no idea that Amelia and Amy were in Boston. So deep had the Earharts sunk, they had lost touch even with their dearest relatives; as far as the Challisses were concerned, they might just as well have dropped off the edge of the earth.

That month Amelia began working at Bournewood Hospital as a nurse-companion, signing on to work until October 1.

Bournewood, a private hospital for the treatment of mental diseases, located on an estate in Brookline, had been founded in 1884 by Dr. Henry R. Stedman, one of the first doctors to devote himself to the new discipline of psychiatry. It was a gracious place, run on the theory that its wealthy patients would get well faster if they were in a homelike setting and were cared for by "companion nurses," accomplished and well educated, who would form close personal bonds with their charges. "Personal attention and influence suitably directed is the sine qua non" was the operating philosophy.

It was an odd choice of occupation for Amelia, considering that she had left her medical studies because the idea of ministering to hypochondriacs, of prescribing "sugar pellets to a patient with an imaginary illness," had "floored" her. But working at Bournewood gave her another perspective: It made her more tolerant. "I did not see then that there was just as much of a problem in curing the somewhat mentally ill as those physically so — even though the methods used might differ." But if it was educational for Amelia, she was much too ambitious for it to be satisfying. Companion nurses were not doctors; they could not control methods of treatment or prescribe medication. Nor was there any chance of advancement, any chance to grow, for to become a psychiatrist meant not just getting a degree in medicine but undergoing psychiatric training — eight long expensive years. For an impecunious woman of twenty-nine, the gulf was unbridgeable.

However attractive the job had first sounded, the reality was that most of the work was menial and much of it distasteful. She lasted only several months before deciding to leave. "Work too confining and pay small," she would later write, but it was the former reason that was of primary importance; her salary was seventy dollars a month — her next job would pay less. She carefully let none of the impatience she felt over her limited role show, and as a result the hospital was sorry to lose her. "She leaves to increase her salary," wrote Dr. Torney, who ran Bournewood. It was the end of summer.

• • • •

There was in Boston a unique, thriving vocational guidance and referral center staffed exclusively by women called the Women's Educational and Industrial Union (WEIU). The first such center for women in the nation, it had been founded by an Englishwoman, Harriet Clisby, "to increase fellowship among women and to promote the best practical methods for securing their educational, industrial and social advancement." It did everything from providing free legal advice to poor workers, to calling attention to the rights of women and children, to running a school of housekeeping, to opening a school for salesmanship for women to train them "to be as competent in purchasing accounting and general salesmanship" as men. Just a few years before, it had set as a condition for the Massachusetts Legal Aid Society to take over the work of its Protective Committee the stipulation that they hire a female lawyer. To Amelia, still gamely pasting clips about female doers in her scrapbook, the way the WEIU had forced the Massachusetts Legal Aid Society to hire a female lawyer would have been a riveting achievement.

There are turning points in people's lives, sometimes little noticed at the time, sometimes never noticed; but going to the WEIU was Amelia's turning point. Through the WEIU, her teaching ability, her intelligence, and her desire to be of service all came together and into focus. She had undoubtedly gone to the Union, as it was called, because it had a reputation for helping women find their calling. She probably did not even know of the similarity between the early career paths of its founder and herself—both had studied medicine at Columbia University (although Harriet Clisby completed her training), and both had ended up in Boston.

There Amelia was, an intensely ambitious woman without any professional training, blocked at every turn. For years her highest priority had been a career. She wanted to succeed on her own—and yet in spite of all her efforts, she wasn't getting anywhere. Instead, she was getting backed into a corner, and it was beginning to look like marriage to Sam Chapman (patiently waiting in Marblehead for just such an eventuality) was what she might settle for. The WEIU was her last hope.

On August 18 Amelia went to 264 Boylston Street in Back Bay to register with the Union for employment and to fill out their forms. Now she was twenty-nine. Two years of short-lived study plans and short-term jobs, two years of going nowhere, had taken their toll. Suddenly Amelia had no professional aspirations at all. She, the keeper of a superachiever scrapbook, now wrote down in the space on the employment form for Work Desired, "Teaching English to Foreigners, Hostess, Anything connected with an Aeronautical Concern." The grit was still there, but the focus was gone. She would settle for a job now; forget a career. And she wasn't sure, given her rootless past and lack of accomplishments, that a job was even in the offing.

"A remarkable man whom I know says, 'Beware of the honest man when he is in a tight place,' " Amelia had written down in the notebook she kept in Los Angeles. It must have stuck in her mind, that an honest person might act out of character when severely threatened. Now, so worried about her credentials or lack of them, she was in just such a tight place. She didn't just gloss over her background, she lied—extensively—on the WEIU job application. She wrote that she had attended Hyde Park High School from 1911 to 1915 instead of just the one winter of 1914–1915, doubled the time she had been enrolled at Columbia to three years rather than a year and a half, and took two years off her age. Then she grossly inflated her professional background, claiming, "I have had five years of tutoring experience as well as class work," when in fact she had had just one.

That last lie gave her a reference problem. Her teaching and tutoring had been done under the aegis of the Educational Service Bureau of Boston, but if she gave the Educational Service Bureau as a reference (and the form demanded professional references), the WEIU would find out that she had been teaching less than a year. For that reason she gave only her two most recent jobs as referrals: the Biddle and Smart Company and Bournewood.

Both places recommended her highly.

She gave Sam Chapman as her character reference. He was either the best she could do, or she thought he would write a superb reference. Instead, he wrote a barely adequate, undistinguished letter. It has no salutation, is undated, is not on proper stationery and is not properly centered, being just a series of lines improperly placed at the top of the page.

> Miss Amelia M. Earhart is
> all right. I have known her four
> years and she is a very dear
> friend of mine. She is a good
> scholar and is capable in any
> field that she may claim.
> Samuel Chapman

"Holds a sky pilots license?" someone scrawled firmly across the form.

The WEIU woke her up—or perhaps it was the alert interviewer who probed, and saw her spark, for she drew her out and formed her own conclusion of Amelia's capabilities. There is another firm scrawl: "an extremely interesting girl—very unusual vocabulary; is a philosopher—wants to write—does write."

• • • •

The best and the brightest women of the time were going into social work. It was the one field where women could achieve positions of authority, the one profession where they could reach the top. Later, career-minded women could go into law or business, run for public office, join the military, become university professors. But in the 1920s those career paths were closed.

Settlement houses and settlement house workers were at the cutting edge of social change. Forward-thinking social activists took part in settlement house work, notable among them Frances Perkins, who would become Franklin Roosevelt's secretary of labor and in that capacity help set Roosevelt's agenda for social programs, and Eleanor Roosevelt, who worked at Rivington House before she was married and introduced her then-suitor Franklin to social work and the realities of poverty. ("My God," he said to Eleanor, "I didn't know anyone lived like that.") The most famous, of course, was Jane Addams. In those early years of the twentieth century, social work attracted the best of the well-educated women of the day. The settlement houses and the social workers who operated them considered themselves a conservative force; they didn't seek to change the social order or to make things any more "classless" than they were. On the contrary, according to Jane Addams, "Hull house was soberly opened on the theory that the dependence of classes on each other is reciprocal; and that as the social relation is essentially a reciprocal relation, it gives a form of expression that has peculiar value."

It is hard, in a later age, to appreciate the power and prestige attached to the early social workers, but what they accomplished was a revolutionary change in social thought. After the founding of Hull House, which was immediately hailed as the leader in the wave of social change, Jane Addams became a widely known lecturer and writer, the author of numerous books, and in 1910 the first woman awarded an honorary degree by Yale—the first acknowledgment by that bastion of the eastern male establishment that a woman (even if she would not be admitted as a student) was worthy of respect. The men and women who had been in the settlement house movement from its inception were looked upon with reverence by their peers, respected by the entire nation, and singled out for honors by the world. In 1931 Jane Addams would be awarded the Nobel Prize for Peace.

Denison House, one of the oldest settlement houses in the nation, had been started in 1892, just two years after Jane Addams founded Hull House in Chicago, by three idealistic college-educated women, Vida Scudder, Katherine Coman, and Emily Balch, who had been "distressed" and "made restless" by a "sense of privileges unshared." They were the ultimate female role models: highly unusual, gifted, respected women. All three were professors at Wellesley.

Vida Scudder, of an old New England family, had gone to Smith; Katherine Coman had graduated from the University of Michigan, class of 1880; Emily Balch, a Bostonian, the youngest of the three, had graduated from Bryn Mawr in 1889. All were pacifists and, at least at the beginning of their careers, socialists. Scudder, who combined a love of literature with a highly developed social conscience, the author of *Social Ideals in English Letters,* had taken a leave of absence from Wellesley to help the staff open Denison House. In spite of the demands Wellesley made upon her, she continued to be the prime mover and supplier of ideas at Denison House.

Katherine Coman, chairman of the Boston Settlement Committee, which superintended the formation of Denison House, was a professor of economics and history at Wellesley; she was as well an English historian and editor of *English History Told by English Poets.* It was she who made Denison House a center for labor activity.

Emily Balch, powerful and effective in every field of endeavor she entered, who would become the most famous of the three, was chairman of the departments of economics and sociology at Wellesley. By the 1920s Balch had left the Socialist Party, become a Quaker, and written a major study of immigrants of eastern and southern Europe. She would go on to become an active organizer and member of the Women's International League for Peace, and in 1946, for her labor for freedom and cooperation among individuals and peoples, she would be awarded the Nobel Peace Prize.

Very much in keeping with the settlement house movement from which it sprang, the philosophy of Denison House was "Not philanthropy but democracy," which was defined as "a free flowing life between group and group." In keeping with that philosophy and in keeping with the settlement house movement, eclectic Denison House provided not only aid, amusements, classes in English and citizenship, and medical care for Boston's immigrants, but also classes in English Literature, Italian art, elocution, Shakespeare, and embroidery, and in the early years of the labor union movement, it provided the space for union meetings.

Amelia was of the second generation of women in the United States whose desire for a career, tempered by a sense of privilege and social obligation, would lead them to social work, just as she was of the second generation of women to attend college. In going into settlement house work she was, as she undoubtedly knew, following in almost the exact footsteps of Jane Addams, who had also first enrolled in medical school and then elected to pursue a more dynamic social role. As she would find out, she was choosing one of the vocations most popular among seven sister college graduates.

The nameless interviewer at WEIU sent Amelia to be interviewed by Marion Perkins, chief executive of Denison House (head worker, as the position was called). Marion, intrigued by her poise and charm, hired Amelia even though she had no background in social work. As she would later write, Amelia walked into her office one day looking for a job, "and a part-time one would do, for she was giving courses in English under the University Extension. . . . She had had no real experience in social work . . . but she wanted to try it, and before I knew it I had engaged her for half-time work at Denison House. . . . I liked her personality and confidence in herself so much that I gave her a position . . . without asking her much about her training."

Thus Amelia, sent by an organization set up and staffed by extraordinary women, came to a place conceived, founded, and run by other extraordinary women. She was on her way—launched—although it would be a while before she knew it.

• • • •

Denison House was located in the south end, on Tyler Street. It started out in a three-and-a-half-story, twenty-foot-wide red brick house at number 93; within a few years it outgrew its home and spilled into the house adjoining. By the 1920s Denison House consisted of five of the red brick row houses joined together with a common entrance at number 93. The settlement house complex stood out from its neighbors on either side because it had whiter steps, cleaner walls, and in the summer, window boxes on the second-story windows; nevertheless it was in keeping with the other mixed-use houses on the busy narrow street. Historically an immigrant haven attracting whatever population flow that world upheavals sent into Boston, the area had once served a primarily Irish constituency. Then the Irish had moved on to be replaced by the Syrians. By the 1920s the Chinese were moving in. From the beginning of the Chinese wave, Tyler Street was its center. When the popular "mayor" of Chinatown, Moy Dow, died one hot August day in 1927, the funeral was held on Tyler Street. As the funeral procession, consisting of automobiles, police, Chinese and American funeral bands, and mourners, went down Tyler Street, it took up the entire breadth and length of the street. There was a Chinese restaurant on one side of Denison House, a Syrian restaurant on the other. Other neighbors on Tyler Street were a Chinese importing house, and the Syrian Roman Catholic church; around the corner was a Tong.

Marion Perkins put Amelia in charge of adult education—which meant teaching English and citizenship to the foreign-born in the neighborhood. The classes, which met in the evening, drew one hundred men and women to the English course alone. Almost immediately, responding to the perceived needs of the Syrian women whose children were in the prekindergarten at Denison House, Amelia organized the Syrian Mothers' Club.

Marion, almost as new at her job as Amelia (she had started that May), saw in her new assistant a kindred dynamic spirit. Over the years the free, open give-and-take between clients and staff—the hallmark of the settlement house in its early years—had succumbed to the exigencies of organizational hierarchy. Marion Perkins sought to bring it back. She formed a council consisting of staff members and children to inaugurate the new policy: "The House is no longer a power outside, granting favors or withholding them. It is a part of each one, and he is not a beneficiary, but a member." Then, seeing how superbly Amelia interacted with the children, she put her in charge of the girls' program.

One of Amelia's tasks was to ferry children who needed outside specialized medical help back and forth from the hospital. Often as she put some child into her sporty car for a trip to the hospital, she first had to explain to the fearful immigrant mother that hospitals were not dreadful places. The parents were as grateful for her patience as were their children.

Wrote one Syrian mother, who baked Amelia meat pies by way of thanks for taking her daughter to Massachusetts General Hospital, "I can still see her, tucking those little meat pies inside her leather jacket. Then she'd be walking down the street and pull one out and nibble on it, that yellow hair all curly and windblown." She drove another Syrian child, a boy blinded by the explosion of a kerosene heater, out to the Perkins Institute for the Blind three times a week for classes in Braille. This remarkable institution, which had trained Annie Sullivan and then recommended Sullivan as teacher for Helen Keller, prided itself on the normalcy of its environment and the diversity of its classes, all of which every year resulted in a "surprising number" of young people who succeeded in making good. Amelia, with her background of teaching trigonometry to blind men—certainly not an easy assignment—was so impressed by the Institute that she thereupon spent several hours a week there as a reader.

Within a year Amelia was working full time at Denison House, and was in charge of the kindergarten, of the girls from five to fourteen, and of so many other activities that they jokingly called her the "official secretary." Her groups were well organized, it was noted, and the children happy. The janitor, who had been there for years and seen good and bad social workers, thought Amelia excellent because the children liked her so. "She never had any favorites, never picked a child out for special attention, and that's what the children consider fair." Under her guidance and in response to the increasing number of Chinese (there were now more than a hundred Chinese families in the neighborhood), two new Chinese girls' clubs, one called the Octopus Club, were flourishing at the settlement house. There were also new home classes in English for the Chinese mothers, who had been living isolated lives in their Boston tenements.

Amelia's Chinese girls soon were enthusiastic basketball players and fielded a team that "had a fine year," even venturing to play a New York City team from Greenwich Settlement House, run by an ex-Bostonian, Mary Simkhovitch. The girls also had a fencing team, popular at the time, a sport Amelia tried and enjoyed. Amelia took it upon herself to open up the American experience to the first-generation Syrian and Chinese girls who were reared by their families "under racial traditions that cut them off from the freedom our American girls enjoy."

Within the year Amelia had moved into Denison House. Her room was on the second floor and simply furnished, but it had windows over-looking the busy scene that was Tyler Street. She took her meals in the dining room with the other resident workers, who usually numbered four, Amelia, Marion Perkins, Vernis Shuttleworth, and George Ludlam, the latter of whom was in charge of the boys. She prevailed on George Ludlam, who became her good friend, to make the boys, who used the linked backyards as their own private gym, to allow the girls to play there too. Vernis, too, became her friend and would eventually buy her car.

The staff were freely encouraged to invite interesting guests to share their repast, for as was usual in settlement houses, there was a housekeep-ing staff who cooked and served the residents. Amelia endeared herself to the other resident workers by braving down the housekeeper, who insisted upon serving the staff breakfast precisely at seven thirty A.M. and then only if they were fully dressed, even though there were days when the residents, working late, were tired. The punctilious housekeeper relented to the ex-tent of telling the residents she didn't care what they wore as long as they were on time. On the first morning after this pronouncement, Amelia, looking terrible, her hair in curlers, dressed in a "disreputable" borrowed bathrobe, and headed into the dining room first; the housekeeper relented on the time, also.

The settlement house, because of its mission and its clients, was neighborhood- and street-oriented and always full of people. Neighbor-hood groups such as the Syrian Ladies' Aid Society, the Syrian Relief Asso-ciation, the Syrian Junior League, the Chinese Students of Greater Boston, and the Loyalist League of America (a group of Greek businessmen) all met at Denison House in the afternoons, evenings, and weekends with some degree of regularity. Friday night was "open night" for adults, as well as the night Mademoiselle DuPont taught French.

Amelia fitted in a visit from Nancy Balis, her sixteen-year-old cousin, in transit to summer camp, late because of a broken ankle. The last time Nancy had seen Amelia had been several years before, when Amelia had pulled up in front of the Balis house in Germantown one day in her long, low, glamorous yellow car with the top folded back ("a marvelous contrap-tion," thought Nancy), accompanied by a beau. Now, teenage Nancy was so dazzled by Amelia and her stay at Denison House that it almost made up for the broken ankle—nothing quite equaled her cousin, who was so nice to her, who "always made her feel like her equal," who, better yet, "insisted we call each other cuz."

Six hundred boys and girls attended classes and activities and clubs ranging from cooper-working and ship-model building to sewing, embroidery, folk dancing, handicrafts, dramatics, choral singing, scouting, table games, and storytelling, which met through the day and into the evening. Sometimes after dinner, for those so inclined, there would be volleyball games in the street with the neighborhood children, or a performance at the Chinese theater. If Amelia found a free moment she could always play the piano—there was an excellent music program, with twenty-four pupils studying piano; twelve, violin; and six, harmony and rhythm.

By 1928 Amelia was a member of an intersettlement committee working on child-study records and, even more impressive, had become a director of Denison House, a signal honor for a new staff worker; she was one of the very few on its board. She was as well made secretary.

It is from this period that Amelia's poem "Courage" dates. It embodies the sentiments of a person who has found herself.

Courage is the price that Life exacts for granting peace.
The soul that knows it not, knows no release
From little things:
Knows not the livid loneliness of fear,
Nor mountain heights where bitter joy can hear
The sound of wings.
How can life grant us boon of living, compensate
For dull gray ugliness and pregnant hate
Unless we dare
The soul's dominion? Each time we make a choice, we pay
With courage to behold resistless day,
And count it fair.

Within a short time her influence in the field of social work spread beyond the confines of Denison House. Regarded by the elders "as one of the most thoughtful and promising of the younger group," she became a Denison House delegate to the Conference of the National Federation of Settlements held in Boston. There she impressed a wider group of social work leaders with her seriousness. She was one of the few of the younger generation who took the time to take seriously a conference questionnaire. Her thoughtful and insightful answers, wrote one of the older social workers, began to cause ripples.

To the question "What keeps you in settlement work?" she answered,

A personal thing which would keep me in any job—i.e., the
feeling that I need more time to make good on several issues I

am not meeting adequately; and the satisfaction of any scientific work which opens unexplored fields and presents problems to solve; and the realization that a thumb must be stuck in the dyke to prevent the flood of ideas and actions which threaten modern living—that is, old ideas of the inevitability of suffering, and many which destroy the happiness and peace of the world. There is a feeling of self-preservation here; for what shuts out happiness for some does so for me and mine.

To the question "How would you replace settlement traditions which you believe no longer have functional values?" she responded with a condemnation of meddling donors.

The philanthropy of the good old days—the tradition of giving clothing, service, etc., free—has to be supplanted gradually. The task is materially helped if responsibility can be shared by House members (in a self-governing body, perhaps) who can be made to see the situation. . . . Cultivating an "angel" and letting him or her dictate policies because of money given is one of the most reprehensible forms of bowing to tradition.

She ended on a brusque note, answering the question, "Have you any suggestion to offer for discussion at next year's conference?" as follows. "Next year's Conference should be a discussion, not an experience meeting. A subject like 'Cooperation' or any topic of interest to staff workers should be discussed in such a manner as to get 'somewhere.' "

Had Amelia been a participant at the 1929 conference, she would have been asked to take a more active part—the older workers were casting their nets, looking for keen young leaders whose thinking was not "paralyzed by their reverence for the pioneers."

Not only did Amelia have Vida Scudder, Emily Balch, and Katherine Coman as role models to help spur her on and reach her potential, she had the climate of Boston itself. Cleveland Amory remarking on the qualities of the proper Bostonian female would touch on "her incredible vitality. . . tradition of hardihood . . . a zeal for reform." Boston gloried in its unique women. Boston women exuded energy. In Boston the notion of "decent" women keeping their names out of the papers except when they were born, married, or died was a truism observed in the breach. Boston women reveled in being news—as long as it was done tastefully. They raised money for charities through publicity in the papers, they partied in the papers, and their sporting exploits were written up in the papers.

• • • •

As it happened, Amelia's two activities—settlement work and flying—dovetailed, and as in Los Angeles, she began to be noticed. It began May 26, 1927, when she flew over the city scattering free passes to the upcoming Memorial weekend country carnival at Cedar Hill in Waltham for the benefit of Denison House. Amelia was merely a passenger—the pilot was Harvard student Crocker Snow, member of the Harvard Flying Club, which owned the plane. Nevertheless as a female pilot, she was news, and photos of her in her flying garb—goggles, helmet, fur-trimmed flying jacket—sitting in the open cockpit of the plane promptly appeared in the Boston newspapers. Amelia had planned to do the stunt incognito, but Marion Perkins, aware of Boston's thirst for female achievers, alert to the publicity a female flier might create for Denison House, talked her out of such an action. Marion was right; the newspapers wrote it up: "Miss Amelia Earhart Flies in a Plane over Boston; Advertises Cedar Hill Carnival" ran one headline, going on to give details of the carnival. "Flies over Boston Despite Rain" ran another.

That summer a new airfield opened on the banks of the Neponset River in nearby Quincy. The ambitious enterprise was started by Harold T. Dennison, an architect from Quincy who had promised himself that when he made his first $100,000, he "would begin to realize his dream" of establishing a great chain of flying fields across New England. Dennison had gone to California looking for planes to sell at his field, met Bert Kinner, and became the Boston agent for Kinner Airsters. Bert suggested he contact Amelia when he returned to Boston. When Harold met her, he was impressed with her assurance and authority (certainly not by her money), for he made her a director and one of the five incorporators of the enterprise, put her on the staff, and sought her help with the interior decoration.

Harold Dennison designed the main hangar in the Spanish style, with an exterior finish of stucco and brilliant tile. There were two airplane showrooms and a tower that served as a classroom for student fliers, on top of which was a revolving beacon that could be seen at night for twenty miles. Dennison instituted an air charter service as well as regular service between Hyannis and Boston. There were two full-time pilots, Allan P. Bourdon and Franklin Kurt; Amelia was on the flying staff, although her duties were not defined, but when the article on the new airport came out, it would have been hard for anyone to guess that Amelia was the only one of the three who was not a full-time employee. Two paragraphs were devoted to her: "Woman on the Staff" ran the subhead, going into her being "social worker at Denison House college settlement, professor of English in the State Extension . . . sportswoman . . . held the altitude record." The men were briefly mentioned.

Among the more unusual jobs Amelia took on at the airfield was decorating the public rooms. She sent off a hastily typed letter to Marian Stabler, vacationing at Lake George. "The field opens on Tuesday next for flying in full force," she wrote. "I am having a great time selecting hangings and furniture for the main hangar. I certainly wish I had you here to consult as the thing will approach the bizazz (Heavens, I am trying to write bizarre) as the colors are orange black and blue, with a few spots of lavender and green thrown in."

The opening on July 2 drew twenty-five hundred spectators. Airplanes—army, navy, national guard planes flying in formation—as well as private planes from the greater Boston area flew overhead throughout the day. The mayor of Quincy ran a flag up the flagpole to signal the official opening of the airport; the ubiquitous Bernard Wiesman gave a speech on behalf of the mayor of Boston. A reporter from *The Boston Herald* sought out Amelia. The language in the interview, obviously one of her first, is stilted, awkward, self-conscious: "New England has some of the best yachtswomen and sportswomen in the world. I am surprised that more New England women have not gone into flying as a sport. . . . when one thinks of all the splendid sportswomen New England has produced . . . I think any normal woman should be able to learn to fly, with planes perfected as they are today, in a very short space of time and with but little application."

· · · ·

That summer, on July 24, Amelia turned thirty. A decade-marker birthday, a jolt to anyone, a really serious birthday for someone who regularly took years off her age, as Amelia did. It was at that time that she moved out of the house at 76 Brook Street, where she had been living with Amy and Muriel, and into Denison House—which must have seemed an act of desertion to Amy and caused her to move with Muriel into a small apartment at 27 Princeton Street in South Medford, near the Lincoln Junior High School, where Muriel taught.

Amelia and Sam Chapman were still engaged. He was working as an engineer for Boston Edison, still patiently waiting for Amelia to settle down and marry him. As far as he was concerned, his courtship, and their relationship continued as before and nothing had changed, even though she had moved into Denison House. He was hopeful because he had before him the example of Amelia's friend from Columbia days, Louise de Schweinitz, and Daniel Darrow. Louise, a doctor, had spent her residency in Boston at the New England Hospital for Women and Children (staffed exclusively by women—not her first choice, but three Boston hospitals turned down her application), while her fiancé, Dr. Daniel Darrow, spent his residency at Boston City. Sam and Amelia had whiled away many hours with them prowling around Boston, listening to Amelia's "enormous" collection of phonograph records, driving out to Marblehead, Sam's territory, in Amelia's Kissell, to swim and picnic on the beach. Clearly Louise's devotion to her work hadn't interfered with their relationship—Louise and Daniel had just gotten married. So there was every reason for Sam to be supportive of Amelia's desire for a career, even if it involved living at Denison House. But still, Sam was a little dismayed by Amelia's move. To him it might have seemed a desertion, even if he wouldn't admit it—and a threat as well—for as it was only too easy for him to see, Amelia's activities were taking more and more of her time. Of course he also knew that if and when they married, he too could move into the House—married couples often did, and there was a married couple living at the House now. But particularly for someone like Sam, trained as an engineer and not, except for Amelia, interested in social problems, it couldn't have held much allure. In any case, he couldn't press her, for the more he did, the more she shied away.

His dismay would have deepened if he had known that Amelia was laying the groundwork for a trip to California the following summer that did not include him. Bert Kinner had delivered a new Airster to Dennison airport, flying it solo across the country to demonstrate the plane's dependability. Maybe, Amelia proposed after he left, she should head west "and spend next summer learning the Kinner motor. It seems such a shame that no one here really knows it."

But then, she was always doing things on her own, so Sam was used to it. It wasn't just the flying and the social work that Sam had to contend with. Her Sunday mornings were taken up horseback riding in Middlesex Fells with Vernis Shuttleworth, her Denison House co-worker. Half in love with her himself, full of admiration for her riding prowess, Vernis would recall she was invariably on time, boots and all, and ready to go no matter what the weather. Her preference was for a tall, prancy horse, and the colder it got, the more the wind blew, the wilder the horses, the more she liked it. "That was *good,*" he remembered her saying, as she grinned and blew on her freezing fingers after one brisk winter ride. Sometimes Amelia even brought Vernis back to Brook Street, and Amy would lay on a breakfast of fruit, oatmeal and cream, wheatcakes, and sausages—"the works."

In fact, now that she was finally on her own and financially independent—not by any means rich, but independent—now that she had at last broken out of the track followed by ninety-nine percent of the women of her day, the track that led straight from parental home to husband's home, just about anything and everything seemed possible. If she had never gotten in a plane again, still she would have made her mark in social work, she would have had as high a profile, as influential a position in Boston as any professional woman of her day.

She was, after all the lean years, fairly bursting with plans. That summer a photo of Ruth Nichols, of Rye, New York, ran in *The Boston Herald*. The famous aviatrix was identified as a member of the Fédération Aéronautique Internationale (FAI) and "the only one of twenty seven commercial pilots in New York state to be licensed by the Commerce Department." In mid-September Amelia wrote to her, "May I introduce myself as a fellow F.A.I. . . . Because your picture has been appearing lately in Boston papers, I make you the victim of an idea which has been simmering for some time. What do you think of the advisability of forming an organization composed of women who fly? . . . If you think the idea worth pursuing, won't you let me know your ideas." It was the first of many letters the two women would exchange.

It was, naturally, the Boston papers that gave Amelia her first notoriety. The perceived moment of change was precipitated by a German girl.

There was a sensational young German aviatrix by the name of Thea Rasche in the United States, touring the Northeast, giving exhibitions of stunt flying. She was good copy—pretty, twenty-three years old, the sister of two German fliers killed in the war, the leading female stunt flier in Europe. On one of her flights earlier that summer in New York, when the engine of her Flamingo suddenly went dead, she skillfully nosedived her plane into the Hudson River. She was such a good pilot neither she nor the plane, which briefly sank before being towed to shore, was much the worse for wear for the experience.

By the time she was scheduled to appear at Dennison Airport the end of September, Thea was such a sensation that more than two thousand people showed up to see her fly. On the appointed day her demonstration was going well until, over Neponset, the Flamingo engine once again went dead. Thea briefly went into a nosedive trying to start the engine (like pushing a car with a dead battery), then banked. Then, having no choice, she put the plane into a glide. She was over the airport, had just cleared the hangar by fifteen or twenty feet, and was in the process of making a dead stick landing—when she saw she was heading straight into the waiting crowd. She veered away and, with no alternative site in view, crashed into the swamp abutting the landing field. But she did it so skillfully that again neither she nor her plane was seriously damaged. The spectators undoubtedly were more shaken up than she.

Thea's dunking in the Hudson had brought forth a spate of articles about women daring to fly and being unprepared. Immediately following Thea's crash landing this time, Amelia climbed into one of the field's Waco 10's and proceeded to entertain the onlookers with what the papers called "an excellent demonstration of flying" to prevent the same negative reaction. Harold Dennison undoubtedly thought the point of her going up was to distract the waiting, worried crowd. That was only his idea, it turned out; Amelia had another goal—to negate any resurgence of antifeminist feeling. Upon landing, she stated her mission to the waiting reporter. "Miss Earhart wanted to prove that Miss Rasche's mishap was unavoidable and no fault of her own; that women are quite as capable pilots as men, and quite as daring" dutifully reported the newsman on the scene. She had finally found her public voice. Soon, the whole world would be listening.

• • • •

In the first months of 1928 Amelia had the clever idea of writing an article about flying for *The Bostonian,* the fashionable magazine that all Boston read, and she had the nerve and self-confidence to charm its editor, Katherine Crosby, into publishing it.

Undoubtedly Katherine gazed approvingly at Amelia's casual style and lack of makeup, so in keeping was her look with that of the proper women of Boston, who were brought up to regard the cultivation of external glamour as cheap artifice, as Cleveland Amory would write. *The Bostonian* was the magazine that kept tabs on the "knowns" of Boston—those whose families had been there for generations. If it reported on the "unknowns," it was likely to be aristocratic unknowns—usually English. The magazine studiously recorded the summer comings and goings of the English diplomatic community, which in those days before air conditioning regularly fled Washington for houses on the North Shore. For an "outsider" like Amelia to be accepted with such alacrity into the sacrosanct inner circle was highly unusual. But Amelia was perfect in looks, unaffected in manner, and modest in demeanor—the ultimate hallmarks of Boston breeding.

Katherine Crosby was effusive—in print; having been charmed, she wanted the rest of Boston to be charmed too. She wrote of Amelia as a "real thoroughbred," her highest accolade, and recounted how it all came about: "a curly headed girl . . . curled up on the couch in *The Bostonian's* sitting room and wondered if she could write us an article about flying. . . . All she wanted was to make flying interesting to women. . . . Amelia Earhart impressed us all at the time as having the least vanity of any girl we had met in a month of Mondays. . . . I had to persuade her to allow her name to be signed to the article." And again her face was before the public—this time a remarkably faithful line drawing of Amelia in the flying outfit in which she had been photographed the previous spring. The article, titled "When Women Go Aloft," appeared in the May issue. In it Amelia gently stated her case.

"While women are hopelessly adventurous, they seem content to take their thrills vicariously, and watch men do things a long time before they attempt to do them. I have hope that this year will see many more women flying. Will it help my bright little hope to blossom into a bouncing reality if I give some aspects of flying from a feminine point of view? In the first place, I shall repeat what I said about beauty. There is the beauty of adventure, as in all sports; and a beauty of the earth, impossible to get in any other way."

She went on to describe the thrills of flying, some common misconceptions of its danger, and closed with a neat encapsulation of her beliefs: "There is no door closed to ability, so when women are ready there will be opportunity for them in aviation."

• • • •

Boston is a small town, but in those days it was even smaller. Amelia was becoming newsworthy enough that in April the aviation department of *The Boston Evening Transcript* asked her to fill out a biography for their files. She contributed the following (as usual lying about her age). "Pilot rating; only F.A.I. [license given out by the Fédération Aéronautique Internationale]. Born July 24, 1898, at Atchison Kansas. Educated, Ogontz School and Columbia University. War Service, V.A.D. Canadian Red Cross. Occupation, social worker. Flying activities, tumbling around a little for sport. Director Dennison Airport Corporation and subsidiary corporations."

Amelia had as a matter of course joined the Boston chapter of the National Aeronautic Association the previous year—part of the "reawakening" of her interest in flying. In this organization too, made up in large part of aviation-minded male "establishment" businessmen such as Gardiner H. Fiske, vice-chairman of the municipal air board of Boston, retired Rear Admiral Reginald Belknap, Harold Dennison, and others involved in flying, she was making an impact. The members were an active, growing group; plans were afoot to begin weekly aviation talks on WLOE, the local radio station.

Her presence at the monthly NAA luncheon meetings in the Chamber of Commerce Building on Federal Street the first Tuesday of each month would have weighed in her favor (a charming, interested, attentive young woman in the midst of all those men), but it was a letter she wrote sometime that spring that particularly marked her out. She was venting her feelings on what seemed to her to be NAA inaction in comparison to Los Angeles, where aviators, including herself when she had been there, were always putting on air meets to publicize themselves and raise money. Here in Boston she was so effortlessly becoming famous; she wanted to put her new-found public relations expertise to work, as she wrote the men. "The cause of the following outburst is the receipt of notice of dues from the N.A.A. I began to think what the organization should stand for and put some of the thoughts down. Notice of dues comes only once a year, so you may feel safe from another attack for some time." She continued, "N.A.A. should co-operate with all types of business men. Perhaps women are chief offenders. . . . Should they have their own organization? There should be advertising. I'd even be in favor of a billboard on a main highway, announcing that Boston was air-minded.

The men were riveted by the activist, competent, good-looking young woman who at one and the same time offered them fund-raising expertise and threatened to resign and form a rival women's organization.

Historically predisposed as Boston was to accept female achievers, what might have been considered an inappropriate letter was taken seriously and weighed on its merits by these Bostonians. Her letter was in fact so well received that on May 29 she was nominated for vice-president because, "with her unusual interest in aviation and her recognized ability, her selection would greatly strengthen the work of the Chapter." It was a great honor; she would serve with Commander Richard Byrd, honorary president; Sumner Sewall, U.S. air ace who held the Distinguished Service Cross, the French Legion of Honor, and the Croix de Guerre, president; and lastly Bernard Wiesman, secretary of the Committee on Aviation for the Boston Chamber of Commerce, as secretary-treasurer. She became the first female officer in the NAA.

Amelia was not the least bit intimidated by the men she would be serving with. Another of her pronouncements was, "The air-mail industry seemed to be as strong a dose of aviation as Boston could stand at the time, and Sumner Sewall was having to hold her nose while he spooned that in." She was on the committee of the National Playground Association chosen to judge the upcoming Boston model airplane tournament. This, too, was a measure both of her industry and of her stature, for such tournaments were major events throughout the country. On the national level, chairmen included all the famous names in aviation, from Orville Wright to Charles Lindbergh; on the city level, all resident aviation luminaries pitched in—and as a result of the enthusiasm of fliers and children alike, the number of young people joining the model airplane clubs and participating in the contests was skyrocketing all across the country.

Two years before, Amelia had been in the depths of despair—unable to get her life going, unable to accomplish anything, unable to even finish a letter to her friend Marian. Now there had been a total transformation. A different person came forward. Her perspective was set, and she was at ease in the public eye; she stepped onto the world stage.

PART TWO

8
Dreams of Glory

•••• While Amelia was becoming more and more attuned to life in Boston, the flying world took a giant leap forward: the North Atlantic—the Mount Everest of flight—was conquered.

It was the spring of 1927 when Charles Lindbergh landed in Paris, having flown the Atlantic in thirty-three hours. His achievement changed the world. "I woke that afternoon," he would later write, "a little stiff but well rested into a life which could hardly have been more amazing if I had landed on another planet instead of Paris." He collected the $25,000 prize Raymond Orteig had put up for anyone who could accomplish the astounding feat. *The New York Times* paid him the unheard-of sum of $125,000 for the story plus $50,000 more for a goodwill tour.

Columbus of the Air, he was called. Fame and riches were instantly his. While he remained abroad, ambassadors attended to his needs; kings and queens, princes and ministers, presidents and parliaments took their turns honoring him. The president of the United States dispatched a navy ship to fetch him home. When he arrived in New York, he was given a ticker-tape parade up Broadway, and the city dissolved into a frenzy not seen since the armistice. He went to Washington next. It, too, went wild. He addressed a joint session of Congress, and was awarded the Congressional

Medal of Honor and the Distinguished Flying Cross. And as he traveled around the country, the adulation never stopped. It was as if aviation were beginning all over again. "An epoch in air history was closed by the flight of Lindbergh and with it an epoch begins," proclaimed *The North American Review.*

Overnight he had become the most famous man on earth. Wrote Walter Lippmann, giving voice to what everyone felt, "Our publicity machine will illuminate whatever we point it at. . . . Point it at Lindbergh and it will transfigure the mundane world with young beauty and unsullied faith."

His flight, according to serious, knowledgeable aviation people, "marked the end of the early pioneering period of aviation and the beginning of the industrial period." But most people didn't care. It was the adventure and the daring that drew their attention.

The challenge of flying the North Atlantic would remain irresistible for years following Lindbergh's achievement. It became, actually, even more irresistible—and much deadlier. In the history of adventuring, to fly the Atlantic must go down as one of the most deadly quests. For an adventurer, it was the supreme adventure; for a seeker of glory, it was the surest path.

Lindbergh's success opened the floodgates. For if the first and greatest challenge had been met—the nonstop North Atlantic crossing—there were still other aerial firsts to be won, other tantalizing prizes. There was the challenge of flying east to west, against the wind—a longer and tougher trip requiring additional gasoline. There was the challenge of winning one of the $25,000 prizes put up by the cities—London, Ontario, to London, England; Philadelphia to anywhere in Europe; anywhere in Europe to Boston.

And finally there was the challenge of being the first woman. The dangers of flying across the Atlantic were perceived as so great, the risks so incomprehensible, the act so brave, that that first woman would become instantly internationally famous.

In the twelve months following Lindbergh's flight, fifty-five air-minded adventurers in eighteen planes attempted to fly the Atlantic. Three planes succeeded, one came close; the rest failed. Out of the fifty-five, eight achieved their goal; fourteen died. Five of these aerial adventurers were women, and in that time span, of the five, three died—either killed on impact, incinerated, or drowned.

It didn't matter that each of the women had men aboard to help her pilot her plane—it didn't really matter to each woman if she failed (as long as she survived)—just daring the impossible, would make her a superstar. These five women made no bones about national honor or scientific achievement. Each was courageous, and each just wanted to be famous. Three tried immediately after Lindbergh, that summer of 1927. The first was an English princess; her plane disappeared. The second was a Viennese actress; her heavy plane never became airborne. The third was an American beauty contest winner; she was rescued at sea. The fourth, a bit later, was another American woman, a niece of Woodrow Wilson, whose plane wasn't ready till winter; she took off two days before Christmas; her plane also disappeared.

The North Atlantic in the throes of winter put a stop to further flights. Spring came reluctantly, that March 1928, as flyers on both sides of the ocean stood poised, waiting for the weather to break.

The fifth to try was England's most glamorous aviatrix, the Honorable Elsie Mackay. The dark-haired daughter of Lord Inchcape, famous for her gowns and jewels and silver Rolls-Royce as much as for her flying escapades, took off from an airdrome in Lincolnshire, England, on March 13 accompanied by one-eyed English air ace Walter Hinchcliffe, who was so good his fellow pilots said that he could just about fly to Paris, Amsterdam, or Cologne with his one eye shut. As the black and gold Stinson Detroiter, powered by a single powerful Wright Whirlwind engine, rolled down the icy field, it threw up spumes of snow; two parallel tracks remained on the white ground as it disappeared to the west.

Front-page headlines on both sides of the Atlantic heralded *Endeavor's* departure and route. *The New York Times* gave it a three column head: "Hinchcliffe Takes Off for America with Daughter of Lord Inchcape; Passes Ireland and Heads Out to Sea."

Fliers were stunned that they had started already because it wasn't cold just in England—the freezing temperatures extended across the ocean to Newfoundland—and ice was a plane's deadly enemy. Excitement grew to a fever pitch. If the fliers made it, they would join the pantheon of the gods, for it would be a double first—not only would Mackay be the first woman to fly the Atlantic, but the two of them would be the first to do it the long hard way, flying against the wind, east to west.

Ships at sea and lighthouses up and down the eastern seaboard of North America signaled and searched the skies. Thousands of people waited at Mitchell field on Long Island. And waited.

It turned out that they had barely begun their quest before disaster struck. Days later, parts of the plane were found, washed up at Donegal on the northwestern coast of Ireland.

• • • •

Mabel Boll, a striking brunette with lots of money and a penchant for publicity, wanted to be the sixth. She came from Rochester, New York, and claimed to be an heiress, but her father, George Boll, was clearly listed as a bartender in Rochester city directories. She was an adventuress, unabashedly ambitious, totally without pretense, searching for fame. She knew that no matter what the world crisis, a woman taking wing across the ocean would always command the banner headlines of newspapers all over the world. "I have no wish to pilot an airplane, for that is man's work," she was quoted as saying. She merely wanted "to have the honor of being the first woman passenger to make the transatlantic trip." Because she usually wore two huge diamond rings, one of 62 carats and the other of 48 carats, as well as other lesser baubles, the press dubbed her the "Queen of Diamonds."

Mabel lived her highly public life in France, where she divided her time between a mansion in Paris and a chateau in the country. Her transatlantic quest, duly chronicled by the newspapers, actually began in August 1927, when she offered 100,000 francs to any pilot who would take her across. She promised reporters she would be wearing a vest fashioned of gold links with buttons made of diamonds and a collar made of platinum. The newspapers loved her gaudiness. As *The New York Times* commented, "Just to be photographed in that sweater on Mitchell Field at the end of the flight over the ocean appears to be her one great ambition." She hoped to fly in the *Columbia,* a Bellanca owned by Charles Levine, the plane that had been Lindbergh's first choice, the only plane besides Lindbergh's *Spirit of St. Louis* to successfully fly the Atlantic that summer. It was still in Europe after its record flight, sitting at Le Bourget. Mabel's proximity to the plane so worried Levine that he had it padlocked. Undeterred, she set out (the press following her progress) to get Levine to change his mind: "Offers Levine $50,000" ran the headline in *The New York Times.* When Charles flew to England shortly thereafter, Mabel followed by boat, first announcing her pursuit to the press, who obligingly printed the story. Gradually and with the press in attendance, she wore him down, and at a joint press conference in September in London, she triumphantly announced (he in silent acquiescence) that she would indeed be a passenger on a transatlantic flight in the *Columbia,* but first the plane had to return to America—she would fly from America to England.

Mabel Boll returned to the United States in October. "Queen of Diamonds Arrives with Gems" ran the headlines. In January 1928 she was at Mitchell field, Long Island, with Charles Levine, talking of an April transatlantic flight. The press, whom she had notified, turned up at the field and obediently reported that she was wearing her two diamond rings, a rope of pearls around her neck, and a diamond pin on her hat. She, in all her finery, and Levine went up for a spin in a Ford trimotor.

On March 5, when Charles and his pilot Wilmer Stultz made the first nonstop flight from New York to Havana, Cuba, in the *Columbia,* a 1,600-mile flight, Mabel Boll was with them. Never mind that she had to sit on an improvised seat in back of the main gas tank; never mind that the crowds at the Havana airport were disappointingly small—she was aboard a first flight, and this time her picture was on the front page of *The New York Times:* she was truly famous.

It was nine days later that Elsie Mackay and Walter Hinchcliffe disappeared. It would have been expected that the tragedy would dampen Mabel's enthusiasm for a transatlantic flight. It certainly dampened Charles Levine's—he abruptly withdrew his plane yet again from her enterprise.

But it turned out that Mabel was courageous as well as bold and was not about to abandon her quest. By the end of March, fourteen days after Elsie Mackay's ill-fated flight, she appeared finally to have a transatlantic trip within her grasp. If she had lost Charles Levine's plane, she had been successful in securing the services of his pilot—sort of. March 28, she and Wilmer Stultz held a joint interview at Curtiss field on Long Island, duly covered by *The New York Times.* Wilmer stated that although he was working with Charles Levine in his attempt to set a new endurance record, "there was an understanding that he would be her pilot if she wished to make the trip . . . that he was negotiating for a larger plane in which to cross the Atlantic if Miss Mabel Boll agrees to his terms for the venture" (not less than $25,000). Mabel Boll, for her part, was more specific—they were "negotiating the purchase of a Fokker from Commander Byrd." The flight would be in May.

Then suddenly everything changed. By the next week, Mabel Boll had lost both pilot and plane. Amy Guest, a very different kind of woman, had entered the lists. She had had enough of Mabel Boll; the Fokker and Wilmer Stultz were hers.

Amy Phipps Guest was, on the surface, an unlikely candidate for such an adventure. A Phipps from Pittsburgh, the daughter of Annie Shaffer Phipps and the enormously powerful steel multimillionaire Henry Phipps, Amy for years had moved in the stately world of wealth and privilege.

It was true that she was unusually competent; she made her mark in whatever she did. She was married to the Honorable Frederick E. Guest, first cousin and close friend of Winston S. Churchill. Her wedding, on June 29, 1905, in St. George's Church in Hanover Square, was one of the most splendid events of that London season. The guest list had included all the great titled names of English society, various European royals, the U.S.

ambassador and his wife (their daughter was one of the eight bridesmaids), plus a contingent of prominent Americans. More than a thousand people attended the reception at the house on Park Lane that the Phippses had taken for the season. Amy's marriage, according to a cousin, was not only grand but "launched the family into a society that was compatible with their growing fortune."

But Amy was neither a passive heiress nor a passive wife. She was energetic, and, like her mother before her, who was an early admirer of Margaret Sanger as well as an early advocate of birth control, she was an independent thinker who never let wealth get in the way of doing anything she felt appropriate. Outwardly conventional, in fact Amy was anything but. In an age when wealthy women traditionally did nothing with their money but spend it, Amy wheeled and dealed. She built one of Manhattan's most luxurious and beautiful apartment houses, One Sutton Place South at Fifty-eighth Street, commanding a breathtaking view of the East River. According to family legend, as the building neared completion, she sold her brother what he thought was the penthouse, then built a floor above him for herself.

She was physically daring—although this was not unexpected in the family, raw courage being a much admired and common Phipps trait. Even those who married into the family conformed to the family mold: Amy's sister-in-law Margarita Phipps, taken on safari in India for her honeymoon by John Phipps, shot and killed a tiger.

Amy, too, would go big game hunting, flying in a seven-seater Bellanca from London to Nairobi with Frederick and their children. The Guest safari on the Serengeti plain, under the direction of white hunter Bror Blixen, was as lavish as any of the day, but it was also—in spite of all precautions—dangerous. Africa was still teeming with game, with herds of wildebeest, zebra, gazelles, eland, and buffalo. Parents and children shot their fill, and since the great trophy in those years, the ultimate sport trophy, was a lion, lion became their quarry. For days they camped in lion country, and for days they were surrounded by prides of lions. One day thirty-eight of the beasts treed Frederick and two of the children. One evening three lions were observed in the moonlight drinking the bath water out of the tub. By the end of the safari, every member of the family had shot a lion, shooting their quarry high in the shoulder as Bror Blixen taught them. Amy, sighting from eighty yards away across open terrain, shot hers a little too far behind the shoulder. Bror had had to finish it off.

In her youth Amy had been an avid tennis player. She was as well a superb rider who fox-hunted wherever she lived—on Long Island, in Virginia, in Leicestershire, England. To her cousin Peggy Phipps Boegner, who saw her once force a borrowed horse over an "enormous" fence riding sidesaddle, she was "absolutely fearless." "Brave as a lion" was how her daughter-in-law appraised her.

But Amy was now stout and matronly, the mother of three children: Winston, twenty-two, at Columbia Law School; Raymond, twenty, at McGill College; and Diana, a teenager at the Shipley School in Philadelphia. And to top off Amy's unsuitableness, she was fifty-five years old. By any standard, flying the Atlantic would be a new level of danger for her. Still, the Duchess of Bedford, the mistress of Woburn Abbey, easily as socially prominent as Amy and as well regarded, had flown for the first time at sixty-two, at which time, in spite of her age, she had fallen in love with flying. Over her husband's objections, the duchess had hired a pilot, bought several planes, and now regularly flew off on exotic long-distance trips—she had just returned from Persia. Amy also knew that the first woman to die in the transatlantic quest, Princess Anne Lowenstein-Wertheim, also an Englishwoman, had been older than she. So there was precedent. Amy had had a great deal of exposure to flying because her husband, Frederick, had served as British secretary of state for air.

From Amy's point of view, Mabel was the quintessential adventuress and as such unassailably loathsome. The prospect of the publicity-hungry "Diamond Queen" becoming the most famous female in the world was simply more than she could stand. Mabel Boll was exactly the kind of person upon whom Guest was determined the mantle of fame would not fall. It "just wouldn't do," as Guest would later tell her daughter Diana, trying to explain her actions: she would go herself.

Amy had to be in London in early June anyway, for her daughter Diana was scheduled to be presented at Court. She would simply arrive by different, more dramatic means.

She told no one, least of all her husband, what she was planning to do, and proceeding with extraordinary speed, she summoned David T. Layman, the Phipps family lawyer, and told him to enter into negotiations with Commander Byrd, whom she knew well, for the use of his plane and as well to enlist his aid in the enterprise. David Layman immediately and efficiently went to work; within a week of the "Diamond Queen's" announcement, the plane was Amy Guest's and so, thanks to the further efforts of Byrd, was her pilot. Then Guest and Byrd began planning the flight. It is worth noting that Amy Guest had to convince Commander Byrd that she was emotionally and physically strong enough to undergo an ordeal in which a great many people had lost their lives. That was apparently no problem. Everything proceeded at a great clip. By the ninth of April, pilot Wilmer Stultz and Louis Gordon, the mechanic-copilot he chose, were picking up *her* Fokker in Detroit. They flew it, as instructed by Byrd, to the new airport in East Boston that lay in an area of newly cindered-over mudflats, away from prying eyes but close to where Byrd lived.

The next week Byrd was visiting Amy Guest at Templeton, her country estate in Roslyn, Long Island; they were deep into organizing the voyage, unhindered by Frederick Guest, who was in England. Amy told no one else except her younger brother Howard, and she swore him to secrecy.

For a variety of reasons, Byrd had decided that the Fokker, a land plane, should be converted to a seaplane, which opened up the dramatic possibility that if all went according to plan, the plane could land in the Thames River, as an airplane had done once previously, and come to a stop right in front of the Houses of Parliament. In anticipation of this event, Amy settled on the name *Friendship* to symbolize the relationship between the two countries.

By that time it was Shipley School spring vacation, and Amy's teenage daughter Diana arrived home for her spring break to find Byrd in residence.

"When the Gods fashioned Dick Byrd," wrote Hilton Railey, who would get to know him better than anybody, "they endowed him, experimentally, with greater charm, better looks, greater shrewdness, better luck than most of his fellows." Not surprisingly, he dazzled Diana—she thought him charming and handsome, as did so many other women and men. That vacation indelibly printed itself in her memory. She would never forget the commander or the many conversations about flying and adventuring—or the fact that at the end of spring break, she went back to Shipley totally in the dark about her mother's plans.

Then, according to Phipps family history, as the days passed and the flight drew nearer, Howard became increasingly worried, and since Amy wouldn't do it herself, he finally told her eldest son what was about to occur. Winston, as he called himself after his Churchillian cousin, having dropped his father's name Frederick, hit the roof. Pointing out to his mother that the trip would be at the same time he would be taking his law school exams, he demanded that she withdraw; he couldn't, he said, possibly study for, much less pass his exams, if she were involved in such an enterprise—she would make him fail. Others in the family were drawn in—undoubtedly Amy's mother, who lived nearby in Westbury, her brother John, and perhaps Frederick. All lined up against her. Against their assembled will, Amy backed down.

But even though she acceded to family pressure, common sense, and quite possibly second thoughts, since death or a ditching at sea had been the fate of every single female transatlantic flyer, she neither retired from the scene nor sold the plane, which the family was also pressuring her to do. Her overriding desire was to make sure that that first woman, who would literally as well as figuratively be flying into the vortex of international acclaim (whether or not she lived to enjoy it), whose name would go down in history, would be a credit to her sex. She was still in charge.

"Keep my ship," she now instructed Layman. "I am determined an American shall be the first woman to fly across to England. Find me someone. Someone nice who will do us proud. I shall pay the bills." She went into detail about what she required in the woman who would be chosen: that she be a lady, educated, and if possible a flier.

"Is that all?" he remembered answering.

· · · ·

Shortly thereafter George Palmer Putnam, the brilliantly successful publisher who had snared Charles Lindbergh and just about every other adventurer of the day for Putnam's, was on his way by ferry to Miller field on Staten Island. Also traveling on the ferry was Bernt Balchen, the Norwegian pilot who had piloted the *America* so brilliantly, who still worked for Byrd, and who had placed his order for a Fokker that past July in Holland. During the ride the two fell into conversation. Putnam, persuasively loquacious, was always on the lookout for new adventures and new stories to publish. By the time the ferry reached Staten Island, Balchen had told him that Byrd had just secretly sold his Fokker to some wealthy woman who was planning a long dangerous flight and that the plane was at the East Boston airport, where it was being fitted out with pontoons.

George Putnam, as he put it, "instantly" saw the possibilities. "And here I had stumbled on an adventure-in-the-making which, once completed, certainly should provide a book."

He went back to his office in Manhattan later that same day and, as it happened, his friend Hilton Railey, a Boston public relations specialist and fund-raiser for philanthropic causes, on his way to catch the five o'clock train back home, dropped in to see him. On such small occurrences are deeds set on course. The expansive publisher told Railey the exciting news he had just heard, and since the Fokker was being fitted out in Boston—supposedly for Byrd—he charged him with the task of checking out the plane and finding out everything he could. (According to Railey, who in his book *Touch'd With Madness* exhibited an irresistible habit of putting words—any words—into people's mouths, George Putnam said, "Pull your chair over. I heard something today that might be of interest to you.")

By midnight that same night, Hilton Railey had tracked down the plane at the East Boston airport, found out that the pilot was Wilmer Stultz and the mechanic Louis Gordon, and that they were lodged at the Copley Plaza Hotel. Pressing on with his sleuthing, he went to the hotel in search of Wilmer Stultz, whom he found still up and drinking. Stultz admitted that he was embarking on a transatlantic adventure, admitted that he was going to have a female with him, but he maintained he didn't know the identity of the woman. He did, however, give out the name of her attorney, with whom he had been dealing: David T. Layman. Hilton turned the information over to George Putnam.

In the meantime, cool, conservative David T. Layman, used to providing legal advice and investment possibilities to the Phipps family, out of his depth in his new assignment, had gotten as far as apprising Byrd of the change in plans—but no further. So when, early one morning, he received a call from George Palmer Putnam, whom he knew slightly, asking him for a conference that the publisher assured him would be "mutually interesting," he was still mulling over his task and had interviewed no one. George's timing (for George) was perfect. "Pretty much at the moment I dropped from the clouds and introduced myself, Layman was wondering what to do next" was George's assessment of the situation. When they met, George filled Layman in on his background in aviation projects and exploration and his unmatched record of publishing triumphs (the latest being the just-released *Skyward* by Richard E. Byrd) and offered his services. David Layman looked "visibly relieved," according to Putnam, at his offer of help in finding a substitute for Amy Guest. The girl who would make the flight, David Layman told him, had to be pleasing in appearance, of a type that would meet with critical English approval, have gone to college, and be a flier.

But if Layman looked "visibly relieved," he was also guarded, for Putnam wanted the exclusive commission to find the girl; this Layman refused to give. Putnam, a brash type, pushed his case—a bit too hard. Layman later recollected that he told Putnam, "All I have to say is that if you should happen to hear of anyone you think might fit such plans we may be willing to consider her. We put ourselves under no obligation or agreement whatsoever to accept her."

Undeterred, Putnam pressed on. Since Hilton Railey had done such a good job of sleuthing, George turned to him again to find a candidate. And since Railey lived in Boston and his contacts were Boston contacts, the first thing he did when he returned was to contact his friend who was involved in the Boston air world, retired Rear Admiral Reginald R. Belknap, who was of course a member of the Boston NAA, and ask him if he knew of a candidate.

"Why, yes," Admiral Belknap said now to Railey. "I know a young social worker who flies. I'm not sure how many hours she's had, but I do know that she's deeply interested in aviation—and a thoroughly fine person. Call Denison House and ask for Amelia Earhart."

When Ruth Nichols found out later that it had all been in the hands of her Rye neighbor George and that he had never even thought of her although she was a well-known pilot, she was furious. Observed Janet Mabie, "She never forgot the slight."

• • • •

At Denison House early one afternoon in April, just as the neighborhood was piling in for games and classes, Amelia was called to the phone and asked by a man if she wanted to do something "aeronautic" that might possibly be hazardous; if so, would she come in for an interview. Since those were the days of Prohibition, Amelia's first thought was that she might be talking to a bootlegger who wanted her to fly some illegal alcohol into the country. She pressed him with questions. It was, of course, Hilton Railey, who later admitted that he had had absolutely no intention of telling her what he was calling about without seeing her first, but he found she gave him no choice. "I had to come out with it because she declined an interview until I stated the nature of my business." Not only that, but after a pause, to Railey's astonishment, Amelia asked him for references—"personal references." Within hours Amelia had checked them out, and later that afternoon she appeared at Hilton Railey's office, taking the precaution of bringing Marion Perkins with her. She was wearing a brown wool suit and hat, under which could be seen the ends of her curly bobbed hair. Kathleen Knight, an associate of Hilton Railey and a director of his company, the Fiscal Service Corporation, didn't see past Amelia's outfit, which she didn't like, noting that her skirt came down to her ankles.

Railey, on the other hand, didn't notice her clothes. He saw her quick flashing smile, her level gray eyes, and her frank, direct way of looking at people, heard her low-pitched, pleasant voice, and took in her five-foot-eight, 118-pound frame. He thought her marvelous—her laugh "infectious," her poise, warmth, and dignity "impressive." He was so bowled over, in fact, that he instantly felt that he had met not just the perfect representative of the American woman that Amy Guest had stipulated but much more: "I felt that I had discovered not their norm but their sublimation." So impressed was he that "I asked forthwith 'How would you like to be the first woman to fly the Atlantic?' " She answered in the affirmative. He told her about the woman (no names mentioned) who, having been talked out of making the flight herself, was looking for someone to take her place, and that George Palmer Putnam had asked him to help in the search.

Amelia understood that she would hear further, she assumed right away, but days went by; she heard nothing. The only development was that Putnam ran her by the Byrds, who had her to dinner at their Brimmer Street house and pronounced her suitable. While she waited, the world went on—the famous flier Floyd Bennett died in a hospital in Canada on April 20; a new experimental giant French seaplane with five motors crashed and sank on a test flight just off the French coast, killing one of the crew; Eleanor Sears, forty-six years old, hiked the seventy-four miles from Newport to her home on Beacon Street, her car and driver crawling behind, in exactly seventeen hours in the rain, the fastest time she had ever achieved; Harvard and Yale began a much-heralded intercollegiate "braintest," each fielding their ten best students for a three-hour examination in English composition and literature. (Harvard would win, mainly thanks to the brilliance of Nathan Pusey, who subsequently became its president.) There was a conference at Radcliffe on the opportunities for part-time work for women.

On April 24 Amelia wrote to Ruth Nichols, with whom she had been corresponding since the previous fall, with some new thoughts on her pet subject: how to set up a women's flying organization. The letter, remarkably detailed, is graphic evidence both of Amelia's enormous capacity for self control and her ability to stay focused:

> . . . let us take up the feminine end of flying with action in view.
> I propose we make three grades of members in the organization
> talked of—Honorary, consisting of F.A.I. inactive flyers, like Kath-
> erine Stinson; Active, of Transport or Private Operators . . . and an
> Associate, or any women who would like to boost aviation. . . . As
> to organization, let us have a governing committee of three, you
> and I and one of the Honoraries. I think we have to be autocratic
> about officers, at first, in order to start something. One of us should
> be chairman, and a secretary and treasurer may be elected later."

Amelia went through her days at Denison House; more people read her article in *The Bostonian*. Still no word came.

May 1 was a Tuesday; she was undoubtedly at the monthly luncheon meeting of the National Aviation Association at Department of Commerce headquarters at 80 Federal Street.

On May 2 she wrote to Hilton Railey:

> It is very kind of you to keep me informed, as far as you are able,
> concerning developments of the contemplated flight. As you may
> imagine, my suspense is great indeed.

Please, however, do not think that I hold you responsible, in any way, for my own uncertainty. I realize that you are now, and have been from the first, only the medium of communication between me and the person, or persons, who are financing the enterprise. For your own satisfaction may I add, here, that you have done nothing more than present the facts of the case to me. I appreciate your forbearance in not trying to "sell" the idea, and should like you to know that I assume all responsibility for any risk involved.

At our next interview—if there is one—I shall have ready the details you ask for.

What made it harder on her was that not only did she not know if she would be chosen, she had been told that there was a possibility that the flight might not come off at all. Not that she let her suspense apparently disturb her life or slow her pace. Quite possibly she slipped off by herself to sit "quietly drinking in the beauty of the sea and shore," which she found restored her equilibrium. But she had a remarkable number of balls in the air in addition to Denison House—and her response to the pressure was to throw up new ones.

She wrote a letter to the Boston Chamber of Commerce, taking them to task for doing what she considered to be an abysmal job of publicizing aviation.

There is a reckless quality in the letter, dated four days after the one to Hilton—the strain was getting to her:

> Why aren't we doing something notable here? You know there are two ways to accomplishment—one, through doing exceptional things, and another by sweeping to it by force of numbers. Aviation needs widespread support. . . .
>
> A social worker always thinks of ways to raise money so I propose a benefit of some sort. . . . I'd ask Will Rogers to come on, and pay him a thousand to fill Symphony Hall.

She addressed the letter to Bernard Wiesman, whom she knew from the NAA luncheon meetings; it was perhaps the combination of both letters that so electrified the gentlemen of the NAA that they would in a very short time vote Amelia into office. (The NAA would announce on election day, June 5, "Today the Boston Chapter of the NAA finds that its nominee for Vice-President has flown away.")

Amelia was also busily trying to become a member of Zonta, a service organization for businesswomen with branches in most of the major cities in the country. Zonta, the first organization for businesswomen in the United States, was founded in 1919 in Buffalo, New York, just as the long campaign for women's suffrage was ending. It filled the need for a women's professional organization for the growing number of such women in post–World War I America. Zonta, whose name was the Sioux word for "honest and trustworthy," was modeled after the Rotary Clubs. Like membership in the Rotary, membership in Zonta was by invitation; like Rotary it was a service organization; like Rotary it met at lunch. "Their luncheon business meetings dealt with the same matters as those of the men in like positions with similar interests who had always been doing business at lunch," according to its early literature. The first president was Mary Jenkins, publisher of *The Syracuse Herald*. Significantly, it was not as a social worker that Amelia rated an invitation to join, but because of her flying activities. On her application for membership, she filled in as her employer the Dennison Aircraft Corporation—as her job she wrote, "A director of the Corporation." She made no mention of her activities at Denison House, listing it only as her home address.

Amelia's application for membership, complete with the obligatory signatures of two "active members in good standing" who were recommending her, was formally dated, signed by her, and submitted to Zonta on May 8, two days after her letter to the Chamber of Commerce, six days after her letter to Hilton Railey.

• • • •

Suddenly she was invited to New York City to be interviewed. She arranged to spend the night before the interview with Marian Stabler in Great Neck. She told the Stablers only that she had confidential business in the city. If the prospect of the flight excited her, it didn't show at the Stablers', but then, Amelia was never visibly excited, *never* appeared anything but calm and collected, according to Marian. (The only thing that betrayed her excitement to Marian was that when she left for Boston, she very uncharacteristically forgot her coat.)

The day after her arrival, Amelia went into the city to see George Putnam, whom she took to be in charge of the search. Over six feet tall, good-looking, with dark brown hair, a rugged physique, a square jaw, and rimless spectacles, the veritable prototype for Clark Kent, he was behind his desk apparently very busy, "making one telephone call after another." He was sizing her up while he talked—a tall skinny girl, probably again wearing her brown wool suit, but she had a certain presence. Just that fall she had described herself as "a social worker who flies for sport, and am on the board of directors of an aeronautical concern. I can not claim to be a feminist but do rather enjoy seeing women tackling all kinds of new problems—new for them, that is."

Her most arresting feature was her direct, wide-set, level gray eyes. Here, as George was just about to learn, was a bluestocking who flew. A girl with a head on her shoulders—he couldn't help but perceive it. She had high cheekbones, a generous mouth (although there was a gap between her two front teeth when she smiled), a high forehead, and freckles on her surprisingly fair skin; her bobbed hair was blond with a blondness almost dark, but still suggesting blond. Boyish looking, many people thought, and looking even younger than the twenty-nine she admitted to. Amelia proudly showed George her pilot's license, the first FAI license granted an American woman, but according to Amelia, he acted unimpressed. Nevertheless he took her over to 787 Fifth Avenue to see David Layman. Of course George was putting on a bit of an act; from the first moment he saw her, he was sure Hilton Railey's discovery would be perfect. David Layman recalled later his first impression of Amelia: a pleasing-looking girl, tall, fair, well mannered, quiet voiced. As they talked in his office, she appeared a little nervous, he remembered, "but that was natural and she was controlling it well." She told him about herself, her career, and her flying. He told her the circumstances of the flight, about Amy Guest, who was financing the trip "from first to last," about the plane, and about the pilot and co-pilot already hired.

"Why do you want to fly the Atlantic?" he asked at one point. Layman said she looked at him for a moment, then smiled. He liked the smile. "It was nice to see," he recalled.

"Why," she replied, "does a man ride a horse?"

"Because he wants to, I guess."

"Well then."

And then, according to Layman, they laughed together. He asked her if she wanted recompense, to which she answered, "No, thank you."

She had won him over, so he took her into the next room to meet John Phipps, who had the final say. She won Phipps over, too, but so entirely and unexpectedly that there was a moment where she almost overdid it; she noticed that he appeared too concerned for her welfare. As self-conscious as she was, as preoccupied as she was with making a good impression, "if I were found wanting on too many counts I should be deprived of a trip. On the other hand, if I were just too fascinating the gallant gentlemen might be loath to drown me. Anyone can see the meeting was a crisis." She had assessed John Phipps correctly; David Layman later said that he had had to allay Phipps's fears for Amelia's safety.

It would have seemed the next step would be for her to meet and be inspected by Amy Guest, but the instigator of the enterprise had left already, according to David Layman. "The Phippses had gotten her a suite on a steamship and waved her 'bon voyage.' She would be in England for her daughter's presentation at Court, but please God by benefit of Cunard liner."

• • • •

So when John Phipps appeared to be satisified, she had passed the last hurdle.

Next, they told her the details: that if she were chosen, she would receive no money even though the pilot and co-pilot were being paid (Wilmer Stultz was to get $20,000 and Lou Gordon $10,000); that she had to sign away any right to damages; that she could lecture and write about the flight and, "consistent with the dignity and integrity of the sponsor and the undersigned," sign contracts about it; but all moneys received had to be returned to Amy Guest to help defray expenses. She could endorse no commercial products "whatsoever." Finally she was told that they would let her know.

She thanked them and, smiling slightly, left.

After the interview Putnam took her to Grand Central Station and put her on a train to Boston. (Much, much later, the careful Amelia noted to her sister that he did not offer to pay her fare and did not seem interested in her.)

Neither David Layman nor John Phipps nor George Putnam saw or made inquiries about anyone else.

David Layman spent the next ten days making discreet background checks, cabling all the information to Amy, and working out the logistics as it became evident that Amelia was going to be acceptable and that the enterprise would definitely go forward. Finally everything was in place; Amy cabled that she wished the personnel Godspeed. He telephoned Amelia. "You may make this flight if you wish under the agreed conditions," he told her. Because she had impressed both David Layman and John Phipps so favorably, Amelia now found out that not only had they decided on her, but that once they took off, she would be in charge.

On June 1 she wrote to Marian Stabler to thank her for letting her spend the night. She was one of Amelia's best friends, but Amelia divulged nothing to her.

• • • •

The Fokker was as powerful as any plane of its day. Byrd thought it the most powerful, reliable plane available. He had used a Fokker, the *Josephine Ford,* for his attempt to fly over the North Pole, and another Fokker, the *America*, to fly the North Atlantic. He had ordered this last Fokker for his forthcoming assault on the South Pole and changed his mind only after Henry Ford offered him a Ford trimotor free if he would use it. (Byrd's use of the Ford would make it instantly famous.) Since a fully equipped trimotor cost $100,000, and $1 million still had to be raised for the expedition, Byrd, after demanding extensive modifications, had accepted the offer and put the Fokker up for sale.

The Fokker was the perfect plane for a transatlantic flight. This model was an F7 that had been modified to give it greater lifting power and enhanced load-carrying ability. It had a larger wingspan than the stock F7, measuring 72 feet from tip to tip, and a stronger undercarriage, enabling it to carry four 95-gallon gas tanks on the wings instead of the usual two, and two additional elliptical tanks in the cabin (shaped to permit passage between cockpit and cabin), each with a capacity of 246 gallons, for a total capacity of 872 gallons. At 6.12 pounds to a gallon, that meant carrying over 5,300 pounds in fuel alone, almost double what the plane itself weighed. It had a cruising speed of 106 and a maximum speed of 129 miles per hour. The skin was plywood, the engine housings aluminum. It was powered by three of what were generally considered to be the best airplane engines of the day, the Wright Whirlwind J5 9-cylinder air-cooled engines designed by Charles Lawrance. Lindbergh had had one powering his much lighter plane; the Wright Aeronautical Corporation claimed that they averaged nine thousand miles to a failure—an incredible record. Lawrance had been awarded the prestigious Collier trophy just that February, which the NAA awarded annually "for the greatest achievement in aviation in America." Amelia must have felt a bit of vindication at the choice of engines and must have commanded the respect of her confreres for having chosen, back in 1921, a plane powered by one of the first engines that the then-unknown Lawrance had turned out.

But accepted as the absolute best in 1928 or not, even air-cooled Whirlwinds were no guarantee of success. Whirlwind engines had powered the two planes carrying American women who attempted transatlantic flights the year before—Ruth Elder's plane had suffered engine failure and landed in the sea near a passing freighter; she lived. Frances Grayson's plane had disappeared; she died.

When Amelia first saw the Fokker, it was in the shadows of its East Boston hangar. Its fuselage was painted bright orange—technically named chrome yellow, as Amelia noted, the color chosen for safety reasons: "it can be seen farther than any other color." She was definitely impressed; she wrote that the golden wings were "strong and exquisitely fashioned."

Because attempts at transatlantic flight generated such hysterical attention, subterfuge became the first order of the day. If the real destination became known, if there was just the merest hint, the merest possibility that a woman—and a pilot at that—was inordinately interested in that powerful plane, the hangar would be besieged, the participants hounded by press and public alike; their lives as normal people would cease. The truth was easy to conceal, since the Fokker was, as far as anybody knew, still part of Byrd's Antarctic expedition—part of his assault force, which was known to include three planes and five pilots, plus scientists, backup crew, supply ships, sleds, tractors, food, and supplies for two years. The personnel were consistent with a Byrd expedition: Commander Robert Elmer, USN retired, Commander Byrd's old friend from Annapolis days was supervising all modifications to the plane. Wilmer (Bill) Stultz had previously worked with Byrd; he was not only eminently qualified to be part of the Antarctic expedition but Byrd had in fact asked him to take part in it. (He had refused because of the extended nature of the enterprise.)

Bill and Louis Gordon were old friends. Both had gone the classic flying route for men of that time—receiving their training courtesy of the U.S. government. Bill, twenty-eight, reassuringly mature looking with his shock of black hair well shot with gray, born in Pennsylvania, had enlisted in the navy in 1919 and trained at its Pensacola flight school, where he became an expert in handling seaplanes, navigation, meteorology, and radio. Upon discharge he had gone to Brazil, where he worked for Curtiss Export, overseeing their forty planes and teaching flying. He subsequently went to work for the Atlantic Aircraft Company, the American branch of Fokker, where he became the test pilot for Byrd's trimotor Fokker *Josephine Ford*.

Louis Gordon, twenty-seven, nicknamed Slim, rangy, happy-go-lucky, often smiling, was from Houston, Texas, and knew more about Fokkers than just about anyone flying. He had enlisted in the Army Air Service at Ellington field, Houston, trained there, and then spent six months studying aircraft engines at Kelly field in San Antonio. After that he had been chief mechanic at the Aberdeen Proving Grounds in Maryland, and following his discharge he flew Fokker trimotors in an air service between Philadelphia, Washington, and Norfolk, Virginia. When Bill called Slim and asked him to join, Slim quit his job and met Bill in Detroit the next day.

• • • •

For her part, Amelia simply had to stay away, with the result that her life in Boston continued on much as before. She had been made head of the summer program at the House, the Vacation program as it was called, and was scheduling its offerings and activities, which mostly would take place, because of the summer heat, in the shady backyard and cooler lower floors of the settlement house.

She had absolutely no idea what forces her flight would unleash. The summer before, when Charles Lindbergh arrived in Boston after his triumphal flight, was just when Amelia had been so caught up in the opening of Dennison airport. The crowds surging to greet him on "Lindy Day" had been so huge that several times the police had had to call for reinforcements, and even so, things got so out of hand on Boston Common that the parade ground resembled a battlefield, with more than a hundred people stretched on the grass. Amelia, absorbed with her projects, must have thought it a momentary phenomenon.

When she wrote Marian Stabler a chatty letter very shortly thereafter, she didn't even mention Charles Lindbergh or the excitement his visit had caused. Now, concentrated as she was on the upcoming challenge itself, undoubtedly assuming that the world had gone wild for Charles only because he was the first, the conquerer, the inventor, so to speak, she gave scant thought to *her* possible postflight fame. She therefore merely asked Marion Perkins for a two-week leave of absence and, worried that her absence might disrupt the vacation schedule, arranged for a staff worker about to leave to stay to cover for her in return for two hundred dollars. She fully expected to be back in Boston July 1 for the opening of the vacation activities. She continued flying, occasionally slipping out early in the mornings in her yellow Kissell roadster across Neponset Bridge to the Dennison airport, flying in borrowed or demo planes out over the nearby cranberry marshes, north and south over the coast, or inland over the Charles and the towns to the west.

Amelia told only four people of the impending adventure: head worker Marion Perkins, George Ludlam, Harold Dennison, and Sam Chapman, her fiancée.

9
Vortex

• • • • Commander Byrd was in charge of all arrangements for the flight; his decisions were the ones that governed the outfitting of the *Friendship*. His judgment was strongly influenced by the harrowing transatlantic flight he had taken the summer before in another Fokker, a virtual twin of the *Friendship* except that it had wheels instead of pontoons, in which he had taken off from Roosevelt field on Long Island and which he ended up ditching at sea off the coast of France.

Richard Byrd was a charismatic, glamorous figure—one of those people who loom large in the eyes of their contemporaries, but who in the light of history become reduced in size and can be seen as flawed. His misjudgments were monumental. Where he went, accidents happened. He recounts the first instance himself—the accident that almost sidelined his naval career. At Annapolis, as captain of the navy gym team, intent on winning the intercollegiate championship in 1911, Byrd devised a splendid gymnastic trick for himself, a "hair-raising" stunt on the flying rings—a kind of double flip that he tried successfully. Once. Then, instead of practicing, he never tried it again until the day before the meet, in a crowded gym. Not surprisingly, he fell, badly breaking his foot.

He barely graduated that June, and because he couldn't physically function properly on a boat, (his ankle didn't work; he fell down a gangway), he was retired by the navy after five years, "retired on three quarters pay; ordered home for good."

World War I saved him. He became a navy pilot, fought his way back on duty. He learned to fly, naturally, on seaplanes.

By 1926 he was a world figure by virtue of the fact that he and Floyd Bennett were the first to fly an airplane over the North Pole (a claim now disputed). To cap that adventure, in pursuit of winning the Orteig prize of $25,000, Byrd next set about assembling plane and crew to fly the Atlantic nonstop from America to France. His aircraft, a Fokker which he grandly named *America,* was ready before Lindbergh's *Spirit of St. Louis* but was involved in an accident caused largely by Byrd's thoughtlessness. Aboard at the time were the plane's designer, Anthony Fokker, Floyd Bennett, George Noville, and Byrd. It was Anthony Fokker, bitter at the needless accident that had ended the chance of his plane becoming the most famous in the world, who pointed the finger at Byrd. He had planned to test the plane alone, but Byrd turned up and not only insisted on going but insisted on Noville and Bennett going also. "I should have refused," Fokker said later to Floyd Bennett, "because without any load in the rear, and with an empty main tank the ship became nose heavy." The Fokker crashed. Byrd had his arm broken, Noville had his stomach muscles torn; Floyd Bennett, the most gravely injured, suffered a fractured thigh and a lung punctured by a propeller fragment; he was in the hospital for months and never did fully recover.

Undeterred, after the airplane was repaired, Byrd got on with his plans, but by that time on May 21, 1927, Lindbergh in the *Spirit of St. Louis* had landed in Paris and won the Orteig, and Clarence Chamberlin and Charles Levine in the *Columbia* had flown nonstop to Eisleben, Germany.

The *America* finally took off from Roosevelt field on June 29, laden down, in addition to what Byrd considered necessities, with 150 pounds of mail—and four in crew, Byrd, Bert Acosta, Bernt Balchen, and George Noville. They hit France, according to Byrd, right on target, then flew over Brest heading for Paris (their destination), but by then it was nighttime and foggy. Byrd later called the trip "a most terrible experience." By his account, they saw bright lights just about the time they expected to see Paris and thought their flight was almost over, but flying a bit further, they realized that the lights were not Paris but a lighthouse beacon; they were lost. They flew on. The compasses had malfunctioned, and again according to Byrd, they tapped them, got them "okay," and headed for Paris again. Then although "I knew we were heading toward Paris," there were no lights. Just blackness. By then, afraid they would run out of gas, they cast out unnecessary equipment in an effort to lighten the plane and headed back for the lighthouse, which they found. As they peered through the rainy night by the light of the beacon, they couldn't clearly distinguish the beach and therefore decided it would be safer to land their land plane in the water as close to the beach as possible. Bernt Balchen, at the controls, made a perfect, incredible landing in the sea, the water shearing off the landing gear "with hardly a jar to the plane." Stunned but not hurt, they all hurriedly climbed out of the plane, inflated the rubber boat, and rowed to shore. They were lucky to escape unharmed. They had landed at Ver-sur-Mer, later to become famous in World War II as Omaha Beach. After the flight, Byrd alone of the fliers always claimed the lights had been Paris.

Just that April 1928, Commander Byrd sent Balchen and Bennett, the pilots who would be going with him to the South Pole, to go rescue German pilots who were stranded on Greenly Island, off the northern tip of Newfoundland, after making the first successful east-to-west transatlantic flight. The rescue mission, sponsored jointly by *The New York World* and the North American Newspaper Alliance, drew public attention to Byrd's upcoming Antarctic adventure. But the Germans had been in no danger. Byrd, with utter disregard for his men, sanctioned Balchen and Bennett to go, even though both were ill with the flu—so ill that when they arrived in Detroit to pick up the plane (as it happened, just a week after Bill Stultz and Slim Gordon picked up the *Friendship*), Edsel Ford took one look at the fliers and clapped them both in the Henry Ford Hospital. Still far from well a few days later, they took off in the specially equipped Ford trimotor bound for Greenly Island. Floyd Bennett, never fully recovered from the first plane crash of the *America* the year before, caught double pneumonia, and in spite of a dramatic flight to bring him serum by Charles Lindbergh, on April 26 he died at the Jeffrey Hale Hospital in Quebec.

A few years later in the Antarctic (with the trimotor renamed *Floyd Bennett* in honor of his dead friend), Byrd endangered the lives of his entire support staff when he insisted on manning an advance weather base alone through the dark Antarctic winter simply because he "really wanted to go for the experience's sake." Rescuing him, his teammates almost died.

Instead of entertaining thoughts to the effect that the *America*'s watery end the previous summer might have been the result of two conditions—that the plane was too heavily loaded and that the navigating had been faulty—Byrd drew the conclusion that flying across so much open water in a plane with wheels was foolhardy. The solution he came up with was to use pontoons instead of wheels.

There had been a mounting number of transatlantic air fatalities since

Lindbergh's successful crossing the summer before. Month after month, the world's top fliers took off to cross the North Atlantic in land planes and were never heard from again. The worst stretch came during the first wrenching week of the previous September—three planes, two taking off from the North American continent, one taking off from England, disappeared at sea; eight fliers died within seven days. The first was the Fokker *St. Raphael,* carrying the English pilot Princess Lowenstein-Wertheim and British air aces Colonel Fred Minchin and Captain Leslie Hamilton, which took off on August 31 from Upavon, England. The second, another Fokker called *Old Glory,* took off on September 6 from Old Orchard, Maine, carrying the aviation editor of the New York *Daily Mirror* and two top pilots, one American and one French. The third was a Stinson, *Sir John Carling,* which took off the next day, September 7, from Harbor Grace, Newfoundland, with two British pilots.

A feeling began to grow that Lindbergh had been lucky rather than smart. Such an august official as the U.S. secretary of the navy, T. Douglas Robinson (who naturally had a built-in bias toward seaplanes) announced: "the departmental policy will in the future be that no naval personnel will be permitted to engage in transoceanic flights in land planes." The Australian government for a time prohibited land planes from flying more than fifty miles over open water within its territory. John A. Wilson, director of civil aviation for the Canadian Air Board, declared: "I deprecate the use of land planes in transoceanic flights." So Byrd touched a chord when he said, "I believe that the flight of the three engine plane that will fly with one engine dead and which is equipped with floats for landing in water is the next step in transatlantic flying." But he should have known better.

When Amelia first saw the Fokker in the shadows that mid-May of 1928, it still had wheels—but mechanics and welders were working on the struts for the pontoons that were shortly to replace them. As she noted, the pontoons were experimental, and "no one definitely could tell in advance whether or not it would prove practicable." Not only was this the first Fokker to be fitted out with pontoons, it was the first pontoon-equipped plane to attempt a nonstop Atlantic crossing. The particular pontoons chosen—made of thin sheets of a new wonder metal, duralumin, a recently developed copper-aluminum alloy a third the weight of steel yet possessing the same strength, constructed by the Junker factory in Germany—were each divided into nine watertight compartments. Each of the huge pontoons, measuring twenty-nine feet in length by four feet in width, could supposedly float, airtight, for weeks in water.

The advantage of a seaplane for a transatlantic flight was obvious: if

there were engine trouble and the plane was forced down at sea, the fliers
stood a chance of survival because the plane wouldn't sink. The disadvan-
tage, more subtle, understood only by experts in the fledgling new world of
planes, was formidable. It boiled down to the fact that a seaplane could not
lift nearly as heavy a load as a land plane, therefore not as much fuel could
be taken, therefore the range of the plane was cut down. Byrd publicly
estimated that pontoons would cut two hundred miles off the range of the
plane. He was way off, as the *Friendship* crew would learn. A second and
related problem, as Commander Robert Elmer, USN retired, whom Byrd
had chosen to supervise the day-to-day fitting out of the Fokker, noted,
was that seaplanes needed a wind to become airborne at all; if there were
no waves and the water was smooth, it was difficult for a fully loaded seaplane to rise, according to Elmer, "because pontoons stick to water much
as a dime sticks to a wet table."

Charles Lindbergh, meticulous planner that he was, knew exactly
why he had chosen a land plane to fly the Atlantic: because flying boats
couldn't take off with sufficient fuel to go the distance. Byrd, on the other
hand, was juggling the safety factor of a plane's being able to land anywhere
on the gray-green sea against its drastically curtailed range. He knew that a
seaplane couldn't make the direct flight from New York to Europe—that
was why he had used wheels on the *America* the summer before. So
whereas Byrd's Fokker *America,* with engines similar to the *Friendship,*
had been able to take off from Roosevelt field on Long Island with four
men aboard and fly nonstop almost to the shores of France, Amy Guest's
Fokker *Friendship,* loaded down, handicapped, as it were, could not even
approach making such a long flight even with one less person aboard—it
didn't have the range. The plan, therefore, was to fly to Newfoundland,
refuel, and then to take off from its easternmost end, from Trepassey Harbor on the Avalon Peninsula, where the navy NC-4's had started off on
their flight across the ocean in 1919—a much shorter flight of eighteen
hundred miles.

In addition to loading the plane down with pontoons, Elmer, under the direction of Byrd, loaded it down with equipment. Lindbergh's
disciplined approach, which had led him to weigh every single necessary
item—to go to the lengths of having a special lightweight seat made out
of rattan, and special boots made of lightweight materials, of cutting out
unneeded sections of charts, of worrying about the few letters he carried,
of deciding against a radio, of deciding to fly alone because "I had
decided to replace the weight of a navigator with extra fuel and this gave
me about three hundred miles additional range"—was antithetical to
Byrd's thinking.

By the time Byrd and Elmer were finished with the *Friendship,* they had equipped it with, as Elmer proudly announced, "everything." They installed the usual instruments, altimeter, gas gauge, speedometer, two magnetic compasses, the newly developed earth induction compass (reliable but having to be reset when a plane changed course), wind drift instruments, smoke bombs to determine wind direction and velocity, flares, a Cardwell, a radio similar to the one Byrd had on the *America,* which had a range of a thousand miles on a 600-meter wave length, and a receiving set designed, built, and installed by Wallace Battison, a Cambridge radio expert. There was also an emergency transmitter with aerial located in the tail of the plane with a range of 50 to 100 miles that would give them ten minutes, in case of a disaster, to send out a call for help to steamers. Battison said it was put on so securely, "you couldn't jar it loose with a charge of dynamite." The Cardwell, all by itself, according to Bill Stultz, weighed a hundred pounds.

Elmer, in spite of his reservations about pontoons, thought he had overseen the fitting out of "the safest and best equipped airplane ever to attempt an ocean flight." Guest and Earhart certainly thought they were in good hands. So did George Putnam. By mid-May the varying load tests, the "countless" takeoffs from the bay, the "brief" flights around Boston, the fine-tuning of the instruments—all of which Amelia was kept apprised of but took no part in—were finished; the plane was ready.

David Layman and his wife came up to Boston hoping to witness the takeoff, as did Amy Guest's two sons Winston and Raymond; Dorothy Putnam came up to join her husband, who by this time had taken to haunting the hangar. An auxiliary pilot, Lou Gower, hired to help out as far as Trepassey, was also present with his wife and waiting patiently. The new problem was the weather—it refused to cooperate. Amelia would remember long gray days.

Still, her life had begun to take on the texture of the future. She had moved into Boston's most elegant hotel, the Copley Plaza (registering as Dorothy Binney, the maiden name of Dorothy Putnam, to avoid discovery) and was at least exposed, if she didn't participate in tea dancing, to the music of Meyer Davis.

• • • •

David Layman had first grudgingly and then gratefully ceded control of the enterprise to George Putnam, whose expertise in mounting expeditions was second to none. Putnam, assisted by Hilton Railey, now addressed himself to the public relations aspect of the flight. Able to present Amelia as a published writer on the basis of her article in *The Bostonian,* he struck a deal with *The New York Times*: they would pay Amelia ten thousand dollars for the exclusive, syndicated rights to her story. (Amelia, of course, would turn this money over to her benefactor.) Then he worked out a deal with Emanuel Cohen, his friend at Paramount News, for an undisclosed sum, giving Paramount News exclusive newsreel coverage in Boston and in Trepassey, Newfoundland. The Paramount News man in New England, considered by all to be the dean of his profession, was Jake Coolidge; he went to work immediately. In the interests of secrecy all of his shots of Amelia were taken on the unused, unfinished roof of the Copley Plaza; there he took a "a great reservoir of shots" of her for future release, assisted by his son Phil. He kept his photographic equipment, in those years so bulky, hidden in a utility closet on the top floor under the roof. (The choice of venue must have been Amelia's; who else would have thought of climbing out onto the roof of an elegant hotel?) It was Jake who deliberately created the "Lady Lindy" image that in later years would stick to Amelia like glue. He posed her mostly in her leather jacket, white-edged helmet, brown broadcloth riding "breeks," high-laced brown riding boots, and goggles. The theme was "Remember Lindbergh." Amelia had bought the jacket at a sale in 1922 for twenty dollars. When new, it had been "an elegant leather coat," a bit too elegant—a bit too shiny for Amelia. Wrinkles, she had decided, were what it needed, so she had slept in it for three nights until it had "a properly veteran appearance." Even then not quite satisfied, she had given it "a last going over—rubbing the sheen off here and there." Now it was to become a fashion statement for the world.

Jake didn't think that Charles and Amelia looked the least bit alike—it was just an illusion he created with his camera. "It wasn't so much that the resemblance was there as that you could make it seem to be there, by camera angles." Later, influenced by the poses and the similar outfits, many people would remark on their resemblance to each other, but just as many thought there was none. George Palmer Putnam, having been part of the magic act, couldn't see it. "She couldn't have resembled the Colonel very much or I would have noticed it," he would write. His wife Dorothy, on the other hand, thought the resemblance "uncanny"; Hilton Railey thought it "extraordinary."

Paramount News sent another of their photographers, Andy Fulgoni, up to Trepassey to wait there for the fliers.

George Putnam arranged with David Layman to provide funds for Hilton Railey to go to England to run interference for Amelia when and if she landed; Hilton set off by boat.

On nice days Amelia drove her confreres around in the battered yellow convertible that George Putnam dubbed at first glance the *Yellow Peril,* not only apt, but also the name of a sleek English plane made by Handley Page.

Her new friends may not have known what kind of a pilot she was, but they undoubtedly noticed that sweet and modest though she was, she drove a car like a bat out of hell. Depending on their temperaments, her passengers were either impressed or scared. Marion Perkins was one of those impressed. Amelia was, she wrote, "an expert . . . handling her car with ease, yes more than that, with an artistic touch." Hilton Railey's wife Julia was one of those who was not. "People got out of the way of it I noticed. Our battered and bedented bus scudded through the traffic like a car possessed. With something of a flourish we drew up at last at the Old France restaurant." (She didn't like the car, either, calling it "the worst looking automobile—hers—I think I ever saw, bar one. Its rear end was cigar-shaped and its ground color a sick canary.")

In spite of the fact that neither Amelia nor anyone else mentions his presence at this juncture, Sam Chapman was still an important part of Amelia's life. She gave him the intimate, delicate job of telling her mother, the type of task a fiancé *would* undertake. There is no doubt they still considered themselves engaged; he, like she, expected her to return to Denison House in two or at the most three weeks.

• • • •

Amelia's actual preparation for the flight was minimal since she was going to wear her everyday flying outfit (which she had been donning for her photos for weeks). In addition to the breeks, boots, goggles, helmet, and leather jacket, she would be taking (and wearing) a light brown sweater, a blouse, a red necktie, fur-lined boots, and, "a single elegance," practically a trademark for pilots of the day, a silk scarf—hers was brown and white. As protection against the cold that they would meet flying at high altitudes, Amelia and the men took fur-lined flying suits, hers borrowed from a friend, Major Charles L. Wooley, commander of the Massachusetts National Guard Air Force, a fellow member of the Boston NAA (she didn't divulge where it was going). The few things she took—a toothbrush, a comb, fresh linen handkerchiefs, a tube of cold cream, a camera borrowed from Layman, field glasses borrowed from Putnam—all fitted into the small knapsack she bought for the occasion at a local army-navy store. She didn't own a watch; Mrs. Layman lent her one, and David Layman loaned her his camera.

She wrote a will of sorts. She itemized her debts that, all told, amounted to slightly over one thousand dollars, most of it owed to a bank, but as a marker of the complexity of her character, it included a $140 debt to Filene's for a fur coat. She suggested that her car be sold to cover the

bills and directed that her interest in the Kinner Airplane and Motor Corporation and the ten shares of stock she owned in the Dennison Aircraft
Corporation go to her mother. ("I hope they will pay and think they will,"
she added.) She concluded, "My regret is that I leave just now. In a few
years I feel I could have laid by something substantial, for so many new
things were opening for me. . . . Selah."

She left letters for her mother and father at Denison House, identifying them, for the unnamed person who would find them (undoubtedly
Marion Perkins), with a penciled note clipped to the envelopes, as "popping off" letters that should be sent out. Her letter to Amy is carefully
upbeat:

> Even though I have lost, the adventure was worth while. Our
> family tends to be too secure. My life has really been very happy,
> and I didn't mind contemplating its end in the midst of it.

But her note to her father, dated Friday, June 1, is even more exuberant and affectionate. She used her childhood name and indulged herself
in deliberate misspellings.

> Dearest Dad:
>
> Hooray for the last grand adventure! I wish I had won, but
> it was worthwhile, anyway. You know that. I have no faith we'll
> meet anywhere again, but I wish we might.
>
> > Anyway, good-by and good luck to you.
> > Affectionately, your doter, Mill

She wrote a letter to Muriel, which she mailed, writing carefully and
honestly, explaining why she had kept her in the dark.

> I have tried to play for a large stake, and if I succeed all will be
> well. If I don't, I shall be happy to pop off in the midst of such
> an adventure. My only regret would be leaving you and mother
> stranded for a while.
>   I haven't told you about the affair as I didn't want to worry
> mother, and she would suspect (she may now) if I told you. The
> whole thing came so unexpectedly that few knew about it. Sam

will tell you the whole story. Please explain all to mother. I couldn't stand the added strain of telling mother and you personally.

If reporters talk to you say you knew, if you like.

She added a postscript, explaining that she had taken care of her affairs. "I have made my will and placed my house in order. I have appointed a girlfriend at Denison House to act as administrator in case of my death."

She had taken care of everything: her job was covered, her will written, farewell letters to her parents in place in case she didn't come back, and Sam delegated to tell her mother. It would have seemed inconceivable to her that Sam could fail to reach Amy before the evening papers were on the streets with the news, but that is what happened.

Clearly she was very much in control of herself. But she couldn't do anything about the plane. The *Friendship* was moored off the Jeffrey Yacht Club in East Boston. The first predawn attempt to take off was a failure. There was not enough wind, and as Elmer had said, the pontoons acted like a dime stuck to the table. The second attempt was aborted because of fog. Amelia loved poetry and had an ingrained habit of retreating into it to handle difficult situations. At Columbia, when she could not answer questions in the weekly physics quiz, she had inserted a little French poetry. Now she quoted Carl Sandburg.

The fog comes on little cat feet and sits on
its haunches
Overlooking city and harbor
And then moves on.

According to Phil Coolidge, with whom Amelia had become friends, both George Putnam and Bill Stultz were beginning to show signs of strain. George "grew irascible," and Bill Stultz so edgy that Phil kept trying to calm him down so that he wouldn't start drinking. There was a disquieting article in *The Boston Globe* on Friday, June 1. The paper reported that more than a thousand gallons of aviation gas and 150 gallons of oil had arrived at Old Orchard Beach, Maine, in anticipation of the arrival of Thea Rasche, who planned to hop off from there on a transatlantic flight. Their two failures to take off took on an ominous meaning.

On Saturday came more inspiring news—the *Southern Cross,* also a trimotored Fokker, had taken off from Oakland, California, and safely landed at Wheeler field in Honolulu after a flight of 27 hours, 28 minutes.

By that time all the support group were staying at the Copley Plaza. That night Mrs. Layman, in the room next to Amelia, heard her padding about late into the night. She knocked and asked if there was anything she could do. "It's like being left waiting at the church. I'll be all right, thanks," fretted Amelia. It was the only display of tension Mrs. Layman noticed. After the long wait was over, Mrs. Layman would take away the indelible memory that of all the participants, Amelia had been the most controlled. As she told Janet Mabie, a great deal of the time Amelia had hardly talked at all: "But you got the feeling, whatever was going through her mind, that she wasn't afraid."

As they awoke on Sunday, June 3, at three thirty, to make a third attempt, the routine was familiar to participants and watchers alike. They breakfasted at an all-night restaurant, drove in the darkness to T wharf, boarded the tug *Sadie Ross,* fat and tidy and bobbing gently just beyond the Eastern Steamship Company docks, and headed out for the big orange and gold plane. If anyone asked what they were up to, they planned to say they were on a fishing expedition. Besides George Putnam, the Laymans, Lou Gordon's fiancée, Gower's wife, Stultz's wife, and the Elmers were there, plus Jake Coolidge of Paramount News and his son. Besides their personal belongings, they had with them a copy of Byrd's book *Skyward* (weighing in at one pound), which the commander had inscribed for Amy Guest, and an American flag. Five hundred gallons of gasoline had already been loaded into the wing tanks and into the elliptical gas tanks in the fuselage, and in addition there were eight auxiliary five-gallon cans in the cabin, making a grand total of 545 gallons. (Amelia alternated sitting on one of the cans and on the bag of flying suits.) The day dawned warm and clear. The sun, she noticed, was just coming over the rim of the harbor, and a few dawn clouds hung about in the pink glow.

The four of them got into the plane, and stowed their gear and supplies. Just before they closed the door, according to Jake Coolidge, they decided to discard Amelia's fur-lined boots and the rubber life raft and oars. "I'll make you a present of the rubber boat," Amelia called out cheerily to Jake, who remembered grinning, a grin tinged with anxiety. As they left, Stultz checked out the instruments, then they saw Slim Gordon hop out onto the pontoons, crank first the starboard, then the port, then the center engine, all of which turned over perfectly, and with a roar the big plane taxied down the bay. Behind the *Sadie Ross* appeared another smaller boat. In it were Amelia's four faithful friends—Sam Chapman, George Ludlam (manager of Denison House), Marian Perkins, and an unidentified woman friend, all of whom Amelia had invited to attend the two earlier abortive dawn liftoffs. This time she had told them not to bother getting out of bed again. They hadn't listened but had gone down to Lewis Wharf the night before and hired a boat for five A.M.

Amelia wondered whether "this day too would . . . flatten out into failure." Off the Squantum Naval Air Station the *Friendship* turned into the light southwest breeze. Stultz gunned the engines; they started accelerating. The huge monoplane had to achieve a speed of fifty miles an hour to become airborne. It raced over the water. Failure. The water wouldn't let them go.

Gasoline is heavy; each gallon weighs over 6.12 pounds. They threw out six of the eight five-gallon cans. Forty-two pounds lighter, they tried again. And again failed. Amelia and Slim Gordon were in the rear of the plane. Now, joined by Lou Gower, they retreated as far back as possible into the hold in an effort to lighten the nose as much as possible. Yet a fourth time they failed. The problem, they all began to realize, was weight. The solution was to remove even more weight. Since they couldn't remove any more gasoline and still reach their goal, the only expendable poundage was the auxiliary pilot. As they turned back preparatory to making yet another run down the harbor, Lou Gower pulled his flying suit from the bag, Slim motioned a boat over, and Lou quietly said good-bye and stepped out of the plane.

Although Gower was thin—Amelia described all the men as having "distinctly Gothic" builds—his 150 pounds made the difference. On the next run the wind freshened, annd the Fokker shook free, lifted, soared, made a brief turn over the *Sadie Ross,* and disappeared into the rising sun. Exultantly, Amelia wrote that the difference in weight turned the *Friendship* into a bird. Still, it took the bird a long time—67 seconds—to become airborne. It was 6:31 when the pontoons shook loose from the water and the *Friendship* headed east into the dawn, destination Trepassey, Newfoundland. The summer before, Byrd's Fokker *America,* identical except that it had wheels, had taken off carrying a full load of gasoline, 800 pounds of extra equipment, and four men. The *Friendship* had not been able to take off with half a load of gasoline, no extra equipment, three men plus 118-pound Amelia. But none of the fliers had time to dwell on that ominous fact because a few minutes into the flight, still in sight of Boston Harbor, Slim Gordon somehow managed to fall against the cabin door in such a way that he broke the spring lock that held it closed. Almost falling out, he tied the door to one of the gas cans with a piece of string. But the gas can was not heavy enough for the job. It began to slide toward the gradually opening door. Amelia dove for it, almost falling out herself, after which, in a joint effort, they tied the door to a brace inside the cabin.

After that, the trip up the New England coast was uneventful. They averaged ninety-six miles an hour. It was hazy; they reached the southern tip of Nova Scotia. Amelia dozed as they headed up its eastern coast, and when she awoke, the clouds beneath them had thickened into fog. She had leisure time to notice what her traveling companions were wearing and discovered, much to her surprise, that though she was in flying clothes, they were not: they had dressed up in city clothes—undoubtedly in her honor.

Land disappeared. Stultz cautiously, figuring they were about fifty miles beyond Halifax, probably over Tangier, decided to turn back and wait it out in Halifax until visibility improved. The trick was to find Halifax, and as Bill Stultz admitted later, it wasn't that easy. He was lost for a while; the *Friendship* dove through the clouds for several hours before finally sighting Halifax Harbor through a rift in the clouds. When he did, he set the *Friendship* down in the Eastern Passage, the easternmost part of the harbor, tying up at the Canadian seaplane station, which he had spotted as he was coming in. Dories came out to greet them, and Stultz and Gordon went ashore to the officers' mess to ask for bearings and a weather report. Amelia meanwhile, to avoid being discovered, stayed out of sight in the plane.

They came back with the news that although the station had not yet received the weather report, it was thought that there was rain and fog ahead; the flight sergeant had told them that if they started out, they might have to return. But Stultz was impatient—they were halfway to their destination—so, Amelia wrote, "Bill says he'll try to make T." Slim cranked up the engines, and they took off without any problem, but within minutes they were again enveloped in fog and forced to turn back. A half hour later they were again taxiing to the seaplane station, tying up behind a Canadian Fairchild seaplane. This time when the flight sergeant came out to help anchor the *Friendship,* they invited him in to discuss the housing situation. The problem was Amelia. They wanted to keep her under wraps, for since midmorning, every flying office at Boston airport and at Dennison airport had been under siege by reporters seeking information. There had been rumors spreading since the day before that Amelia was to make the flight; now newspapers had the story, and reporters were working their way up the coast.

Stultz and Gordon went ashore with the flight sergeant to see if he could arrange for Amelia to stay with a government official, leaving Amelia again in the plane; again, because of circling boats, forced to stay away from the windows. They had no luck with private lodgings, however. They all set out for the Thorndyke Hotel in the town of Dartmouth, located across the harbor from Halifax, where they were booked into adjoining rooms on the third floor. Amelia immediately went up to her room and stayed there to avoid the reporters, although she found it little to her liking: the straw was coming out of the mattress, the window wouldn't stay open, and both the single bedsheet and the pillowcase were dirty. Slim and Bill repaired to a Chinese restaurant, only to be spotted by reporters and photographers who followed them back to their room at the hotel. Amelia heard the newsmen trying to persuade the fliers to get dressed and have their picture taken. She was furious at the inconsiderateness (it was midnight) but said nothing for fear they would discover her next. They arose early, at five thirty A.M., but by the time they breakfasted at the hotel, they were surrounded by newsmen.

All the morning papers had the story and were going wild. *The New York Times* proclaimed on its front page in a four-column-wide head that dominated the page, "Boston Girl Starts for Atlantic Hop, Reaches Halifax, May Go On Today," followed by reams of copy and photos of the three of them. The *Herald Tribune* was more optimistic: "Girl and Stultz on Atlantic Flight Halt at Halifax; Going On Today." "Girl Hops from Boston to London, Forced Down at Halifax on First Leg" ran the headline in the *Boston Herald*.

They finally took off at nine thirty. The liftoff took just sixty seconds "in a perfectly calm sea"—a very good sign. It was a sparkling clear cool day, 52 degrees outside, 58 degrees inside the cabin. They flew along the coast at 1,800 feet and by 11:55 they were over Cape Canso, the northeasternmost point of mainland Nova Scotia. Stultz relinquished the controls to Gordon, and Slim headed northeast across the open sea. They climbed to 3,200 feet, and the temperature inside the cabin dropped to 53 degrees. "The sea," Amelia wrote, "looks like the back of an elephant, the same kind of wrinkles." At 12:50 they nosed down and sighted Newfoundland, the Burin Peninsula, to the left. Amelia set her watch ahead an hour. It was hazy, they were just under a cloud bank, flying at 3,000 feet, when they saw land—Peter's River at the entrance to St. Mary's Bay, which meant they were on target. Their destination, Trepassey, lay on the other side of Cape Pine, ten miles to the east.

10
Trepassey

• • • • The *Friendship* circled Trepassey twice before putting down in the choppy water of the harbor after a flight of 4 hours, 24 minutes. As the big monoplane taxied slowly toward the small cluster of houses on the eastern shore that was the town of Trepassey, dories full of men whirling ropes (Amelia called them maritime cowboys), each evidently hoping to guide them in, surrounded the *Friendship*. Slim Gordon, standing out on one of the pontoons as they came in toward the shore, was almost knocked into the water by one of their lines. It was only after Paramount News cameraman Andy Fulgoni circled the plane in his launch and urged the townspeople to stand clear that Stultz could head for the mooring arranged for them, a few hundred yards from the Trepassey town dock.

The town magistrate, Fred Gill, and his two sons, waiting near the monoplane in a dory, secured the honor of giving Amelia and Bill Stultz a ride to the dock, where the fliers were officially greeted, photographed, and interviewed by members of the press; Slim Gordon came later, after tending to the plane. The children of Trepassey, who had been watching and waiting at the windows of the convent school facing the harbor, ran down to the shore en masse. Amelia "had a vision of many white pinafores and aprons on the dock," and was under the impression that school had let out early so that the children could greet them. In fact, the children had simply fled without permission, for which they were made to stay late. (She went up and visited with the children later at the convent school; the nuns were scandalized at the sight of a woman in pants.)

It was arranged that the three fliers would spend the night at a small frame two-story house with attached general store belonging to Richard and Fanny Devereaux a few hundred feet from the water's edge, just opposite where the *Friendship* was moored. Mrs. Devereaux too, at first sight of Amelia in her "breeks" and boots was "quite overcome, and felt me to be sure I was present in the flesh." To make room for the visitors, the Devereauxes sent their children off to relatives.

Trepassey was a fishing community of some six hundred souls, all Catholic, who eked out a living on the "lean and bony" shore. It was a bleak place; the life was so harsh that all the energy of the townsfolk went to maintaining their precarious existence—there was nothing left over for amenities of any kind, either inside or outside their houses. Literally the only spots of color inside the houses, as Amelia noticed, were the religious pictures, which hung "everywhere." Indoor plumbing didn't exist, and most families, including the Devereauxes, didn't even have a bathtub. Each wooden house, enclosed by its picket fence, stood starkly on its rocky piece of land; not a flower, not a shrub, not a tree punctuated the landscape. The shoreline was black gravel, occasionally interrupted by a sand beach.

The men went off fishing for weeks at a time, leaving the women to tend to the livestock and run the life of the island community. Most families, including the Devereauxes, kept a milk cow, chickens, and a few sheep. Fresh vegetables and fruit were almost unknown. The rocky land was so poor that except for a few hundred acres with adequate topsoil, nothing grew, and so those precious acres had to be devoted to subsistence crops—hay, potatoes, turnips, radishes, and cabbage.

The biggest excitement for the villagers was watching who got off the twice-weekly train from St. John's. Not that any of these things at that point made any impression on the fliers; the flight up from Halifax had gone beautifully, taking half an hour less than the five hours Bill Stultz had predicted, and buoyed up, they expected to be off the next day.

They had planned to spend that first afternoon refueling the *Friendship* and get an early start the next morning, but as they proceeded with the refueling, the northwest wind began blowing down the harbor, stirring up such a sea, it became impossible to load the gasoline safely, so they had no choice but to wait and finish the next day.

Amelia walked to the telegraph office located a few houses down from the Devereauxes, where telegraph operator Mike Jackman lived and worked, and sent George Palmer Putnam a telegram. "Good trip from Halifax. Average speed 111 miles per hour. Motors running beautifully. Trepassey Harbor very rough. Three hundred gallons of gasoline were loaded today. Everybody comfortably housed and happy."

The Boston Evening Globe, coming out only hours after the plane landed, told the world in inch-high headlines running straight across the front page: "Boston Girl's Plane Landed at Trepassey, NF, at 12:55."

In it Amelia gave a slightly awkward interview.

> The flight from Halifax here was really delightful, and I feel proud of being the first woman successfully to make the trip. . . . Really a delightful idea is this trans-Atlantic flight. . . . Gliding through the air at almost two miles a minute with the boisterous ocean beneath and the air above is thrilling but that is the bright side. The dangers, terrific contest with the storm swept Atlantic fogs, rains are the reverse side of the picture. . . . I am entering the contest with confidence in both the plane and the men in charge and for the issue I trust in Providence. I think the best and most delightful way to come to Newfoundland is by seaplane.

By the next morning they realized that, Commander Byrd notwithstanding, Trepassey Harbor was a very bad place for them to be. They would get to know the configurations of Trepassey Harbor well—the long narrow sliver of water, the inner harbor one and a half miles long protected from the sea by an elbow of Powles Peninsula, at its narrowest less than a half mile wide, at its widest a mile. Facing the town across the harbor on the western shore were hills 360 feet high. At the head of the harbor the hills rose to a height of 120 feet. It was so narrow that the *Friendship* could take off only on a southwest course, going down its length. That morning they awoke to find the wind still from the northwest—no good for them, since they needed a northwest wind once they were airborne, not before. But at least it was clear and they could see about them; there would be many mornings when the hills wouldn't be visible; twenty-one out of the thirty days of June, Trepassey Harbor was fog bound.

Byrd had undoubtedly picked Trepassey because it was the only harbor on the Avalon Peninsula—itself the closest point to Europe—with which he was familiar. He had been to Trepassey in May 1919 with the navy's three huge Curtiss flying boats, the NC-4's, which had started out from Trepassey Harbor to make the first transatlantic crossing by air (in hops because they were heavy and had a range of only fourteen hundred miles), guarded by sixty-five warships strung across the ocean in case they went down. Those planes had had problems taking off, and but for the swells, they would have been towed out of Trepassey Harbor, around Powles Point, and into nearby wide Mutton Bay, where they would have been able to take off into the northwest wind.

But Byrd had been too preoccupied with getting a place on one of the planes to assess the qualities of Trepassey as takeoff point. He had been in on much of the navy's planning for the crossing and desperately wanted to be a part of it, but he had been refused permission (several times) to go: "But soon after our arrival Towers handed me a radio from Captain Irwin which specifically directed that I should not accompany the expedition." His energies while at Trepassey were directed toward trying to change his orders. For Byrd, each day of delay at Trepassey had not been a problem to be analyzed but a day of opportunity—another day to change the navy's mind. The *Friendship* crew would pay the penalty. For them each day was a new trial to be endured. Amelia would enter in her log, "All of us are caged animals."

That first morning dawned clear and cool, a welcome change after sweltering Boston. Stultz and Gordon worked on the plane, repairing the radio, which had been cutting out, and the oil tank, which had developed a small crack. They managed to put some gas in the tanks, but the wind was gusting to thirty knots, and by afternoon, when Bill had finished closing the crack with cement and adhesive tape, the northwest wind was "a howling gale."

Telegrams were pouring in "every few minutes" for Amelia. One was a gallant cable from her mother, wishing her daughter success and regretting that she was not one of the party. Some unsettling ones had to do with an article that had appeared in the Boston papers to the effect that her family had recently fallen on hard times and that Amelia was flying the ocean to recoup the family fortune. Before the day was out, using the opportunity presented, Amelia cabled George Putnam:

> PLEASE GET THE POINT ACROSS THAT THE ONLY STAKE I WIN IS THE
> PRIVILEGE OF FLYING AND THE PLEASURE OF HAVING SHARED IN A FINE
> ADVENTURE WELL CONDUCTED WHOSE SUCCESS WILL BE A REAL
> DEVELOPMENT AND PERHAPS SOMETHING OF AN INSPIRATION FOR
> WOMEN.

George saw to it that the cable itself was included in the next day's news stories.

• • • •

The fliers knew there was a spoiler on the horizon, knew that delay might open a window of opportunity for others. Amelia viewed herself—naturally, since she was flying in Amy Guest's plane with Amy Guest's pilot—as a lucky substitute for her benefactress. Mabel Boll saw things very differently. Even though her negotiations with Commander Byrd for the Fokker had never been finalized, and even though Bill Stultz had flown down to New York especially to tell her that he was withdrawing from her enterprise, as far as Boll was concerned, Amelia was in *her* plane with *her* pilot, and she was determined to get even. The moment she heard about the *Friendship* taking off from Boston Harbor on Sunday, she set to work doing what she did so well—getting publicity. She called *The New York Times* so speedily that the same edition that broke the story of Amelia's flight the day after she took off, on the streets that Monday, June 4, even as the *Friendship* was winging its way from Halifax to Newfoundland, carried her story as well. The one column head had run: "Miss Boll, in Tears, Finds Herself, Left." "I can't understand it," she told the *Times.* "Wilmer was down here only a few days ago and I asked him when he was coming back to fly the *Columbia.* He said in just a few days."

But Mabel already had a pilot, and a good one—Canadian war ace Oliver Le Boutillier, and she appeared to have won over Charles Levine again—her plane was the *Columbia.* Nor had she overlooked the *Herald Tribune,* which reported that "Miss Boll challenged her woman rival from Boston to a race across the Atlantic." (*The Boston Globe* carried essentially the same tale.) By the next evening, when Amelia was going over the telegrams in Trepassey, the Newfoundland paper in St. John's had picked up the story. The real news was that the only thing stopping the *Columbia* was that it had been raining so much that the long narrow runway at Roosevelt field, the only runway long enough for the heavy plane to take off from, was too soft to be used.

• • • •

The next morning, Wednesday, June 6, it was again sunny, clear, and brisk; the wind was still blowing from the northwest, although not as hard, and was occasionally beginning to veer south. Amelia, Bill, and Slim went aboard *Friendship* at eight thirty A.M., finished refueling the plane to seven hundred gallons, and tested the radio by successfully raising nearby Cape Race. Following that, they made a tour of the harbor in a motorboat to figure out the best place to start the takeoff. Then they heard from Dr. James Kimball at the Weather Bureau in New York—there was heavy rain, dense fog, and east winds off the English coast; they couldn't start. Blocked, they took the rest of the day off, getting to know the tiny house well as they began to spend unwanted time in it. Upstairs there were three very small bedrooms—one for the Devereauxes, one for Amelia, and the third that Bill and Lou shared. Downstairs there was the kitchen and living room. The ceilings were so low that when, out of boredom, Amelia lay on her back on the downstairs couch and carefully stretched her long legs straight up, she could plant the soles of her boots on the ceiling.

As she found out, wrecks were an integral part of Trepassey life. The small luxuries, the few bits of silver in the homes, even some of the furniture, came as a result of shipwrecks caused by the turbulence of the great polar current that dipped in close to the Trepassey shore as it swept westward around the island. English mariners came to call that stretch of Avalon the fatal iron-bound coast. The French knew it as a place of death and called it so. Trepassey is a corruption of the French verb trépasser, which means "to die." Through the passage of time and their incurious nature, the townspeople had completely forgotten where the name came from. If Amelia had only known, as the days dragged on and she felt as if it *were* the end of the world, she would have remarked on its appropriateness.

Late in the day Frederick Ryan, the *New York Times* reporter who had arrived on the scene, told them of Mabel Boll's preparations—that she was planning to take off from Roosevelt field the next morning. What made it worse was that they all knew that the *Columbia* was virtually unbeatable. Not only had Bill Stultz just flown it down to Cuba with Mabel Boll and Charles Levine eight weeks previously, but it was the plane Clarence Chamberlin and Charles Levine had flown nonstop 3,911 miles from Roosevelt field to Eisleben Germany. Not only did the *Columbia* have a greater range than the *Friendship,* but as Stultz admitted to Ryan, it was faster. If they were to start at the same time, Mabel Boll would easily beat them across. The only consoling thought for Amelia, Bill, and Slim was that although the *Columbia* had flown nonstop from Long Island to Germany, it couldn't this time because Le Boutillier was taking a co-pilot, Captain Arthur Argyles—and with two men and Mabel Boll in it, the plane was too heavy to go the direct route to Europe. It too would have to refuel in Newfoundland, giving them a twelve-hour lead.

The news, naturally, galvanized them. In spite of not altogether reassuring weather reports from Doc Kimball, they held a ten P.M. press conference at which they announced that they would rise at six the next morning, put an additional 200 gallons of gas aboard (bringing them up to 900 gallons), and make a start at about nine. Amelia's suggestion that they "get out of this trap and into the next harbor" at four A.M. when the wind died down, fell on deaf ears. Her last entry in her log: "perhaps we may make it." And so they went to sleep on their third night in Trepassey. In London Amy Guest, horrified at the turn of events, was reduced to having someone state on her behalf, "The *Friendship*'s flight is in no sense a stunt. Safety is the governing consideration." It didn't sound very convincing.

• • • •

Byrd, Guest, and Putnam had made careful and elaborate plans to ensure that the *Friendship* would have the most extensive weather information it was possible to assemble. Dr. James Kimball of the New York Weather Bureau was in charge of the effort. He collected weather data from ships at sea and from weather stations in the United States, Canada, Bermuda, the Arctic, Greenland, and the Grand Banks. In addition, England sent him information covering the eastern Atlantic and Europe. He took all this data and, standing at his high desk in the Whitehall building in lower Manhattan, sometimes watched by George Putnam, plotted it out on an outline map of the North Atlantic. Each day when he had assimilated all the information, he sent it on to Trepassey. Bill and Amelia then took this data and in turn plotted it out—the storms, the winds, the low and high pressure centers—on Stultz's navigation chart. But Kimball was more than weather report coordinator; as the person who knew more about weather patterns than anyone else, he was in a real sense in charge of the expedition. It was he who had picked the takeoff day for Charles Lindbergh and Commander Byrd. As Amelia wrote "We shoved off only when he said go."

That Thursday, June 7, dawned clear and warm, 60 degrees in Trepassey, with a perfect wind for takeoff, west-southwest—perfect flying weather. Kimball had wired them that the transatlantic weather was good enough for them to start, so for the first time since they had arrived on Monday, they could positively look forward to resuming their journey. But thoughts of a nine A.M. start evaporated when Bill noticed that the right-hand float was lying deeper in the water than the left. Slim went out to check and found fifty gallons of water in it. It took until noon to plug the leak, pump out the water (at seven pounds a gallon, that would have been a deadly 350 pounds), and finish loading the gasoline.

By then, the eagerly awaited southwest wind had died down and the water was almost a little too smooth, but highly charged, spurred on by the specter of the *Columbia,* they decided they would attempt a liftoff anyway. They hadn't been able to take off from Boston Harbor with themselves plus Lou Gower and only five hundred gallons of fuel. Aboard they now had nine hundred gallons—an additional 2,800 pounds. Would they be able to lift this heavier load? They went ashore, quickly ate what they hoped would be their last Trepassey meal, refilled their thermos bottles, packed up some sandwiches, and said brief good-byes to local residents and reporters. Amelia notified Mike Jackman to send off a telegram if they actually became airborne. At 12:22, all motors turning over, they started. The big trimotor gathered speed and roared off down the harbor for more than a mile but never got close to liftoff. Three times in the light wind they tried, three times the pontoons remained glued to the sea. Not willing to give up, they announced they would try again later, at four o'clock, when the wind was expected to freshen. But the wind didn't freshen, and finally, defeated, they taxied back to the mooring. They went ashore fearing the worst, but encouraging news awaited them: the *Columbia* had indeed taken off from Roosevelt field at six fifteen that morning, but it ran into bad weather, got lost in fog, and finally was forced to turn back, landing at noon. It was reported that when Boll returned to Roosevelt field, she stepped from the plane weeping.

Later yet in the day, back checking over the plane, the fliers found a leak in the oil tank. They dismantled the tank, and took it to the shop of local carpenter Joseph Hewitt, who soldered closed an inch-wide hole, caused, they thought, by a dory boat hook. In the end they couldn't consider it an altogether bad day—in fact, they considered themselves lucky, for they realized that if they had succeeded in becoming airborne and started out for Europe, they would have run out of oil and crashed in midocean.

• • • •

That same day the St. John's afternoon paper, *The Evening Telegram,* carried news of the German aviatrix, Thea Rasche. The Bellanca she had bought, a twin of the *Columbia* powered by a Wright Whirlwind engine, was being delivered to her at Curtiss field on Long Island, "and within the next three days," she informed the Newfoundland paper, *she* would take off and fly to Berlin.

On Friday Amelia appeared cheerful, *Times* reporter Ryan said— they were all looking forward to getting a long night's rest, their first, really, because finally "they think everything aboard their craft is in the finest condition." They seemed unfazed by evening weather reports of no change for the better over the Atlantic, which meant they probably wouldn't start till Sunday, figuring the weather would hold up Boll as well.

Thea Rasche's new Bellanca arrived at Curtiss field, and respected transatlantic pilot Clarence Chamberlin took it up for a test flight and declared it "handled very well." Fräulein Rasche reiterated her plan to fly to Germany by way of Newfoundland as soon as she could.

Saturday June 9. It was still cold, in the forties. The little wind there was came from the east; a dull, foggy day. The *Friendship* swung idly at its mooring.

George Putnam tried to lighten the situation with a telegram: SUGGEST YOU TURN IN AND HAVE YOUR LAUNDERING DONE.

To which Amelia replied, THANKS FATHERLY TELEGRAM NO WASHING NECESSARY SOCKS UNDERWEAR WORN OUT SHIRT LOST TO SLIM [GORDON] AT RUMMY CHEERIO AMELIA.

The next evening Kimball reported that from Cape Race across the ocean a series of low-pressure areas extended nearly to the coast of Ireland, with fog, storms, and easterly winds all the way across the great circle route. As night fell in Trepassey, the wind veered west, and fog rolled in. They thought the fog was just their bad luck—they didn't realize they were in one of the most persistently foggy areas of the world, or that June was one of the worst months, fogbound most of the time. Mariners knew that the fog brooded over that stretch of shore almost "incessantly" in summer, but Byrd had not consulted with mariners.

By this time it was finally getting to Amelia. She wrote in her log that evening, "We have had a cruel day." The worst of it was that while they were stuck, "our competitors are gaining on us by delay. Rasche is the one to fear. I wish we'd have a break."

And indeed, Rasche was getting closer. At Curtiss field on Long Island mechanics spent the day installing instruments in her new Bellanca. There was no activity in the *Columbia*'s hangar. The plane and its fliers were ready—they had done everything there was to do—now they were waiting for a green light on the weather.

• • • •

Sunday, June 10, was a bad day—cold, with easterly winds. But it wasn't just the weather that was wrong. The scenario Amelia feared most had happened—the men all got drunk.

The second day they were in Trepassey, Amelia had discovered to her horror, driving around with one of the newspaper reporters and Andy Fulgoni, the Paramount photographer, that some of the reporters had liquor with them. She did what she could, exacting a promise from Andy not to let Stultz and Gordon see it, but during the week the fliers and the reporters had gathered in Andy's room, and that was the end of it. "I wish I were a Catholic and could turn over the responsibility of the moment to some deity or demon," she wrote, "the boys went after bad booze and got it last night." They didn't get back until six A.M. Bill woke up at twelve thirty, but Slim slept until five P.M. She was bitter about the reporter who had made it all possible. "I could choke Frazer. It doesn't matter if *he* drinks."

Amelia's log ended on a rare note of despair. "Fog has come in thick and woolly, and rain is now accompanying. Job had nothing on us. We are just managing to keep from suicide."

To the southwest, in New York, the weather broke; Mabel Boll announced late in the day that she would take off early the next morning.

• • • •

Monday, June 11, started hopefully in Trepassey. As dawn broke, it was raining and still foggy, but as the morning progressed, the rain stopped, the fog lightened, and it seemed to be warming up. While they waited for the morning report, the wind freshened and hopes were high, but when the telegram came from New York, it was bad news, they couldn't start— "the Atlantic wasn't inviting," "mayhap tomorrow noon." The only consoling thought was that the bad weather now extended south down the coast and would hold the *Columbia* up too.

Charles Levine, evidently to keep them twisting, made the announcement, which the Newfoundland papers picked up, that *had* the *Columbia* taken off, it would have headed "directly" for Europe. Apprised of this, the *Friendship* crew discounted it as a deliberate attempt to mislead them. To pass the time, the trio went exploring, going to see the old cannon at the mouth of the bay, and did some much-needed shopping. They spent the evening working puzzles. Amelia had read the few books and wished for more. By nightfall it was cold again, and she was grateful for a borrowed flannel nightgown. They went to sleep without knowing Mabel Boll had taken off.

The next day the wind was right, the fifteen-knot southwest wind was in fact "the wind we had been praying for," as Amelia wrote, there was not a trace of fog, and Kimball gave them a green light to go. They loaded their things onto the *Friendship,* and again said their goodbyes. Just past one P.M. Slim Gordon started the motors and they were off, taxiing into position. Stultz gunned the engines, and they went roaring down the harbor. Again the pontoons refused to rise from the water. Stultz tried and tried to get the big monoplane airborne, tried from various parts of the harbor—tried for four heartbreaking hours before he quit. Bill hoped the problem might be water in the pontoons and had Gordon open every single one of the eighteen compartments, only to find that they were watertight and contained less than a gallon in all. Before the last attempt, Amelia wrote, they unloaded everything they could into a waiting rowboat—the moving picture camera, Amelia's leather coat, her boots, bags, even a thermos—in their attempt to make the craft lighter. A watching reporter was not impressed. He thought the small pile indicative of "the desperate straits to which the flyers were reduced."

As she got off the plane at the end of the day Amelia kept her feelings to herself, merely saying, "What rotten luck," to the reporters. In the log Amelia blamed their failure on a receding tide that roiled the sea and threw the spray so high, it drowned the outboard motors. Many of those watching believed the plane was too heavy to ever lift off, according to *Times* reporter Ryan. Amelia was so upset by their failure, she couldn't read the newspapers and letters waiting for her. Then came more bad news—Boll and the *Columbia* had reached Newfoundland. It was, Amelia wrote, "the worst day." Little did she know that worse was to come. Much worse.

At eight P.M. the *Columbia* circled Harbor Grace, seventy-five miles to the northeast, and landed there on the pebbly airstrip built the summer before, to be greeted by Judge Casey, airport officials, and crowds of townspeople. They had been buffeted by winds, almost forced down by the weather, and they were tired after the ten-hour flight, but Mabel Boll's first question upon alighting was "Has the *Friendship* hopped off yet?" Told no, she had exclaimed, "Great. Our chances are even." She and her pilots went immediately to the Cochrane House, dined, and then, tired or not, strolled about before retiring. Oliver Le Boutillier was quoted as saying that the plane had averaged 120 miles an hour. That was ten miles an hour faster than the *Friendship*. But—a ray of hope for the Trepassey crew—he also said they would spend a day or two resting before tackling the Atlantic. Mabel Boll said they would start Thursday.

On Wednesday, June 13, it was overcast but at least clear of fog. Again Amelia, Bill, and Slim received a go-ahead from Doc Kimball. They rose at six and began their preparations. Again, gamely, they loaded on supplies, said their good-byes to the now few onlookers, and started out. They tried twice to take off that morning. The first time they taxied a full three miles without being able to lift off from the water before giving up. The second time they skimmed along the water for two miles, only to fail again. In the afternoon they taxied the *Friendship* to the head of the harbor, the extreme northeast corner, and, starting from there, tried four more times. Between runs, keeping all curious boats at a distance, apparently to keep the amount a secret from watching newsmen, they jettisoned gas. The frustrated newsmen, watching from afar, could not tell how much was taken off, but Amelia later wrote in her log that they took off three hundred gallons. Then yet again they tried and failed. To at least one spectator, it became clear that the plane just didn't have the power—that the fault wasn't the engines, or the salt spray, or unfavorable winds: "the real fault in this case is with the ship itself."

By the end of the afternoon, the left motor was cutting out, and while working on it close to shore, they suddenly found themselves stranded on a sandy ledge as the tide ran out. Luckily the wind had died down during day, so they finished repairing the motor and went ashore, returning at midnight, when high tide allowed them to float the *Friendship* off the ledge. Boll sent a taunting telegram suggesting that the *Friendship* come to Harbor Grace and that they start out from there at the same time.

Amelia was in charge of communications in Trepassey; George Putnam, installed at the *New York Times* office in Times Square in Manhattan, was in charge of the New York end. Desperate to get off, even if it meant flying to Europe in stages, Amelia had sent a cable to him there inquiring about refueling facilities in the Azores. Apparently after being informed that that was indeed possible, thoroughly discouraged by their plane's inability to carry as heavy a load as they had expected, they announced to the press that the Azores rather than Europe might have to be their goal.

Even the prospects of a partially successful flight were now uncertain. Theirs wouldn't be the first trimotored seaplane unable to take off for a transatlantic flight. That previous fall, a trimotored Junkers, a twelve-passenger plane reconfigured in the Junkers factory to accommodate the huge amount of fuel required for a transatlantic flight, carrying Viennese actress Lilli Dillenz and a crew of four, also equipped with Junkers pontoons, had, as the world waited on tenterhooks, tried unceasingly for two months to lift its load and was finally forced to abandon the effort. "The days grow worse," Amelia wrote in the log. ". . . None of us are sleeping much any more. . . . I think each time we have reached the low but find we haven't. . . . We are on the ragged edge." Amelia's cables were reflecting something more than her frustrations, for suddenly David Layman, worried, wired Amelia, PLEASE SEND PUTNAM CONFIDENTIAL REPORT WHAT GOES ON ARE YOU SATISFIED THERE CAN WE HELP MORE THERE OR HERE.

The problem was Bill Stultz's drinking. That previous fall he had been through a protracted, dangerous, and frustrating effort to fly Frances Wilson Grayson across the Atlantic. Now he was involved with what looked like another problem plane that might never make it, and sitting at a nearby airfield was the *Columbia,* the proven plane he knew so well, the plane he had flown to Havana. He suddenly looked and felt like a bit of a fool. Newspaper articles had referred to him initially as Grayson and Boll's pilot. (*Herald Tribune* headlines first identified him as "Mrs. Grayson's Ex-Pilot.") Because of Boll's sobbing calls to the newspapers, everyone the world over knew he had dumped her for Amelia. To make matters worse, his ex-client and flying companion on the Havana trip was now publicly taunting him. As the days stretched out in Trepassey and the *Friendship's* prospects became increasingly dim, it began to look as if he had made the wrong choice. Alcohol was his friend even in the best of times, but it was his refuge in bad. The first time Hilton Railey ever laid eyes on him—that night at the Copley Plaza, when he had spilled the beans about the flight—he had been drunk; or as Hilton delicately put it, "tight and talkative."

Amelia later told George Putnam she had become so worried about Bill's condition that she came very close to wiring him and Layman to replace Stultz—possibly with Lou Gower, the pilot who had been forced to disembark when they had started out in Boston. Her motives in not doing so were mixed. For one thing, she didn't know her backers very well. She couldn't be sure that Putnam and Layman would believe and trust her; she was afraid their response might be to call off the whole enterprise—expensive and costing more with each passing day—what with the costs of the plane, the daily weather reports, for which they were paying the Weather Bureau, Hilton Railey's expenses in London, the daily expenses of the three of them in Trepassey, the endless cables back and forth: "How could she know that we'd not simply think that here was a girl whose inexperience had caught up with her, or whose courage had failed." Amelia had another reason—she knew that if she fired Stultz, she would irrevocably ruin his career; she didn't want to be the cause of that.

Amelia was certainly not without experience with drinkers; she had had ample time to observe that even during her father's drinking stretches, there were intervals when he was sober and able to function perfectly well. Now, she had no doubt of Bill's abilities when *he* was sober; he had done an excellent job bringing them to Trepassey. She was banking that once airborne, once absorbed in the flight, seated in the finite, controllable space that constituted the interior of an airplane, he would be constrained by his environment and his training would take over. She resolved to stick with Stultz—to keep him sober and see it through.

While Amelia and Slim and Bill were desperately and repeatedly trying to take off in the *Friendship*, Mabel spent the day resting at her hotel. The *Columbia*, meanwhile, surrounded by curious townsfolk at the airfield built the summer before on the high plateau above the town of Harbor Grace to the northeast of them, was being carefully checked out by its crew. In the evening Mabel attended a reception given in her honor by the Knights of Columbus. During the reception, which was followed by dinner and a dance, she was eulogized by local dignitaries. If Amelia, Bill, and Slim were spared the details, they certainly knew that the *Columbia* and her crew were ready and waiting. The *Columbia* crew, for its part, was getting hourly updates on the *Friendship*. Mabel, informed that her rival had abandoned plans to fly to Europe direct, smiled and announced *her* new goal: Italy. And as the day turned into the uncertain twilight that is the night in those northern climes in June, it became Thursday, June 14.

• • • •

The wind that greeted the fliers that morning in Trepassey was north northeast. In the balmy 65-degree air the morning fog, earlier so thick it kept a large number of schooners bound in port, finally cleared out, and it turned into a fine, fresh day. The weather in Europe, however, was extremely bad. The worst was in Paris, where storms caused four planes to crash. The big event of the day, of which there is no mention in Amelia's log, was that her companions went for a test flight without her, probably the only time such a thing happened, and that it was successful. Aboard they had some six hundred gallons of gasoline, just a partial load, and a male stand-in for her. According to observers who watched the plane, the *Friendship* taxied and took off "almost immediately" with its lightened gas load, and flew for thirty-four minutes. It was the first time since it landed at Trepassey that the *Friendship* was actually airborne. The radio kicked up again, and Bill was unable to raise nearby Cape Race—but still, they were all so elated, they announced they were rejecting the Azores as their goal; their destination would be Ireland. Now, again eagerly, they waited for Kimball to tell them they could start. But when the cable came it was bad news.

Kimball reported a storm off the Irish coast; neither the *Columbia* nor the *Friendship* could start. Nevertheless the Trepassey fliers, buoyed by the *Friendship*'s successful flight the day before, attacked that Friday with optimism. They digested the news in the flying world: Belgium was offering $30,000 for the first airman flying New York to Ostend; a Swedish geologist was planning a flight following the Viking route—Norway, Iceland, Greenland, Labrador, and Canada; the Canadian National Railway was naming its four new stations after four fliers—Fitzmaurice, Lindbergh, Alcock, and Hinchcliffe—and would name the next one Endeavor, to honor Elsie Mackay. The *Southern Cross* had successfully flown the Pacific. The big monoplane had started out from Oakland field, San Francisco, May 31, a few days before the *Friendship* left Boston and, with stops at Honolulu and Fiji, had landed in Brisbane, Australia, covering the

7,800 miles in an elapsed flying time of 83 hours and 38 minutes—the first time the Pacific had been bridged. The *Friendship* crew were happy that their confreres had safely flown halfway around the globe, but they also felt a twinge of frustration—the *Southern Cross* was a Fokker F7 with Wright Whirlwind engines—"practically identical with the *Friendship* except that she was not equipped with pontoons," Amelia noted. And the *Southern Cross* had had no problems taking off, even though she carried more fuel than the *Friendship* (they considered 880 gallons of fuel a "light load") *plus four in crew*. Still, they had made it, and, as Amelia wrote later, "so could we. Their accomplishment was a challenge."

They had a musical evening. Stultz and Andy Fulgoni played "Jingle Bells" on the guitar harp. Observed Amelia, "Two are required for the feat and I am terribly amused." Perhaps part of her amusement was relief that at least one of her rivals appeared stopped—Thea Rasche was having problems over the ownership of her Bellanca and was reportedly forced to abandon her attempt at a transatlantic flight.

Mabel Boll spent the day at her usual pursuits, dining and shopping. She went to a luncheon in St. John's given by the colonial secretary, Sir John Bennett, bought herself a "beautiful" Labrador silver fox fur, and went on a tour of the city.

On Saturday there was a slight west wind in Trepassey, and although it was warm, it was as usual overcast; flying conditions over the Atlantic were still bad. At Amelia's urging, even though the wind was freshening, the *Friendship* was reloaded with some of the gasoline taken off. All told, 120 gallons were put back. The weather report from Kimball was that there was a storm center slightly to the south of their route, moving east; the midocean areas were still troubled. Still, he gave them a conditional okay to start the next day. Amelia went to bed without making any entry in her log—highly unusual, the only day not accounted for. It was just too painful, for as she later told George Putnam, Bill Stultz spent the day drinking heavily.

• • • •

By Sunday, June 17, it was clear, and the wind was a brisk twenty knots at nine A.M., coming from the west. The remaining gas was loaded, packaged as usual in the five-gallon cans that could be dumped out as needed to lighten the plane. As George Putnam later recounted, Amelia had made up her mind—they had to go that day if they wanted to beat the *Columbia* across. Never mind that Bill was suffering a hangover and didn't like the weather; never mind that the weather over the Atlantic was at best borderline. As the person whom George Putnam and David Layman had put in charge, Amelia had the authority to force the issue; she also had the moral strength. Amelia was sure that once airborne, Bill's instinct and ability would come to the fore, and he would act like the professional he was. George Putnam would later call her decision "either the bravest or the silliest act of her whole career." There was no doubt that Bill Stultz did not want to go; four men, Burnham Gill, the son of the town magistrate, stringer for the Associated Press; Joey Smallwood of *The Evening Telegram;* Frederick Ryan of *The New York Times;* and Andy Fulgoni, of Paramount News, watched Amelia, dressed in breeks, boots, and leather coat, carrying knapsack and camera, coerce Bill into the dory and out to the plane. To all four of them, Amelia appeared firmly in control, which didn't make them worry any the less. Burnham watched Amelia and Bill at ten A.M. arguing as they walked along the rocky beach. Smallwood approached them to talk to them and reported Amelia as saying, "We have a dandy breeze behind us and we are going in spite of everything." "Stultz," he added, "appeared worried and agitated." He said that if they came down in a heavy sea, they would not "live a minute." Ryan was also on the scene. "Miss Earhart said the wind was favorable and she was confident of success. 'We are going today in spite of everything,' " he reported. To Andy Fulgoni, snapping pictures, Amelia repeated what she had said: "We're going today, and we're going to make it." Andy, being a photographer and therefore a skilled observer, thought Stultz "precariously nervous"—and not sober. One could only hope for the best, he decided.

Amelia had given the agreed-upon telegram to Mike Jackman to send to George Putnam a half hour after they left: "VIOLET CHEERIO AMELIA," the signal for their successful departure. As they boarded the dory at 10:50, Andy Fulgoni, the Paramount cameraman, took their picture. There weren't many townsfolk about—the *Friendship* had set off too many times before, only to return, for them to turn out. Slim Gordon climbed onto the pontoons and cranked the engines; they sprang to life. At 11:10 he cast off the mooring lines, taxied slowly to the head of the harbor, dumped a can of gas, and tried but failed to take off. The engines were then stopped and examined, then the fliers were observed to dump out more gasoline and taxi back to start again. Again the *Friendship* roared off down the harbor, and again the pontoons remained glued to the water. It looked as if the day was going to be a repeat of other days. On the next try, however, the plane rose slightly. Then more cans of the gas, so carefully loaded the day before, went overboard. Now only seven hundred gallons remained. On the next attempt, taking off from the head of the harbor and heading southwest toward the open sea, after about a mile the seaplane lifted off the water, then slumped back down, but kept going. Amelia described it.

I was crowded in the cabin with a stop watch in my hand to check the take-off time, and with my eyes glued on the air speed indicator as it slowly climbed. If it passed fifty miles an hour, chances were the *Friendship* could pull out and fly. Thirty—forty—the *Friendship* was trying again. A long pause, then the pointer went to fifty. Fifty, fifty-five—sixty. We were off at last.

It was a dangerous takeoff; it took a full three minutes. She later told George Putnam that the takeoff was the most dangerous part of the flight; the plane had "rocked and staggered" as it plowed through the water, both outboard engines sputtering from the salt spray. Observers watched the plane disappear out to sea, then reappear a few minutes later, and circle very low over Trepassey Harbor at a height of about fifty feet as they made one final check of the Whirlwind engines and got their bearings. Then finally the *Friendship* straightened out and again disappeared, this time for good, heading northeast.

Mike Jackman could finally send Amelia's cable.

When she found out that the *Friendship* had actually taken off, Mabel, still sitting in St. John's, was stunned. Stunned because, faced with the same weather reports, her pilot, Oliver Le Boutillier, had decided against taking off, and his decision prevailed on the *Columbia*; on Charles Levine's plane, the pilot was in charge. Le Boutillier was quoted as saying that as he had reports of two storms approaching on the Atlantic and as his ambition was to be the oldest living aviator, he would not take any chances; he would await more favorable weather reports.

With ill grace Mabel promptly charged that Dr. Kimball had sent the *Columbia* a different and more ominous weather report than he had sent the *Friendship*—a charge Dr. Kimball vehemently denied, declaring the weather information given was "precisely the same in each case." Dr. Kimball further infuriated Mabel by announcing that although he had freely given her enterprise weather information, since it had been gathered at the expense of Miss Earhart's backers, now that the *Friendship* was airborne, no previous financial arrangements having been made, he would do so no longer.

• • • •

The *Friendship* was airborne—but with only seven hundred gallons of fuel. It was the beginning of twenty anxious hours.

It was 12:21 P.M. Newfoundland time when the *Friendship* finally inched its way into the air. To plot their course, they had Bill Stultz's original and only navigation chart, upon which each day in Trepassey

Amelia and Bill had plotted the Atlantic storm and weather patterns as they received the information from New York. It was not in terribly good shape—"with its endless erasures and new markings it was almost worn through."

Their hoped-for destination was Southampton, England. Commander Byrd had made their flight plan. Byrd's decisions were in large part a response to the problems he had encountered flying the Atlantic the summer before. He and his companions, following the example of Lindbergh before them, had flown the great circle course to Europe because it was the shortest route. But unlike the *Spirit of St. Louis,* Byrd's *America* had gotten lost; he had ended up ditching his land plane in the sea off the coast of France. Flying the great circle course took finesse; it involved periodic resetting of compasses and course changes that eventually threw his plane off course. The commander wouldn't ever admit that the *America* had been off course, but nevertheless the flight plan he decreed for the *Friendship* provided for flying the rhumb line (the same compass heading from start to finish) rather than the great circle course, obviating the necessity of altering course and resetting compasses. Bill would simply have to steer 106 degrees and adjust for wind direction and drift.

But there was a drawback—following a compass heading (a rhumb line) was always longer than following a great circle course. Using it meant adding forty miles to the *Friendship's* flight.

At first the visibility was good, as the *Friendship* winged its way northeast over nearby Mutton Bay, then Biscay Bay. The rivers and lakes of Newfoundland—"wonderful greens and blues"—appeared beneath; soon they flew over Cape Ballard on the eastern shore, and then they were over the open sea, where for the first hour the visibility was good.

Then the weather closed in.

They had hit a storm system and were in the midst of thunderclouds—tall threatening cumulonimbus clouds rising straight up, topped by ice crystals. Bill climbed to 2,500 feet to try to find clear sky, then to 3,300 feet. At 5,000 feet, Amelia wrote, visibility momentarily improved, but then they flew into the storm. There was no way over it. Below them there were snow flurries, ahead more fog. The temperature in the cabin was a brisk forty-two degrees. They dropped to 4,000 feet, into the teeth of the storm. It was the heaviest storm Amelia had ever flown through. However, it was no more than they had expected; it was the stormy weather Kimball had predicted and that had kept Le Boutillier from taking off. They were also bucking headwinds.

Bill Stultz radioed Cape Race that they had left the banks of snow, fog, and hail behind and were now flying in clear weather. That evening he made contact with two ships, each of which gave him a bearing, which enabled him to fix his position. He found out that he was only ten miles off course. He was pleased; he had no idea that it would be his last radio fix.

Amelia wasn't terribly comfortable. The warmest place, as far forward as she could get to the cockpit, which was heated by the exhaust from the engines, involved perching between the gas tanks. Back in the cabin it was cold, and there was no comfortable place to sit because the lifesaving cushions, along with the rubber raft, had been left behind and they were wearing their flying suits. There was a small window on either side of the cabin. On the port side in front of the window was the chart table; the radio was next to it. Amelia took several photos northward kneeling beside the chart table. So long did she kneel looking out that she complained she was getting housemaid's knee. Occasionally she went forward, trading places with Slim or Bill. When Bill came back to send or receive messages, she would look up the call letters. Once, trying to overcome a headache, she fell asleep.

When she woke up, it was morning and the radio had quit. They were enveloped in fog as they would continue to be for almost nineteen of the twenty hours of the flight. As Amelia wrote later, "We might as well have been flying over the cornfields of Kansas for all we could see of what was beneath." At one point Bill climbed to 11,600 feet to try to get over the clouds that "reared their heads like dragons in the morning sun," but the fog rose still higher. In fact, they were flying in the midst of towering cumulus clouds—clouds that are large, dense, tall towers with a height of anywhere from 3,000 to 20,000 feet, sometimes with merged bases and separate tops in the shapes of puffs, mounds, and towers—impossible to rise above.

Occasionally the wet weather made the outboard engines, slightly caked with salt, turn over roughly, but each time they recovered. Amelia wrote of her pilot, "Bill sits up alone. Every muscle and nerve alert. Many hours to go. Marvelous also."

What she did not mention in her log was that she had found a bottle of liquor that Bill had stashed away.

As the hours of flying continued, the tension increased. Seven hundred gallons of fuel was barely enough to get them to Ireland; if they were off course, they would be in serious trouble.

The air speed indicator didn't give them actual speed but only speed through the air—how fast a stream of air was passing the wing of the ship. If a plane was going 80 miles per hour and there was a 20-mile wind against it, the indicator would register 100 mph—and if a plane was going 120 and there was a 20-mile following wind, it would still register 100 mph.

Wind drift indicators were used to figure out wind speed and direction, but they worked only if they could be seen. If they vanished into the fog, if the waves were never visible (another way to judge the wind was by watching the whitecaps), there was no way to estimate wind speed, and if there was no way to estimate wind speed, there was no way of knowing how many miles they had gone.

The view from the *Friendship* was zero. All those hours had passed, and the only thing they knew for sure was that they should have reached Ireland long before. In hopes of sighting land, Bill nosed the plane down between the fog layers, at first gently, then steeply—so steeply Amelia's ears hurt. Water began dripping into the window, the port engine started to cough. Then the other two began to sound ragged. At three thousand feet the descent eased, Amelia's ears felt better, and she thought the motors sounded better, although "not so good." They began to see patches of ocean; then after a half hour, through a break in the clouds, some five miles to the south of them, they saw a steamer. It was the *America,* although they couldn't see its name. They were happy to see the ship, for it meant that they were flying over the shipping lanes, which, that close to Europe, was exactly where they should have been. But if they were on course, the steamer should have been on the same course as they were. Instead, it was going directly across their path, which threw them into confusion. Since their radio couldn't send but might possibly receive, they tried to drop a note on the *America*'s deck asking it to radio its position.

Dropping things onto boat decks was not an uncommon thing to do in those days. As late as 1933, Ernest Grooch, a Pan Am pilot, as a lark, successfully dropped the Sunday papers onto the deck of the liner *President Hoover* when he sighted it in the China seas. The *Friendship* crew now expected the steamer would either radio them or paint the latitude and longitude on the deck, a common courtesy that ships extended in those years. So they weighted their query down with one of the remaining Boston oranges, and Amelia tied it with a silver cord, then dropped it down through the hatch; it missed the ship by two hundred yards and sank immediately. Using more precious fuel, they circled and tried again with their one remaining orange, only to miss again by several hundred yards.

They had some thoughts of giving up, of landing in the sea near the steamer and being picked up, as Ruth Elder and George Haldeman had been when they landed six hundred miles off the Azores the summer before. That way, at least, they would live to tell the tale. But Bill simply said, according to Amelia, "Well, that's out," then swung the plane back on course and kept straight on.

Their situation was precarious. They had started out with 700 gallons of fuel. At full power each engine burned 20 gallons an hour; Lindbergh had figured that his one Wright Whirlwind engine would burn 16 gallons per hour and had actually averaged just under 11. If each of their three engines performed as well as Lindbergh's and there were no leaks, they would be using up 33 gallons each hour, which gave them an estimated 21 hours and 40 minutes of flying time before their fuel ran out. That meant there was no margin for error. And they had detoured twelve miles off course when they sighted the ship—and then circled it—in all wasting some twenty-five minutes and at least fifteen precious gallons of gas.

As Amelia learned later from the ship's captain, they had left the scene too quickly. When the *America* realized the plane was the *Friendship,* they at first tried, fruitlessly, to communicate with them by radio. Then Captain Fried ordered the ship's name and course to be chalked on the deck, but by then the *Friendship* was gone.

In point of fact they were only a mile off course and didn't know it. The fog was so thick that it had obscured the land beneath them. The *Friendship* had flown right over Ireland, passing over Valentia and Dingle Bay, their first checkpoint in Europe as it had been Lindbergh's. When they sighted the *America* they were already over the Irish Sea, which was why the ship seemed to be going the wrong direction.

Now Bill, really worried, kept the *Friendship* at five hundred feet, flying just beneath the fog, so that they could continue to see the sea. They began to see small craft but, like the *America,* apparently going in the wrong direction. They kept thinking they saw land (a common occurrence; Lindbergh mistakenly thought he had seen trees) and kept being disappointed. Bill was at the controls, and Slim, beside him, was gnawing at a sandwich, when out of the mists he saw a blue shadow. He looked at it for a while, then pointed it out to Bill. The sandwich flew out the window as Slim realized that this time it was land.

• • • •

Bill thought it was an island off the Cornwall coast, "as I could see from the map that it was not Ireland." He was under a great deal of pressure to set down—the *Friendship* was so close to being out of gas, the engines were sputtering unless the plane was flying level, and even then the port motor was coughing a bit, according to Amelia. So he couldn't fly over land in his seaplane—he had to follow the coast, where he could set down.

Just then Bill saw what looked like a break in the coastline. He followed it, peering through rain and a leaden sky up to what turned out to be a bay, and past a factory town they would learn later was Burry Port, Wales. Then he circled back, dipped around the Burry Port Copper Works chimney stack (passing, according to one observer, only a few yards from it), and then landed. Bill wrote, "I picked out the likeliest looking stretch and brought the *Friendship* down in it."

They tied up to a buoy near some railroad docks.

It was lunchtime when the *Friendship* landed, but because of the steady drizzle, there were not many people about. Workers looking out their windows saw the plane tied up to Number 10 buoy, but it took a while for the townspeople to react. Eventually Ernest Bevan, an accountant at the Crown Colliery, who had seen the plane fly by and circle back called up Cyril Jefferies, junior clerk at the Great Western Railway Company, whose desk was in front of a huge window overlooking the water and who could plainly see the craft. He was at that moment staring excitedly at it out his window and suggested Bevan get help to the plane. Just then railway official C. H. Owen walked in and, taking charge of the situation, called Norman Fisher, head of the Frickers Metal Company also nearby, who had a rowboat tied up at the docks, and told him to get out to the plane; Fisher grabbed one of his employees and finally did just that. It was dead low tide and rather a long row; Jefferies, watching them make their way slowly out, had time to eat his sandwich, dig up some newspaper accounts of the flight (he had not been aware that the *Friendship* had finally become airborne), and walk to a spot on the beach opposite the plane—at low tide, it was more mud flats than anything else—before Fisher reached it.

By the time Norman Fisher arrived, Amelia, Slim, and Bill, who had been waving to attract attention (according to Amelia, for nearly an hour), had closed the plane's door. Fisher knocked on the side of the plane, perhaps too timidly; there was no response. Possibly exhausted and still deaf from the sound of the engines (possibly Amelia still was wearing the ear stoppers given her by Marie Byrd), they didn't hear the knock. But after a few minutes the door finally opened, and a long conversation ensued. Fisher was explaining to the fliers that the island they had seen was Lundy Island at the entrance to the Bristol Channel, and that they had landed on the coast of Wales, not the coast of Cornwall or Ireland. Not that they really cared by that time exactly which shore they had reached. "No one," Bill said later, "was more thankful than I was to see the Welch coast. . . . I saw the estuary which I now know to be Burry Port, and after circling to make sure everything was clear I landed on a strip of water and fastened up to a buoy."

Having doffed the flying suit he had been wearing over his everyday clothes, Bill set about making himself presentable, then went off in the boat, stunning the waiting Cyril Jefferies when he alighted on dry land, who observed, "He was dressed in a grey trilby, at a nonchalant angle, a light macintosh coat, and a dark double breasted suit, just as if he was going for a stroll down Broadway. His appearance enhanced my respect for him. The normality of his appearance suggested the coolness of a man of courage."

Under the circumstances, Bill's aplomb was all the more remarkable, considering he had gone ashore in search of two things—a telephone to notify the group waiting for them at the Imperial Airways slipway in Southampton that they had landed, and another more pressing one, fuel for the plane. Not altogether surprisingly, the *Friendship's* three Whirlwind engines had not been as efficient as the one Whirlwind engine that had powered the *Spirit of St. Louis*. As Bill admitted in his first interview, "I came ashore to see about gasoline. At the moment I have not enough to let us rise again."

The *Friendship* was out of gas.

11
Golden Girl

• • • • Amy Guest was waiting impatiently with her family in London. She had a lot riding on the outcome. It was her dream, her creation, that the world waited upon. She had chosen Byrd, she had set the standards for the woman who would take her place, she had passed on all plans, including the choice of the Fokker. And she had extended herself financially. Not only had she bought the plane and financed its refitting and new equipment, paying the agreed-upon sums to the pilots, paying the living expenses for Amelia, Slim, and Bill for the duration of the adventure—picking up the tab in Boston, in Halifax, in Trepassey, and (hopefully) in England—her commitment extended to paying for the transportation, hotel and peripheral expenses of Hilton Railey and his assistant, now into their ninth day of waiting in Southampton, where the *Friendship* was expected to land. And she would have to get them all home.

It was in Southampton that Bill Stultz found Hilton to report that they had landed in Burry Port and that Amelia was waiting aboard the plane. Hilton requested that Bill ask Amelia to remain aboard the *Friendship* until he could join them. Now Amy Guest, exhibiting her usual style, gave the nod to Hilton Railey to charter a seaplane from Southampton-based Imperial Airways so that he and Allen Raymond of *The New York Times* could immediately fly to Burry Port.

Three hours after the *Friendship* landed, the Imperial Airways plane glided to a stop a few hundred yards away, and the two men saw Amelia seated cross-legged in the doorway of the plane, apparently oblivious to the clamor caused by the two thousand astounded inhabitants of Burry Port lined up at the water's edge, talking among themselves and staring at her.

They went ashore to find, as would happen again and again all over the world, that the assemblage only had eyes for Amelia. As she stepped on land, the crowd surged toward her—some to touch her flying suit, some to get her autograph, some to shake her hand, some just to see her up close. Fingers grabbed a corner of the bright silk scarf sticking out from under her flying suit, tugged it off her neck, and moments later the scarf was a souvenir being distributed among the onlookers. She was almost crushed. At which point the high sheriff of Carmarthenshire, Burry Port's three policemen, plus helpers, locked arms to form a ring around Amelia and slowly fought their way into the offices of the nearest building a hundred yards away, locking the doors behind them. They stayed there until more policemen and the motorcars Hilton Railey had arranged for arrived to take them to the Ashburnham Hotel, a ways outside the town, where they could safely spend the night.

The next morning they motored back, and quickly boarded the *Friendship,* bound for Southampton, their original destination. Carrying only the fifty gallons of gas Bill had put aboard the afternoon before, the big plane took off effortlessly, even with the added poundage of Hilton Railey and the *Times* reporter.

Southampton went wild when the *Friendship* came into view. The ships waiting in the harbor let loose their sirens, and as the fliers stepped onto the landing platform, there was again a wild outburst of enthusiasm among the eager throng, some of whom surged forward, almost pressing people into the water.

There on the dock amidst the various local officials—everyone from the mayor (who happened to be female) on down—waited Amy and Frederick Guest. There on the dock Amelia and Amy met for the first time. One can imagine them forthrightly shaking hands and congratulating and thanking each other, but the words are lost to posterity. Together they all escaped into waiting cars and were driven to London.

There the continuing tumultuous interest initially stunned Amelia. In her wildest imaginings nothing came close to the appalling furor the trip had created; she could find no place to hide. Even with Hilton Railey running interference, the first twenty-four hours in London were rocky indeed. For a fleeting moment she was overwhelmed, bursting out, "I am caught in a situation where very little of me is free. I am being moved instead of moving. . . . It really makes me a little resentful that the mere fact that I am a woman apparently overshadows the tremendous feat of flying Bill Stultz has just accomplished. But having undertaken to go through with this trip I have to go through with it." Reporters even managed to gain entrance to her room at the Hyde Park Hotel that first morning, catching her, as they carefully noted, wearing a too-large borrowed silk frock as she plowed through the mountains of telegrams and cablegrams. Escape became imperative. At this juncture Amy Guest again stepped into the breach, offering Amelia forthwith the hospitality and privacy of her home, and so Amelia moved into her house in Mayfair.

• • • •

Part of Amelia's outburst of course was due to exhaustion. As the world marveled at the sheer nerve of the exploit, without ever learning about the crucial role Amelia had played in getting the plane off the ground in Trepassey, it also conferred fame upon her without appreciating the amazing grit, the unusual tenacity that enabled her to write about it. All anyone knew was that they couldn't get enough of her. What was helping to fuel the excitement was Amelia's personal achievement: she had scooped the world press. Even though fighting exhaustion, Amelia didn't collapse in the plane in the three hours she had waited for Hilton in Burry Port. She had a ten-thousand-dollar contract with *The New York Times* and *The London Times* for her story, and showing remarkable composure, clear-sightedness, and detachment, she had written the first installment of the story of the flight while she waited—an incredible achievement for someone who had barely slept in over twenty-four hours. So that by the time they arrived in London, the newspapers were full not just of the facts of the achievement and the profiles of the participants—her story under her own byline was running simultaneously in *The London Times* and *The New York Times*.

She had truly hit the ground running. "I have arrived and I am happy—naturally. Why did I do it?" was how Amelia opened her first article. Then she went into details of the trip, and plainly and carefully stated the obvious before everyone forgot: that she had been merely a passenger and that the men deserved the credit. And each day for the next several days, no matter how full her schedule, Amelia wrote a sequel. The second article started with a wonderful hook. "Some day women will fly the Atlantic and think little of it because it is an ordinary thing to do"—in its day a totally mind-boggling notion. The articles were all anyone could hope for—readable, accurate, and informative.

And novel. No other adventurer—for that was what she had become, the first female adventurer—had pulled off such a clever feat, for the simple reason that no other adventurer could write. Even if she hadn't laid a hand on the controls, she was a flier and brought to her writing the informed perspective of a flier. It immeasurably enhanced her image.

And so, because it was such a scary accomplishment, because the fear factor was still so high, because people still didn't want to fly—wanted rather to see the planes and read about the exploits but stay on the ground—all the world's great lined up to sing Amelia's praises. President Coolidge was just one of many who sent her a congratulatory telegram; Henry Ford put a limousine at her disposal. *The London Times* editorialized that the flight was "A Woman's Triumph" and reported virtually every word she uttered. When she was discovered sitting in the royal box at one of the big movie theaters, she was given a ten-minute ovation. She had lunch at the American embassy, took tea with the prime minister, was guest of honor at a dinner given her by the Guests, saw Helen Wills Moody play at Wimbledon, was Lady Astor's guest in the House of Commons, and was invited for Sunday lunch at Cliveden. She attended Ascot, where she was photographed looking very chic and feminine in an elegant frock, and laid a wreath at the Cenotaph and a bouquet of roses in front of the statue of Edith Cavell.

Hilton Railey, meanwhile, kept hiring secretaries (he stopped at four) to help him deal with the onslaught, and still he could not keep up with the telegrams, letters, and offers of everything from jobs to marriage that were pouring in. By the second day Amelia had gotten her second wind. "I don't want to be known always merely as the first woman to fly the Atlantic," she was quoted as saying, and took pains to remind everyone she was a social worker. "Aviation is a great thing, but it cannot fill one's life completely. . . . I am bringing a message of good will and friendship from American to British settlement houses."

• • • •

As Amelia hit her stride, she began to do more things her own way. She went to visit Toynbee Hall, the famous settlement house in the East End of London started by a group of Oxford men that, she reminded everyone, was the model for all the settlement houses in the United States and most particularly Denison House. She also took the time to visit a Denison House friend of hers in Sheffield.

She spoke, along with Winston Churchill, Lady Astor, and the Duke of Sutherland, at a luncheon given by the Women's Committee of the Air

League of the British Empire. She was perfectly at ease both in one-on-one conversations with these famous people and on her feet speaking before them—so much so, it was a subject for commentary: "She spoke calmly and with perfect poise," summed up one observer. Instead of talking about the flight, her speech dwelled upon how much farther ahead England was in popularizing flying, both in number of air passengers carried and in developing new light airplanes and the pilots to fly them, and what steps the United States should take to catch up.

In spite of her protestations, she suddenly didn't sound like a social worker.

She sailed for home on the steamship SS *President Roosevelt,* arriving on July 6 to another tumultuous frenzied welcome. New York City's official welcoming yacht, the *Macon,* full of august officials, steamed out to meet the *President Roosevelt* to transfer her to shore, and as it approached the pier, circling fire boats pumped streams of water into the air and blew off their whistles. The trio was given a triumphal parade up Broadway, followed by a reception at city hall; Commander Byrd, who continued to act like the proud father (and, with the Guests still in London, with even more success) gave them a star-studded luncheon.

The pattern established in England—that Amelia, the passenger, was accorded more acclaim than the crew—held true as well in her own country: "City Greets Miss Earhart; Girl Flier, Shy and Smiling, Shares Praise With Mates" ran the banner headline in *The New York Times,* reflecting national sentiment.

In spite of it all, Amelia managed to be lionized with a minimum loss of control. One thing that softened the blow was that she still didn't quite realize that her life as a social worker was over. She kept telling New Yorkers she would be going back to Denison House "if I haven't been fired." She enthusiastically submitted to the lunches and dinners, teas and receptions George Putnam set up for her those first few days, most of which, at her direction, were heavily weighted toward women's organizations and social work: she attended and spoke at a lunch at the Women's City Club and at a reception at the United Neighborhood House, and she always talked up the roles of Lou Gordon and Bill Stultz, who were usually by her side.

But it was summer, and it was sweltering hot in the grand limousine that ferried her around the baking streets, and on her second day in New York, emerging from the children's ward at Columbia Presbyterian Hospital at 158th Street, instead of getting back into the limousine with Dorothy and George Palmer Putnam, she calmly climbed into the empty sidecar of one of the police motorcycles escorting them and blasted off. The patrolman, Officer Minnett, obligingly opened up his siren, and, it was observed, "the flier's tawny curls became a snarled cluster of yellow as the motorcycle picked up speed." With the siren's wail opening up traffic before them, Minnett streaked down Riverside Drive, down Broadway, turned onto Seventy-second Street, fled past the lawns and trees of Central Park, and then roared down Fifth Avenue, to the Biltmore, at Forty-fourth Street and Vanderbilt Avenue, where Amelia was staying. When she got out, it was observed that her cheeks were pinker than usual and that there was "a brighter light" in her eyes. "It was wonderful," she said, "I'd sneak out any time for a ride like that."

Her trip to Boston for the great reception planned for her there was like a royal tour. The Ford Company provided her with a Ford trimotor and pilot. A second plane took Bill and Lou. Also on the plane was a Paramount News photographer and three reporters, one of whom breathlessly datelined the resultant story "Aboard the Earhart Plane"—plus of course the Putnams. Unfazed, she napped a little, sat in the cockpit with the pilot, Nathan Browne, asked him questions about the trimotor, so similar to the Fokker, and tried her hand at flying it for a little while. Porter Adams, the clean-cut ex-naval officer, improbably the nation's first aerial policeman (in Los Angeles in 1916), now a Boston banker and august president of the NAA, was standing on the tarmac to greet her, flanked by more than a quarter of a million people waiting to catch a glimpse of their hometown girl. Among all the scheduled events—the NAA lunch honoring their newest Boston vice-president, at which she impishly held up three five-dollar bills she had just extracted for signing up three new members, and the speeches at the state house and city hall and to the thousands gathered on Boston Common—she fit in a visit to Denison House. She thrilled all the families—the parents and the children whom she knew so well, greeting them as naturally as she had ever done, picking up where she had left off. "What did she say? What did she think of the flight? How did she like her reception in Boston?" asked a reporter of one of the women. "That I don't know" was the reply. "I don't know those things. She didn't say. She just asked about us."

Nevertheless Amelia was acutely aware of the uproar her appearance created, and after that she made no more statements about returning to Denison House to work.

The extraordinary attention continued. Wherever she went, she was mobbed; whenever she traveled, she was treated like royalty. When she left Boston, the president of the railroad gave her his private car and had the train make a special stop at Rye, where she was visiting the Putnams.

• • • •

Besides the reception in Boston, George Putnam had picked, among the many eager supplicant cities who wanted to throw triumphal receptions for the three of them that summer, Chicago, Pittsburgh, and Bill Stultz's hometown, Williamsburg, Pennsylvania. Chaperoned by George and Dorothy Putnam, Amelia, Bill, and Slim traveled by private railroad car, and at each station, as their train ground to a halt, bands played, crowds cheered, and cameramen gathered.

Chicago claimed her as its own. Amelia visited her old school, Hyde Park, spoke to the assembled students, then stepped from stage to piano to reach the audience, much to the horror of the principal and the delight of the audience. She went to the race track and presented a bouquet of roses to the winner of a six-furlong sprint named in her honor, saw three innings of a Giants–Cubs baseball game, made a brief radio speech, and in the sweltering heat, managed to fit in a swim in Lake Michigan. She also visited Hull House.

Pittsburgh was the next stop, a two-hour layover on the trip back east. Upon their arrival they were driven to city hall so that Amelia could be given the keys to the city. It was still sweltering, and after the hot limousine ride back to the railroad station, instead of getting into the private car with her group, she pulled another switch on her companions—she calmly requested, received, and donned overalls, cap, and goggles and climbed into the cab of the engine at the front of the train. As the train rolled out of Pittsburgh, there is a marvelous photo of her leaning far out the cab window of the locomotive and waving a final adieu. But it wasn't an experience she would repeat—it was much hotter, standing above the firebox, and much dirtier than she expected; when she got out in Altoona, she had to scrub down before rejoining her companions.

By the last weekend in July, Amelia was again ensconced at the Putnams' house in Rye working on the book of her flight that Putnam's would shortly publish. It was an easy place to take. Dorothy and Amelia got on famously; Dorothy was as taken with Amelia as her husband, and in fact the scarf that had been torn from Amelia's neck at Burry Port had been a gift from Dorothy.

By this time Amelia knew both Putnams as well as anyone else in the world. Both of them had been her constant escorts, shepherding her to every function: in New York sitting with her in the limousine and reduced to watching her take off in the motorcycle sidecar; flying with her in the trimotor to Boston; and going on the train to Williamsburg, Pennsylvania, where Dorothy and Amelia had sneaked off and gone shopping. They had also been her companions on the long train ride to Chicago and back.

Yet if Dorothy had any idea that her husband was falling in love with

Amelia, she didn't show it. Amelia settled down in the spacious Putnam home in Rye across from the eleventh hole of the Apawamis Club and in two weeks finished the manuscript that Putnam's would almost immediately publish. She dedicated the book to her hostess: "To Dorothy Binney Putnam under whose roof tree this book was written." George gave it the title of *20 Hrs. 40 Min., Our Flight in the Friendship,* very much in his usual style—which leaned to the tongue-in-cheek-informational. When he wrote his own autobiography, he called it *Wide Margins: A Publisher's Autobiography.*

· · · ·

Time magazine profiled George Palmer Putnam as a person with a dangerous combination of literary ability, business acumen, and energy; brash, effusive, unstoppable, and very bright. From a conservative family, he had grown up in Rye, New York, the son and grandson of publishers. His grandfather, for whom he was named, had started G.P. Putnam's, a publishing house that, by progression, by the time George was growing up, had become G.P. Putnam's Sons and was run by George's father and his two brothers.

Washington Irving had been one of the early Putnam writers. (The "Irving Table," upon which the author had written many of his works, resided in the Putnam library; Amelia undoubtedly used it too.) Putnam's had published the early editions of Poe, Lowell, Fenimore Cooper, Hawthorne, and Parkman, and their volumes lined the walls of George's family library. Yet George was proud to boast that although the atmosphere in his home was decidedly literary, he was not: "Just as ministers' sons are supposed to go bad . . . I fell from literary altitudes early, and often." More than anything else, he loved the great outdoors—the untended, untouched, if possible unexplored parts of the world. As a child, he favored adventure books about daring boys and the great outdoors, with titles such as *Cab and Caboose* and *Canoe and Saddle.* And when he grew up, his tastes were the same—the only substantive difference being that his adventurers were now daring adults.

He attended the Gunnery School in Washington, Connecticut, where, interested as he was in trout fishing, rock climbing, and hunting and uninterested as well as untalented in the team sports that were so important to the school, he found himself a loner. He went to Harvard, where he found himself similarly out of sync, stayed for just a short time, then went adventuring—heading for what was then the fringe of the desert south of Los Angeles in a fruitless attempt to acquire gold mine claims. Undoubtedly pressured by his father, he then enrolled at Berkeley, lasted just one term, and then again succumbed to the call of the wild. He was, he said, "an easterner in the far reaches of the roaring west" who wanted to find the "roar." He chose to settle in Bend, Oregon, because it was in the center of the largest area in the United States not penetrated by the railroads.

Bend in 1909 was a town of twelve hundred mostly unruly people, who supported twelve saloons and countless gambling and whore houses. When the mayor, in the midst of a brawl, fell to his death out the window of one of the houses, George, by then married to Dorothy Binney, a Smith girl with a taste for adventure and the great outdoors herself (they had met at a Sierra Club outing) and the father of a baby boy, became mayor. He succeeded in cleaning up the town to some extent, then became publisher and editor of the Bend weekly newspaper *The Bulletin* and, from 1914 to 1917, secretary to the governor of the state. He cut such a wide swath in Oregon history that he was deemed worthy to be the subject of a college thesis *(Frontier Publisher)* in 1966. He enlisted in the army when World War I started, and by the time the war was over, his father as well as his elder brother had both died, as a result of which, instead of heading back out west after the armistice, he moved back to Rye, New York, and took his elder brother's place in the family publishing firm. By that time he had written four books—two about Oregon, one about his travels in Central America, and one about Field Artillery Training School.

Ensconced in New York, he gave publishing his all. He concocted a bit of literary pastry for which he wrote a detailed plot and then corralled Louis Bromfield, Rube Goldberg, Frank Craven, Alexander Woollcott, and various other authors each to write a chapter. *Bobbed Hair,* as the finished work was called, appeared first as a novel serialized in *Collier's* magazine, then as a book, then as a movie. He published Alexander Woollcott's first book and collected for the Putnam imprint Heywood Broun, Louis Bromfield, Edward Streeter, and James J. Corbett. Having established his credentials with the literary community (or at least made them take notice), he went back to his métier—adventure stories by real-life adventurers. He became more than just a publisher of adventurers' tales—he became a participant. And if their dreams needed organizing or their expeditions required financing, he was there ready to help out. His great friend from childhood was the artist Rockwell Kent. As a young man, he had done Kent an unusual favor—he had masqueraded as Rockwell's wife when Rockwell had built himself a house on Monhegan, an island off the coast of Maine, where tradition decreed that after a bachelor built a house, he brought home a bride. Rockwell brought George, dressed in bridal finery, whisked him into the house, and kept him "under wraps" inside until the islanders' attention turned to something else and the presumed bride could disappear to the mainland—forever. So it was quite natural that when Rockwell Kent needed financing for a trip to Alaska, George would arrange it in return for the rights to the chronicle of his life there. Rockwell's Alaska years evolved into the book *Wilderness*—published, naturally, by Putnam's.

His brashness, energy, intelligence and showmanship soon made him the most talked-about publisher in New York. His métier was the adventurers—the explorers of the far reaches of the planet and the new explorers of the skies who were unlocking the secrets of the world; they were his greatest success. He cornered the market in heroes, as it were. He published (and wrote the foreword for) *Winged Defense* by General William Mitchell, head of the U.S. Air Force as well as a famous pilot. He published Roy Chapman Andrews's treks into the Gobi desert, and the explorations of William Beebe, Knud Rasmussen, Lincoln Ellsworth, Bob Bartlett, and Fitzhugh Green. He was responsible for the publication of *Skyward,* the account of the flight over the North Pole (since disputed) by then–Naval Lieutenant Richard E. Byrd. (He put the plane on display at Wanamaker's department store in New York and Philadelphia, and it drew thousands.) Nor did he neglect his first love, boyhood adventurers. He sent his twelve-year-old son David off to the Galapagos with William Beebe and published David's journal as *David Goes Voyaging,* the first of a string of books Putnam's published by boy explorers that would also include *Among the Alps with Bradford* by the then-young and unknown explorer Bradford Washburn, and *Derek Goes to Mesa Verde* by the son of the superintendent of Mesa Verde National Park.

Nor did he neglect himself. Having organized another adventuring expedition, in which David would accompany Bob Bartlett, Peary's skipper to the North Pole, aboard a hundred-foot fishing schooner bound for Greenland to collect live specimens of narwhal, walrus, seal, and other Arctic fauna for the American Museum of Natural History, George succumbed to the lure of the wild and signed himself on.

Addressing his restless, unconventional mind to the problem of rounding up specimens, he drew on what he had learned in his western days and came up with the novel idea that the best way to capture the animals would be to lasso them. He then persuaded his old friend, Carl Dunrud, a western guide whom he had met on pack trips through Yellowstone who was a crack artist with a lariat, to come along to rope the sought-after animals. Carl thus became the first and possibly the only man ever to successfully lasso musk ox, polar bears, and walrus.

In a nod to Carl Dunrud, George titled the resultant book, by expedition historian Edward Streeter, *An Arctic Rodeo;* his son's second book was *David Goes to Greenland.*

Adventuring was simply in his blood. The summer before he entered Amelia's life, George organized and went on an expedition to Baffin Island, off the west coast of Greenland, that given his irrepressible nature, became known as the George Palmer Putnam expedition. The result of his energy and the well-trained team of workers he had assembled was that the expedition corrected numerous errors in the map of Baffin Island. Just that past winter he had chosen to spend Christmas on top of Mount Washington, the highest mountain in New Hampshire, with Bradford Washburn and David.

The most impressive feat he had performed for Putnam's was snaring the greatest hero of the age, the courageous sky explorer who had conquered the Atlantic and flown into the hearts and imagination of the world, Charles Lindbergh. For that coup George became a celebrity in his own right.

George had snared Charles Lindbergh by the seemingly simple expedient of prevailing on the Paris office of *The New York Times* to place his telegraphed request for publishing rights into the hands of the harassed and still-exhausted flier. One of George's virtues, as far as his adventurers were concerned, was that he made things as painless as possible for them by finding, at the drop of a hat, suitable ghostwriters to flesh out their tales. In his highly unusual but for him normal fashion, efficient George had the writer for Lindbergh's book, with an already partially written manuscript, on the ship Lindbergh took home. George assumed that Lindbergh, like Richard Byrd and the others, would accept the finished work presented to him—but he didn't know his man. Lindbergh didn't like having words put in his mouth. He decided to write the book himself. Bound by the terms of his contract, Lindbergh holed himself up at a friend's and wrote the agreed-upon forty-thousand-plus words. The book went on sale the month after the flight.

For George this was the normal way of doing things; he himself wrote his book about the tragic death of the balloonist Salomon August Andrée in the space of ten days. George didn't think it was anything special to crank out a book with such speed—he had the whole thing down to a formula; in the normal course of events, without rushing, start to finish, he would get a book out in two or three months. When pressed, he did it in less. Bradford Washburn, boy mountain climber, was astonished in later years to recollect that under George's guidance he actually wrote his first book in fourteen days. The secret to the speed was very little editing and almost instantaneous printing by the Knickerbocker Press, the Putnam printing plant in nearby Yonkers (for which George had designed as logo Henry Hudson's ship the *Half Moon*, which appeared on all frontispieces). The books were beautifully illustrated, superbly promoted, and efficiently distributed. In that heady era when the oceans were being flown across for the first time, great mountains scaled, deserts spanned, and the hitherto mysterious poles explored, these bare-bones accounts—pedestrian, unadorned—of the doers, usually beefed up with a little autobiographical information, were all that was needed. The haste of his publications sometimes showed, but George didn't care.

Amelia's book must be seen in this light; it is very much of a piece with all George's adventure books. For the foreword George efficiently lifted, verbatim, the description of Amelia by Denison House headworker Marion Perkins that had just appeared in the July issue of *Survey* magazine. More to the point, he prevailed on Amelia to write the text in a matter of weeks. She returned from England on July 6, and did not have a chance to settle down to work on the manuscript until after the midwestern tour. But she had *20 Hrs. 40 Min.* finished by mid-August. "My book goes to press very soon," Amelia self-mockingly wrote her friend Marian Stabler. "I should like to have made it better but time was short and I done as good as I could." She phrased the same thought more elegantly in the foreword:

> In re-reading the manuscript of this book I find I didn't allow myself to be born. May I apologize for this unconventional oversight as well as for other more serious ones—and some not so serious? I myself am disappointed not to have been able to write a "work"—(you know, Dickens' Works, Thackeray's Works), but my dignity wouldn't stand the strain.

Even in the brief time she supposedly was devoting herself exclusively to the manuscript, she was doing other things. There was the odd matter of her endorsement of Lucky Strike cigarettes (even though she didn't smoke). Hilton Railey and George Putnam, both involved with Byrd, who was poised to embark on his expedition to Antarctica, cooked the idea up between them. Hilton had become Byrd's public relations adviser, fundraiser, and general manager; George had the contract to publish his book on the expedition. Now Hilton arranged for Amelia to be paid fifteen hundred dollars to endorse Lucky Strike cigarettes, the brand Bill and Lou had smoked on the trip, specifically so that she could publicly donate it to the Byrd expedition—which would give added hype to his trip. Amelia agreed to the arrangement in gratitude for Byrd's unstinting public and private support of the *Friendship* enterprise. She wrote a formal, lengthy, gracious letter to Byrd that George and Hilton released to the newspapers simultaneously with his equally lengthy reply. The timing was perfect: the gesture received more press coverage than President Coolidge's vacation activities in Wisconsin.

Amelia's gesture had two consequences, both of which also took time to deal with. Otis Wiese, editor of *McCall's,* had come out to Rye to see if Amelia would write for his magazine, and she had enthusiastically agreed, but he was put off by the Lucky Strike endorsement and withdrew the offer. David Layman, too, was dumbfounded, although for a different reason when he read about the endorsement. In his eyes she had broken word never to endorse a product; he wrote her a "stiff" letter to which she never replied.

After the *McCall's* disappointment George arranged a meeting with Ray Long, the dynamic, dapper editor of *Cosmopolitan,* at his office on Fifty-seventh Street and Eighth Avenue, out of which came a contract for Amelia to be aviation editor of the magazine—the first ever; she was to devote her time to writing about "the popular phases of aviation." On top of these activities, there was her social life—suddenly very full, what with lunches, dinners, theater performances, fascinating people to meet, groups to talk to, and old friends to see. In addition she agreed to fly to Sea Girt, New Jersey, the second of August, to be present when the governor awarded Wilmer Stultz a major's commission in the national guard, so there was another day gone.

It was a miracle the book got written at all.

• • • •

Amelia seemed to have no trouble coping with George or with anyone else. She appeared to have walked into the eyes of the world fully formed, so relaxed and at the same time so in control did she appear. Only to Amy did she admit how triumphant she felt, and how vindicated. A letter that fall to her mother opens, "The night's activities. Byrd's dinner, Theater, Jimmy Walker's. Hooray."

She felt triumphant about her new financial state as well. The long dark days of penurious living had weighed her down—and only with the burden lifted did she admit how heavy it had been. Now, with her earnings as an author and editor, she paid off her debts—and still there was money left over. Caring and family-minded as she was, she saw to it that Amy and Muriel shared in her good fortune; whatever Amy—and in the beginning Muriel—wanted from then on, they could have. She notified Amy, "Sent package to P [Muriel]. If you know something she wants get it for her and I'll pay. Also you. My treat, at last." And a short while later, in the same vein, she is imploring her mother, "Please throw away rags and get things you need on my account at Filene's. I'll instruct them. I can do it now and the pleasure is mine."

She even had a plane again. At the various social functions in England, Amelia had met England's most famous aviatrix, Mary Heath, the wife of Lord James Heath. Lady Heath, a formidable woman who held the first transport license ever granted to a woman in England (the law was changed for her), had just returned from a long and difficult twelve-thousand-mile flight: solo in her Avro Avian, she had flown from Croydon, England, to Cape Town, South Africa, and back, returning to England that May. The year before, she had set a new altitude record for light planes in the Avian. Lady Heath had rushed home after meeting Amelia to send her her address and phone number and assure her that "if you phone me I'll throw down whatever I'm doing to come and fly with you or talk."

As they finally arranged it, Amelia slipped out to Croydon early one morning to try out the famous plane, its fuselage covered with plaques and medals from its travels. The flight was a great success; Amelia thought it the best machine of its kind in the world. To her delight, Lady Heath offered to sell it to her. Such a sale was a leap of faith on both their parts, for by no stretch of the imagination could a settlement house worker (over a thousand dollars in debt) come up with $3,200—the price they agreed upon. What they both must have had in mind was a different future for Amelia—one much more lucrative than her past. It bothered Lady Heath not at all that Amelia had agreed not to profit from the flight and would turn over the money *The New York Times* paid for her story to her benefactor—through syndication they would earn $12,460; it established her earning power. And so it was decided—Lady Heath had one more plaque made and affixed to the Avian before it was shipped. It read, "To Amelia Earhart from Mary Heath. Always think with your stick forward."

The British registration for the little plane was G-E Bug. Avro Avians were highly respected both for dependability and performance. This particular plane, manufactured in 1924 by the A.V. Roe Company of Manchester, was powered by an 85-horsepower, 4-cylinder air-cooled Cirrus engine. Amelia would have felt quite at home in it, for like her old Airster, which it rather resembled, it was a 2-seater open biplane. It was almost as small, at 24 feet 3 inches only 5 feet longer, with a wingspan of 28 feet, just 1 foot wider, and at 880 pounds almost as light.

The Avian was crated and shipped to the United States, and by the end of July, as Amelia returned from the West, it was being assembled at Curtiss field on Long Island. Amelia was flying under her 1923 FAI certificate issued by the NAA. In those years it wasn't really necessary for a pilot to have a license—one could fly for sport, non-commercially in a plane, as long as the plane was unlicensed. But if the plane was licensed, then the pilot had to be too. The Avian was not licensed in the United States. George asked Porter Adams, vacationing in Thetford, Vermont, to help, and particularly to see if a license for the plane and a new pilot's license for Amelia could be issued without any publicity. As the director of aeronautics informed Porter, Amelia could simply identify the Avro Avian and fly it "non-commercial" as an unlicensed plane, in which case she wouldn't need a new pilot's license, or she could opt for licensing the Avian, which involved submitting complete engineering data in accordance with Air Commerce regulations, in which case she would need a new license for herself.

Amelia decided the time and circumstances demanded a new pilot's license and therefore a license for the plane as well. While waiting for the registration, a complicated and lengthy procedure, Amelia applied for a simpler but more restrictive Department of Commerce identification for the Avian that would at least let her fly it legally. On the application Amelia made one significant change: she scratched out the "his" underneath her signature on the affidavit, changing the phrase so that it ran: "Amelia Earhart, being first duly sworn, says that the foregoing statements are true of [her] knowledge."

• • • •

While Amelia had been in Boston for her triumphal homecoming, she had told her friends at Dennison airport to prepare for the arrival of the Avian, then still on the high seas. She had said it with the full intention of returning there herself, picking up her old life at Denison House, and flying out of her old airport. Then she had holed up in Rye and realized that her life had changed and that she was never going back, so she had sent it to Curtiss field on Long Island to have it assembled and hangared. Whether from embarrassment or oversight or a combination of both, she neglected to tell Harold Dennison of the change in plans, with the result that into the beginning of August, Dennison airport officials were still waiting for the crated ship and anxiously inquiring of the Department of Commerce as to its classification.

In the meantime she had flown it to Rye, and, assigned the number 7083 by the Department of Commerce, it sat less than a mile away from the Putnam home at the Westchester Country Club. Finally Amelia got to do what she had been itching to do for two months—get her hands on the controls of an airplane. She had no trouble getting used to the Avian. By the end of August, she was giving demonstration flights, taking off and landing on one of the carefully mowed country-club-immaculate grass polo fields. It must have reminded her of California four long years before, to be giving demo flights in her own plane. On the last Friday in August, a sizzling hot day when the temperature reached into the nineties, Amelia took up several passengers, including the intrepid David Putnam, taking the opportunity to gun the plane into the cooler air high above Long Island Sound.

Amelia had by that time decided that the time was ripe to fulfill her ambition of 1924: to fly across the country. This time there were no obstacles—she was in superb health, it was the right time of the year, and the material she gathered could be used in her brand-new job as aviation editor of *Cosmopolitan*. The veteran plane, its fuselage studded with medals from many of the towns and cities where it had been, made it easier, reminding one and all as it did that in it Lady Heath had end-to-ended Africa—which made flying across the continent seem tame and eminently achievable. Even though Amelia had five hundred flying hours under her belt, she had never done serious long-distance flying.

• • • •

She left on Sunday, August 31. With her was George, off on another adventure, as usual unable to resist playing hooky if there was an exciting event he could take part in. This time he got more than he bargained for. The realities of flying kicked in when Amelia tried to land the Avian at Rodgers field outside Pittsburgh. It was not a polo field—so highly prized by fliers because they knew that a field where horses wheeled and galloped had to be flat and true—but a normal farm field, with rocks and gullies, stumps and ditches. The plane rolled into a shallow ditch hidden in the grass. An incredulous George Putnam couldn't believe such a bizarre thing had been allowed to occur, insisting, "Miss Earhart had made a perfect landing and was taxiing to a stop when the plane struck an unmarked ditch on the field and went into it. The plane made what is called a ground loop and nearly turned over."

In 1928 (and for many years following) in the world of flying, ground loops were so unavoidable that pilots thought of them in the same way that car drivers did flat tires: as one of the unpleasant breaks of the game. Amelia wasn't upset, although she did blame herself for not having first "taken the precaution of flying low over Rodgers Field to examine it," as she admitted in an article later that fall.

But the plane was a mess; it needed new landing gear, a new propeller, and probably a new lower left wing. A distressed George Putnam, faced with the grounding of his star performer, got to work and in record time found the parts needed—but parts for the English plane were hard to come by in the United States, he had to buy a whole new plane to get them. He arranged for a pilot from Air Associates to fly out an identical Avian from Curtiss field within twenty-four hours of the accident. Then four mechanics worked night and day, and forty-eight hours after the accident, Amelia's plane was fixed. Who bore the expense is not known. What is known is that George was more distressed at being caught out, as it were, accompanying Amelia sub rosa, and having his idyllic little outing not only discovered but ruined. He tried to be jaunty about it and almost succeeded.

> Miss Earhart had visited my home and while there, we decided
> to take a little jaunt. As she was just "playing around" with no
> particular object in view, she headed her ship for Pittsburgh. We
> had a lovely trip, stopping at Bellefonte Field. We had lunch there
> and then headed for Pittsburgh. There was no incident of any kind
> to mar the journey until we ran into that ditch in Rodgers Field.

As for Amelia, she used her enforced layover time to buy a sufficient number of white flags to mark the length of the ditch so that, she said laconically, "maybe there won't be so many that run into it." George originally had planned to head back home after Pittsburgh, but he used the accident as the excuse to continue with her as far as Dayton, Ohio.

There is a prophetic 1928 photo—undoubtedly snapped on the roof of the Copley Plaza by Jake Coolidge—of the two of them before the *Friendship* flight. Amelia, in boots, breeks, and leather jacket is smiling into the distance; George, tall, handsome, in a well-cut business suit, is staring adoringly into her eyes. Right after the *Friendship* had taken off from Boston Harbor, he had given the following remarkably prescient interview:

> No money in the world could induce her to go upon a stage or
> in a film. She would shrink from that sort of exploitation. She
> might consider writing or a short and carefully selected lecture
> tour, but I know that she would not give a moment's consideration
> to anything of a theatrical nature.
> Indeed she thinks right now that when the flight is over she
> is going back to Denison House settlement far from crowds, for-
> gotten. She won't be able to, of course, we all know that. But she
> honestly thinks that no one will pay any attention to her after it
> is over. She is an extraordinary girl. She has captivated all who
> met her.

In truth, from the beginning of June on, Amelia was rarely out of George's sight, and as compulsive as he was to keep busy, as driven as he was to always have several projects going at the same time, she was never far from his thoughts. He was forever writing to her, forever offering her bits of advice. Now he even managed to convince her to let him, as well as her mother, know where she was every day of her transcontinental flight. If there were telegraphic facilities available, both got telegrams. And she signed the telegrams to him, those fall days, in a way that was meaningless to anyone but him—"A.E." To no one else was she known by her initials.

But no matter his attention, his planning, or the long reach of his influential arm, the flight across the country was for Amelia an exercise in self-reliance, as she had intended it to be. Later, when she wrote it up for *Cosmopolitan,* she called it a vagabonding trip, and it was; some stops were planned, most were not. "I'm just a tramp flyer now," she said at one airport. The first night after George left her was one of the planned stops, giving him no excuse to worry. She went to Belleville, Illinois, where two friends from college days, Annabel Hoppe and Dr. Elizabeth Conroy, arranged a dinner for her at the local country club, and she stayed with the Hoppes.

A surprising number of times she managed to avoid hotels, lodging instead in private homes, even when nothing had been arranged beforehand. She turned into an expert at coaxing food and lodging invitations out of perfect strangers. After she landed unexpectedly at some airfield, she would sigh and murmur how tired she was of hotel rooms (absolutely true), and before the person knew what had happened, a woman (always a woman and usually married) would timidly proffer her home, thrilled to be able to protect Amelia from a night in a hotel, and from crowds and questions. "She said she hated to go to a hotel, that she knew she'd be bothered all the time there," said her hostess in Muskogee, Oklahoma, who was at the field looking for her husband, the field manager, and happened to see her land; in Casa Grande she even found a woman with whom she had acquaintances in common. Nor did she ever get into trouble this way, for a further talent she found she had was a knack for picking the right people; she enjoyed herself, and inevitably so did her hosts.

Once, toward the end of a morning, in some unnamed place, hungry, Amelia dropped down and landed on an isolated farm and was invited in for a chicken dinner. The plane, so small and easy to handle, with a propeller she could crank by herself standing on the back side (and then quickly hop into the cockpit), made such independent actions possible. But the realities of flying kept kicking in with a vengeance. A woman or a man traveling alone across the continent in 1928, in the still-not-quite-perfected-air machine, was bound to find trouble, particularly since there was no such thing as a pilot who had not had at least one forced landing. That was where luck and skill came into play—with both on your side, the trouble would be minor. It had gotten to the point that *Popular Aviation* magazine gave away a hundred dollar watch for the best forced landing story it received each month.

Navigation was a serious challenge. This was Amelia's first long-distance flight, and she learned how hard it was to navigate (or avigate, as aviators called it back then) with the inadequate maps of the day and the lack of defined fields. And it got harder as the populated East gave way to the less populated Midwest and the more sparsely settled Southwest, and even harder as cities gave way to featureless towns, towns became smaller and then became hamlets—just clusters of houses really; and harder still when the empty spaces between the settlements grew, and the farms turned into the endless plains of the Southwest. She learned dead reckoning; she had no choice.

The open cockpit made it even more challenging. The wind rushing about made the maps blow around. Amelia resorted to pinning the map she was using to her knee with a safety pin, but the pinning and unpinning as she flew off the edge of one map and onto another was never easy and became difficult when there were other things to do. West of Fort Worth, Texas, heading for Pecos in bumpy air, she was pumping gas from the reserve tank and didn't, momentarily, pin, and suddenly the map of west Texas blew away. She followed her last compass course southwest, but then in pursuit of signs of life, and needing gasoline, she followed cars on a road going northwest, followed the road and the cars into the purple haze of the setting sun, and finally saw a small cluster of houses grouped around an oil well, one road running through. She had to land before darkness fell and rolled right through the town on its one road, its Main Street, to find out that she had flown clear across Texas and was in Hobbs, New Mexico. The townspeople helped her fold up the wings of the little Avian and move it to a safe place for the night (an overhelpful cowboy managed to put his foot through a wing; a piece of tablecloth was glued down over it), fed her at the Owl Cafe, found her some gasoline, and gave her a bed. The next morning she took off down Main Street, with more help from her new friends, but still without a map, heading southwest as instructed, looking for the Pecos River and a railroad line, her markers for the town of Pecos.

It was a short flight, only a hundred miles. The engine started to sound rough, but she thought it would work its way through and ignored it. She set down in Pecos, where she ended up at a Rotary Club lunch, then took off for El Paso, and then suddenly real trouble—the engine started kicking up badly—and she had to put down in the desert amidst the mesquite bushes. Friendly passersby helped her tow the plane, its wings again folded, down the highway back to Pecos. It turned out the Hobbs gasoline was bad and had ruined the engine valves. She remained there for the five days it took the mechanics to bring the engine back into working order.

Pecos was one of the control stops in the cross-country flights of contestants for the National Air Races, on their way west to Los Angeles. Amelia had planned to slip in and out of Pecos before the contestants ever landed, but that plan went up in the smoke of her engine. Instead, there she was watching as the forty-odd planes piloted by the top fliers in the country clocked in.

She had, of course, let George know where she was, and he had a surprise in store for her: a first copy of her just-off-the-press book, delivered to her there in Pecos.

Several days later she landed at Fly field in Yuma, Arizona, to gas up for the final leg of her journey to Los Angeles. As often happened after fueling, onlookers helped push the plane into position for takeoff. This time among the helpers was the Union Oil man who serviced the plane, who should have been able to control things but couldn't, or didn't—perhaps it was the excitement combined with the 104-degree heat. Suddenly the Avian was nose down in the sand. Later headlines and stories by reporters not on the scene turned it into another drama and had Amelia hammering out a bent propeller prior to takeoff, but it wasn't true. This time no damage was done. Later still, near Long Beach, California, she did make a forced landing in a field of five-foot grass and turned completely over.

On September 14, the seventh day of the National Air Races and Aeronautical Exposition at Mines field in Los Angeles, fliers were still straggling in from their cross-country odysseys. Amelia arrived that day in between George Haldeman, who had been forced down in Albuquerque by lack of fuel and bad headwinds, and Jack Iseman, who, flying Charles Levine's *Columbia,* had been forced down in Amarillo by a leaky fuel valve. She was given a standing ovation, and later, while many in the crowd had eyes only for Charles Lindbergh, flying in formation with two military aviators, Amelia took the opportunity to spend the afternoon examining the hundreds of different planes parked on the field, the latest and best of the day. Compared with them, she said, hers was just a toy, with no commercial possibilities—a plane for an amateur. She was boning up on aviation information; she didn't intend to stay an amateur forever.

Amelia took the more northerly route east on her way home. It was a first for her, flying so high, and she had carburetor trouble in the high altitudes that the Continental Divide demanded. The motor sounded so bad that a hundred miles south of Salt Lake City, just east of Tintic, Utah, she had to make a forced landing in a plowed field; the earth was soft, the wheels sank, and again the Avian nosed over; and again the propeller broke. ("I am going to find out all about carburetors immediately," she told a waiting reporter.) She spent that night in Eureka, Utah, with Maude Hillsdale, which would have been an interesting experience because Maude had driven an ambulance in World War I, for which the French government awarded her the Croix de Guerre.

The following day, none the worst for wear, Amelia went to Salt Lake City and assumed her public relations persona—George Putnam had booked her into various speaking and social engagements. She talked to three high school groups, led a discussion on social work and social problems at a meeting of the board of the Salt Lake Community Chest, spoke before the Ladies' Literary Club, was taken on a tour of a copper mine, visited a settlement house, and was guest of honor at a dinner.

It was not until Tuesday, October 9, nine days later, that she finally climbed into the cockpit of the Avian and took off over the Wasatch Mountains for Cheyenne and points east. She had indeed learned about mountain air—how it thinned and reduced engine power and affected the carburetor, how it sucked up and down and switched directions and suddenly turned to fog. This time she threaded her way through the high peaks of the Rockies without incident.

• • • •

In the 1920s *Cosmopolitan* was a magazine for forward-thinking "modern" young women but it had a general audience as well. It published topical articles and fiction reflecting the fashionable currents of the day. At that time it was a fabulously successful magazine, publishing Theodore Dreiser, Sinclair Lewis, Emil Ludwig, and Damon Runyan, among others. When Calvin Coolidge decided to explain himself, his article, "Why I Did Not Choose to Run," appeared in the May 1929 issue. Amelia was signed on because she was a "hot" commodity doing the most exciting thing a woman could do: fly. Ray Long was just jumping on the bandwagon; flying was arguably "the" hot media topic—newspapers were creating aviation sections, radio stations were scheduling aviation hours in prime evening time. Now, with Amelia, *Cosmo* had the first aviation editor.

She was presented as daring, ultrafashionable, chic, beautifully dressed, and apparently wealthy. Photos of her in that first issue show her dressed for riding, flying, and tennis, and with a fur draped about her shoulders dressed for a ball; every outfit is beautifully fitted, her hair is perfectly coiffed, she is wearing makeup, and a bemused smile plays about her lips.

If Ray Long's object was to present her as the most glamorous woman of the moment—the Cosmopolitan girl to end all Cosmopolitan girls—he succeeded. He turned her into the Renaissance woman.

In the 1920s the boyishly slender figure had become the object of every woman's ambition, and nowhere was that more evident than in the pages of *Cosmo*. Amelia was exactly what he wanted the *Cosmo* girl to become. She was tall, slender, with gray eyes and short, apparently curly hair, a nice little round nose with freckles, the Harres family high forehead, white teeth, pale complexion, quick flashing smile. She looked the perfect heroine of the age; she had the perfect figure. She had long legs and walked with a long-legged, loose-jointed stride, usually wearing slacks, an exciting new fashion statement that *Cosmo* wanted its readers to note.

No one knew that Amelia wore pants to hide her thick ankles. Not even becoming the most famous and most photographed woman in the world assuaged her self-consciousness about her legs—she had hated her legs as a child, and fame made absolutely no difference to the adult woman, she still hated her legs. But such was her charisma that even though she wore her trademark pants from sheer vanity, to hide her ankles, as the world's newest fashion plate, with her innate sense of style, she turned pants into a fashion alternative.

As the chic, glamourous aviation editor, Amelia, of course, was limited to writing about flying. In the first articles she wrote about how she had gotten into flying, how much she enjoyed it, the planes she had owned. The thrust of all her articles was that flying was safer as well as easier than the general public believed it to be. She answered readers' questions, published their poetry, and described her trip vagabonding about the country. She told how to go about getting a license, how to make sure of getting a good instructor, how much it all cost. She stressed the safety factor always. She urged women to let their daughters learn to fly and proclaimed that "the year of 1929 is ushering in the Flying Generation." She wrote about Anne Lindbergh, who was a pilot, and about Amy Earhart, whom she had taken flying so many times that she was bored and now always took a book with her, usually a mystery story.

But *Cosmopolitan* was not the right place for articles urging women to be pioneers, to open up new fields of endeavor to other women, or to further the cause of aviation for all by forming aviation country clubs, Amelia's new interest. A gentle prod not to be scared was about all that *Cosmopolitan* could handle. *Cosmo* was for playgirls—it was about image rather than accomplishment. If Amelia was perfect for *Cosmo,* it was not perfect for her—its subject matter was too limited.

Although Amelia had made the decision to become a member of

the staff of *Cosmopolitan* and live in New York, in her own mind she still thought of herself as a social worker—perhaps one temporarily on assignment, but a social worker for all that. Indeed, years later, when a reporter asked her if she missed social work, she replied that she had never left it. Actually, from the first day, she had been a bit self-conscious about working for such a high-profile magazine as *Cosmopolitan*. In early December, in a letter to a social worker she had known in Boston before the *Friendship* flight, she admitted as much. She had spoken at a New York State dinner for social workers, she informed her friend: "I talked at the Better Times dinner the day before yesterday in order to pay, if I could, the debt I feel I owe to social workers. I know it was not adequate, but it seemed as much as I could do."

At some point before she flew west, Amelia had written to Mary Kingsbury Simkhovitch—head of Greenwich House, a settlement house in Greenwich Village, who had come to the July settlement house reception given Amelia—asking if she could become a member of the Greenwich House staff, explaining that it wasn't feasible for her to go back to Denison House. Mary recalled that Amelia had had it in her mind to maintain an association with social work, "as active as her altered way of life would permit." Simkhovitch, knowing Amelia's reputation as one of the most promising and respected of the younger social workers, undoubtedly aware of the dilemma Amelia found herself in, said that Greenwich House would consider itself privileged to make a place for her there, that she could be a resident. This situation allowed her to maintain as active an association with social work as her altered way of life would permit and be a member of the staff. So for the rest of 1928 and most of 1929, Amelia made her home in the handsome six-story brick Georgian house designed for Mary by Delano and Aldrich at 27 Barrow Street in the East Village.

Mary was an exceptionally capable as well as charming woman. A member of one of the Boston Brahmin families, which had been pillars of the church, public servants, and part of the literary establishment of the city for generations, she had graduated from Boston University (refusing to be shut up in a women's college), studied at Radcliffe, then had gone to Berlin for further training. While in Germany, she met her future husband, Vladimir Simkhovitch, and Denison House founder Emily Balch. Mary, a contemporary of Emily and Vida Scudder, founded Greenwich House at roughly the same time as they founded Denison House. In the 1920s it was the most dynamic settlement house in New York. It reflected Mary's vision of an unstratified society, a vision that extended even to the board, which was composed of workers and neighbors as well as the traditional wealthy upper-class donors that usually comprised all board members.

Amelia was a very unusual resident, the only person permitted by Mary Simkhovitch to use Greenwich House somewhat as a hotel. It provided her with the constant challenge of interesting company, the comforting presence of a world she knew, and perhaps more important, it shielded her from an overly curious world.

The needy and the interested, the sick and the well, literally in the thousands each week, came to the settlement house. Children flocked to Greenwich House to attend the public school Mary ran on the premises, then stayed to be part of the after-school clubs; the elderly came to be taken care of and to have their health checked by the nurses; the able came to acquire skills in the shops; all came to listen to Mary. Under her stewardship the house became such a catalyst for change that the movers and shakers of society were irresistibly drawn to its side and contributed funds. She had just launched a campaign to raise $150,000 for the Greenwich House Music School, and before she started, she already had $27,000 in hand from generous benefactors. The long arm of Mary Simkhovitch even extended to protect the illegal Patsy's Barn, two blocks away, where behind a green door lived a horse, a goat, and chickens, which the settlement house children loved to visit.

Mary achieved a high degree of competence in all projects. She prevailed on the dean of American education, John Dewey, to set up the education department and be its first head; it remained affiliated with Columbia University and Teachers College, with four representatives on the Greenwich House board. The workshop-apprentice programs that Mary set up, based on those she had seen in Florence, flourished. The pottery workshop was so successful, it became self-supporting, selling wares at its own store on Madison Avenue—its pots were acquired by the Metropolitan Museum for its permanent collection as well as by J.P. Morgan. There was an equally professional stone-cutting shop. The music school students held recitals, and their choral groups competed successfully in city-wide songfests. The children's theater gave Christmas performances on Broadway.

When Amelia moved in, the workshops were operating out of their own buildings down the street, as did the music school. What she encountered at 27 Barrow Street were the core residents: basically the administrators, headworker Mary, whose life was seamlessly intertwined with her work, her husband Vladimir, their children, and the staff. But leading social thinkers of the day from all over the world also came, to exchange ideas and see the life of an American city, or to attend a conference. They stayed for dinner or for several days or several weeks, which meant that Amelia would as likely as not end up talking to a leader of the

British labor movement, a social worker from Japan or Russia, or a Russian revolutionary or Frances Perkins, then New York State commissioner of labor down from Albany for a lecture, or Emily Balch—any and all of whom might drop in for breakfast, lunch, or dinner. It was all quite civilized; nor did the extra guests cause the slightest ripple, since as was traditional in settlement houses, meals were cooked by a cook and served by a butler who both took great pride in the settlement house.

• • • •

Amelia felt at home and fitted in. Her impact on the children and adults alike was incalculable; she inspired them all and continually "got involved," causing Mary to comment approvingly that she had "a very tender heart" and was "sensitive to injustice." She was, however, a slow, careful writer who "sweated out her sentences," observed Mary, herself a prolific writer, author of several books, who routinely dashed off perfect letters and statements to newspapers in record time.

Amelia found companionship not just with Mary but with Vladimir, a professor at Columbia who had a fine collection of ancient art. She could drop her defenses and relax with him. He was fascinated by her—and worried about her future. He admired her sincerity, honesty, and gaiety of spirit; but he thought she gave too much of herself to the public side of her career and wanted her to concentrate on social work. He wasn't sure she was tough enough, that she had the emotional fortitude to endure the notoriety that her new high-profile life demanded. "I felt scared for her, watching her lose her priority in herself. She seemed to have no plan for self-protection," he told Janet Mabie; life on the outside would be very different. He was aware of how complex Amelia was, aware that she was driving herself to become a top pilot, the spokesperson for her generation of women, and at the same time had a great need to make money, and it made him apprehensive. If she had stayed in social work, he mused, "she wouldn't have made so much money, but then, a lot of it never did her any good anyway." But the world was almost sucking her out of social work; she would move on.

It was to Vladimir that Amelia opened up a side to her personality that rarely showed: her restless desire for new challenges, wanting him to understand what drove her on. "Are you interested to know I shall try a parachute jump next week? I've tried to analyze my desire and find it's the seeking of a new sensation. Why do we use the same ones over and over again? We hold hands in the moonlight—and then spend the rest of our lives trying to repeat the moment."

Amelia didn't do a great deal at the settlement house, but her presence was enough to energize everyone, and she did her bit and made it count. She spoke at the children's annual club council awards dinner and, to everyone's delight, presented the cup to the senior Greenwich House basketball team, which defeated Denison House in the big annual grudge game. The junior girls' basketball team, with Amelia watching over them, came out first in their local contest. She mesmerized a neighborhood gathering with a description of her transatlantic flight. She became a member of the committee for the children's theater annual Christmas production at the John Golden Theater. She also arranged for her mother to give ten dollars to be a member of the settlement house—a respectable sum, not as much Eleanor Roosevelt gave that year but the same amount contributed by Condé Nast.

It seemed as if her life were in perfect balance: she was earning her living as a writer, flying when she had the opportunity, and contributing to the social work movement by living in a settlement house.

12
Dreams Come True

•••• On July 1, 1929, Bill Stultz died.

He had been stunting in his own plane, a taper winged Waco that he had just bought from his employer, the wealthy sportsman John Hay Whitney, when he crashed. He had crammed two passengers, young men from Long Island who wanted some thrills, into the forward seat of the two-seat plane and taken off from Roosevelt field just past noon.

He started stunting at an exceptionally low altitude, but those on the field thought nothing of it because Bill was considered the most skillful pilot around. Then an observer in nearby Mineola saw the Waco dive at a house and pull up just before crashing into its roof. The next moment, back over the field, the plane started fluttering down tail first, leveled off at about fifty feet, then dove straight down into the grass. All three men were killed.

Because knowledge of Bill's drinking was widespread, the wrecked plane was examined with particular care. It was discovered that Bill had not cut the switch, the procedure used to avoid fire, that the throttle was wide open, and that the passenger controls had not been disconnected, a violation of federal regulations. And, a bizarre touch, two shoes of different sizes and colors, twisted out of shape, were jammed under the rudder bar; it was impossible to move the bar until they were taken out. The shoes spoke of moments of sheer terror. Also because of Bill's drinking, an autopsy was performed. A few days later everyone knew the chilling truth. He had been "very drunk," the autopsy revealed. He was twenty-nine.

Amelia attended the funeral the next afternoon at three o'clock at the Reformed church in Manhasset, as did Lou Gower, the pilot who had gathered his gear and left the *Friendship* in Boston Harbor. After it was over, Amelia went into New York City to take her part in the radio show on station WRNY at five fifteen P.M., lending her voice to the aviation industry effort to calm people's fears—real enough, since there had been two other accidents at Roosevelt field in less than a week. It would have taken great self-control for her to talk calmly; she must have thought over those days in Trepassey, and how they might have ended, then, for all of them.

• • • •

The era of airline travel was just beginning. Jack Maddux had started Maddux Air Lines in July 1927, with one plane, a Ford trimotor, flying between Los Angeles and San Diego. By the end of 1928 the line had thirteen trimotors, two Lockheed Vegas, and two Travel Airs and had flown 9,443 passengers 386,736 miles all over the West. In the Midwest, Transcontinental Air Transport (TAT), put together by C. M. Keys, was growing even faster. In the summer of 1929 Keys and Maddux joined forces and started the first transcontinental service, with Jack Maddux as head of the western division. Maddux hired Charles Lindbergh to lay out the route (the line became known as the Lindbergh Line), and it was a combination air-rail trip—passengers flew during the day in sixteen-passenger Ford trimotors and slept at night in Pullman cars—in the East belonging to the Pennsylvania Railroad, in the West belonging to the Santa Fe. The planes flew between New York and Columbus, Ohio, and between Amarillo, Texas, and Los Angeles. It took a full forty-eight hours to span the continent from New York to Los Angeles. The total fare varied from a minimum of $337 to a maximum of $403 one way, depending on the standard of comfort on the trains. Special aero-cars transported the passengers from plane to train for the night rides.

Maddux hired Amelia as assistant to the general traffic manager, to work out of the TAT office at 959 Eighth Avenue in Manhattan, but he thrust her back into a traditional woman's role: her job was to supply the "woman's angle," which meant seeing that women's comforts, luxuries, and needs were addressed. It was vital to fill those needs so that women would begin to buy tickets and travel by airlines. Ninety-five percent of airline passengers were men—and if the women didn't join them, the airlines would fail. So since the trimotors had no toilet facilities and made fifteen-minute stops every two hours, a great deal of thought had to go into making the waiting rooms at airports attractive; airline officials ran the preliminary plans and color schemes by Amelia for her opinion. Each stopping area had to be perfect, each landing field and lounge a "show window" of aviation.

No effort was spared to make air travel seem like ocean voyaging or traveling by train. The planes were carpeted, there were curtains at the windows, the seats were deep, comfortable, adjustable, and upholstered in green leather. A male cabin attendant decked out in a white uniform served meals on a folding table set up for each passenger, complete with a lavender linen tablecloth and napkins. A typical menu consisted of tomato surprise, assorted cold meats, sandwiches, fruit cup, cake, and hot coffee. Passengers were offered a map of the route, postcards of places along the way, and writing paper.

In a flurry of publicity on Sunday, July 9, 1929, the line inaugurated service. On the East Coast, in Pennsylvania Station, Amelia christened the brand-new Ford trimotor the *City of New York,* hauled into the cavernous interior of the station for the occasion, while simultaneously on the West Coast America's sweetheart Mary Pickford christened the *City of Los Angeles.* Then the next day Amelia got on the train and headed west, to join up with the Lindberghs on the last leg.

It was hoped that passengers would flock to TAT for the glamorous trip, but in spite of the excitement and interest (a crowd estimated at a hundred thousand watched Charles take off on the first flight from Los Angeles), it was a rocky road, fraught with accidents to the passengers and ultimately bankruptcies for the investors. Combining her two jobs, Amelia devoted a *Cosmopolitan* article to TAT and the other new airlines crisscrossing America. They all needed help; in spite of the elaborate planning TAT had done, there were soon empty seats. With reason: On the first day, as one of the trimotors taxied across the field at Albuquerque, it was hit by an unexpected gust of wind that caused it to ground-loop and brush a wing against the hangar office. No one was hurt, but the seven passengers had to continue on in another plane.

By the time Amelia's *Cosmopolitan* article on the wonders of the airlines came out in October, TAT's the *City of San Francisco* had crashed into a mountain sixty miles east of Albuquerque in broad daylight, killing all aboard. Amelia fretted that the press overplayed accidents, but there was nothing she could do about it; news was news. Scarcely had 1930 begun than Keys, in an effort to increase passenger traffic, slashed the price of a ticket almost in half. The effect was largely negated, however, because the week after the fare cut another TAT plane crashed, this time in bad weather, at Oceanside, California, again killing all aboard. Had the public known that the insurance industry considered flying so dangerous they wouldn't write policies for pilots, there would have been even more empty seats.

• • • •

It had been announced that for the first time ever a women's race would be one of the feature events of the 1929 National Air Races and Aeronautical Exposition. The reasoning behind this surprising development was eminently practical: it would promote aviation. If women flew, it might seem safer, and if it seemed safer, more people would fly. As Frank Copeland, the marketing director of what came to be known as the Women's Air Derby, put it:

> If the feminine is considered the weaker sex and this weaker sex accomplishes the art of flying, it is positive proof of the simplicity and universal practicality of individual flying. It is the greatest sales argument that can be presented to that public upon which this industry depends for its existence.

The derby was an exciting prospect for the fliers. The women would start out August 18 from Santa Monica and end in Cleveland, Ohio, where the National Air Races would be in progress. It would be a real race—a true test of navigational and piloting prowess, the first ever for women. The winner would get real money, for thousands of dollars of prize money were being put up. But then various men on the race committee and some male members of the National Aeronautic Association began to have second thoughts. The specter of accidents bothered them; they didn't want to shoulder the blame if a woman got killed. It was suggested that every woman carry a male navigator with her, and that the race start somewhere east of the Rockies, so that no women would crack up in the mountains. It began to look like it wouldn't be a real race at all.

• • • •

By this time Amelia had obtained a transport license, the mark of a professional pilot. She was only the fourth woman to pass the rigorous test—the others being Ruth Nichols, Phoebe Omlie, and Lady Mary Heath. This, added to her unique popularity, made Amelia the obvious person to voice everyone's anger. She weighed in with the following blast, calculated to hit the newspapers and subject the race committee to public pressure:

I for one and some of the other women fliers, including Elinor Smith, Lady Heath and Mrs. Louise McPhetridge Thaden, think it is ridiculous to advertise this as an important race and then set us down at Omaha for a level flight to Cleveland. As for suggesting that we carry a man to navigate our own course through the Rockies I, for one, won't enter. None of us will enter unless it is going to be a real sporting contest.

How is a fellow going to earn spurs without at least trying to ride?

The idea was dropped. Those in charge decided the race would take place as planned and that the same rule for eligibility would be applied to women as to men; every pilot had to have flown a hundred solo hours, twenty-five of which must have been cross-country flights of more than forty miles from home port. It was a great victory for the women.

So then Amelia had to start looking for a plane, for her Avian was in the toy class, and the race, the first cross-country race sponsored for women alone, would be the event of the year. If she were to make a good showing, she needed something new and powerful. As aviation editor of *Cosmopolitan,* as a star of the lecture circuit, as a vice-president of TAT, she was already right up there in the public eye: she had to take the next step. She had to go for the gold.

The Vega was the hot plane of the late 1920s and early 1930s. Vegas didn't even *look* like other planes—they looked like speeding bullets, they were so sleek and streamlined. There were no connecting wires, no exposed controls; the fuselage, built of plywood, was curved instead of angular—the engine was covered by a cowling. And Vegas were fast. By the time Lockheed finished building the six different single models that made up the line, they were the benchmark against which all other planes were measured. It was in a Vega that Captain George Wilkins flew over both the North and South poles in 1928. It was in a Vega that Arthur Goebel set a transcontinental speed record, and it was in a Vega that Frank Hawks broke Goebel's record. Everyone wanted one for its speed, but Vegas had other attributes that appealed even to the fledgling airlines, who coveted them for their passenger-carrying capability as well as the long distances they could fly without refueling.

And so on July 30, when Amelia sold her Avian to the Whittelsey Manufacturing Company and that same day took possession of a new plane, it would have been surprising, given her instinct for the newest and best, if she *hadn't* chosen a Vega. She settled on a five-passenger model that

Lockheed was using as a demonstrator in the East. Reportedly it had been flown by Charles Lindbergh, had ferried New York City mayor James J. Walker about, and was reputed to be a fine plane. Eighteen days before the race was to start, Amelia, accompanied by Lieutenant Orville Stephens, an army pilot on leave, uncomplainingly flew it west to Burbank, California, to have Lockheed fine-tune it. But when Wiley Post, then merely one of the Lockheed test pilots, a year away from fame and his round-the-world flight, took it up for a spin, he pronounced it the foulest plane he had ever flown. Lockheed officials, appalled that the Vega was so bad, impressed with Amelia's prowess at being able to fly it across the country without incident, thereupon traded Amelia a brand-new plane for hers, a five-passenger Vega with a 220-horsepower J-5A Whirlwind engine, and scrapped the original one within the year. It was a handsome gesture on the part of Lockheed, but it meant that Amelia had to get used to another new plane.

• • • •

"A chance to play the game as men play it, by rules established for them as flyers, not as women" was Amelia's delighted description of the Women's Air Derby. The "Powder Puff Air Derby" was the derogatory name the male press gave the race, and it stuck, but nothing could take away the fact that the contest put women's flying on the front pages of the newspapers and captured the imagination of women all over the country. It was an epochal event, the spectacle of so many women flying across the country.

Forty women qualified to compete for the honor of winning one of the lap races put up by the towns along the route—$200 or $250—or winning a piece of the big prize, the $8,000 jackpot for the first overall finishers. Nineteen women, fourteen in the heavier plane class and six in the lighter weight class, actually started out from Clover field, Santa Monica, on August 18. Sixteen reached Cleveland nine days later.

The women all flew solo, although as the rule was finally written, it was permissible to carry another woman as mechanic as long as the mechanic had never soloed, but "no male person will be allowed to ride in this derby race." Because long-distance flying was still so chancy, another rule stipulated that every entrant had to carry a three-day supply of food and one gallon of water for each occupant. (Ruth Nichols as a matter of habit always carried extra food and water, as did most other pilots.)

The race schedule was complicated. Leaving from Santa Monica, there were overnight stops at San Bernardino, Phoenix, El Paso, Abilene, Dallas, Wichita, St. Louis, and Columbus, with at least one and usually two timed stops at specified places every day. For the daytime stops the rules were first in, first out; for the overnight stops it was last in, first out. By unanimous vote, the women changed the layover times twice, once for Amelia, who on the second day, landing at Yuma toppled her plane against a sand bank (in which a six-inch piece of concrete was embedded and hidden) and bent the propeller and needed double the stipulated hour and a half to fix it; and once at El Paso, where they voted to delay starting until a storm that would have penalized only the smaller planes with limited gas supplies had passed by.

By the time the women had flown the entire 2,350 miles over the Rockies, across the deserts of the Southwest, and the wheat fields of Kansas, Marvel Crosson, a fine pilot, holder of the women's altitude record, was dead, the victim of a failed engine and a defective parachute. There were other less serious accidents: Ruth Nichols struck a tractor upon landing on a runway that was being graded, destroying her plane; Pancho Barnes overshot a field and totaled hers; Bobbi Trout, the twenty-three-year-old Californian who had held the altitude record until Marvel Crosson took it away from her, drifted into Mexico and flipped her plane over upon landing, destroying her landing gear and propeller. Blanche Noyes found a fire in her plane and successfully put it out; and Opal Kunz got lost, ran out of gas, and landed in a creek bed but managed to take off without damage.

Many papers and many people had a field day reporting on the accidents, and some took it as proof that women shouldn't be flying such difficult races. Only Amelia seemed to think it significant, as she pointed out, that the sixteen women who crossed the finish line represented the highest percent of "finishers" in any cross-country race for men or women up to that time. First-place winner was Louise Thaden of Pittsburgh, and second place, Gladys O'Donnell. Amelia, flying her hot plane rather gingerly, came in third, not a bad showing, for knowing she had the fastest plane, she had loaded herself down with some of the personal baggage of her derby rivals, which started to shift around inside as she came into the Cleveland airport and necessitated her making several abortive passes before she could land. The fliers won $3,600, $1,950, and $875 respectively—excellent prize money; even Amelia's share was more than most women earned in six months.

Huge predominately female crowds waited at the fields, curious to see what female pilots looked like and what kind of planes they flew. Twenty thousand were on the field at Columbus, Ohio, the last stop before Cleveland, waiting to greet them.

• • • •

The race had a stirring effect on the pilots. All, even those who hadn't had problems, had endured nine long days of dawn takeoffs, tough flying, and dangerous landing fields. More than piloting came into play. At each air-port layover they had had to see that their planes were serviced, supervise the fueling, and check out that the NAA agents who were supposed to guard their planes from the curious, who sometimes poked holes through the fabric-covered wings trying to learn what planes were all about, were indeed in place and watching. No matter how exhausted they were at each stop, they had to endure speeches and luncheons and long evenings of dressing up and socializing at the fried chicken banquets the local Chambers of Commerce and booster organizations in each town put on. The final night was black tie, so they at last got to put on the dinner dresses they had been toting across the country for the jammed-to-overflowing dinner in the ballroom of the Hotel Statler in Cleveland, which drew the affair to a close. The derby was a grueling experience—a trial by fire—and it welded the women together into a group the way a shared experience can do.

Amelia had been interested in forming a women's flying organization at least since the fall of 1927, when she had written Ruth Nichols, then better known than she, outlining the idea to try and enlist her support. They had been refining the idea ever since, and before the start of the Derby in Santa Monica, they had discussed it with others. As they talked up the idea, other pilots began to see the need also. In Cleveland those finishers who had formed such close personal bonds—among them Amelia, Ruth Nichols, Bobbi Trout, Phoebe Omlie, Louise Thaden, and Blanche Noyes—who were gathered under the bleachers watching the events at the National Air Races decided a women's flying organization was an idea whose time had come; they began to make plans.

Back in New York, Clara Studer, the head of the women's department of the Curtiss Flying Service in Valley Stream, Long Island, who wrote a weekly newsletter for women pilots, gave out the first call to organize. She rounded up the four pilots then flying out of Curtiss field: Neva Paris, Frances Marsalis, Margaret Brown, and Fay Gillis, and they signed the letter she wrote on Curtiss stationery and sent out to all the female licensed pilots in America, asking them to attend a meeting on November 2 at Curtiss field. On the appointed day twenty-six women showed up at the Curtiss hangar—one, Viola Gentry, so eager, she hobbled in on crutches, having just been discharged from the hospital; thirty-one absentees sent their enthusiastic support.

The major concern at the meeting was not what kind of organization it would be—that was fairly self-evident—but what to name it. Suggestions ran the gamut from Climbing Vines, Homing Pigeons, and Lady Buzzards to Queens High, Lady Birds, and Cloud Chasers. The issue was finally settled when Amelia's suggestion was adopted: that the name be the final number of charter members who signed up, whatever it would be. Amelia and Neva Paris then sent letters out to the 117 licensed pilots; ninety-nine joined, so the organization became the Ninety-Nines.

They set out the basic goal: "To provide a close relationship among women pilots and to unite them in any movement that may be for their benefit or for that of aviation in general." As one of the charter members said, summing up the general feeling, "There is something about flying that inspires sex loyalty in women."

The fliers decided that at least for the present they would operate informally and have no president, only a national secretary, Louise Thaden, and a treasurer, Blanche Noyes, and regional representatives. At least one flier, Edna Gardner Whyte, remembers that Amelia, although having no formal title, presided over the early meetings. When, in 1932, it was decided to have a more structured organization, Amelia became the first president; Louise became vice president.

Under Amelia's direction the Ninety-Nines published a monthly magazine, *The 99 News,* chronicling news of the members; within a short time Clara Studer, who was later let go by Curtiss because of the Depression, on Amelia's suggestion was its editor. Amelia helped defray her expenses.

• • • •

Having set in motion the formation of a women's flying organization, Amelia next turned her attention to living arrangements for herself. The old progression of a well-brought-up woman moving from her parents' house to her husband's house was no longer set in stone: there could be a few years solo in between. But where to spend them? Her option as an ex-social worker, to live in a settlement house, could be only a temporary solution for her, and no answer at all for others.

It was still unthinkable for young women to live in hotels — unthinkable and dangerous — and the boarding houses of an earlier generation had disappeared. The women flocking to the cities needed proper places to stay: women needed women's residences. There was one place, the Martha Washington Hotel in New York City, dating from 1904, the first hotel to open its doors solely to women. It was so strait-laced, no males were allowed on the staff: no male bellhops, no doorman; everything was done by women. The suffrage pioneers stayed there.

Next, in New York, came the Barbizon and the Panhellenic, elaborate club hotels offering a wholesome environment in addition to rooms. They screened their clientele, made them fill out detailed forms, and actually asked for references. These hotels provided musical afternoons, teas, bridge parties, lectures, dances, and sports facilities. The Barbizon boasted a swimming pool, a gymnasium, and even a fencing instructor.

But still, they were for-profit hotels, not real clubs.

The American Woman's Association (AWA) bridged the gap. The AWA had a membership of more than three thousand business and professional women headquartered in New York, and when they announced they were going to build a clubhouse in the city that would be as lavish and complete as any men's club in existence, the initial response was overwhelming. When the AWA held its first fund-raising meeting at Carnegie Hall in April 1925, so many women appeared they had to call the police to maintain order.

Ten thousand women showed up for the grand opening of the clubhouse April 13, 1929. The building, at 323 West Fifty-seventh Street, was a wonder: twenty-eight stories high, faced with brick, built around a courtyard that contained four fountains, it boasted 1,250 rooms, each with bath. It was lavishly decorated, its public rooms were filled with antiques, it had roof gardens, solariums, a library, a music room, a cafeteria, dining rooms, an auditorium, and a fully equipped gymnasium with swimming pool. *The New York Times* called it a temple to the spirit of emancipated womanhood. To the women it meant they finally had a place where they could live in comfort and safety, freely able to take advantage of club dinners, musicales, and professional meetings—a complete social calendar. One of the first galas at the AWA was for Margaret Sanger, who was awarded the AWA medal before an audience that included John Dewey and other famous educators of the day. The rooms were quickly taken.

Amelia couldn't live forever at Greenwich House, no matter how accommodating Mary Simkhovitch and her husband were. By this time she had a secretary, Nora Alstulund, living with her. Instead of taking an apartment of her own, she became the AWA's most illustrious tenant, moving into the new residence with Nora. It was perfect for her—so easy, and given her hatred of all forms of housekeeping, so appropriate—as well as being so convenient to the *Cosmopolitan* offices, located just east of the AWA on Eighth Avenue. She could walk to work. She stayed there till she married, adding her luster to the address.

• • • •

In November 1929 Amelia was again winging west in her Vega. This was her third transcontinental flight in three years, and its differences from the others showed her transformation. She was no longer vagabonding in a toy plane like the Avian, no longer flying a Vega whose characteristics were a mystery to her; this time she was in her light green Vega, which she knew like the back of her hand and flew with assurance. She was bound for Los Angeles to stay with Jack Maddux, her boss, the new president of the TAT. She stopped along the way to try and drum up support for the still-unnamed women's flying association. One such overnight stop was in Allentown, Pennsylvania, to stay with and enlist the support of pilot Dorothy Leh. With her was Nora Alstulund, her secretary, for she needed to keep current with correspondence and articles as she went.

Jack, a rugged adventurer, ex-Lincoln car dealer, ex-bus line owner, and his wife Helen, who kept the books for Maddux Air Lines, lived in a house notable for having the latest and best in labor-saving and mechanical devices—radios, appliances, and plumbing, as well as, according to Anne Lindbergh, the worst taste in furnishings: a lighted red and green glass parrot, heavy dark plush curtains, sconces in the semblance of candles dripping over the edge. But the Madduxes were generous hosts, totally caught up in the flying world, and thought nothing of having Amelia plus her secretary staying with them for weeks on end. Nor did they mind the fact that she was constantly picking up and leaving for short periods to fulfill speaking engagements elsewhere. Their warm hospitality was a measure of Amelia's standing: in January she would share her guest quarters with another Maddux employee, America's most famous couple, the Lindberghs, perfectly comfortably. In the meantime Amelia's capacity for work and play was impressive. She was still sporadically writing articles for *Cosmopolitan,* although she was spending more and more time at TAT and had been given responsibility for making sure everything ran smoothly on the western division as well as the eastern, and she was working on the Ninety-Nines and doing public relations for the Pennsylvania Railroad.

When she had been in Santa Monica signing up at Clover field for the derby, Amelia had run into Bobbi Trout, a twenty-three-year-old slim, boyish Californian who had once briefly held the unofficial women's altitude record and was then holder of the women's unofficial endurance record of seventeen hours. Bobbi had been asked by a Los Angeles promotion company, Ullman and Associates, if she would be interested in going for the first women's endurance-refueling flight if Ullman bankrolled it and handled the publicity. Bobbi, who had agreed as long as the flight would be after the derby, was looking for a co-pilot. She didn't know Amelia but Amelia had written her a nice congratulatory letter in February. ("May I add my congratulations for your endurance mark, seventeen hours? I am, of course, very much interested in what women are doing in the air.") Now Bobbi decided Amelia would be the perfect co-pilot and asked her.

Amelia was intrigued—the flight would be a great feather in her cap if it was successful, and Bobbi was a top pilot. An endurance record involving in-flight refueling would, as she said, be a "terrific" new type of record for women. But Ullman and Associates was a Los Angeles firm, the attempt would be made on the West Coast after the derby, Bobbi was going for the *world* endurance-refueling record, which stood at four hundred hours—over two weeks in the air. Just getting organized would take months, the flight itself would take weeks, and she was committed to *Cosmopolitan* and TAT—all of which meant she had a lot of work cut out for her in New York City. Amelia thought it over, checked it out with George Putnam, and regretfully demurred. (She was carefully encouraging Bobbi in the process, however, and kept her as a friend; Bobbi ended up asking Elinor Smith, although "I don't know why I didn't ask Louise Thaden," she remarked years later, regretfully.) On November 26 Bobbi and Elinor took off, but after forty-two hours their refueling plane developed engine trouble and they had to abort the flight, much to Bobbi's disappointment, and after having devoted all of October and most of November to the effort, she called it quits. Even so it was a new women's record.

By the time Bobbi and Elinor took to the air, Amelia was back out in California at the Madduxes'. A few days before Bobbi and Elinor took off, however, Lockheed gave Amelia a chance to make a record of her own. They put a gleaming white Vega Executive two days out of the shop at her disposal to play with—and asked her if she wanted to use the plane, equipped with a powerful 425-horsepower Wasp engine (almost twice the power of hers) to try and beat the existing women's speed record of 156 miles an hour. She couldn't refuse such a tempting offer. With bespectacled Joe Nikrent of the NAA as her official timer, on November 22 she ripped around the three-kilometer course at Metropolitan airport in Van Nuys averaging 184.17 miles an hour; on one leg she went much faster, writing jubilantly in her logbook, "Speed run, 197 mph on one leg. Hooray!"

It was an especially satisfying performance because she had been fighting for recognition for special records for women every chance she got (as she had mentioned in her congratulatory letter to Bobbi Trout) and had gone to Washington to appear before the NAA Contest Committee earlier in the year to press her case for their official imprimatur. Her argument had been that since there were separate women's tennis, high-jumping, running, swimming, and golf records, separate aeronautical records made sense as well, "inasmuch as women haven't traveled so far as men aeronautically." Her point of view had prevailed; Joe Nikrent's presence was necessary if the record was to be officially recognized.

There was a small ceremony at the new Grand Central Air Terminal in Glendale—a gathering of noted pilots to celebrate the new women's speed record, probably organized by Lockheed. Amelia's old friend Waldo

Waterman attended, along with Pancho Barnes, Bobbi Trout, and Elinor Smith. For the event, which garnered newspaper coverage, Amelia was photographed standing holding a huge bouquet of flowers and wearing a cloche hat, chic dress, and scarf. She looked altogether feminine and demure, very much in keeping with the public relations image that airlines were fostering—that flying was such a cinch that a slip of girl could excel.

• • • •

Her brief taste of flying the powerful recording-setting Vega Executive whetted Amelia's appetite for a more powerful model of her own. On March 17 she traded in her plane to Lockheed for a five-passenger Vega powered by a 425-horsepower Wasp engine. It was state of the art. By April, as the weather warmed and she became used to her plane, she began thinking of the next Women's Air Derby. She wanted the derby to be better run, naturally, and at the request of the Contest Committee (quite possibly she put the idea in their head), she began gathering thoughts from the other contestants and Ninety Nine members so that everyone who wanted to would have input, there would be consensus on the changes, and this time it would be run more to their satisfaction. The suggestions, Amelia noted, helped paint a picture of what the women had gone through the previous summer, racing in the first derby. The public relations demands had put them under too much strain. The women wanted at least two hours to be allowed at midday for rest and servicing their planes, "without scheduled entertainment" (no luncheons to attend), two free hours on the field before dinners, and dinners that ended by nine P.M. Finally they wanted a provision that not all the contestants had to turn up at each town's entertainment in return for the prize money that local businessmen put up: they could rotate. A knottier problem to solve, as Amelia wrote Ruth Nichols, was how to divide the field into separate classes, so that no matter what kind of plane was entered—a powerful big model or a small, light displacement model—everyone had a chance at a prize. Amelia was chewing it over, undecided.

In the end, as she learned to her bitter disappointment later in the summer, all the work, all the time, all the effort she had put in was for naught. The men's race committee decreed that this year the women had to fly planes with engines severely restricted in size. That meant Amelia, with her Vega powered by a 425-horsepower Wasp engine, was ineligible, as were Blanche Noyes, Elinor Smith, and Ruth Nichols, who also flew powerful planes. The race committee also decreed that two army pilots and a flight surgeon had to accompany the planes on their flights east—another slap in the face. The race committee turned a deaf ear to the objections of

Amelia and the other fliers. Again delegated to be spokeswoman, speaking for Blanche, Louise Thaden, Elinor Smith, and Ruth Nichols as well as herself, Amelia went public in early August, announcing to the media that all five of them "definitely refused to compete" in the race, scheduled for later in the month. As *The New York Times* reported, "Miss Earhart explained that the women have outgrown the small craft used in last year's race and take great pride in their ability to perform to higher standards of piloting ability." The idea of being chaperoned she dismissed out of hand; it was "not welcome among women competitors unless similar precautions are taken with the men's races." The race was run, but with no one of interest competing, it was ignored as an event.

• • • •

TAT began to have problems. The grandiose TAT style cost a great deal of money; coast to coast by train and plane in forty-eight hours did not appeal to enough passengers to begin to pay expenses. As a result, in spite of all the hoopla and glamour, in the first eighteen months of operation the company lost $2.75 million. Amelia continued working for TAT through the summer, but by October 1930 it had ceased operation.

By that time Amelia was working for the New York, Philadelphia and Washington Airway Corporation (NYPWA). It had been started by two wealthy Philadelphians, Charles Townsend Ludington and his younger brother Nicholas. She was made a vice-president, along with Gene Vidal and Paul Collins, her two good friends, both of whom had also worked for TAT, Paul as superintendent of operations and Gene as a member of the technical staff. Gene was general manager and Paul vice-president of the new line. The NYPWA flew between three high-volume cities—Newark, Camden (servicing Philadelphia), and Washington—every hour on the hour from eight to five, in Lockheed Vegas, Stinson trimotors, and Consolidated Fleetsters. The first flight was September 1, 1930. Stations of the Pennsylvania Railroad were used for picking up passengers and selling tickets.

The airlines were beginning to face the fact that they were not going to make money until and unless women flew; women—and their babies and young children—*had* to fill the seats, there was no alternative. Amelia, as the most famous female pilot, therefore became a valuable asset to an airline and was treated more seriously. Now she was given real responsibility, as opposed to being an adviser, as she had been at TAT. She was in charge of publicity and the complaint department. One reason behind making her the head of the complaint department was that passenger comfort and discomfort were two sides of the same coin and could be dealt with most efficiently by the same person. A woman's touch, especially such a famous woman's touch, could only help. Amelia flew over the line at least once every two days, doing everything from chaperoning a bird, to selling two seats for a pony (which rode standing partly in the aisle), to trying to placate a gentleman who insisted they accept him and his thirteen bags, to dealing with a woman who claimed she would be traveling with a lapdog and showed up with what onlookers described as a young heifer, as well as dealing with the most common complaint—an oversold plane. She had to exercise good judgment, according to Paul Collins, "and get along with men; not only those who had never flown before and were petrified but the kind who wrote letters saying 'I'm an old army flyer myself and yur engines sound punk to me.' "

• • • •

The NYPWA was an immediate success, being the first airline to operate with the frequency and dependability of trains; the public loved it. Amelia's bulletins of its progress were given maximum visibility. *The New York Times* even wrote a laudatory editorial on the new line and carried her letter on its progress, in which she stated that in the first thirty days of service, the line had carried 4,884 passengers, that weather had caused the cancellation of only eight flights, and that the ten daily scheduled flights had been increased to eleven because of demand. On the last day of 1930 Amelia happily announced to the press that in the four months the line had been in operation, it had carried 17,106 passengers, completed 2,150 trips, and flown 430,200 miles—all without problems.

She decorated the walls of her office with amusing old prints of the aircraft of long ago and collected articles on early attitudes—scorn, amusement, fear—that the first steam engines had caused before they became the accepted, normal, safe alternative to horsepower. In the spring of 1931 she gave up line responsibility for publicity and stopped dealing with complaints altogether, for she found her mail depressingly one-sided: "It is the disgruntled one who takes pen in hand and writes and writes and writes."

From then on she did only publicity projects—writing articles, doing interviews, giving speeches where she thought she could be effective. Her salary was adjusted downward from the five hundred dollars a month she had been getting to whatever percentage of the month she expended on behalf of the airline. It was all very informal, and it was up to her to say what the amount, plus expenses, should be. "If you have spent one-fifth of your time on NYPWA work you will receive $100," Gene Vidal, who adored her, wrote, leaving it up to Amelia to figure out what she should be paid.

The main reason she gave up line responsibility was that she just didn't have the time. At the end of March she was off on a one-month lecture tour in the Midwest: one-night stands, each day a new city and a new speech. She started in Hamilton, Ohio, and ended in Meadville, Pennsylvania, twenty-five speeches and thirty-one days later.

By that time she was sufficiently worn down and bothered by sore throats to check into a hospital and have her tonsils out. The operation left her "almost inarticulate. Also the knees are a bit wobbly," as she wrote her mother. But to the world she gave no quarter; she wanted to appear tough, and she did. When the press found out about the operation, a few days had already passed. They finally located her at noon on Thursday, April 30 in Washington, D.C., and thinking it was just the day after her operation (she didn't disabuse them), they reported admiringly that she was recuperating by giving a speech—on "The Modern Woman"—to a Kiwanis Club there.

A week later she gave a no-holds-barred speech to 250 Barnard College students—far different from her usual diplomatic utterances. She told the assembled coeds they were as physically qualified for aviation as men but would have to work twice as hard to get the same amount of credit. She told them the educational system was based "on sex, not on aptitude," and many girls therefore found themselves shunted off into cooking and sewing simply because they were girls. "As a matter of fact, I know a great many boys who should be making pies—and a great many girls who would be better off in manual training. There is no reason why a woman can't hold any position in aviation providing she can overcome prejudices and show ability," she told the rapt coeds.

There was a special reason for the forcefulness of her speech: it was exactly six years since she had left the Columbia-Barnard campus—broke, untrained, and facing an uncertain future. Returning brought back the pain, but it also brought home to her how far she had traveled. She wanted others to make the same trip.

13
Courtship and Marriage

• • • •   Amelia was still engaged to Sam Chapman, but in fact she had been drifting apart from him for some time. With the move to New York and her busy life, Sam hardly got to see her. Nevertheless he was waiting patiently—had been waiting patiently since the California days—and would have taken her on any terms, in spite of the fact that they had never set a wedding date. In the twilight days of the relationship, Amelia had burst out to her sister her annoyance at Sam's continually putting her needs before his. "He should do whatever makes him happiest. I know what I want to do and I expect to do it, married or single." Not even Muriel, in her heart, ever thought Amelia would marry him. The question, for Amelia, was how to tell him.

Amelia had arranged to be in Boston on November 13, 1928, following the *Friendship* flight, for a Zonta meeting (her first; she had received a radiogram aboard ship that she had been admitted to membership) and, the following evening, to speak at a fund-raising benefit for Denison House at Symphony Hall. It was at some point during this trip that she broke the news to Sam. She let two weeks pass to give him time to adjust; then, since she was such a celebrity, she announced her change of plans to the world via the newspapers. "I am no longer engaged to marry. You never can tell what I will do. If I was sure of the man I might get married tomorrow. I am very sudden, you know, and make up my mind in a second."

Sam Chapman, stunned, would live out his life in the Chapman family home in Marblehead and never marry; he never got over Amelia. They would remain friends for the rest of her life.

George had been pursuing Amelia—for professional reasons, then for personal reasons from the moment they met. He thought she was perfect, the height of chic. He was mad about everything to do with her, including "her beautifully tailored gabardine slacks." He adored her hands and included a full-page photograph of them in his posthumous biography, writing, "The tapering loveliness of her hands was almost unbelievable, found in one who did the things she did." (Gordon Selfridge thought the same, saying of her hands, "the most beautiful I think I ever saw, the hands of an artist.")

George also wrote, "I think she really did not realize that often she was very lovely to look at (You're prejudiced! she would jeer at me), and often felt sure that she was actually unattractive. . . . Perhaps her most notable physical characteristic was her slimness—a Washington newspaperwoman once commented on her: 'incredibly slim hips and great femininity'—but evidently people seeing for the first time a woman who flew oceans and tinkered with motors expected a massive, mannish individual, big-footed and heavy-handed, and with a deep bass voice. And then when the anticipated Amazon turned out to be a graceful, lithe person, with a Peter-Panish figure, gray eyes with laughter lurking in them, her sensitive features lit with intelligence and friendliness and a placid, low voice, and hands notable in their beauty, it was all a little confusing."

Not only was she the apotheosis of everything he admired, she was his creation—for if it had not been for him, Amelia would not have been on the *Friendship*. Not that Amelia's fame turned his head; he was used to dealing with celebrities; but he had discovered her, and he was directing her business life.

With his irresistible energy and instinctive eye for public relations George became Amelia's chief buffer and counselor, particularly since the moment Hilton Railey returned to the United States Byrd had snared him away to organize his Antarctic expedition.

George was simply always there for Amelia. He was part of the welcoming committee aboard the *Macon,* always by her side as she went to the various functions in New York. He was master of the small gesture as well as the large. He arranged and was on the Ford trimotor that flew her, the reporters, and a photographer from New York to Boston for that triumphal reception; he arranged to have her car (which he had christened on first sight the *Yellow Peril* after the sleek 1910 English Handley Page monoplane of the same name) brought, which she hadn't seen since she had left. She needed someone to help her cope with her new status, and he was only too delighted to be that person. When she was traveling, he sent her reams of information. As he explained it, "In this period when our association was primarily a business matter, there were long intervals of communication only by letter or telegraph; a voluminous correspondence it was too! That is, it was from my end. The answers to my letters were usually my letters returned, with notations in pencil on the margin."

Nothing she did escaped his eye, nothing she did was too trivial for him to comment upon. A few months after the *Friendship* flight, their relationship had progressed to the point that he could write, "Your hats! They are a public menace. You should do something about them when you must wear them at all! Some of them are cataclysms! But I hasten to add the Pittsburgh bonnet is a peach, as are several of the floppy ones with bits of brims."

Their courage and prowess drew them together; their characters were very different; early on they took each other's measure. Amelia enjoyed doing things thoroughly and carefully and calmly, one task at a time, whereas he rushed around from one project to the next. Following Amelia's penchant for bestowing descriptive names on people, she had immediately dubbed George "Simpkin"— after the cat in *The Tailor of Gloucester,* for he reminded her of Simpkin who, not content with keeping only one mouse in reserve to toy with, always kept several, each under an inverted teacup, "against the danger of having time idle on one's hands." As George wryly admitted, "She early perceived that, important as the project of which she was the center became, it was really just then one of a group of enterprises in which I was engaged. One mouse was not enough."

And indeed, involved as he had been in the *Friendship* flight during April, May, and June—coordinating the various aspects with Amy Guest, David Layman, Richard Byrd, the flight crew, the press, and Hilton Railey; rushing back and forth from Boston to New York, dazzled by his newfound Galatea—he still found time to talk his new friend David Layman into bankrolling a trip to hunt big game in Africa for three fifteen-year-old Boy Scouts, which would result, when the Scouts returned in September, in another book for Putnam's to publish. He even had another "first flight" project going at the same time he was organizing the *Friendship*—the Australian Hubert Wilkins, also under contract to Putnam's, on April 15 began the first west-to-east crossing of the Arctic. Wilkin's saga, the story of the 2,200-mile flight, would also come out in the fall of 1928. And these two other projects were not all; George was also writing the occasional article as roving correspondent for *The New York Times.* This level of activity was, for him, nothing unusual; as he admitted, "My interests are usually plural."

So that by the time the *Friendship* was airborne, the validity of being called Simpkin (as well as the affection implied in the tease) was so firmly stuck in George's mind that he signed some of the cables he sent to Trepassey "Simpkin."

In New York in November, George gave a dinner for Amelia at the Heigh Ho, a fashionable East Side restaurant. It was a classic George guest list: mostly famous adventurers. Present were the explorer Roy Chapman Andrews, back from the Gobi Desert; pilot Clarence Chamberlin and his wife; the Connecticut senator-elect; and balloonist William Beebe and his wife. And of course George's own wife, Dorothy.

George wrote a promotional article of his publishing triumphs for Putnam's entitled, "An Intimate Review of Aviation's Best Sellers," that appeared in the July 1929 *Sportsman Pilot.* Although he mentioned Lindbergh, Byrd, Clarence Chamberlin, and Sir Hubert Wilkins, among others, he devoted the most words and by far his most effusive prose to Amelia's recent slim effort: "the most dramatically interesting bit of manuscript that has passed over my desk was written under unique circumstances. To date it is in a class all by itself—and likely will remain so for some time to come. This particular manuscript was written in a plane as it winged its way over the Atlantic. . . . That author, of course, is Amelia Earhart. . . . It's a humorful, modest volume, set down with unusual literary skill." And so on.

The summer of 1929, in an effort to impress Amelia, George decided to try a "first flight" of his own—to Bermuda. Superb organizer that he was, he hired the best of the best to assist him. In addition to a state-of-the-art plane and an excellent pilot, he signed on as navigator world-acclaimed Lieutenant Commander Harry Lyon, who had guided the flight of the *Southern Cross* on its epochal transpacific flight the previous summer. But in spite of all George's excellent preparations, just about the only thing that went according to plan was their takeoff, from an airfield on Long Island. The trip was a disaster. He later confessed, "In the end I nearly broke my neck. Even so, it was something to have seen A.E. staying on the ground, while I flew. . . . Our undertaking lost no time in becoming a comedy of errors. Midway along the Jersey Coast the engine conked and we squashed into a gummy mass of mud. Rescued from that we finally made Atlantic City, after a spanking descent on the hillside of a heavy wave that bounced us back into the air a hundred feet or so and nearly broke the plane in pieces. . . . Between Atlantic City and Norfolk, believe it if you can, Lyon got lost and . . . the thought did just cross my mind that something was being mixed with the navigation which was not water."

George had discussed the proposed flight with Amelia and had kept her apprised of the flight's nonprogress. She saw him off and it was she and not Dorothy who met him when he returned, by train, to New York City. When she met him at Pennsylvania Station, she was very gracious, according to George. "She never once said: I told you so. She had, and I should have listened."

Amelia was in demand all over the United States. George was her agent, her manager, and her publicist. He set up her schedules, contacted the newspapers, organized her speeches, and sent her endless suggestions as to how to make them better. "You are apt to take less time than you think you will take. Have plenty of spare ammunition on cards to fill in the gaps. To this end I suggest your mapping out your talk on the small cards I am having handed you together with your films. Remember you will be working with a pointer (get a pointer!) with the slides. You will have a tendency to turn your back on the audience. This is a difficult trick. You really have to remember always to talk into the microphone; walk over to the slide, point out what you want to, and then return to the microphone and explain." As a good coach, he pointed out her weak points. "Remember too your tendency is to let your voice drop at the end of sentences. And perhaps the most vital of all is the necessity of ending matters crisply and definitely." Sometimes he was pompous, as when he told her, "Many a good speech, like a railroad, is ruined by lack of adequate terminal facilities."

• • • •

In December 1929, in Reno, Nevada, Dorothy divorced George. The divorce was amicable as divorces go; Dorothy had a beau of her own. Still, Amelia was certainly a large factor. It was during a party at which Amelia was one of the guests that Dorothy packed up her trunk and left the Rye house for good. Dorothy, like George, was drawn to adventurers—she married Captain Frank Upton, the hero of a North Atlantic steamship rescue, less than a month after her divorce. The fact that the end of the Putnam marriage had been mutually desired by both partners and that by the terms of the divorce George set up a joint trust to provide for Dorothy and the children went a long way toward enhancing George's image in Amelia's eyes.

She had lunch with Marian Stabler shortly after the divorce became final. "Of course everyone wants to know if I'm going to marry George," Amelia burst out, at which point Marian asked, "Are you?" "NO," replied

Amelia, giving as the reason that she liked Dorothy Putnam and thought the divorce "was a shame."

Then George's life took an unexpected turn. In February 1930 his uncle, George Haven Putnam, the respected head of G.P. Putnam's Sons, Civil War veteran, author of thirteen books, champion of international copyright agreements, died at the age of eighty-five. George, who had been working at Putnam's since 1919, fully expected to buy out his uncle's holdings and become president, particularly since that had been George Haven Putnam's wish as well as his own, and his uncle had drawn up a contract establishing the basis for George's purchase of his holdings after his death. But, unexpectedly, George Haven's son Palmer Putnam, a mining engineer, returned from Africa and decided he wanted to run Putnam's, in spite of the fact that he had no background in publishing. He bought out George's interest, put himself in charge and George out to pasture. Within a short time Palmer was bankrupt and Putnam's, spiralling downward, had been taken over by Walter Minton and Earl Balch—all of which left George out of a job.

By summer George had joined Brewer and Warren, a new publishing house, with the particular charge of developing an adventure and travel list. No matter how much he liked his new partners or how well he got along with them—and the firm shortly thereafter became Brewer, Warren and Putnam—it would have been a traumatic, uncertain time for George. Even given his highly vaunted ability to juggle countless balls in the air at the same time, it probably was this distraction, as much as Amelia's foot-dragging, that kept him single for a year after his divorce.

On the other hand, there is certainly no doubt that Amelia did not rush into marriage. She was in the full flush of an incredible career. She had been catapulted onto center stage, and for herself and American woman-hood she dearly wanted to stay there. Her instinct was that marriage, even to George, would throw her off balance. But George was persistent. By his own admission, he proposed and was turned down "twice, at least." Never one to give up, he kept on trying and began to wear her down. She was still struggling, as she wrote to a friend, long after George's divorce had come through.

> I am still unsold on marriage. I don't want *anything,* all the time. . . .
> A den. . . . Do you remember in "If Winter Comes" how Mabel
> was always trying to get her husband a "den" and how he hated it?
> He said he wasn't a bear. A den is stuffy. I'd rather live in a tree. . . .
>
> I think I may not ever be able to see marriage except as a cage
> until I am unfit to work or fly or be active—and of course I
> wouldn't be desirable then.

But before the year was out, she changed her mind. She had, after all, been listening to George and following his advice for over a year. She knew he knew what he was doing. She respected him. The press sensed the coming nuptials and pursued George for information. "To marry Miss Amelia Earhart would be swell," George said to one interviewer, then went on to inject a note of caution: "But nothing in this vale of tears is certain."

On the eighth of November 1930 they applied for and were granted a marriage license in a Connecticut town near where George's mother lived. Two more months would go by. She was filled with misgivings.

• • • •

George pressed his case. Amelia's mind began to wander. She became interested in a newfangled airplane, the autogiro—possibly dangerous, certainly distracting. Invented by a Spaniard a few years before, the first American production model, made under license at the Pitcairn plant in Willow Grove, Pennsylvania, made its first test flight just the week before they applied for the marriage license. Within several weeks Amelia was up in the PCA-2 to see what all the fuss was about, liked what she found, and soloed. The strange craft, which had the fuselage of a conventional plane but had four large rotor blades mounted on a mast above it, could take off in a short distance—and land on a dime. Never mind that it was slow and awkward, and that on landing it settled down awkwardly like an old hen, as Anne Lindbergh observed; it didn't need a landing field. The possibilities seemed endless. Thomas Edison called it "the greatest advance that could have been made in aviation."

Before too long the smitten George evinced an interest in autogiros, and the next time she drove out to Willow Grove to fly a Pitcairn giro, on the Friday before Christmas, he was with her. He spent most of the day hanging around waiting for her. She took off and landed so many times, a watching observer lost count. As the afternoon wore on George decided he might as well go up himself. Amelia kept at it, piloting the PCA-2, experimenting to see how stable it was—until darkness forced her to call it quits. George's reward was to spend the weekend with her at her boss's house—at C. T. Ludington's, head of the Ludington line, in Philadelphia. No doubt he was fitting in with her plans. No doubt they were traveling together in the most open manner; even *The New York Times* knew they were both spending the weekend at the Ludingtons'.

By January Amelia was entertaining thoughts of backing out of the marriage—and in an uncharacteristically frantic action, she was driven to ask her male friends their opinion. She called up her good chum Carl Allen, aviation editor of *The New York World Telegram,* and asked him to round up their mutual friend Deacon Lyman of *The New York Times* and meet her. "I need advice badly and I need it today if possible," she said to Allen. Allen was one of her great admirers. The two men dropped everything and within twenty minutes were knocking at her door. According to Allen, she was vacillating about the marriage—she was afraid it would wreck her glittering career. The meeting was awkward, the men stunned. As Allen remembers it, he said to her, "In my opinion, Mr. Putnam excels in and relishes this essential role from which you instinctively shrink; he basks in the reflected public glorification which you receive, telling himself, truthfully, his role helped create this acclaim and can do much to give it still greater dimensions. And he is probably right. *It may be that you need him as much or more than he needs you.*"

Amelia had always cherished her freedom, always held a deep-seated ambivalence toward marriage. Swinburne's Atalanta could have still been speaking for her.

". . . a maiden clean,
Pure iron, fashioned for a sword; and man
she loves not; what should one such do with love?"

"wherefore all ye stand up on my side,
If I be pure and all ye righteous gods,
Lest one revile me, a woman, yet no wife,
That bear a spear for spindle, and this bow strung for a web woven."

Should she or shouldn't she? It was a difficult decision.

• • • •

Being a wife and mother and pursuing a career would involve trade-offs and sacrifices, particularly in those times when the labor-saving devices now taken for granted were just a promise for the future: fulfilling the duties of mother and wife was a full-time job. Running a home and working (we are talking here of the upper-middle-class home) was like trying to pat your head and rub your stomach at the same time. A contemporary Radcliffe study of wives who worked would conclude that it was almost impossible. The WEIU did a study of Simmons College graduates in the first quarter of the twentieth century: of the 1,102 who had married, a grand total of 93 were gainfully employed. Even of this small number, eleven were widows and two divorced, which meant that of the more than one thousand married Simmons graduates, only fifty-three managed to work while living with a husband. Even in 1989 historian William O'Neill, in *Feminism in America: A History,* looking at it from a different perspective, would conclude that "it seems evident that the institutions of marriage and family, as presently conceived, are among the chief obstacles to feminine equality."

Since childhood, Amelia and Lucy and Katch Challiss had been lukewarm toward the notion of marrying: they were afraid a man would stand in the way of their careers, interfere with their lives. It was of course not an idle fear: men often did. Aversion to marriage seemed to be a common thread running through the women in Amelia's family in her generation. From childhood on, Amelia, Lucy, and Katch had dreamed grand dreams of exciting careers, not exciting marriages. As teenagers they didn't think the two matched up—but on the other hand they liked men, the unsolvable dilemma. It was Katch who had formulated the most specific career plan: she decided she was going to be a newspaper reporter and live in Paris. Both she and Lucy went to college to prepare for their careers, Katch to Kansas State where she graduated Phi Beta Kappa, Lucy to Wheaton. Lucy, pursued by suitors, had gone off to Paris after graduation and found a job teaching at the American School in Neuilly. There she had a social whirl and taught many children of note, including Price Phillip of Greece. Lucy, great fun, loved by everybody, who "lit up a room," it was said—so close to Amelia and so attractive—couldn't bring herself to marry, but she also had great trouble saying no to her suitors. Four times Lucy became engaged—twice sending out wedding invitations—and four times she backed out. She took a variety of jobs throughout her life, and she enjoyed an incredibly busy social life—breakfasts, lunches, teas, cocktails, dancing evenings—to the hilt. Extremely competent, at one point in the 1930s she became head of *Vogue*'s school directory department. When World War II came, she enlisted in the Red Cross, went to Italy as an ambulance driver, and ended up organizing and running USOs (servicemen's clubs). After the war she worked for a textile design firm in New York City. Her life was still a constant round of activity; she was always on the go, and because she was so charming and entertaining, she was always busy. And always single.

Katch, it was true, had married in 1929, but only after a considerable struggle, and under duress as it were. On the boat to Paris to join Lucy and become a teacher at the American School, Katch had met Bill Pollock, a tall, handsome, wealthy, kind, intelligent student at Yale University who fell head over heels in love with her and proposed. On her way to France to live out her dream, then, she had had the bad luck to meet her dream man. She stalwartly refused him, and he returned to college, but for three summers running Bill returned to Paris to be with her and try and make her change her mind. The fourth summer, when he said he was going to marry someone else if she turned him down again, she had grudgingly accepted.

But all her life Katch was doubtful about the rightness of her choice of committing to marriage, never sure the role of wife and mother was right for her. Her large house, situated in the rolling farm country of eastern Ohio, became a showplace for that part of the world: there she lived out her life as the gracious hostess, the conscientious mother of one daughter, an active participant in all the community philanthropic activities. But in her bones she felt was missing something, stuck out there in Ohio while her sister and cousin went gallivanting around the world, and it made her fretful. Her daughter Patricia could feel it as she was growing up.

Amelia wasn't all that sure that she would have the strength of character to continue her career, as her friend Louise de Schweinitz had done. There was always the possibility that she would gradually succumb to the demands of marriage and throw in the towel, as her smart Phi Beta Kappa cousin Katch had done.

"A woman's best protection is the right man," says a character in Clare Booth Luce's play *The Women*; perhaps that, in the end, was the overriding reason that decided Amelia.

On February 6 George and Amelia telephoned George's mother Frances Putnam at her house in Noank, Connecticut, on Long Island Sound and told her that they were driving up and would spend the night, and that the ceremony would be the next day at her home. On Saturday, February 7, acceding to Amelia's wishes that there be an absolute minimum of fuss and trappings, they were married in Frances Putnam's cream-colored two-story house—Square House, as it was called. George's description of his bride: "She wore something as simple and forthright as herself, and not new, bought for the occasion. A brown suit, I think, and a casual crepe blouse with a turndown collar and, as I remember it, brown lizard shoes. No hat, of course." He even adored her matter-of-factness.

Her choice of clothes for her wedding was amazingly similar to that of her mother, thirty-six years before: both wore brown traveling suits, brown shoes, and stockings. It was also remarkably similar to what she wore every day. Following the ceremony, Amelia, as her mother had a generation before, donned a brown hat and a brown fur coat.

The New York Times had an article on the event, probably supplied by George himself—it has his touch.

> The ceremony itself, performed by Probate Judge Arthur Anderson of Groton, Ct, [a family friend] consumed but five minutes. The only witnesses were Mrs. Frances Putnam, Mr. Putnam's mother; Charles Faulkner, his uncle; Robert Anderson, the judge's son, and twin black cats.

As Mr. Putnam slipped a plain platinum ring on Miss Earhart's finger the cats, coal black and playful, rubbed arched backs against his ankles.

Just before the ceremony, Amelia's fear of finding herself tied down by marriage resurfaced. She borrowed some of Mrs. Putnam's stationery, slipped off by herself, and put her thoughts down for George. The resultant letter doesn't seem to have bothered him:

Dear GP;

There are some things which should be writ before we are married. Things we have talked over before—most of them. You must know again my reluctance to marry, my feeling that I shatter thereby chances in work which means so much to me. I feel the move just now as foolish as anything I could do. I know there may be compensations, but have no heart to look ahead. In our life together I shall not hold you to any medieval code of faithfulness to me, nor shall I consider myself bound to you similarly. If we can be honest I think the difficulties which arise may be best avoided. . . .

Please let us not interfere with the other's work or play, nor let the world see our private joys or disagreements. In this connection I may have to keep some place where I can go to be myself now and then, for I cannot guarantee to endure at all the confinements of even an attractive cage.

I must exact a cruel promise, and that is you will let me go in a year if we find no happiness together.

I will try to do my best in every way. . . .

AE

George hid the letter away, only revealing its existence after she died, then writing that it was "a sad little letter, brutal in its frankness, but beautiful in its honesty. At length I have decided it has a place, contributing to these pages something of the structure of a character and a gallant inward spirit."

He may have hoped, that morning of the marriage, that she didn't mean what she wrote—that it was an excess of apprehension and plain fear that drove her to make such a dramatic statement. He may well have thought that, for his later analysis—that it was a sad little letter—is so far off the mark: there is nothing sad about demanding sexual freedom. It was in fact a breathtakingly independent statement, couched in diplomatically acceptable terms, which George accepted.

Amelia wanted to make sure that George didn't take her to be an ordinary bride. The letter is not so much a declaration of the rights of a married woman, as a declaration that although married she would continue to behave as if single—when it pleased her. It is hard to believe that any bride or groom, when handed such a letter the day of the ceremony, would go through with the ceremony. But George did. Her career first, over him, she wrote: marriage may "shatter" chances in work "that mean so much to me," so he better watch out. Sexual freedom was obligatory—a fascinating and radical notion: she demanded the right to be unfaithful. He acceded, of course, at what cost to himself one can only guess. For the rest, she demanded that each had their own spheres of work and play, and if everything became too much, she might need a private bolt hole.

It is an extraordinary statement. It rips her mask off and shows her as a much stronger, much more fearless, much more self-assured person than she let on. It shows the steely hand in the velvet glove, the raw power that lay at the heart of her soul; it shows that her emotional courage was the equal of her physical courage. It becomes apparent at this point that she in fact really didn't know the meaning of fear. Of failure, yes, but not of fear.

Some of her biographers maintain that Amelia's and George's was not a love match from the start, that she had simply married her manager, as Gore Vidal phrased it. But as her wedding statement makes clear, nothing could have been further from Amelia's mind than the thought that she was entering into a marriage of convenience—a "smart" marriage. Far from assuming that one of the pluses to matrimony would be having George's constant professional help, she was afraid that his constant presence (read: demands) would "shatter" her career. And if she wasn't marrying him for practical reasons, then she was marrying him for love. Certainly, to agree to such terms, George had to be truly mesmerized. He was a man who loved women, who loved the marital state—he had married at a young age, divorced and remarried, was single long enough to attract Amelia, remarried eighteen months after she disappeared, and remained happily married till he died, but for Amelia he abdicated the ordinary male role and put up with the conditions she imposed.

A companion gesture to Amelia's written declaration of rights—a small gesture but equally significant—was her refusal to wear her wedding ring. She never wore the platinum band that George put on her finger at their wedding.

And yet with it all—her unusual strength of character, her deeply feminist beliefs—she still managed to be the likable, supportive, gutsy, intelligent person that everyone wanted as their friend. Carl Allen would describe her admiringly as "a curious mixture of boyish naivete and feminine guile." As their lives meshed, George became the fall guy of the team. He was the one who had to keep her on schedule, who fended people off to give her space and a little peace and quiet, who was delegated to say no. That was one reason he was nowhere near as well liked as she, but there were plenty of others. Where she was reserved, he was bold; where she was thoughtful, he was careless; photographers noticed that he always tried to put himself into the pictures they took; reporters noted that he was always trying to manage the angle of their stories and then get rid of them, while Amelia, left to her own devices, would like as not invite them to share a meal with her. George loved celebrities above ordinary people; her friends disliked him on that score. He was forever (brusquely) rushing her off from one event to another. The result was that whenever anything went wrong, *he* was assigned blame. What *was* true was that the irrepressible George couldn't seem to leave her alone: he was always getting involved in her affairs. But she was the one in control.

She did enjoy living in a real house, and as she began thinking of her family's possessions, she pestered her mother to send her the family heirlooms. "I should like the old quilts etc. and the things which were Grandma's," she wrote Amy shortly after the marriage, directing her mother to send her grandmother's old music books. (A bit later she berated her mother for sending only two of Amelia Otis's music books when "I remember three.") She also asked for and received the family silver and linen, some family books, a walnut table that had been in the Otis family, and various other objects. "The candlesticks were sweet. I've had 'em on the table ever since they came," she wrote, thanking Amy. And she softened to the extent of buying herself two canaries, something she had wanted "for ever so long."

One has the impression that if ever she thought of having a baby, it was now, right after her marriage. She was never again quite so home-minded as when she first moved into George's house in Rye.

Within a year she was working on a second book. She wrote about her youth, giving the reader a cheery look at the uneventful childhood of an adventurous tomboy, and about her early flying adventures. She included a bit of history about famous women fliers and tried to gather information (not too successfully) on women who managed to make a living out of flying. Certainly it was because of George that her thoughts were so directed.

He delighted in playing the injured husband role.

When Ninety-Nines' business seemed to consume too much of Amelia's time, George announced that he was forming the 49.5 Club, composed "of the lesser halves of the 99 Club." When Frances Marsalis and Helen Richey broke the women's world endurance record in 1933, George sent them a teasing telegram.

> CONGRATULATIONS TO YOU BOTH. NOW THAT YOU HAVE DEMON-
> STRATED HOW LONG WOMEN CAN STAY UP IN THE AIR, WILL YOU ENTER
> ENDURANCE CONTEST TO BE UNDERWRITTEN BY 49.5 CLUB? OUR OR-
> GANIZATION PROPOSES OFFERING APPROPRIATE TROPHY FOR WOMEN
> FLYER WHO ESTABLISHES 1934 ENDURANCE RECORD OF LONGEST CON-
> SECUTIVE SOJOURN IN HER OWN HOME.

Many people—including many of Amelia's pilot friends—didn't like George Putnam. They didn't think he was "good enough" for her. They didn't like the way he always puffed her up—sometimes at the expense of others. They didn't like his brusque manner and his rather obvious lack of interest in other women pilots—he literally only had eyes for Amelia. He even gradually centered his business life on her, to the point that he lost interest in his own projects—while he was married to her, his own authoring came to a stunning halt. He was a prolific writer and the author of twelve books in his lifetime, but three were published before he and Amelia were married, and nine afterward. He published nothing from 1931 until she disappeared.

He was an unusual combination: a huckster, but one with impeccable taste. What he was pushing was his favorite person in the world. He arranged Amelia's lectures, published her books, promoted her interests, and last but far from least, cultivated important people. Nor was he self-effacing; a bit of a ham, he craved center stage for himself as well as for her. He had always lived in a world of celebrities and excitement, and ordinary people leading pedestrian lives simply bored him. In a word, he was spoiled.

There were those who thought Amelia put up with him merely because she needed him to showcase her. But in fact observers of their home life indicate that it was much more than a marriage of convenience. They had fun together. They enjoyed the same things. It would be said in later years that she had grown tired of George and the busy schedule he set, And yet no one, certainly none of her Ninety-Nine friends, none of the students and faculty at Purdue, where she later spent so much time, would have thought of her that way. For she had an aptitude for handling people and handling her husband, and the way she handled the pressure he put upon her was just an indication of that. Quite obviously, like any relationship, theirs had its moments of strain. But Amelia was sufficiently independent to balance her personality and wishes against his wishes, as he appreciated: "No client of any counselor ever received counsel more reasonably—or on occasion, refused with more firmness to act on it. For, endowed with a will of her own, no phase of her life ever modified it—least of all marriage."

George was always nearby, always joshing, always part of the action. He was always intimately concerned with every detail of her flights and usually was the last person to say good-bye to her and the first to greet her when she landed. Moments before takeoff in Oakland for Honolulu, with the Electra ready to go at the end of the runway, Paul Mantz had to throttle down the powerful engines so that George could climb up on the wing "for a final farewell with his wife," and even after the farewell George and William Miller, of the Bureau of Air Commerce, in Miller's car, chased after the plane as it roared down the field. After the accident, the first thing she did was call him. And yet he learned to share her with others.

After the wedding, Amelia was back at work the following Monday. To be fair, she had announced immediately that Monday would find them *both* back at their desks. They were.

14
The Lindbergh Trail

• • • • Ruth Nichols had been news for most of 1931; that was the year she became the top American aviatrix. In March she flew her Vega to 28,140 feet, taking the altitude record away from Elinor Smith. In April she flew it 181.157 miles per hour, taking the speed record away from Amelia—25 miles an hour faster.

In the spring of that year she announced that she was "going to follow the Lindbergh trail" and be the first woman to fly solo across the Atlantic to Paris. From then on Ruth was definitely front-page news.

Ruth's aeronautical adviser was Clarence Chamberlin, the pilot who flew Levine's Bellanca to Germany in 1927 right after Lindbergh. Chamberlin put a new, powerful 600-horsepower Wasp engine in Ruth's Vega and, to save weight, replaced the landing gear with a gear that was ultralight but had a safety factor of only three to one. Clarence's flight plan called for Ruth to fly to Harbor Grace, Newfoundland, the favorite jumping-off spot for transatlantic flyers, the closest point to Europe, and take off from there.

From the day in April when the story hit the papers, Ruth was dogged by reporters and overwhelmed with fan mail, to such an extent that she hid away for several days to adjust. She gave optimistic, detailed interviews, telling one reporter that she believed her chances were "98 percent" in favor of success, and that "at Newfoundland I will await definite word of good weather from Dr. Kimball." She decided it would be a good idea to have Hilton Railey at her side to help her cope in Europe.

Hilton sailed for France. Ruth took off on the afternoon of June 22 for Harbor Grace, with a light load of gasoline, planning to make one stop along the way. After flying four hours, she found herself over the St. John's airport in New Brunswick as scheduled. She circled the small, rock-enclosed field, studying it none too happily, only too aware of her delicate landing gear and the tight landing pattern the field demanded. She had no choice but to land—it was getting dark, and she didn't have enough fuel to go further. She made her approach and, worried about her landing gear, touched the wheels down too gently and too late—and couldn't stop before hitting the cliffs at the end of the field. She wrecked the plane and broke five vertebrae in her back.

She was tough. Her plane was repaired, her back mended in a cast, and as fall approached, she was flying again. She and her orthopedist worked out the optimum posture angle for her cockpit seat, and she hoped to make another attempt before fall storms began. But by the time she and the plane were ready, the weather was getting dicey, so instead of flying the Atlantic, she decided to rack up the women's long-distance record—the only one she was missing. She won that handily, flying the 1,950 miles from Oakland, California, to Louisville, Kentucky, her broken back encased in a steel corset. When spring came, she and Clarence Chamberlin were ready for another transatlantic attempt; by mid-May it appeared that she would take off any day.

Elinor Smith planned to beat her out. Three years before, as a photogenic seventeen-year-old brunette, she had hit the headlines in New York when she flew, on a dare, under each of the East River bridges. It had been easy, she said at the time, but there was a navy destroyer right in her path as she flew under the Brooklyn Bridge, and she had to make a quick vertical bank to get through. Actually, pilots flew under the East River bridges all the time, and the George Washington Bridge as well. But they didn't do it dodging ships; they waited for clear space. And they didn't have newsreel cameras photographing it. The Department of Commerce, definitely not impressed, grounded Elinor for fifteen days for the escapade.

Now she was twenty, seasoned, with a commercial license under her belt; she announced on the eighteenth of April in an NBC radio interview with Grantland Rice that she was going to fly from Harbor Grace, Newfoundland, to Dublin, Ireland, sometime in early May in her Wasp-powered Vega. She had been preparing for a transatlantic flight since the previous August. In fact, she too was on the Lindbergh trail—her flight plan, filed with the Department of Commerce, was to fly to Newfoundland, Ireland, and France—but by announcing for Ireland she took some of the pressure off herself.

Laura Ingalls, another expert pilot, was also in the running. She was an aerial acrobat—so fearless, she had casually set a record of 714 consecutive barrel rolls over St. Louis and 980 loops over Muskogee, Oklahoma, explaining, "the chamber of commerce paid me a dollar a loop, expecting me to make maybe fifty or sixty, so I just kept looping until I ran out of gas." Her backer, the Atlantic Exhibition Company, had chosen Laura as the most likely candidate to successfully fly their Lockheed *Air Express* from New York to Paris to win the title "Lady Lindbergh." She too spent the winter of 1931–32 getting ready.

Amelia, serenely leading her life in Rye, enjoying her luxurious home and married life, was off on a different tack. She spent 1931 flying Harold Pitcairn's autogiro.

Harold Pitcairn knew that if he could seriously interest Amelia, future sales would be assured, so in early December, just weeks after the first production models rolled out of his plant, he arranged for her to come out to Willow Grove, Pennsylvania, and take a ride with Jim Ray, his chief test pilot. On December 19 she soloed, stating that she found the craft easier to handle than she expected.

She and Pitcairn and George, getting along so well, decided that Amelia would go for an altitude record in the autogiro, a challenge for Amelia and great publicity for the PCA-2. On a spring day in April, while her confreres were concentrating on emulating Lindbergh, Amelia was back at Willow Grove, having accepted Harold Pitcairn's invitation to establish a "ceiling" for the new windmill plane. Not a "stunt altitude flight," she hastened to say, because such things were unpopular, but that is exactly what it was. Luke Christopher, there as official observer for the NAA, installed a sealed barograph, and there was an oxygen tank, but otherwise it was a standard PCA-2. Shortly after noon she took the autogiro aloft and in an hour and a half nursed it up to 18,500 feet, but at that altitude trouble developed in the fuel line, and she came down. She had a light lunch and a nap while one of the Pitcairn test pilots worked over the engine, then decided to make another attempt. Loaded with forty-two gallons of gasoline, she took the autogiro aloft and held it ascending until it wouldn't go any further—at which point her altimeter registered 19,500 feet. The actual record, when the barograph was examined, was 18,415 feet, which became the official altitude record for autogiros and stood for years.

With the enthusiastic backing of George, Amelia now proceeded to order an autogiro for herself, planning to make the first transcontinental flight of an autogiro ever—which would make another record. A few days later it was announced that Harold Pitcairn had won the prestigious Collier trophy for 1930, given for the year's highest aeronautical achievement, for the revolutionary new safe autogiro. It was a major event in the flying world, as well as a dramatic media event: he accepted it on the south lawn of the White House, flanked by one of his autogiros, which had just landed on the White House lawn. Orville Wright as well as everyone else who mattered in the flying world watched as President Hoover did the honors.

One result of all the publicity was that various American companies began eyeing the autogiro as a possible vehicle to publicize their products. The Beech-Nut Company placed an order. Probably on George's initiative, they entered into negotiations with Amelia: they would sponsor her on an epoch-making flight across the country, and she could use the plane thereafter, if she would fly their model with their name printed in large letters on the fuselage. She agreed.

On May 29 she took off from Newark. But autogiros were not by any means perfected, so with her was Eddie Gorski, a mechanic, and with him was a hundred pounds of spare parts and tools to deal with the heavy maintenance that the experimental craft required. She took the northern route, crossing the Rockies over Colorado, and arrived June 6 in Oakland without incident, only to find, to her chagrin, that a professional pilot from Poughkeepsie, New York, had beaten her to the coast by a week. By June 22 she was back in Newark, having flown 11,000 miles in a total of 150 air hours.

Amelia turned the autogiro into one of her best *Cosmopolitan* articles. Titled, appropriately, "Your Next Garage May House an Autogiro," it appeared in the August issue. She predicted the day would come when country houses would have wind cones flying from their roofs to guide guests to the front lawn landing area (Harold Pitcairn's home, Cairncrest, already did), and she held out a future for the autogiro for weekend fishing and hunting trips and quick sorties to golf and aviation country clubs, as well as a new painless way to commute to work.

But the autogiro in fact gave Amelia a lot more trouble than she admitted to the world.

She dumped the Beech-Nut autogiro at least three times. En route home, taking off from Abilene, Texas, she was suddenly engulfed in a windstorm, known locally as a "dust devil," that dropped the air pressure underneath her, thus causing the autogiro to drop. Avoiding spectators, she managed to bring the autogiro down in a nearby parking lot, but not before she damaged it and several cars. Amelia stepped out unhurt; the autogiro needed serious repairs. Not that she was anything but inconvenienced; before the day was out pilot Paul Lukens was taking off from the Pitcairn factory and winging west in a new autogiro for her; Pitcairn Aviation and the Beech-Nut Company thought too much of the publicity she generated for them to even think of her not flying.

Paul Collins and his sister witnessed the second accident. After a "rather erratic" autogiro flight she made after taking off from the airfield in Camden, New Jersey, she "finally landed on a fence. Amelia stepped out frustrated and furious, and announced, 'I'll never get in one of those machines again. I couldn't handle it at all,' " according to Helen Collins MacElwee.

The third was in September. Attempting a slow landing near the grandstand of the Michigan State Fair grounds, Amelia failed to level off soon enough, and the autogiro dropped twenty feet to the ground. The landing gear was demolished, a wing crumpled, and the plane ground looped, but she emerged unhurt and unruffled from the cloud of dust that surrounded the wrecked craft. "It was all my fault, and I'm not injured at all. I just didn't level off soon enough," she told the waiting crowd, according to the newspapers. But writing to her mother, she had another explanation: the landing gear had given way "from a defect," causing her to ground-loop. And when she was quoted as saying "it was all my fault," she went on to say in her letter to Amy, she had been addressing George, who, while running to her side, somersaulted over a guy wire he didn't see and ended up in the hospital, much to his embarrassment. Pitcairn Aviation as usual came through with another machine, and within a few hours Amelia was on her way to Saginaw, Michigan, to fulfill her exhibition flying engagement there.

Other major drawbacks to the autogiro, besides its quirky landing characteristics, that Amelia made light of at the time effectively curbed her interest. One was its lack of range; on the round-trip flight to the coast, she had had to stop seventy-six times to refuel—at least once every two hours. The other was its lack of power—it cruised at only eighty miles an hour, and if there were headwinds, it was considerably slower. That meant that taking an autogiro on a long trip got you there only marginally faster than driving a car, and in fact one traveler tracked her in his automobile on a hundred-mile section in Nebraska and almost beat her.

By fall she and George had hatched the idea that it was time for her to write a second book. She still seemed seriously uninterested in entering the Lindbergh contest. She was concentrating on the book, writing to all her friends for information, for she wanted to mention the top fliers, what they were achieving, and how they were financing their plans. Over the winter she wrote of Elinor Smith, "these days she has a fast Lockheed, such as Miss Nichols has used, and no one knows what is up her sleeve," a not-particularly-sly reference to Elinor's plans to fly the Atlantic. By the time winter was over, Amelia had finished the book and had decided to beat Elinor to the punch.

She didn't let the project take over her life, however. She remained remarkably in touch with all her usual interests. At the end of March she wrote her father's widow, Helen Earhart, to make sure Helen had enough money to pay the property taxes on the house she had lived in with Edwin: "Dear Helen, Now that spring is rolling round again and taxes are due, I am writing you to find out if you are all right as concerns this important matter. . . . As you know I am much interested in what you do, who were so fond of ESE, and what becomes of the home he cared so much for."

Life was particularly pleasant for Amelia just then because her secretary, Nora Alstulund, was leaving to go to Argentina, and she had prevailed on her cousin Lucy Challiss, who happened to be between jobs (she would shortly become schools editor of *Vogue*) to come up to Rye and take her place. Lucy had been a hard sell; Amelia had made the initial call to her to come to Rye, then both Amelia and George worked her over — it was a team effort to sell the job. Lucy had gone to George's office at five one evening, and he and she had walked to meet Amelia on Park Avenue, where she was attending a meeting of the Society of Woman Geographers, a select group of women with published works to their credit. The three of them drove to the country, dined, and talked by the fire. "Nora to leave — they ask me to come," Lucy cryptically wrote in her diary, initially reluctant. She went home, thought it over for a few days, and then agreed. George called to check on her travel arrangements. She arrived in Rye two weeks later, on Saturday, April 16, 1932.

Once ensconced, she had a good look at Amelia's life and wrote down her impressions in her diary, day by day. The things that stand out in her account: that Amelia and George were very much a couple and planned most things out together; that Amelia looked and acted as if she hadn't a care in the world; that the house was always full of people, of whom one was often Eugene Vidal; and that through it all there was always a sense of order and tranquillity. Who was responsible for that feeling? Certainly the sense of order flowed from impeccable planning, and Amelia and George were both excellent planners, but the sense of tranquillity — that was Amelia's special gift. She was soon to get into her Vega and fly alone across the ocean, but it didn't show. Lucy didn't even know that it was thirty-two days to liftoff. Gardening and houseguests seemed to come first.

Sunday morning Lucy joined them at nine thirty for breakfast, after which she lazily read the papers and went ouside to garden. Most Saturdays and Sundays for the next months were spent gardening or raking and burning leaves, even if the day was blowy or cold. And interestingly, aside from possible time spent on a rowing machine upstairs in the loggia, which Lucy mentions seeing but never mentions Amelia using, raking leaves was Amelia's only physical exercise.

People flowed through the house in a steady trickle, growing heavier on weekends: business associates, writers, celebrities, explorers, neighbors, fliers—all found a cordial welcome at Locust Avenue. It was an unusual weekend that didn't find houseguests in residence. George likened the house to a hotel, noting that "the roster in any month might include aviator, actor, arctic explorer, big game hunter, balloonist, cowboy, correspondent—and so on pretty well through the alphabet."

Amelia, acting as if nothing major were about to happen, carried on a variety of activities. She spent Monday afternoon going over the final galleys of her book *The Fun of It,* by that time complete except for the hook—the final chapter. To guarantee maximum sales, George had arranged for Amelia to dash off the last chapter, "Across The Atlantic—Solo," after she landed and for the book to go on sale throughout the United States within weeks of her return.

She filled Lucy in on her job, which was primarily to keep Amelia organized and run interference for her. She didn't expect Lucy to write letters for her as Nora had done; someone else came in to do that. Lucy's first task was to unpack and arrange the family books, still in boxes, that Amy had sent down at Amelia's request. Books were put everywhere, particularly in each guestroom; even George occasionally pitched in and helped.

Lucy was in the house a full week before Amelia told her about the proposed flight. Late Friday evening, while she was eating a grapefruit, Amelia told her her plan. Lucy watched for the pace of life to change, to quicken, but it didn't. The next morning Amelia went off to Teterboro, New Jersey, to fly while Lucy raked and burned leaves; she was back in time for lunch. Several people came for dinner; several stayed overnight. Sunday morning Amelia and George burned leaves. At teatime Amelia's friend, *World Telegram* reporter Carl Allen arrived with his wife.

Amelia spent Monday and Wednesday at Teterboro, flying the Vega, but she returned well before dinner. The other days she spent in New York and at her desk working over her Ninety-Nines list with Lucy. (The organization now numbered more than 275 members.) There was no hanging around the airport for her.

Amelia did fly on Saturday, but on Sunday, May 1, a gray, rainy day, she went with George and Lucy to dig up plants at "the old Day garden" for later replanting in their own garden.

Amelia appeared so carefree both because she and George had already made all the plans with great care and intelligence and because she was a naturally tranquil, calm person. The seeming inattention and lack of focus was a screen; the flight was being planned down to the last detail. The key to the master plan, the most important part of the puzzle, was to choose the right adviser.

Amelia and George chose well when they chose the laconic Norwegian Bernt Balchen. In 1928, when Charles Levine had hired Clarence Chamberlin to pilot his Bellanca to Germany (the flight that made Chamberlin famous; it was the second plane to span the Atlantic after Lindbergh), Clarence had turned to Bernt to prepare his charts and flight plan. Bernt was also a pilot—it was he who had bellyflopped Byrd's *America* in the sea off the coast of France so superbly that no one had been injured.

Bernt was not only a fine flier and a seasoned navigator but an engineer as well. The modifications he made to Amelia's Vega were basic, well thought out, and effective. He took no shortcuts, made no unnecessary changes, and didn't shave the safety margin too close, as Chamberlin had done when, to save weight, he installed the too-fragile landing gear that contributed to Ruth Nichols's crash. To increase the Vega's range, he and Eddie Gorski, chief mechanic and former maintenance supervisor for Fokker, who lived near the field where he had worked before, ran braces from one side of the fuselage to the other to strengthen it, replaced the upholstered wicker passenger seats in the cabin with fuel tanks, and added smaller fuel tanks in the wings. In its original configuration, the Vega had two wing tanks and could carry a total of a hundred gallons. When the retrofitting was complete, the Vega had eight gas tanks that could hold a total of 420 gallons—enough to give it a cruising range of 3,200 miles—and a new 500-horsepower supercharged Pratt and Whitney Wasp D engine S/n 3812, ordered from the East Hartford plant. Bernt added a drift indicator, an aperiodic compass, a magnetic compass, and a directional gyro. Then the tests began. Bernt and Eddie would load the plane with sandbags to simulate the weight of the fuel Amelia would be carrying, then fly around over the Meadowlands, checking out the plane "for hours on end," recalled Eddie. Then, because they could not land with all that weight, Bernt would fly around in circles while Eddie pushed the bags out. "People thought we were dropping bombs," remembered Eddie.

• • • •

Bernt, consulting with Major Edwin Aldrin, another flier at Teterboro, decided that Stanavo gasoline and oil should be used, so Stanavo fuel was sent to up to New Brunswick, where the plane would land first, and to Harbor Grace, Newfoundland, Amelia's jumping-off point for the transatlantic flight. There would be a landing in New Brunswick because Eddie Gorski and Bernt would be traveling with Amelia, but with their added weight the Vega couldn't carry enough gasoline to make Newfoundland: Eddie was going along to make sure the plane was perfectly serviced, thereby lessening the chances of a mechanical problem over the ocean; Bernt's mission was to pilot the plane to Harbor Grace so that Amelia could rest and be fresh when she started, but also to help deal with an emergency, if one arose.

Bernt and Eddie both lived near Teterboro, so the long hours were easy for them. Bernt was also a friend—the person who had set George on the trail that led to Amelia in the first place—set George in motion as it were, for it was he who had told George about the *Friendship* on that epochal day they had both ridden the Staten Island ferry.

The second consideration was to keep Amelia's life as normal as possible so that she would not be subjected to the intolerable pressures that inevitably fractured concentration and drained energy. That meant total secrecy—no one, not even family, not even her mother was to be told, as had been true as well of the *Friendship* flight. That part was easy—Amelia simply wrote Amy a chatty letter and enclosed pictures of the house and the garden, as it looked then. But making sure there were no reporters hanging around pushing her for details about flight plans; no photographers running over fuel lines and bothering her, as there had been for Ruth Nichols, who had been besieged by the press at the Jersey City airport and overwhelmed with a spate of fan mail; no questions about when and why and what for to disturb her thinking or trouble her sleep—that part was harder.

They resorted to the subterfuge that had worked so well with the *Friendship* flight—they let everyone believe the plane was part of someone else's expedition. It was widely known that Bernt was working with Lincoln Ellsworth on his upcoming South Pole flight, so they chartered Amelia's Vega to Bernt and let everyone assume that he was testing and changing and modifying it with the intention of using it in the Antarctic. It wasn't a big yawn, but at least there were no reporters circling.

With perfect trust in Bernt, Amelia had no need to watch as the fuselage was modified, the controls checked and rechecked, and the instruments installed, tested, and calibrated. She left everything in his hands. She had one major task; to learn to fly blind, so that if fog closed in, she would not lose her course. It was a task that demanded concentration but not exhaustive hours. Nor did she have to spend time gathering weather data. George was working with James Kimball, still the meteorologist upon whom ocean fliers relied.

Nor did she, now in command of her transatlantic flight, make any postflight plans at all. There would be no Hilton Railey trip to Europe as there had been for *Friendship* and for Ruth Nichols the year before; there were no plans, even, for George to meet her abroad. So there was no pressure on that score. Her eyes were focused only on the prize.

Bernt and she worked out the route. He came over to Rye one evening for dinner, and they worked over the maps and charts. He found the house full of the flowers Amelia and Lucy had picked that morning.

On Wednesday, May 11, two fine fliers, the Scots aviator James Mollison and the English aviatrix Amy Johnson, who had just become engaged, announced that they were going to attempt to fly the Atlantic. Two days later, on Friday the thirteenth, Lou Reichers took off from Harbor Grace bound for Paris—he too was on the Lindbergh trail. He was flying a Lockheed Altair, a newer, faster plane than Amelia's, with a powerful 625-horsepower Wright Cyclone engine. An ex-army flier, he was bankrolled by physical fitness multimillionaire Bernard Macfadden, who had promised him a ten-thousand-dollar bonus if he could cut Lindbergh's time in half. Lou planned to fly the Atlantic in daylight, which had never been done before. He left Newark airport shortly after midnight, reached Harbor Grace a little after six A.M., refueled, and took off. It was a bad plan. He had been tired before he started. He rationed himself to a big swallow of hot coffee every half hour and tried to navigate. By the time he figured he should be over the Irish coast, night was falling, it was raining, his thirsty engine was getting low on gas, and all he could see was water. When he spotted a ship, the SS *President Roosevelt*, he frantically blinked an SOS with his navigation lights and bellyflopped his plane near it, totally out of fuel. The plane hit the water so hard that those on the ship said it sounded like the firing of a gun; Reichers's head was thrown forward onto the cowling with such force, his nose was broken, his face lacerated, and he was knocked unconscious. He came to as the lifeboat from the ocean liner was taking him off his plane; he was treated by the ship's doctor and put to bed, where he stayed two days.

On Sunday evening Ruth Nichols came for dinner. She and Amelia discussed the various problems that ocean flying presented—in a general way—but Amelia was vague about her own plans, although friendly and helpful. Ruth was always looking for support and help and good ideas, and it didn't occur to her that Amelia wasn't too, but Amelia, made of sterner stuff, was looking for none of those things. Ruth described the modifications just being completed on *her* Vega, and particularly the safety factors that had been added, sure that Amelia was focused on safety considerations as she was, but Amelia was confident that she and Bernt had thought of everything. She just didn't think in terms of negatives. "I don't bother to go into all the possible accidents that might happen," Ruth remembered her saying. Amelia didn't even pack a parachute, figuring it wasn't worth the weight. Nor did she query Ruth about the St. John's airfield, the field where Ruth had crashed into the cliff, Amelia's first destination now—so supremely confident was she that Bernt was right and that the problem had been Ruth and her plane. And yet Amelia had to have been more than just a little curious. She dissembled, giving Ruth the impression that *if* she was planning an ocean flight, it certainly wasn't imminent—there was no need for Ruth to rush her preparations. And anyway, Ruth told their mutual friend Carl Allen, her impression was that *if* Amelia took off on a solo flight, it would be "across the South Atlantic."

It wasn't that Amelia was ultrasecretive, it was just that she was competitive and wanted to get off first. Actually, the only thing holding her back was the weather. A front was passing, according to Dr. Kimball: "Not to go *just* yet," wrote Lucy.

On Tuesday a Fox MovieTone crew showed up at the field, so instead of flying she marked time by picking up a barograph in Newark and checking in with Doc Kimball. She headed back to Rye for dinner.

She took the next day off, driving out to Long Island for a ride in the new Goodyear blimp *Resolute.*

Lucy's diary entry for Thursday, May 19, 1932, begins, "Breakfast as usual, Mill to fly." However, it really wasn't "breakfast as usual" at all—it only seemed that way to Lucy because Amelia had been her usual calm self. They had all been counting down the days waiting for the right weather—and because, as everyone in the flying world knew, May 20—the next day—was the fifth anniversary of Charles Lindbergh's flight. If Amelia were to take off for Europe exactly five years to the day after Charles had, which was her intention and which would add immeasurably to the excitement and significance of her flight, she had to get to Harbor Grace by Friday. That meant that the dawn of the nineteenth was the dawn of the last day Amelia could start out from Teterboro. They—Amelia, George, Bernt, and Eddie Gorski—all knew that if the weather gave a promise, even a hint of breaking, it would be D-day. And that morning dawned with a clearing sky, a northwest wind, and temperature in the low sixties. The weather would have been foremost in Amelia's mind.

But Lucy was unaware of the significance of May 20 as a starting date, and lulled by Amelia's ordinary manner into assuming that if she went out to Teterboro with Amelia, it would be just another day of flying for Amelia and waiting around for herself, Lucy decided to stay home, do "bits and pieces," and lunch with a friend. To her misfortune: upon returning from lunch, she found that Amelia had returned briefly to the house and left her a cryptic note—"Came to fetch you." A bit later George called to tell Lucy that Amelia had taken off from Teterboro at three fifteen.

In fact Amelia had returned to Rye not just to "fetch" Lucy, as she so considerately wrote her friend, but to don her jodhpurs and yellow silk blouse and retrieve her windbreaker, her flying suit, and some miscellaneous maps and charts.

Twenty minutes after Amelia returned to Teterboro, the trio were airborne. With Bernt at the controls, Amelia, in the fuselage with Eddie Gorski, tried to rest. Bernt flew for three and a half hours, arrived at St. John's at dusk, and landed without incident; the airport where Ruth Nichols had cracked up held no surprises for them. They stayed the night, took off the next morning, and arrived at Harbor Grace at 2:01 Atlantic Time (one and a half hours later than Eastern). Bernt again did all the flying so that Amelia could save her strength.

The airfield at Harbor Grace, running east-west, lay between the town and Conception Bay to the southeast and Lady Lake to the north. Fred Koehler from Stinson Aircraft, sent looking for a place to put an airfield for transatlantic flights, had spotted the location in 1927 and talked the townspeople into building the field. It was a high natural plateau, a natural elongated plain, four thousand feet long, two hundred feet wide, with a stone and gravel surface, a dream field. Best of all, there was a hill at its eastern (starting) end that made the field slope downward for half its length, which greatly helped the heavily loaded transatlantic planes gather speed as they took off. It was here that Mabel Boll and the *Columbia* had waited four years before.

Immediately upon their arrival in Harbor Grace, Amelia was taken into town to the customs and immigration offices. Then she and Bernt went over the latest weather information from George: the outlook was not perfect, but it was "promising." On the assumption that she would take off at dusk, Amelia went to Archibald's Hotel and took a nap while Eddie and Bernt supervised the servicing of the Vega. Several hours later she returned to the field.

In the meantime more telegrams arrived from George, giving them Kimball's final weather forecast, based on reports from weather stations in the United States, from some forty vessels scattered from Iceland and

Greenland, from Labrador and Baffin Land, from England, France, and Germany. It all pointed to not perfect but reasonably good weather. Amelia made the final, irrevocable decision to go.

Twenty-four miles away at Holyrood, Captain Christensen, the skipper of the greatest plane in the world, the Do-X, had planned to precede Amelia and help her by flashing wireless weather reports of the weather she would encounter, made the opposite decision and stayed on the ground, waiting for better weather.

Amelia appeared very calm. The AP reporter Bill Parsons, watching her as she returned to the airfield, wrote that "there seemed to be an aura surrounding her. Even though everyone wanted to get as close to her as possible, to shake hands, to wish her well, to touch her, she was very patient, and showed no signs of anxiety or fear." Her confidence was so palpable, "it just oozed."

Was she really as cool as everyone thought? She was, for she suddenly remembered she had forgotten to pass on to someone else a job she had had no time for, and now she tended to it. At 6:11 she sent a telegram to Louise Thaden:

> WESTERN FLYING WANTS FIVE HUNDRED WORDS ON NINETY NINES
> STOP PLEASE COVER PURPOSES FORM OF ORGANIZATION ACTIVITIES
> MEMBERSHIP REQUIREMENTS OFFICERS NAMES STOP THINK OPPOR-
> TUNITY TO STRESS OLDEST BROADEST PILOT CLUB ALSO IMPORTANT
> TO MENTION PREPAREDNESS COMMITTEE CAN COVER SAME GROUND
> STRICTLY MILITARY GROUPS STOP SEND TO RANDALL IRWIN MANAGING
> EDITOR
>
> AMELIA EARHART

Five hours and thirty minutes after landing at Harbor Grace, one hour and nine minutes after sending off the telegram, carrying with her some canned tomato juice and a thermos of Rose Archibald's soup, Amelia climbed into her Vega. Bill Parsons snapped some final pictures, and when he pleaded for "just one more," she paused obligingly and smiled. Then she settled herself down into the Vega, gunned the engine, and waved good-bye to Eddie and Bernt and the small watching crowd. The chocks were removed, and she roared off down the field.

The plane gathered speed nicely as it roared down the field and took off into the southwest wind. Then it climbed into the twilight sky, made a wide turn over Lady Lake and out across the town and the blue waters of Conception Bay, and disappeared. Weather reports indicated that there was a storm to the south of her proposed course but nothing serious between her and France.

Amelia was now on the Lindbergh trail, her destination Paris. "They gave me clearance papers, and I filled a blank space saying I was going to Paris," the AP reporter quoted her as saying. It would have been a nice touch, exactly five years after Lindbergh, to land, as he had, at Le Bourget.

It was such a clear evening that from an altitude of twelve thousand feet, Amelia could see icebergs and a fishing boat on the water's surface. One hour out, as clouds began to scud over the waves, the altimeter failed, but the visibility was still good; the moon came out, and the stars, so she had time to adjust to the fact that she would have to rely on her eyes to see how far above the sea she was flying. After three hours she smelled burning oil and, looking out, saw that a small blue flame was licking through a broken weld in the manifold ring where the hot exhaust gases from the cylinders went. It was worrisome: weighing the alternatives, she decided it was safer to continue than to turn back, try to find the unlit Harbor Grace field, and land there still carrying a heavy load of gasoline.

There was a cold front over the North Atlantic. As she continued flying, the weather began to deteriorate; she ran into a storm that, according to Kimball, should have been to the south. Ahead she saw black cumulus clouds that extended from the ocean to "very very high"—too high to fly over. Four hours out she plunged into the black clouds, found herself in a rainstorm, then saw that the rain on the windshield was turning to ice—and then felt the ice as the controls froze and the Vega went into a spin: "How long we spun I do not know. I do know that I tried my best to do exactly what one should do with a spinning plane, and regained flying control as the warmth of the lower altitude melted the ice." She skirted "too close for comfort" to the whitecaps. Twice more she ventured higher, only to encounter ice; twice more she came down and flew just above the breaking waves, which she could not always see. She was using the fuel mixture control and the carburetor to give herself some sense of altitude. It gave her her lowest low-level limit—warning engine sputters—but it was a delicate process requiring maximum concentration, staying high enough to require a little leaning of the engine to get it to operate properly. (When Ben Howard, another fine pilot, heard about it later, he said, "I thought, doggone it, I don't know many pilots—that is many men pilots—who would have sense enough to do that, let alone a gal.") As dawn broke, she found herself between two layers of clouds, then eventually climbing, flying in brilliant sunlight on top of white clouds that looked like endless snowfields.

More hours out, she turned on some of the reserve tanks of gasoline, only to find that a cockpit fuel gauge was defective; gasoline started trickling down the side of her neck.

At two in the afternoon the American ambassador to France, accompanied by most of the staff of the U.S. embassy, arrived at Le Bourget to wait for Amelia.

Charles Lindbergh had had a twenty-five-mile-an-hour following wind pushing him along; but as the day progressed, Amelia did not. What had been a light southerly breeze turned into a strong southwest wind. And it was turning against her.

Again she came down to sea level, and this time saw a small fishing boat; she realized by its size that she was near land. Continuing, she saw two more boats. She had been flying a fixed-compass course all night—not the harder-to-plot-but-shorter great circle course—but because she had run into a storm and Kimball's weather reports had shown a storm to the south of her route, she worried that she, not the storm, was off course. The thought that she had drifted south was reinforced now when she saw by the waves that the wind had come around to the northwest. Concerned about the manifold, concerned about the defective fuel gauge, concerned that the engine was beginning to sound rough, and lastly uncertain about her exact location, she gave up hope of France and turned her thoughts to Ireland. She flew over a rocky island (probably one of the Aran Islands) and found herself over Ireland; started south but didn't like the look of the sky ahead; turned north, picked up a set of railroad tracks, followed them north away from the storm, and landed in a pasture. She had reached Culmore, outside of Londonderry, in northwestern Ireland. She had made landfall exactly on the course Bernt Balchen had set for her, a little north of the center of Ireland.

"Tell my friends in New York I am very glad to have come across successfully but I am sorry I didn't make France," she said cheerfully in her first statement. Nobody really cared. They were just glad she was safe and sound.

She was the first person to cross the Atlantic twice in an airplane.

She had landed on James Gallagher's farm hard by his cottage at 1:46 P.M. British time. She explained who she was to the startled farmers, then went into Londonderry to telephone. She also called the airport at Croydon outside London, thinking she might fly there. But the Croydon officials advised against it.

So, refusing all offers of hospitality from the townspeople, she calmly returned to Gallagher's thatched cottage to be near her plane, accepted the Gallaghers' offer to spend the night with them, went to the room they gave her, and fell asleep.

The next day, after posing with the Vega, Paramount News flew her to London. The American ambassador, Andrew Mellon, was waiting in the clubhouse at Hanworth air park in Middlesex in a thunderstorm. He brought her to London, and she spent the night at the U.S. embassy.

And the world lined up to sing her praises. She had become the most famous, most celebrated woman in the world. Wrote American columnist Walter Trumball, "So now Charles Lindbergh and you are the only two who have ever flown the ocean alone, and the championship, as John L. Sullivan would say, remains in America." The English felt the same: "Her glory sheds its lustre on all womanhood," trumpeted *The Sunday Express*. When she returned to America, she would learn that the new theater in Radio City, the glitziest new movie theater in Manhattan, had incorporated her feat in the glass mural they commissioned to decorate the lobby.

She did her best to defuse the adulation with humor. In her first radio speech she said that the rumors that she had killed a cow upon landing were false "unless one had died of fright." A while later she remarked, "When there is a traffic jam on Fifth avenue men always comment, 'Oh, it's a woman driving.' So I determined to show them."

For fear of disturbing her preflight focus, Amelia had made no postflight plans. That left her alone in England to deal with all the consequences of the flight. It was too much; George was anxiously awaiting her request that he join her, in the interim keeping himself busy lining up lucrative deals. (He would bring a line of hats and sport clothes picked out by Lucy with him on the *Olympic* for Amelia to endorse—she said no to the hats.) Finally she asked him to join her; he sailed for Cherbourg on the twenty-seventh.

By that time much had happened to her. She had visited the Prince of Wales at St. James's Palace at his invitation, and they had gotten along so famously that the prince kept her an extra fifteen minutes past her scheduled time—a very unusual occurrence that caused much comment and later led to press stories (untrue) that she had danced with the Prince of Wales; and she had received a telegram of congratulations from his father, the king. Her plane was on display on the ground floor of Selfridge's department store in London, drawing thousands. She had been entertained at the House of Commons, taken by Lady Astor to Epson Downs to see the derby, been "towed" to meet George Bernard Shaw, and had given so many speeches that her voice was down to a whisper.

She was wearing clothes from Selfridge's at the urging of Gordon Selfridge, a pilot himself and the brother of Violette de Sibour. It was the easy way out; she had brought no change of clothes with her and was wearing a dress loaned to her by Ailsa Mellon, the daughter of the American ambassador. Still, she had been a hard sell; she wasn't in the mood, according to Gordon Selfridge, even for the pleasure of having her plane displayed. She was uncomfortable with the quid pro quo of free clothes for free publicity for the department store. "My first impression of Amelia," he recalled, "was a sort of comical paradox. She was determined she wouldn't select any clothes just to get herself, easily, on the front pages. But she submitted."

By Wednesday she had finished the final chapter, "Across the Atlantic—Solo." In a special pocket inside the back cover, George included a recording of her speech upon landing in John Gallagher's field; *The Fun of It* was on sale within weeks of her return to the United States.

Because her original destination had been Le Bourget and so many preparations had been made for her there, Amelia felt that it was only right that she visit France before returning home. She made the Channel crossing on aircraft manufacturer C. R. Fairey's yacht *Evadne,* met up with George in Cherbourg harbor, and then they both went to Paris. There the crowds were, if anything, more enthusiastic than in England. She was awarded the Cross of the Knight of the Legion of Honor by the minister of air, Paul Painlevé, who had awarded the same medal to Lindbergh five years before. "And now I have the honor to bestow this cross upon the Colonel's charming image," he was quoted as saying, to which she replied dryly, "I can find no words to express my appreciation." She was received by the French Senate and dined with Lady Mendl at her Villa Trianon, which had just been wired for sound by Douglas Fairbanks.

From Paris they went to Rome upon the invitation of Mussolini, and then to Brussels, where the king and queen of Belgium asked them to dine. (The queen pulled out a camera and snapped *her* picture; King Albert awarded Amelia the Cross of the Chevalier of the Order of Leopold.) They sailed for home on June 15 on the *Ile de France.*

The United States continued the unprecedented shower of honors. The National Geographic Society awarded her the special gold medal they had given Charles Lindbergh five years earlier. The award, made in Constitution Hall, the auditorium of the Daughters of the American Revolution, by President Hoover, was the first the society had ever bestowed on a woman. More than ten thousand requests for tickets to the 3,800-seat auditorium were received. If a bomb had gone off, the government of the United States would have ground to a halt, for present was the president; the chief justice of the Supreme Court and his wife; the secretaries of state, treasury, and commerce; the attorney general; the postmaster general; enough members of Congress to form a quorum of each House; high officers of the army, navy and marines; and diplomats from twenty-two countries. The president of the society spoke, followed by the president of the United States, followed by Amelia. She limited herself to an account of the flight, straying only to say in closing that although her flight had added nothing to aviation, still she hoped that the flight had meant something to the women in aviation. "If it has, I shall feel it was justified."

She had entered a realm beyond stardom.

• • • •

That summer Amelia wrote a piece for a magazine that probably came closest to expressing her feelings on the whys and wherefores of the flight:

> Have you ever longed to go to the North Pole? or smell overripe apples in the sunshine? or coast down a steep, snow-covered hill to an unknown valley? or take a job behind a counter selling ribbons, and show people how to sell ribbons as ribbons have never been sold before? or take a friend by the arm and say, "Forget it—I'm with you forever?" or, just before a thunderstorm, to turn ten somersaults on the lawn?

The year before, the American Woman's Association had given its first annual award to Margaret Sanger as the woman who had made the most outstanding contribution to society. Now, in the fall of 1932, at a dinner arranged by the Women's Press Club in which forty women's organizations took part, Amelia became the second recipient. The award was made by Dr. Lillian Gilbreth, the industrial psychologist whose picture, sitting in the huge touring car surrounded by her husband and their eleven children, was one of those Amelia had neatly pasted in her scrapbook of women achievers all those years before. Now she had the pleasure of hearing Dr. Gilbreth say, "Miss Earhart has shown us that all God's chillun got wings."

15

Having Her Cake

•••• Up until she took off on her transatlantic solo flight, Amelia seems to have been content and happy with George. When not traveling, their routine was to spend the work week in New York City at the Seymour Hotel and go to the country on weekends. There were usually people around, but Amelia and George enjoyed puttering around their home alone together. Lucy's diary chronicles plenty of quiet times, hours spent together working in the garden, relaxing, and working over flight plans.

But after the Atlantic solo there was a change in Amelia. She began looking beyond George.

Literally the moment he received word she had safely landed in Ireland, George went to work setting up licensing deals for clothes manufacturers to cash in on her fame—he gave a lunch for clothes manufacturers, visited clothes designers, and had Lucy picking out hats at Farrington and Evans, visiting an agent for sports clothes, and trying on jodhpurs prior to choosing a maker. He and Lucy were very busy on the project, which Amelia must have agreed to before she took off, and he was also negotiating a very important deal for himself at Paramount Studios. And then Amelia asked him to drop everything and come to Europe and help her deal with the world. He did. Lucy helped him pack, and he was off by boat to France on May 27. "I thought I couldn't face coming home alone," Amelia wrote her mother. Several weeks later they returned on the *Ile de France*; while they were on the high seas George's appointment as chairman of the editorial board of Paramount Pictures was announced. He had managed to fit everything together—his life and hers.

He was so proud to be with her. He later recounted how he had given Amelia a twenty-dollar bill at Teterboro just before she, Bernt, and Eddie took off for Newfoundland. "Generous allowance for a trip to Europe," she had teased him. She used it to pay for the telegram she sent upon landing in Londonderry. Then she went to the trouble of retrieving the bill, which necessitated borrowing English pounds from someone with which to replace it. She signed the retrieved twenty-dollar bill and gave it back to George. It became one of George's "most treasured" souvenirs. It is hard to reconcile this gesture of Amelia's with anything that went before. By retrieving it, Amelia shows she knew how epochal her flight was, how significant and valuable that twenty-dollar bill was, or she wouldn't have thought of doing it—and then signing it.

No one realized more than Amelia that her piloting skills had not been proven by the *Friendship* flight and that her celebrity status was based not on achievement but on the lucky accident of having been in the right place at the right time. Now she had changed all that. She had earned her spurs. Now she knew she would go into the record books—knew that she was a celebrity.

She was on such a high because she had learned something: she had a gift. She didn't get sleepy on long-distance flights; she had incredible built-in endurance. Realizing her gift, she now concentrated on breaking long-distance records. She began right away; she decided to try to be the first woman to fly nonstop across America. Because she neither smoked nor drank, the parties and social life, the constant round of people, had not tired her: she was as ready as ever.

Transcontinental record flights at that time originated on the West Coast because of the prevailing winds: that meant she had to start out from Los Angeles. She wanted to do it as soon as possible. It was July 1, and even though she had been traveling and partying for a month, and had returned home only on June 20, she was in top form. And since everyone wanted to do what she wanted, everyone changed their plans: George rearranged his schedule so he could go west with her; Lucy, about to go to Ohio to visit Katch and Bill Pollock, instead prevailed upon them to come and stay and keep her company at Locust Avenue to deal with all the things happening there. Ten days after her return to America, on July 1, Amelia, George, and his son David flew to Los Angeles. She hoped to beat Frank Hawks's record of 17 hours 38 minutes, coast to coast.

On July 10 she took off from Los Angeles, had good following winds, and was making very good speed, but she then had fuel feed trouble and was forced to land in Columbus, Ohio. She was on the ground for an hour and a quarter before it was fixed, but still she landed in Newark 19 hours, 14 minutes after she started. The time was good enough to establish a new women's transcontinental speed record—she beat Ruth Nichols's record by almost ten hours, and since her flight time was 17 hours 59 minutes, she had flown almost as fast as Hawks. She went home to Rye disappointed.

Because Amelia was scheduled to be back out in L.A. later in July for the opening of the Olympic games, where she would be awarded the Distinguished Service Cross by Vice President Charles Curtis, George decided to stay on the West Coast until she returned and begin his new job at Paramount. It was a serious error, as it would turn out.

• • • •

It was a fact of their life that Amelia was constantly surrounded by men. George was used to it. She had a particular ability to make men take her seriously without making them feel threatened. And that attracted them. She didn't divide the world up by sex, as most women did in the 1930s, treating women friends one way and men friends another. She took and gave advice and help where she found it. Thus she had gone to men—Carl Allen and Deacon Lyman—for an opinion on her impending marriage.

As she became involved with men in joint ventures, they became her friends—which meant, perforce, they became George's friends, too. But one case was different: her deepening relationship with Gene Vidal, the handsome son-in-law of the powerful blind senator from Tennessee, Thomas Gore. Gene was special. He had everything: looks—blue eyes, a handsome face, a powerful spare build, abundant dark hair, a winsome smile—plus intelligence, character, and incredible athletic ability. He had gone to the University of South Dakota on an athletic scholarship, earned varsity letters in football, baseball, basketball, and track, and still managed to graduate first in his class with a degree in civil engineering. At West Point his athletic prowess was the stuff of legend: he was captain of the football team, drop-kicked a forty-seven-yard field goal to win a fiercely contested game against Notre Dame, made the winning touchdown against Navy in 1916, was the star of the basketball team, and won the award for being the best all-around athlete—coming in first in the discus, high jump, broad jump, and hammer throw. Following graduation, Gene served in the Corps of Engineers, then in the Air Service, and then became West Point's first flying instructor. While in the army he was named to the 1920 U.S. Olympic team, placed both in the pentathlon and the decathlon, played on the rugby team as well, then went on to coach the U.S. pentathlon team in 1924. He was by far the brightest star of his era.

Gene's marriage to Nina Gore in 1922 had been a glittering affair attended by most of official and social Washington. In 1925 their son, Gore, was born, but before the 1920s were over, their marriage was on the rocks. The Vidals lived with the Gores in their large Rock Creek house. Living with one's in-laws is never a menu for happiness, and it wasn't in this case, although the circumstances were unusual—it was Nina rather than Gene who disliked it most. The senator and his wife began to share the parenting of Gore with Gene, for their daughter was a fun-loving, party-going socialite who drank too much and, as even her parents could not help observing, was a neglectful mother at best. Gene, bright and charming, was not interested in the endless round of parties, nor particularly interested in making money. He was in love with flying and wanted to be with people who, like himself, were in love with flying. That left arguably the most attractive man in Washington free to go where he pleased, and where he pleased was where Amelia was. He would appear alone or with Gore in Rye on countless weekends: the Putnam house in Rye became his home away from home. Nina divorced him in 1935. (By that time they had drifted so far apart that he learned from reporters that she was on her way to Reno.) Her attentions had shifted to Hugh D. Auchincloss, who possessed an abundance of money and a love of parties; they would marry that same year. Gene was, if anything, relieved.

• • • •

Gene and Amelia had worked together at TAT, and then when Gene organized the Ludington line, he had persuaded her to become vice-president. There, thrown together even more, she had a chance to see the hard-working, resourceful, and efficient Gene in action. He and Paul Collins, shouldering most of the administrative duties, and Amelia, capably performing hers, made it almost immediately the most efficient and popular airline in the country, with the result that in the first year of operation, it showed a profit of over $8,000—something unheard of in the industry. The Ludington line was so efficient, it flew passengers for twenty-five cents a mile, while it cost Eastern Air Transport, which also flew the lucrative Washington–New York route, eighty-nine cents a mile. Nevertheless Postmaster General Brown, the czar in such matters, operating on the idea that competition was bad rather than good, awarded Eastern Air Transport the U.S. mail contract for the route, knowing that without the contract, Ludington could not survive. Their backs to the wall, the Ludington brothers sold out to Eastern in February 1933. But a small victory for Amelia, Gene Vidal, and Paul Collins, all of whom quit, as well as for the Ludingtons, was that the ensuing outcry against Brown triggered a government investigation of his high-handed, arbitrary policies, which resulted in Brown's public disgrace and resignation. The battle created a bond between Amelia, Paul, and Gene.

Gene and Amelia were powerfully attracted to each other. Gene was a fine pilot and a fine athlete; he possessed superb hand-eye coordination, and excellent reflexes—qualities particularly necessary for pilots of the early planes: "When you see a pilot dance you can tell if he or she is a good pilot. A good pilot will betray the rhythmic coordination of the good dancer, that unconscious balance and freedom of motion," Amelia and other good fliers discovered. George was a rugged outdoorsman but not well coordinated, not a natural athlete.

Now Gene would visit Rye whether George was present or not, and when Amelia returned east alone after her transcontinental solo, she immediately invited Jack Gillies, a pilot friend, and Gene to Rye. She was glowing, so transformed from the Amelia of old that her cousin Katch, companionably house-sitting with Lucy, was "perfectly astonished" at the change in her. She had blossomed, saw Katch; "she looked so lovely, tall, and slender, in shiny silk pants and long jacket." On Sunday after Jack Gillies left, she and Gene drove off by themselves to a dinner party, leaving her cousins behind.

Gene was due back the following afternoon. There was Ninety-Nines business to attend to, and no matter what her personal activities, Amelia always kept on top of it, so that Saturday morning, July 23, 1932, she had her secretary come over and she wrote all the governors to remind them that they had to have their membership lists up-to-date and correct. That done, she tended to Gene. He was no ordinary guest, to arrive by train and be picked up at the station—Amelia drove into New York City to pick him up.

Soon afterward Amelia was due out in Los Angeles again, where George and David were patiently waiting for her. This time Lucy and Gene were flying out too. By the time they arrived, Lucy had a crush on the dashing Gene, and after he took her to the Brown Derby for dinner, then for a drive to Santa Monica where they sat by the sea, Lucy was in love. Soon she was huddled by the phone waiting for his call: the waiting went on for days. Finally Lucy "found Gene who explained last night poorly." When she "found Gene," he was with Amelia, and he departed with Amelia for the Olympic stadium, leaving Lucy behind stamping letters. Lucy did not confide any further anguish to her diary—it was not her style—but it seems obvious that although Gene was Amelia's, they had been so circumspect that it took Lucy a bit of time to get the message. It was all very civilized, and nothing broke the mirror surface of Lucy's friendship with Amelia, then or ever. Like Amelia, Lucy was emotionally strong. Her diary from then on is an unbroken impersonal record of events.

• • • •

After a few weeks of watching the Olympics from Douglas Fairbanks's box, hobnobbing with Hollywood celebrities, and being squired around by Gene as well as by George, all dutifully noted by Lucy, Amelia, undeterred by all the distractions, was ready to span the continent again.

On August 24, at 12:26 P.M., with a minimum of fuss, after downing a bowl of soup, and packing away hard-boiled eggs, cocoa prepared by Lucy, and some tomato juice, her old standby, after posing for the waiting Paramount photographers, after getting the green light from Standard Oil that the tanks were topped off, Amelia took off from the Los Angeles municipal airport. She set down in Newark, New Jersey, 19 hours, 7 minutes, and 56 seconds later, with another record under her belt: first woman to fly nonstop coast to coast. She also broke the two-thousand-mile long-distance record that Ruth Nichols had set flying between Oakland, California, and Louisville, Kentucky.

"Perfect flight, no stops," she shouted to the mechanic, who climbed up to the cockpit and was the first person to greet her in Newark. Her gray eyes looked strained, naturally, but other than that she looked remarkably well and remarkably well dressed. Her hair blew in the breeze above a bronze and yellow silk scarf draped around her neck; her short-sleeved tan silk jersey shirt matched the color of her jodhpurs; she was smiling. No, she wasn't particularly tired, she said, just hot and thirsty.

This flight had been totally without incident, as stress free as such a journey could be, and only two minutes off the time she had estimated it would take. However, it wasn't particularly fast, which Amelia said was due to the lack of favoring winds. "If I'd had as good weather as I had before, I'd have broken all the records," she said. "But you might have to wait a thousand years for that." It was, in fact only seven minutes less than she had taken the first time, and 1 hour and 27 minutes longer than Frank Hawks had taken in *his* Vega. Realistically, she admitted that she didn't think she could better Hawks's time, "not in this plane." It wasn't her style to compete directly—to pursue head-to-head competition with men in any case. She had achieved her main goal, so she hung up her spurs knowing that the number of male pilots who had flown the country nonstop was few and that she had joined their number. It was just nine years since two army pilots, Lieutenant John A. Macready and Oakley G. Kelley, had spanned it nonstop for the first time, stunning the world and leading Major Henry "Hap" Arnold to say, "The impossible had happened." Now Amelia had done the impossible, too.

In mid-October 1932, back in Rye, Gene was visiting again. Paul Collins was also there (Amelia appeared Saturday, October 15, with both of them in tow), and Lucy notes, they had a grand old time, playing cards after dinner late into the night. The next day Lucy drove Paul and Gene to the train, and she noted in her diary, "George low." It was certainly understandable. It was also understandable that Lucy decided to throw in the towel: she quit and on October 19 sailed for Europe on the RMS *Berengaria*. Helen Weber, who had been performing many of the secretarial duties—while Lucy concentrated on flowers, Amelia's clothes, and the books—moved in to fill her place. It would be several months before Lucy returned.

• • • •

Amelia and Eleanor Roosevelt had first met at a curiously low point in the latter's life, the end of November 1932. The euphoria of Franklin Roosevelt's election to the presidency earlier that month had worn off, for Eleanor, within a matter of days, whereupon she fell into an acute state of depression, notes the historian Doris Kearns Goodwin, sure that her life would soon shrink to arranging and attending endless teas, luncheons, and receptions—that she would be, finally, trapped within the ceremonial side of government. Lorena Hickok, her closest friend, called the book she wrote about Eleanor *The Reluctant First Lady* because the last thing Eleanor wanted to do was perform the ceremonial duties required of a president's wife. She couldn't bear the thought of being just his appendage. She wanted to be out and active and accomplishing things, as she had always been, whether it was making speeches for Franklin while he recovered from polio, organizing the Women's Division of the Democratic Party with Mary Dewson, or teaching literature, drama, and American history to girls at the Todhunter School in New York as the governor's wife. She had always sought out and was happiest in the company of women who worked: she was not a social animal. "I think that every woman has a right to 'a life of her own,' " she started out an article for *Cosmopolitan* written just after Franklin was elected. Her closest friend was Lorena Hickok, arguably the brightest and certainly the most widely known female journalist in America. Her other women friends were also successful in their own right—gainfully occupied. Running a beautiful house, even if it *was* the White House, was Eleanor's idea of a nightmare. She was looking—desperately—for a role she could play that wouldn't be at cross-purposes either with her own beliefs and inclinations or with the demands of her husband.

Amelia and Eleanor had so much history in common: they both had alcoholic fathers, both had been largely brought up by grandparents. There were the physical similarities—imagined and real: they both believed themselves to be ugly ducklings, too tall, with bad teeth (Amelia had a gap between her two front teeth that she tried to hide), and bad legs, and both had unexpectedly long, graceful fingers. They had the same outlook, the same high sense of moral purpose that had led them both into social work, the same fierce need for independence, the same desire to open doors for women that would shortly lead Eleanor to institute weekly White House press conferences in the Treaty Room for women reporters only. (They would be limited to women in order to force editors to hire female reporters if they didn't already have any on their staff, but limited also because Eleanor thought she'd get better coverage if the stories were written by women. Both women were very practical feminists.) There was, as well, the shared dislike of ostentation and ceremony.

It was, significantly, Eleanor, not Franklin, who cabled congratulations to Amelia after her solo transatlantic flight, and it was to Eleanor that Amelia directed her brief reply: "Thank you very much for your message. . . . It was kind of you and Governor Roosevelt to think of sending it."

The two women met on November 20, 1932, just weeks after Franklin was elected president. Amelia was giving a routine talk and showing movies at the local public high school in Poughkeepsie, a half hour's drive from the Roosevelt home at Hyde Park. The newspaper notices of her lecture, billed as "Flying for Fun," mention that Amelia would show movies as well as talk. Nancy Astor, the lone female member of Parliament who had entertained Amelia in England, was spending the weekend with the Roosevelts. Before the publicized lecture, Amelia and George were invited to Hyde Park to dine with the Roosevelts and to renew old ties with the outspoken Nancy. Eleanor Roosevelt always had a special place in her heart for achieving women—and here was the superachiever who had flown the Atlantic. Eleanor went to the lecture and introduced her. By her remarks it was apparent that while other people may have admired *her,* there was no doubt whom Eleanor admired: "I hope to know Miss Earhart more and more but I never hope to admire her more than I do now. She has done so many things which I have always wanted to do."

At the Poughkeepsie lecture, Amelia described her solo transatlantic flight; ran movies of her incredible receptions in London, Paris, and Rome; and diplomatically praised Poughkeepsie hometown boy Lieutenant John Miller, who had beaten her across the continent in his autogiro. When she finished, she was given a standing ovation. Nancy Astor, never one to be left out, made some concluding remarks. Poughkeepsie and the Women's City and County Club got more than they had bargained for.

That had been the beginning of Amelia and Eleanor's friendship. Eleanor's introductory remarks had not been idle words. The life of a pilot spoke to her: the freedom, the mastery of the air, the aloneness. It appealed to Eleanor at this critical juncture in her life: she could learn to just fly away. She was a gutsy woman: she took her first airplane ride in 1930 at the age of forty-five, she rode a bobsled at the 1932 Winter Olympics, and as notations in the White House ushers' diaries show, she rode horseback virtually every morning in all the years she was in Washington. She was taught to shoot by the national guard a few years later and usually carried a pistol when she was by herself on car trips. Now she spoke of her desire to fly to Amelia. The timing was perfect—Amelia offered to be her instructor and arranged for the use of a plane at a secluded field and for her friend, Dr. Henry Templeton Smith, to give Eleanor the general physical examination, plus the eye color test, depth perception test, and the equilibrium test that were required for a student pilot permit. Eleanor passed, and the doctor signed her permit. Six weeks later, Eleanor enclosed the permit to her flying mentor, Amelia, with the notation "The question now comes as to whether I can induce my husband to let me take lessons. I will let you know if I am successful with him. I haven't had a chance even to talk to him about it." But when she did, the answer was no. Not that Franklin forbade her, of course, as she wrote Amelia later; their relationship was much too complicated for that "My husband convinced me that it was a waste of time to learn when I could not afford to buy a plane." And of course it was out of the question that she would ask him to ask his mother, who held the purse strings.

Eleanor gracefully—perhaps with a tiny sigh of relief—gave up the project, but she remained gamely air-minded. She once stated to reporters that she only took trains when her secretary accompanied her, so she could get work done: "But I always fly when I travel alone." And her admiration for Amelia continued to grow.

She put Amelia on the White House invitation list. She invited Amelia to a small luncheon with Frances Perkins, Franklin's new secretary of labor, the first woman appointed to a Cabinet-level job, shortly after the inauguration, then invited her and George for dinner and to spend the night, on the evening before Amelia's lecture to the Daughters of the American Revolution (DAR) on April 21, 1933. A few days before, Eleanor had been made honorary chairman of the United States Amateur Pilots Association. Now Amelia arranged for Eastern Airlines to loan her a plane—a Condor—and flight crew and after dinner, having waited to make sure the sky was clear and the stars brilliant, asked Eleanor if she wanted to taste the experience of night flying for the first time. She did. So not bothering to change, in their elegant satin evening dresses, fur coats, and white kid gloves, accompanied by several reporters, Eleanor's brother Hall, and George, they went up in the Condor. Amelia had the cabin lights turned out so that Eleanor could savor the full beauty of the night. Amelia spent a bit of time demonstrating that she could fly the plane, and Eleanor took a turn in the cockpit so that the captain could explain the controls to her.

They were all on a high after the flight, particularly Eleanor. When they got back to the White House, the new car Hall had driven east for his sister, washed and shining, was standing just beyond the portico. "Amelia, lets see how it rides!" Eleanor exclaimed, and they hopped in and took a spin before calling it a night.

The next day in her talk to the DAR, Amelia praised Eleanor's spirit: "The example set by the first lady of the land has done more to advance aviation among women, I think, than any other factor."

Eleanor thought so much of Amelia that she kept her poem "Courage Is the Price" in the desk drawer where she kept special items that gave her strength and inspiration. Later she would also keep a photograph of Amelia in her sitting room. Franklin, too, enjoyed Amelia's company, appreciated her fresh good looks, her sense of humor, her flying ability, and her intelligence, and didn't hold her project of teaching Eleanor how to fly against her. He thought highly enough of Amelia's input to grant her that most-highly-prized commodity in Washington, time with him whenever she requested it. He held her in such high esteem that she had but to ask Louis Howe, Franklin's liaison in the early years, for an appointment for the request to be immediately granted. For example on April 5 she sent a telegram to Howe, requesting a three minute interview with the president, "tomorrow, Thursday or Friday." It wasn't quite done on those days, but it *was* arranged for Wednesday, April 12, at 3:30 P.M.. At the time when Franklin was debating the merits of forming an umbrella organization (a department of transportation) to regulate rail travel, flying, roads, and the nation's waterways, he listened to what Amelia had to say on government regulation of flying and how the department could operate most efficiently—she thought an umbrella organization was a good idea.

• • • •

The Bendix race was without a doubt the most exciting annual event in American aviation—the Kentucky Derby of the air world. Two generations of fliers would struggle to win the Bendix, promoted by Clifford Henderson to spur pilots, plane designers, and manufacturers to ever-faster speeds in ever-more dependable machines. Held annually since 1931, it was a free-for-all cross-country race designed by Henderson to "force airplane designers, builders and pilots to really get down to business." It always ended at the airport where the National Air Races were held and served as its opening event. The race was named for Vincent Bendix, the tough, bright, high-profile inventor, pilot and head of Bendix Aviation, who each year donated half the cash prize, $15,000 (Henderson put up the other half), and the trophy. Ex-army pilot Jimmy Doolittle, the first person to make a landing flying blind (cockpit hooded over) won the first race in a Laird, flying the route from Los Angeles to Cleveland at an average speed of 223 miles an hour. In 1932 Captain James Haizlip, former air corps test pilot, flying a Wedell-Williams, flew the same course at 245 miles an hour.

The third year, 1933, Henderson suddenly decided that women could enter. June 30 was the race date and Henderson waited till the beginning of the month before announcing his decision. It wasn't nearly enough time to get a plane up to racing speed, nevertheless, Amelia thought it was important to enter, as did Ruth Nichols, even though both knew they couldn't win against the men who were flying planes equipped with engines twice as powerful as theirs that they had been fine-tuning for months. They were the only two women to enter.

After her solo flight Amelia had sold her plane, minus its engine, to the Franklin Institute in Philadelphia for $7,500 for exhibition in their new Hall of Aviation, presumably because she felt that it had seen its best days. Indeed, Clarence Belinn, an engineer whom she knew from TAT, who examined it sometime after her transatlantic and cross-country flights thought it was in dangerously bad shape. Dot Leh, another Ninety-Nines friend of hers, has suggested that as a replacement she buy the Vega that Elinor Smith had once owned, which Elinor had sold to William W. Harts, Jr., a few weeks after Amelia's transatlantic flight—not having any use for it after Amelia had bested her—which was languishing in dead storage at Floyd Bennett field on Long Island. Amelia had taken possession of the plane and its license number 965Y in April "hanging" into it her 500-horsepower Wasp engine, which was still in excellent shape. The plane was quite similar to her old one but in much better condition.

That year the Bendix was revamped and the direction reversed, for the National Air Races were being held at Mines field in Los Angeles. The start was from Floyd Bennett field. There Amelia, with George's aid, got ready for the transcontinental endurance contest. Ruth Nichols, even with Clarence Chamberlin helping her, had the bad luck of running into serious problems with her borrowed Vega. As a result she started a day late (with Henderson's permission) but the retractable landing gear kept giving her trouble, and it took her three days to complete the course. She was overlooked by the media; very few people even realized she was a contestant.

Amelia as usual drew a crowd—close to two thousand people gathered on the evening of June 30 at Floyd Bennett field to see her take off. It was planned for shortly before midnight, but at dusk a violent electrical storm suddenly rolled in, bringing with it pelting rain and powerful wind gusts. As it became obvious that her departure would have to be postponed, the numbers of onlookers dwindled, Amelia retired to a lounge at the airport and, as was her habit, quickly went to sleep. George was in his element, keeping everything organized, gathering the weather reports, bustling about. Some three hours later, when all the turbulence had blown out to sea, he woke her up, and at 3:50 A.M. she was the first contestant off, zooming down the long concrete runway in her Vega, leading a field of six. The men waited longer, more cautiously letting the weather settle down even further: a prudent move, rationalized the *New York Times* (male) reporter, because *their* ships "were faster and harder to control." Roscoe Turner was second off, over an hour later; followed by Lee Gehlbach, flying Haizlip's plane, which had won the Bendix the year before; followed by Russell Thaw, in a Gee Bee racer; followed by Russell Boardman in another Gee Bee.

Boardman had trouble taking off. His Gee Bee yawed, slipped off the runway and hurtled through the tall grass for a hundred feet before he finally got control and pulled it safely into the air. At Indianapolis, where he stopped for fuel, he was not so lucky. On takeoff, as he swept away at the end of the runway, having gained an altitude of about forty feet, the Gee Bee again went out of control, flipped over, and fell upside down to the earth. Boardman, pinned under the wreckage, suffered a fractured skull, a punctured lung, and a broken shoulder; he died the next day.

Thaw too had trouble at Indianapolis. His Gee Bee suddenly dropped a wing and ground-looped, damaging the plane to such an extent that he was forced to drop out of the race.

Gehlbach had problems with a clogged gas fuel line, and while making a forced landing at New Bethel, Indiana, he crashed through a fence in a field; he was not seriously injured, but he was out of the race.

Amelia, somewhere west of Wichita, Kansas, reported that her motor was heating up badly in the headwinds, causing her to make such poor time, she was "hopelessly" out of the race; as a result she decided to spend the night on the ground and not even try to make the deadline. She continued westward the next day and then had the misfortune to have the hatch cover of her plane blow open; she landed in Winslow, Arizona, to have it repaired. When she arrived at the Los Angeles municipal field (Mines field), it was at a peak moment of interest. The stands were jammed, for the Thompson trophy race, a fifty-mile free-for-all—probably the most exciting contest at the National Air Races—was in progress: Amelia couldn't land. She circled the field for half an hour until the race was over. Tired and frustrated as she was, she undoubtedly enjoyed the idea that all those thousands of people sitting in the stands had a chance to see her pretty red machine silhouetted against the canopy of blue, for by the time she landed, everyone knew she was up there. And even though she hadn't finished by the 6 P.M. Bendix deadline, everyone knew she, the first woman to dare fly in the Bendix, *had finished,* proving her particular toughness of character and her competence and by extension the "rightness" of allowing women to enter the race. She won an extra bonus—a two-thousand-dollar prize—for being the first woman to finish.

The winner, Roscoe Turner, also had had problems. Finding himself low on fuel after crossing the Alleghenies in darkness, he had had to make an unscheduled and therefore dangerous stop in Columbus, Ohio. The only pilot who had an uneventful flight was James Wedell, who came in twenty-eight minutes after Turner.

Amelia's calm demonstration of competence was lost in the furor created by a tragedy two days later. Florence Klingensmith, twenty-six, of Fargo, North Dakota, a fine flier with a solid competitive record in closed-course racing, the only woman entered in the hundred-mile Philips trophy race, had completed three-quarters of the race, was in the middle of the pack holding fourth place, and was leading four of the ablest men pilots of the country when the fabric of one wing of her Gee Bee gave way, and she crashed to her death.

Cliff Henderson, who had only grudgingly allowed women to compete in the Bendix and the National Air Races to start with, used Klingensmith's death as the excuse to reimpose the ban on women flying competitively. The idea being bruited about by misogynists (starting with him) was that Florence had died only because she lost her head; if Florence had *kept* her head, he asserted, she would have pulled up and bailed out. It was a patently absurd idea. Gee Bees were known to be dangerous planes. Florence's was the third Gee Bee to crash in three days, but no disparaging comments had been made about the men who crashed—Boardman, who died, and Thaw, who didn't. Nor, earlier, had anyone cast aspersions on the flying skills of Lowell Bayles, killed when his Gee Bee crashed in 1931, or on Jimmy Haizlip, whose Gee Bee's wings broke off, followed by both wheels, as he came in for a landing, throwing the plane end over end before it came to rest. Nevertheless Henderson was not to be denied: he wanted the women out of his hair, and he decreed that none would fly in the Bendix or in the National Air Races in 1934.

Within three days Amelia was again trying to better her long-distance Los Angeles-to-New York record. Typically, she told inquiring reporters that she had little hope of breaking her previous time. Then, taking off from Los Angeles and landing in Newark 17 hours and 7 minutes later, she did just that, flying 1 hour and 56 minutes better than she had done before and maintaining an average speed of 165 miles an hour. But she made two stops, having announced she would make none. The first, in Amarillo, Texas, was to fix the hatch, broken again, that she had been holding closed with her right hand for some seventy-five miles. The second, in Columbus, Ohio, was for gasoline. When she appeared finally at Newark, her white coveralls streaked with grease, she apologized for looking dirtier than usual. Compared to Roscoe Turner's time flying against the wind, her time was slow, but for a Vega driven by a 500-horsepower engine, it was very respectable indeed.

When she and George, who was at the airport waiting for her, walked to their car to go home, she got in on the driver's side, gunned the engine, and set off for home. She was still not sleepy.

• • • •

George had business in Europe and was pushing Amelia to go with him. She refused to go. "It is a business trip and I don't look forward to a stuffy ride over for a week there and a stuffy one back," she confided to her mother. George put off the trip in the face of her intransigence, hoping that later he could prevail upon her to change her mind.

But life was just too pleasant for Amelia in Rye. There was entirely too much going on. Lucy was there, Katch was visiting again—they would spend leisurely days swimming at the Manursing Island Club. Amelia took them all with her to dine at the palatial estate of Helen and Ogden Reid, owners of *The New York Herald Tribune,* in nearby Purchase, on Sunday evening. It was while they were there that they heard that Amy Mollison, England's star flier, and her husband James, overdue from England, had crash-landed in a marsh near Bridgeport, Connecticut. (Amelia had hoped to welcome them to New York upon their arrival, but instead saw them first in the Bridgeport hospital on her way to Boston the next day. She invited them to visit, which they did the following weekend, both still swathed in bandages. She took them to visit the Roosevelts in Hyde Park.)

Lucy went to visit friends in the Hamptons but had to return to Rye: "Call for help from Amelia. She picked me up and we drove out in time

for dinner. George arrived from Washington. He to go abroad next week."
The next afternoon Amelia left for Boston, to meet Paul Collins and Gene
Vidal. Was there a full-blown fight, or the threat of one, between Amelia
and George over Gene? Was Lucy summoned to be a buffer between them?
While Amelia was in Boston, Lucy and George dined alone. "We talked
on terrace" was all she told her diary.

The following day Amelia returned—with Gene and Paul.

• • • •

Later in the week Amelia was in New York generating publicity for the
Boston-Maine Airways, where David Binney Putnam had just started
working. She posed with David, who had been diamond-hunting in British Guiana, and his dead tarantula, on the occasion of his being hired by the
Boston-Maine Airways as a dispatcher, an event that resulted in a charming
story (with picture) that appeared in *The New York Times*. David took the
dead tarantula out of its jar, but when he tried to pour boiling water over its
legs to make them extend to normal length, "Miss Earhart, who was guid-
ing him through the intriciacies of an interview, advised against it." Amelia,
in her element, started to tell various tall tales, such as when she and friends,
trying to find out who was taking bites out of the fruit in her dining room,
outwaited a chipmunk one night and watched the animal waddle in and get
to his task; how a Ludington Airways plane had had a live pigeon sitting between the cylinder heads when it landed at Washington D.C., which meant
the bird had passed through propeller blades that were turning at fifteen
hundred revolutions a minute. When she was finished, she suggested that
the reporters tell some stories, which they did. "At 4 o'clock Miss Earhart
was elected president of the Monday Afternoon Exaggerated Narratives
Club, which was founded on the spot. She adjourned the meeting 'until
the next time' and promised to brush up on tall tales," the *Times* reported.

George, finally realizing there was no hope of getting Amelia to go
with him, left for France—by himself. It was a cliff-hanger, as Amelia
wrote to Dot Leh: "After all I did not go to Paris with the honorable husband. We decided at the last minute I had so much to do that it was better
to stay at home."

George was abroad for most of September. Gene came to visit
Sunday, September 10.

• • • •

Amelia had become a force to contend with in Washington by way of her
friendship with the Roosevelts. Her influence was put to the test as she
championed Gene. He wanted to become a major player on the U.S. avia-

tion scene, and when Franklin Roosevelt was elected to the presidency, it looked as if his time had come. One of the first things Roosevelt did after assuming office in March 1933 was to reorganize the Aeronautics Branch of the Department of Commerce, which had jurisdiction over all civil aviation matters, under a new director. That was the job that Gene wanted. So did many others, forty-three candidates in all, some powerful and qualified, some political hacks, some just well-connected Washingtonians—a formidable field. Gene was a clear front-runner with his West Point background, his flying experience, his years of organizing and running airlines, his powerful Democratic father-in-law, and Amelia's active sponsorship. Still, faced with finding solutions to the enormous problems involved with getting the economy on its feet and with such a plethora of politically well-connected candidates pressuring him (even John Nance Garner, the vice-president, was pushing a candidate), FDR backed off and decided not to fill the post right away. Instead, he divided up the duties three ways: he appointed J. Carroll Cone chief of the aeronautical development division, Gene chief of the regulation division, and Rex Martin chief of the airways division. All summer Gene and the other two chiefs jockeyed for the vacant post.

As the summer progressed it became obvious even to President Roosevelt that an overall head was needed. Amelia had been championing Gene both to Franklin and to Eleanor since spring. She even had George pushing for the appointment.

But June turned to July, July to August, August to September and still no word, the president had a great deal on his mind, and he would not be rushed. It was not till late September that he finally made his decision. By that time the president was in Warm Springs, Georgia. He summoned Gene down and on September 20, 1933, with Gene at his elbow, called a press conference at which he announced that he was making Gene the new Director of the Aeronautics Branch. (The following year there was a name change and Gene found himself the Director of the Bureau of Air Commerce.) It was all very satisfying, and one of the nice perks that went with the job was the second-floor corner office, with its big windows shaded by a row of pillars looking down on Pennsylvania Avenue. Gene left Warm Springs later in the day, headed straight to Rye and Amelia to tell her all about it, and again spent the night. The next day Amelia drove him the two hours to Newark, New Jersey, turned around, and drove home.

Amelia watched over Gene's career like a mother hen. On November 5 she sent the president a newspaper clipping favorable to Gene, together with a note: "Because I ventured to urge upon you the desirability of appointing Gene Vidal, I am naturally delighted to find a Republican paper giving such praise to what Vidal is already accomplishing." The article had the desired effect on FDR. He wrote her back, "because it comes from the *Herald Tribune* it is high praise indeed." Little did the president realize that the article was less a commentary on Gene's ability than a marker of Amelia's wide sphere of influence: the writer of the article, Carl Allen, was Amelia's old and close friend, whom she had consulted about the advisability of marrying George; further, Allen had been hired by the *Tribune* at least partly on Amelia's recommendation to the Reid family, the publishers.

Amelia and Nina Vidal remained on speaking terms. They even had lunch together early in January 1934 at the Hotel Seymour. Gene was nervous enough to stop by—Nina was unpredictable at the best of times and occasionally had a drinking problem.

By all accounts Gene Vidal did a very good job as director. Faced with a severely slashed Depression budget, he still managed to restore night operations to the country's lighted airways and continued other navigation aids slated to be discontinued; he also reorganized and streamlined department operations and simplified the regulations governing the licensing of private fliers. So well did he do that *Time* magazine made him the subject of a story and put his picture on the cover, a signal honor in those years, one that not even Amelia ever achieved. His was a highly visible job, and his photogenic face, in and out of an airplane—he flew himself everywhere in his small Stinson, having divested the department of its fleet of expensive planes—became almost as familiar in the newsreels as Amelia's and Charles Lindbergh's.

One of his department projects, his dream, was to develop a small, easily operated low-priced all-metal airplane that would sell for seven hundred dollars—the price of a car—and be as safe; at his request $500,000 was set aside by the Public Works Administration (PWA) for the project. It was launched with much fanfare. Amelia did her bit: she was photographed with various other well-known airminded people (all men except for her) to announce and publicize the PWA funding. However, it was not a popular project with certain members of Congress who felt that the government should not be funding such an undertaking—that private enterprise should—and various legislators pressured Gene to concentrate on more traditional civil aviation concerns and the smooth facilitation of departmental policy. Gene had another problem as well: when FDR had made him director, Carroll Cone and Rex Martin, the two men who had been co-chiefs with him, became assistant directors. It would have been better administratively if they had been transferred out, for both of them, and particularly Cone, spent their time trying to undermine Gene and secure the top post for himself rather than doing their jobs. As Nick Komans reported in his book *Bonfires to Beacons,* which gives a blow-by-blow description of the bureau's growing pains, Vidal had two assistants, "but damn little assistance."

Then a series of flying accidents—the last being an airline crash in May 1935 that claimed the life of Senator Bronson Cutting of New Mexico—focused the eyes of the nation and Congress on the airways. It became known that at the time of the accident, Cutting's pilot had been groping for the Kansas City airport in thick fog because the Kansas City radio beacon was turned off. The Senate formed a committee to investigate the general safety of the airways and specifically why the beam wasn't working.

The question was raised as to whether the director was wasting his time and energy on extraneous projects such as the "poor man's airplane" rather than tending to the overall needs of flying in the United States. Senator Copeland of New York, who directed the investigation, wondered whether Gene was "too amiable" for the job. Inevitably, there were calls for Gene's resignation, which came to naught, but which were worrisome.

• • • •

Amelia was the most important nonrelative in Gore Vidal's young world. He preferred her to his own mother. He remembers his first night in the "jungle" guest room in Rye as petrifying—the foreboding greens and dark browns, the monkeys, strange birds painted on the walls; he had been put to bed in the dark and woke up screaming. And he remembers that the next morning, when he told Amelia how frightened he had been, she thought it very funny. He remembers walking with her on the boardwalk in Atlantic City and being gawked at by thousands. He remembers her visiting him when he was sick and, while talking, taking some modeling clay and modeling a head in the hour or so she was there—doing "an awfully good job." He loved her "beautifully modulated" speaking voice and remembers how much she loved poetry. She would read poetry with Gore—hers, his, and others'. She encouraged his poetry-writing efforts and tried to steer him toward Amy Lowell and away from Edgar Allan Poe. ("I was in the Edgar Allan Poe stage at the moment," he recalls.) He remembers Gene telling him that she wore men's underwear when she flew, and that although George thought it was his boxer shorts she wore, Gene boasted to his son that she had actually been wearing *his* new jockey shorts for several years. Some years after her last flight, it was reported that a Russian sailor had seen a white woman signaling from a small island dressed in jockey shorts. George told Gene that the outfit was wrong—it couldn't be Amelia, because "she always wore my shorts when she flew, but I wore boxer shorts." Gene thought that was very funny. Katharine (Kit) Vidal, whom Gene married in 1939, would corroborate that Amelia wore Gene's shorts. "Gene used to buy them for her. She was too embarrassed to buy them herself." "She adored my father," Gore recalls, and "Gene's affection for Amelia was not equal to her love for him." He, of course, had his own childhood crush on her. He thought she would make a perfect mother—in fact, he proposed for his father, so anxious was he for Gene and Amelia to be married. When he blurted this out, he remembered, Amelia was delighted; his father blushed. To his disappointment and Amelia's, nothing came of the suggestion.

Gene was an excellent pilot and made his way around the country in his Stinson monoplane, often with Gore in tow. One unexpected result was that Gore logged so many hours in the air accompanying his father that by the age of ten, he had learned how to fly, with his father's blessing. Gore was such an apt student that Gene put him behind the controls of his prototype Hammond flivver plane—the one that, at seven hundred dollars would be within the reach of the working man—to show the press that it was so "foolproof," even a child could handle it. (Since Gore was too young to solo legally, and the director couldn't be seen to be breaking the law, Gene installed a nonflying adult in the rear seat.) Gore took the Hammond up, circled the field, and landed without incident. Amelia, too, flew the Hammond, giving it more much-needed publicity.

During this period of his life Gene carried three pictures in his wallet: one was of the kindly landlady who helped advise him about Gore; one was of Gore; the third was of Amelia.

Part of Gene's job was to foster the development of equipment that would make flying safer. To that end, in 1935, he enlisted Amelia as a dollar-a-year technical consultant, announcing that she, along with Captain Albert Hegenberger, on loan from the army to the department, would be testing the new Lear radio directional-finding compass.

Gene knew her well. "She used to practice flying all the time and I think never really reached the self-set top of what she considered proficiency," he told Amelia's biographer, Janet Mabie. He noticed that she began to shy away from shaking hands. She just wouldn't do it whether from hygienic considerations or not he didn't know, if she could avoid doing so without seeming rude. Particularly with understanding friends would she avoid it. Gene was also one of the few people who could tease Amelia and get away with it. The tight-fistedness that her years of poverty had fostered never left her, and it amused him. Once, he remembered, they were eating at an airport counter and she ordered the seventy-five-cent lunch. He knew she wanted ice cream and, teasing her, asked her why she didn't order it.

"Because it isn't on the seventy-five cent lunch," she answered, frostily. Jack Gillies, another of Amelia's friends, put it differently. "She was a cheap little girl to feed. You could keep her happy quite a long time, just supplying her with apples." But both knew that frugality was only one side of her personality, and that she was also generous to a fault. In 1930, when she could ill afford it, she had given Jack's brother and new bride Betty Huyler, a Ninety-Niner, a dozen sterling-silver demitasse spoons as a wedding present.

In spite of Amelia's attraction for Gene, she never fell into the trap of letting him set the direction of their relationship. She was always in control. Indeed, he didn't even dare hire air-marking pilots, those women whose job it was to have signs painted on top of buildings so pilots could identify towns from the air, without first getting Amelia's approval. Shortly after agreeing to take the dollar-a-year job as technical consultant, she resigned "personally" to the director. It seems to have been a matter of discretion and served to delink their names in the public eye. In her straightforward manner she issued a press release: "I wish to be free to pursue my commercial activities without any possibility of embarrassment or misunderstanding which might arise from this official connection, informal and insignificant as it is."

George didn't have any choice except to put up with Amelia's conduct, if he wanted to stay married to her. He had, after all, agreed to it. And throughout the years he and Amelia definitely maintained a closeness. Helen Weber, who came on the scene in the fall of 1932 after Lucy left, looking out a window of the house in Rye one day, saw Amelia sitting in a wheelbarrow, roaring with laughter and squealing with delight as George careened her back and forth across the lawn. At one point George devised a way to have Amelia all to himself, at least for a little while, on a dream vacation. His old friend Carl Dunrud, the Yellowstone ranger who had accompanied him to Greenland to lasso northern specimen wildlife (he successfully roped two polar bears and a walrus, which eventually ended up in the Bronx Zoo), had settled down in northwest Wyoming with his wife and children and ran a dude ranch, the Double Dee. In the summer of 1934 George arranged for himself and Amelia to spend time there, to motor out in Amelia's little black Franklin: a nice long vacation just for the two of them. It would be the first time in a long while they would be alone, unaccompanied by friends and business acquaintances, and he would be in control.

They spent five days at the Double Dee, a three-thousand-acre spread just east of the Rockies, and then Carl (thirty-two-year-old Vera was six months pregnant with her third child), with the help of his Minnesota cousin and a young boy wrangling at the ranch for the summer who later became a pilot, loaded up eight packhorses with tents, duffels, a stove, fishing gear, bedding, clothes, and food, and they rode into the Absaroka Mountains for two weeks of riding, fishing, and hiking. Amelia loved it as much as George hoped she would. "She talked of the joy of living in the stillness, the quiet beauty of the mountains. She spent hours with field glasses, watching young lambs of mountain sheep romp and play on distant mountain tops," he wrote. Fully at home on the ranch, comfortable with the Dunruds (Vera remembered her as a very nice, modest, retiring, "very lovely" person), full of plans for the future, she filed a claim on some land she fell in love with on the pack trip, a site in a steep valley between Mount Crosby and Mount Sniffel, a stone's throw from a waterfall on the Wood River, near the Double Dee but a mile higher. She promised the Dunrud children, Richard and James, that she would be back. She asked the Dunruds to do discovery work on the claim and arranged for Carl to build her a four-room log cabin. For each of the two summers following, she and George made plans to return to the ranch, but the next summer Amelia's sinuses kicked up and she landed in Cedars of Lebanon Hospital, then got pleurisy, and the summer after that her amazing new plane swallowed up the time. By 1937 the cabin, still unseen by Amelia, was four logs high.

George went so far in his quest to spend time with Amelia as to accompany her on lecture tours. Even after the summer and fall of 1933, when he had endured Gene at Locust Avenue for what must have seemed like an eternity of weekends, he was available in November when Amelia needed him. She was going, not too enthusiastically, to speak in New England and eastern Canada. At her request, he was going with her. "George is going with me to the most northern points as I do not like the territory very well and need moral support," she wrote Amy.

• • • •

Gene and Amelia were undoubtedly lovers. Only two people knew the situation well enough to have an opinion, and they were very discreet. One, Katharine (Kit) Vidal thought so from the way he talked about her. The other was a child—and he thought so too: the child was Gore.

> To touch your hand or see your face, today,
> Is joy. Your casual presence in a room
> Recalls the stars that watched us as we lay.
>
> I mark you in the moving crowd
> And see again those stars
> A warm night lent us long ago.
> We loved so then—we love so now.

George found this poem, one of the few Amelia wrote that was not destroyed by a smoke fire that destroyed much in their Rye house in the fall of 1934. If she had written the poem for him, George would have known about it. Of her passion there can be no doubt: Could the subject be other than Gene?

On the surface Gene and George continued to be friends.

Try as he might, George was sometimes only on the fringe of Amelia's business interests, where Gene was central. Amelia was also a good friend of Paul Collins, a superb pilot, one of the few who flew the U.S. mail in the early years and lived to tell about it, who was also a close friend of Gene's from the Ludington line days. Ernie Pyle described him as tall, well set up, with coal black hair, light skin, "great" eyes. Six years older than Amelia, like Amelia looking years younger than his age, and like her intelligent, he had made the transition into the business world and was perfectly at home behind a desk. He was a fine organizer, had been general superintendent of TAT and helped Gene set up the Ludington line. When Pan American Airways pulled out of New England, where they had been managing Boston-Maine Airways for the Boston and Maine Railroad and the Maine Central Railroads, railroad officials approached Paul to provide the management, equipment, and service in their place. Paul came to Rye to visit Amelia, Gene Vidal, and Sam Solomon, a very astute businessman involved with aviation who, among his other enterprises, managed Washington, D.C.'s, Hoover airport. The four of them sat on the floor (because, as Sam remembered, Amelia liked sitting on the floor) tossing around various business plans and finally decided that they would go into the airline business as equal investment partners. Each invested $2,500; that was sufficient financial muscle to form National Airways, Inc., their new corporate name for what was still called the Boston-Maine Airways, whose route was from Boston northward; it would eventually become Northeast Airlines. Paul was president, Amelia first vice-president, and Sam Solomon second vice-president. (Gene, already director of aeronautics, was a director but had no title.)

The first meeting with the railroad officials to hammer out details of the route and other organizational matters was held on Monday morning, July 24, 1933, Amelia's thirty-sixth birthday. Paul and Amelia left Rye at four thirty A.M., and in a marathon meeting they settled on the general schedule: the railroad wanted to have plane service to Portland, Rockland, Bangor, and either Waterville or Augusta, Maine. With the meeting concluded, it remained for Paul and Amelia to physically survey the route, for as the railroad officials pointed out, "How do you know that you can fly from the towns we designate as stops on the line with safety?" Paul asked for a car and driver and twenty-four hours. Then he and Amelia took the train to Portland, where the driver picked them up, and drove the 80 miles to Rockland; they checked out the field, then drove the 63 miles to Bangor, checked its field, drove 55 miles to Waterville, then 20 miles to Augusta (which they found had too small a field), then 60 miles to the Scarborough field south of Portland, took the train back to Boston, and sat down with the railroad people as promised at two P.M. and settled the last detail: it would be Waterville. Then Paul raided Eastern for personnel—former Ludington workers unhappy at Eastern—Clarence Belinn, whom he put in charge of maintenance, and three pilots. On August 7 Paul took delivery from Eastern on two ten-passenger Stinson trimotors, which he had gotten for a very good price.

Amelia went to Boston periodically to work with Paul and tend to public relations and sales, her special responsibilities. She also helped him peg mileage tariffs, for which she had a good feel. By August 9, a sunny, cloudless day in Boston, everything was ready to roll. Sam Solomon and his wife Alma, Paul Collins, Amelia, the chief executive officer of the railroad, the general traffic manager, and three reporters stepped into the Stinson and flew to Portland, Rockland, Bangor, and Waterville. Advance notice had been given that Amelia was on the plane, and gratifyingly large crowds turned out at each airfield to see her and to hear her speak on the wonders of flight.

Two days later was the formal opening of the airline. One Stinson was at Logan airport in Boston, the other at Portland. Amelia, Gene, and eight first-time passengers flew the ninety miles to Portland and then went on to Bangor. The following weekend Paul and Gene were both with Amelia in Rye.

By October the line had added a feeder service through Burlington, Vermont, and by March 1934 the Burlington route was extended to Montreal. But it was hard for the airline—the first to continue service in that part of the world in winter. All the hangars, including the one the line used at Logan airport, were unheated. Every night the temperature dropped below 32 degrees, newspapers had to be stuffed into the engine exhaust stacks to block moisture and prevent freezing; the oil had to be drained out and stored in a heated office; and each engine had to be wrapped up. Each morning the procedure had to be reversed. The public was apprehensive, therefore business was slow. With public relations executive Herbert Baldwin, Amelia visited the cities, talked up air travel, and contacted civic groups. On Saturdays when only one plane flew (because of lack of business), the other was used to visit cities along the route and offer free ten-minute flights. But there were few takers—until Amelia began focusing on women's groups, in the hope that if she could convince the wives that flying was safe the husbands would follow. It worked: the demonstrations became more popular. When the Bangor Chamber of Commerce held a Women's Day, ten thousand women turned out; two hundred went up in the air. Nothing could quite beat having her, all dressed up in mink coat, chic boots, and hat, standing on the tarmac prior to one of the line's pioneering flights. With Amelia standing next to the Stinson on a bitter cold icy day at the Portland airport, apprehensive fliers never even thought to question why there were automobile tire chains on the wheels—something of a necessity when plowing wasn't possible and the runway was slick with ice. Because of her, Burlington, Vermont's, number-one citizen, William Appleyard, sold $10,000 worth of tickets before the airline made its first flight there, on February 7, 1934.

Still later, intent on expanding, Paul and Amelia formulated a plan for Boston-Maine Airways to fly from LaGuardia airport, then called North Beach airport, to a racetrack eight miles from Boston that they knew they could easily convert into a field. That one the company didn't buy.

Amelia's business interests were prospering, but her home life was giving her a bit of trouble as 1934 drew to a close. That Christmas the card George and Amelia sent out had a somber note. Their ship was the "George and Amelia" and the text ran, "Although no models ourselves, at least we're still afloat."

16
Role Model

• • • • When Amelia started flying at the beginning of the air age, she and all the other women fliers wore modified semimilitary (U.S. Infantry version) riding clothes. Then in the late 1920s, as women pilots tried to show a timid world that flying was easy, effortless, and safe, they took to wearing normal street clothes to drive home the point. For that reason, when Amelia was the aviation editor of *Cosmopolitan* vagabonding west in 1928, she was often photographed in a light tan suit with conventional skirt and low-heeled two-tone oxfords. Then women's flying clothes caught the eye of the fashion industry. The great Paris couturiers began including one or two flying suits in their collections, although usually tarting them up so badly, they were unwearable. English and American fliers looking for something to wear began designing their own. Louise Thaden, winner of the 1929 Women's Air Derby and vice-president of the Ninety-Nines under Amelia, designed a clever dress with a zippered jacket and front and back panels concealing a divided skirt; it was so attractive that golfers began snapping it up. Another pilot, Edith Folz, also veteran of the derby, designed a combination pilot and street outfit with a removable zippered skirt, the "Folz-up suit," which won fourth place in the inventors' meet at the Century of Progress the summer of 1933. By the 1930s flying outfits were available or could be special-ordered at many department stores. One-piece coveralls called monkey suits, usually made of gabardine, often trimmed with flannel, were also available.

Amelia's interest in designing clothes began with flying clothes for the Ninety-Nines. She had become the first president in 1932, at which time she was promoting the adoption of a members' coverall that was both good-looking and rugged. She sent a sample suit around the country to be voted upon by the regional governors. She hoped that when adopted, it would be a consciousness-raising tool for the members as well as a moneymaker for the organization, for Flying Field, the trademarked material of which it was made—*Vogue* obligingly described it as "sturdy and gabardine-like"—would, if it sold well, give the Ninety-Nines a nice revenue stream. But the Ninety-Nines were a democratic, decentralized organization, and there was endless debate instead of decision making; the goal of adopting one version began to fade. *Vogue* did a two-page photo spread on the "First Lady of the Sky" in January 1933 showing, on one page, Amelia posing in the original flying suit. It sported loose trousers, a zipper top, and big pockets, with the material nipped in at the wrists and ankles, but since it hadn't been adopted by the Ninety-Nines, it wasn't identified as "theirs," much to Amelia's frustration. The facing page shows Amelia in a brown jersey sports suit, suitable, according to the text, for traveling in a closed-cockpit plane (as opposed to a sporty open-cockpit model or other mode of "conventional" transportation).

Nothing came of the Ninety-Nine coverall, but Amelia decided to pick up the ball and design her own line of clothes "for the woman who lives actively." Contrary to what many thought, Amelia was very interested in style and fashion. When she was a little girl, according to Amy, she used to pester her grandmother to give her scraps of material to sew into new dresses for her dolls—indeed, Amy hadn't been sure whether Amelia enjoyed playing with dolls as much as making them new clothes. In St. Paul as a teenager, when her family was short of money, she had taken some drapes down from the attic and created hobble skirts, the fashion of the day, so that she and Muriel would have new clothes to wear for Easter.

She had bought her first fur coat in her Denison House days on her social worker's salary, and she now owned a becoming mink coat and a beaver coat as well. She had learned from Ray Long and *Cosmopolitan* how to dress, and how important it was. People accustomed to seeing her in flying clothes were continually surprised at how elegant she looked in "normal" clothes. Mary Welch, the *Time* magazine reporter who later married Ernest Hemingway, would remember seeing Amelia sweeping elegantly through the Chicago airport wearing a beige suit with a matching fox fur thrown about her shoulders. Well-cut silk lounging pajamas, of which she had a closetful, were her clothes of choice for the evening. *Christian Science Monitor* reporter Janet Mabie was struck by her fashionable ice-blue-satin evening pajamas. A Purdue student at a graduation banquet thought unforgettable Amelia's sleeveless midnight blue evening dress "covered with silver stars as if the gods had sprinkled them on her," set off by "a cloudlike collar" of white mink.

She worked at her image. Just as her hair seemed artless, so her clothes, her look, presented a consistent image of understatement and casualness that was deliberate. She often wore colorless nail polish. She liked facials and found them soothing; she liked "health afternoons"—spending time in a steam room, followed by a cold hosing down, followed by a massage, particularly when Lucy Challiss would do it with her. She was very conscious of the image she projected. Even when she had been stuck in Trepassey, Newfoundland—anxiously, fretfully waiting to take off in the *Friendship*—even then she had taken the trouble to painstakingly heat up a curling iron and curl her hair.

Her seeming casualness was deceptive. The functional slacks she had worn when she was in her twenties were now custom made, often gabardine, perfectly tailored; the windbreaker was now usually soft suede; and the shirt was often parachute silk, which she favored because it was light, very strong, and could be laundered with impunity.

George had presented her with business deals in the past, but they were his, not hers. This time she would be totally in control. Now a deal was struck with several New York garment manufacturers to make an Amelia Earhart line; one department store would be given the exclusive in each city; in New York it was Macy's, in Chicago Marshall Field's. In all, thirty department stores scattered from coast to coast carried the line. Marshall Field's set up a special Amelia Earhart shop with pretty young mannequins in aeronautical outfits in charge, filled their prime State Street windows full of Amelia's clothes, and gave her a tea to which they invited all Ninety-Nine members as well as other pilots.

She passed on every detail. She installed a dressmaker's dummy in the apartment at the Hotel Seymour, pored over swatches of material and, working with a seamstress, created outfits using her old sewing machine. The line included good, wearable sport dresses, separates, and coats, as well as flying clothes. She used scaled-down screws and bolts and miniature oil cups for buttons, belt buckles made of ball bearings, and belts that closed with cotter pins and parachute clasps. Amelia took parachute silk—gossamer thin, pale of color, incredibly strong—and turned it into blouses and shirts, adding tails to the shirts—at that time a feature exclusive to men's shirts—explaining, "I made up my mind that if the wearers of the shirts I designed took time out for any reason to stand on their heads, there would be enough shirt *still* to stay tucked in." She insisted that her clothes be comfortable and branched out into simple silk dress and jacket combinations. She sent Lucy off to plumb Elizabeth Hawes, a fashionable designer of expensive clothes, for information. The most interesting of the women's magazines of the era, *Woman's Home Companion*, which gave a page to Eleanor Roosevelt in each issue and published Edna Ferber and other top novelists, did several spreads on her, one showing her looking particularly chic in a silk print dress. In another issue, featuring designs by the leading French and American couturiers such as Mainbocher and Lanvin, Amelia was given equal editorial space. The magazine, referring to her as "Amelia Earhart, Designer," showed her dressed in another of her two-piece dresses, the signature silk scarf she wore flying casually tossed around her neck, caught into an elegant soft bow. Her designs had now been made into patterns that the reader could buy through the magazine.

She even designed hats, to everyone's amusement, even though by that time she had stopped wearing them and her tousled mop of curly hair was famous. Then she started a Ninety-Nine "Hat Contest," the purpose of which was to recognize something important accomplished each month by a Ninety-Nine member and award the winner with one of her hats. It was decided that landing in strange airports was good practice, and a point system was worked out that was announced in the *The 99 News*: "For each airport, 1 point; for an honest to goodness forced landing without damage (verified by Department of Commerce inspector), 2 points; if cows in pasture, 3 points. (If cows eat fabric before rescued, damage not counted as resulting from crackup.)"

Amelia specified how the contest would run:

1. Candidate must furnish proof of landing by having signature of airport-manager or some other responsible person to verify the landing. 2. The report forms must be sent to the sectional governor by the last day of the month. The governor will check and select the highest ranking hat-chaser in her section within five days, sign and send her report slip to Clara Studer, editor of the *99'er,* who will send it on to Amelia to be countersigned. Slip in hand, the winner will then go to the nearest store carrying the Amelia Earhart line and select her hat.

But the clothing enterprise ran into a problem: Amelia spent too much time working on it, without pulling back on either her lecturing or her flying. She wore herself down getting everything just right. Given her life, she couldn't be a full-time clothes designer, and temperamentally she was couldn't do it part time. The strain began to show: before she knew it, she was losing weight, beginning to look gaunt, and had to add fat to her diet—eating waffles "just soaked in butter," to get back some of the weight, according to Amy, who loved having something she could finally scold Amelia about. (Amelia would write her, in irritation, "I have been drinking cream and gained ten pounds, so that's that.") She gave it all up after a year.

• • • •

"It's a routine now," she once said. "I make a record and then I lecture on it." That was certainly true—lecturing paid the expenses, made the records possible, took most of her time, and were best attended when she had just done something newsworthy.

But when she walked out onto a lecture stage, audience members often reacted with disbelief. The woman that everyone had in their mind's eye and expected to see was the woman they saw in the newsreels and newspapers—the aviatrix emerging from her plane after a record-breaking flight: drawn face, disheveled hair, slightly grimy, dressed in wrinkled workaday blouse and pants. The Amelia who stood in front of them looked totally different: slender, pretty, fashionably dressed (more often than not in shades of brown), wearing high-heeled shoes, fragile. Altogether taller, slimmer, more beautifully groomed—more feminine—than they had expected. Right away it gave her an edge, put her in the good graces of her audience, that she looked so charmingly normal and had such a disarming appearance.

She was in fact very relaxed when she spoke. She spoke without notes, and it was second nature for her to joke about her notoriety, exhort women to stand up for themselves, and thrill them with her adventures. By the mid-1930s she was a professional—she could capture an audience and hold them riveted. Joan Thomas, who wrote for *Popular Aviation,* held her to be the equal of the great diva Madame Ernestine Schumann-Heink—both spellbinders, in a class by themselves. She talked as casually of her historic solo Atlantic and Pacific flights, wrote another correspondent, "as though they had been the imaginative flights of troubled sleep." A reporter watched her talk for over an hour and ten minutes in late 1935, "without a sound coming from the audience except that of laughter and applause." She had learned, as well, to be dryly humorous.

As she described the sensation of flight, which she always did rather poetically, she raised her arms and curled her long tapering fingers toward each other, as though she were holding a globe. Then as she stood and talked to her audience, if she was relaxed and everything was going well, and it invariably was, she would drop her hands and clasp her fingers together in what looked like the overlapping grip of a golfer.

Her appearance—so unthreatening, so much like their own—was an effective tool. Like everything else to do with Amelia, it was not left to chance but was the result of planning. She made it a point to dress conservatively and yet with style—to look like the very "best" of her audience, to appear as one whom the men and women listening would accept as "their" social equal, someone with "their" values. For then they might suspend preconceived ideas and listen to what she had to say about women and flying. For evening lectures she usually got quite dressed up, as was the custom of the time. "Smartly tailored evening ensemble" wrote a reporter of her attire in one southern town, while another noted her jacketed dinner gown of purple taffeta "relieved only by a broad white collar and bow of taffeta," and another wrote of her charming semiformal brown satin dress. She thought that donning traditional attire made the radical things she was saying go down more easily—seem less radical—and she was right.

• • • •

Like a politician, she gave the same speech over and over, merely changing nuances, altering details. She generally started by brushing away her fame. A favorite opener was the story of the young boy who took her for Lindbergh's mother. Having broken the ice, she next usually asked how many in the audience had ever been in a plane.

Another subject she always touched upon was the importance of allowing and making arrangements for children to go up in a plane: "If you forbid your children to fly they'll get a bootleg ride, and a cheap ride is seldom safe."

Somewhere along the line she usually asserted that flying was safer than driving, particularly at speeds above forty miles per hour, and threw in some statistics. Sometimes she threw in her "transportation sermon," the gist of which was that periodic physical examinations for those who drove automobiles would cut car accidents by fifty percent.

And then if she were speaking to a women's group, she would get to the guts of her speech: that women had to stand up for themselves. She would go into the career possibilities for women in the fledgling air industry and urge women to consider trying to break in—in any capacity, hostess, pilot, navigator, factory worker, public relations—wherever they saw an opening. Usually she was quite sanguine about the possibilities, but sometimes she was not: "In aviation as a whole, women are outnumbered forty to one, but I feel that more will gain admittance as a greater number knock at the door. If and when you knock at the door, *it might be well to bring an ax along; you may have to chop your way through,*" she told one group in 1934.

She would urge women of all ages to break out of their "platitudinous sphere" (one of her favorite phrases), asserting that unlike the prisoner at the bar who is innocent until proven guilty, the woman is guilty until she proves that she can do the things men do. Or she might say that machines were too much man-made—made for men, as she did to one YWCA.

• • • •

Naturally, when she was talking to a mixed audience, such as the Chicago Geographic Society, or a branch of the national Civic Federation, or a men's group, such as the Men's Club of Temple Israel in Paducah, Kentucky (October 19, 1933), she discussed the possibilities that the future held for flying rather than dwelling upon women's concerns. One of the ideas she threw out was for the government to experiment with midocean sea dromes that could gather weather information, with the possibility that if they worked, a chain of them could also be landing places for transoceanic air service—giant stepping-stones across the sea, which had been the dream of many for years. A usual charge to attend a lecture was $1.50—more than a moving picture but not an inordinate amount for the day. Sometimes the speech was sponsored by the local women's city club and more often than not was held in the local high school auditorium. There would be introductory remarks by the mayor, the head of the city club, and the head of the local Zonta chapter. Sometimes Amelia would have a movie camera set up and show her exploits and those of other fliers: after her transatlantic flight she showed pictures of the receptions given her in London, Paris, and Rome as well.

She would usually stand chatting until the committee rescued her from the enthusiasm of her admirers, cheerfully autographing programs and answering questions. She was as well unfailingly polite to reporters, going out of her way to let them interview her. As she tried to explain once to Katch, furious because a reporter was interrupting their lunch, the reporter should not only be treated with patience but given lunch, too. "Ask her to come in. She has her living to earn, too," Katch remembered Amelia saying to her, and Katch grudgingly had been forced to set a place for her at the table.

Amelia was just as patient with young people. A St. Paul newspaper reporter, watching her field questions from the young representatives of high school weekly papers, watching her give them kindly, courteous

There was a round window just about this size in their house in Rye that must have given Amelia and George the idea for this picture.

Courtesy of the Schlesinger Library, Radcliffe College, and Muriel Earhart Morrissey.

Amelia with some of the other entrants in the First Women's Air Derby. From the left: Mary von Mach, Maude Keith Miller, Gladys O'Donnell, Thea Rasche, Phoebe Omlie, Louise Thaden, Amelia, Ruth Elder, Blanche Noyes, and Vera Dawn Walker. Courtesy of the International Women's Air and Space Museum.

Boston gave Amelia a royal welcome after the Friendship *flight. Here she is greeting her mother, Amy.* Courtesy of Corbis-Bettmann.

With Gene Vidal, father of Gore. They were the closest of friends. Amelia helped convince Franklin Roosevelt to appoint Gene the Director of the Bureau of Air Commerce. Courtesy of Corbis-Bettmann and Gore Vidal.

Working on a dress for her line of designer clothes for active women. The line was carried by thirty department stores across the country.

Courtesy of Corbis-Bettmann.

At the beginning of the Bendix transcontinental race, Floyd Bennett field, June 30, 1933. Amelia and Ruth Nichols were the first women to fly in the race. Amelia had problems with her plane, but beat Ruth by over a day. Courtesy of Corbis-Bettmann.

Amelia M. Earhart, first woman to fly the Atlantic by aeroplane

says—

"Lucky Strikes were the cigarettes carried on the 'Friendship' when she crossed the Atlantic. They were smoked continuously from Trepassey to Wales. I think nothing else helped so much to lessen the strain for all of us."

"It's toasted"

No Throat Irritation-No Cough.

© 1928 The American Tobacco Co., Manufacturer

Two of Amelia's endorsement endeavors. Above: 1928. Amelia posing before a Plymouth. Chrysler hired her to be their first celebrity spokesperson. Left: 1928. Amelia agreed to do this Lucky Strike ad because she wanted to donate the proceeds to Commander Richard Byrd's expedition to Antarctica. The editor of McCall's, Otto Wiese, was so put off by the advertisement that he withdrew his offer of employment, and Amelia went to work for Cosmopolitan.

Courtesy of Corbis-Bettmann.

After announcing that he was going to rest at Hyde Park, his Hudson river estate, and would have no visitors, Franklin Roosevelt invited Amelia and George and their houseguests, Amy and James Mollison, for Sunday brunch. Amy and James, English aviators, were still recovering from a crash landing in Bridgeport, Connecticut after having flown the Atlantic. July 30, 1933. From the left: Eleanor Roosevelt, Amelia, James, Amy, FDR. Courtesy of FPG International Corp.

Amelia and Eleanor Roosevelt, on the occasion of the National Geographic Society lunch honoring Amelia in Washington, March 2, 1935. Courtesy of Corbis-Bettmann.

The famous portrait by
Edward Steichen, taken
for **Vanity Fair** *magazine,*
May 1932.

Courtesy of Vanity Fair. *Copyright ©
1931 the Condé Nast Publications, Inc.*

*Amelia took delivery of the Electra on July 24, 1936, her 39th birthday. Shortly
thereafter, she flew it to Purdue. Here she is at the Purdue airport, her students
lined up in front. Courtesy of Purdue University Libraries, Special Collections & Archives. Copyright © 1997
by Purdue Research Foundation.*

*Helping promote Gene's $700 airplane. The occasion is the granting of $500,000
for the project from the Public Works Administration. From the left, sitting:
Amelia; Ewing Mitchell, assistant secretary of commerce; J. Carroll Cone, assistant
director, Bureau of Air Commerce; Edward P. Warner, Society of Automotive
Engineers. In rear: Dr. George Lewis, National Advisory Committee for
Aeronautics; Leighton Rogers, Bureau of Air Commerce; Gene Vidal; Fred L.
Smith, National Association of State Aviation Officials; Robert Renfro, editor of*
Sportsman Pilot; *Al Williams, American Petroleum Institute.*

*Just after the fateful crash in Hawaii. By the time the plane was repaired, world
weather patterns had changed and Amelia had to change the direction of her world
flight from west to east.* Courtesy of AP Wide World Photos.

Amelia and Fred, with a map showing the Pacific stretch of the flight. They finally took off May 21 from Oakland, California.
Courtesy of AP Wide World Photos.

Amelia and Fred in Jakarta (then called Batavia).
Courtesy of AP Wide World Photos.

One of the last photos of Amelia and Fred, taken in Lae, New Guinea (with them is F.C. Jacobs, manager of a New Guinea gold mine). They took off for Howland Island and were never seen again. Courtesy of AP Wide World Photos.

attention even though their questions were long, distracting, and silly, declared she should get a special record for patience.

The amount of time she spent on the circuit was awesome, the schedules (often two speeches in one day) incredible, the distances she traveled amazing. The stamina that allowed her to fly such long distances is apparent in the more mundane pursuits of her life as well. She could spend a month doing one-night stands and not appear tired. She could drive a car astonishing distances with no ill effects. The day she started out on one jaunt, at the beginning of October 1933 in the Midwest, she took her mother, in Chicago visiting the Shedds, shopping for clothes at Marshall Field's. Then in early afternoon she got into her car and drove to Sioux City, Iowa, a distance of almost six hundred miles, where she was due the next day at 12:15 for lunch prior to giving a lecture at 1:30 at the Sioux City Women's Club. "I drove here all the way and arrived about 4:30 A.M.," she wrote Amy. "It was a gorgeous night and I thought I'd rather sleep for a few hours after I reached Sioux City than to get up at an early hour and drive." She spent the next two weeks crisscrossing Iowa, Nebraska, Minnesota, Kansas, and Missouri, giving speeches at four more women's clubs, three college groups, two men's clubs, and an automobile association, ending up back in Chicago, where she gave two speeches on the twentieth. During the tour she spent a night in Atchison with the Challisses, taking the time to visit her uncle Theodore and the mothers of some of her childhood friends whom she felt close to, and giving an interview to *The Atchison Globe.* Starting October 21, she spoke in Oak Park, Rockford, and Janesville, Illinois; Whitewater, Wisconsin; Danville, Illinois; South Bend, Indiana; Toledo, Ohio; Lansing, Michigan; and Springfield, Illinois, ending up with two lectures—afternoon and evening—at the Detroit Institute of Arts, thirteen speeches in twelve days. Later she was off to Texas. Nor did she slow down as the years went by. Fourteen days in January 1936 saw her give lectures in South Carolina, Kentucky, Texas, Oklahoma, and Arizona.

The amazing thing was that the curiosity of the public remained unabated; it was matched by Amelia's continuing enthusiasm to the task at hand. No matter that in 1935 she spoke before 136 groups totaling 80,000. She was telling men and women about a brave new world where people would hop on planes the way they hopped on trains, where Europe would be just hours away. And she was telling them it was theirs for the taking. She was telling the women—thirty years before Betty Friedan wrote *The Feminine Mystique,* forty years before Gloria Steinem launched *Ms.* magazine—that they should fulfill themselves and be more than wives and mothers. She saw every lecture as a new opportunity to win people over.

She probably would have done it for nothing—being paid to give advice was *almost* irresistible.

• • • •

In the fall of 1934, as the result of a speech, Amelia met Edward C. Elliott, president of Purdue University. He looked conservative—stiff collar, proper suit, graying hair slicked down and parted in the middle—but he was not. He was a college president committed to educating women for a life outside the home, an extreme view for his time. More typical was the traditional mindset of Henry Moore, president of Skidmore College, who made sure Skidmore coeds concentrated on art and good manners, dressed well, and developed a taste for music, since their goal in life was to maintain beautiful households. Elliott, head of a coed land grant college—he liked to refer to himself as a Hoosier schoolmaster—would cite the opening of the first Purdue residence hall for women, South Hall, as giving distinction to the year 1934 at Purdue. He wanted women to have careers and saw his job as giving them the necessary training. He was so forward looking and so committed to his vision and at the same time so practical that he realized he had to change the culture of Purdue if his ideas were to have impact. Nebraska born, his father, like Amelia's, had worked for the Union Pacific. He was bright and disarming, a brilliant talker, and an original thinker who delighted in unconventional solutions to problems. He was also interested in flying, with the result that Purdue boasted a flying field, planes, a new hangar, and a curriculum that included aeronautics as a subject of study.

The occasion of his meeting with Amelia was the fourth annual Conference on Current Problems sponsored by *The New York Herald Tribune* in September 1934, which took place shortly after the new hangar was completed and the women's residence opened. The audience at the conference—three thousand strong—filled every seat in the Grand Ballroom of the Waldorf Astoria in New York City. It seemed as if everyone important in American public life was seated on the dais, each in turn expounding their pet idea on how to rescue America from the doldrums of the Depression. Eleanor Roosevelt spoke about bettering relations between capital and labor; Mayor of New York Fiorello LaGuardia spoke about defending the Constitution; Dr. Glenn Frank, president of the University of Wisconsin, spoke about the changes being wrought in Washington. Everyone, including the superintendent of New York schools, spoke in generalities.

Elliott spoke about young people. His ideas were direct and basic: that government must take inventory of occupational facts relating to young people because the economic recovery of the country depended on harnessing their energy, that the young needed guidance to find the direction and location of their goals. His speech over, he sat down and listened to the next person on the program—Mrs. Nicholas Brady, head of the Girl Scouts of America—stress the importance of the scouting program because it prepared women to become competent to manage their future household affairs. How women should prepare themselves to be good wives was exactly what he least wanted to hear. His mind began to wander; he intended to slip out, and would have, except for "this rather personable creature sitting on my right," whom he decided to stay and listen to. It was Amelia. She spoke about the future of aeronautics and the part women were to play, of the need to pay attention to "young ideas" and the difficulty women were having in obtaining positions in the aviation industry—they were outnumbered forty to one by men, she said. What she did not say—but undoubtedly knew, for it was a painful fact that her friend Clara Studer, editor of *The 99 News*, was writing about—was that many women were giving up flying, vanquished by the Depression. The past year had seen a devastating decrease in female pilots: where there had been six hundred in 1933, now, in 1934, the number had dropped by almost half. So many just couldn't afford to keep up their licenses.

Elliott was impressed by everything about Amelia, from the way she looked to the words she spoke. In his eyes the most important immediate problem to be solved was how to effectively educate young women. He knew that to solve the problem, he had to bring new forces into play. He needed teachers who could be role models for his Purdue coeds, and he realized he was looking at the role model to end all role models. His first thought was that she would be perfect as a speaker at the upcoming vocational conference that the women at Purdue were organizing. The following day Helen Rogers Reid gave a luncheon and again, as Edward Elliott remembered it, "I had the very good fortune of being seated next to Amelia. During the luncheon I learned that she had an abiding interest in the problem of the education of women. Our ideas as to the nature of this problem and its solution fitted." Elliott, determined to get her on his campus, arranged a dinner with Amelia and George at the Coffee House Club, a mid-Manhattan club frequented by the theatrical, publishing, and magazine movers of the city, one of George's favorite places. Surrounded by books and paintings, originals of sketches in *Vanity Fair*, a grand piano, and theatrical mementos, they talked, waited upon by club maître' d, Williams, "steward extraordinary," according to George. After dinner Amelia and George sat on a couch beneath the club's Maxfield Parrish bulletin board, Amelia with her feet tucked up underneath her like a little girl. Edward Elliott, facing them in a chair, came to the point.

"We want you at Purdue," he said, smiling wisely at Amelia.

"I'd like that," she said as simply and as directly, "if it can be arranged. What would you think I should do?"

What, as Amelia brought up, could she, with no degree or qualifications for teaching, contribute? Elliott assured her that she could inspire women. He proposed that she make Purdue the center of her interests, that she work there to find the best way to properly prepare women for the modern world. The conversation continued for another two hours as he told her about Purdue and they sounded each other out. Almost immediately after they parted company, Elliott completed the essential phone calls, and Amelia rearranged her schedule. Three weeks later she was on the Purdue campus in Lafayette, Indiana, giving an address on "College and Careers" at the Conference on Women's Work and Opportunities organized by the Women's Self-Government Association of the college. As the featured speaker, she made her address at the luncheon in the ballroom the second day.

It was probably unclear to many interested educators what kind of collaboration Amelia and Edward Elliott had in mind. The initial assumption would have been that Purdue was beefing up its flying offerings—and that that was where Amelia would fit in to the curriculum. By then a growing number of colleges had flying clubs and gave aeronautical courses, including William and Mary, where Amelia spoke in 1932. Indeed, competition among colleges for aviation was becoming as keen as it was for conventional sports. There were now national intercollegiate meets that were hotly contested. But it wasn't aeronautics that Amelia was interested in teaching—then or ever, as Elliott grasped. She had a special message for young women. She was intrigued that Elliott believed that the effective education of young women was vital to the health of the country. She herself had heretofore concentrated on inspiring young college women—something in itself—but Elliott connected the effective employment of women to the economic well-being of the country. A few years before, she had told Barnard College students that the educational system as then constituted was based "on sex, not on aptitude," that there were a great many boys who would be better off making pies and a great many girls who would be better off in manual training, and further, that the trick was to overcome prejudice and *show* ability.

She was becoming increasingly focused on identifying and lifting the barriers that held women back, as time and experience showed her just how intractable those barriers were for the vast majority of young women. The shift wasn't readily apparent; she was never rude, still accepted speaking engagements at men's clubs, and hardly ever was overtly feminist. But she would now give neither time nor funds to aid even deserving men. So singleminded was she becoming that even when Marion Perkins asked her for money to fund studies for an unusually bright young boy at Denison House, she refused; she would in fact no longer give money to Denison House at all unless it was used "for *girls* in some way," as she wrote, underlining "girls" by way of emphasis. As Elliott would observe, "her primary interest in life was not in this career of adventure upon which she had embarked, but rather in an effort to find and make some additions to the solution to the problem of careers for women." Now President Elliott was giving her the chance to push her message further.

It took until the following May before Elliott worked out something more specific. Then, in a letter dated May 18, he outlined his plans for creating a department for the study of careers for women:

> The department would be energized by people who had been
> successful in their careers. Miss Earhart would be the first appointee
> to this new center, and could serve as either Department Head
> or nonresident professor or lecturer on careers for women. She
> need only spend two weeks out of each semester at the University,
> giving addresses, classes, or conferences.
>
> Miss Earhart would also be free to advise university officials on
> constructive modifications in the various programs, and also help
> in selecting other professors for the new program. Her campus
> schedule would be worked around her other professional duties,
> and she would also be chief consultant for the University work in
> aeronautical engineering.

He offered her a salary of two thousand dollars a year—at a time when the Indiana legislature had reduced Purdue's funding by twenty percent. With a minimum of deliberation Amelia accepted the offer.

It was a huge challenge. Neither the university staff nor the engineering students themselves were nearly as committed as their president. To the contrary, there was active opposition to the idea. The same year Elliott set out to hire Amelia, 1934, the Purdue personnel department secured 84 jobs for graduating men and arranged for the industry representatives who came on campus to recruit 38 more. In contrast personnel found only four jobs for women that year and arranged for zero industry representatives to visit the campus to recruit women. The next year the department found

96 jobs, and industry reps provided 73 more for graduating men. The numbers for graduating women were the same as the previous year: four and zero. The contrast is particularly striking because over ninety percent of Purdue women worked after they graduated; only three percent listed themselves as housewives.

Unfortunately the jobs these female graduates secured, as Amelia readily found out, were overwhelmingly in home economics—because that was what Purdue traditionally trained them for. There *were* usually a few women in the freshman class who enrolled in engineering, a pitifully small group of eight or ten, but by the end of their junior year all had usually quit—overwhelmed, "counseled" out by their male professors, and made to feel uncomfortable and unwelcome by the male students. Amelia wanted to change that. She wanted to break down the boundary lines between the schools as a way of breaking down the condescending attitude of the professors and the male students towards the coeds. "Today it is almost as if the subjects themselves had sex, so firm is the line drawn between what girls and boys study," she observed.

What Amelia left unsaid was that the male faculty sexualized their courses as a way of making them off limits to women. It was a highly effective tactic, for if women were discouraged from studying engineering, they wouldn't learn that it was as much within their grasp as any other discipline. The subtle, pervasive push on the part of the professors to keep the girls in home economics and out of agriculture and engineering worked like a charm.

In a way it was understandable. In January 1935 there were still several million young people between the ages of 16 and 24 on relief. With jobs so hard to find, it didn't help, many conservative men felt, for women to start competing for the plums.

Complicating the problem for Amelia was that the head of the School of Chemical Engineering and the head of the School of Civil Engineering had been there for twenty-five and thirty years respectively. They were of the same mindset as the Yale students who, just a few years previously, had paraded behind a banner bearing the inscription, "Marry Them Early; Tell Them Nothing, Treat Them Rough." Professor Peffer, professor of chemical engineering, didn't think girls should even be visible—he called his staff together one morning to tell them how upset he was to behold one of his best students holding hands with a girl "for all to see." Even A. A. Potter, the engineering professor considered by contemporaries to be "the most kindly dean of all," was also unalterably opposed. Nor did time blunt his opposition. When he was interviewed at ninety-four, he stated that he still believed

Purdue had been wrong to hire Amelia because "she was a very courageous woman, but very poorly educated. After a woman was educated, she thought they should fix typewriters and washing machines. She thought an engineer was a mechanic. She was not a help in improving education."

Not surprisingly, a number of the Purdue faculty wives followed the mindset of their husbands and were "mortified" by a report that one afternoon Amelia had strolled into the village in slacks, unescorted, mounted a stool at Bartlett's Drugstore, and ordered a soft drink. A rumor was floated that Amelia had been seen smoking. That summer *Fortune* magazine pontificated, "The fact is that the Woman's Movement started because women, for the first time in history, were bored to death." Amelia and President Elliott were fighting an uphill battle.

• • • •

Amelia gave afternoon talks for day- and part-time coeds and the girls who lived in sorority houses in the Memorial Union, the campus meeting place where the students gathered to snack and socialize. There, in a large, closed-off area on the second floor that was so informally furnished it resembled a living room, Amelia, usually perched on the grand piano, swinging her legs a bit, talked and answered questions. Most of the students kept coming back for more.

Study whatever you want, was her message; don't let the world push you around. The discussions—for there was always discussion and a good deal of interaction after her talk—encouraged such thinking. It took courage and commitment for a young woman to transfer from home economics to engineering, and it took money, which meant that besides running the gauntlet of professors and male students, the girls also had the herculean task of convincing their families that such a course was wise.

Don't get married right away Amelia hammered. Graduate, then have a career, then get married. "You're going with that senior," she would say. "When you graduate be sure you go on and have a career; don't get married as soon as you get out of school." She irritated many of male Purdue students with that message, and with her "outspoken" ideas. And they were not at all bashful in saying so. As glamorous a role model as she appeared to the students (and most were surprised at how much more feminine she looked in person than in the newsreels), in her well-tailored brown slacks, small figured matching shirt, and brightly colored scarf knotted at the throat, or attired in evening dress addressing a dinner meeting looking gracefully feminine,

she was a definite threat to the men: a superstar advocating independence.

> Many divorces are caused by the complete dependence of the
> female. At first there is the strong sexual attraction that sometimes
> masquerades as love. Everything goes well until the first financial
> crisis jars the man's confidence and threatens the woman's secu-
> rity. The woman can't help. All she can be is dependent, because
> that is what she has been trained to be. Instead of standing beside
> the man, giving him encouragement by contributing her own
> efforts, she becomes accusatory and sullen and the sex drive that
> passed for love is no longer enough to satisfy either of them. If
> we begin to think and respond as capable human beings able to
> deal with and even enjoy the challenges of life, then we surely
> will have something more to contribute to marriage than our
> bodies.

Besides her talks with students she circulated a questionnaire among them,
from which she learned that their goals were her goals, too: 92 percent
wanted careers. It encouraged her, "crystallized" her thinking.

A prestigious men's senior student honorary group was annoyed
enough to request a face-to-face meeting with Amelia to complain about
the advice and counsel she was giving. She asked them why they objected.
"It's hard enough to get the girls to marry us as it is" was their reply. On
the other hand, the male students who were working their way through
Purdue by waiting on tables during banquets and dinners, presumably from
lower-class homes where women worked, had an entirely different view.
After a small dinner for twelve that included Amelia and President Elliott,
after she had finished her buttermilk and everyone else had finished their
coffee, she walked into the kitchen and introduced herself to each of the
three male waiters. She "chatted with us for several minutes, and left all
of us feeling much—well, greater than before and extremely flattered to
think she took the time to do that."

The coeds normally vied for the privilege of sitting at the head
table presided over by Helen Schleman, director of the hall; they tried even
harder when Amelia was on campus, for she ate there too. By this time
Amelia was a confirmed buttermilk drinker, and that became the favorite drink in South Hall. After dinner Amelia and Helen Schleman and as
many girls as could fit would go into Schleman's suite and continue the
conversation.

After the Schleman sessions the girls, by then dressed in pajamas and bathrobes, followed Amelia into her suite, held rap sessions sitting on her bed, or sprawled on the floor. The college had had no regular dormitory rooms for five of the girls and had put them in a first-floor guest room; initially unhappy with their lot because they were cut off from the rest of the students, they now found, living next door to Amelia, they had a relationship with her that the others didn't have and felt privileged. "We were indeed fortunate," recalled Marian Fitzgerald, who remembered that they would purposely leave their suite door open to entice her to come in and visit. "She was very outgoing."

At the same time as she was espousing feminine independence, she was giving, by example, a lesson in how to handle married life. George phoned every evening. "But George would *always* call," remembered Audria Soles, sometimes even during dinner. "Now George," Amelia would say, "I don't know when I'll be back. I'll try to be back by [such and such a date,] but I'm not sure. I'll be home as soon as I can finish." At least once he was so lonely, he sent her roses. Once when she missed his evening phone call, she sent him a telegram, "SEE YOU SOON."

• • • •

At the beginning of September 1935, just before Amelia started at Purdue, the glass ceiling came crashing down on all airwomen. Helen Richey, the first woman to secure a job as a pilot on a scheduled airline, was pressured into resigning.

Richey was intelligent, young, pretty, and a brilliant flier—an unbeatable combination that quickly brought her to the top of the flying world. Born in 1909 in McKeesport, Pennsylvania, in love with flying, she took lessons when she was twenty and after only six hours of instruction got her license. At twenty-one she had a limited commercial license that enabled her to take passengers sightseeing and fly charters in her own plane, a four-passenger Bird given to her by her parents. At twenty-four she had a full transport license. In 1933 she and Frances Marsalis set a new women's endurance record by remaining in the air ten days. The following year she won the featured event at the Women's National Air Meet, coming in first in the fifty-mile closed-course race around pylons.

After that she was famous. Her goal in life was to become a regular airline pilot flying air mail and passengers, so in December 1934, when Central Airlines, a new airline serving Detroit, Cleveland, Pittsburgh, and Washington, started up—so near her she didn't even have to move—she promptly applied and was accepted for the position of co-pilot. All the Ninety-Nines shared in her excitement.

James D. Condon, Central Airlines' aggressive president, had just underbid Pennsylvania Airlines for the contract to carry mail and was looking for ways to increase passenger traffic. He thought that hiring a female pilot would be a perfect way to publicize his new company. And Helen was the perfect female: she had a superb record, having flown more than a hundred thousand miles in the air with never a scratch, and was photogenic, modest, responsible. All of the line's twelve-passenger Ford trimotors plying the Washington to Detroit route required two pilots. She would be flying every other day.

Helen's first flight was on December 31. It was everything it should have been—uneventful, fun, and well covered by the reporters and photographers waiting at the fields, who watched her make neat three-point landings and were favorably impressed. Virtually every newspaper in the nation did a piece on her. "Helen Richey today has conquered the last masculine stronghold of aviation, the cockpit of a passenger airliner," exulted a Cleveland newspaper in a typical headline. The magazines followed suit. *Time* wrote about "Miss and Mail" on January 14; *Air Woman's* "Reason to be Proud" was in their January issue; *Collier's* "Ladybird" appeared March 30; *McCall's* "She Flies Like a Man" appeared in June. She was sought after to do testimonials for coffee, for motor oil, and for various other products. The public couldn't get enough of her.

Edna Gardner Whyte, a navy nurse as well as a fine pilot, had been waiting years to fly for an airline—and when she heard about Helen, she too applied to Central Airlines for the position of co-pilot. She was "rejected flatly," to her acute discomfort. Another pilot, Johanna Burse, suffered the same fate. It was apparent that one woman pilot was as much as Central would stomach. Before long it became apparent that one woman pilot was one too many.

Women had flown passengers before. Edith Folz had been co-pilot on a special trip for West Coast Air Transport in 1930. Ruth Nichols had flown as a reserve (nonscheduled) pilot from Jackson Heights, Long Island, to Hartford, Connecticut, in 1932 for the New York and New England Airways inaugural flight. In 1934 Amelia had been instrumental in arranging for Amy Mollison to be the co-pilot on a TWA flight to the West Coast. But there was a significant distinction: Edith Folz had been co-pilot on just one special trip, as was Amy Mollison; nor was Ruth Nichols a "regular" pilot on a scheduled airline. Helen Richey was different—the first woman hired to fly a regular mail and passenger route. And it raised hackles all over the male flying world. They came down on her—hard. The Airline Pilots Association summarily turned down her application for membership and on January 22 sent the Department of Commerce a strong letter detailing their reasons: that the idea was preposterous, that it was dangerous because women didn't have the physical strength to handle an airliner in bad weather, and finally, the real reason: "If the practice of hiring women to pilot airliners continued, where would that leave the men?" Leaving nothing to chance, the Airline Pilots said they would call a strike if Helen continued flying. James Condon, faced with losing his pilots, backed off and lamely told Department of Commerce officials (and the Pilots Association) that he had hired Helen "purely for publicity purposes" with the intention of firing her after a week or two.

But Condon knew that public opinion would be on Helen's side—and that if he fired her, his airline would get a black eye and lose business. So instead of firing her, he had her spending her time giving speeches at luncheon clubs, posing for publicity photos, giving tours of the Allegheny airport—and very, very occasionally flying. By the end of August she had made fewer than a dozen round trips between Washington and Detroit, when the number should have been over a hundred. And she was always on call. Frustrated and bored, as August drew to a close, Helen finally resigned.

Amelia and Helen were good friends. Amelia often stayed with Helen as she crisscrossed the country lecturing. Once she even left her car in her care. Now Amelia was angry, even angrier than Helen, at Condon's shoddy treatment of her. She had been very proud of her friend's achievement, had gone so far as to publicly say that the daily flights Helen Richey was making as co-pilot on Central Airlines' run from Detroit to Washington were doing more to further women's place in aviation and were more significant than her own recent Pacific flight.

Now she looked for a forum—a platform—that would command attention for her objections. She didn't want to call a press conference, however—that was not her style. In the end, she accomplished her aim with great delicacy: she wrote a letter to a women's group in Hawaii that had raised money to erect a marker in Oahu to commemorate the airfield she had taken off from on her flight to Oakland suggesting that if they had any money left over, they should set up a fund to help women break down barriers and attain their rightful place in aviation. She carefully explained in the letter what had just happened: that Helen had been fired because the Airline Pilots Association refused to take her in, "not because of lack of ability—all her co-workers admitted she was okay as to flying—but because she was a female. The result of this action was that the Department of Commerce refused to let her fly passengers in bad weather, so the poor girl could not do her part at all and had to resign."

The result was all she hoped. The Pan American press bureau got hold of the letter and published it, and Amelia's remarks were heard around the world. By November 7 the story was front-page news. Department of Commerce officials, sorely pressed, acted surprised and insisted they hadn't even heard of Helen's resignation. "The only thought was that it was too much of a physical job in rough weather," said Fred Neely, chief of the department's aeronautical information section. "It was not an order, not an attachment to her transport license. It was just an informal suggestion made to the airlines," thereby admitting complicity. The Airline Pilots Association admitted innocently that it was true that Helen had been turned down because membership was restricted to men but that "it had been suggested that Helen re-apply for membership at their next meeting, but she had not done so." Condon weighed in with "Miss Richey's father called me shortly before Labor Day and said his daughter's health was poor. He said she wanted to resign so she could go to California to rest. We agreed to release her, of course."

Then Alice Paul, the famous suffragette who had picketed the White House in Woodrow Wilson's time, took up the cause. "Certainly Miss Earhart herself has demonstrated the fallacy of that old idea of women's physical inferiority which we meet on a thousand fronts every day." That comment, too, hit the front pages.

Said Helen, "Miss Earhart has told the story better than I could."

A number of newspapers sought out comments from Ruth Nichols and Ruth Haviland, both of whom held transport licenses, and used them out of context so that the women seemed to imply that females didn't have the requisite strength, when what they said was that muscular energy *was* indeed necessary. Ruth Nichols, in fact, was unequivocal about Helen. "I thought that it was outrageous," she fumed from the hospital where she was recovering from another crash. "High discrimination. . . . There is no reason why she could not be a co-pilot."

Clara Studer, editor of the *The 99 News*, took some grim satisfaction in the fact that it took the Pilots Association eight months to get rid of Helen. Apparently it was this event that led Amelia to back the Equal Rights Amendment to the U.S. Constitution. If prejudice extended even into government agencies, there really was no other choice.

· · · ·

November 7, the day Amelia's letter appeared in the papers, was Amelia's first official day at Purdue, and instead of all the negatives she could have thrown at the young women, she chose to point with pride to the progress women were making in their pursuit of meaningful careers. For of course, Helen Richey, co-pilot for Central Airlines, *had* been a breakthrough, she *had* cracked open the door, nudged the glass ceiling, at least for a little while. An upbeat Amelia chose to dwell on that thought for her first speech on the Lafayette, Indiana, campus: "Things are changing so rapidly and the field is broadening so much for women that the opportunity for employment upon graduation from college is better than it has been, and promises to expand even more," she announced, more upbeat than ever. A few weeks later Gene Vidal hired Helen as an air-marking pilot for The Bureau of Air Commerce, to work under Phoebe Omlie.

It had been known for months that Amelia would be at Purdue that fall, and the knowledge had been a galvanic force: fifty percent more freshmen women enrolled than had enrolled the year before; it was for that reason that the year-old South Hall ran out of rooms and put coeds in what were supposed to be guest quarters.

President Elliott, ever sensitive to people, publicity and promotional schemes, had a real flair for the dramatic. Seeing Amelia so happy and so hard and effectively at work, he asked George about Amelia's immediate goals "beyond academic matters." George, no amateur himself at seeing all angles, replied that she wanted a bigger and better plane—not just to go faster and farther but to use as a laboratory for research in aviation education and for technical experimentation. But presumably because President Elliott agreed so easily, George later wrote that he thought the idea had been in Elliott's head from the first moment he heard her speak at the *Herald Tribune* conference. If they considered her pioneering feats to be "the most potent single influence today in encouraging American air travel," as Purdue authorities were on record as saying, then the purchase of an Earhart-Purdue plane was almost inevitable.

President Elliott, a very resourceful man, was not one to overlook the possibilities of any situation. One of his more brilliant creations was the Purdue Research Foundation. It grew out of an idea of David Ross, president of the Board of Trustees of Purdue and a wealthy industrialist alumnus, that there should be a connecting link between the university research labs and Indiana industries. Ross's aim was for Purdue, with its strong engineering department, to give the fruits of its wisdom and its inventions to Indiana industry. What drew Elliott's enthusiastic support was that if it worked, the plan would benefit the university as well, for it would attract industry funds to academe. The connecting link they devised was the Purdue Research Foundation. Pragmatic as Elliott was, he turned it into a perfect symbiotic relationship in which everyone was enriched. Soon the foundation was involved in myriad projects. Within a few years it was exchanging gifts, such as property, from wealthy alumni for tax-exempt annuities, thereby greatly increasing alumni giving, as well as issuing tax-exempt Purdue bonds to finance the building of dormitories. It had become a free-wheeling, successful entity that attracted wealth, attention, and students to Purdue, much to the satisfaction of President Elliott, who was delighted at its stunning and wide-ranging results.

The hundred-acre Purdue University airport, the first airport owned by a university, was donated by Ross to the Foundation in 1930 in its first year—the first tangible fruit of this labor. A new sports stadium was another early product. There would be many others through the years.

Now, in the fall of 1935, President Elliott arranged a dinner party at Purdue, at which Amelia spoke of her dreams for a flying laboratory. Present were David Ross and J. K. Lilly, both wealthy alumni associated with the foundation. Many figures have been bandied about, but according to Purdue Research Foundation records, before the evening would be out, Ross and Lilly had each offered her an outright donation of $20,000 to make her dream come true. Another $33,000 in equipment and cash would be invested in the plane by the Bendix Corporation, Western Electric, Goodrich, and Goodyear, bringing the fund total to $73,000. In April Elliott announced their gift, the purchase of the plane, and the Foundation's creation of the Amelia Earhart Fund for Aeronautical Research, which would receive all future contributions. The purpose of the fund, according to the university, "was to provide ways and means for pure and applied aeronautical research backgrounded on the facilities already established at Purdue." It was understood by Amelia that although the new Electra airplane would be registered in her name and was hers to use, it belonged as much to the foundation as to her, and that although she could benefit from her writings, the proceeds would be shared with Purdue.

Unbeknownst to everyone until much later, it was Amelia's plan from the beginning to fly around the world, according to Robert Topping, who wrote the official history of Purdue. "Upon her return she was expected to write a book on her flight and the research activities that were part of it. Her plane was then to become the property of PRF [Purdue Research Foundation]. Income realized from the book and exhibitions of the plane were to be used to advance applied research in aeronautics."

PART THREE

17
New Records

•••• By 1934 Amelia had become so involved in her various projects—lecturing, fashion designing, starting airlines, running the Ninety-Nines, encouraging flight competitions, and signing on to teach at Purdue—that she barely had time to fly. She hadn't set a record since her second transcontinental flight or done any noteworthy flying since the Bendix.

In September 1933 she had been held in such awe that on the occasion of the official opening of the Franklin Institute Aviation Hall in Philadelphia, the twin attractions were Orville Wright standing next to the engine that had powered his epochal flight at Kitty Hawk, and Amelia standing under the Vega in which she had flown the Atlantic. There was no one to touch her—then—but other, younger women had since then been making incredibly difficult "first" flights, for which they were quite properly being lionized. Dashing and pretty New Zealander Jean Batten flew from Kent, England, to Darwin, Australia, in May 1934 in 14 days 22 hours, beating Amelia's friend Amy Mollison's record by almost five days; Laura Ingalls, whom Amelia had beaten out to be the first solo female pilot to fly the Atlantic, flew solo clear around South America and was internationally acclaimed. The popular young German pilot Elly Beinhorn had more recently flown solo around the continent of Africa.

There was one great "first" left: the Pacific Ocean had still not yet been tackled—solo—by man or by woman. Its time had come. It had been the hope and goal of Ruth Nichols to be the first to fly solo across that broad expanse of water, broader than the Atlantic, but ever since her crackup in New Brunswick, she had been dogged by ill luck, and so far she had not been able to raise sufficient money to mount the challenge.

Bobbi Trout, co-holder of the woman's endurance record, came very close to mounting the challenge. It had been almost within her reach; she had made the most meticulous plans. She had secured the financial backing of soap manufacturer Gordon Davidson and hired a promoter-manager, and with much fanfare, in 1931 Davidson ordered an Altair from Lockheed for her. Advertising contracts were drawn up for *Miss Commerce,* as the plane was to be called, for in addition to Davidson's backing her manager planned to sell advertising space on the side of the plane for $100 to $2,500 depending on the size of message, to have NBC carry her live broadcasts as she made the flight, and to sell the specially printed first-day air covers she would carry with her. The project made headlines all over the country and seemed to be on track—and then Davidson backed out, the other advertisers drifted away, and the enterprise folded. Bobbi was sidelined.

The Pacific had been flown a few times by pilots with crews—twice by the Australian Charles Kingsford-Smith. He did it the first time with a crew of three from Oakland, California, to Honolulu the same summer Amelia crossed the Atlantic in the *Friendship.* (He too had been flying a trimotored Fokker.) With a co-pilot, Kingsford-Smith flew it again, reversing the course, in early November 1934. Kingsford-Smith's 1928 transpacific flight took 27 hours and 28 minutes; his 1934 flight took 14 hours and 59 minutes. The time difference is a startling indication of how quickly planes were improving, but still, everyone was wary of the Pacific. Seven fliers—one of them a woman—had died in other attempts.

Sometime in September 1934, before Kingsford-Smith's flight, just about the same time she was working with Elliott to fit Purdue into her schedule, Amelia made the decision: her next big flight would be from Honolulu to California. She worked out the details with Paul Mantz, her new technical adviser, upon whose shoulders would fall the logistical and mechanical details; he visited them in Rye the first weekend in October. The final decisions made, on Saturday, October 6, she dropped the bomb on Lucy Challiss: "Amelia told me new plans—oh dear!" wrote Lucy in her diary.

Shortly thereafter Janet Mabie and her fourteen-year-old son Kenneth came to visit Amelia in Rye. Even though Amelia had spread out her parachute, so that it billowed like waves from end to end in the huge living room, covering the piano, lamps, and bookshelves, and smothering the room "like a blanched London fog," she did not guess that something epochal was about to happen. Mabie later reflected that the reason, of course, was that Amelia acted as if she examined it every week. "The last person on this earth from whom you would hear that Amelia Earhart was going to make a Honolulu–California flight would be Amelia Earhart," she consoled herself later. And Amelia had indeed been calm. Mabie's son was listening when the talk at one point touched on the honors Amelia had received and where she kept them. Much against her will, she was persuaded to show them to Kenneth. She scuffed upstairs in her old soft slippers, according to Janet, and scuffed back down again carrying her treasures. So they looked in awe at the velvet and tooled-leather boxes holding the orders from France, Belgium, Italy, Romania, and Sweden, and the medals from scientific organizations. The Legion of Honor gleamed in the palm of her hand.

"Gee," said Kenneth.

" 'Gee' is right," said Amelia, snapping closed the suitcase. "I'd better see what there is in the house to eat, or you and I won't get any supper."

• • • •

They closed up the Rye house soon after and rented a house at 10515 Valley Spring Lane in Hollywood. Amelia got in her car and drove west on a lecture tour that would end up in California, leaving Lucy, who was again in residence and helping out, and George to tend to final details. So final was the decision to move west that Amelia even took herself out of the Manhattan directory, which listed her as living at the Seymour Hotel as of November. (George, however, continued to give the Seymour as his business address.) Her mother agreed to visit, for a while; she would hold down the Hollywood house while Amelia was in Honolulu.

The plans and preparations for the flight were made efficiently and seemingly effortlessly. One of the decisions made was that since radios were now more powerful and lighter, Amelia should take one. She filed an application and on November 21 received FCC approval to install radio equipment in her Vega. Probably because hers was the first civilian plane equipped with two-way radio telephone equipment for a long-distance flight, and because the government was involved, in the time-honored way that interesting government news manages to leak, enterprising reporters found out that the FCC had specified that the equipment must be used "only for communication with ships and coastal stations when in flight over the sea." So they knew she was about to fly an ocean—which could only be the Pacific—and started paying close attention.

George did his best to throw them off: on November 22, accosted by a reporter, he baldly stated that Amelia was on a lecture tour of California and was "not contemplating any long flight." In fact, of course, all the final decisions and fitting out were just about completed, as was the flight plan, which called for flying from Honolulu to California, since it was commonly accepted wisdom that it is easier to hit a continent than an island.

Ten days later, in California, Amelia had her picture taken with the Australian Charles Ulm who had been the navigator for Kingsford-Smith on the 1928 flight. Ulm was about to take off from Oakland bound for Honolulu with two in crew on the first leg of a flight to Australia. On December 3 Ulm did take off from Oakland—he disappeared to the west and was never seen again. The coast guard cutter *Itasca* was sent out to search and rescue the fliers, it spent weeks combing the most promising areas but found not a piece of his plane. That brought the total number of fliers killed flying that stretch of water to ten.

• • • •

It became impossible to hide from reporters the fact that not just Amelia, George, Paul Mantz, and his wife Myrtle were sailing to Hawaii on the *Lurline,* but the plane and a mechanic as well. By December 18 George was admitting it. She "may" fly back, he grudgingly conceded.

Reporters met them in Honolulu, asking whether Amelia would fly to California. She answered coolly, "I thought I would do some flying over the Hawaiian Islands." But then, as leis were placed around her neck, she was asked, "If you fly to the California coast will Mantz fly with you?"

That broke through her reserve. "If I fly to the coast I will not take a *cat* along," she snapped back. They had her—they knew it was just a question of when.

Their headquarters was the home of Fleischman Yeast heir Chris Holmes, a friend of Paul Mantz's who lived on the beach at Waikiki in Honolulu. The absent owner had instructed his manager to put the facilities of the house and the culinary arts of his Chinese staff at the disposal of Amelia's entourage. Meanwhile, the U.S. Army was making sure everything was in readiness for her at Wheeler field. The facilities at Wheeler, in fact, had been put at her disposal; army mechanics, engineers, and guards tended to her plane from the end of December to January 11, when she took off, giving all possible support to Paul Mantz and mechanic Ernie

Tissot as they worked over the plane. Army personnel mowed a pathway on the unpaved field and placed white flags along its edge. As she was readying to depart on the flight, Major Everett Clark, commandant at Wheeler, "attested to the mechanical excellence of [the] plane." In addition, Major Halstead Dorey, commander of the Hawaiian Division, accompanied by the acting commander of the Hawaiian Department, arrived and inspected it. The U.S. military wanted to make sure nothing bad happened to the heavily loaded plane. No other fliers were accorded such special treatment.

Not everyone, however, thought the flight was a good idea; the Ulm disaster had cast a pall on derring-do. *The Honolulu Star-Bulletin* thought the enterprise foolhardy. "There is nothing intelligent about flying solo from Hawaii to the mainland in a single-engined land plane, which is very poor equipment for a long across-water flight," they wrote, claiming that her radio could only carry three hundred miles. To disprove it, Mantz took the plane up to an altitude of twelve thousand feet over Honolulu and established two-way voice communication with Kingman, Arizona.

There was also some question as to whether Amelia should have funded the flight with $10,000 from Hawaiian business interests—put up to promote good will and closer ties between Hawaii and the United States. The Hawaiian businessmen who were putting up the money were suddenly accused of trying to buy favorable tariffs for Hawaiian sugar. The last thing they expected (or needed) was adverse publicity. They had hoped the tie-in with Amelia would promote legislation that would bring Hawaii closer to the United States—something that was of the utmost importance to Hawaii, since it was not yet a state. Now, their influence was being called into question, on top of which, if something happened to Amelia, they would be blamed. They tried to renege. Four days before the flight, dressed in leather jacket and jodhpurs, Amelia drove in from Wheeler field to the posh Royal Hawaiian Hotel on Waikiki, marched into the dining room where the men were meeting, and blasted them: "Gentlemen, there is an aroma of cowardice in this air. You know as well as I do that the rumor is trash, but if you can be intimidated, it might as well be true. Whether you live in fear or defend your integrity is your decision. I have made mine. I intend to fly to California within this next week, with or without your support."

They decided to stand by her. It was the first time that Amelia had ever been subjected to public criticism, and she took it hard. She later said that she felt "physical strain" during the flight that was "more difficult than fatigue"—the only admission on record that outside opinion affected her. Once again, she left behind "popping off" letters, as she had before the *Friendship* flight—this time two perfectly proper and straightforward ones, everything spelled correctly, for as she knew, if she did "pop off," they would go into the public domain.

Amelia's plane was still the Vega once owned by Elinor, now painted Fokker red with gold trim edged with black, so that NR 965Y looked very much like the Vega that had preceded it. Various other changes had been made. The engine was the 500-horsepower engine that had taken Amelia across the Atlantic in 1932, which she had removed from the Vega before it was donated to the Franklin Institute. The metal fuel lines were now encased in rubber to prevent leaks. The newest Hamilton "constant speed" controllable-pitch propeller, enabling a pilot to maintain constant engine revolutions irrespective of altitude, had been installed; and the wheel pants had been removed to reduce weight. Because of the radio a trailing wire antenna jutted out of the bottom center of the fuselage, and there was an antenna mast on each wingtip, as well as a centerline antenna ending at a short mast halfway back to the tail. Fuel tanks instead of passenger seats took up the interior of the fuselage, which, together with tanks installed on the wings, gave a total capacity of 520 gallons. Amelia sat on the left side of the cockpit, on a cushion; to her right was the radio, "a large black box, with the dials on top so I could reach them easily." The radio and the generator that powered it weighed eighty pounds; the 50-watt radio, made by Western Electric, covered a range of 210 to 500 kilocycles. In the cockpit were also backup hand-pump handles with which Amelia could manually switch from one tank to another in case the automatic system failed. (It didn't.) There were also backup instruments; three clocks—one set at 12:00 so that she could see elapsed time—three compasses, and two altimeters.

Considering the added weight of the 520 gallons of gasoline she was carrying and the wetness of the field, she made a superb takeoff. The Vega tore down the muddy runway tail high and streaked into the air. George was relieved, but so weary when the takeoff was over that he remarked to no one in particular that he "would rather have a baby than go through this again." The remark was overheard, misinterpreted (that he wanted Amelia home having babies), and given widespread media attention, much to his discomfiture.

Amelia took off at four thirty P.M. so that the flight would start and end in daylight. She was in the air 18 hours, 16 minutes—a huge stretch of time. Exactly one hour into the flight, she radioed, "Everything okay," and during the course of the flight sent out twenty-four similar messages, at a quarter to and a quarter past the hour. She never gave her position or course, evidently not wanting to give an approximation and not being able to chart it and fly at the same time. Her chart, actually, was some two and a half feet long and eight inches wide. It was marked off into sections, each section representing one hour's flying. At the end of each section were the compass headings she was meant to follow for the next hour.

Everyone was pulling for her: all ships traveling between Honolulu and the mainland that night were ablaze and kept on their searchlights, and she had a chart showing their course and probable position. When one saw her, it was prepared to radio her position to the world at large.

She tuned in to station KGU, the Honolulu commercial broadcasting station, and was rewarded with a complaint from her husband, waiting at the radio station (addressing her, as he usually did, by her initials): "A.E., the noise of your motor interferes with your broadcast. Will you please try to speak a little louder so we can hear you." She said that hearing him "was really one of the high points of the flight." It was another first—the first time there was two-way radio contact on a civilian flight.

"It was a night of stars," she wrote, "of tropic loveliness. Stars hung outside my cockpit window near enough to touch." During the flight she sipped hot chocolate, tomato juice, and water.

After the sun came up, fog rolled in, and after staring through fog for three hours, she said in one of her radio messages, "I am getting tired of this fog." (The message was received as "I am getting tired," which so alarmed listeners that a nurse and physician were dispatched to the airport, which would later annoy Amelia immensely.) After the morning fog dissipated, looking down at the water, she saw the Dollar Liner *President Pierce*—San Francisco bound, she knew, from Honolulu. She circled, lined herself up with the wake of the vessel, and noting that her course and the ship's course were the same, knew she was on target. A radio check with San Francisco giving the location of the ship as three hundred miles from San Franciso told her exactly how much farther she had to go. She came in low over the coast, flew straight in over San Francisco Bay, and landed.

Her eyes were bloodshot, which she attributed to a faulty ventilator (the code was to never admit you were tired), and when a policeman tried to shoo away reporters who were clamoring that they were on deadline and had to talk to her immediately, she was steady enough to stop him: "But officer," she said, "deadlines are important." And she went on answering questions—tired but still functioning. One reporter asked her if she was now ready to give up long-distance flying. "Not while there's life in the old horse left," she replied. Her time, compared with Kingsford-Smith's, was very slow, a personal disappointment, but no one cared. It was the first solo by man or woman, over that part of the Pacific.

The world went wild again. Even the staid old *New York Times* threw away its reserve and reached for Keats to sing her praises, exulting, "She now holds the fair planet in her hands." A crowd estimated at between 10,000 and 14,000 waited for her at the Oakland airport. (Said Amelia later, "I thought there might be some kind of meet going on when I first saw it.")

She flew briefly to Los Angeles, and when she returned to Oakland for the huge celebratory dinner being given in her honor, the navy sent up eleven planes to escort her down. President Roosevelt, the secretary of war, and the secretary of the navy sent greetings; Amelia was given a bracelet of California gold nuggets. Everyone of importance in the city was there, including former president Herbert Hoover. *The Nation,* acting a bit prim, grudgingly allowed as how $10,000 was not much for risking one's life to cross an ocean for the first time, that all she had agreed to do "against the shining background of that magnificent achievement, [was] parrot a puny phrase to the effect that Hawaii was part of the United States" (hard to argue with).

Eleanor Roosevelt was one of those absolutely dazzled by Amelia's latest exploit. She extended Amelia a carte blanche invitation to the White House. ("When you come to Washington will you and your husband if he is with you stay with us? Let us know as much ahead as you can.") In the face of such honor, Amelia made a special detour to Washington on January 31 to breakfast with Eleanor and have a private audience with the president.

There was a moment just then, when Eleanor's career was sputtering and Amelia's career was so brilliant, that the president's wife, like every other American woman, looked to Amelia as a role model; she couldn't get enough of her. Indeed, a week after Amelia left for New England (she was addressing the joint legislatures of Vermont and Maine—at each state house she wound up with a stirring plea to build more airports), Eleanor was writing with more fervor than manners called for that Amelia was a perfect guest except in one respect: "you need not always feel that you have to be out for every meal. We all feel we did not see enough of you." When Eleanor *could* catch her, she asked her for advice on furthering her own career, which at that point was not going as well as she thought it should. *Woman's Home Companion* had just dealt her the stunning blow of discontinuing her monthly column, a staple of the magazine since FDR became president. Her weekly newspaper column had not yet reached its later prominence. She was in search of a new, professional, effective agent.

Amelia, good wife and good friend, offered up George, who had just been separated from his job as head of the editorial board at Paramount Pictures in the wake of the firing of Emanuel Cohen, his boss and sponsor at the movie studio. "Would you like GP to try to find a substitute for the woman's magazine work you have been doing? He is in constant contact with writers and editors and other people. . . . I know he would be only too glad to stir up something interesting," she wrote Eleanor. (To her mother she wrote, "GP has left Paramount and is in a state trying to decide what alley to run down.") George, being inventive, entrepreneurial, and full of energy as well as at loose ends, took just a few days to come up with the idea of a weekly joint broadcast by Amelia and Eleanor—radio conversations "touching on matters of basic interest to American women today." Irrepressible huckster that he was, he loved the challenge and offered himself up to be her agent and arrange it. Eleanor shot this down. ("I am not particularly anxious to get tied up for the whole summer, besides the fact that I have an agent who has more or less made my radio contacts.")

Within a few days George came up with another thought: Would she like to write a piece for Ray Long, formerly of *Cosmopolitan* and now running "the best of the movie magazines *Photo Play*"? Ray Long, according to George, wanted an article about the movies the president and the family watched: "No discussion of specific pictures, of course, but a general informal article on the kind of pictures which are liked best." Eleanor considered it, but what she really wanted was for Amelia to fly her around the country—just the two of them—in a little two-seater plane, as she told George in her letter to him in mid-March, so she could gather information on the New Deal Federal Emergency Relief projects and particularly the Arthurdale project in West Virginia that would kick off the Subsistence Homestead Act and provide housing and employment for two hundred desperately poor familites. What better way to travel, and what an incredible publicity coup to have Amelia as her pilot. Her letter went on that she was looking for a plane to borrow "if Amelia is free." George leaped at her suggestion like a fish to a fly, but he had more grandiose ideas: "Definitely a plane is available. It is a new four place closed ship. It has very fine equipment, including telephonic radio receiving and sending apparatus, plus the new radio 'homing compass.' " It might have worked out, and both women were looking forward to the trip (whether they were two or four). But the relief programs were just about to be reorganized with the undersecretary of agriculture, Rexford G. Tugwell, as their new administrator, and Tugwell felt Eleanor was jumping the gun—he advised against it. He wanted them to wait six months, he wrote Eleanor, until the various programs were coordinated and running smoothly.

Eleanor was quite taken with the idea, however, and continued to pursue it: possibly an autumn tour, she thought, and offered suggestions for dividing up the funds that would accrue from radio talks and magazine articles.

By the end of May, much to George's disappointment, Eleanor had decided to work not with him but with another agent, George Bye. Unfazed by the rejection, George wrote her back that he thought her decision "admirable," that Bye was an old friend, indeed, had worked for George for several years "at the beginning of his agency career." Within a short time Bye had signed her up with United Features Syndicate for a six-day-a-week column of five hundred words. Called "My Day" it became staple reading for millions. Eleanor became almost as popular and well known as her husband.

• • • •

That spring the Mexican government had inaugurated a radio campaign over NBC in an effort to promote goodwill and the all-important United States tourist trade. Noting all the good publicity that Amelia's flight had churned up for Hawaii, it decided to invite Amelia to fly to their country in hopes she could generate as much good will for them.

To tempt her, the Mexican government offered, through the Mexican consul general Eduardo Villasenor, a small but colorful issue of 780 air-mail stamps of December 1, 1934, showing the Aztec emperor Cuauhtemoc contemplating the snowcapped volcano Popocatépetl, which would be overprinted with "Vuelo de Amelia Earhart, Mexico, 1935." Amelia was to be given 200 of the stamps to carry home with her to sell, the remainder were to be put on sale in Mexico. The terms would cover the costs of the flight, and Amelia decided a nonstop, California-Mexico flight would be an interesting challenge. George, warned about corruption in Mexico, went down to Mexico City to oversee the stamp operation himself. He actually took with him the electro and the violet ink to be used in the overprinting—necessary to prevent copying—because the Mexicans did not have such equipment, and he was savvy enough to pick up Amelia's allotted two hundred stamps at the post office department on April 18, the day before she was scheduled to take off. His caution was rewarded: Mexican officials tried to talk him into accepting only 140 stamps, giving as the excuse that 60 stamps were needed for a library. He held firm. As the *Diario Official* of the Mexican government put it, he was "highly irritated at the failure of the Post Office Department to comply with the agreement" and threatened to call off the flight. The stamps were found and put in his hand, and Amelia proceeded as scheduled. (Their sale, some reputedly for as much as a hundred dollars apiece, covered the costs of the flight.)

She took off on a moonlit night from the Burbank airport on the nineteenth of April. So clear was the air that the moon gilded the hills, but as she traveled south over the coast and the Sea of Cortés, a white haze blended sandy coast and water into a muddle. Her engine seemed to be overheating, which she rectified by resetting the propeller. She was again following a chart that gave her hourly course headings. She successfully located Tepic and Guadalajara, but at the hour she was supposed to be over Mexico City (if her dead reckoning was correct), as she was hand-pumping gasoline, she saw a railroad beneath her—which according to her chart shouldn't have been there. Just then something—a speck of dirt or an insect—irritated her eye, and she decided to set down. It is possible that she was feeling a bit light-headed as the combination of her lack of sleep and the altitude (she was flying at ten thousand feet) took their toll.

Looking down, Amelia saw a flat dry lakebed beneath her and set down. Mexicans appeared, speaking Spanish to her, which she didn't understand. She pulled out her chart, and although there was a language barrier, a "bright, dark-skinned boy" established her location on it as Nopala, and after the cowboys cleared a path through the children, goats, and cattle that had gathered and she had mentally marked off clear space free from the cactus and prickly pear dotting the landscape, she took off for Mexico City, some sixty miles away.

At the Mexico City airport the largest crowd since Lindbergh flew in 1927 was gathered and wildly applauding as she drew to a stop. *The New York Times* and most other newspapers again put her safe arrival on the front page. The flight raised her reputation another few notches, but she was disappointed and, interviewed shortly after landing, called her flight "unsuccessful" and vowed to "do a better job of flying non-stop to New York."

She was declared an official guest of Mexico, given a private audience with President Lázaro Cárdenas, and invited to a presidential garden party, and she took part in the regular Foreign Office Sunday radio show. She received a platinum medal from Amalia de Cárdenas, wife of the president, inscribed, unfortunately not to Amelia Earhart but to Amelia Earhart Putnam. A gold medal from Aida de Rodriguez, wife of the ex-president, was also presented to her with a degree of pomp. Both ceremonies left her underwhelmed—she felt frustrated at not getting an opportunity to talk to less privileged women or find out what Mexican law and tradition permitted them to do outside the home.

Having set down in Nopala on the way down, Amelia's resolve to make the return trip to Newark nonstop was uppermost in her mind. Because Mexico City is at 7,500 feet and the air at that elevation is thin, taking off with sufficient gasoline—470 gallons, weighing thousands of pounds—necessitated a very long runway that would enable the Vega to get up to a speed of a hundred miles per hour or better. None existed; both the civil and the military fields were too short. The heavily loaded Vega needed three miles to become airborne.

Again a government put an army at her disposal. Mexican soldiers under the direction of Colonel Roberto Fierro, chief of Mexican Military Aviation, filled ditches and shaved off hummocks on the mud-caked but mostly level flats of what had been Lake Texcoco, until they had fashioned a three-mile runway, which they even staked out with flags. The Mexican government also transported the requisite drums of gasoline to the lakebed, located six miles outside Mexico City, and provided soldiers to guard them and her plane. The soldiers would remain on duty to clear the area of cows, people, horses, and goats when she was ready to take off. Pan American Airways also helped: Her plane had been housed in the Pan Am hangar at the Mexico City airport and worked over by Pan Am mechanics.

Her stay in Mexico City stretched to eighteen days before weather permitted her to take off. James Kimball, at his post in New York, was in charge, as usual. Amelia was impatient to get off and made more than one abortive trip to the field. Her comment after an unexpected weather delay forced her to return to the hotel can be taken as a commentary on the too-elaborate ceremonies the Mexican government was putting her through: "Nature does as thorough a job as man." George did leave, by means unknown; the following day he was in Dallas, on his way home.

A few days later, finally the weather cooperated. Casasolo, Pan Am's star mechanic, drove out to the makeshift field for the last time, and by the light of automobile headlights, gave the Vega's engine a final check. General Samuel Rojas, commander of the First Air Regiment, not to be left out of any ceremony, bade her a formal good-bye, as did Mexican foreign affairs officials. The leavetaking was interrupted when Amelia noticed that for some reason there was only one gasoline pump at the field and dashed off in a car to the nearest airport to borrow another.

The takeoff itself, at just after six A.M. went smoothly, although it took almost four minutes and most of the length of the dusty lakebed before her wheels lifted off the ground; Amelia was relaxed, almost ecstatic to be airborne—finally. "Slowly I climbed to 10,000 feet, to skim over the mountains that hem in the high central valley where the city lies, separating it from the lands that slope down to the sea. Majestic Popocatépetl raised its snowy head to the south, luminous in the rays of the rising sun. A fairyland of beauty lay below and about me—so lovely as almost to distract a pilot's attention from the task at hand, that of herding a heavy plane out of that great upland saucer and over the mountains that make its rim."

• • • •

Wiley Post practically dared Amelia to fly over the Gulf of Mexico on the Mexico City–Newark leg—a distance of some seven hundred miles—by saying to her that she shouldn't.

Wiley, onetime barnstormer, parachute jumper, oil field roustabout (where he had lost an eye), and superb flier, so casual, confident, and thorough that on long-distance flights he habitually drained each tank until the engine quit before switching to another ("that way, I know exactly how much gas I've got in each tank," he explained), who with Harold Gatty had flown around the world in eight days in 1931, did not make idle comments about important things.

"Did Wiley Post, the man who had braved every sort of hazard in his stratosphere flying, really regard a simple little flight from Mexico City to New York across the Gulf as too hazardous? If so I could scarcely wait to be on my way," declared Amelia. After the Atlantic and the Pacific, it seemed to her eminently feasible. She didn't give it too much thought and, following the Pan American Airways route, headed northeast for Tampico, on its western shore, where she shot out over the Gulf.

Six hours and ten minutes later she was over New Orleans, where she made radio contact with the Department of Commerce radio station. "Everything O.K.," she reported. From there north she followed the air route of Eastern Air Lines. The manager of Eastern, Eddie Rickenbacker, the famous World War I ace, had broadcast instructions to all landing fields of the system to be on the watch for her and to have weather reports ready. Tuning in, she heard the Eastern radio operators reporting adverse winds below 7,000 feet, so she was flying at 10,000 feet, where the wind was behind her. Mobile, Alabama, reported her over the city at 3:02. Two hours later she passed over Atlanta, 305 miles away, going 150 miles an hour. She was over the Spartanburg, South Carolina, airport, a distance of 169 miles, one hour later.

Charles Lindbergh had flown nonstop between Mexico City and Washington in twenty-seven hours seven years before. Others had tried to fly from Mexico to the New York area nonstop, but heretofore the rarefied atmosphere of Mexico City had prevented fliers from loading their planes with enough fuel to make it possible. As Amelia's progress north was broadcast, a crowd gathered at Washington's Hoover airport. She roared across Hoover airport 13 hours 6 minutes after takeoff—cutting nearly fourteen hours off Lindbergh's time. As her green and red navigation lights flashed overhead, Gene, waiting and watching below, radioed her to land, even though as he and everyone else knew, if she made it on to Newark, it would be a big first. "You've done a splendid job, so come down," Gene pleaded, to which Amelia composedly replied, "Thanks for the invitation. I'm going through."

By nine P.M. when it became apparent that she would be the first person to fly from Mexico City to Newark, a line of cars headed toward the Newark field to join the hundreds of cars already parked and waiting there. One hour and 23 minutes later, the Vega appeared over the airport and made a great half circle. The floodlights caught it in their beam, and she made a perfect three-point landing. Fourteen hours and 18 minutes after takeoff, having covered a distance of 2,100 miles, she was down.

The huge, excited multitude broke through police lines and rushed onto the field. Police cars tried to cordon off the plane, but when Amelia emerged from the cockpit, tousleheaded and smiling, she was entirely surrounded by the onlookers. There was an incredible amount of jostling. Policemen grabbed her, almost pulling her apart in the process; then, protected by the policemen and flanked by police cars, she walked, laughing, toward the hangar reserved for her; George met her partway there. Reporters noted that he was upset and "raged vainly" at the aviation fans who appeared bent on tearing Amelia limb from limb. But Amelia appeared to be enjoying every minute. Observers found it hard to believe that she had just finished such a punishing flight—"her face was tanned and ruddy but there were no lines of fatigue." She had set three new records: a new intercity nonstop record between Mexico City and Newark, a new women's nonstop speed record for the distance, and a new speed record from Mexico City to Washington, where she was timed at 13 hours, 5 minutes, 52 seconds. Paul Collins was at the field with George. "That's a *flier!*" he said softly, to no one in particular.

Never had her stamina shown more clearly. The energy and conditioning that allowed her to go without sleep for long periods of time—that allowed her to be fully functional rather than overcome with fatigue—made this, her third long flight, look almost easy.

"No one should undertake a long flight who becomes fatigued after staying up just one night under normal flying conditions," she wrote.

• • • •

The newspaper coverage of the flight eclipsed the message King George sent to Adolf Hitler, on the occasion of the king's silver jubilee, promoting the interest of peace.

18
New Frontiers

•••• The day after Amelia landed, she gave an interview sitting in her flower-bedecked suite at the Hotel Seymour. Still smarting from the criticism she had endured for the Hawaiian flight, she wished to clearly explain why she had accepted money at all—why there had to be a commercial aspect to her flights. The country was still in the grips of the Depression, and practicality was the order of the day. After all, $1,348 was the average income, and ninety-eight percent of American families lived on less than $5,000 a year. "Flying with me is a business. Of course I make money. I have to or I couldn't fly. I've got to be self supporting or I couldn't stay in the business," she told the reporters.

But the "business" she was referring to was the lecture tours, magazine articles, and books she had written. The reporters still poked at her, asking if the Mexican flight was a setup similar to the Pacific flight. "I received an invitation from the Mexican government. I spent my own money to get there. I wasn't paid a cent. They were most charming and gracious. They issued a special stamp in my honor" was her reply.

It wasn't that there was any disapproval of pushing products—that kind of commercialism was an accepted part of flying and adventuring. All the famous fliers, including Lindbergh, endorsed the tools of the trade.

Admiral Byrd, the acknowledged master fund-raiser of them all, endorsed everything from Grape-Nuts cereal to bacon. At various times Amelia endorsed Chrysler cars, Essex Terraplane cars, Longines watches, the Eastman Kodak movie camera, and of course Beech-Nut, when she flew their autogiro. Newspaper and magazine advertisements as well as radio commercials were at the time extolling the sturdy virtues of lightweight Amelia Earhart air travel luggage. And as everyone was aware, after the solo transatlantic flight, she endorsed the plane, the engine, the propeller, the engine's spark plugs, its fuel and oil, and its radio and navigational instruments.

The reporters just wanted to make sure that she was still the straightforward, adventurous, uncomplicated standard bearer of her sex—that she wasn't being used by special interests to push hidden agendas. Promoting products for money was acceptable to the American public: promoting causes for money was not, particularly foreign causes. After all, she was *America's* heroine, as female heroes were then called.

The problem was, of course, made infinitely worse because the standards for women were arbitrary and foolish. Thus *McCall's* magazine had refused to hire Amelia after she endorsed a cigarette (even though she didn't smoke) because "nice" women didn't smoke—although every man could.

Plenty of men, as well as plenty of women, still weren't at all sure that females should be doing long-distance flying in the first place. There were those who thought Amelia *might* be an anomaly. There were those who thought she merely hid the "female" problem: the menses. In the 1930s and on into the 1940s most men and many women thought that menstruation impaired a woman's mental as well as physical performance. In 1941 two army doctors wrote a handbook called *Fit to Fly,* in which they set forth the accepted thinking: "During the menstrual period women tend to become emotionally upset and it is believed that several aircraft accidents have been due to this cause. It also should be obvious that a woman who is pregnant should not be allowed to pilot an aircraft."

In 1942 the Civilian Aeronautics Administration put out a *Handbook for Medical Examiners,* in which it is stated, "All women should be cautioned that it is dangerous for them to fly within a period of three days prior to and three days after the menstrual period." In 1943 the Air Transport Command ordered its women pilots grounded for the week they menstruated. The order only became moot, according to Sally Keil, who wrote their history, because the men were afraid to ask. It would take the United States Army until 1945 to do a study demonstrating that menstruation had no effect on pilot performance.

Amelia had already begun working on the problem of men's misperception of women's ability to function during the menses. A great deal of the male opposition to Helen Richey serving as a regular pilot for Central Airlines could be laid to this one cause. The knowledge that girls with menstrual problems didn't choose a career where such a disability would sideline them, and that women who did choose such careers had no problems of any kind was, in those years, shocking to men.

Amelia was assembling evidence. She had the statement of Dr. Alexis Carrel that there was no more reason to assume that menstruation threw women off balance "than there is for assuming that men, being men, are always nervously and mentally on an even keel." She had the statement of the wardrobe mistress of a circus, who in her youth had been a trapeze artist, whose daughter was a trapeze artist then working in the circus, that trapeze and high-wire women worked without regard for their periods: "Good gracious. If my life depended on it I couldn't remember when any of my girls had to take any time out for *that!*" She had the statement of Florence Rogge, ballet mistress at Radio City Music Hall: "We never think about it. It has been my experience that any such periodic handicap in a girl comes from a structural cause and that such a girl would naturally not enter a career of dancing. I would think the same thought would apply to a woman who wanted to be a professional pilot. The girl with any important deficiency wouldn't attempt to be a pilot."

But providing anecdotal evidence and proving something beyond the shadow of a doubt are two very different things, particularly when the conclusion not only flew in the face of accepted wisdom but challenged a major rationale for keeping women out of the workplace. Amelia thought Purdue coeds would be the perfect subjects to study—she would be able to go before boards of medical officers and prove that women's performance was not affected by menstruation and that strictures against women serving as airline pilots were baseless. As it was, unchallenged, the medical establishment took a long time to change its mind.

Another less serious problem that air women had was how to relieve themselves. When Gore Vidal revealed that Amelia wore men's underwear when she flew, it indicated a practical approach to the situation. (Ladies' underwear—usually silk—was not only impractical but uncomfortable under slacks.) Women on long-distance flights urinated through a funnel into a pail, according to Jacqueline Cochran. Wearing men's underwear made it slightly easier. But with Purdue coeds as willing collaborators, Amelia could pull together studies and statistics that would demolish the menstruation myth, and as practical as she was, she would probably have fine-tuned women's flying clothes in an effort to make the problems they faced in relieving themselves less onerous.

• • • •

1935 was Amelia's most productive and most hectic year. In between her solo flights she spoke 136 times before eighty thousand people. At $300 a lecture, that meant she was grossing some $40,000 a year—at a time when the average stenographer was being paid $20 a week, telephone operators $15, and when half of the men and two-thirds of the women in the country earned less than $1,000 a year. And in spite of the endless number of times she spoke about women seizing job opportunities when and where they could, still the men who listened tuned out her feminist message—simply didn't seem to register it. Even George.

By summer she was run down, understandably. At the end of June her sinuses were kicking up so badly, she landed in Cedars of Lebanon Hospital in L.A., then got pleurisy. It threw all their plans off schedule and meant they would not get to the Double Dee ranch that summer after all.

Meanwhile another man had entered Amelia's life: Paul Mantz. It was he who had tuned up her Vega for the transpacific and Mexican flights. It wasn't a love interest—purely professional.

Paul Mantz, a superb flier, six years younger than Amelia, was the best-known and most successful stunt pilot in Hollywood. But he was also a supersalesman, a promotor, and a very different kind of person from those Amelia usually chose for friends. With dark brown eyes, slick black hair, and a cropped, narrow moustache, he had a penchant for brilliant ties, loud sport coats, gold jewelry, cigars, frosted martinis, and women. He was also, according to fiction writer Irving Wallace, empty-headed and shallow, a man of no real perceptions or sensitivity. And yet he and Amelia got on very well, at least in the beginning.

He had watched the famous flier Lincoln Beachey, whom Orville Wright had called "the most wonderful flier I ever saw," put his plane into the dive he never came out of and end up dead in San Francisco Bay. As a young man in love with flying, he watched his instructor, in a Jenny, go into a controlled spin that suddenly became uncontrollable and deadly the day he was to solo. He gave up flying for five years after that; then, after Lindbergh flew the Atlantic, he decided it had to be his life. He lied about his academic background and sneaked his way into the army aviation training program. He broke into the movie business by flying a biplane clear through a small hangar when no one else would; for another movie, *When Willie Comes Marching Home,* he ripped both wings off a Stearman biplane flying between two trees. He would do anything, but careful planning underlay his stunts. In pursuit of movie stunt work he had picked up various vintage planes, then branched out into the charter business; in a typical Mantz touch he called his charter plane the *Honeymoon Express.* It was famous for taking stars to Yuma for impulse marriages

(California had a three-day cooling-off law), gambling sprees, and illicit weekends.

Paul Mantz thought he was a law unto himself. The day before he was to graduate and get his wings from the army, he was thrown out for buzzing a train and missing the locomotive stack by inches. That was in 1928. In September 1934 he buzzed Redwood City, "in memorable fashion," to cheer up his bedridden mother—in the process scaring everyone else and earning a reprimand from the Department of Commerce. Once he landed on and then quickly took off from the deck of an aircraft carrier he saw steaming along beneath him in San Francisco Bay, for which he was lucky not to be put in jail. While testing Amelia's Vega he dive-bombed on film star William S. Hart's ranch; again he was reprimanded by the Department of Commerce. Later he would almost crash a twin of Amelia's Lockheed Electra, losing control of a spin for a movie called *Lockheed*.

Amelia took all this in stride. When Paul dive-bombed Hart's ranch, the retired film star had roared out of the house and gotten the number of the plane. Amelia ended up accompanying Paul to visit and apologize. ("Damn near shook the bricks out of the chimney," Bill Hart later grumbled.) It resulted in a new friendship; Amelia and George spent many hours at his Horseshoe ranch east of Hollywood, among treasures such as Charles Russell's finest Western paintings, shoes from every horse Bill had ever owned, and his two enormous dogs, Minnie and Prince, who insisted on chasing rabbits across the lawn and put Amelia in mind of Daudet's rabbits, who "warmed their paws in the moonlight." So she couldn't stay mad.

She had stayed with the Mantzes in their Toluca Lake home in North Hollywood twice, once for approximately a month, once for a few days, before she and George rented a house for themselves. By then the Mantz marriage was breaking apart, and when Myrtle sued for divorce (the divorce was granted in July 1936), she used those visits to name Amelia as co-respondent. There was never evidence that Amelia and Paul were interested in each other, particularly because Paul was head over heels in love with another woman, Terry Minor, whom he had recently met and who would shortly become his wife. It was more annoying than serious—"the silly accusations fell of their own weight," Amelia assured Amy. Amelia had decided to go into business with Paul, putting her plane in with his for charter, making plans for a flight school, thinking of putting on an air circus—she wasn't sure just what, after her record flights, but the commercial possibilities seemed very attractive. Paul seemed to have the big business commercial touch. Amelia was looking to enhance her income stream, and the income potential of linking their names seemed like too good a deal to pass up. She could give United Air Services greater visibility, more customers, and respectability and benefit financially at, she hoped, no great investment of time, for Paul appeared to be immensely successful. They rolled over the possibilities, as did George, who after some hesitation agreed that it was a sound business idea. She bought into United Air Services. In September Paul and Amelia would sign a business agreement to form the Earhart-Mantz Flying School.

Meanwhile Boston-Maine Airways was just beginning to do quite well. FDR had opened up the bidding for airmail contracts and the B&M won the contract for mail service north of Boston. Amelia and Gene now had the opportunity to sell their stake in Boston-Maine and took advantage of it, doubling their investment: each got twenty thousand dollars.

In June Amelia and George bought a house of their own in the Toluca Lake district, one of the fastest-growing townships in North Hollywood. Amelia had decided to move to California earlier that fall, but it had taken George, a bit left out in the beginning, some prodding to fall in with her plans. Amelia expected that he, of course, would be handling the publicity for any Earhart-Mantz enterprise; she hoped he would also supply ideas. One of the projects she and Paul were talking about was an air circus; George was, she told her mother, "all hep about this too." Not having been given a great deal of choice, he caved in, went house hunting, and was the one to find the house at the end of Valley Spring Lane in North Hollywood. The house was on a square lot, with two sides on the golf course of the Lakeside Country Club and the rounded California hills beyond. The house was too small but well situated; by the time they did it over, it would have nine rooms: four bedrooms, four and a half baths, and a sun deck.

• • • •

Amelia had never let up on what aviation historian Don Dwiggins called her "constant hammering" at Cliff Henderson and Vincent Bendix to rescind his ban on permitting women to enter the Bendix. Her pressure, in combination with her most recent record-breaking long-distance flights, which demonstrated more clearly that women could safely fly long distances, plus the crash of more Gee Bees (all with male pilots), decided the issue; the men had no choice except to readmit women into the race. But since Vincent Bendix shared Henderson's basic attitude that women didn't measure up to men as pilots and therefore couldn't possibly win, he put up a $2,500 "consolation prize" for the first woman who finished. Amelia waited until the last minute to submit her entry, and when it was announced, it moved the Bendix onto the front pages of the country's newspapers.

The Bendix race that year, 1935, would start out on the Friday of Labor Day weekend at the Union Air Terminal in Los Angeles and end in Cleveland at the opening of the National Air Races. It was no longer a solo race.

Roscoe Turner, who held the Los Angeles-to-New York speed record of 10 hours and 2 minutes was flying a powerful Wedell-Williams capable of speeds in excess of three hundred miles an hour. Jacqueline Cochran, newcomer to the aeronautics scene, was flying a 1,000-horsepower Northrop Gamma plane, as was Russell Thaw; Roy Hunt was flying a fast Lockheed Orion low-wing monoplane; Earl Ortman had an R-3 Silver Bullet powered by a 750-horsepower Wasp engine; Benny Howard, a vacationing United Airline pilot, accompanied by his wife Maxine "Mike" and Gordon Israel, both pilots, were in a Wasp-motored monoplane of Howard's design. Royal Leonard was in Q.E.D., a plane that had crash landed at least once.

Amelia knew her plane—"the old family bus," with its 500-horsepower engine—was dependable but not fast enough to win, unless—and the possibilities were always there in those years—unless mishaps took out the rest of the field. But she couldn't very well not enter, given her status as the best female long-distance flier and the champion of the right of women to enter. Paul decided to fly with her as a passenger, and an engineer friend, Al Menasco, owner of an up-and-coming engine company, joined up for the ride.

Henderson had planned to have starting times and they were tentatively set, but when fog rolled in, the idea was abandoned, and it was decided that the first plane ready would take off, mainly because several of the pilots said they wouldn't take off unless the fog lifted. Amelia, again less intimidated than others, was again the first contestant off, her wheels beginning to roll at 4:53 A.M. on the foggy morning of August 30. Roy Hunt stayed on the ground another hour, and then took off at six o'clock, followed almost immediately by Howard. Turner, remarking that "any man is crazy to take off in this kind of weather," waited till almost eight. One pilot, Seward Pulitzer, withdrew rather than take off in such thick fog. Cecil Allen and Jacqueline Cochran were the last to take off.

Cecil was flying one of the unreliable Gee Bees, and this one too now killed its pilot as it went out of control on takeoff. Jacqueline Cochran, following him, missed the end of the runway by three hundred feet and caught her trailing antenna in a fence, thereby knocking out her radio; she pulled out of the race upon landing in Arizona. Ortman in his Silver Bullet landed at Kansas City and decided to remain there; Leonard was forced down at Wichita by a broken fuel line. Benny and Mike Howard and Roscoe Turner were in a dead heat to the finish line, but Benny and Mike managed to win by twenty-three seconds. Russell Thaw came in third, Roy Hunt fourth. Amelia, who stayed at the controls for most of the race (Paul and Al played cards in the rear), piloted her cargo to fifth place and picked up the five-hundred dollar prize, which would pay for gas and incidental expenses. For her it was just one more flight most of the way across the country; she had lost count of the exact number she had made.

After the race was over, Amelia and Paul formalized their agreement to open the Earhart-Mantz Flying School with a contract. Then Amelia went off on the lecture circuit, visiting thirty cities in thirty days in Ohio, Michigan, Minnesota, Nebraska, Iowa, Illinois, Indiana, and Kansas.

• • • •

Two days after the Bendix, Laura Ingalls, the pretty New Yorker who had flown around South America, got into her Lockheed Orion and flew non-stop from Burbank to Floyd Bennett field in 13 hours, 35 minutes—breaking Amelia's nonstop coast-to-coast record by more than five and a half hours. Laura Ingalls had destroyed her record not only because she was a good flier but because the *Auto-da-Fe,* her sleek black Orion with the zodiac sign painted on the cowling, was new.

"I'd like to find the tree on which new airplanes grow. I'd certainly shake myself down a good one," Amelia had said a few weeks later. George evidently was listening, and reported it to President Elliott.

The Lockheed Electra, named after a star in the Pleiades, was Amelia's dream plane. It was the first fully pressurized plane, could carry twelve, had a wingspan of 55 feet, was almost 39 feet long, could fly to an altitude of 19,000 feet, and had a range of 4,000 miles.

But why did she want a huge twin-engined plane?

Part of the answer lies in tragedy. The summer of 1935, her good friends Wiley Post and Will Rogers, were planning a tour of the Yukon, the Northwest Territories, and Alaska in Wiley's Vega. Amelia gave Wiley gas tanks from her Vega—traded them for his wheels.

Wiley, a year younger than Amelia, brought up on a hardscrabble farm in east Texas, a school dropout at the age of fourteen, was fearless. An oil field roustabout in Oklahoma, Wiley became a parachute jumper for a flying circus that worked the town and jumped ninety-nine times in two years, along the way learning how to fly. Later, back in the oil fields to earn enough money to buy a plane, he lost an eye through another worker's carelessness. Undeterred, he taught himself to estimate distances with one eye and became such a good pilot that he became a test pilot for Lockheed. It was while working there that he met Amelia.

Will Rogers, the part Cherokee Oklahoma cowboy, probably the most popular man in America, certainly the most popular film star, had done more to popularize aviation than anyone except Lindbergh, Amelia felt. The Sunday before Wiley and Will left, Amelia and George had lunch at Will's ranch in Santa Monica.

Wiley, who loved pushing equipment to the limit, was always changing and experimenting with his planes. For this Yukon tour he had modified a Lockheed Orion. He not only exchanged the wheels for floats and added Amelia's fuel tanks, he substituted wings from the Sirius, another Lockheed design, for the ones designed for the Orion. The biggest change he made, however, according to Kelly Johnson, design engineer at Lockheed, was to put in a more powerful engine—the biggest engine he could—the biggest propeller, and a different gear box. Johnson disapproved because the additional weight of these changes made the plane so nose-heavy that the only way the plane could take off was to be rocked fore and aft on its floats with the power on until finally the nose came up and it bounced into the air.

"Wiley, you'd better watch this. You'll have trouble on takeoff," Johnson argued, "because I doubt that there is enough elevator power to get the nose up." Johnson didn't think the CAA (Civil Aeronautics Authority) would certify the altered plane, but they did, although later they would say they didn't know about all the design changes.

Wiley Post and Will Rogers started out on their voyage. They were having a splendid time, were three hundred miles from the Arctic circle, when Wiley set down in an Eskimo encampment, landing in a sort of lagoon to make some repair to the engine and make sure where he was. When Wiley took off again, on August 15, he managed to get the plane into the air and was climbing steeply, but suddenly the engine stalled, everything went wrong, and they crashed to their deaths. Amelia was devastated.

Wiley was every flier's hero. His first solo round-the-world flight in 1931 in a Vega had taken just eight days—an incredible achievement. He wrote a book about it. But he always had ambitious plans and was always short of money. Now he had met his death trying to soup up the engine of a single-engine plane to force it to give higher performance. If he had been in a twin-engine plane, it might not have happened. The big leap for Amelia was the crucial one of going from one engine to two. The death of her two good friends pointed the way; she made her decision.

The choice was clear if—and it was a big if—one had sufficient funds. And now, with the Purdue Research Foundation behind her, Amelia did. As for the particular choice, Amelia and most of the fliers she respected flew Lockheeds. They made the best land planes, as Sikorsky made the best seaplanes. And having moved to North Hollywood, the center of the nation's aircraft industry, Amelia had moved to within ten miles of Burbank, where Lockheed built its planes. The Electra was in the final stages of development: it was Lockheed's bid to capture the next generation of fliers. The Electra won hands down. It first flew on February 23, 1934. It was the fastest multi-engine transport in the world, the first able to cruise faster than two hundred miles an hour, the first plane with an all-metal surface to go into production in the United States. Northwest Airlines bought the first one off the line in July 1934; Braniff followed suit. Paul Collins, too, thought they were the new airplane of choice. He wanted them—badly—for the Boston and Maine, and knowing banks would turn a cold shoulder, he turned to fellow director Sam Solomon, a friend of Lockheed's president Robert Gross, who negotiated a deal so that the Boston and Maine could buy them on the installment plan.

• • • •

The Electra was the first plane to carry the unmistakable imprint of Clarence L. "Kelly" Johnson, a genius whose designs would include World War II's P-38 fighter-interceptor, the F-80, the first American operational jet fighter, the first planes to fly at three times the speed of sound, and the U-2, in which Gary Powers was shot down over Russia.

A big bright lad, son of Swedish émigrés, well coordinated enough to win a football scholarship to the University of Michigan, Johnson cut his teeth on the Lockheed Electra. His first day at Lockheed, he announced that the company's prototype new-model transport—which he had tested for his professor in the wind tunnel at the University of Michigan the year before—was unstable. To give the plane stability, he put a double vertical tail on the Electra, a touch that made it distinctive looking and turned it into a winner right away.

There were four Electra 10 models, all the same size, all built to hold ten passengers and two in crew: the 10A, with two Pratt and Whitney Wasp Jr. engines rated at 400 horsepower each; the 10B, with two Wright Whirlwinds rated at 420 horsepower each; the 10C, powered by two Wasps, rated at 450 horsepower; and the 10E, equipped with two Wasp engines, rated at 550 horsepower each. As the engines increased in horsepower, the weights varied from 6,300 pounds empty and 10,000 pounds gross on the 10B to 7,100 pounds empty and 10,500 pounds gross on the 10E.

Once she had decided, Amelia bought the 10E. Lockheed was so delighted with the idea of Amelia flying the Electra that they pulled out all the stops to have it ready for her birthday, even to the point of putting pressure on their suppliers. John Diehl, a B.F. Goodrich tire design engineer, remembers that it was of such importance that the plane be ready for delivery on July 24 that all rules at the plant were waived. The National Recovery Act, Roosevelt's law limiting workers to a forty-hour work week so that more jobs would be available in the Depression-ridden country, was in effect. Diehl had been told that if he spent any more time at night working on experimental tires, his pass would be lifted, but then he received a call late one afternoon asking him to come that evening and build three tires for Amelia, because no tires of the right size were in stock. "My boss called me and said, 'We make rules and now they must be broken. Would you please come in tonight and build three tires for Amelia Earhart?' " He and his crew worked straight though the night, and at eight the next morning the tires were finished.

She took possession of the Electra on her thirty-ninth birthday, July 24, 1936. It was a breathtaking plane. She was one of two individuals to own one; the other was the multimillionaire flier Howard Hughes, who acquired his Electra at about the same time.

Acquiring the plane meant getting to know Kelly; he helped Amelia break it in and work out various problems. He thought she was a very good pilot, "sensible, very studious, and paid attention to what she was told."

On August 29 she flew the Electra nonstop from Burbank to Kansas City, accompanied by Paul Mantz and Bo McKneely, her mechanic. She was contemplating entering the Bendix solo, she told the ever-present reporters at the field.

When she arrived at Floyd Bennett field, she was more than satisfied. "I could write poetry about this ship," she said to some mechanics.

She was flying east to enter the Bendix; 1936 was one of the years the race was run from New York to Los Angeles. Don Dwiggins, author of *They Flew The Bendix Race,* thought of the 1936 race as sort of an off year, probably because only seven planes were entered and three of them were piloted by women: Amelia, who had asked Helen Richey to be her co-pilot; Louise Thaden and Blanche Noyes, Amelia's friends whom she would recommend to Gene for the air-marking program, who were flying a 420-horsepower C17R Stagger-wing Beech demonstrator, loaned to them by Olive and Walter Beech; and Laura Ingalls in a sleek new Lockheed Orion. First off in the blackness at Floyd Bennett field at 1:37 A.M. on September 4 were William Gulick and Buster Warner in a 750-horsepower Vultee, followed by George Pomeroy at 2:03 in a Douglas DC-2, followed by Amelia and Helen in the Electra at 2:47, followed by Joe Jacobson in his Gar Wood *Gamma* at 3:12, followed by Louise Thaden and Blanche Noyes, followed by Ben and Mike Howard in *Mister Mulligan.* Last off at 6:11 was Laura Ingalls.

Moments after Amelia and Helen took off, a bolt in the hatch cover over their heads worked loose, and the big hatch—big enough to provide access—popped open. Only after the automatic pilot kicked in could Amelia, who was at the controls, help Helen wrestle it closed. At one point, "the wind almost sucked us right out of the cockpit," according to Amelia. It took them two hours before they got it securely into place. When they made their refueling stop in Kansas City, precious time was lost while it was wired shut. Later they had to deal with a cabin door that worked loose—all very time-consuming. They came in fifth. Their problems paled, however, beside those of Benny Howard, the 1935 winner, who flying with his wife, cracked up in New Mexico when the propeller blade just "let go," and Joe Jacobson, who narrowly missed being killed as he parachuted to safety after his plane suddenly exploded over Stafford, Kansas.

Laura Ingalls, flying solo, was making good time until she made her refueling stop which, because it was unplanned, took much longer than it should have. George Pomeroy in his DC-2 (his crew were playing cards in the back) also lost precious time refueling.

Louise Thaden and Blanche Noyes, meanwhile, were having problems with their directional gyro as well as with their radio, which conked out halfway across the continent—providentially *after* enabling them to learn that of their two refueling sites, only Wichita was clear and fog free. They went in dodging thunderstorms. They were sure, when they landed their trim blue Beechcraft at Mines field near Los Angeles, that they were in last place, sure they were, in Louise's words, "the cow's tail" of the race. They landed only to show they had gotten through and were puzzled to be greeted by the crestfallen faces of Vincent Bendix and Cliff Henderson. Then they were stunned when Cliff said to petite, blond Blanche, as she squeezed out of the plane handsomely attired in blue-green culottes and green flannel shirt, "I'm afraid you won the Bendix race. I wish you hadn't but if it had to be a woman I'm glad it was you." Then, to add insult to injury, Laura Ingalls in her Lockheed Orion followed them in to claim second place.

Louise noted with amusement that by evening the press releases referring to Bendix's prize for the first women to finish no longer called it the "consolation prize," as they had before, but the "special award." It added $2,500 to the $4,500 Bendix prize that Louise and Blanche walked away with. Their time of 14 hours and 55 minutes set a new east-west speed record that would stand for two years, until Alexander Seversky finally broke it. Their victory stilled the voices of those fanatics who leaned on the strength argument to hold female pilots back, for petite Blanche Noyes, ex-actress, ex-star of *White Cargo,* weighed all of eighty-five pounds.

It was a moment of great satisfaction to all the women pilots—a vindication of their prowess, and another step forward. Two years before, Cliff Henderson had said they weren't good enough pilots, safe enough pilots, strong enough pilots, to compete. Now they had walked off with the first and second prizes. It made no difference to Amelia that she had been bested by her good friends. They could sense her pride. "I don't think there was a jealous bone in her body," mused Blanche later. "She was just a fine woman all the way through." Amelia took her time wandering about the field, watching the races, seeing people, among them Gene.

• • • •

A few days later she had something else on her mind: Beryl Markham, attempting to fly from England to New York, crashed in Nova Scotia, nevertheless becoming the first woman to fly the Atlantic alone from east to west. Naturally, Amelia was asked if *she* had any inclination to try the flight from that direction. "I don't know—you know I've seen that ocean twice, and it doesn't get any prettier," she replied. But she was already planning her round-the-world flight, had been since August, when the Department of Commerce granted her a license, "restricted for long distance flights and research."

The next week all thoughts of transatlantic flights were crowded out of her mind by her concern for Gene Vidal. In spite of the large chunks of time spent with Paul Mantz, Purdue, and her new plane, there had been no change in her relationship with Gene. They were as intimate as ever. She had been asked to testify before the Senate Air Safety Committee and turned her appearance into a spirited defense of Gene and of bureau efforts to make the airways safe. She was "obviously nervous" as she sat down, according to the *Washington Post,* probably because she knew she was going to be walking out on a limb. Senator Copeland, chairman, seeking to put her at ease, said that the committee "wanted to find out all we can in answer to the question of air safety." Instead of replying to that point, according to the paper, Amelia "vigorously defended Federal airways personnel, whom," she declared were "on trial." She went on for several minutes in that vein. The headline over her picture was all she could have hoped for: "Amelia Earhart Lauds Bureau of Air Commerce," as was the caption that ran underneath: "tells Senate Air Safety Committee there was 'no group more loyal, interested and conscientious' than the Bureau of Air Commerce." Having made her point, she then went into an assessment of various airports and navigation aids, and ended up returning in the afternoon with a receiving set tuned into the Washington airport so that the senators could hear what a radio beacon sounded like.

When Amelia and Paul were making plans to fly to Denver for the Fourth of July air races, Amelia had wanted Gene to come, too. How to do it discreetly? Like a politician, using her people skills, Amelia had proceeded by indirection: She asked Paul to ask him. Paul wrote to Gene, "Amelia has consented to fly her ship up there, and I am wondering if it will be possible for you to come over and join us. Amelia mentioned particularly she would like so much to see you." Gene answered to Amelia, sending her a telegram that he couldn't do it: "Still can't leave here." It seems probable that there were two reasons he turned down the invitation: one was Paul Mantz, and the other was the demands of his job.

Laura Ingalls had applied to Gene for a position in the Bureau's air-marking program. What did Amelia think? queried Gene. Not a good idea. "After your note Ingalls out," Gene replied. Amelia then asked Gene to hire Blanche Noyes, who was in need of a job after her husband Dewey was killed, for the air-marking program. He authorized it the end of July.

• • • •

Things were *too* quiet in Washington that August as far as the Bureau of Air Commerce was concerned, quiet even by summer-doldrums standards. As Gene wrote Amelia, "it is the quietest period we have had since I have been here—whatever that means." He needed to find out.

It was the calm before the storm.

In mid-September came a Washington bombshell: it was announced that by executive order the bureau was going to be reorganized. Gene and his two assistant directors were to be fired, and a new director, a lawyer with sweeping new powers, would be appointed in his place. Amelia plunged in to the fray in support of her man.

Roosevelt was about to run for his second term. He had made Amelia a member of the advisory committee of the National Youth Administration, along with such heavyweights as the president of the NEA (National Education Association), the president of the biggest labor union in the United States, the president of Howard University, and others of the same caliber; Amelia had enthusiastically agreed to campaign for him and up to that point she had been letting Gene arrange the particulars of her support, for it was not only appropriate but politically helpful to him to act as her spokesman. Roosevelt not only liked her but needed her voice for the Democratic party.

Amelia decided to work through Eleanor, even though FDR was in Washington. She sent a remarkable telegram to the First Lady threatening to desert a planned campaign event and refuse to support FDR publicly if

Eleanor didn't make Franklin change his mind about firing Gene. It was a powerful threat; Amelia pulled out all the stops.

SEPT. 15 1936

MRS. FRANKLIN D. ROOSEVELT,
THE WHITE HOUSE.

I AM WIRING YOU CONCERNING A MEAN AND UNFORTUNATE
INSTANCE OF POLITICAL SCHEMING BECAUSE OF MY PROMISE TO YOU
TO JOIN THE NEW YORK STATE AUTOMOBILE CARAVAN NEXT WEEK
AND ISSUE A STATEMENT FOR THE NATIONAL COMMITTEE. AVIATION
IS MY VOCATION AND AVOCATION. I SHOULD RATHER HELP THE
INDUSTRY PROGRESS THAN PROGRESS MYSELF. THUS I FEEL THE PRE-
EMPTORY DISMISSAL OF THE DIRECTOR OF AIR COMMERCE AND TWO
ASSISTANTS SUBSTITUTING LEGALLY TRAINED INDIVIDUAL FOR ONE
OF PRACTICAL EXPERIENCE IS ALMOST A CALAMITY. THERE IS LITTLE
USE OF MY TRYING TO INTEREST OTHERS IN THE PRESIDENT'S CAUSE
WHEN MY HEART IS SICK WITH THE KNOWLEDGE THAT AN INDUSTRY
CAN BE JEOPARDIZED AND AN INDIVIDUAL'S CAREER BLASTED BY WHAT
SEEMS A PERSONAL FEUD. MAY I HOPE THAT BEFORE ANY SCALPS ARE
ATTACHED TO ANYONE'S BELT THE PRESIDENT WILL PERSONALLY
ASCERTAIN THE TRUE SITUATION FROM MR. VIDAL. SURELY ONE
DAY'S NOTICE OF DISMISSAL CAN ONLY RESULT IN CONFUSION IN A
BUREAU LONG A TARGET OF ATTACK AND IS POOR REWARD FOR LOYAL
SERVICE. PLEASE BELIEVE THIS MESSAGE IS NOT INSTIGATED BY ONE
OF THOSE AFFECTED INSTEAD IT IS SENT PERSONALLY AND SOLELY
IN THE INTERESTS OF FAIR PLAY. IF YOU WOULD LIKE TO QUESTION
ME PLEASE WIRE INSTRUCTING WHEN I MAY TELEPHONE YOU.

That was on a Tuesday. Amelia knew that Eleanor, a strong Vidal supporter, would share her outrage. Eleanor showed Franklin the telegram, and according to Janet Mabie, Amelia's overly warm defense of Gene made Franklin burst out laughing. "He admired her spirit and he laughed and laughed." The next day he had lunch with Secretary Daniel Roper, head of the Department of Commerce, Gene's boss. Secretary Roper informed the press that he and the president discussed the makeup of the Federal Maritime Commission during the meal, but they discussed the bureau also, for the next day its reorganization was canceled. By the time FDR left Washington the next evening on his special train bound for Cambridge, Massachusetts, to speak at Harvard's three hundredth anniversary cele-bration, it had all been solved—Amelia had been notified and was wiring thank you.

SEPTEMBER 17

MRS. FRANKLIN ROOSEVELT.
THANK YOU SINCERELY FOR YOUR HELPFULNESS IN THE MATTER ABOUT
WHICH I WIRED YOU. AM INFORMED OUTCOME NOW PROMISES TO BE
SATISFACTORY TO VIDAL WHOSE LOYALTY MERITS THE FAIR TREATMENT
WHICH YOUR INTERESTS SECURING. I AM SURE YOU UNDERSTAND I
WAS ACTUATED BY DESIRE TO SERVE THE INDUSTRY, THE INDIVIDUAL
AND THE ADMINISTRATION. GRATEFULLY, AMELIA EARHART

It had taken the two women just forty-eight hours to change FDR's mind. Eleanor had acted decisively, even though she was undoubtedly feeling poorly, for by Saturday she was feverish and in bed with the flu, necessitating FDR's unexpected return to Washington. So powerful was the combination of the two women that FDR permanently shelved his plans to reorganize the bureau. Gene, meanwhile, was madly trying to get in touch with Amelia and, knowing she was flying her Electra to Purdue, was preparing to travel there to see her.

His cable dated the eighteenth: ARRIVING BY RAIL INDIANAPOLIS SEVEN THIRTEEN SATURDAY MORNING WILL PHONE YOU ON ARRIVAL

On the following day, the nineteenth, from Indiana, for the first time efficient Amelia endorsed the president. If FDR had wondered even for a moment whether it was all that important to keep her happy, his doubts were permanantly laid to rest: Amelia's endorsement was headline news. Still under the circumstances it is hard not to find double entendres in the statement itself: "I am aligned with President Roosevelt because of his social conscience. Throughout his term of office he has fought against odds to reduce human misery. He has realized that obsolescence can affect parts of the machinery of government just as it does the machinery of industry," ran Amelia's endorsement.

A week later Amelia and George took their conspicuous place in the Democratic Caravan, a parade of cars carrying prominent people that was rolling through upstate New York. When she spoke in the tiny town of Mechanicville, it was reported on in the national press. It was also noted that she, not George, was at the wheel of their car.

The Caravan, along with the rest of the Democratic Party, was heading for Syracuse for the opening of the Democratic State Convention in the Armory on Monday the twenty-eighth, where, in his home state, FDR was scheduled to give his first political speech to kick off the campaign. As the president spoke, Amelia was prominently seated nearby with Mrs. Herbert Lehman, wife of New York's governor, and Frances Perkins, secretary of labor. Later, Amelia, too was put on the schedule.

Earlier in the day she had made a campaign speech over the NBC radio network for her Rye neighbor and friend Caroline O'Day, the state's only woman representative, whom Amelia had first supported when she ran in 1934. O'Day was one of the friends that Amelia and Eleanor Roosevelt had in common: she had been one of the founders of Eleanor's Vall-Kil furniture factory in 1927, along with Marian Dickerman and Nancy Cooke. Now at the end of the afternoon, dressed in a knitted blue two-piece suit with bright scarlet and white kerchief at the neckline and a blue camel's hair coat, Amelia stepped to the podium and seconded O'Day's nomination for a second term. As she did so, the delegates, particularly the women, many of whom had remained through the entire session just to hear her and Mrs. O'Day, raised a loud cheer.

Gene Vidal wasted no time, once his department was saved, in consolidating his position with the Democratic powers-that-be by demonstrating his position as Amelia's confidant and adviser. He immediately wrote Mary Dewson, vice-chairman of the Democratic National Committee, that Amelia would now campaign for the president not just in New York State but all over the country: "she plans to include her thoughts as to The President in some 28 lectures which she will give during the next months. I feel that it is a good break that she is lecturing in both Ohio and Michigan. Please let me know if there is anything further I might do for you."

Mary Dewson gracefully replied, "We really are very grateful to you for what you have done in getting Miss Earhart interested in working for President Roosevelt."

• • • •

The annual army-navy football game at West Point was scheduled for the twenty-eighth of November. Gene was planning to take Gore and invited Amelia to join them. As the teams fought up and down the field, Gore was impressed with Amelia's "good working knowledge" of football; she and Gene were having a great time together. During the half she devoted herself to Gore: "What *color* is a crowd—pink or gray or what?" he remembers her asking him, and as it got later and colder and furs looked more and more attractive, "How many animals go into making the average complement of clothes?" They traveled back by train and, Gore remembered, "as her fans peered excitedly into our train compartment, she described how she planned to fly around the world."

Going around the world had been a rite of passage since Magellan, who in 1519 was the first to try—and the first to die in the attempt. A Circumnavigators Club for those who circled the globe dates from 1902. The first person to race around the world was Nellie Bly, an ambitious, talented reporter who worked for Joseph Pulitzer's *New York World*. In those pre-airplane times, her goal was to beat Phineas Fogg's fictional record, as dreamed up by Jules Verne, of eighty days. She did it with time to spare. Nellie left New York City in November 1889, crossed the Atlantic and the Mediterannean, proceeded to Aden, Ceylon, Singapore, Hong Kong, Tokyo, and San Francisco, then returned to New York 72 days, 6 hours, 11 minutes later. It won her fame and fortune, parades and book contracts.

So began a new challenge for intrepid adventurers, most of them American, of which there seemed an endless number. It was as if Americans, so newly having conquered their own continent, having made heroes of Daniel Boone, Lewis and Clark, and John Fremont, in the past century, had the energy to spare and the mindset to just keep going until the world was as familiar as their own country. As travelers got the hang of foreign shipping and train schedules, the times kept dropping: 67 days, 60 days, 54 days, 40 days—until in 1911 a one-legged Frenchman by the name of André Jaeger-Schmidt circled the earth in 39 days, 19 hours, 42 minutes. By 1913, ten years after Kitty Hawk, the time was down to 35 days, 21 hours, 36 minutes, achieved by another American, John Mears. He made the last forty miles of that trip sitting on the wing of an airplane.

Naturally that started everyone thinking about doing it entirely by plane. In 1914 a company seeking publicity put up a prize for an airplane race around the world—the winner to get $100,000—but before anyone could even begin to get excited, World War I put an end to the quest. It would be another ten years before the first flight around the world, in 1924, when again it was done by Americans: U.S. Army fliers in four Douglas World Cruisers, open-cockpit single-engine seaplanes, aided by the navy, which stationed ships along the ocean routes. One plane crashed in Alaska, another was damaged and abandoned at sea, but two returned 175 days later. The fliers had a terrible time.

"Would you do it again?" one of the men was asked. "Not for a million dollars—unless we were ordered to" was the reply.

Major Jimmy Doolittle and his wife went around the world in 1933, partly by plane and partly by boat, to study aviation developments and foreign commercial airlines. The Lindberghs made their second survey flight, which took them around the world, that same year. As Amelia was preparing to start, they were surveying India.

Wiley Post and Harold Gatty, an Australian navigator who had flown with Charles Kingsford-Smith, were the first civilians to fly around the world in a plane. They took off in Wiley's Lockheed Vega *Winnie Mae* on June 23, 1931, from Roosevelt field. Wiley thought he could circle the globe in ten days, but they did much better than that, completing their circle in 8 days, 15 hours, and 51 minutes. It was a sensational accomplishment, even though their circumnavigation covered only 15,474 miles, barely more than half the circumference of the globe. Wiley was lionized and given parades, and he wrote a book about the trip. Then he flew solo around the world in 1933 in 7 days, 18 hours, handily beating his previous record. Fifty thousand people were waiting at Floyd Bennett field when he landed.

According to Harry Bruno, the pilot and public relations genius who raised the money for Wiley's flights, twice around the world wasn't enough for Wiley. When he and Will Rogers took off in the summer of 1935, their real destination was another round-the-world jaunt—the North Pole was just the first step. Wiley wanted to be the first person to do it three times. He thought it was a wonderful way to raise money, have fun, and stay in the public eye. It never occurred to him that he would crash and be killed.

Now Amy Mollison was studying celestial navigation to prepare herself for her own globe-girdling flight; she thought she would be ready in 1938.

Amelia planned to do it around the earth's waist. It was the longest way to do it, of course, 27,000 miles, and would involve crossing the equator four times. But it had never been done that way at all, meaning Amelia had no need to hurry to beat someone else's time. "My frosting on the cake," she called the flight one day. Why circle the globe at all? Her explanation was clearly rendered, carefully thought out:

> Here was shining adventure, beckoning with new experiences, added knowledge of flying, of peoples—of myself. I felt that with the flight behind me I would be more useful to me and to the program we had planned at Purdue.
>
> Then, too, there was my belief that now and then women should do for themselves what men have already done—and occasionally what men have not done—thereby establishing themselves as persons, and perhaps encouraging other women toward greater independence of thought and action. Some such consideration was a contributing reason for my wanting to do what I so much wanted to do.

Of course there was more to it than that—more than the fact that she had already flown the oceans and there was "just" the world left; more than the fact that the achievement would have been the capstone of her career, that she would be the first woman to fly the Atlantic, the Pacific, and the world. Her internal clock was urging her on: her fortieth birthday was coming up July 24, 1937. She had to rack it up by then, then she could relax and turn her mind to less taxing but no less interesting tasks. She was very aware of time breathing down her neck—she always had been. In Boston in 1926, having passed her twenty-ninth birthday, highly aware of how close she was to hitting thirty, with her career still going nowhere, she had been so driven, she had lied on her job application to the WEIU. Now, no one realized that she was about to turn forty because of the one lie she always told—the lie about her age. She had been habitually taking off one year since she was a student at Columbia. Her friends would have better understood the pressure she felt if they had known her real age. 1936 had seen only a series of shakedown flights. Now she was ready, the plane was ready, and she was restless to start.

19

The Plan

• • • • Many people, over the years, have thought that Amelia's desire to fly around the world was foolish. Even Hilton Railey, who had helped her cope with her first Atlantic passage in 1928, didn't understand it. "She was caught up in the hero racket which compelled her to strive for increasingly dramatic records," he wrote soon after she died, trying to exonerate her from her decision, to make it seem as if it were external forces that had pushed her on. Louise Thaden, however, who was close to Amelia, was closer to the truth when she observed that "it is the only major flight she ever attempted for purely selfish reasons. She wanted to fly around the world, because it would be fun."

There was no doubt what women across the country thought of Amelia's proposed circumnavigation when they found out. In the spring of 1937 *McCall's* kicked off a new series of covers to sell the magazine—a gallery of great women, starting in March with Anne Lindbergh, followed by Katharine Cornell in April. They put Amelia on the cover of the May issue, roughly coinciding with the beginning of her trip. It was a wonderful likeness: the smile, the tousled hair, the white silk scarf. "Amelia Earhart has dared to blaze the earth's uncharted skyways, spanning a continent, an ocean's vastness, the globe we call the world. She is America's Number One

Aviatrix and it is fitting therefore, that her portrait be included in *McCall's* gallery of Great American Women," ran the text.

Purdue also liked the idea. The Purdue Research Foundation statement was that they expected the flight would "develop scientific and engineering data of vital importance to the aviation industry." She had asked for a formal leave of absence from the university in April 1936, and they open-handedly gave it to her, authorizing Elliott to grant her a leave "at such time and for such duration as may be necessary to permit her to make proper preparations for said flight, and to undertake same." They must initially have been worried that they *might* be criticized for backing such an undertaking, for they concluded that the university and the PRF could "become associated in the cooperative research project without fear of correctly being charged with sponsoring a publicity stunt."

Purdue had already been involved in practical flight research in scientific aeronautics, doing experimental work in aviation for the Department of Commerce, putting down a runway system composed of various types of runway materials to determine their suitability for airport purposes. Experimental work was also under way in applying television and shortwave radio to low-visibility flying.

Originally, Amelia intended to work within this aeronautical program with the Electra, then afterward fly around the world testing the effects of long-distance flights on pilots and equipment, in a "flying laboratory." But then she decided she wanted to do the flight first, then hang up her spurs and work with Purdue. By August reporters were sniffing around, looking for a story, asking questions. Amelia told them: "I'm nearly sold on the idea of flying around the world because I'd like to do it, but I'm a busy person this year. I have a lot of things to do. Next year? Well, one never knows."

Even as she prepared to take leave from Purdue, she made some parting shots to keep women focused on their future.

> The most important subject today is modern economics. I am referring to social economics. When women really know about economics, take the long view of the subject, they will abandon this sentimental attitude about protective legislation for women, minimum hours and minimum wages for women. Limited hours and limited pay only prolong the infantile period of women and work to the disadvantage of those who want to progress. Wages should be based on work, not sex nor any other consideration. The problem should be, not minimum scales for women but minimum scales for everybody.

While Amelia tended to her new plane, the university considered plans for expanding the PRF into a permanent Amelia Earhart Fund for Aeronautical Research, or possibly funding a two- or three-year scholarship to be given to a girl interested in aviation, as well as working with Amelia's proposed future experimental flights.

As always during preparation for a flight, Amelia's life went on as before. George tended to getting the new house finished and furnished. He arranged for a leading mail-order house to lavishly equip the kitchen—in return for permission to advertise the fact. The furnishings were contemporary in feeling—simple pieces of good quality and clean lines. Amelia must have been thinking of returning to her first love, the piano, for there was a piano in the living room. It was a light, cheery house, with sliding-glass doors and tall windows. The stone patio faced a golf course, but was separated from it by shrubs and a low stone wall.

Amelia had sent out from Rye the most precious of her books, some dating from her school years; an *Ivanhoe* she had doodled in, books of verse, a three-volume edition of Kipling, the sonnets of Edna St. Vincent Millay, and a signed first edition of *Lazarus Laughed* by Eugene O'Neill. There were books on aviation as well, including *Air Babies* by her friend Elvy Kalep, and many others. All were arranged on the shelves of her study. During her flight, Amy was going to live in the house. A special luxurious bathroom was installed for her, "The bathroom is a Roman dream of elegance, of which I am particularly envious," wrote George.

Besides her usual lecturing, Amelia was dealing with her mother and Muriel. Although Amelia was always scolding her mother for being such a soft touch for all her relatives, in fact Amelia was an even softer touch. She had just discovered, to her chagrin, that although she herself was helping out Nancy Balis's sister and husband—Amy was sending them money as well. Muriel's marital problems, of several years' duration, had worsened. Amelia and George continued to help Muriel in spite of their strong negative feelings about her husband, Albert. Amelia made no bones about calling Albert not only a bad businessman but a selfish person who neglected his family. At one point, while Amy was staying with Muriel and him, he would have had Amy paying room and board, if Amelia hadn't squashed the idea. Albert habitually put his own activities and interests before Muriel's. Unable to meet the payments, they had lost the house that Amelia and George had helped them buy. Then Albert lost a substantial amount of additional money that they had given him. ("I am deeply sorry to hear further reports of your unhappy domestic situation. I had hoped that the money which George and I advanced would help Albert grow up. However, it appears just to have aggravated the petty side of his nature and made him really mean. I was so hopeful he would make good, I did not exact any moral guarantee," wrote Amelia.)

Moreover, Muriel's dependence on Albert ran against everything Amelia believed in; visiting her sister in recent years had been enough to set her teeth on edge. Because of Albert's profligate spending, Muriel was always doing housework—sometimes with Amy's help—much to Amelia's irritation. In the fall of the previous year Amelia had accepted a dinner invitation from Muriel—and then reneged, put off by the idea of her sister slaving over preparing a dinner. She wrote to Amy to apologize: "Please tell Pidge when I wrote her about cancelling a dinner she was planning in Cambridge, I did not mean that George and I would not eat at home with just the family if she wishes. That is, if she will have a maid come in for whom I will gladly pay." Her sister exemplified everything in male-female relations that Amelia hated: housework, dependency, unquestioning obedience to a husband. All the things from which Amelia was trying to free women still bound her sister. It made her, in the case of the dinner, unreasonable, for it would have brought no pleasure to Muriel to have had a maid come in and cook the meal.

Now Amelia decided to do as much as possible for her sister before her trip. She wrote Muriel in January, deeply worried, advising her not to sign any legal papers, not to move out of her house, "no matter how tough things may get," and to come out to California so that they could talk. Muriel did. It was the first time in years that the two sisters had spent time together. For the moment all was well. It was as much as Amelia could do for Muriel before she left.

The effort to help her sister didn't deflect Amelia from her flight preparations. The living room of the North Hollywood house, according to Muriel, "was just completely covered with equipment. They had three different types of rubber rafts they were testing, one that you had to inflate yourself; another that was supposed to be automatic; then there was still another shape that could be used upside down as well as rightside up, and it still wouldn't capsize; and all things of that kind."

There was so much to consider. The Department of Agriculture was supplying the Electra with aluminum cylinders to take air samples at various altitudes in different parts of the world. For her own part Amelia intended to keep an accurate record of every detail to establish the fatigue point on long-distance and high-altitude flights: she planned to track the performance of the plane, and the magnetic, meteorological, and radio variables of the upper air in different parts of the world—data sorely needed before international air travel could become safe.

She wanted of course to find out whether altitude affected digestion, and whether some foods were easier to digest than others. "Also I should like to know the rate at which fatigue is induced by the myriad instruments a modern pilot must use. Are men and women different in their reactions to air travel? If so, how?" Eye fatigue was also on her mind. (Her red-rimmed eyes had been commented upon several times after long-distance flights.) To prevent eyestrain—another "vital aspect"—she was planning to take a "battery" of sunglasses made up especially for her. All aspects of mental and physical fatigue, a pilot's major problem, interested her. She originally planned to test the products of several manufacturers, including a sort of fog-dispelling product that she was supposed to use over San Francisco.

Planning for the flight actually started even before Amelia accepted delivery of the Electra. Everything had to be thought out in advance and dealt with. The nitty-gritty work—requiring hundreds of phone calls and letters and cables—was done by George, whose job it was to turn all Amelia's needs and requests into reality. Among other things, he had to organize caches of gasoline and oil—more than thirty—at various points along the route. He did this through their friend Count Jacques de Sibour, a pilot (as was his wife), whose book he had published who now worked for Standard Oil. Then they had to decide at what stops the plane would be overhauled—no plane could go 27,000 miles without considerable maintenance—and send the necessary engine parts and mechanics to those places. But that was the easy part.

The hard part was to figure out the logistics and involve the U.S. government in the project. That required Gene. George worked through Gene's department (The Bureau of Air Commerce) and, whenever necessary, through Gene personally. Would Gene find out about the navy field in Honolulu? asked George in August. We need, he said, "an exact description of the new runways, the total length of the pavement, the extra run and the nature of the approaches . . . what the condition will be as of, say, February. I do so hope you can get the information from the Navy Department."

Every country over which Amelia was going to fly and/or in which she would land had to grant permission. Here the crucial person was Gene's assistant, J. Carrol Cone, in charge of regulations. George gave Cone the proposed route of the flight, and Cone set up the permitting procedures. The original proposed route was San Francisco–Honolulu; Honolulu–Manila; Manila–Allahabad; Allahabad–Karachi; Karachi–Aden; Aden–Khartoum; Khartoum–Dakar; Dakar–Natal; Natal–New York. Cone informed George that he had passed the information on to the Department of State, and that department would seek the necessary permits. He also, almost apologetically, informed George that Amelia's license had lapsed, and that the department wouldn't concern itself about it but that she should renew it.

The next request to Gene: would the Bureau of Air Commerce ask the navy for relevant weather data over the Pacific? Forthwith. Six days later the information—"Climactic Features of the Pacific Island Region"—and the relevant hydrographic charts were in the hands of the bureau, even though the navy was not too happy about it and asked that it be returned when Amelia was finished with it. . . .

• • • •

The job of seeking international permissions devolved onto the chief of protocol, Richard Southgate. Lest Southgate have any thought of shrugging off the gargantuan task, George, probably at Amelia's suggestion but quite possibly on his own, wrote to Eleanor Roosevelt asking for her help. Eleanor had her secretary, Malvina Schneider, write a superbly manipulative letter to the chief of protocol: "Mrs Roosevelt, upon her return to Washington the other day, found Mr. George Palmer Putnam's letter to her and learned that you had kindly consented to take care of the things he wished done in the State Department. . . . She is sure you will be *very* nice to him."

Every single country over which Amelia planned to fly had to be contacted by the State Department—and notified that the installation of the necessary fuel tanks meant that the weight of the plane, when fully fueled, would exceed by several thousand pounds the approved gross weight for commercial aircraft of this type, and that as a result a certificate of airworthiness could not be granted, although the bureau "considers the plane to be satisfactory for the purposes of this flight." As 1936 turned into 1937, the letters turned into day letters and telegrams, which were so numerous and so expensive, the State Department opened a charge account for George; just these costs alone mounted into hundreds of dollars. The arrangements dragged on interminably. The State Department file, declassified in 1972, is three inches thick. Every single country to be overflown had to signify its assent. Every single one did—except the Sultan of Muscat. "There is no hope of permission being obtained from the Sultan at present for private flights over that territory," George was informed, so the route had to be changed.

George was so deep into handling Amelia's correspondence that he now took on the job of telling Amy what was happening. "Dear Mrs. Earhart," he wrote in January, "Amelia is feeling grand. Her plane and her plans are developing splendidly. Incidentally, so is our house. In the final stages now."

In its later version, the proposed route, in its first leg, was from Oakland to Honolulu, then to New Guinea and Port Darwin in northern Australia (instead of Manila); the second leg extended from Australia to the west coast of Africa by way of Arabia; the third leg was the South Atlantic; the fourth was from Brazil north to home.

The biggest problem that Amelia had to solve was how to fly the long stretch of the Pacific Ocean. The absolute maximum range of the Electra was 4,000 miles; but Honolulu to Tokyo was 3,900 miles; and Honolulu to Manila was 5,800 miles. No matter what route she took, Amelia would have to refuel along the way. Pan American had established fueling stations at Wake, Guam, and Midway, but these were fueling stations for seaplanes, useless to Amelia in the Electra. The best solution seemed to be to do an aerial refueling over Midway Island. That would involve the navy. So George went to work to enlist its cooperation. He started at the top, with the secretary of the navy, to whom he proposed the project. The navy, according to internal memos, had done this once, in San Diego in 1930, when "a fleet patrol plane in flight was fuelled successfully, both by day and by night." Just once—but then, Amelia was not an ordinary personage. If the navy had done it once, that was enough, thought Admiral Cook, and he decided that subject to successful completion of preliminary preparations and trials, the navy could refuel Amelia's plane; A PBY-1 seaplane could be used. No modifications of the plane would be necessary; all that was required would be to make up the necessary hoses and a suitable reel, similar to a target reel, to raise and lower the hose. Cook bumped his report up to Admiral Standley, chief of U.S. Naval Operations. And there it sat.

Amelia anxiously awaited word; then, taking no chances, she wrote the president, who had been an assistant secretary of the navy and knew intimately its byzantine workings. Obviously possessed of insider information as to the status of the request as well as having more detailed information about the state of naval aviation than the navy appeared to have, she wrote President Roosevelt an artful letter. It helped that she and Roosevelt were such good friends and that she had told the president about the flight when they spent the night at the White House the previous spring.

> Dear Mr. President; Some time ago I told you and Mrs. Roosevelt a little about my confidential plans for a world flight. . . . The chief problem is the jump westward from Honolulu . . . This matter has been discussed in detail by Mr. Putnam with Admiral Cook, who was most interested and friendly. Subsequently a detailed description of the project, and request for this assistance, was prepared. It is now on the desk of Admiral Standley, by whom it is being considered.

Some new seaplanes are being completed at San Diego. They will be ferried in January or February to Honolulu. It is my desire to practice actual refueling operations in the air over San Diego with one of these planes. That plane subsequently from Honolulu would be available for the Midway operation. I gather from Admiral Cook that technically there are no extraordinary difficulties. It is primarily a matter of policy and precedent.

In the past the Navy has been so progressive in its pioneering, and so broad-minded in what we might call its "public relations," that I think a project such as this (even involving a mere woman!) may appeal to Navy personnel. Its successful attainment might, I think, win for the Service further popular friendship.

Within days Admiral Standley agreed to refuel the Electra: the navy agreed to pay most of the costs of deploying the tender and the two airplanes involved; and Amelia's expenses were limited to reimbursing the navy for the gas and oil they would transfer to her plane.

But Amelia lacked expertise in aerial refueling: as the admiral in charge of the fleet aircraft informed his superior, there remained the problem of "airmanship"—"The ability of the pilot of the receiving plane has not been demonstrated." Amelia would require "considerable" special training, according to the admiral, to learn the procedures involved in the approach and departure phases of refueling, to avoid fouling the hose in the propellers of her plane. He did not think the navy should bear the expense of this, "either in cost of time of pilots and airplanes."

Here Gene stepped back into the picture with another idea. Sitting in Washington, D.C., Gene had been so anxious about Amelia as she flew up from Mexico City the year before, so worried that something might happen to her, that he had gone to the airport and had gotten on the radio and pleaded with her to quit and land in Washington—after she had been in the air for only thirteen hours. What was he to think of this scheme of Amelia's to refuel her plane—but not get any rest herself? To fly four thousand miles nonstop over water—a twenty-six-hour flight if everything went perfectly, and longer if it didn't. It was certainly fraught with danger. Why not find a place where she could land, refuel, and rest? Suddenly the Bureau of Air Commerce instituted a new policy.

Starting in 1935, the U.S. government, in response to a military buildup by the Japanese, began taking steps to protect its West Coast and "prove up" its sovereignty in the Pacific in as low key a way as possible against Japanese encroachments. The army had developed plans to build the largest military air base on the Pacific Coast at Tacoma, Washington.

Coincidentally, Pan American was asking for stepping-stones across the Pacific for its seaplane Clipper service to the Orient, which was planned to carry U.S. mail as well as passengers. The two plans fitted in so perfectly together that the Bureau of Air Commerce gave permission to Pan Am to erect supply bases on Guam, Midway, and Wake Island with alacrity. Pan Am immediately sent supply ships to the islands, began to construct the hangars and other buildings that would be needed for its seaplanes to refuel, and set up communications facilities. The navy went out of its way to help. At Guam the navy unloaded all supplies, and ferried Pan Am personnel from ship to shore when necessary; the naval governor of Guam invited top Pan Am personnel to dinner. Within six months all was ready. The first China Clipper left Alameda airport on a Friday at the end of November 1935, with Captain Edward Musick as chief pilot and Fred Noonan as chief navigator, and landed in Honolulu 21 hours and 3 minutes later. The Clipper continued on to Midway, Wake, Guam, and the Philippines, landing in Manila the following Friday.

At roughly the same time, Gene was suggesting that Jarvis, Baker, and Howland, the so-called Line Islands south and west of Hawaii, should be claimed by the United States for use as bases for land planes flying to Australia and New Zealand. Baker was forty miles to the south of Howland, half a degree north of the equator, while Jarvis lay more than a thousand miles to the east. These islands needed to be clearly staked out as "American," because of the Japanese but also because Gene was sure that the future of air travel across the Pacific surely belonged to land planes rather than to the lumbering seaplanes then favored. The islands, tiny but big enough for landing fields, had been claimed by the British, in the guano-digging days of the last century and subsequently abandoned. When he informed the State Department of their strategic importance, he was told that they already belonged to the United States, although England "might" raise a conflicting claim, and that "whoever first moved to colonize them would gain undisputed possession under the provisions of international law."

So Gene proceeded to colonize them. He picked Bureau of Air Commerce aide William Miller, an ex-navy pilot whom he used for special projects, and put him to the task in January 1935. Operating at first with the utmost secrecy, Miller chose twenty young men of Hawaiian blood from the famous Kamehameha school in Hawaii as colonists. In March the Coast Guard cutter *Itasca,* with Miller, the young men, tents, food supplies, steel drums of fresh water, and other equipment set out for the islands. The young Hawaiian men stayed on the islands, usually four to an island, for nine or ten months, went home for a few months, and then returned. After a year the State Department decided to make the colonization clearly permanant and to install meteorological equipment. Supervision was turned over to the Division of Territories and Island Possessions of the U.S. Department of the Interior. Miller returned to Washington, Richard B. Black of the Department of the Interior took over, and the project was given much local publicity. A prefabricated house consisting of a living room, a radio room, a bedroom, and a kitchen with a large front porch opening off the living room was put up on each island.

The next step Gene undertook was to build a landing field on one of the islands, where land planes could refuel in midocean—in time for Amelia's trip. Howland Island, eighteen hundred miles from Hawaii, was the most suitable. Carl Allen would write that "there is gallantry even in government and Miss Earhart was the first flyer to suggest putting the country's new 'conquest' of these islands to practical use." But of course the only way Amelia would have known about the size and suitability of Howland Island would have been if Gene had told her. It was a Gene Vidal production from start to finish.

"During the late part of 1936," recalled Richard Black, "I received a Trans-pacific telephone call and later a score or so of letters from my Division Headquarters in Washington requesting that I set up a project to build a scratch-grade runway. First they considered Jarvis Island and later Howland Island. It was revealed to me, and it was considered more or less confidential at the time, that this station was to be used by the famous aviatrix Amelia Earhart for her round-the-world flight in what was called a 'flying laboratory.' "

Gene sent Robert L. Campbell, another Bureau of Air Commerce aide, to help Black do the job (having more or less assigned Miller to Amelia), and Campbell and Black and eight additional young Hawaiians, some World War I tractors, graders, scrapers, and rollers, left Hawaii on January 12 to begin construction, with the assistance of the regular colonists, of three scratch-grade runways on the treeless mile-and-a-half-by-half-mile island. Eventually, a cache of some eighteen drums of 87 octane gasoline were deposited on the island for her.

Amelia knew about the airstrip on Howland before the president, for on January 8 she sent FDR a wire that threw various aides into convulsions and resulted in the following memo to FDR from the acting director of the Bureau of the Budget.

> She wrote about her proposed round the world flight this spring
> and hoped for Navy cooperation in refuelling west of Hawaii,
> which was subsequently kindly arranged by Admiral Standley. Says
> since then the necessity for such difficult and costly maneuvers

has been obviated and instead she hopes to land on Howland Island where the Government is about to establish an emergency field. Says Dept. of Commerce approves her plan and the Interior Dept. is very cooperative as is the Coast Guard. Says all details are arranged and the construction party with equipment due to sail from Honolulu next week. Says she is now informed that apparently some question re WPA [Works Progress Administration] appropriation in amount of $3000 which covers all costs other than those borne by her for this mid-pacific pioneer landing field which will be permanently useful and valuable aeronautically and nationally. Understands its moving requires executive approval and asks that it be expedited.

On January 11 Amelia learned that the president had released WPA funds to the Bureau of Air Commerce to build the field on Howland Island. Richard Black, Air Commerce aide Robert Campbell, the additional workers, and the machinery left Hawaii the next day. So that most vexing problem was taken care of, courtesy of Gene.

The next Bureau of Air Commerce intervention for Amelia involved the army—the only branch of the armed services not yet helping the flight. Here, too, George relied on help from Gene's bureau. George wrote a letter to the secretary of war saying that he was looking for housing for the Electra, and for maintenance work by army aviation mechanics, "competent aviation mechanics to service her plane, check her Wasp H engines, and Hamilton constant speed propellers," when she landed at Wheeler field in Honolulu. "We are fortunate in having the kindly cooperation of the Department of Commerce and the Navy and the Coast Guard," he baldly wrote. To insure that the secretary of war actually issued the specified instructions, George requested that ubiquitous Commerce aide William Miller personally deliver the letter.

• • • •

Amelia knew she needed a navigator for the over-water portion of the flight. Several were under consideration. George, with his restless, creative mind, inevitably had a suggestion: Brad Washburn, whose book he had published ten years before, in the boy explorer series; Brad had gone on to make a great name for himself as an explorer and was now a professor at Harvard. George knew Brad had been in Alaska and had taken the first photographs of Mount McKinley while flying an Electra. Brad received a phone call from George one day asking him to come and talk to them. Although he had known George well, he didn't know Amelia except by reputation, but he felt as if he knew her, for before she was married, his wife had worked at Denison House and had lived in Amelia's room. When Brad arrived, it was to see Amelia sprawled on the floor with her maps lying around her. They had supper and talked all evening. She showed him the itinerary, marking out the first two legs, Hawaii to Howland Island, Howland to New Guinea. She traced the lines on the maps with a finger, mentioning the distances between points. Brad spent most of the evening next to her on the floor, talking about the flight, with George in a chair next to them. She charmed him—and probably knew instantly that he wouldn't do.

Brad asked what radio signals there would be on Howland for them to home in on and was told there wouldn't be any. He thought that was unwise, since her 50-watt radio wouldn't be powerful enough to pick up ground stations. He knew he didn't have the navigational experience to hit such a tiny island as Howland: "I backed out of it with their clearly not having asked me to be navigator. She would naturally have wanted someone who agreed with her plan, and I didn't. I would have turned it down anyway because my navigation experience was not adequate to handle that kind of a job. Very frankly I knew all about how to get it done, but I couldn't do it."

Another prospective navigator whom Amelia consulted in the early stages was Paul Collins. He, too, remembered spreading maps on the floor and discussing the feasibility of the routes, but he now ran an airline—he couldn't up and leave. She finally settled on Harry Manning, who had been captain of the *President Roosevelt,* the ship that had brought her home from England after the triumphal flight of the *Friendship.* He too was a pilot; they had talked during the crossing of possibly someday teaming up for a flight.

Harry Manning graduated from the Marine Academy, worked his way up from able seaman, and rose rapidly in rank. He was awarded the Congressional Medal of Honor in 1929 for rescuing thirty-two passengers from a sinking ocean liner. When Amelia asked him to be her navigator as far as Port Darwin, Australia, he agreed and arranged a leave of absence.

· · · ·

In mid-February 1937, with all the decisions for Amelia's flight having been made, the only thing left for Gene to arrange was the smooth execution of the flight itself. He assigned William Miller to officially interface with the navy and coordinate the plans for Amelia's flight. The navy was notified by telegram. MR. MILLER AIRWAYS SUPERINTENDENT DEPARTMENT OF COMMERCE WILL COORDINATE PLANS FOR FLIGHT. HE WILL ARRIVE OAKLAND ABOUT TWENTY FIVE FEBRARY AND WILL CONTACT NAVAL

DISTRICT AUTHORITIES KEEPING ADDRESSEES ADVISED REGARDING DEVEL-
OPMENTS. All the big decisions had been made. It was a rare moment in
history—Amelia had wrapped the entire U.S. government—up to and
including President Roosevelt—right around her finger. She was planning
to take off within two weeks.

Gene's unprecedented step of assigning one of his best men, Miller,
a government employee, to a nongovernmental project, was one of his last
acts. His final act was to issue a bureau directive requiring all commercial planes to have radio direction finders and antennae shielded against
snow, rain, fog, and dust static. Radio direction finders had become operational just that spring. DFs, as they were called, had been developed
by Bendix Aviation at the behest of Pan Am for the Clippers. Then, on
the last day in February, tired of government infighting, too entrepreneurial to be happy in bureaucratic Washington, probably realizing that
his dream of building planes for the common man would continue to
be blocked, Gene threw in the towel and resigned. He would be visiting
his mother in Santa Barbara, he announced, and flew out to California a
few days later, to be met at the Burbank airport by Amelia, with George
in tow.

There was much speculation about Gene's plans. Rumors floated
about that he was going to form a connection with a company that
would set up sea dromes in the ocean and fly land planes across the sea
in competition with the Pan Am Clippers. Other rumors had it that he
would join Bendix Aviation. The idea of forming a new airline resurfaced;
there was talk that he would join Amelia, George, and Floyd Odlum,
head of the immensely powerful Atlas Corporation, in the formation of
a transatlantic air service. Gene did nothing to dispel the rumors, saying, "I can say this much, however. It'll be something quite unusual in
the way of aviation. Airline operations will enter into it." Theirs would
have been a natural alliance, fueled by his closeness to and respect for
Amelia, the powerful financial aid of her friend Floyd Odlum, and the
enmity that existed between Gene and Juan Trippe, the head of Pan
American.

Gene's orders to William Miller to facilitate naval aid to Amelia once
she had left the United States provided for the following: that a seaplane
tender would take a station midway between Honolulu and Howland and
return to Pearl Harbor after she had landed at Howland; that the coast guard
cutter *Duane*, with two aviation mechanics, would proceed to Howland
to service Amelia's plane while she was there; that weather information
would be collected from the governor of Samoa and other points; that the
USS *Ontario* would take up a station midway between Howland and New

Guinea; and that personnel would be available on Howland Island to scare away the birds.

. . . .

The countdown to the world flight had begun. By Tuesday, March 9, ever-present reporters noted food, maps, and a hodgepodge of other necessary articles piled on a small table in the hangar next to the plane. On Thursday, March 11, Amelia flew the Electra into Oakland, the takeoff point, ac-companied by George, Bo McNeely, her mechanic, and a representative of Bendix Aviation, who was checking out both the direction finder and the radio. Amelia was undoubtedly the first private pilot to receive a ra-dio direction finder—indeed, a Bendix official had made a special flight from Washington at the end of February so that Lockheed could install it on the plane. It had a loop, carried on the outside of the plane just above the cockpit (Amelia posed with the loop: it was just a circle big enough to frame her face), which the pilot could turn to face the direction of a radio signal. Pan American relied heavily on radio direction finders—in fact, they would not start service until the direction finder at each refueling stop was up and calibrated and ready to guide them in. The new system was unerring, according to Amelia's friend Carl Allen, as he wrote in one of his columns, coming to point "as unerringly as a bird dog questing a quail-scented breeze."

Upon their arrival in Oakland, she and George moved into the Oakland Airport Inn along with Allen, her chosen observer who was syndicating the story for the *Herald Tribune*. She was planning to leave Monday, she announced, "unless the weather goes against me." In fact, if the weather permitted she planned to take off on Sunday, shortening the agony of ex-pectation by one day. It was raining that Thursday. The next day it was also raining, and the weekend prospects were for heavy rain. Friday saw the lowest barometric reading in seven years for San Francisco. Amelia was handling the waiting better than George. As usual before one of her flights, he was wound up tighter than a drum. As newsreel photographers were asking Amelia for yet another pose, he startled them by taking center stage and asking, "What's the idea of flying around the world? Don't you know a woman's place is in the home?" He immediately laughed and promised to say something nice, and the scene went off according to the best of newsreel intentions, according to the newsmen present. But the day before when he was asked if he wanted to go too, he replied, "Well, between 185 pounds of husband and 185 pounds of gasoline, there's a lot of difference—and the gasoline wins."

On March 13 Pan American announced the imminent opening of

its aerial service to New Zealand. The Pan Am plan was to fly from San Francisco to New Zealand in four travel days. Captain Musick was poised to make the first survey flight over the seven-thousand-mile route in one of the new Sikorsky Clippers, to check out weather patterns, seaplane landing facilities, and the new direction finders. He also had to see if the refueling station—actually a six-thousand-ton motor ship, the *North Wind,* anchored next to the coral outcropping of tiny Kingman Reef—would do to fuel, provision, and service the seaplanes. Pan Am was also surveying and planning to begin a run from someplace on the East Coast to Bermuda, as well as airmail service from Manila to Hong Kong. Captain Musick was twiddling his thumbs at Alameda waiting for the weather to break so he could set off across the Pacific on the first leg of the trip to New Zealand. To Gene and the others, it seemed like the perfect time to challenge Juan Trippe and his still-nascent airline with some heavyweight competition.

Amelia had been practicing blind flying with Paul Mantz, who had equipped his flying school with a Link trainer—an earthbound zero-view cockpit that simulated blind flying. On the thirteenth an Air Commerce inspector tested her blind flying skills and passed her after flying with her in the Electra for an hour with the cockpit covered. "She can do it," he said as he stepped from the plane. Someone asked Amelia if she had been scared. "Scared?" she repeated. "No just thrilled."

George didn't like Paul Mantz; the feeling was returned. Paul thought he was "a boor," while George treated him quite casually. Paul was, nevertheless, Amelia's hundred-dollar-a-day technical adviser, and perforce they got along. Indeed, Paul had flown George from Los Angeles to Oakland and back in the Electra so he could observe the various instruments and the Bendix direction finder in action. He had worked out the installation of fuel tanks and helped with the design of the instrument panel, as well as advising which instruments should be installed; he had also suggested other special gear Amelia would need. (On the other hand, he suggested that the Electra be painted orange or red—a suggestion that Amelia simply ignored, as she disregarded George's thought that the plane should sport Purdue's colors. Its aluminum skin remained gleamingly unpainted, except for black, orange, and red stripes painted on the backs of the wings to increase visibility.) In his capacity as Amelia's advisor, Paul himself had needed help: he enlisted the aid of Amelia's old friend Clarence Belinn, still working for Paul Collins and the Boston-Maine Airways in Boston, who was an authority on debugging gasoline tank cross-feed problems and laying out auxiliary gas tanks, to help him plan the Electra's tank configuration. He went to Kelly Johnson at Lockheed, the young engineering genius who translated all the plans into actuality. Kelly, although Paul didn't admit it, instructed Amelia on the use of wingflaps on takeoff. Kelly would say, "She was very sensible, very studious, and paid attention to what she was told." She didn't drive him crazy cross-checking on every single thing, the way his neighbor Laura Ingalls did.

The Electra cockpit was four feet eight inches high, four feet six inches wide, and four feet six inches fore and aft, with dual controls and two seats. Amelia had found that having to observe instruments on an angle, out of her line of vision, was a large factor in eye fatigue, particularly at night. So the instrument panel had been planned with particular care: there were some fifty dials and gauges altogether, but the most important and most often used were placed directly in front of Amelia's eyes. There were two groups of instruments, those having to do with the engines (duplicated for each one) and the flight and navigation instruments. The flight instruments included turn and bank indicators, rate of climb, air speed, and artificial horizon. The navigation instruments included two magnetic compasses, directional gyros, the Bendix radio direction finder, the Western Electric radio, and the cuplike microphone that hung beside the window to the left of her head, which transmitted at 500, 3105, and 6210. Amelia planned to broadcast on 3105 and 6210. As far as Harry Manning was concerned, however, the 500-kilocycle band, the standard frequency used by ships, was "the most important of the frequencies . . . because ships at sea and shore stations operating in code on this wave length [would] be practically his sole source of radio assistance after leaving Honolulu." In the center of the instrument panel was the Sperry gyro pilot.

The navigator's station was in the rear of the plane, behind the six fuel tanks, on the right side of the plane, adjacent to the aftermost window. A window had been added in the cabin ceiling, and the normal windows had been replaced with panes of flat, distortion-free glass so that the navigator could take star sights through them also. The chart table was wide and low, about eighteen inches off the floor. Beneath it under a glass inset was visible the face of a master aperiodic compass. Next to the table was an altimeter, an air speed indicator, and a temperature gauge. A Pioneer drift indicator, which measured the direction and distance of markers dropped into the sea to indicate wind direction, had been installed in the rear, near the navigator's station, in the cabin door, which by an ingenious arrangement could be held open four inches. The markers were presumably similar to the ones Pan Am used: by day, when the sky was clear and the sea visible, thin glass jars filled with aluminum powder that when dropped into the water burst upon impact, creating twenty-foot-long metallic spots. By night, canisters of acetylene gas were dropped—which ignited as they hit the sea. Communication between navigator and pilot was via a cut-down bamboo fishing pole; a paper clip at its end held cards upon which messages were written. There was also a catwalk over the tanks connecting the cabin to the cockpit, providing awkward but adequate access.

Amelia and George and Harry had daily conferences with Pan Am meteorologist John Riley, Paul Mantz, and Willis Clover, the Oakland airport weather forecaster, as well as William Miller. G. M. Turner, superintendent of the Oakland airfield, who was personally supervising the arrangements to make sure everything went perfectly, was also usually present.

First-day covers were all the rage and not just among stamp collectors. When the China Clipper made the first transpacific airmail flight the year before, the public went wild, buying a record 277,728 of the new twenty-five-cent airmail stamps the first day. Because demand was so great, to help pay for the flight, Amelia signed as many of the coveted covers as she could. George had provided for ten thousand in all—and each cover that was signed meant five dollars, twice the amount of an unsigned cover. The stamps were to go on sale at Gimbel's in New York, so the more Amelia signed, the more money it meant. But either signing the covers was a last-minute thought or they were late being delivered, because days before her planned liftoff, there were still a mountain of them to be done; as Amelia and George took their meals in the airport restaurant, usually with Carl Allen in attendance, between courses Amelia signed her name in the upper-left-hand corner of each envelope. In fact, according to Carl Allen, she and George had it down to a system: in the morning ten autographs before orange juice, fifteen before the bacon and eggs, then a few more in any spare moments, then twenty-five before she turned in at night. "She and Putnam exchanged conspiratorial grins as though they were letting me in on an amusing secret," wrote Allen much later, when he began to blame George for everything. "Their little joke, if that was what was intended to be, had all the sprightliness of the proverbial lead balloon." But as he noted at the time, "as she writes she carries on conversations about her forthcoming flight or on any other topic with complete detachment from what her hands are doing." It was undoubtedly the most effortless but the most boring task extant. Signing all ten thousand would have taken her something on the order of sixteen hours, but writing ten signatures before orange juice took just one minute. In spite of the covers, noted Carl Allen, Amelia was as patient as ever with autograph seekers who broke through George's interference—"she hardly ever refuses a signature once someone reaches her side." George, on the other hand, was succumbing to the pressure and was decidedly impatient. Just as Jake Coolidge had found George "irascible" in the final days in Boston before the *Friendship* took off, so now Allen found him hard to take. Allen himself was there taking meals with them and staying at the inn because George had sold the rights to the round-the-world voyage to the *Tribune,* knowing that Allen was the one reporter whom Amelia thoroughly enjoyed having around and also that Allen was an excellent observer as well as a first-rate writer. "He was good company, never preyed on her nerves with importunate questions, never waved any deadlines in front of her, often had suggestions to contribute out of his excellent knowledge of aviation," wrote George, not having the slightest idea what a huge role Allen had played in Amelia's decision to marry him.

Pan American's Pacific Division head, Clarence Young, was also working with Amelia. The previous January, when Pan Am had inaugurated service from Miami to San Juan, Puerto Rico, she had lent her presence to the event. Now Juan Trippe ordered Pan Am personnel to put every facility that Pan Am possessed, as well as every bit of weather information they collected, at Amelia's disposal for the duration of her flight. It was hoped, wrote Allen, that the Pan Am long-range direction finders could track her as far as Port Darwin. To this end Pan Am personnel had been instructed to stand watch twenty-four hours a day while Amelia flew the Pacific. Manning, meanwhile, was more intent on working the standard steamship radio channel of 500 kilocycles, which would enable him to communicate with ships at sea and most of the shore radio stations, including the coast guard radio station near San Francisco. He planned to rely on it almost exclusively.

On Friday Paul Mantz took Manning up for a last-minute radio check, but Manning was "perturbed" to find that he could not raise the San Francisco coast guard station on the 500-kilocycle frequency. The other two frequencies, 3105 and 6210, worked perfectly, but Manning was only interested in the 500-kilocycle band. A radio expert was summoned.

On Saturday Amelia and Mantz and Manning took the plane up for a two-hour radio and compass check and flew almost a hundred miles out to sea; the radio equipment and the direction finder worked perfectly. "All were in high spirits when they landed," according to Carl Allen.

Before she left Burbank, Amelia had also been working with Kelly Johnson of Lockheed. He was a hands-on engineer, who believed in flight-testing all his "babies." Only twenty-seven, he had already worked with all the great pilots—Jimmy Doolittle, Wiley Post, Sir Charles Kingsford-Smith, and Roscoe Turner. Amelia learned from him to master a device called a Cambridge analyzer, which by analyzing exhaust gas allowed the most efficient use of fuel: "You used it repeatedly, resetting mixture control and leaning out engine fuel to get maximum miles per gallon." Flying together, he and Amelia worked out the absolute maximum mileage that could be gotten from the plane. She was as thorough as he, according to Kelly: "The two of us, she as pilot and I as flight engineer, would fly her Electra with different weights, different balance conditions, different engine power settings, different altitudes." Kelly listed distance, fuel loads, and gross weight for each leg of the flight, and from them Amelia knew that she could add one or even two people for the California-to-Honolulu segment.

If she had worked well with Kelly Johnson, she was beginning to have doubts about Harry Manning's ability. As she told Carl Allen, Manning said that the double duty of acting as navigator and radio operator "imposed a greater physical strain than any one man should be expected to stand." This factor was accentuated when it was decided that the "flying laboratory" should send out periodic signals as focal points for Pan American Airways' long-range direction finders, since this arrangement and the necessity of receiving the position fix radioed back by the airline's operators added still another job to the already overworked Captain Manning's list of activities.

"Miss Earhart said," he continued, "that with Captain Manning trying to do the work of a radio operator and navigator it kept him 'jumping around all the time.' "

Knowing she had no weight problems, she decided to add another navigator, Fred Noonan.

• • • •

Pan Am navigators were regarded with respect by everyone in the flying world. They were the best, so good that a few years later, when the U.S. Air Corps decided to teach its cadets serious navigation, it sent them to Pan Am's facility in Coral Gables, Florida, to learn. Now it was announced that Pan Am's Fred Noonan would be relief navigator as far as Howland Island.

A tall dark Irishman, Noonan had started out a sailor, had rounded Cape Horn three times on a windjammer, and four times on a steamship, and was torpedoed three times while in the Royal British Naval Service in World War I. He became a transport pilot with New York Rio and Buenos Aires Airlines, flying from New York to Buenos Aires.

When Pan Am bought NYBRA, it moved Fred to Alameda, California, the Pan Am headquarters and jumping-off place for the new China Clippers, with which Pan Am was about to span the Pacific. The company put Noonan in charge of its navigation school. He was the navigator on the epochal first flight of the *China Clipper.* The planning and execution of the flight were virtually flawless; everything went like clockwork, not only on that first flight but on all the ones that followed. By the end of

1936, Noonan had made eighteen air crossings of the Pacific. According to Page Smith, one of the youngest, at twenty-three, pilots working for Pan American, he was regarded by all the Clipper personnel with awe—they thought him the world's top celestial navigator.

But something went wrong in his life; he had started to drink—and Pan Am let him go. Since the circle of fliers in those years was so small, "everyone" knew about it. Amelia certainly knew about it; Clara Livingston, a member of the Ninety-Nines, a pilot and a friend with whom she and Fred would later stay with in Puerto Rico, "didn't think he was a great risk" as Amelia's navigator. "He was a pleasant person, you know. . . . He had tried so hard to reform." Not everyone was convinced that he had succeeded. Gene Vidal thought that including Fred Noonan on Amelia's flight was a great mistake, and he told her so. She then asked Gene to go in his place, but Gene demurred on the grounds that he wasn't a good enough navigator.

Pan Am pilots, who presumably knew what they were talking about, believed that although Noonan "might have missed a trip or something," he *never* drank on the job. It was planned that he would leave the flight at Howland, having done the "lion's share" of navigating up to that point, letting Manning mainly concern himself with operating the radio. But he had had an automobile accident in the recent past. Amelia wasn't bothered by this knowledge; she knew that he was in the process of changing his life, that he and his first wife had gotten divorced just that spring, and that he had a new, serious lady friend.

Once Noonan had signed on, he made one request: for an octant to shoot the sun and stars—it was his principal tool. Amelia asked the naval station at San Diego to loan her one. "Amelia Earhart urgently requests air station loan Navy octant for projected trans Atlantic flight and shipment air express to Oakland immediately," they cabled Washington. Clearance was granted on Tuesday, March 16, by the secretary of the navy.

Amelia hadn't any thought of bringing Paul Mantz to check things out in Honolulu, but there he was sitting it out with her in California because of the weather, and at the last minute he asked to come—to help her out, he said, but also to join his fiancée, Terry, who was on her way by boat to Hawaii. Amelia could hardly refuse. He could be co-pilot for the first overnight flight, allowing her to rest and be fresh for the difficult Honolulu–Howland passage, and he could be counted on, as Carl Allen noted, "to assume complete responsibility for preparing the 'flying laboratory' for the next stage of the trans-Pacific flight." Obviously Allen thought including Mantz was a splendid idea, or he wouldn't have mentioned it.

In light of later developments, it is instructive to make particular note of Allen's thoughts. Amelia made a similar assessment: "By the end of this first long hop any incipient mechanical troubles should show up. It will be fine to have him on hand for a final check before I shove off westward."

Government vessels were on the move. Richard B. Black, of the Department of the Interior, was aboard the coast guard cutter *Shoshone* at Howland Island and reported that the three runways there were ready and waiting. The navy minesweeper *Whippoorwill* was steaming into position between Honolulu and Howland Island; the navy tug *Ontario* was moving into position between Howland and Lae, New Guinea.

In hopes that a Sunday takeoff might be possible, loading began. Between two and three hundred pounds of equipment was weighed and stowed in the plane as Amelia watched and made mental notes so that she would be able to locate anything without effort. Five vacuum bottles for hot drinks, water canteens, a desert waterbag for keeping water cool in hot climates, a life preserver for each person, a rubber life raft with oars and a kite sail (which could serve as an emergency radio antenna), more chocolate bars, raisins, canned tomato juice, standard army emergency rations, fishing tackle, a hand-operated battery charger for use if the motor-driven generator failed, a spare tail wheel, and the small package of "no-fog" that she was supposed to test for its ability to dissipate fog (which Fred Noonan would eventually make her get rid of).

All the activity heightened the tension and public's interest. A crowd estimated at nearly ten thousand camped behind the steel fence near the navy hangar that housed her plane.

American women waited nervously, impatiently, proudly, for Amelia to take off. The Oakland airport switchboard was being bombarded with hundreds of calls each day, of which at least seventy-five percent were from women, "who seem to feel Miss Earhart is a champion of their sex's ability to accomplish feats of flying equalling those of any man," according to C. A. Weaver, who presided over the switchboard.

In the Hawaiian Islands, hundreds of outlying islanders gathered on Oahu to attend the unveiling of a plaque for Amelia that was to take place on her arrival.

The headwinds that had kept the Pan Am Clippers from starting out earlier in the week built up again on Sunday, forcing one Clipper that had finally taken off and was a third of the way to Oahu to turn back. In the face of the adverse weather, Amelia postponed her start by twenty-four hours, to the delight of Oakland airport personnel; for them the extra day and the high winds, which would help dry out the field, were a gift from Providence. Paul Mantz, after driving his car up and down the hard surface apron to test it, had found that the unending drizzle had made it much too soft for the Electra, and airport superintendent G. M. Turner had been working frantically with a crew of men and trucks, scrapers, and a steamroller to fill in the soft spots, afraid Mantz would opt for Mills field across the bay in San Francisco.

At a Monday-morning conference at the Pan Am base on the Bay at Alameda with John A. Riley, the Oakland airport government weather forecaster, and Willis Clover, the chief meteorologist for Pan Am's Pacific Division, Amelia and Paul learned that the low-pressure areas and adverse winds were still sitting some five hundred miles off the California coast and that Pan Am had grounded their Clippers till Wednesday. They had no choice but to do the same.

By Wednesday, March 17, the winds had finally changed; Pan Am prepared to send off its planes, and Amelia began her final preparations. It was St. Patrick's Day, and from somewhere Amelia obtained a collection of shamrocks. She pinned one on each member of the Electra flight crew, including herself. "Her husband was similarly decorated by the smiling airwoman," reported the newspapers. They ate a quick lunch perched on stools at the lunch counter, then Amelia repaired to her room for a short nap. Meanwhile, Bureau of Air Commerce executive William Miller and Superintendent Turner staked out the runway Amelia would use with a series of cardboard placards, placed on alternate sides of the takeoff strip every 150 feet.

The crowd, uncertain about Amelia's departure time, was down to a more managable five thousand or so. She smiled and waved at the friends who were waving at her from the edge of the runway. She appeared relaxed as always and was dressed "as usual," wrote Carl Allen, in brown slacks, and a brown, gray, and blue plaid shirt, with a brown linen scarf knotted loosely around her throat and a tan leather jacket.

At 3:13 in the afternoon sunshine broke through, and Captain Dahlstrom piloting the Pan Am Hawaiian Clipper took off. At 4:19 Captain Musick, piloting the Clipper on the survey flight to New Zealand, took off. At 4:36 Amelia was in the air. All three planes were bound for Honolulu. Amelia, of course, was taking off from a muddy field, whereas the Clippers, being seaplanes, took off across the water of the bay.

As Amelia moved down the field, George couldn't resist bidding her one last farewell; as he approached the plane, Paul throttled down the powerful engines. (It must have been at Amelia's request, for it was not the kind of thing he would have done on his own.) George climbed up on the wing for some final words with his wife—it was, after all, the last time he expected to see her for a long time. Then he climbed back down and got into William Miller's car, and they chased behind the plane as it roared down the field. The field was still very wet. As the Electra approached the red flags marking the halfway spot, it was throwing up a wake like a hydroplane. Still, it managed to get off in a little over eighteen hundred feet. Pan Am officials purportedly instructed both Musick, bound by way of Kingman Reef, Pago-Pago, and Samoa, and Dahlstrom, in another Pan Am trans-Pacific Clipper Manila bound by way of Wake, Midway, and Guam, both of whom would also land in Hawaii, to reduce their normal cruising speed by fifteen knots so that Amelia would pass them easily and there would be no speculation about a Pacific "race." An excellent public relations move, it made Pan American look good and obscured the truth about the planes: that Amelia's was faster.

Back at the field, Bill Miller sent off the cable containing his carefully detailed notes on the beginning of the flight to naval headquarters, and he alerted all ships along the route as well. Some reporters told George that there was a move in Congress to award a congressional medal to Amelia for her flying achievements. He smiled and expressed his hope that he would receive one too.

20
The Beginning

• • • • The Electra made the passage from Oakland to Honolulu in 15 hours, 47 minutes, setting a new speed record. Amelia flew fifty minutes of every hour; Paul kept track of fuel consumption. Manning worked the 500-kilocycle band—so long, noted Amelia, that he blew out the generator. For the last few hundred miles Noonan and Amelia set their course with the aid of the Bendix radio direction finder: Fred directed Amelia to locate the Makapu beacon with the DF and keep it ten degrees to starboard. It worked like a charm. Eighty miles from Makapu, "Fred says start down." She turned over the controls to Paul Mantz.

Paul circled the field twice; airport personnel watching the plane feared that the winds were causing trouble. Paul admitted to wrapping the plane around "in a steep bank" in order to check the wind sock. The landing was terrible—so hard, in fact, that the impact weakened the landing gear. Amelia was not happy.

Paul would later tell his biographer that Amelia complained about his landing because she was exhausted, "very fatigued and kind of exuberant," but it was actually he who was in a high state of bother. He landed the plane without cutting the engines on the ramp, as was expected; instead he taxied into the hangar, thereby leaving the welcoming committee, which included three generals plus a squad of men, waiting in the drizzle, according to First Lieutenant K. A. Popers, Station Engineering Officer at Wheeler field. Paul was actually in such a state that he left the field without giving comprehensive instructions: "Mr. Mantz departed with the rest of the crew with no word whatsoever as to what was to be done to the plane in the way of service and check-over. Mr. Thomas, the Pratt and Whitney engine man for this territory, was present and he and the Engineering officer took it upon themselves to do what is usually done to put an airplane into suitable condition for the continuance of such a flight," according to army records. Paul flung out as he left that for the last six hours of the flight, the right-hand Hamilton constant speed propeller had been frozen in position. And yet he didn't bother to mention it in his flight log. He also told them, "insisted," that the generator had blown because the control box was "out of order," but the mechanic traced the trouble to a blown fuse—a piece of information Paul should have relayed to Amelia, but never did.

Certainly Amelia exhibited no fatigue. Immediately after they landed she made the photographers who were intent on snapping her with Paul wait until Harry Manning and Fred Noonan were also standing alongside. Then she went off and ate a huge breakfast. "And speaking of breakfast, a bright particular memory . . . were the so-fresh scrambled eggs miraculously awaiting us," she recollected.

Paul and Amelia were not getting along, and within a very short time, Amelia had all but fired him—in her own fashion, which is to say, she referred to him in *Last Flight* as still being her technical adviser but in fact was consulting him only when it was absolutely necessary. Paul took great pride in being her adviser as well as her business partner; he wasn't used to such treatment, and from then on he never spoke of Amelia except condescendingly. The wound, the rejection, rankled for the rest of his life, causing him, after she died, to tell a number of untruths about her, denigrating her intelligence and competence, with the aim of inflating his role and his guidance. There is no other explanation for the studied lies and the amazing male chauvinist tone that exists in his biography—Ruth Nichols called it the last grumblings of a jealous colleague. None of which would be worth mentioning if so many people hadn't swallowed it whole and used his comments as the basis for an assault on Amelia's piloting skills.

Amelia went off to Christian and Mona Holmes's house at Waikiki to rest and to write her story for the *Herald Tribune*; it appeared next day on the front page. Before she left Oakland, Amelia had given George an estimated flight time; her prediction turned out to be almost on the nose—she was only five minutes off. (After she landed, George sent her a teasing cable, "Please try to be more exact.")

Army mechanics disassembled the self-adjusting pitch mechanism on the propeller and found that an improper lubricant had been used that had congealed when the Electra had briefly hit icing conditions. Since they didn't have the necesssary tools at Wheeler to fix the problem, both propellers were removed, and taken to the Hawaiian Air Depot at the navy's Luke field, where they were worked on through the night. It took hot kerosene to loosen the frozen blades. At two A.M. the propellers were returned to Wheeler and reinstalled on the plane, working perfectly.

Mantz showed up at eleven o'clock accompanied by his fiancée Terry Minor and Christian Holmes, and took off in the Electra with his companions, first announcing that he would land at Luke field to see if the concrete runway there would be better for the final takeoff than Wheeler's dirt runway. This, of course, seriously affected all the armed forces' preparations, but responding to the situation, the Luke group operations officer immediately recalled all planes and cleared his field. After landing at Luke, Paul decided its runway was preferable to that at Wheeler and that Amelia should take off from there. He ordered the plane to be gassed up. Then he left, according to government records. Lieutenant Arnold, the Luke depot inspector, was watching as Standard Oil began the refueling, which was being executed as usual through a chamois strainer. The lieutenant immediately noticed "considerable sediment" on the chamois and ordered the gas flow stopped. Military aviation fuel was subsequently used.

By the time the plane was loaded it was after seven P.M. Nine hundred gallons of gasoline were now in the Electra, slightly less than the plane had lofted into the air at Oakland. Even that was more than Amelia needed for an eighteen hundred mile trip; Howland was six hundred miles closer to Honolulu than Oakland, and the Electra had had four hours' worth of gas left when it landed at Honolulu, but Amelia was simply taking normal precautions; weather patterns could always change, and she wanted enough gasoline aboard to be able to turn around eight hours out "if it became necessary."

Amelia had called up during the afternoon to say she would either leave at eleven that evening or at dawn. At nine-thirty the decision was made to start at dawn. Depot personnel who remained to work on the plane spent the night on cots in the final assembly hangar at Luke.

At 3:45 A.M. the officer-of-the-day reported with a guard detail of twenty men and established a rope barrier around the plane. Another officer was sent with sixteen men to establish a line of sentries at two-hundred-foot intervals along the west side of the runway and to relight and relocate certain of the lights. Sometime between four and four thirty, Amelia, Paul, Fred, Harry, Chris Holmes, and Terry Minor arrived. It was still dark; Amelia ordered the runway lights on, surveyed the field, and then announced that she would wait till daylight to start. At Howland Island, the coast guard cutter *Itasca* waited.

At five thirty the motors were started, and Captain Manning and Noonan took their places, and at five forty Amelia taxied out to the northeast end of the runway, preceded by Paul in a car.

As the Electra roared down the runway gathering speed, it swung slightly to the right, whereupon Amelia throttled down the left engine. The plane then started swinging left, and as it did, it tilted outward, throwing all the weight onto the right wheel. Suddenly the right-hand landing gear collapsed, and "The airplane spun sharply to the left sliding on its belly and amid a shower of sparks from the mat and came to rest headed about 200 degrees from its initial course."

The official crash report described the accident. But the official report did not mention that army aviators thought the wet runway had added to the problem, that after the heavily loaded plane began skidding, it would have been almost impossible to straighten it out.

Amelia immediately shut down the engines, thereby preventing a fire. She would later write that the plane was moving so easily down the runway "that I thought the take-off was actually over. In ten seconds more we would have been off the ground, with our landing gear tucked up and on our way southwestward. There was not the slightest indication of anything abnormal." She studied the accident, naturally, and listened to the comments of witnesses who said the tire blew, but she thought the fault lay in the landing gear, weakened by Paul's hard landing. "Possibly the landing gear's right shock absorber, as it lengthened, may have given way," she wrote for publication. Her first intimation that something was wrong was when she felt the plane pull to her right: "I reduced the power on the opposite engine and succeeded in swinging from the right to the left. For a moment I thought I would be able to gain control and straighten the course. But, alas, the load was so heavy."

It was a disaster of the first magnitude—and totally unexpected. All the preparations, all the people, all the hoopla—there was nowhere to hide. The first thing she did was call George.

"It is amazing," she said later, "how much can happen in one dawn."

• • • •

Amelia left the next day at noon aboard the SS *Malolo,* having given brief statements to reporters that she would resume her flight later. A week later the air force put the plane aboard the SS *Lurline;* "based on the written request and authorization of Miss Earhart," its destination was the Lockheed plant at Burbank.

The mechanics at Lockheed found that the the right wing, both engine housings, the right-hand rudder, the underside of the fuselage, and both propellers were seriously damaged. The oil tanks ruptured. In the process of repairing the plane Lockheed strengthened the landing gear—tacit acknowledgement that a full load of gasoline subjected it to "excessive" strain.

The accident was such a stunner that many just couldn't cope with it, least of all Amelia and George. Back in California, they were faced not just with the fact of the accident, as unsettling as that was, but with the incidental expenses, which were huge. Six mechanics were on the verge of setting out for various parts of the world to service the plane, at least one had left; their travel expenses and salaries had to be paid. Then arrangements had to be made to safeguard the supplies and the fuel that were in place. Then the Air Corps demanded that George pay $1,086 to the Hawaiian Air Depot as payment for the materials used in the overhauling, repairing, and preparing for shipment of the plane. Then there was the cost of transporting the damaged plane back to Lockheed, and the cost of the steamship tickets for Amelia, Harry Manning, and Fred Noonan. And there was the plane itself; Lockheed's bill came to $14,000.

Amelia and George needed help to get back on track; they went to Harry Bruno, pilot and public relations adviser—a genius at raising money. Harry had been Charles Lindbergh's press agent in 1927 and had gone on to represent everyone in the flying world from Anthony Fokker to Richard Byrd.

Amelia visited him first, and told him how sorry she was that the accident had happened "because she thought it would mean a lot to aviation." The next day George went to see Harry and asked him to help raise money, which Harry quickly did—$20,000 from Vincent Bendix and $10,000 from Floyd Odlum. That kept the project alive.

"On the prosaic dollar-and-cent side friends helped generously, but even so, to keep going I more-or-less mortgaged the future. Without regret, however, for what are futures for?" wrote Amelia in *Last Flight.* It was charmingly put, but still, it was one of the rare times when she talked about money. She dedicated her book to Floyd Odlum, who opened his deep pockets to her; he, too, wanted to keep the project alive.

Then Harry Manning pulled out, for the repairs would take till mid-May and he had to get back to work. Rumors had it that Amelia was relieved. She took to spending hours every day at the Lockheed plant, keeping herself "busier than ever before." She had again started working with Kelly Johnson, getting his take on the causes of ground looping and working to get the most out of the Cambridge analyzer, which was so crucial to fuel consumption.

Then she made a big change in plans: she decided to fly east around the world instead of west. The reasons were several. First, if she proceeded west, the delay meant she would reach the Caribbean and Africa—the last leg as planned—at the start of the monsoon season, but if she reversed, she could fly through before they started. Second, changing direction would afford her the luxury of flight-testing the plane as she flew from Oakland to Miami, the revised jumping-off place, thereby saving the time of running such tests in California. And a third, a huge advantage, she would be flying around the world with the prevailing winds instead of against. Many pilots agreed that this route was more sensible, but the change also meant that she would be taking the most difficult navigational stretch—the long Pacific hop to tiny Howland Island—at the end instead of the beginning. But that meant another adjustment: Fred Noonan had to be along for the entire flight, for to fly the Pacific and hit such a small island required celestial navigation, and it wasn't possible to pilot and take sun and star sights at the same time. Nor was she trained to do it.

Paul Mantz was not consulted.

She sent off mementos: to Gore, the blue-and-white-checked leather belt he had often seen her wear; to Gene, her old watch. She sent the flight coat in which she had flown the Atlantic, plus a fine buffalo coat that William Hart had given her and other personal belongings to Carl Dunrud to store for her. She attached a note to the buffalo coat: "To you Carl. I know of no one that can put this to better use than you."

On the way home from the army-navy game at West Point with Gene and Gore the previous fall, she had talked about her round-the-world flight. Gore had asked her what part of the flight most worried her. "Africa," she had answered. "If you got forced down in those jungles, they'd never find you." At that point Amelia was envisaging a solo flight across Africa, having dropped her navigator after landing in Australia and being alone above the jungle. Gore and his father each responded with worries about the Pacific. Amelia, though, planning to have a navigator aboard on that leg and in love with Gene, answered "Oh, there are always islands," then continued, "Wouldn't it be wonderful to just go off and live on a desert island?" Marooned on an island, she added, she could finally write the two books she had in mind. One, based on learning at Denison House that sometimes parents got it all wrong, was going to be about bringing up children; the other one—she had an aversion to bankers—would be on the capitalist system. Gene was quite dubious, according to Gore. "Then," Gore remembered, "they discussed just *how* you could survive; and what would you do if there was no water? and if there was no water, you would have to make a sunstill and extract salt from sea water and how was that done?" So there was no doubt such thoughts were in her head.

Carl Allen thought the flight was a dangerous undertaking. It wasn't that she wasn't well prepared or skillful enough, he told her when she asked him what he thought her chances were. She was as well prepared as anyone, and her flying equipment just as good. Still, he answered, he thought her chances of completing the flight successfully were fifty-fifty. She replied:

> I hope your guess is a good one . . . No one really could expect
> better chances on such a flight. Actually, I'm not worried about
> the percentages except for my navigator. As far as I know, I've got
> only one obsession—a small and probably typical feminine horror
> of growing old—so I won't feel completely cheated if I fail to come
> back.

She never talked about God. Once she was asked by another pilot, who admitted to praying "like crazy" when she was in a tough spot, if she ever prayed in like circumstances. "No-o-o I don't believe so," Amelia replied slowly, a ghost of a smile flickering across her face. "I guess I think it would be a little unsportsmanlike, to wait and only send God a hurry call when I was in a jam."

• • • •

On Thursday, May 21, 1937, at 3:50 P.M., ten years and one day after Charles Lindbergh had taken off on his solo flight across the Atlantic, five years and one day from the time Amelia had taken off on hers, Amelia lifted her Lockheed Electra off the runway of the airfield in Oakland, and officially began her flight around the world. The sky was clear and the temperature was mild as she winged her way toward Tucson.

A key player—Bill Miller of the Bureau of Air Commerce—was no longer working with Amelia. His absence was not Amelia's choice, however: Gene Vidal was no longer head of the Bureau of Air Commerce, and Bill had been sent off on another assignment. Nor was Paul Mantz with her; he was in St. Louis, flying competition acrobatics. He hadn't even known she was going to start. He was furious he hadn't been in on the plans and called it a "sneak departure."

• • • •

Because the plane had just come out of the Lockheed plant in Burbank, Amelia was able to get away with calling what was her first leg a "shakedown" flight and keep all publicity to a minimum, much more in keeping with all her earlier flights. With her were George, Fred Noonan, and Bo McKneeley, flight mechanic; the plan was to fly eastward cross-country and if all went well, if they could shake out all the bugs, to take off from Miami for the first transoceanic leg. And bugs there were: after landing in Tucson, when Amelia restarted the engines to taxi to the fuel pumps, the left motor, still hot, backfired and, in the afternoon heat, burst into flames. The fire went out almost immediately; the damage was "trivial, mostly some pungently cooked rubber fittings." Amelia shrugged it off as due to the Arizona summer weather. The engine was cleaned and the plane hosed down, and the next day they started out into the teeth of a sandstorm.

They put down that night in New Orleans, their landing unannounced. The first anyone knew of her presence was when she radioed ten miles out at Plaquemines that she was approaching. Then she "streaked out of the setting sun, circled Shusan Airport three times, set down on the runway at 5:55 P.M. . . . her hair tousled as usual." "I've never been on the ground at New Orleans," she told the reporters waiting for her at Shusan disarmingly. "I've flown over your airport here numerous times, and it looked so nice from the air that I decided to land and see how it looked from the ground."

• • • •

It was partly cloudy and in the seventies when they took off the next morning at 9:10, bound for Florida. They landed just after midday at Miami municipal airport. The landing was a hard one because the shock absorber fluid had leaked out of the landing gear—another bug to correct. The next week or so would be spent preparing, checking, and fixing the Electra, working out minor adjustments in components and radio, and waiting for parts. They had brackets fitted to the side of the fuselage just behind the door to hold a "sky hook," into which the metal rods supplied by the Department of Agriculture were fitted that trapped air and microorganisms for study. (Fred coughed in one and would have thrown it away, but Amelia insisted it be put with the others, because "I thought it would give the laboratory workers something to ponder when they came upon its contents among the more innocent bacteria of the equatorial upper airs.") Maintenance work was done by Pan American mechanics. Amelia, George, and Fred moved into a two-bedroom suite at the Columbus Hotel, the Putnams having a bedroom off one end of the living room, Noonan off the other.

Amelia spent most of her time at the Pan Am hangar with the plane, although she did accept one offer to go deep sea fishing. She also attended a reception honoring Captain H. T. Merrill and his co-pilot Jack Lambie, held across from the hotel in Bayfront Park, who had just completed, in a sister ship to Amelia's Electra, the first commercial transatlantic round trip from New York to London. Carl Allen, conscientious reporter, still on the job for the *Herald Tribune,* accompanied Amelia on a tour of the big hangar-workshops at Pan Am's Dinner Key facility, where the Sikorsky Clipper ships were hauled out and inspected after each flight. Both Carl and George observed that Pan Am personnel changed their opinion of Amelia for the better after observing her firsthand. Many at Pan Am had been feeling sorry for their former confrere, Fred Noonan, whom they all respected, reported Carl, but after they observed Amelia in action, "they were willing to concede that 'poor old Fred' needed no sympathy, that he evidently had signed up with the pick of the lot of women aviators." Carl went on: "she knew exactly what she wanted done, and had sense enought to let them alone while they did it. There was an almost audible clatter of chips falling off skeptical masculine shoulders"

When Allen first arrived in Miami and caught up with Amelia at the airport, one of the first things he did was to go over the equipment list to see if there had been any changes since Oakland. He noted one change that he wasn't sure he approved of—the elimination of the marine frequency radio that operated on the 500-kilocycle bandwidth. "Oh," she said, "that was left off when Manning had to drop out of the flight. Both Fred Noonan and I know Morse code but we're amateurs and probably never would be able to send and receive more than 10 words a minute. . . . The marine frequency radio would have been just that much more dead weight to carry and we decided to leave it in California." That made sense to Carl, for as a pilot he knew useless weight could mean the difference between life and death: between having enough fuel and not having enough to complete a journey against unexpectedly adverse winds.

A new, powerful antenna had been installed to maximize the 6210 to be used during the day and the 3105-kilocycle frequency to be used at night. But Pan Am radio technicians decided to replace the antenna with yet another one after she was unable to communicate with either the local broadcasting station or with the Bureau of Air Commerce airways station at the field in a test flight. She planned to broadcast every half hour, fifteen minutes before and after the hour, all the way around the world.

• • • •

Fred Noonan had a friend in Miami by the name of Helen Day. An attractive young businesswoman, she knew him from the time he had lived in Coconut Grove, Florida, and flew for New York Rio and Buenos Aires Airlines, the line Pan American had bought. He had spent a considerable amount of time with Helen, then a college student, and with her circle of friends. Helen was now the accountant for a chain of stores. With time on his hands, even though he had recently remarried, Fred called her up and asked her to dine with him and to come early to meet Amelia.

She went up to the suite the last afternoon and met Amelia and George. She found George much as Edna Whyte described him: tense and preoccupied. He ventured a brusque and minimal "How do you do" and "Good-bye" to her as he wrestled with final arrangements. His immediate problem, according to Helen, was that Amelia had no cash, and the banks were closed—a problem that was solved when someone thought of asking *The Miami Herald* whether they would cash a check, which they did. Then Helen listened as the plans for where they would spend the next night changed. Clara Livingston, a pilot, one of the original Ninety-Nines and a friend of Fred and of Amelia, called up and offered to put them up at her sixteen-hundred-acre sugar plantation in Puerto Rico, promising, according to Fred, "not to have a party. . . . It would be a quiet restful evening. . . . You can believe her. . . . She doesn't have a reporter up her sleeve." Amelia and George and Fred discussed it and decided it was a great idea.

Helen found Amelia very relaxed; if the the imminent departure weighed heavily upon her, it didn't show. Amelia wore a light chocolate brown housecoat that had two stripes, one ivory and one orange, that went from shoulder to hem—an outfit Helen thought very attractive. It speaks volumes about Amelia's mindset, as well as her relationship with Fred Noonan, that Amelia now queried Helen about her blind mother, about whom Fred had told her a great deal, who was unusual for her alertness and interest in life. Then Amelia's social work training came to the fore—she wanted to know what the Lighthouse for the Blind was doing for the blind people of Miami.

Helen and Fred went out for an early dinner at a restaurant up the boulevard a little way from the hotel. During dinner he told Helen that he had had a drinking problem, but that it was over, he had stopped, and that he viewed this trip as his opportunity to show everybody else that he'd turned his life around. He also told her that he was being paid "considerable" money. She came away feeling that he had indeed turned the corner, and didn't think there was a great risk in having him for navigator. Nor did Clara Livingston. Nor, evidently, did Amelia.

He did feel, however, that it was a dangerous adventure. He said, Helen recalled, "Amelia can take care of herself; if we were forced down anyplace I don't feel that she would lean on me unnecessarily—you know—she would carry her own weight. You know, I wouldn't fly across the Mississippi River with Laura Ingalls."

Helen told him that there had "been some stuff in the papers about romance." "Forget it," he said. "There's no romance going on—just two people doing a job."

Helen, being the local with a car, drove him back to the hotel and on the way offered to drive him out to the airport the next morning. Fred declined, thinking it too much of an inconvenience. She dropped him back at the hotel and drove on home, only to find out upon arrival there that he had been calling her. It transpired that Amelia wanted Helen to have breakfast with them and so Fred decided it was a wonderful idea to add Helen and her car to the entourage. So at three A.M., pushing her way through the knots of reporters jammed in the lobby Helen gave her name and was allowed up the elevator to their suite, where she found Amelia, George, George's son David and wife Nilla, Eustace Adams, an author and old friend of the Putnams' who lived in Florida, and Fred Noonan, all busily gathering equipment. Helen helped them carry down their things—various items that included pith helmets, thermos jugs, and a machete in case they were forced down in the jungle. Someone carried Amelia's small suitcase, which contained five shirts, two pairs of slacks, a change of shoes, a light working coverall, a weightless raincoat, linen, and toilet articles. Fred carried only his octant.

They went down and pushed their way through the lobby, then drove to a Greek restaurant and had breakfast. Helen listened, fascinated, as Amelia asked for hot tomato juice to be put in two of the two-quart thermos jugs, and asked Fred, "Are you going to drink that stuff?" To which he replied, "No, she is."

They arrived at the airport just after four A.M. It was still dark when they got to the small hangar; a light was burning. The mechanic Bo McKneely was there, having spent the night with the plane. Since except for Bo there was no one about to help get the plane out of the hangar, everyone got out of their cars and pushed. By the time they were finished, police had arrived to cordon off the area, and a crowd estimated at five hundred were sitting in their cars with their headlights beamed at the hangar. Helen had said good-bye and was some distance away when Fred called her back and gave her letters and three dollars in money orders for her to send on to the postmasters of Hollywood and Oakland for his July rentals for two post office boxes in those cities, "in case he was late." By four thirty the small amount of luggage carried by Amelia and Fred had been loaded into the plane, together with the thermos bottles of hot tomato juice and, for Fred, coffee. Amelia, exercising the utmost care, warmed up the ship's two engines. Then she shut them down, another glitch: a thermocouple, which registered cylinder-head temperatures from the left motor, refused to work. Bo McKneely set about repairing it. The rising sun was brushing back the silver gray of dawn, Amelia noted.

Just before takeoff, George as usual couldn't resist another good-bye. He climbed up, leaned into the cockpit for a last kiss, and shook Fred's hand. It could be seen that Amelia "exuded confidence and smiles." George did not.

At 6:04 Amelia closed and fastened the hatch; thirty seconds later, the Electra was airborne. Standing on the roof of the administration building with David, George paced nervously back and forth until the silver plane rose and wheeled and disappeared to the southeast.

21
The Flight

• • • • They were off on June 1, the pilot who was afraid of nothing, who just wanted to make the first globe-girdling flight touching the Southern as well as the Northern Hemisphere and knew it had to be done before she was forty, and the navigator out to show the world that his life was back on track.

They started out in easy stages. The flight to San Juan took a little over eight hours. Their mutual friend Clara Livingston met them at the airport and drove them out to her sugar plantation to spend the night at Mi Casa, her dramatic colonial hacienda with its twin staircases curving down to the beach.

They were up and at the airfield before dawn for the planned flight to Paramaribo, Dutch Guiana, but they had to settle on Caripito, Venezuela—much closer—because construction work at the field shortened it too much to allow them to take off with the planned fuel load. When they landed in Caripito, the general manager of Standard Oil took care of them and put them up in his home. From Caripito they flew the 1,330 miles to Paramaribo, which Fred knew well from his Pan Am days, and they stayed at the hotel where he had stayed then. Their next stop was Fortaleza in northeast Brazil. In both of these places they were, Fred wrote happily to Helen, "besieged" with invitations of hospitality and showered with kindnesses—to the extent that when they went shopping in Fortaleza for sponge rubber and liquid cement to plug a small leak in the cockpit, the shopkeeper wouldn't let them pay, insisting they take the items as his gift.

He was pleased, Fred wrote, that Amelia had flown the most direct routes rather than the established trade routes to reach Fortaleza, even though that meant they were flying over impenetrable jungle, for it gave him a chance to brush up on celestial navigation.

Gradually he and Amelia became friends. Wrote Amelia, "little by little I came to know my shipmate's full story." As they crossed the equator (the first time for Amelia), they were so busy that Fred forgot to dunk her with the thermos of cold water he had been saving for the purpose. He wrote to Helen of this part of the flight:

> Those routes took us across hundreds of miles of unexplored dense virgin jungles. Nothing visible but solid carpets of tree tops, with frequent wide winding rivers cutting through them. The weather was uniformly good—over the Orinoco River we encountered a few heavy tropical downpours, but we were able to circumvent them.

They were planning to spend an extra day at their next stop, Natal, so that the plane could be serviced before the long overwater hop to Africa, but the facilities were so good in Fortaleza that they decided to change and have it done in Fortaleza instead.

Two mornings later they took off at 4:50 A.M. and were in Natal—only 275 miles distant—by seven. Air France used Natal as its jumping-off place for the South Atlantic and had two ships permanently stationed in the ocean to give them weather updates. The airline offered to make the information available to Amelia; at the same time advising her that it was already too late in the day to start across the ocean.

They took off from the pitch-black field at three fifteen the following morning—destination Dakar. The flight went smoothly for most of the way. While over the ocean Amelia broadcast her position every half hour. She and Fred tended to the air canisters, sealing and labeling more than a dozen with the place and time of exposure and stowing them away.

But they didn't land at Dakar, because Amelia second-guessed Fred, thinking him wrong. Fred's instructions were to head south—"change to 36 degrees"—but a thick haze was obscuring the African coast, "and for some time no position sight had been possible," as Amelia explained, so when she received his note (by way of the bamboo pole), she turned north instead, and they landed at St. Louis, Senegal.

The next day, June 8, they flew the 163 miles south to Dakar, the capital of French West Africa. There they were taken in hand by the governor-general. They ate his French food. ("Where Frenchmen are, there is also good food . . . the meals were delicious.") They attended a reception in their honor given by the Aero Club. Local mechanics fixed a broken fuel meter. They spent the night in the governor-general's mansion. Weather reports showed threatening tornadoes in their path the next day, so they laid over and then altered course slightly north for Gao on the Niger River, a flight of 1,140 miles, which they made in 7 hours and 50 minutes, at an average speed of 143 miles per hour. They slept in the open desert at Gao because it was so hot and both liked the experience "immensely." Dakar had been another day lost, but Amelia was in no hurry.

The morning of June 11, flying low enough to be enveloped in the steam rising from swampy forests, they flew down the Niger, following the French Air-Afrique route marked by beacons. They spotted a herd of hippopotami in the Chari River and flew on to Fort-Lamy in French Equatorial Africa, 989 miles distant. There the heat was so intense, the ground crew waited until after sunset to refuel the plane. The next day they took it easy, their destination El Fasher in the Sudan, only 690 miles and a three-hour flight away. El Fasher was truly exotic—the airfield was surrounded by an eight-foot thorn hedge to keep the animals out, their lodgings were in a former sultan's palace, and no one spoke English.

Flying over Africa, Amelia's thoughts strayed back to Bogie, the game she had played as a child in the barn with her cousins and sister. Senegal, Timbuktu, Ngami, El Fasher, Khartoum—places whose names had seemed so mysterious and exotic and tantalizingly far away when she was a young girl dreaming up trips in the old carriage—now lay beneath her as she flew eastward almost straight across Central Africa. Those "imaginary journeys full of fabulous perils," had a hold on her mind: she was living out her fantasy.

Once they left behind the rivers and recognizable landmarks, Fred found the navigating difficult because the African maps were so inaccurate. He finally gave up on maps altogether, yet his navigation skills were so good, they were never more than half an hour off course, according to Amelia. They continued ever eastward across Africa, stopped briefly at Khartoum, junction of the Blue and White Nile, then crossed the Red Sea.

Amelia was certainly feeling well as she prepared to leave Africa, for on the last stop there, in Assab, she mentioned that she was so hungry, she felt "as hollow as a bamboo horse." By the time they left Africa, they had been the guests of the governors of Senegal, French West Africa, and French and Anglo-Egyptian Sudan, as those countries were then called.

The only serious problems they had encountered were linguistic, and with Amelia's French and German, and Fred's Spanish and Portuguese, they muddled through. Wrote Fred, of Africa, "We had a glorious time."

England was waxing rhapsodic at Amelia's progress. *The Daily Telegraph* proclaimed her the spiritual descendant of Sir Francis Drake: "The air, it seems, is breeding such a race of men and women as the civilized world has not known since the sixteenth century."

The flight from Assab was longer than it should have been because the Sultan of Muscat had refused them permission to fly over Muscat, on the southeastern shore of the Arabian Peninsula, which meant they had to fly out along the edge of the Gulf of Aden. Amelia and Fred could see desert in the interior, treeless, parched, dry river canyons, and mountains and hills along the shore. The manual mixture control lever for the starboard engine jammed, which meant Amelia could not regulate the flow to that engine; to compensate and to economize on fuel, she reduced speed. As a result, averaging 147 miles an hour, they took a little over thirteen hours to travel the 1,920 miles to Karachi. Still, long flights were becoming routine.

In Karachi, waiting for them, was Jacques de Sibour with a supply of new maps and relevant data. Jacques was later quoted as saying that Amelia exhibited in Karachi a "whole attitude almost frighteningly different from what he had known." Unfortunately that brief observation merely adds a spot of mystery; without defining what her new "attitude" was, it is a tantalizing but not helpful piece of information, particularly as the reports Amelia was filing each night about this time indicate the activities and observations of a fit person. The first morning in Karachi, she rode a camel, likening the first moments to the first symptoms of a flat spin. Fred, too, was in good spirits. Watching the camel's antics, he shouted, "Better wear your parachute." Amelia went "cameling" a second time. She and Fred were checked out by British doctors who found their "robust healthfulness beyond question."

Another, stronger indicator of Amelia's good health and the pleasure she was taking in the trip is a recording of her telephone conversation with George, who telephoned her in Karachi on June 15. The conversation was mechanically recorded in the office of *The Herald Tribune,* from whence it was placed.

George asked her how she felt, and Amelia answered, "Swell! Never better."

The plane, too, was fine, she told George, except for a problem with the fuel flow meter and analyzer, which she expected would be fixed in Karachi.

He wanted to know how long she would stay in Karachi—two days, she thought. Where was she headed? "Probably Calcutta." Was she having a good time? "You betja! It's a grand trip. We'll do it again, together, sometime," she replied. The enthusiasm is unmistakable and genuine. Fred, too, "is fine."

Slightly over halfway around the world, Amelia was now on the home stretch and seemingly on schedule. She was obviously relieved to be where she was, pointing out that "Karachi airdrome is the largest that I know." It was the main intermediate point for all the traffic from Europe to India and the East, so Imperial Airways (British), KLM, Air France, and Pan American all were there, and their mechanics as well. The engine parts from Pratt and Whitney were there as specified. She had the Karachi post office stamp the covers. She even had a telephone conversation with George. *Everything* was going like clockwork.

It is from Karachi that we have a detailed description of the cockpit—Amelia gave its exact size in feet and inches, the layout of instruments, and so on, in response to a reporter's casual question.

Fred felt upbeat, too. He was having a wonderful time, as his letters show. In a letter to his wife he praised Amelia as "a grand person for such a trip. She is the only woman flier I would care to make such a trip with because, in addition to being a fine companion she can take hardship as well as a man, and work like one." It seemed as if Amelia had chosen the perfect person to accompany her.

She was sending George a steady stream of notes penciled on pages ripped out of her logbook or from a scratch pad, then stuffed into any old envelope. Most of them concerned chores for him to do concerning the flight—little courtesies like writing, on her behalf, to those who had been hospitable to her. That showed discipline, for every evening, no matter how long the day, after seeing to the maintenance of the Electra and to the refueling (the gasoline had to be inspected) and after the socializing, Amelia then had to make sense of the day and telephone or cable her story to the *Herald Tribune*. She also kept a log of the trip. Not all her notes to George concerned the tasks at hand. From India she wrote, "I wish you were here. So many things you would enjoy. . . . Perhaps some day we can fly together to some of the remote places of the world—just for fun."

From Karachi Amelia and Fred flew to Calcutta, 1,390 miles distant. On that flight they were surrounded by black eagles, "giving its pilot some very bad moments."

About this time, Amelia made a telephone call to George. As it had been arranged ahead of time, George asked Gene Vidal and Paul Collins to wait for it with him in his suite at the Hotel Seymour. Paul made notes of what he heard—of both sides of the conversation.

This conversation has caused great puzzlement and confusion about the actual state of affairs on the Electra. "I'm starting to have personnel trouble," Paul heard Amelia say, to which George replied, "Stop the flight right there and don't take any chances." To which Amelia answered, "I have only one bad hop left and I am pretty sure I can handle the situation."

Paul was sure he heard right, that Amelia had without doubt said "personnel trouble." Both he and Gene were amazed at the clarity of the telephone connection and the conversation. "We could both hear plainly what she was saying to her husband."

George, naturally worried, asked Amelia to call him when she reached New Guinea. Gene and Paul concluded that Fred had started drinking again.

· · · ·

Even though they had reversed direction, the delayed start of the flight had still left them at risk of being caught by monsoons, which started in June and ran through October; now, just as Amelia and Fred were making their way from India to the South China Sea, the monsoons hit. It was June 17. "We hoped to squeeze through before they struck their stride," wrote Amelia. They just missed. In Calcutta it had rained all night, turning the field to mud. But advised that more rain was coming, which would render a takeoff totally impossible, they left at dawn with only a partial load of gasoline so that the plane would not be too heavy—and even then they only just got off the field. They flew only the 335 miles to Akyab in Burma. There the monsoons hit them hard, so hard the rain beat patches of paint off the wings. Badly wanting to put that weather pattern behind them, Amelia took off but was forced by the rains to turn back. Fred, using dead reckoning, got them back over the Akyab airport "after two hours and six minutes of going nowhere." They had to spend another night there. They took off the next morning, June 18, for Bangkok, necessarily flying at eight thousand feet to stay clear of mountains, but after flying blind for two hours in heavy rain, they called it quits and decided to settle for Rangoon, half the distance. The sheets of water lost their force near sea level, and the sight of mere clouds caused Amelia to burst into poetry—so happy was she to see some break in the unrelenting rain—and quote Longfellow:

> The hooded clouds, like Friars,
> Tell their beads in drops of rain.

She put down in Rangoon as the sun's rays touched the golden roof of the great Shwe Dagon Pagoda on the outskirts of the city.

Austin C. Brady, the American consul, put them up and lent them his car; the Standard Oil representative acted as their guide. Amelia visited the pagoda. She had time to note the condition of women in the Burmese city: that although men and women were segregated in streetcars, there were many women in business, and they had had the vote for many years. It was all very pleasant, but Rangoon was only four hundred miles from Akyab; they had fallen behind schedule by another day.

Singapore was the next stop, a flight of just over twelve hundred miles, made without a hitch. She collected twenty-five dollars from the pilot of a KLM airplane for beating him to Singapore. (They had taken off at the same time from Rangoon.) That was followed by a flight to Bandung, in what was then called the Netherlands East Indies.

An hour after their arrival in Bandung that Monday, June 21, Amelia received a telephone call from New York, presumbably from George. Unfortunately the only knowledge we have of what was said is Amelia's version, which she sent off to be printed as part of her daily story in the *Herald Tribune.*

She and George spoke about the arrangements being made with the navy and the coast guard for the overwater flights from Lae, New Guinea, to Howland Island, and from Howland to Honolulu: "There were details to settle about radio frequencies, weather reports and the like," she wrote.

Unfortunately it was George who was seeing to all these details for Amelia. As energetic and efficient as he was, when it came to radio frequencies and direction finders, he didn't really know what he was talking about: he was a publisher, a promoter, not a pilot. In the past Bill Miller, who was a pilot, had taken care of all weather and communications details with the coast guard and the navy, but Gene was no longer at the Bureau of Air Commerce, so they no longer had Bill Miller to ask the right questions, no one who knew the intricacies of radio communication and could make sure that there was no snafu. Amelia thought everything was settled and organized, but it wasn't, as she would later find out.

Some minor instrument adjustments had to be made on the Electra, so Amelia and Fred planned to stay in Bandung an extra day to take advantage of the expertise of the KLM mechanics, who were familiar with the Electra's instruments because their Dutch Douglas DC-3s were equipped with similar ones. The hotel was good; Amelia's room was "filled with flowers." Amelia and Fred went sight-seeing. They walked on the rim of a volcano, were entertained by yet another American consul-general, took a three-hour car trip to Batavia (Jakarta) to visit some close friends of Fred's, and flew back to Bandung on a local airline. While in Batavia, Amelia telephoned New York to say that KLM mechanics had "licked a small trouble with my fuel regulator."

Wednesday at 3:45 A.M., the usual time they started, Amelia was warming up the engines to take off and noticed that one of the instruments refused to function. It was not until two that afternoon that they got off, reaching Surabaja at sunset. But, Amelia wrote, "certain further adjustments of faulty long-distance flying instruments were necessary." There were no good mechanics there, so she turned back to Bandung. They remained there in total from Sunday, June 20 to Saturday, June 26.

When George talked with Amelia again, she told him she believed she would get off the following day, and be in Kupang by evening. As a result, he announced, from Oakland, that Amelia would reach Howland Island Sunday, Hawaii on Monday, and be back in Oakland on Tuesday, June 29, or Wednesday the thirtieth. He had lined up various broadcasts, and Amelia was supposed to be the speaker at the dinner concluding the Institute of Technology program at Purdue on Friday, July 2. But although Amelia took off as expected, that was the day she had to return because of instrument malfunctions.

Biographers have speculated that the purpose of the Bandung layover was for Amelia to recuperate: from exhaustion, from stomach ailments, from whatever. But from reading Amelia's account, and more to the point, from reading a letter Fred wrote to Helen at this time, the picture that emerges is of the two of them being no worse for wear. The letter to Helen is seven pages long, and Fred makes no mention of Amelia begging off a shopping or sight-seeing trip, no mention of her being other than a good companion. Besides the sight-seeing trip to Batavia, Fred wrote, they both made several sight-seeing trips "to nearer places." They both had had problems digesting the twenty-one courses of the rijst tafel but nothing serious. The climate was excellent; the days not too warm, the nights cool. "We had a most enjoyable time," he wrote, even though they spent considerably more time in Java than expected, due to

> some minor, but important, instrument adjustments to be made. . . .
> Took off once and got as far as Surabaya—about three hundred and
> fifty miles—only to have the instruments fail again—so returned
> to Bandung. They are functioning perfectly now, thank goodness
> for the Dutch mechanics.

Amelia, too, felt that the instruments were finally fixed for good. She placed a call to George from Surabaja to tell him; she caught him in Cheyenne, Wyoming, where the United Airlines plane he was flying west had put down to refuel; it was on the ground only twenty minutes. George included only the end of the conversation in his book, stating that it was "the last conversation" he had with her.

"Is everything about the ship OK now?"

"Yes. Good night, Hon."

"Goodnight. . . . I'll be sitting in Oakland waiting for you."

• • • •

Amelia and Fred took off on Sunday, June 27, planning to refuel at Kupang, on Timor Island, and continue on to Port Darwin in Australia. But their start was late, and the day short. (Flying directly east meant they lost almost two hours of daylight each day.) They landed at 12:07 P.M. After dealing with customs and the local greeting committee, inspecting the plane carefully, and refueling, so much time had passed that Amelia, deciding that prudence was the better part of valor, decided to spend the night and get an early start the next day. Facilities were quite primitive on the island. There was no hangar for the plane, so they staked it down and put covers on the engine and propellers. There was no hotel, either, but there was a government guest house where they could stay, staffed by native cooks who set before them an "astonishingly splendid lunch," as Fred wrote Helen. As usual they went sight-seeing, to get the feel of Kupang, "perched as it is on cliffs with winding paved roads," then returned to the guest house for tea, bath, and a rest. Advised that Amelia and Fred would be leaving before dawn, the staff set to work to provide an early dinner, which was announced as Fred was closing his letter to Helen. "I hear the dinner gong—or its equivalent—and Amelia is calling—so I must close."

The next day they were driven out to the field at five A.M. Amelia, it was noted, thanked everyone gracefully for the help they had given her; the Electra took off at six thirty. They reached Port Darwin, their destination in Australia, in 3 hours and 29 minutes. As they approached Port Darwin, Amelia and Fred kidded each other about a small boat they saw in the distance, which Amelia insisted was a pearl-fishing lugger. Fred replied (via a scrap of paper), "Once aboard the lugger and the pearl is mine." They landed just after ten A.M.; it was Monday, June 28. Australia was a new landscape, observed Amelia, "endless trees on an endless plain." She began thinking of the long flight facing them over water. Their parachutes would be useless, she decided, and arranged for them to be shipped back to the United States.

A telegram from Jean Batten, Australia's top flier, was waiting for her; Amelia hoped finally to meet her, but because of time constraints it couldn't be arranged. She also received a query from the Australian government direction finding wireless station. They wanted to know why there had been no radio communication from the Electra to them. Amelia informed them that her DF receiver was not functioning, whereupon airport personnel arranged a ground test and discovered that the fuse for the DF generator had blown. They replaced it, ran a ground test that was satisfactory, according to A. R. Collins, Aircraft Inspector and officer-in-charge of the airport, and advised her to inspect the fuse in the event of further trouble.

At dawn they took off into headwinds "as usual." Collins reported that during the Electra's journey from Darwin to Lae, communication was established with Darwin for a distance of two hundred miles from this station, "radio phone being used by Miss Earhart."

Seven hours and 43 minutes later, Amelia and Fred landed in Lae, New Guinea, a flight of some twelve hundred miles, mostly over water. It was Tuesday, June 29.

22
Lost

•••• Longitude and latitude are imaginary lines drawn on the globe. The equator is the beginning point of latitude, from which all degrees of latitude are measured. All other latitudes run parallel to it. It is also the only great circle of latitude—the only one that passes through the center of the earth. So circling the earth at its waist means traveling at zero degrees latitude. Put another way, it means, roughly, always flying east or west.

Longitude is harder to pin down. The meridians of longitude are not parallel; they are all great circles that pass through the North and South poles. That makes the distance between them zero at the poles and the maximum at the equator.

As Dava Sobel points out in *Longitude,* any sailor worth his salt can gauge latitude—that was how Columbus sailed straight across the Atlantic in 1492. Latitude depends on taking sights on the sun, or "shooting the sun," measuring the angle between the sun and the horizon when it is highest in the sky at noon. Time is not a factor. Fred had no trouble figuring latitude.

But figuring longitude is much more of a problem because time is a factor. Zero degrees longitude is an arbitrary line. Navigational aids calculating longitude began when the Englishman John Harrison perfected the chronometer, so the meridian passing through Greenwich, England, became zero degrees. Likewise, the measurement of time was based on the observatory in the town of Greenwich. Greenwich Time—GMT—became the universal benchmark from which times all over the world are calculated.

Longitude is measured in degrees, but to plot one's position the navigator must know the time—exactly. The earth makes one complete spin—one 360-degree circle—every twenty-four hours. Every hour is 15 degrees of longitude, always. But the distance between the meridians is greatest at the equator and least at the poles. One degree of longitude always equals four minutes of time, but only at the equator does one degree stretch for sixty nautical miles. Latitude, by contrast, is always the same—one degree of latitude equals sixty miles no matter where on earth you are.

When navigating by the sun and stars, the only tools available on ocean passages in 1937, longitude—that is, the distance traveled around the earth—was determined by consulting the Greenwich Hour Angle, a detailed compilation of star positions, upon which Fred Noonan also relied. The *Air Almanac* gave the Greenwich Hour Angle—the geographic position of the important celestial bodies for every day, hour, minute, and second of the year. Using his octant to "shoot" heavenly bodies, Fred could locate the spot on the earth, the geographic position, that was directly under a given celestial body—it's splash-down position—and work out the plane's distance from that spot. Then he could enter the Electra's probable position on his chart. But to do this he had to know what time it was—exactly—for each minute of error would result in a fifteen-mile miscalculation. That was why radio communication was so important to Fred: he had to check the rate of his chronometers.

• • • •

Amelia kept the Electra at an altitude of eleven thousand feet for most of the way to Lae, to stay above a heavy cloud layer. Proceeding by a combination of celestial navigation and dead reckoning, Fred positioned them perfectly; they came down, as planned, on the western flank of New Guinea's mountain range, reached the coast, found Lae, and set down.

Lae was by no means a hardship stopover. More than a thousand Europeans lived there, and it was the headquarters of Guinea Airways. It had a three-thousand-foot-long airstrip, a new hotel, and excellent communication with the rest of the world. After seeing to the airplane and getting radio and weather reports, Fred and Amelia went their separate ways. Amelia went out to dinner with Eric Chater, the manager of Guinea

Airways; Fred went out drinking with some locals, including James A. Collopy, district superintendent of civil aviation. Fred "had some drinks and sat talking airplanes" and didn't turn in until well after midnight, according to Collopy.

The next day Amelia got on the telephone and called her story into the *Herald Tribune*. She was aiming to get off the next day at noon, she reported, if everything could be done by then: "Everyone has been as helpful and cooperative as possible—food, hot baths, mechanical service, radio and weather reports, advice from veteran pilots here."

But the plane was having radio difficulties again, according to Amelia, just a day after being fixed by the Australians. "Captain Fred Noonan, my navigator, has been unable, because of radio difficulties, to set his chronometers."

Later in the day, she sent a telegram to George, which has been the subject of much speculation. She sounded worried.

RADIO MISUNDERSTANDING AND PERSONNEL UNFITNESS PROBABLY WILL HOLD ONE DAY HAVE ASKED BLACK FOR FORECAST FOR TOMORROW YOU CHECK METEOROLOGIST ON JOB AS FN MUST HAVE STAR SIGHTS ARRANGE CREDIT IF TRIBUNE WISHES MORE STORY.

"Radio misunderstanding" probably refers to the fact that Amelia had thought that *Itasca* could take radio bearings on her on 3105 kilocycles until they informed her that they could not "due to lack of suitable calibrated equipment on that frequency." The coast guard on June 18, just prior to the *Itasca*'s sailing, said they informed her of that.

The words "personnel unfitness" remain a mystery. Gene Vidal told Gore that he as well as George had been at the *Herald Tribune* office, that "personnel trouble" was code for Fred's drinking, and that both he and George advised her to abandon the flight. But she told them she thought "personnel" were improving. Since Amelia's views on alcohol had gone from laissez-faire to negative—there was no liquor served in her new house—she was being strangely mysterious if the problem was a clear-cut case of too much alcohol. Paul Collins, a close friend of Gene's, corroborates this conversation. Gene told Paul, "Amelia stated that she was still having personnel trouble and had had to delay her takeoff for Howland Island for two days though the weather pattern was good." George never divulged to anyone what he thought, and, it must be noted, he never mentioned that he had spoken to Amelia in Lae.

One can only speculate. Possibly Fred went on a bender. Possibly the word in the telegram is misspelled and Amelia meant "personal" unfitness.

The only thing that can be said with certainty is that *something* was wrong, or Amelia wouldn't have sent the telegram. The real question is, did it affect the flight? And the answer, of course, is that we don't know. The enforced delay certainly annoyed Amelia though, for she wrote, "Denmark's a prison and Lae . . . appears to two fliers just as confining."

With an extra day on their hands, Amelia and Fred used the time to repack the plane and discard various things that were no longer of use. Amelia noted that she and Fred were making the repacking a joint effort, and that when that task was finished, they went off sight-seeing—together—and that Fred was the driver: "We commandeered a truck and with Fred at the wheel . . . we set out along a dirt road. We forded a sparkling little river. . . . We turned into a beautiful coconut grove." It doesn't sound as if she is dragging around a disagreeable companion with a hangover, as some biographers have speculated, or that she was ill, under the weather, or feeble, as others have put forth, but it cannot be ruled out.

There was no partying the next evening, according to James Collopy. Both went to bed early. There are several pictures of them taken in Lae. In most Amelia has a camera in her hand. Contrary to later reports, she looks fit and healthy. So does Fred.

• • • •

Fred Noonan was a fine navigator. Pan Am had thought so highly of his abilities that they made him chief navigator and gave him the job of training individual navigators for the Clipper runs. William Grooch, a fellow officer at Pan Am wrote about the beginning of Pan Am's transpacific service:

> Several junior flight officers were assigned to each flight. Their
> work was supervised by the navigation instructor, Fred Noonan.
> In flight, Noonan directed them as to the proper use of navigation
> instruments. Later he corrected their paper work and pointed out
> mistakes. Training was tedious work but it was absolutely necessary.
> All of us realized that while the radio direction-finder was a great
> aid it was not infallible, and our navigators must be able to find
> their way without it if necessary.

Fred was regarded with something close to awe: "The crew maintained that he could 'shoot the sun' standing on his head."

The big problem in navigation was still longitude. What was true about longitude in the fifteenth century still held true in the twentieth: it was more difficult to figure than latitude. On that first Clipper flight that Musick skippered and Noonan navigated, one night Noonan got seven fixes from the stars and received forty-one radio bearings; he was dead on course but was making a bit faster speed than he had figured. That meant his longitude calculations were off.

Fred was very good, but on the Electra he was missing navigation aids that he had become used to on the Clipper flights, namely the radio bearings beamed to the Clippers by Pan Am operations, and the ability to communicate with ships at sea. It was because he couldn't send and receive messages in Morse code, necessary to communicate with ships, any better than Amelia, that they had jettisoned the trailing antenna; he was also aware that Howland Island was not reachable by Pan Am radio because it was too far from their route. Perhaps he didn't even realize himself just how crucial the constant stream of information was to his navigational prowess. Amelia certainly knew how hard it was to find an island. After she, Fred, Harry Manning, and Paul landed in Hawaii, she had written, "Making the landfall that morning was even pleasanter than my first of California's shore line two years ago. After all, it would require ingenuity to miss a continent, which I was aiming for then. Hawaii, however, is something else again and we all knew how easily it could be passed by." Compared with Howland, Hawaii was a continent.

• • • •

Richard Black, whom George was in contact with, was point man for Amelia for the South Pacific, in charge of gathering the weather information as well as coordinating the ships that would help guide her in. He saw to it that the Fleet Weather Central forecast for July 1 for Amelia's route, based on information gathered from all British and American stations and ships in the South Pacific reached her:

> For Earhart, Lae, accurate forecast difficult account lack of reports
> your vicinity. Conditions appear generally average over route, no
> major storms apparent. Partly cloudy skies with dangerous local
> rain squalls about 300 miles east of Lae and scattered heavy showers
> remainder of route. Winds ESE about 25 knots to Ontario and
> then E to ENE about 20 knots to Howland.

Black, in hindsight, would later say that he thought she shouldn't have taken off in the face of such a forecast. But five years before, while waiting at Harbor Grace, Amelia had been faced with a doubtful weather report that kept the captain of the greatest plane in the world, the Do-X, on the ground; she had taken off and triumphed. It didn't particularly bother her that she would have the wind on her nose; she would have been expecting it. Southeast trade winds blowing at twenty-five miles an hour were the norm in June, according to Clarence S. Willaims, who mapped portions of the flight.

Nor did the report seem dangerous compared with the storms that she and Fred had already flown through, the monsoons that had forced her back twice to Akyab. The thought undoubtedly was that if a serious storm developed before the point of no return, the Electra could do what it had done in the past: retrace its route back to Lae. The most important factor was Fred's ability to set their course by the sun and stars—and nothing in Fleet Central's forecast cast doubt that he would be able to do so.

The standard navigation operating procedure that Fred set up for the Clipper flights was as follows: the navigator received a weather report every thirty minutes; every sixty minutes he "shot the sun"; and every 120 minutes the plane dropped down near the surface of the water so that he could make a drift site from which he could compute the exact wind direction and intensity. Fred would have been following this procedure on the flight to Howland, at least in the beginning—shooting the sun and the stars, dropping down to the sea to take drift sights. He would have depended also on dead reckoning. He would have been flying a great circle course, as was Pan Am practice. If he was following the procedures he had instituted at Pan Am, he would be plotting longitude and latitude every half hour, as well as altitude, speed, and direction of the wind.

There would later be theories that there was confusion as to time, because the flight crossed the international date line. But standard operating procedure at Pan Am was to send time messages based on Greenwich time, precisely to obviate this error. Indeed, every Pan Am Pacific flight crossed the date line, and knowing about it was one of the tricks of the trade.

• • • •

The navy and coast guard thought they were prepared to render every aid. The *Itasca* was waiting at Howland Island, with Richard Black aboard, backed up by a staff of nine military personnel. Black had juggled the schedule of *Itasca*'s regular three-month tour to replenish supplies at Howland, Baker, and Jarvis so that it arrived in plenty of time to get Howland set up for Amelia. Now, under the supervision of Army Air Corps Lieutenant Daniel Cooper, the runways were marked off with red flags by the young Hawaiian settlers. The short 2,400-foot runway running east-west, the one Amelia was expected to use because of the prevailing easterly winds, got special attention, but the other two, the 4,100-foot northeast-southwest runway, smooth and hard, which would be used in a crosswind, and the 4,100 foot north-south runway, the longest of all, which would be used if the wind shifted, were also carefully checked out and marked. Since there was a huge bird population—10,000 frigates, 8,000 boobies, and 14,000 terns on the tiny island—numerous birds had been forcibly removed from the runways. The small house with a living-radio room, kitchen, and bedroom had been tidied up for her, and the bed made. Beach and offshore patrols had begun, and a radio-telephone connection was set up between the island and *Itasca*. The USS *Ontario* assumed a position halfway between Lae and Howland Island to help guide her in. The USS *Swan* took up a position midway between Howland and Honolulu, to guide her home on the final leg. They began waiting.

According to navy records, a final weather report to Fred Noonan showed that the winds had abated; they were estimated to be between twelve and eighteen miles per hour beginning east-southeast and changing to east-northeast, with squalls to be detoured. It seemed as if the weather was improving. The radio must have been fixed—they wouldn't have dared take off otherwise.

The Electra, loaded to the maximum—with 1,100 gallons of gasoline and 75 gallons of oil—began its roll down the runway at precisely zero Greenwich time, ten A.M. Lae time. As the plane reached the road that crossed the unpaved runway near the seaward end, it bounced into the air, went over the drop-off and then flew so low over the water that the propellers threw up spray, according to observers. The flight to Howland Island was 2,556 miles, or 2,201 nautical miles, a very long way, but no one—certainly not Fred's peers—expected that Fred would have any trouble finding Howland.

A cable went out to the *Herald Tribune* that she had finally taken off. The world began waiting.

> Not much more than a month ago I was on the other shore of the Pacific, looking westward. This evening, I looked eastward over the Pacific. In those fastmoving days which have intervened, the whole width of the world has passed behind us—except this broad ocean. I shall be glad when we have the hazards of its navigation behind us.

So ends Amelia's narrative.

The fact that they left at zero Greenwich time made it easier for Fred to work out their position from the celestial sights, for now his watch time and GMT were the same. For everyone else waiting to hear from the plane—notably the navy and the coast guard—it made it easier to follow the Electra's progress: for even though the Electra would be crossing the 180th meridian, the international date line, they didn't have to make allowances for all the time changes and the date change as well.

The chart of the area then in use, #1198, published at the Hydrographic Office within the navy, contrary to assertions that it showed Howland Island wrongly placed, in fact was reasonably accurate. According to the last chart correction made by the U.S. Government dating from 1995, the coordinates to the day beacon on the west side of Howland are: latitude, 0 degrees 48 minutes, 19 seconds north; longitude, 176 degrees 37 minutes west. The chart Fred was using showed Howland within half a mile of those coordinates. When, years later, emulating Amelia's world flight, Anne Pellegreno used the latitude and longitude coordinates that Fred Noonan had used for Howland, she found they were correct.

Seven hours, 20 minutes into the flight, Lae received a report from the plane that their position was 4 degrees 33 minutes south, 159 degrees 7 minutes east. That meant they were on course flying east-northeast, coming up on the equator but still south of it by some 277 miles, with 1,390 nautical miles to go before they would reach Howland. But it also meant that they had covered, by Fred's computations, only 785 miles in 7 hours, 20 minutes and were therefore making a ground speed of only 107 knots (nautical miles) per hour. Flying at that rate, it would take them another thirteen hours to reach Howland. That meant slightly over twenty-one hours in the air. That longitude reading meant that the headwinds they were encountering were stronger than had been predicted. The flight from Oakland to Hawaii was only some hundred miles shorter, and they had made that flight in 15 hours, 47 minutes. This was going to be different.

Sunrise at Howland was at 1745 GMT. If the headwinds stayed steady on the nose, they would get there about two and a quarter hours after sunrise. Flying into the sun, all Fred had to figure was longitude: he knew they were heading in the right direction—he just didn't know how far they had gone, for the effect of wind, often variable on a plane over water, is hard to determine.

• • • •

The *Itasca,* 250 feet long, painted white, was lying off the northeastern side of Howland Island. It was sending up a plume of black smoke to serve as a signal for the fliers that could be seen for miles. The low-lying island, two miles long by half a mile wide, was marked by a lighthouse erected by the U.S. Lighthouse Service. At sea level the lighthouse could be seen ten miles away. Mariners figure that they are two miles from a shore when they can see a building's windows, but for aviators, visibility at sea changes in the blink of an eye. An island can disappear under a bank of clouds.

Visibility at Howland Island was good that morning, according to the *Itasca*—the sky was clear to the south and east, the direction from which Amelia was approaching, although it was somewhat overcast about twenty miles to the northwest. There was an east-northeast wind ranging between fourteen and thirty miles per hour.

And so began the tragic last act. Amelia was supposed to contact the *Itasca* at fifteen minutes before and after the hour. They were supposed to send her a steady stream of weather information and position fixes.

• • • •

Fourteen hours and 15 minutes into the flight, the *Itasca* reported that they had recognized an Earhart voice message, but that it wasn't clear except for the words "Cloudy weather cloudy." One hour later, 15 hours and 15 minutes into the flight, the *Itasca* heard Amelia asking them to broadcast on 3105 kilocycles on the hour and half hour. She reported it was overcast. Sixteen hours and 24 minutes into the flight, the *Itasca* reported that they could hear Amelia but that her voice signals were "unreadable" with five people listening. Twenty minutes later she broadcast again, and this time her message was clear: she wanted bearings on 3105 frequency and said she would whistle into the microphone. A few minutes later she called again. "About 200 miles out," the *Itasca* radiomen heard, and she whistled briefly into the microphone. A half hour later, back on the agreed-upon schedule, 17 hours and 15 minutes into the flight, Amelia was back on the radio:

> Please take bearing on us and report in half hour I will make noise in microphone about 100 miles out.

During this time the *Itasca* had been transmitting weather reports to Amelia on the hour and half hour on 3105 kilocycles, as she had requested. She had received none of their transmissions.

It was 17:45 GMT; 17 hours, 45 minutes into the flight: sunrise at Howland Island. There was now enough light so that Amelia and Fred would have been looking to *see* the island, as Amelia's next transmission, nineteen hours into the flight, makes clear:

> We must be on you but cannot see you but gas is running low have been unable reach you by radio we are flying at 1000 feet.

Twenty-seven minutes later, at 19:27 GMT, the radiomen heard:

We are circling but cannot see island cannot hear you go ahead on 7500 kilocycles with long count either now or on schedule time on half hour.

Nineteen hours 33 minutes into the flight—for the first and only time—Amelia received a transmission.

Earhart calling *Itasca* we received your signals but unable to get minimum please take bearings on us and answer on 3105 kilocycles.

The *Itasca* then reported that they heard long dashes for a brief period but that the high-frequency direction finder could not cut her in on 3105 kilocycles.

Twenty hours and 14 minutes into the flight, Amelia radioed the *Itasca* the following message:

We are on the line of position 157 dash 337 will repeat this message on 6210 kilocycles. We are now running north and south.

And then there was silence.

• • • •

Fred was good at estimating distance covered, he thought he knew how far east they had traveled, and he felt secure using his octant, looking up the Greenwich Hour Angle of a star, then figuring their position from it. "This was a trick that Noonan had used in Pan American navigation many a time. He would make the longitude by time and then he would start looking north and south for the island objective," recalled Richard Black. But what if during the night the winds had increased, slowing them down more than he expected, and the skies had been too overcast to get a good star fix? As Amelia mentioned twice, it was cloudy. They were, Fred had to have thought, far enough east, so he had started looking north and south for Howland. They had gone the required distance, he would have figured: that was the significance of the communication that they were running north and south. To the southeast, just thirty miles from Howland, was Baker Island. Other than that, there was nothing for hundreds of miles.

The *Itasca* waited in disbelief. At 21:45 GMT—an hour and a half after Amelia's last transmission—they reported Amelia's nonarrival to fleet headquarters, at the same time giving the weather: "Sea smooth visibility nine ceiling unlimited."

Ceiling unlimited. And yet Amelia and Fred hadn't seen the plume of smoke, the boat, or the island.

They had never even been close.

23
Later

•••• Prior to her Hawaii–Oakland flight two years before, Amelia had gone over the procedures for landing a land plane in the ocean with Paul Mantz so she knew it could be done successfully. As she had noted at the time, "a craft of that type has been known to float for eight days before the crew were rescued." For that solo overwater flight, Amelia had worn an inflatable rubber vest and of course carried an inflatable life raft. Now, in 1937, she was a much more seasoned flier than she had been in 1935. She and Fred had a Very pistol to shoot rockets and balloons to raise a flag, and they would have believed that they had a fighting chance of coming out alive even if they did run out of gas and land in the sea. And because the gas tanks on the Electra were empty, they would have acted as floats—another reason to think there would be enough time for them to get out of the plane and into the inflatable raft. The odds of making it with the inflatable, which was stocked with food, were pretty good.

On the other hand, assuming that she made as good a landing as possible under the circumstances, two things could rule against survival: waves, which could break up the plane before they had a chance to get out, and sharks. The crew of the *Itasca* had been catching sharks since their arrival at Howland on June 23. The sharks and barracuda, observed Air Corps Lieutenant Daniel Cooper, were "plentiful."

• • • •

Search efforts began. Going on the assumption, as they reported to fleet headquarters, that "if the plane had been close to Howland it was believed the island or the *Itasca* would have been easily seen except from the north-west" (the overcast area) and also because Baker Island lay thirty miles to the southeast and Amelia had not mentioned sighting it, *Itasca* began search-ing to the northwest. As night fell, the search continued; lookouts were posted, and sailors swept the seas with high-powered searchlights. They found nothing.

There were navy PBY seaplanes in Honolulu capable of making the 1,660-nautical-mile flight to Howland to mount an immediate air search—but only one plane at a time could go because only one plane at a time could land in the sea, be refueled and stay on a towline for the night behind the *Itasca*. Upon hearing the news that Amelia was overdue, Lieutenant Sidney Harvey, the senior officer in charge of the navy flight squadron, with a crew of eight including himself, immediately made ready to fly a PBY to Howland to begin the search. But it took the whole day before the plane was ready.

Harvey and his men left at seven P.M. that evening, planning to arrive at Howland in daylight, spend the next day searching, and that evening land in the sea and tie up behind the *Itasca*. As they proceeded, the radiomen kept requesting Amelia to send her carrier wave—that is, press down on her microphone button. "The pilots received three dashes," recalls Page Smith, one of the pilots, adding that such a sound was inconclusive evi-dence and quite possibly it was from someone other than Amelia. As the men strained to hear, the weather deteriorated, and soon they were flying in snow, sleet, and lightening. *Itasca* radioed that a tropical front had moved in causing ten-foot waves that would make it impossible for a plane to tie up to a towline. That clinched it—the PBY turned back, reaching Hono-lulu twenty-four hours and ten minutes after it had taken off. Well before then, the navy, worried that the plane would run out of gas, had sent four ships steaming out in the PBY's flight path to keep watch for the fliers.

At Howland there was still only *Itasca* on the scene.

Itasca kept monitoring the airwaves in the hope that the plane had landed on a reef or island—the radio would have been silenced almost immediately if it had landed in the sea. And they kept thinking they heard something. False lead followed false lead. Three days after its disappear-ance, *Itasca* radiomen heard a transmission they thought was so promising, they cabled Washington that they were going to check out an area 280 miles north of Howland. It turned out to be another false lead. By Tuesday, July 6, the *Itasca* had searched three thousand miles in daylight and fifteen hundred miles at night. But it was the only ship on the scene.

George's first thought was that Amelia was down in the Phoenix Island region southeast of Howland. The battleship *Colorado* catapulted three planes from its deck to inspect the region's islands. The planes skimmed over Gardner Island, also called Nikumaroro Island, McKean Island, and Carondelet Reef, but saw only ruined guano works and the wreck of a tramp steamer. By then it was Wednesday; five days had passed.

On the premise that the ocean current ran west and the winds south-southeast, it was decided to intensively search the Gilbert Islands, six hundred miles due west of Howland. But it was not until July 13 that the minesweeper *Swan,* which had been midway between Hawaii and Howland, actually checked out Onotea in the Gilberts, subsequently continuing to Taputcouea, Nukinau, Peru, and Nonuti, also in the Gilberts. The *Itasca* followed, reaching Tarawa in the Gilberts two days later. Crew members interviewed the British administrator, who assured *Itasca* personnel that there was no sign of the plane. Nevertheless the *Itasca* continued to search various islands in the group. The Japanese embassy in Honolulu was also questioned.

The *Lexington,* the fastest aircraft carrier in the navy, had put into Santa Barbara, California, on July 3 and given its men liberty, according to J. J. Clarke, air officer on the ship. At about four P.M. they got a message to get ready to go to the South Pacific and make a search for Amelia. They hoisted the recall flag, sent out search parties to try to get as many men back as they could, and that night went down to San Diego so they could load the squadrons early the next morning. They made quick work of loading the planes, sixty-two in all, but needing fuel, the ship had to make first for Honolulu. Running at a speed of about thirty knots, it reached the Hawaiian Islands in four days, something of a speed record. Three destroyers, the *Lamson,* the *Drayton,* and the *Cushing* accompanied the *Lexington* and stayed with it during the search.

Fastest ship in the navy or not, it took, in total, eleven days for the *Lexington* to reach Howland Island. While the carrier was under way, the fliers organized their planes into groups and drew up a search plan so that when they took off, they would have "an eye on every mile." The information they had was that Amelia had passed over the Gilbert Islands on course and on speed and had only had about four hundred miles to go to Howland.

Once at their destination, the naval pilots took a point north of

Howland and drew a circle in the outer range of the amount of gas the Electra could have carried. They searched that circle—150,000 square miles. They found nothing. They concluded that Amelia and Fred never even got into their life raft, because if they had, there would have been some sign of it, but there was no sign of anything. But then, they didn't begin the search until two weeks after Amelia's disappearance.

There had to be a reason for the tragedy, everyone said. Carl Allen had agreed with Amelia in Miami that jettisoning the trailing antenna and the marine frequency radio "made complete sense," since neither she nor Fred were proficient in Morse code, and extra fuel "could spell the difference between life and death." He concluded, after reading the *Itasca's* radio log, that the key to the tragedy lay not in the jettisoning of the marine radio but in the lack of knowledge of that fact aboard the ship, for they kept asking her to tune in to the 500-kilocycle marine frequency and pick up their direction finder. To add to the mystery there was *another* direction finder on Howland that operated on 3105 kilocycles, although it wasn't properly calibrated, according to Lieutenant Daniel Cooper, stationed on the island.

One thing was sure: Bill Miller, as a former navy pilot, would have been knowledgeable about radio frequencies. Had he been coordinating everything for Amelia, it might have made a difference. More important he would have known—because he would have been on the scene in Miami—that Amelia had dropped the trailing antenna, and he would have notified the *Itasca* and Richard Black at the outset. If Gene Vidal hadn't resigned, Miller would still have been on the scene.

There is also the strong possibility that it wouldn't have mattered what frequency Amelia's communications equipment was operating on, because the equipment wasn't working. A blown fuse had knocked out the generator on the Oakland–Honolulu flight in March, air force mechanics had discovered after they landed. A blown fuse was the culprit in the lack of functioning of the direction finder receiver on the Kupang–Darwin flight, Australian authorities reported. The day after that there may have been another short circuit in the receiving equipment, according to Amelia's last cable from Lae: "my navigator has been unable because of radio difficulties, to set his chronometers" (although there was also a report of a line breakdown at the Malabar radio station, making it impossible to receive time signals). Fuses are easily replaced. But when fuses blow it is an indication of an underlying electrical problem, and means that the problem will recur. The *Itasca* had asked Amelia to broadcast on 500 kilocycles to make use of its ship direction finder, but they also kept communicating on every frequency they could think of. They asked her on every transmission that she acknowledge. Only once through that long morning did she indicate that she had received any signal from them, yet *Itasca* would later find out that they were heard all over the Pacific on 3105, 7500, and 500 kilocycles. So it is quite possible that the lack of communication was not due to confusion as to kilocycles but to a fault in the Electra's wiring.

• • • •

Before Amelia took off, George had moved into the coast guard station in San Francisco so that he would be able to give out bulletins on Amelia's progress from Lae. He simply stayed there, spending days and nights without sleep in the copper-walled radio room with the coast guard radio operators, hoping against hope that word would come that Amelia was still alive, wearing himself out listening to every false message—and there were many—reporting that she was. Each time a new hopeful report came in, he offered suggestions as to search quadrants to the navy and he suggested that the Department of Commerce pressure England and Japan to mount rescue operations of their own. He tried to keep the U.S. Navy search from winding down. Finally, exhausted, he went into seclusion at the San Francisco home of Dr. Harry Clay, an old friend.

But he didn't give up on finding Amelia. Nor did Gene Vidal. At the end of July Gene succeeded in meeting with President Roosevelt and Under Secretary of State Sumner Welles and convincing them that "a thorough surface search" of the Gilbert Islands—British possessions— should again be made.

George offered a two-thousand-dollar reward for any information. Sumner Welles wrote countless letters on behalf of both Gene and George.

When not a scrap of the plane turned up after more than a year had passed, George finally, reluctantly, came to the conclusion that she had died.

• • • •

On December 7, 1941, the Japanese attacked Pearl Harbor.

Ever since, there have been people who thought the Japanese were hiding something. The idea began to grow that Amelia had been on a mission to find out what the Japanese were up to in the South Pacific. In 1943, when the United States and Japan were two years into the war, Hollywood made a movie, "Flight to Freedom," starring Fred MacMurray and Rosalind Russell. Amelia and Fred, the movie script went, were working for the government: they agreed to get "lost" in order to give the U.S. Navy an excuse to search Japanese waters.

Harry Manning was tracked down and denied that they were on a spy mission. Charles Edison, assistant secretary of the navy at the time and later secretary of the navy, in an interview, remembered that the matter had been "thoroughly discussed" at the time. "I am satisfied," he stated, that "Amelia Earhart was not flying on any Navy mission."

As the war progressed and the United States began to retake islands that had been in possession of the Japanese, speculation about Amelia's fate surfaced in another form. Servicemen began hunting for and finding evidence that she had been captured by the Japanese: executed, tortured, imprisoned. All the stories had one thing in common: she had suffered a horrible fate.

Fred Goerner, a CBS reporter, spent six years and mounted four expeditions in search of Amelia and Fred. He was sure that they had been found by a Japanese fishing boat, transferred to either the *Kamoi* or the *Koshu,* and transported first to Jaluit, then Kwajalein, and finally to Saipan, where they were imprisoned and died. There have been countless other expeditions, and every group that travels to a South Pacific island comes back with something that they try to turn into enough money to pay for the expedition: a generator, a piece of a shoe, part of a box; but in the end nothing matches.

What do the Japanese think of being made the villains of the piece? In 1981 the Japanese writer Fukiko Aoki, who would three years later become bureau chief for the Japanese edition of *Newsweek,* decided to find out what really happened and if possible lay the Japanese demons to rest. The result of her investigation was first published in an article that appeared in the April 1983 issue of the Japanese magazine *Bungei Shunju,* titled, "Was Amelia Earhart Executed?" In 1984 she published a book, *Searching for Amelia.* Her work is not known in this country because neither the article nor the book has been translated.

Her judgment, based on the evidence she found, should (hope springs eternal) lay to rest all of the "captured by the Japanese" stories in the English-speaking world. Her conclusion, based on hard evidence and exhaustive research over the years, is the same as that of most knowledgeable contemporary fliers: that Amelia and Fred's plane must have sunk to the bottom of the sea.

Aoki found that there were indeed only two Japanese ships in the area on July 2, 1937, the battleship *Koshu* and the carrier *Kamoi,* as the Japanese said, and she thoroughly investigated the movements of both ships. She interviewed Kozu Yukinao, who had been communications officer of the *Koshu,* and saw copies of the *Koshu's* log for the days concerned. The *Koshu* left the island of Palau in the Carolines on June 26 and arrived at Grinich, the southernmost of the Japanese Mandated Islands, on July 3, the day after the Electra went down. The men aboard the ship were watching for the plane, so it was no surprise to them when they received orders to search for it a few days after it was reported missing. The *Koshu* headed south, out of Japanese and into United States waters, fully aware of where they were. But Japanese superiors, uncomfortable at the idea that they were trespassing, as it were, ordered the ship back north. The *Koshu* arrived at Jaluit Island in the Marshalls on July 13, having seen nothing, stayed at Jaluit till the nineteenth and then went back to Truk and Saipan.

The second Japanese ship, the *Kamoi,* was docked in Saipan but did not join in the search. According to Yuichi Wada, a sailor on the *Kamoi* whom Aoki interviewed, the *Kamoi* left Saipan on July 3 and headed straight for Japan without joining in the search. Aoki saw copies of the *Kamoi's* newspapers for the days concerned that corroborate these facts.

This is important because all the various Westerners who maintain Amelia and Fred were captured by the Japanese, killed, and/or tortured have one of these two ships picking them up at various places and transporting them to an island—usually Saipan in the Marianas—because there was no other means of transportation.

Aoki tracked down every person still alive in Saipan whom Fred Goerner and others said had seen Amelia and Fred in the hands of the Japanese. There was Josepa Reyes Sablan, quoted as seeing two white people taken into the military police headquarters in Garapan. She told Aoki she remembered only having her picture taken with an American, "but says she doesn't know anything about whether it was a white pilot or not." Josephine Blanco, cited extensively, wasn't believed by her brother-in-law. He told Aoki, "she was really young at the time." No Japanese inhabitant of Saipan—and there were 20,000 according to Aoki—ever saw or thought they saw Amelia. Said one islander Aoki questioned, "About once a year a foreigner comes here to ask us that same question They always have this expression like we are hiding something here. Unfortunately we aren't."

Aoki's conclusion, after "exhaustive research," was that Fred Goerner had gone around the island suggesting a possible scenario, and the islanders, happily, suddenly important, at the front and center of the world and wanting to stay that way, agreed with their newfound friend and made up stories that they thought would please him.

But her main point is that at this stage there would have been no point in interning Amelia and Fred, because no matter where they landed, there would have been nothing of a military nature for them to see. A bit later would have been a different story, but in July 1937 Japanese eyes were still focused on Manchuria, which they invaded five days after Amelia's plane went down. They had indeed begun to build airfields on their islands, but none on the order that the U.S. Navy thought, and they had as yet built no fortifications. It was still peacetime, and there weren't yet even soldiers on the island, let alone a military prison. Japanese construction on their islands was roughly the equivalent of the American government improvements on Howland, Baker, and Jarvis, combined with Pan Am's island docking facilities. Like the combination Bureau of Air Commerce/Department of the Interior colonization effort with airfield funds supplied by the WPA, the Japanese had civilians building airfields, and by 1937 they had four: on Saipan, Palau, Yap, and Truk. The *Kamoi's* mission in July 1937 was to drop off two engineers to design and build more airstrips in the Mandated Islands.

The most notable fact about the Japanese navy in that part of the South Pacific in June and July 1937 according to Aoki, was its absence. The *Koshu* was a slow, refitted German cargo ship. Yet this was the ship that Japan was relying on to gather information on ocean currents and prevailing weather patterns and at the same time to patrol their waters.

The day after the attack on Pearl Harbor, on December 8, 1941, four Japanese Mitsubishi planes attacked Howland and Baker. Two of the four Hawaiian boys on Howland were killed, and two others managed to hide in a thicket and were taken off the island by navy destroyers. A short while later Japanese submarines surfaced off the islands and shelled them flat, destroying everything including the lighthouses. The Japanese did it because they thought there were underground storage tanks as well as other crucial equipment on the islands. They thought America was hiding something.

Things would change shortly for both countries—six months would make a huge difference. Japan would step up its activities in the South Pacific, as would the United States. In February 1938 Black received orders to set up permanent American stations on two more islands, Canton, four miles wide by eight miles long, and Enderbury, both in the Phoenix group, to the south of Howland and Baker, which he did even though the British flag flew over Canton. Black landed, met the British, announced his intentions, and carried out his orders, which were to "raise our flag on a pole a little taller than theirs and to fly a little larger flag and build our foundations a little more solidly than theirs, all of which we did." He left colonists—more young Hawaiians—behind.

Canton, only 421 miles to the southeast of Howland, as well situated to be a mid-Pacific refueling station as Howland and so much bigger, was within a few years transformed into an air force base. During the war, it would figure as the destination for a B-17 bomber that went down somewhere in the Pacific with Captain Eddie Rickenbacker aboard. Rickenbacker was on a mission to deliver a secret message from the secretary of war to General Douglas MacArthur, then in Port Moresby, New Guinea. Rickenbacker and an air force crew of five left Honolulu bound for Canton Island, eighteen hundred miles distant. Those aboard the plane never figured out exactly how they went wrong, but they never found Canton—or any other island. As the time for their arrival approached and passed, Canton fired off their antiaircraft guns with shells timed to go off at seven thousand feet, and sent up search planes; the Canton radio wasn't working but the fliers were in radio contact with nearby Palmyra Island. After many hours the B-17 ran out of gas and landed in the sea. They managed to get out and into rubber rafts, floated unseen for 22 days, and were finally sighted and rescued. They were luckier than Amelia and Fred.

• • • •

There will always be speculation about Amelia Earhart's death. It is hard—heartbreaking—to lose a major icon so abruptly, so inconclusively, and it is so tempting to try to write another ending to the grand adventure.

Jake Coolidge, the photographer who made her "Lady Lindy," said, "She was great; Amelia made herself. She got a break handed to her sure. The *Friendship* was one of those things that can happen to a person. But what she did with the break was *her*."

So this pilot, this woman who, when asked if she missed social work, replied that she had never left it, ended up suffering the same fate as other pilots who died making epic flights: Charles Nungesser and François Coli attempting the North Atlantic in their legendary plane *L'Oiseau Blanc* in 1927; Frances Grayson attempting the North Atlantic in 1927; Princess Anne Lowenstein-Wertheim attempting the North Atlantic also in 1927; Elsie Mackay and Walter Hinchcliffe attempting the North Atlantic in 1928; Charles Ulm, whose hand Amelia shook just before he took off, attempting the Pacific in 1935; Sir Charles Kingsford-Smith and his navigator Thomas Pethybridge somewhere over the Bay of Bengal in 1935; Wiley Post and Will Rogers, near Barrow, Alaska in 1935; Jean Mermoz who once said, "It's worth it, it's worth the final smash-up," attempting the South Pacific in 1936.

Amelia came into the public eye because she was an adventurer, but she was more: she was America's sweetheart, America's shield. She did everything better than everybody else—beckoned us on, and set more records, and she did it seemingly effortlessly. She made us so proud to be American. Perhaps because she was cut down in her prime—perhaps because she did not quite have time to fulfill her potential, we can't let her go. She is thirty-nine forever. She has become America's dream woman.

She is if anything more revered now than she was immediately after her death. The Boston-based Women's Educational and Industrial Union annually gives an Amelia Earhart award to a prominent Boston woman for expanding the economic and career opportunities for other women. Logan Airport has an Amelia Earhart terminal. Atchison, Kansas, has made her birthplace and childhood home into a museum; their airfield is named after her. Most of the places she lived have named streets after her.

The Zonta International Foundation awarded 35 women $6000 each for graduate study in aerospace-related science and aerospace-related engineering in 1997. They will join the 522 women from 51 countries who have already received Amelia Earhart Fellowship awards. The Ninety-Nines now number over 6,500 women. Every year they give out Amelia Earhart awards to women for advanced flight training: over 300 since inception. Beginning in 1992 corporate America has been contributing funds to the program.

Two women have made commemorative flights retracing Amelia's route in Lockheed Electras: Ann Pellegreno in 1967 on the thirtieth anniversary of Amelia's flight, and Linda Finch thirty years later on the 100th anniversary of Amelia's birth. The Vega in which Amelia flew the North Atlantic hangs in the National Air and Space Museum in Washington. Now novels as well as biographies are written about her.

Amelia wrote an epitaph for her friend Wiley Post:

So close was he to his profession that he could not know the sheen on his own wings.

It could well serve as hers.

Notes

Abbreviations Used in Notes

AE	Amelia Earhart
AOE	Amy Otis Earhart
GPP	George Palmer Putnam
JM	Janet Mabie
KCP	Kathryn (Katch) Challiss Pollock
LC	Lucy Van Hoesen Challiss
MEM	Muriel Earhart Morrissey

AG	*Atchison Globe*
BET	*Boston Evening Transcript*
BG	*Boston Globe*
CITP	*Courage Is the Price*
ET	*Evening Telegram*
FOI	*The Fun of It*
LF	*Last Flight*
LITHW	*Lady in The High Wind*
NYHT	*New York Herald Tribune*
NYT	*New York Times*
PA	*Popular Aviation* magazine
SW	*Soaring Wings*
WM	*Wide Margins*
20H	*20 Hrs. 40 Min.*

Columbia OH	Columbia University Oral History Collection
DH	Denison House
FDRL	Franklin D. Roosevelt Library

IWASML   International Women's Air and Space Museum Library
NASM   National Air and Space Museum
NYPL   New York Public Library
SLRC   Schlesinger Library, Radcliffe College
WEIU   Women's Educational and Industrial Union

Preface

page xii: "I advise them all . . .": *The Purdue Alumnus,* December 1975.

Colonial History

page 3: "in the midst of a heat wave . . .": *AG,* July 24, 1897.

page 3: dubbed the "Queen": Ruth Martin, *Family Tree: Challiss, Harres, Martin, Tonsing, Otis,* account of W. L. Challiss.

page 4: half a block away . . .: Robert L. Tonsing, letter to author.

page 4: "The sky turned . . .": JM, *LITHW,* SLRC.

page 4: At eleven thirty P.M. . . .: AOE, baby book, SLRC.

page 5: When the Episcopal minister . . .: Records of Trinity Episcopal Church in Atchison.

page 5: "I baptize thee . . .": *Book of Common Prayer of 1892,* in use in Atchison in 1897, according to the Rector Max T. Tracy, in letter to author.

page 5: This baby was the first . . .: Martin, *Family Tree.*

page 5: in the way she entered . . .: AOE, baby book, SLRC.

page 6: "But Saturday's bairn . . .": Ibid.

page 6: Maria Grace Harres was born . . .: Martin, *Family Tree.*

page 6: "He thought Grandmother . . .": Ibid.

page 7: "The religious severity . . .": Frances Trollope, *Domestic Manners of the Americans,* p. 275.

page 7: large three-story house . . .: Martin, *Family Tree.*

page 7: "a natural born nurse": Reminiscences of AOE in Martin, *Family Tree,* p. 4.

page 7: "delicacy and good taste": Trollope, *Domestic Manners,* p. 261. Mark Twain said of Trollope that she, "alone of them all, dealt what the gamblers call a strictly 'square game.' She did not gild us; and neither did she whitewash us," Alfred Knopf edition of *Trollope,* frontispiece.

page 8: Alfred's forebears, . . .: *Otis Family in America,* New England Historic Genealogical Society.

page 8: "taxation without . . .": Barbara Tuchman, *The March of Folly,* p. 131.

page 9: "As to my course . . .": Alfred Otis, letter to George Otis, March 6, 1852, given to author by Nancy Balis Morse.

page 9: "Come on then, gentlemen . . .": Seward quoted in David McCullough, *Truman,* p. 27.

page 10: on the September day . . .: Frank Blackman, *Kansas: A Cyclopedia of Kansas History,* vol. 1, p. 109.

page 10: "to kill a baby . . .": Leverett Spring, *Kansas: The Prelude to the War for the Union,* p. 124.

page 10: "but for the hotbed plants . . .": Ibid., p. 33.

page 10: "From these facts . . .": Eli Thayer, *A History of the Kansas Crusade,* p. 57.

page 10: his "ideal" settlers: . . .: Ibid., p. 179.

page 11: We cross the prairies as of old . . .: Whittier quoted in Ibid., p. 69.

page 11: southern mob tarred and feathered . . .: Spring, *Kansas: The Prelude,* p. 82.

page 12: Even David Rice Atchison . . . .: Blackman, *Cyclopedia of Kansas History,* vol. 1, p. 113.

page 12: "The grand jury indicted . . .": Alfred Otis, letter to George Otis, Nov. 16, 1856, given to author by Nancy Balis Morse.

page 12: "His capital stock was . . .": *Genealogical and Biographical Record of North-Eastern Kansas,* Chicago: The Lewis Publishing Company, 1900, p. 38.

page 12: a photograph of Amelia Otis . . .: Martin, *Family Tree,* p. 83.

page 13: *Cold* and *remote* . . .: Pat Antich, interview with author. Alfred's physical description, given by Janet Mabie, came from either Amy or Amelia.

page 13: The part of going to church . . .: Alfred, letter to George, Oct. 21, 1953. The sect was the Campbellites.

page 13: "It presents a very fine . . .": Burton Williams, *Senator John James Ingalls,* p. 25.

page 14: from gunpowder to coal oil . . .: Advertisement, *Freedom's Champion,* NYPL, April 1862.

page 14: "In winter time . . .": White, *Story of a Kansas Parish,* p. 9.

page 14: Atchison passed a law . . .: *Freedom's Champion,* NYPL, July 8, 1862.

page 14: the last thirty southern families . . .: Mrs. W. L. Challiss, *The Story of the First Baptist Church of Atchison, Kansas,* pp. 9–11.

page 15: The early records . . .: White, *Story of a Kansas Parish,* pp. 9–11.

page 15: "Glorious victory . . .": *Freedom's Champion,* NYPL, July 18, 1863.

page 15: A short while later . . .: Martin, *Family Tree.*

page 15: his custom to return . . .: *Biographical and Genealogical Records of North-Eastern Kansas,* p. 41.

page 16: One of the first of Atchison's . . .: Challiss, *Story of the First Baptist Church.*

page 16: "When we first came . . .": Flo Menninger, *Days of My Life,* p. 186.

page 17: Mark Twain wrote . . .: E.W. Howe, *Plain People,* p. 146.

page 18: "were the undisputed leaders . . .": MEM, *CITP,* p. 20.

page 18: "Among the best stories . . .": AE, *FOI,* p. 4.

page 18: diphtheria epidemic . . .: MEM, *CITP,* p. 19.

page 19: persuaded her parents . . .: JM, *LITHW,* II, p. 21, SLRC.

page 19: "My mother had wanted . . .": Nancy Balis Morse, interview with author.

page 19: Amy embroidered . . . .: Martin, *Family Tree;* Philadelphia city directories for those years.

page 19: She even fibbed about . . . .: Morse interview.

page 20: Amy's denial mirrors . . . .: KCP, interview with author. Alfred and Amelia always claimed that Amy's youngest brother, who was obviously slow, had been injured at birth. Yet it was clearly understood within the family, even by the cousins, that Theodore was retarded.

page 20: The ball, "the way she told it," . . .: MEM, *CITP,* p. 23.

page 20: He said: "This is Edwin . . .": Ibid.

page 20: Johann Earhardt, . . .: Sue Nunes, *Tree Top Baby,* p. 208. Material is from Pennsylvania Archives.

page 21: The chronicle of his descendants . . .: David Earhart, *A Brief History of the Ancestors and Near Kindred of the Author,* unpublished ms., Jan. 1, 1898; SLRC.

page 22: Taking note of his proselytizing nature, . . .: Lillian Hickman, *The History of Midland College,* unpublished thesis, Luther Library.

page 22: He picked a disastrous year.: Earhart, *Brief History.*

page 22: 27,000 civilian lives . . .: Essay by David McCullough; Walter Zinsser, ed., *Extraordinary Lives,* p. 45.

page 22: "None labored . . .": Hickman, *History of Midland College,* p. 13, Midland Lutheran College, Fremont, Nebraska.

page 22: it was a life of hardship . . .: Earhart, *Brief History.*

page 23: On a Sunday when Edwin . . .: MEM, *CITP,* p. 17.

page 23: having secured a pastorate . . .: Earhart, *Brief History.*

page 23: Harriet Earhart Monroe . . .: Hickman, *History of Midland College.*

page 23: Edwin became the first head . . .: *Midland College Catalogue 1887–1888,* Luther Library.

page 24: would permanently look down . . .: KCP interview. Speaking of the Tonsings, Katch would express it thus: "No style, that family."

page 24: "Energetic" and "useful," . . .: *AG,* June 2, 1885.

page 24: three of whom listed themselves . . .: listed as roofpainters in the 1888 Atchison city directory, Atchison Public Library.

page 25: This minister's son . . .: KCP interview.

page 25: The wedding was held . . .: *AG,* Oct. 17, 1895.

page 26: only twenty feet wide . . .: 1887 plat of Ann Street, provided by the Wyandotte County Museum.

page 26: "lifted the lid . . .": AE, *FOI,* p. 5.

page 26: saw a bear . . .: JM, *LITHW,* SLRC.

page 26: "hoped for many a day . . .": AE, *FOI,* p. 5.

Kansas Girl

page 27: "I . . . was lent . . .": AE, *FOI,* p. 5.

page 28: orphaned granddaughter . . .: Morse interview.

page 28: "Dignified and of aristocratic . . .": Obituary in *AG,* May 7, 1912.

page 28: a complete mental breakdown . . .: Ibid.
"and it seemed for a time that he had reached the period of life when the grasshopper becomes a burden . . . but eminent physicians who were consulted . . . assured the family that such incidents were common to men of about that age . . . that nature was tired." Ibid.

page 28: fully expecting to die . . .: Ibid.

page 28: "He realizes fully, . . .": Arthur G. Otis, letter to Charles Otis, Apr. 18, 1906; given to author by Nancy Balis Morse.

page 28: "It grieves me to tell you . . .": Alfred Otis, letter to Charles Otis, Dec. 15, 1899.

page 29: Mary Brashay, the Irish cook, . . .: KCP interview.

page 29: She finally gave them . . .: AE, *FOI,* p. 18.

page 29: the tales of Beatrix Potter, . . .: AE, *FOI,* p. 5.

page 29: the hollyhocks, phlox, . . .: MEM, *CITP,* p. 61.

page 29: its huge window . . .: Louise Foudray, curator, Amelia Earhart Birthplace Museum, Atchison, Kansas.

page 30: two great-great-grandchildren . . .: Martin, *Family Tree,* p. 69.

page 30: Amelia's first word . . .: Amy Otis, *Queer Doings and Quaint Sayings,* Amy Otis collection, SLRC.

page 30: Amy kept a baby book . . .: Amy Otis, *Queer Doings and Quaint Sayings,* Amy Otis collection, SLRC.

page 30: "Don't go near . . .": *AG,* July 21, 1963; Mrs. Paul Tonsing.

page 31: "Why doesn't he . . .": JM, *LITHW,* II p. 18, SLRC.

page 31: a sign had been put up . . .: Frank Baker, interview with author.

page 31: The most exciting . . .: Ibid.

page 32: golden wedding anniversary . . .: Martin, *Family Tree,* p. 10.

page 32: her second cousin Orpha . . .: Ibid., p. 82.

page 32: "Such a kind, thoughtful . . .": KCP interview.

page 32: "getting me up there . . .": Ann Park, interview with author.

page 33: her own Indian pony . . .: AOE interview, SLRC.

page 33: "Amelia was much too kind . . .": KCP interview.

page 33: "this horse opened . . .": AE, *FOI,* p. 9.

page 33: putting up "beware" signs . . .: Ibid., p. 14.

page 33: "you don't realize . . .": Ibid., p. 11.

page 33: "I think" . . .: JM, *LITHW,* II, p. 5, SLRC.

page 34: "Cousin Annie is just . . .": JM, *LITHW,* II p. 9, SLRC.

page 34: wanted to hunt snakes . . .: JM, *LITHW,* III p. 10, SLRC.

page 34: she decided to build her own roller coaster . . .: Muriel has this taking place in Kansas City (MEM, *CITP,* p. 30). But Balie Waggener didn't live there; he lived in Atchison, and in an interview July 21, 1963, in *AG,* he said the roller coaster had been built in the barn of Judge A. G. Otis.

page 35: "We thought being . . .": KCP interview.

page 35: "She could get as rough . . .": *AG,* July 21, 1963.

page 35: "Until the eighth . . .": Waggener interview, AE, *20H,* p. 29.

page 35: "our home, creaking . . .": GPP, *SW,* p. 12.

page 35: AE, *FOI,* p. 4.

page 35: I watch the birds . . .: GPP, *SW,* p. 169.

page 36: Katch's favorite voyage . . .: KCP interview, Oct. 9, 1986.

page 36: "dashing wildly . . .": AE, *American Magazine* (Aug. 1932).

page 36: "We weighed . . .": AE, *LF,* p. 144.

page 37: "To mine angel cousin . . .": KCP interview.

page 37: But her favorite poem . . .: Ibid.

page 38: the private College Preparatory School . . .: AE *FOI,* p. 5, Muriel, who wanted to do everything Amelia did, loved it, too, and wanted to go there but was, to her regret, "never enrolled," as she admitted to me.

page 39: "Amelia's mind . . .": GPP, *SW,* p. 29.

page 39: Macaulay's *Lays* . . .: On the flyleaf of the book is inscribed: "To Millie Earhart—For Writing The Best Theme." Sarah Walton wrote on the flyleaf, "The joy of achievement was uppermost in Amelia's mind. The prizes at school as the plaudits and awards of the world were secondary to her personal satisfaction in a job well done." SLRC.

page 40: "We girls would like to play," . . .: Baker interview.

page 40: Under Amelia's guidance . . .: Park interview; MEM interview.

page 40: heading straight for a junkman's . . .: AE, *FOI,* p. 12.

page 40: she played with Ann and Katchie . . .: Park interview; MEM interview.

page 41: "Millie was always . . .": Park interview.

page 41: "I just adored . . .": KCP interview.

page 41: Blanche Noyes, friend and . . .: Columbia OH

page 42: "Amelia had her *own* . . .": MEM, interview with author.

page 42: "I thought that my father . . .": AE, *FOI,* p. 7.

page 42: "We watched, wide-eyed, . . .": MEM, *CITP,* p. 26.

page 43: a girl named Lily . . .: MEM, *CITP,* p. 53. Muriel puts the Orphan's home in Kansas City, but the Soldier's Orphan's Home was in Atchison, according to NYPL records.

page 43: "This particular elevator . . .": JM, *LITHW,* III, p. 6, SLRC.

page 43: the dress code in Atchison . . .: Baker interview.

page 44: "though we felt terribly . . .": AE, *FOI,* p. 11.

page 44: "pretty much like a sieve": MEM, *CITP,* p. 65.

page 44: had hinged backs. . . .: JM, *LITHW,* III p. 12, SLRC.

page 44: she held worm races. . . .: GPP, *SW,* p. 29.

page 44: she also tried to make manna, . . .: AE, *FOI,* p. 16.

page 44: "concluded then that overgrown radishes . . .": AE, *FOI,* p. 16.

page 45: created imaginary playmates . . .: GPP, *SW,* p. 13.

page 45: "We always waited . . .": Katherine Dolan O'Keefe, *AG,* July 20, 1976.

page 45: "All I knew . . .": GPP, *SW,* p. 24.

The End of Childhood

page 47: the three men would retire . . .: Patricia Antich interview.

page 47: "I didn't like him,": KCP interview.

page 47: what manner of man . . .: Ibid.

page 48: "the happiest of times.": MEM, *CITP,* p. 26.

page 48: still he needed more money . . .: Ibid., p. 28

page 48: "This news is a terrible . . .": Ibid., p. 27; Edwin's letter is dated May 12, 1903.

page 49: a vacation spot . . .: GPP, *SW,* p. 31.

page 49: Lucy called them horse pies . . .: GPP, *SW,* p. 31.

page 49: calling her Dr. Bones.: GPP, *SW,* p. 10.

page 50: "Dear Madam: . . .": Edwin Earhart, letter to MEM, Aug. 2, 1909.

page 50: contingent on moving . . .: Des Moines city directory, 1908; Edwin Earhart is listed as a claims agent living at 1443 Eighth Street.

page 50: after "Millie" Earhart left . . .: interview with Orpha Tonsing, Martin, *Family Tree.*

page 50: they lived in four houses. . . .: Des Moines city directories for those years. Muriel, writing many years later, claimed that they had lived in only the one house on Cottage Grove Avenue, but she was writing fifty years after the fact. The Cottage Grove house was the last happy home for her and her family for many years.

page 51: "He bore on his nose . . .": AE, *FOI,* p. 8.

page 51: "an end to the pinchpenny days . . .": MEM, *CITP,* p. 55.

page 51: "Bring the girls . . .": JM, *LITHW,* III p. 7, SLRC.

page 51: They traveled in it . . .: *AG,* July 20, 1976.

page 51: a sumptuous dinner . . .: MEM, *CITP,* p. 72.

page 52: The same year the Earharts . . .: Drake Neighborhood Association, *From Keokuk On: The History of the Cottage Grove Area,* p. 27, published by the Association.

page 52: They found Von Sol . . .: GPP, *SW,* p. 28.

page 52: silk party dresses . . .: MEM, *CITP,* p. 77.

page 52: she liked the German composers . . .: AOE interview, SLRC.

page 53: an expensive set of Kipling's . . .: MEM, *CITP,* p. 69.

page 53: "wrote him the most hysterical appeals . . .": Mark Otis, letter to Charles Otis, Sept. 17, 1913: "It is only two years ago that he left her and although Mother offered to make suitable provision for her and the children at the time, she would have none of it and wrote him the most hysterical appeals to return, one of which he was graceless enough to send to me." Forwarding the letter to Mark backfired—badly. Mark had thought little of Edwin to start with and even less now—he thought him contemptible for committing such a "graceless" act. And he thought less of his sister. He would later use the information to undermine her credibility with the family.

page 54: "although Mother offered to make . . .": Ibid.

page 54: "It is a great deal more . . .": E. W. Howe, *Country Town Sayings,* p. 294.

page 54: Theodore, who sat all day . . .: KCP interview.
"It is my *will* that only the net income of the shares of my estate devised to my children Amy O. Earhart and Theo. H. Otis shall be paid over to them annually and that the entire principal and capital thereof shall be managed and controlled by my said Trustee Mark E. Otis for the said period of fifteen years after my death upon the trust hereinbefore described."

page 54: she dictated a letter: Letter given to author by Nancy Balis Morse.

page 55: the terms of her will . . .: On file, District Court, Atchison County, Kansas.

page 55: *The Atchison Globe* printed . . .: *AG,* Feb. 24, 1912.

page 55: wasn't totally accurate . . .: Exhibit A, case #11220; District Court, Atchison County, Kansas.

page 55: Ephraim even agreed . . .: AOE, letter to Charles Otis, Mar. 18, 1913. ("I felt sure uncle Eph would not have spoken as he did about them if they had not been thoroughly trustworthy.") Mark Otis, Margaret Balis, and Amy "agreed by and between the parties hereto that all necessary and proper steps be immediately taken for the appointment of said The Northern Trust Company [of Chicago, Illinois] as such Successor in Trust." Given to author by Nancy Balis Morse.

page 56: On the first Sunday in May, . . .: *AG,* May 7, 1912.

page 56: "he sat on the porch . . .": *AG,* May 8, 1912.
Mark Otis, letter to Charles J. Conlon, Apr. 17, 1912: "I am also enclosing herewith the bond required by the State of Kansas duly signed by my father, the Northern Trust Co. and myself." Given to author by Nancy Balis Morse.

page 56: the family members who attended . . .: *AG,* May 11, 1912.

page 56: a lengthy document . . .: was filed in Probate Court in Atchison County, June 28, 1912.

page 57: "All the old bitterness . . .": MEM, *CITP,* p. 83.

page 58: raced to meet him . . .: Ibid., p. 79.

page 58: "It was our 'old' Dad, . . .": Ibid., pp. 82–83.

page 58: "I am now safe . . .": Ibid., p. 84.

page 59: Before long . . .: Ibid., p. 83.

page 59: "We did have such a delightful . . .": Charles Earhart, letter to AOE, May 22, 1912; given to author by Nancy Balis Morse..

page 60: I cannot depend . . .: AOE, letter to Charles Otis, Jan. 21, 1913; given to author by Nancy Balis Morse. The text of this letter is as follows:

> My dear Uncle Charlie
> I had expected to run in and see you for a little while tomorrow, but at the last moment some housekeeping matters prevented my coming to St. Paul with my husband, so I am asking him to leave some papers with you which I wish you would look over for me, and see if everything is being done as it should be. I cannot depend on my husbands opinions in this matter as the feeling between Mark and himself is so bitter than an unbiased opinion would be impossible while when I ventured to ask Mark for explanations of certain things, he immediately felt that I had been incited to ask by my husband, and has been suspicious and angry ever since.
> I have no intention of breaking dear mother's will, and while I cannot help feeling that she would have been far more careful about guarding poor Theodore's and my interest if she had been her normal self when the will was writ-

ten, I understand only too well her great anxiety that we be
protected from the dangers that seemed to threaten me especially but on the other hand I spent so many years of my life
near her and was with her weeks and months at a time, and
knew so well her opinions of the business ability of each of
us children that I know it was only in a spirit of desperation
that things were left as they were. Mark does not realize and
has blamed me for an atmosphere of seeming distrust of his
business ability, which he had found lately in Atchison but
Dear Uncle Charlie I have absolutely nothing to do with it,
and have myself had letters urging me to look out for Theodore and myself as at the end of fifteen years there would be
nothing left for either of us. I have been very careful not to
say anything that would at all show any distrust to anyone and
even to my husband I do not dare show any anxiety but there
seemed such discrepancies between the appraisement of the
properties at first and the reports to the State Department and
the Trust Company that I felt as if I would like you to look
over the papers for me and tell me whether it is only that
I do not understand the statements that make them seem at
variance.

page 60: I know truly . . .: AOE, letter to Charles Otis, Mar. 18, 1913; given to
   author by Nancy Balis Morse.
page 60: "Plain, modest, . . .": *St. Paul History and Progress* (Pioneer Press Co.,
   1897), p. 167.
page 60: Charles had at various times . . .: Biographical reference data filed by
   Charles Otis for *The Dispatch and Pioneer Press,* St. Paul Public Library.
page 61: "the combination of a sick maid . . .": AOE, letter to Charles Otis, Mar.
   18, 1913; in author's possession.
page 61: Mark, in a preemptive strike, . . .: Mark Otis, letter to Charles Otis, Sept.
   9, 1913; records of Atchison County Court. She gave 1021 Ann Street
   as her residence in 1916.
page 61: "While the same is on the order . . .": Mark Otis, letter to Charles Otis,
   Mar. 12, 1913; given to author by Nancy Balis Morse.
page 62: the chauffeured Rolls-Royce . . .: Morse interview.
page 63: Dear Mark; You will be . . .: AOE, letter to Mark Otis, Sept. 3, 1913;
   given to author by Nancy Balis Morse.
page 64: "this will be supplemented . . .": Mark Otis, letter to Charles Otis, Sept.
   9, 1913; given to author by Nancy Balis Morse.
page 64: Now, about Amy, pray . . .: Mark Otis, letter to Charles Otis, Sept.
   17, 1913; given to author by Nancy Balis Morse. The text reads:

I am just in receipt of a long letter from Amy which I have
only had a chance to hastily glance over, but which points out

most distressing conditions. It seems that E. lost his position last October and has done nothing scarcely for the family support since. She writes that she is penniless and speaks of a grocery bill and woman-like says nothing about any judgements or liens that may be outstanding against her interests under the trustee-ship. I immediately wired her to see you, as you have full power to act for me and as I stated in my first letter, any sums that you may advance for her temporary needs will be promptly repaid by myself immediately upon knowledge of the amount advanced. . . .

>   Hastily and sincerely yours,
>   [signed] Mark E. Otis

page 64:   He took another day to . . .: Mark Otis, letter to AOE, Sept. 19, 1913; given to author by Nancy Balis Morse. The text reads:

My dear Amy:

   I have your letter and can assure you that there is no bitterness in my heart towards you and the children; I only regret your present straits and trust through the good offices of Uncle Charlie some means may be devised to intelligently assist you. You had better see him at once and give him the true statement of all your debts and promises to pay for rent, etc., any papers you may have signed relating to your interests under the trusteeship, then a statement of what is necessary for your immediate needs. Those together with your last reports from The Northern Trust Co. as to the amounts they let out at interest for you. This, then will enable him to determine how I can assist you in my capacity as President of The Otis Real Estate Co. or personally. However, from whichever source, it must be in the nature of a secured loan to be repaid in manner and time to be specified.

   Amy would never know that it wasn't her uncle's fault but her brother's, never know just how devious Mark had been, how he had smeared her reputation with her uncle. Thus years later Muriel would write: "Mother's wealthy and prominent uncle and his family paid us one surreptitious 'duty call.' They then ignored us completely. This was a bitter pill for Mother, who had never been treated as an unwelcome poor relation before." So painful was Charles's snub that when I asked Muriel, some seventy years later, for the name of the uncle, she set her lips and refused to answer.

page 66:   Forty years later Muriel . . .: MEM, *CITP,* p. 88.
page 66:   the church provided Amelia . . .: JM, *LITHW,* III p. 14, SLRC.

page 66: friends and activities: . . .: Patricia D. Brynteson, parish secretary, St. Clement's, letter to author; Marion Blodgett, interview with author.

page 66: Blessings on thee . . .: AE, letter to Virginia Park, Mar. 6, 1914, SLRC.

page 67: Her 91 grade point average . . .: Transcript, St. Paul Central High School.

Teenage Years

page 68: Upon arrival Edwin went . . .: MEM, *CITP,* p. 94.

page 69: The family rolled around . . .: AE, *FOI,* pp. 17–18.

page 69: She arrived at the train station . . .: Katch Challiss, diary, Aug. 6–Sept. 7, 1914.

page 71: over a glass of milk . . .: GPP, *SW,* p. 26.

page 71: Its student body . . .: All material on Hyde Park High School, including *The Aitchpe,* the yearbook, was provided by Tom Staniszewski.

page 71: Amelia participated in none . . .: *The Aitchpe,* 1915. All school activities are noted beside each student's picture; Amelia's is blank.

page 72: In *The Aitchpe,* . . .: Many books, starting in 1937 with George Palmer Putnam's *Soaring Wings,* give the yearbook caption as "The girl in brown who walks alone." Putnam presumably got it from Muriel; whether she made it up out of whole cloth is not known. But most biographies since have faithfully reprinted it, without ever seeing the yearbook.

page 72: She kept so much to herself . . .: *Hyde Park Weekly,* vol. 25, no. 1 (Sept. 14, 1928).

page 73: (She laughingly remarked . . .: Ibid.

page 73: attempted to resurrect his law practice . . .: St. Paul city directory, 1915.

page 73: he moved to Kansas City . . .: Kansas City directories, 1915–1918, in Kansas City, Missouri, Public Library.

page 73: Edwin joined them. . . .: Address given on court documents, Atchison, Kansas.

page 73: Amy had never given up . . .: Records of District Court, Atchison County, Kansas.

page 73: In September 1915 Amy . . .: Petition #11220, District Court, Atchison, Kansas.

page 74: "a very silly place . . .": KCP interview.

page 74: Nor did Ogontz appeal . . .: Morse interview.

page 75: she alone claimed the house . . .: AOE quoted in Martin, *Family Tree,* p. 5. Philadelphia city directories for the years locate the house of Gebhard Harres, "cabinetmaker," on South Third Street.

page 75: When Muriel wrote . . .: MEM, *CITP,* p. 71.

page 75: she was almost totally deaf . . .: Morse interview.

page 75: Margaret was undertaking . . .: Starting in the fourth grade Nancy and Jane would go to Germantown Friends, as their elder brothers had.

In later years Margaret would extend her hospitality to Charles Otis's grandchildren.

page 76: "I remember Mother wearing . . .": Morse interview.

page 76: Ogontz was a school . . .: Abby Sutherland, *100 Years of Ogontz,* p. 72.

page 78: I don't have a minute . . .: AE, letter to AOE, October 25, 1916, SLRC.

page 78: "I played hockey yesterday . . .": Ibid.

page 78: "Amelia was always pushing . . .: GPP, *SW,* p. 34.

page 79: "Dearie, I don't need . . .": AE, letter to AOE, March 1917, SLRC.

page 79: "Her style of dressing . . .": GPP, *SW,* p. 35.

page 79: the Orpheus Club . . .: AE, letter to AOE, March 1917, SLRC.

page 79: a scrapbook that she called "Activities of Women . . .": AE, scrapbook, SLRC.

page 80: "The boys have been lovely . . .": AE, letter to AOE, postmarked August 14, 1917, SLRC.

page 80: "The general age . . .": AE, letter to AOE, October 3, 1917, SLRC.

page 81: "It is a sweeping blow . . .": Ibid.

page 81: "very few people understand . . .": AE, letter to AOE, November 1917, SLRC.

page 81: she was one of five . . .: Ibid.

page 81: "It has been rather . . .": Ibid.

page 81: In a close-up picture . . .: GPP, *SW,* p. 38.

A Life of Purpose and Action

page 82: The student body resolved . . .: *The Mosaic,* the Ogontz school publication.

page 83: "Returning to school was impossible, . . .": AE, *20H,* p. 31.

page 83: the St. Regis . . .: JM, *LITHW,* V p. 2, SLRC.

page 83: "Muriel and I sent Miss Macdonald . . .": AE, letter to AOE, Feb. 21, 1918, SLRC.

page 84: I *am* a busy person . . .: AE, letter to AOE, "a spring Sunday," SLRC.

page 84: on her first day . . .: JM, *LITHW,* SLRC.

page 84: staining germs . . .: AE, letter to Edwin Earhart, SLRC.

page 84: "It was a thing of rusty wire . . .": AE, *LF,* p. 5.

page 85: "frankly unimpressed . . .": Clarence Chamberlin, *Record Flights,* p. 186.

page 85: "full sized birds . . .": AE, *20H,* p. 37.

page 85: "the next best thing" Ibid., p. 38.

page 85: "He was bored . . .": AE, *LF,* p. 6.

page 85: reached Canada in June. . . .: Eileen Pettigrew, *The Silent Enemy: Canada and the Deadly Flu of 1918.*

page 86: She went on the night shift . . .: AE, *FOI,* p. 20.

page 86: a long, debilitating course of treatment . . .: Ibid., p. 21

page 86: "the lovely country roads . . .": MEM, *CITP,* p. 106.

page 86: "If only I were over there . . .": AE, letter to Kenneth Merrill, in SLRC, quoted in Mary Lovell, *The Sound of Wings,* p. 28.

page 86: Charlesbois taught the girls . . .: A Smith College publication in Smith College Archives, p. 12; given to author by MEM.

page 87: "The life of the mind, . . .": Louise de Schweinitz, interview by JM, 1945; quoted in *LITHW,* SLRC.

page 87: "very poetic, . . .": Marian Stabler, interview with author.

page 88: She could, according to Marian, . . .: Ibid.

page 88: "to afford extraordinary educational opportunities . . .": John Burrell, *A History of Adult Education at Columbia University,* p. 19.

page 88: In the fall of 1919 . . .: *Columbia University Annual Report for 1919–1920,* p. 183.

page 88: Among the famous professors . . .: Burrell, *History of Adult Education,* p. 72.

page 89: "some dump," . . .: AE to AOE, datelined "Saturday, NY," SLRC.

page 89: She then signed up . . .: Records Division, Columbia University.

page 89: Louise, three weeks younger . . .: Louise de Schweinitz, letter to author.

page 89: This interest, he recalled, . . .: Dr. James McGregor, interview by JM; quoted in *LITHW,* VI p. 6, SLRC.

page 89: "so capable she could have done anything" . . .: Louise de Schweinitz, interview with JM, quoted in *LITHW,* VI p. 5, SLRC.

page 90: on a mild May afternoon, . . .: JM, *LITHW,* VI p. 9, SLRC.

page 90: slippery leather soles . . .: Louise de Schweinitz, letter to author.

page 90: At the end of spring term, . . .: Columbia University records.

page 90: "after a year of study . . .": AE, *20H,* p. 44.

page 90: "It took me only a few months . . .": AE, *FOI,* p. 23.

page 90: Amelia was on the receiving end . . .: Ibid., p. 24.

page 91: "aviation caught me.": Ibid., p. 24.

California

page 92: "for several reasons . . .": Donald Glassman, *Jump,* p. 1.

page 92: "never forget . . .": The Curtis Standard JN4-D Military Tractor Handbook, Aviation Publications, p. 48

page 93: "like a falling leaf,": *NYT,* June 6, 1920.

page 93: "greatest of all daredevil fliers,": *Ace,* Sept. 1920.

page 93: Of the first forty: Paul Collins, *Tales of an Old Air-Faring Man,* pp. 88–90.

page 93: "I stopped counting . . .": George Vecsey and George Dade, *Getting Off the Ground,* p. 255.

page 93: "In those days . . .": Antoine de Saint-Exupéry, *Wind, Sand and Stars,* p. 13.

page 94: "It's the fashion . . .": *Ace,* Dec. 1920.

page 94: 500 feet wide and 4,000 feet long . . .: Ibid.

page 94: It was there that Amelia . . .: AE, *20H,* p. 44.

page 94: The meet featured . . .: *Ace,* Dec. 1920.

page 94: "characteristically fair,": AE, *20H,* p. 46.

page 95: "local air thrill maker": Frank Hawks, *Speed,* p. 125.

page 95: she "knew" she had to learn . . .: AE, *FOI,* p. 25.

Amelia's diffidence . . .: AE, *20H*, p. 70. She would admit as late as 1928, "If it be car or plane, my inclination is to be absolutely sure of myself before I whisk anybody else's body around in it. . . . As a matter of fact, I have never asked any men to take a ride. I think I have always feared that some sense of gallantry would make them accept, even though they did not trust me. So my male passengers have always had to do the asking."

page 95: That fall she had leased . . .: *Ace,* Dec. 1920.
page 95: She was wearing a brown suit . . .: Snook, *I Taught Amelia,* p. 1.
page 96: "so in a few days . . .": AE, *20H,* p. 49.
page 96: "I knew I could fly.": Snook, *I Taught Amelia,* p. 81.
page 97: "Wilshire Gasoline" . . .: Ibid., p. 95.
page 97: "a beautifully tailored outfit,": Ibid., p. 104.
page 97: That book and the many others that followed . . .: Ibid., p. 105.
page 97: her fat ankles. . . .: KCP interview; Nancy Balis Morse interview.
page 98: "We were not quite sure . . .": GP, *SW,* p. 39.
page 98: "looked thoroughly feminine.": Quoted by Doris Rich, *Amelia Earhart,* p. 31.
page 98: what always stuck in Amelia's mind . . .: AE, *FOI,* p. 33.
page 98: "to nose down on a right-hand turn . . .": Curtiss Aeroplane, *The Curtiss Standard JN4-D Military Tractor Handbook,* p. 52.
page 99: It rained mightily . . .: *Los Angeles Examiner,* Feb. 16, 1921.
page 99: By the end of February . . .: Snook, *I Taught Amelia,* p. 106.
page 99: The first prototype, . . .: *Ace,* June 1920.
page 99: By June . . .: Ibid.
page 99: "Speed kings of the board bowl . . .": *Los Angeles Examiner,* Feb. 27, 1921.
page 99: The Washington's Birthday extravaganza . . .: *Ace,* Feb. 1921.
page 100: Bert dropped out . . .: Ibid.
page 100: going against the advice . . .: AE, *20H,* p. 62.
page 100: "It was like a favorite pony. . . .": AOE, AOE papers, SLRC.
page 100: a job she kept for several years. . . .: Los Angeles city directory, 1921 and 1922, "Earhart, Amelia M. clerk."
page 100: "wiped out my indebtedness, . . .": AE, *20H,* p. 67.
page 101: Charles Lawrance, . . .: *Who Was Who in America,* vol. 3, 1951–1960, Chicago: C. N. Marquis, 1963, p. 503.
page 102: "the prettiest plane . . .": Neta Snook, interview with author.
page 102: "I remember thinking, . . .": Snook, *I Taught Amelia,* p. 138.
page 102: "a few times.": Ibid., p. 121.
page 102: "periodically became clogged.": Ibid., p. 122.
page 102: So scary did Neta find the plane . . .: Ibid., p. 122.
page 102: Will Rogers's definition . . .: Collins, *Old Air-Faring Man,* p. 23.
page 102: Amelia gave her some soothing explanation . . .: Snook, *I Taught Amelia,* p. 122.
page 103: "She'd look at me with her winsome half smile, . . .": Ibid., p. 125.
page 103: "We have to look nice . . .": Ibid., p. 126.

page 103: "Crashes were frequent . . .": AE, *20H*, p. 82.

page 103: "I was almost angry . . .": Snook, *I Taught Amelia*, p. 124.

page 104: Amelia, whose loyalty to friends . . .: "The visit in 1924 was the last time I saw Amelia." Snook, *I Taught Amelia*, p. 158.

page 104: Amelia thought dating . . .": Ibid., p. 110.

page 104: "Sowing wild oats . . .": AE, black book, SLRC.

page 105: I refused to fly alone . . .: AE, *20H*, p. 54.

page 105: he had as well become financially involved . . .: "W. B. Kinner and J. G. Montijo are making a number of improvements on their Long Beach Boulevard Field and report business good." *Ace*, Nov. 1921.

page 105: Under John's instruction, . . .: AE, *FOI*, p. 35.

page 105: "thoroughly rotten landing.": AE, *20H*, p. 56.

page 106: On November 3 . . .: *Ace*, Dec. 1921.

page 106: "The Pacific Coast Ladies Derby . . .": Ibid.

page 106: It was at this first rodeo . . .: Ibid.

page 107: In reporting the fatal accident, . . .: Ibid.

page 107: On December 17 . . .: *Ace*, Dec. 1921; *Los Angeles Examiner*, Dec. 18, 1921.

page 107: During the afternoon . . .: *Los Angeles Examiner*, Dec. 11, 1921.

page 107: Amelia had turned up . . .: AE, *20H*, p. 75.

page 107: At that stage . . .: *Los Angeles Examiner*, Dec. 4, 1921.

page 108: "the chatterers never knew . . .": AE, *20H*, p. 75.

page 108: She was full of plans . . .: *Ace*, Dec. 1921: "Miss Earhart has placed an order for one of the new 1922 model Kinner Airsters and will fly to New York in the spring to compete in the eastern events during the 1922 flying season."

page 109: "I lingered on . . .": AE, *20H*, p. 86.

page 109: "I am sure . . .": Letter, June 23, 1920, SLRC.

page 109: In 1921 they had moved . . .: Los Angeles city directory, 1921, Los Angeles Public Library.

page 109: On her suggestion . . .: MEM, *CITP*, pp. 119–21.

page 109: "Peter is drowned, . . .": MEM, *CITP*, p. 121. Sometime in February 1922 Muriel was informed by letter by Amelia while she was at Smith that all was lost. She never went back after finishing the term, according to Smith College records.

page 110: Amelia began dropping his name . . .: MEM, *CITP*, p. 117.

page 110: keep a belaying pin . . .: AE, *FOI* p. 176.

page 110: Amelia had been investigating . . .: Snook *I Taught Amelia*, p. 105.

page 111: "I can't name all the moods . . .": AE, *FOI*, p. 48; AE, black book, SLRC; notes on color negatives. Amelia wrote in *FOI* (p. 48) that she took a photography course at the University of Southern California, but no courses in photography were given at USC in the years 1920–24, according to the registrar's office, neither in summer, undergraduate, nor graduate school, nor was she listed as a student.

page 111: "nearly became bankrupt.": AE's WEIU job application.

page 111: She began driving . . .: AE, *FOI*, p. 49; *American Magazine*, Aug. 1932.

page 111: was famous for . . .: Advertisement in *Los Angeles Examiner,* Feb. 20, 1921.

page 112: 5314 Sunset Boulevard, . . .: Los Angeles city directory, 1923.

page 112: putting money aside . . .: GPP, *SW,* p. 43.

page 112: The prototype engine, only 50 horsepower, . . .: *Ace,* Apr. 1922.

page 112: "The greatest pleasure . . .": AE, *20H,* p. 88.

page 113: It too was none too safe; . . .: John Underwood, *Madcaps, Millionaires, and "Mose,"* p. 32.

page 113: As *The Ace* somewhat pompously . . .: *Ace,* Apr. 1923.

page 113: On September 1, 1927 . . .: *NYT,* Sept. 1, 1927.

page 113: marked by an air rodeo . . .: *Ace,* Mar. 1923.

page 113: just taken delivery . . .: Ibid.

page 114: "If weather conditions . . .: *Ace,* Mar. 1923.

page 114: lose it in July to Bertha Horchem . . .: *Aeronautical Digest,* Aug. 1923.

page 114: On May 16 . . .: photocopy of AE's license from NASM.

page 114: The test, under the aegis of the Aero Club of America, . . .: Adopted Oct. 13, 1919; *1922 Aero Club of America Rule Book,* chap. 4, p. 176.

page 114: In June Amelia . . .: *Aeronautical Digest,* July 1923.

page 115: "has declared its intention . . .": Ibid.

page 115: Tis a wonderful thing . . .: Fragment of unidentified newspaper.

page 115: Bert Kinner was so successful . . .: *Ace,* Feb. 1924.

page 115: When her old friend . . .: Ibid.

page 115: had agreed to be engaged.: AE quoted in *NYT,* June 8, 1928: "We have been engaged for four years."

Breaking Through

page 117: Three days after their arrival . . .: AE, *20H,* p. 89.

page 117: It was not until the spring term, . . .: Columbia University records.

page 117: so severely debilitated . . .: Stabler interview.

page 118: "It seems odd that a family . . .": Ibid.

page 118: to watch the eclipse of the sun . . .: The eclipse was January 25.

page 118: Now Amelia enrolled in only two, . . .: Columbia University records.

page 119: she had received a letter . . .: AE, letter to Lloyd Royer; given to author by Vivian Smedad; the date AE received it is noted on envelope.

page 119: she knew he was equally strapped, . . .: John Underwood, *Madcaps, Millionaires and "Mose,"* p. 31.

page 119: "I inserted a little French poetry.": AE, *FOI,* p. 22.

page 119: "conditional on . . .": Columbia University records.

page 120: earning three credits . . .: Harvard University records.

page 120: the pioneer investigator . . .: Barbara Sicherman and Carol Hurd Green, eds. *Notable American Women,* pp. 303–306.

page 121: "No, I did not get into M.I.T . . .": AE, letter to Marian Stabler, IWASML

page 122: 27,759 foreigners . . .: Massachusetts Department of Education. AE was employed by the Educational Service Bureau, at 100 Boyston Street, according to WEIU files, SLRC.

page 122: "an office class . . .: WEIU collection, SLRC.

page 122: That month Amelia began working . . .: Ibid.

page 122: Lucy Challiss passed through Boston . . .: LC, diary, June 1926.

page 122: founded in 1884 by Dr. Henry R. Stedman, . . .: Obituary, Dr. H. R. Stedman, May 29, 1909, unidentified newspaper, Bournewood files.

page 122: "Personal attention and influence suitably directed . . .": Dr. Henry R. Stedman, "The Art of Companionship in Mental Nursing," paper presented at the Boston Psychopathic Hospital, Bournewood files.

page 122: sugar pellets to a patient . . .: AE, *FOI*, p. 23.

page 123: "I did not see then . . .": Ibid.

page 123: "Work too confining . . .": WEIU files, SLRC.

page 123: "She leaves to increase her salary, . . .:" Ibid.

page 123: history of the WEIU: Ibid.

page 123: "to increase fellowship among women . . .": history of the WEIU by Diane Goldman and Mary Hilderbrand who assembled the collection for the SLRC.

page 123: "to be as competent . . .": WEIU files, SLRC.

page 123: still gamely pasting . . .: AE scrapbook. Two articles dated 1925, SLRC.

page 124: "Teaching English to Foreigners, . . .": AE's registration card, WEIU.

page 124: "A remarkable man . . .": AE, black book, SLRC.

page 124: I have had five years. . . ": AE's registration card, in WEIU.

page 125: she gave only her two most recent jobs . . .: Letter dated Aug. 10, 1926, from Biddle and Smart to the WEIU, SLRC.

page 125: Miss Amelia M. Earhart is . . .: WEIU files, SLRC.

page 125: "Holds a sky pilots license?" . . .: Ibid.

page 125: "My God," he said to Eleanor . . .: Doris Kearns Goodwin, *No Ordinary Time,* p. 96.

page 126: "Hull house was soberly opened . . .": Jane Addams, *Twenty Years at Hull House,* p. 90.

page 126: Information about Vida Scudder, Katherine Coman, and Emily Balch.: Barbara Sicherman and Carol Hurd Green, *Notable American Women, The Modern Period: A Biographical Dictionary,* pp. 41–45, 636–638. *Who Was Who, in America,* vol. I, 1897–1942, p. 247.

page 127: "Not philanthropy but . . .": Denison House records, 1891–1961, SLRC.

page 127: "and a part-time one would do, . . .": Marion Perkins, introduction to AE, *20H.*

page 128: When the popular "mayor" . . .: *Boston Herald,* Aug. 22, 1927, SLRC.

page 128: Chinese restaurant on one side . . .: Boston Atlas, 1928, Rare Books Room, Boston Library.

page 128: in charge of adult education . . .: DH report, Oct. 1927–28, SLRC.

page 128: "The House is no longer a power outside, . . .": Ibid.

page 129: One of Amelia's tasks . . .: AE, *FOI*, p. 15.

page 129: "I can still see her, . . .": *Boston Sunday Advertiser,* Mar. 23, 1975, SLRC.

page 129: This remarkable institution, . . .: Annual Report 1926, Perkins Institution and Massachusetts School for the Blind.

page 129: she thereupon spent several hours a week . . .: John Burke, *Winged Legend*, p. 70.

page 129: "She never had any favorites, . . .: "Notes from the Field," *Neighborhood: A Settlement Quarterly*, no date.

page 129: Under her guidance . . .: *Neighborhood: A Settlement Quarterly*, Jan. 1928.

page 130: "under racial traditions that cut them off . . .": *Cosmopolitan*, Nov. 1928.

page 130: simply furnished, but it had windows . . .: Barbara Washburn (who lived in the room after Amelia), letter to author, Sept. 11, 1989.

page 130: She prevailed on George Ludlam . . .: JM, *LITHW*, VII p. 15, SLRC.

page 130: The punctilious housekeeper . . .: JM, *LITHW*, VIII p. 14, SLRC.

page 130: Amelia fitted in a visit from Nancy Balis, . . .: Morse interview.

page 130: Six hundred boys and girls . . .: DH report, Oct. 1927–28, SLRC.

page 131: It is from this period . . .: AE, *20H*, pp. 16–17.

page 131: "as one of the most thoughtful and promising . . .": "New Settlement Leadership," *Neighborhood: A Settlement Quarterly*, July 1928.

page 132: Cleveland Amory remarking on . . .: Cleveland Amory, *Proper Bostonians*, p. 98.

page 133: Amelia had planned to do the stunt incognito, . . .: Marion Perkins, introduction to AE, *20H*, p. 13.

page 133: the newspapers wrote it up: . . .: *Boston Herald*, May 26, 1927.

page 133: "Flies over . . .": Undated clipping, DH file, SLRC.

page 133: Two paragraphs were devoted to her; . . .: *Boston Herald*, July 3, 1927.

page 134: "The field opens on Tuesday . . .": AE, letter to Marian Stabler, Aug. 1, 1927, IWASML.

page 134: "New England has some of the best . . .": *Boston Herald*, July 3, 1927.

page 134: It was at that time . . .: Marion Perkins, introduction to AE, *20H*, p. 14.

page 134: had spent her residency . . .: JM, *LITHW*, VIII p. 9, SLRC.

page 135: "and spend next summer . . .": AE, letter to Bert Kinner, Nov. 27, 1927, in Muriel Morrissey and Carol Osborne, *Amelia, My Courageous Sister*, p. 77.

page 135: Amy would lay on a breakfast . . .: JM, *LITHW*, VIII pp. 8–9, SLRC.

page 136: a photo of Ruth Nichols, . . .: *Boston Herald*, Aug. 27, 1927.

page 136: "May I introduce myself . . .": Ruth Nichols, *Wings for Life*, p. 94.

page 137: stated her mission to the waiting reporter. . . .: *Boston Herald*, Oct. 2, 1927.

page 137: Amelia was perfect . . .: Amory, *Proper Bostonians*, p. 281.

page 137: "a curly headed girl . . .": *Bostonian*, May 1928.

page 138: "While women are hopelessly adventurous, . . .": AE, *Bostonian*, May 1928.

page 138: asked her to fill out a biography . . .: *BET*, June 4, 1928.

page 139: "The cause of the following . . .": Julia Railey, in *BET*, June 23, 1928.

page 139: "with her unusual interest . . .": Boston chapter, National Aeronautic Association (NAA); NAA file in NASM.

page 139: serve with Commander Richard Byrd . . .: *Aeronautic Review*, June 1928.

page 139: "as strong a dose . . .": AE, *20H*, p. 90.

Dreams of Glory

page 143: "I woke that afternoon, . . .: Charles Lindbergh, *The Spirit of St. Louis,* p. 501.

page 144: "An epoch in air history . . .": Augustus Post, reprinted in *Aviation for Boys.*

page 144: "Our publicity machine . . .": Walter Lippman, 1927, quoted in *Vanity Fair: A Cavalcade of the 1920s and 1930s,* p. 121.

page 144: "marked the end . . .": Harry F. Guggenheim, *The Seven Skies,* p. 216.

page 144: In the twelve months following . . .: Edward Jablonski, *Atlantic Fever.*

page 145: famous for her gowns . . .: *Boston Herald,* Aug. 31, 1927.

page 145: Front-page headlines . . .: *NYT,* Mar. 14, 1928

page 146: "I have no wish . . .": *NYT,* Oct. 17, 1927.

page 147: On March 5, . . .: *NYT,* Mar. 6, 1928.

page 147: "there was an understanding . . .": *NYT,* Mar. 28, 1928.

page 148: "launched the family . . .": Peggy Phipps Boegner and Richard Gachot, *Halcyon Days.*

page 148: By the end of the safari, . . .: Bror Blixen, *The Africa Letters,* p. 34.

page 148: To her cousin Peggy Phipps Boegner, . . .: Peggy Phipps Boegner and Richard Gachot, *Halcyon Days,* p. 192.

page 149: "Brave as a lion . . .": Mrs. Pope Guest, interview with author.

page 149: regularly flew off . . .: Judy Lomax, *Women of the Air,* p. 50.

page 149: It "just wouldn't do . . .": Diana Guest Manning, interview with author.

page 149: summoned David T. Layman, . . .: The plane cost $62,000; the buyer of record was the Mechanical Science Corporation. Richard S. Allen manuscript, NASM.

page 150: By that time . . .: Manning interview.

page 150: "When the Gods fashioned Dick Byrd . . .": Hilton Railey, *Touch'd with Madness,* p. 110.

page 150: according to Phipps family history, . . .: Manning interview.

page 151: "Keep my ship, . . .": JM, *LITHW,* IX p. 4, SLRC.

page 151: on his way by ferry to Miller field . . .: GPP, *WM,* p. 292. George had snared for Putnam's, Charles Lindbergh's *We,* Billy Mitchell's *Skyways,* Richard Byrd's *Skyward,* Sir Arthur Whitten Brown's *Flying the Atlantic in Sixteen Hours,* and Captain George Wilkins's *Flying the Arctic.*

page 151: "instantly" saw the possibilities. . . .: GPP, *WM,* p. 293.

page 151: "Pull your chair over. . . .": Railey, *Touch'd with Madness,* p. 100.

page 152: "Pretty much at the moment . . .": GPP, *WM,* p. 293.

page 152: "visibly relieved," . . .: GPP, *WM,* p. 293; JM, *LITHW,* IX p. 77, SLRC.

page 152: "All I have to say . . .": JM, *LITHW,* IX p. 7, SLRC.

page 152: Undeterred, Putnam pressed on . . .: Hilton Railey, *Touch'd With Madness,* p. 100; GPP, *Soaring Wings,* p. 52. Putnam and Railey give different versions of how this came about; this is Putnam's. According to Railey, Putnam knew only that there was a plane in East Boston; Putnam told Railey to find it, pumping the pilot until he gave him Layman's name, at which point they went to Layman.

page 153: "Why, yes," Admiral Belknap said . . .: Railey, *Touch'd with Madness*, p. 101.

page 153: "She never . . .": JM, *LITHW,* SLRC. MEM writes in *CITP* that Nichols's health was the reason, but there was nothing the matter with her, by Nichols's own account.

page 153: "I had to come out with it . . .": Railey, *Touch'd with Madness*, p. 103.

page 153: Amelia asked him for references . . .: AE, *20H,* p. 97.

page 153: She was wearing a brown wool suit . . .: Kathleen Moore Kennedy, interview with author.

page 153: "I felt that I had discovered . . .": Railey, *Touch'd with Madness*, p. 102.

page 154: On April 24 Amelia wrote to Ruth Nichols, . . .: Ruth Nichols, *Wings for Life*, pp. 94–95.

page 154: On May 2 she wrote to Hilton Railey: . . .: Railey, *Touch'd with Madness*, p. 104.

page 155: Why aren't we doing something notable . . .: Mary Lovell, *The Sound of Wings*, pp. 51–52.

page 155: "Today the Boston Chapter of the NAA . . .": *BET,* June 6, 1928.

page 155: Zonta, a service organization for businesswomen . . .: Zonta history, from Zonta Souvenir Book, 1980.

page 156: Amelia's application for membership . . .: Files of Boston Zonta.

page 156: "a social worker who flies for sport . . .": Nichols, *Wings for Life*, p. 24.

page 156: "making one telephone call . . .": AE, *LF,* p. 9.

page 157: Nevertheless he took her over to 787 . . .: JM, *LITHW,* SLRC; AE, *20H,* p. 100.

page 157: "Why do you want . . .": JM, *LITHW,* IX, SLRC.

page 158: "The Phippses had gotten her . . .": JM, *LITHW,* SLRC.

page 158: So when John Phipps appeared . . .: JM, *LITHW,* IX p. 8, SLRC. There are very slight variations in the manuscript. This seems the earliest and therefore most reliable version.

page 158: Next, they told her the details: . . .: JM, *LITHW,* IX p. 8, SLRC.

page 158: "You may make this flight . . .": JM, *LITHW,* IX p. 10, SLRC.

page 158: On June 1 . . .: AE, letter to Marian Stabler, IWASML.

page 159: "strong and exquisitely fashioned.": AE, *20H,* p. 101.

page 160: Both had gone the classic flying route . . .: AE, *20H,* pp. 311–14.

page 161: The crowds surging to greet him . . .: *Boston Herald,* July 23, 1927.

page 161: merely asked Marion Perkins . . .: JM, *LITHW,* SLRC.

Vortex

page 162: He recounts the first instance himself . . .: Commander Richard E. Byrd, *Skyward*, pp. 27–28.

page 163: "I should have refused, . . .": Bennett repeated it to Bernt Balchen, who related it in *Come North With Me.*

page 163: "I knew we were heading toward Paris, . . .": Byrd, *Skyward*, p. 267.

page 164: "really wanted to go . . .": Byrd, *Alone*, p. 3.

page 165: "I deprecate the use . . .": *NYT,* June 28, 1928.

page 165: "I believe that the flight . . .": Byrd, in *Boston Herald,* Sept. 3, 1927.

page 166: "because pontoons stick to water . . .": *NYT,* June 5, 1928.

page 166: "I had decided . . .": Charles Lindbergh, *We,* p. 202.

page 166: By the time Byrd and Elmer . . .: *NYT,* June 6, 1928.

page 167: "everything.": *NYT,* June 19, 1928.

page 167: The Cardwell, all by itself. . . .: Ibid.

page 167: "the safest and best equipped . . .": *NYT,* June 19, 1928.

page 167: music of Meyer Davis.: *BET,* June 4, 1928.

page 168: In the interests of secrecy all of his shots of Amelia . . .: JM, *LITHW,* IX p. 13, SLRC.

page 168: "It wasn't so much . . .": JM, *LITHW,* IX p. 13, SLRC.

page 168: "She couldn't have resembled . . .": GPP, *SW,* p. 176.

page 169: "People got out of the way . . ." *BET,* June 23, 1928.

page 169: hers borrowed from a friend, . . .: *Aeronautic Review,* Jan. 1928.

page 169: a will of sorts. . . .: AOE papers, SLRC.

page 170: "popping off" letters . . .: GPP, *SW,* p. 57.

page 170: I have tried to play . . .": *NYT,* June 5, 1928.

page 171: The fog comes on . . .: AE, *FOI,* p. 66.

page 171: According to Phil Coolidge, . . .: JM, *LITHW,* X p. 12a, SLRC.

page 171: On Saturday . . .: *BG,* June 2, 1928.

page 172: "It's like being . . .": JM, *LITHW,* IX p. 16, SLRC.

page 172: "But you got the feeling, . . .": Ibid.

page 172: The sun, she noticed, . . .: AE, *20H,* p. 120.

page 172: Just before they closed the door, . . .: JM, *LITHW,* IX p. 33, SLRC.

page 173: Exultantly, Amelia wrote . . .: AE, Flight Log, Seaver Center in Western History Research, Los Angeles County Museum of Natural History.

page 173: a few minutes into the flight, . . .: AE, Flight Log, Seaver Center.

page 174: the *Friendship* dove through the clouds . . .: *NYHT,* June 4, 1928.

page 174: There had been rumors . . .: *BET,* June 4, 1928.

page 174: little to her liking: . . .: AE, Flight Log, Seaver Center.

page 175: "Girl and Stultz . . .": *NYHT,* June 5, 1928.

page 175: "The sea," Amelia wrote . . .: Ibid.
(The evening edition of *The Boston Globe* would proudly report that their stringer was the first reporter to talk to the fliers.)

Trepassey

page 178: "Good trip from Halifax. . . .": *NYT,* June 5, 1928.

page 178: twenty-one out of thirty days . . .: Weather for Cape Race, June 1928, from Stu Porter, Canadian Scientific Services Meteorologist.

page 179: Those planes had had problems . . .: Richard K. Smith, *First Across.*

page 179: "But soon after our arrival . . .": Commander Richard E. Byrd, *Skyward,* pp. 91–92.

page 179: "a howling gale.": AE, *20H,* p. 147.

page 179: Amelia cabled George Putnam: . . .: *NYT,* June 4, 1928.

page 181: "get out of this trap . . .": AE, *20H.*

page 181: Her last entry . . .: AE, Flight Log, Seaver Center for Western History Research.

page 181: In London Amy Guest, horrified at the turn . . .: *NYT,* June 7, 1928.

page 182: "We shoved off . . .": AE, in *Cosmopolitan,* May 1929.

page 182: Slim went out to check . . .: AE, Flight Log, Seaver Center.

page 183: encouraging news awaited them: . . .: *NYHT,* June 8, 1928.

page 183: "and within the next . . .": *Evening Telegram,* June 7, 1928.

page 183: Amelia appeared cheerful, . . .: *NYT,* June 9, 1928.

page 183: "Rasche is the one to fear. . . .": AE, Flight Log, Seaver Center.

page 184: "I could choke Frazer. . . .": Ibid.

page 185: Before the last attempt, . . .: JM, *LITHW,* SLRC.

page 186: "the desperate straits . . .": *NYHT,* June 13, 1928.

page 187: "the real fault . . .": *NYHT,* June 13, 1928.

page 188: Amelia later told George Putnam . . .: GPP, *SW,* p. 61.

page 190: "so could we. . . .": AE, *20H,* p. 169.

page 190: "Two are required . . .: Ibid., p. 168.

page 190: spent the day drinking . . .: GPP, *SW,* p. 60.

page 191: Burnham watched Amelia . . .: F. Burnham Gill, "First Woman to Cross the Atlantic in a Flying Boat," *Newfoundland Quarterly,* vol. 60, no. 4 (1961–62).

page 191: "We have a dandy breeze . . .": *ET,* June 18, 1928.

page 191: "precariously nervous" . . .: JM, *LITHW,* X p. 7, SLRC.

page 192: "I was crowded in the cabin . . .: AE, *FOI,* p. 73.

page 192: Observers watched the plane . . .: *ET,* June 18, 1928.

page 192: only seven hundred gallons of fuel.: AE, *20H,* p. 170.

page 192: To plot their course, . . .: *Cosmopolitan,* May 1929.

page 193: "wonderful greens and blues": AE, in *NYT,* June 19, 1928.

page 194: "Bill sits up alone. . . .": AE, *20H,* p. 187.

page 195: "Well, that's out," . . .: *NYT,* June 21, 1928.

In spite of the uncertainty of their position, Amelia had the presence of mind to take a picture of the ship before closing the hatch in the bottom of the fuselage; it was probably at this time that, inspired by the oranges, she dropped Bill Stultz's bottle into the sea.

page 196: The sandwich flew out . . .: AE, *20H,* p. 196.

page 197: called up Cyril Jefferies, junior clerk . . .: Cyril Jefferies, *I Was There,* reprinted in the Golden Jubilee Program, June 18, 1978; reprinted in *The Mansion,* June 1983, Blair County Historical Society bulletin, Blair County, Pennsylvania.

page 198: "I came ashore . . .": *NYT,* June 19, 1928.

Golden Girl

page 200: There on the dock . . .: *NYT,* June 19, 1928.

page 201: "I am caught . . .": *NYT,* June 21, 1928.

page 201: managed to gain entrance . . .: *NYHT,* June 21, 1928.

page 202: kept hiring secretaries . . .: *NYT,* June 28, 1928.

page 202: "I don't want to be known . . .": *London Times,* June 20, 1928.

page 203: "She spoke calmly . . .": *NYT,* June 26, 1928.

page 204: "It was wonderful," . . .: *NYT,* July 8, 1928.

page 204: tried her hand at flying . . .: Nathan Browne, Columbia OH.

page 204: "What did she say? . . .": *BG,* July 7, 1937.

page 205: As the train rolled out of Pittsburgh, . . .: *NYT,* July 25, 1928; AE, *20H,* p. 289.

page 206: "I fell from literary . . .": GPP, *WM,* p. 27.

page 207: He was, he said, "an easterner . . .": GPP, *WM,* p. 49.

page 207: cut such a wide swath . . .: Mary Lovell, *Sound of Wings,* p. 372.

page 209: Just that past winter . . .: Bradford Washburn, interview with author.

page 209: was astonished in later years . . .: Ibid.

page 210: "My book goes to press . . .": AE, letter to Marian Stabler, postmarked Aug. 16, 1928, IWASML.

page 210: In re-reading the manuscript . . .: AE, *20H,* p. 9.

page 211: received more press coverage . . .: *NYT,* July 31, 1928.

page 211: wrote her a "stiff" letter . . .: JM, *LITHW,* SLRC.

page 211: "the popular phases of aviation.": GPP, *SW,* p. 196.

page 211: "The night's activities. . . .": AE, letter to AOE, Aug. 12, 1928, SLRC.

page 212: "Please throw away rags . . .": AE, letter to AOE, Aug. 26, 1928, SLRC.

page 212: Lady Heath had rushed home . . .: Mary Lovell, *Sound of Wings,* p. 127.

page 212: a leap of faith . . .: *Cosmopolitan,* Jan. 1929.

page 212: they would earn $12,460; . . .: GPP, *SW,* p. 190.

page 212: "To Amelia Earhart . . .": AE, *FOI,* p. 88. "Always think with your stick forward" is a reminder that if the mind wanders and the nose goes up, the plane goes into a stall.

page 212: was almost as small,. . .: C. A. Sims, *British Aircraft.*

page 213: . . . opt for licensing the Avian . . .: Porter Adams, letter to Major Clarence Young, July 31, 1928; Major Young, letter to Porter Adams, Aug. 3, 1928; NASM files.

page 214: On the last Friday in August, . . .: *NYT,* Sept. 1, 1928.

page 214: "a perfect landing . . .": *NYT,* Sept. 1, 1928.

page 214: "taken the precaution . . .": *Cosmopolitan,* Dec. 1928.

page 215: Miss Earhart had visited . . .: *NYT,* Sept. 1, 1928.

page 215: number of white flags . . .: *Muskogee Daily Phoenix,* Sept. 5, 1928.

page 215: There is a prophetic 1928 photo . . .: AE, *20H,* p. 298.

page 215: No money in the world . . .: *NYHT,* June 6, 1928.

page 216: It had gotten to the point . . .: *PA,* Aug. 1928.

page 216: "She said she hated . . .": *Muskogee Daily Phoenix,* Sept. 5, 1928.

page 217: She followed her last compass course . . .: AE, *Los Angeles Times,* Sept. 18, 1928.

page 218: Suddenly the Avian was nose down . . .: *Yuma Morning Sun,* Sept. 15, 1928.

page 219: "I am going to find out . . .": *Salt Lake Tribune,* Oct. 1, 1928.

page 219: how it thinned . . .: Mariana Gosnell, *Zero 3 Bravo.*

page 219: Amelia was signed on . . .: for the November issue.

page 219: "the" hot media topic . . .: WABC had a Friday-night "Aviation Hour."

page 220: "the year of 1929 is . . ." *Cosmopolitan,* Mar. 1929.

page 220: usually a mystery story.: *Cosmopolitan,* Jan. 1931.

page 221: Indeed, years later, . . .: JM, *LITHW,* SLRC.

page 221: I talked at the Better Times dinner . . .: AE, letter to Mr. Hesley, Dec. 10, 1928, Special Collection Manuscripts, Wald Collection, Columbia.

page 221: that she could be a resident.: JM, *LITHW,* XII pp. 9–10, SLRC.

page 221: came to the settlement house. . . .: Records of Greenwich House, Tamiment Library, NYU.

page 223: If she had stayed in social work, . . .: JM, *LITHW,* XII pp. 10, 12, 13, SLRC.

page 223: "Are you interested to know . . .": JM, *LITHW,* XII p. 12, SLRC.

page 224: She spoke at the children's annual . . .: Records of Greenwich House, Tamiment Library, NYU; Mary Simkhovitch, *Neighborhood: My Story of Greenwich House.*

page 224: She also arranged . . .: AE, letter to AOE, Aug. 9, 1929, SLRC.

Dreams Come True

page 225: He had been stunting . . .: *NYT,* July 2 and 3, 1929.

page 226: "very drunk," . . .: *NYHT,* July 6, 1929.

page 226: a combination air-rail trip . . .: R. E. G. Davies, *Airlines of the United States Since 1914,* p. 85.

page 227: No effort was spared . . .: Dorothy Binney Putnam, in *Sportsman Pilot,* Aug. 1929.

page 227: By the time Amelia's . . .: *NYHT,* July 30, 1929; John Underwood, *Madcaps, Millionaires and "Mose,"* p. 46.

page 227: another TAT plane crashed, . . .: Anne Lindbergh, *Hours of Gold,* p. 122. The accident was January 19.

page 228: She weighed in with the following blast, . . .: *NYT,* July 12, 1929.

page 229: She settled on a five-passenger model . . .: Aircraft registration 6911 NASN, Historical A/C Listing, NASM file.

page 230: the foulest plane he had ever flown.: AE, *LF,* p. 14.

page 230: "A chance to play the game . . .": *Woman's Journal,* Oct. 1929.

page 230: the $8,000 jackpot . . .: Glenn Buffington, "History Relived 60 Years Later," IWASM.

page 231: second day, landing at Yuma . . .: Bobbi Trout, interview with author.

page 231: she had loaded herself down . . .: C. B. Allen, "The Vindication of Amelia Earhart," NASM.

page 231: The fliers won . . .: Doris Rich, *Amelia Earhart,* p. 94.

page 232: She rounded up the four pilots . . .: Fay Gillis Wells, interview with author.

page 233: "There is something . . .": Margery Brown, Ninety-Nine files, Will Rogers Airport, Oklahoma City, Okla.

page 233: Amelia helped defray . . .: Wells interview.

page 233: There was one place, . . .: *NYT,* Feb. 24, 1929.

page 234: membership of more than three thousand . . .: "Oak Trees from Acorns," American Women's Association collection, SLRC.

page 234: Ten thousand women showed up . . .: *NYT,* Apr. 13, 1929.

page 236: "I don't know why . . .": Trout interview.

page 236: writing jubilantly in her logbook, . . .: Richard S. Allen, *Revolution in the Sky,* p. 94.

page 236: as she had mentioned . . .: Bobbi Trout, *Just Plane Crazy,* p. 87.

page 237: A knottier problem to solve, . . .: AE, letter to Ruth Nichols, Apr. 18, 1930, IWASM.

page 238: As *The New York Times* reported, . . .: *NYT,* Aug. 6, 1930.

page 238: by October 1930 . . .: Davies, *Airlines of the United States,* p. 93.

page 238: The NYPWA flew between . . .: Ibid., p. 154.

page 239: Amelia flew over the line . . .: AE, *FOI,* p. 115.

page 239: "and get along with men; . . .": JM, *LITHW,* XIII, SLRC.

page 239: On the last day of 1930 . . .: *NYT,* Jan. 1, 1931.

page 239: amusing old prints . . .: Helen Ferris, *Five Girls Who Dared,* pp. 7–8.

page 239: "It is the disgruntled one . . .": AE, *FOI,* p. 112.

page 239: "If you have spent . . .": Eugene Vidal, letter to AE, University of Wyoming, American Heritage Center.

page 240: She started in Hamilton, . . .: AE itinerary 1931, SLRC.

page 240: "almost inarticulate. . . .": AE, letter to AOE, SLRC.

page 240: just the day after . . .: *NYT,* Apr. 30, 1931.

page 240: "As a matter of fact, . . .": *NYT,* May 9, 1931.

Courtship and Marriage

page 241: Not even Muriel . . .: MEM interview, Aug. 7, 1988.

page 241: "I am no longer engaged . . .": *NYT,* Dec. 23, 1928.

page 242: "The tapering loveliness . . .": GPP, *SW,* p. 215.

page 242: (Gordon Selfridge thought . . .: JM, *LITHW,* XIV p. 7, SLRC.

page 242: George also wrote, . . .: GPP, *SW,* pp. 91–92.

page 243: "In this period when . . .": Ibid., p. 77.

page 243: "Your hats! . . .": Ibid., p. 78.

page 243: As George wryly admitted, . . .: Ibid., p. 59.

page 244: "My interests are usually plural.": GPP, *WM,* p. 288.

page 244: So that by the time . . .: GPP, *SW,* pp. 58–59.

page 244: In New York in November, . . .: *NYT,* Dec. 2, 1928.

page 244: George wrote a promotional article . . .: *Sportsman Pilot,* July 1929.

page 244: in an effort to impress Amelia, . . .: GPP, *WM,* pp. 284–86.

page 245: "You are apt to take less time . . .": GPP, *SW,* p. 80.

page 245: It was during a party . . .: Mary Lovell, *The Sound of Wings,* p. 153.

page 245: "Of course everyone . . .": Stabler interview.

page 246: I am still unsold on marriage . . .: GPP, *SW,* p. 74.

page 247: "To marry Miss Amelia Earhart . . .": *BG,* Feb. 8, 1931.

page 247: even the *New York Times* . . .: *NYT,* Dec. 20, 1930.

page 248: "I need advice badly . . .": Carl B. Allen manuscript draft of a review of *The True Amelia Earhart Story*, in NASM, courtesy of Doris Rich.

page 248: Swinburne's Atalanta . . .: Charles Swinburne, "Atalanta in Calydon."

page 248: A contemporary Radcliffe study of wives who worked . . .: "The six requisites for the happy combination of a professional pursuit with married life are 1) a husband's active cooperation, 2) health to stand the strain of conflicting interests, 3) adequate household assistance, 4) training and experience before marriage, 5) work with short or adjustable hours, 6) complex arrangements for the children." WEIU file, SLRC.

page 249: Both she and Lucy went to college . . .: Antich interview.

page 250: "She wore something as simple . . .": GPP, *SW,* p. 75.

page 250: "The ceremony itself, performed by . . .": *NYT,* Feb. 8, 1931.

page 251: There are some things . . .: GPP, *SW,* p. 76.

page 251: "a sad little letter, . . .": Ibid., p. 75.

page 253: "a curious mixture . . .": Carl Allen, "The Vindication of Amelia Earhart," NASM.

page 253: share a meal . . .: Once, to Katch's horror, she asked a reporter into Katch's house to have lunch with them; KCP interview.

page 253: "The candlesticks were sweet. . . .": Jean Backus, *Letters From Amelia,* p. 116.

page 254: be underwritten by 49.5 Club . . .: AP news, Dec. 29, 1933.

page 255: "No client of any counselor . . .": GPP, *SW,* p. 88.

page 255: PLEASE TRY . . .: *NYHT,* Mar. 19, 1937.

The Lindbergh Trail

page 256: "follow the Lindbergh trail" . . .: *New York World Telegram,* Apr. 21, 1931.

page 257: "at Newfoundland I will await . . .": *NYT,* May 16, 1931.

page 258: on the Lindbergh trail . . .: Clarence Young, letter to the secretary of state, Sept. 19, 1931, giving department approval "to Miss Elinor Smith's request for permission to make a flight to Newfoundland, Ireland and France," NASM.

page 258: Her backer, . . .: Don Dwiggins, *They Flew the Bendix Race,* p. 82.

page 258: great publicity . . .: The *NYT* promptly ran an article, Dec. 20, 1930.

page 258: On a spring day in April, . . .: There is some confusion about when Amelia soloed because she erroneously claimed in *The Fun of It* that she took that first flight "on a bright spring day" and soloed later the same day, making it all sound much easier than it was. Perhaps, given her marriage, she was uncharacteristically distracted and forgot about the December flights.

page 258: not a "stunt altitude flight," . . .: *NYT,* Apr. 1, 1931.

page 258: Shortly after noon . . .: GPP, *SW,* p. 208; *NYT,* Apr. 9, 1931.

page 259: a professional pilot . . .: Frank Kingston Smith, *Legacy of Wings,* p. 188.

page 259: a windstorm . . .: *NYT,* June 13, 1931.

page 260: the second accident. . . .: Helen MacElwee, letter to author.

page 260: But writing to her mother . . .: AE, letter to AOE, Sept. 17, 1931, SLRC.

page 260: within a few hours . . .: *NYT,* Sept. 13, 1931.

page 261: At the end of March she wrote . . .: AE, letter to Helen Earhart, Mar. 26, 1932, SLRC.

page 261: The three of them . . .: LC, diary, for Apr. 16 and the following days.

page 263: To increase the Vega's range, . . .: Eddie Gorski, in *Spotlight,* July 1987; FAA records; Harvey H. Lippincott (corporate archivist, United Aircraft), letter to Richard S. Allen, Oct. 18, 1974; NASM files, original Department of Commerce documents.

page 263: "dropping bombs,": Gorski, in *Spotlight,* July 1987.

page 265: knocked unconscious. . . .: Richard S. Allen, *Revolution in the Sky,* pp. 61–62.

page 266: "across the South Atlantic.": C. B. Allen, "The Vindication of Amelia Earhart," NASM.

page 267: talked the townspeople . . .: Bill Parsons, *The Challenge of the Atlantic,* p. 14.

page 268: Twenty-four miles away . . .: *NYT,* May 22, 1932.

page 268: made the opposite decision . . .: *NYT,* May 22, 1932.

page 268: "it just oozed.": Bill Parsons, letter to author.

page 268: WESTERN FLYING WANTS . . .: telegram from AE to Mrs. H. V. Thaden, sent on May 20, 1932; Ninety-Nine files.

page 269: weather began to deteriorate; . . .: Stuart Porter (scientific services meteorologist, St. John's), letter to author, Sept. 3, 1987: "It is not surprising that she would pick up icing in this cloud at 12,000 feet."

page 269: (When Ben Howard . . .: Ben Howard, Columbia OH.

page 269: As dawn broke, . . .: GPP, *SW,* p. 108. Her barograph showed an almost vertical drop of three thousand feet, marking the moment her plane iced up and went into a spin.

page 269: fuel line was defective . . .: *NYT,* May 22, 1932.

page 270: "Tell my friends . . .": Ibid.

page 271: Wrote American columnist . . .: GPP, *WM,* p. 295.

page 271: A while later . . .: *Literary Digest,* June 4, 1932.

page 271: Finally she asked . . .: LC, diary, 1932.

page 272: "My first impression . . .": Gordon Selfridge, interview by JM, SLRC.

page 273: She had entered a realm beyond stardom.: Gore Vidal.

page 273: Have you ever longed . . .: AE, "Flying the Atlantic," *American Magazine,* Aug. 1932.

page 273: "Miss Earhart has . . .": NYHT, Nov. 7, 1932.

Elinor Smith never forgave Amelia for beating her out, and from then on she tried to smear Amelia's reputation. In fact, she denied there had ever been a race to be the first woman to fly the Atlantic. She may have been unaware that her request to the State Department for permission to fly to Newfoundland, Ireland, and France had been filed with other information about the Vega, which had indeed been hers. She claimed her plan had been to fly to Rome across the Alps and that it hadn't come off because her backer didn't have sufficient funds to buy the latest instruments. "The odds against making a safe crossing of the Alps at night without an earth inductor compass were just too great in my mind," she wrote in her book *Aviatrix,* which wasn't true—when she bought the plane, one of its unusual pieces of equipment had been an earth inductor compass. She also claimed she had sold the plane to Amelia, which was also not true: a month after Amelia's flight, she sold the plane, by then in her husband's name, to William W. Harts, Jr. *He* sold it to Amelia, after she sold her own Vega to the Franklin Institute, FAA Registry files, Oklahoma City, Okla.

Having Her Cake

page 275: "I thought . . .": Jean Backus, *Letters from Amelia,* p. 128.
page 275: "most treasured" . . .: GPP, *SW,* p. 115.
page 276: stuff of legend: . . .: Obituary, Eugene Luther Vidal, Class of November 1918, West Point, West Point alumni publication.
page 277: their marriage was on the rocks.: Gore Vidal, *Palimpsest,* pp. 67–71.
page 278: "When you see a pilot dance . . .": JM, *LITHW,* VI p. 8, SLRC.
page 278: She had blossomed, . . .: KCP interview.
page 278: Amelia drove . . .: LC, diary, July 15, 1932.
page 278: By the time they arrived, . . .: LC, diary July 23–Aug. 1, 1932.
page 279: Her hair blew . . .: *New York World Telegram,* Aug. 25, 1932; photo just after landing in Newark.
page 280: "The impossible . . .": Joseph Corn, *Winged Gospel,* p. 14.
page 280: "George low.": LC, diary, Oct. 16, 1932.
page 280: notes the historian . . .: Doris Kearns Goodwin, *No Ordinary Time,* pp. 89–90.
page 280: "I think that every woman . . .": *Cosmopolitan,* Apr. 1933.
page 280: Her closest friend . . .: Doris Faber, *The Life of Lorena Hickok.*
page 281: (They would be limited to women . . .: Hickok, *Reluctant First Lady,* p. 108.
page 281: "Thank you very much . . .": Papers of Eleanor Roosevelt, FDRL.
page 281: "I hope to know . . .": *Poughkeepsie Eagle-News,* Nov. 20, 1932; *Sunday Courier,* Nov. 20, 1932.
page 282: rode the bobsled . . .: Faber, *Life of Lorena Hickok.*
page 282: taught to shoot . . .: *NYT,* Feb. 21, 1934.
page 282: "The question now . . .": GPP, *SW,* p. 132.
page 282: "My husband convinced me . . .": Eleanor Roosevelt, letter to AE, April 4, 1933.
page 282: "But I always fly . . .": *PA,* Apr. 1934.
page 283: "Amelia, lets see . . .": GPP, *SW,* p. 130.
page 283: "The example set . . .": AE, speech before the Daughters of the American Revolution, April 21, 1933.
page 283: Eleanor thought so much . . .: JM, *LITHW,* XVI p. 6, SLRC.
page 283: it *was* arranged . . .: AE, telegram to Louis Howe, Apr. 5, 1933, asking for a three-minute interview with the president "TOMORROW, THURSDAY, OR FRIDAY" and arranged for Wednesday, Apr. 12, at three thirty; FDRL. George did not have the same access; he had to write to

Basil O'Connor and ask him to put his ideas before FDR (as he did May 19, 1933).

page 284: "force airplane designers . . .": Don Dwiggins, *They Flew the Bendix,* p. 16.

page 284: named for Vincent Bendix, . . .: Ibid.

page 284: languishing in dead storage . . .: FAA Aircraft Registry files, every change of ownership, noted as well as other detailed information.

page 285: The men waited longer, . . .: *NYT,* July 2, 1933.

page 286: The only pilot . . .: Ibid.

page 286: Florence Klingensmith, . . .: *PA,* Nov. 1933.

page 286: known to be dangerous planes.: Only seven were built. When Don Dwiggins wrote his history of the Bendix races, *They Flew the Bendix,* he titled one chapter, "Gee Bees—Born to Kill."

page 287: white coveralls . . .: *NYT,* July 9, 1933.

page 287: driver's side, . . .: Doris Rich, *Amelia Earhart,* p. 167.

page 287: "It is a business trip . . .": July 13, 1933, in Backus, *Letters from Amelia,* p. 147.

page 287: Amy Mollison, . . .: LC, diary, July 23, 1933.

page 287: "Call for help . . .": Ibid., Aug. 14, 1933.

page 288: "We talked . . .": Ibid., Aug. 16, 1933.

page 288: Later in the week Amelia was . . .: *NYT,* Aug. 22, 1933.

page 288: "After all I did not . . .": AE, letter to Dot Leh, Sept. 8, 1933, Ninety-Nines files.

page 288: Gene came . . .: LC, diary, Sept. 22, 1933.

page 289: Instead he divided . . .: Nick A. Komons, *Bonfires to Beacons.* The two assistant aeronautical directors, Carroll Cone and Rex Martin, were both eager to expand their powers.

page 289: nice perks . . .: Gore Vidal, in *New York Review of Books,* Jan. 17, 1985.

page 289: The next day Amelia drove him . . .: LC, diary, Sept. 22 and 23, 1933. Shortly thereafter Lucy became school editor for *Vogue.* The intimacy of Amelia and Gene's relationship is fixed by Lucy's diary entries; Lucy spent the next months visiting schools, not in Rye.

page 290: "Because I ventured . . .": AE, letter to FDR, Nov. 5, 1933; C. B. Allen, in *NYHT,* SLRC.

page 290: on Amelia's recommendation . . .: Rich, *Amelia Earhart,* p. 181.

page 290: They even had lunch . . .: LC, diary, Jan. 8, 1934. "Gene came in" was Lucy's cryptic entry.

page 290: he still managed to restore . . .: C. B. Allen, in *NYHT,* Nov. 5, 1933.

page 291: "but damn little assistance.": U.S. Air Services, Nov. 1936, quoted Nick A. Komons, from *Bonfires to Beacons,* p. 233.

page 291: "too amiable": *NYT,* Feb. 28, 1937.

page 291: modeling clay . . .: JM, *LITHW,* III p. 4, SLRC.

page 291: toward Amy Lowell . . .: JM, *LITHW,* XVI p. 5, SLRC.

page 292: "she always wore my shorts . . .": Vidal, *New York Review of Books,* Jan. 17, 1985.

page 292: "Gene used to buy them . . .": Katharine Vidal Smith, interview with author.

page 292: "She adored my father," . . .: Gore Vidal, interview with author.

page 292: childhood crush . . .: Vidal, *New York Review of Books,* Jan. 17, 1985.

page 292: When he blurted this out, . . .: Gore Vidal, *Palimpsest,* caption above picture of Amelia and Gene.

page 292: During this period . . .: Rich, *Amelia,* p. 230.

page 292: "She used to practice . . .": JM, *LITHW,* XII p. 5, SLRC.

page 292: shy away . . .: JM, *LITHW,* XII p. 15, SLRC.

page 292: hygienic considerations . . . .: Gene did tell JM that she became a "bug on health." JM, XII p. 13, SLRC.

page 292: "Because it . . .": JM, *LITHW,* III p. 2, SLRC.

page 293: "with apples.": JM, *LITHW,* XII p. 15, Jack Gillies, the husband of flier Betty Huyler Gillies, would tell JM.

page 293: "I wish to be free . . .": *Washington Evening Star,* Aug. 6, 1935.

page 293: roaring with laughter . . .: Rich, *Amelia,* p. 153.

page 293: he successfully roped . . .: Mrs. Jack Logan, article in unidentified magazine, sent to author by Vera Dunrud.

page 293: They spent five days . . .: Carl M. Dunrud, "amelia earhart in wyoming," *In Wyoming,* Jan.–Feb. 1974.

page 294: "George is going with me . . .": Backus, *Letters from Amelia,* p. 137.

page 294: Only two people . . .: Katharine Vidal Smith, interview with author; Vidal interview.

page 294: To touch your hand . . .: GPP, *SW,* p. 171.

page 295: The four of them . . .: James Haggerty, *Aviation's Mr. Sam,* p. 28.

page 295: left Rye at four thirty . . .: LC, diary, July 24, 1933.

page 296: Paul asked for a car . . .: Paul Collins, *Tales of an Old Air-Faring Man,* p. 134.

page 296: a good feel.: JM, *LITHW,* XIII, SLRC; Paul Collins interview in Haggerty, *Aviation's Mr. Sam:* "We stopped in at a wayside lunchroom during an inspection trip. Amelia borrowed a pencil and piece of paper from the waitress and started to figure. Pretty soon she came up with thirty cents a mile. It was right for the situation and showed the clarity with which her mind worked."

page 296: By October . . .: R. E. G. Davis, *Airlines of the United States Since 1914,* p. 51.

page 297: Because of her, . . .: Collins, *Old Air-Faring Man,* p. 138.

page 297: That Christmas . . .: Christmas card, Atchison Public Library.

Role Model

page 298: Louise Thaden, winner of . . .: Joan Thomas, *PA,* May 1934.

page 299: She sent a sample suit . . .: Ninety-Nines files, Will Rogers Airport, Oklahoma City, Okla.

page 299: clothes "for the woman who lives actively.": GPP, *SW,* p. 205.

page 299: In St. Paul as a teenager, . . .: MEM, *CITP,* p. 90.

page 300: "covered with silver stars . . .": Sally Keil, *Those Wonderful Women in Their Flying Machines,* p. 31.

page 300: when Lucy Challiss . . .: LC, diary, July 12, 1932.

page 300: often parachute silk, . . .: JM, *LITHW,* SLRC; *Christian Herald,* Feb. 1938.

page 300: In all, thirty department stores . . .: Thomas, *PA.,* May 1934.

page 301: "I made up my mind . . .": GP, *SW,* p. 205.

page 301: "Amelia Earhart, Designer," . . .: *Woman's Home Companion,* Aug. 1934.

page 301: a Ninety-Nine "Hat Contest" . . .: Thomas, *PA,* May 1934.

page 302: "I have been drinking cream . . .": AE, letter to AOE, Jan. 27, 1933, AOE papers, SLRC.

page 302: "It's a routine . . .": Doris Rich, *Amelia Earhart,* p. 155.

page 302: held her to be . . .: Thomas, *PA,* May 1935.

page 302: "as though they had been . . .": *Brockton Daily Enterprise,* Dec. 11, 1935.

page 302: "without a sound . . .": Ibid.

page 302: As she described . . .: JM, *LITHW,* III p. 4, SLRC.

page 303: "Smartly tailored evening ensemble": *News Herald* [Rock Hill, S.C.], Jan. 1, 1936.

page 303: "relieved only by . . .": *Brockton Daily Enterprise,* Dec. 11, 1935.

page 303: another wrote . . .: *St. Paul Pioneer Express,* Oct. 8, 1935.

page 304: "In aviation as a whole . . .": AE, "Choosing a Career," 1934.

page 304: Or she might say . . .: AE, speech to Winthrop College students, Rock Hill, S.C., *Evening Herald,* Jan. 17, 1936.

page 304: machines were too much man-made . . .: *PA,* Oct. 1931.

page 304: "Ask her to come . . .": KCP interview.

page 305: "It was a gorgeous night . . .": Backus, *Letters From Amelia,* p. 149.

page 305: She spent the next two weeks . . .: AE, lecture schedule (mismarked as probably 1932), SLRC.

page 305: Fourteen days . . .: AE, 1936 lecture schedule, SLRC.

page 305: The amazing thing . . .: Joan Thomas, *PA,* June 1934: "The curiosity of the public seems unabated after 2 years of almost constant lecturing."

page 306: It seemed as if everyone important . . .: *NYHT,* Sept. 27, 1934.

page 307: he intended to slip out, . . .: JM, *LITHW,* XVI p. 13, SLRC.

page 307: her friend Clara Studer, . . ." Clara Studer, "Donne Pilota Americana," manuscript, Oct. 1934, NASM.

page 307: He knew that to solve . . .: Robert Topping, *A Century and Beyond,* p. 233.

page 308: "We want you . . .": GPP, *SW,* p. 242

page 308: make Purdue the center . . .: Todd Fruehling, in *Purdue Alumnus,* Dec. 1975; sent to author by the Purdue Research Foundation.

page 308: the effective education . . .: Topping, *Century and Beyond,* p. 233.

page 308: A few years before, . . .: *NYT,* May 9, 1931.

page 308: "her primary interest . . .": *NYT,* Nov. 28, 1937.

page 309: The department would be energized . . .: Fruehling, *Purdue Alumnus,* Dec. 1975.

page 309: The next year . . .: *Where They Go and What They Do,* Purdue University publication, pp 16, 17.

page 310: "Today it is almost . . .": Fruehling, *Purdue Alumnus,* Dec. 1975.

page 310: In January 1935 . . .: William Manchester, *The Glory and the Dream*, p. 127.

page 310: "Marry Them Early; . . .": Dorothy Thompson publicized the incident, in *NYHT*, Sept. 27, 1934.

page 311: "she was a very courageous . . .: Fred Cavinder, in *Indianapolis Star Magazine*, Dec. 12, 1976, Purdue Research Foundation files.

page 311: A rumor was floated . . .: Topping, *Century and Beyond*, p. 234.

page 311: That summer . . .: *Fortune*, July 1935.

page 311: Amelia gave afternoon talks . . .: Ellen Carter Bossong (Purdue alumna), letter to author.

page 311: "When you graduate . . .": Audrie Soles (Purdue alumna), letter to author.

page 311: "outspoken" ideas: Marian Sharer Fitzgerald (Purdue alumna), letter to author.

page 312: "Many divorces . . .": John Burke, *Winged Legend*, p. 161.

page 312: 92 percent . . .: GPP, *SW*, p. 247.

page 312: A prestigious men's senior . . .: Helen Schleman, speech, Nov. 26, 1984.

page 312: On the other hand . . .: Orin A. Simpson (Purdue alumnus), letter to author.

page 313: "We were indeed fortunate,". . .: Fitzgerald letter.

page 313: "But George would *always* . . .: Soles letter.

page 314: She was hired to be co-pilot . . .: Glenn Kerfoot, *Propeller Annie*, p. 43.

page 314: She was sought after to do . . .: Ibid., p. 50.

page 314: "rejected flatly,": Edna Gardner Whyte, *Rising Above It*, p. 176.

page 314: Edith Folz . . .: *PA*, Jan. 1930.

page 314: Ruth Nichols had flown . . .: Ruth Nichols, Columbia OH.

page 315: "not because of lack of . . .": Kerfoot, *Propeller Annie*, p. 57.

page 316: "It was not an order, . . .": *NYT*, Nov. 7, 1935.

page 316: "Miss Richey's father . . .": Kerfoot, *Propeller Annie*, p. 58.

page 316: "Certainly Miss Earhart herself . . .": *NYT*, Nov. 8, 1935.

page 316: "Miss Earhart has told the story . . .": *NYHT*, Nov. 7, 1935.

page 316: "I thought that it was . . .": Ruth Nichols, Columbia OH.

page 317: "Things are changing . . .": AP article datelined Lafayette, Indiana, Nov. 7, 1935.

page 317: fifty percent . . .: Office of the Registrar, Purdue University.

page 317: George, no amateur himself . . .: GPP, *SW*, p. 272.

page 317: "the most potent . . .": Purdue publicity release from the Office of the President, Apr. 19, 1935.

page 318: Present were David Ross . . .: This account is based on information sent to me by W. D. Griggs, assistant treasurer, Purdue Research Foundation.

page 318: The purpose of the fund, . . .: Purdue publicity release from the Office of the President, Apr. 19, 1935.

page 318: "to provide ways and means . . .": article by Priscilla Decker based on the three official reports labeled "Amelia Earhart Fund for Aeronautical Research," that appeared in *Campus Copy,* Oct. 1962, a Purdue publication.

page 318: "Upon her return . . .": Topping, *Century and Beyond,* p. 235.

New Records

page 321: twin attractions . . .: *NYT,* Sept. 18, 1933.

page 322: It had been almost within her reach; . . .: Bobbi Trout, *Just Plane Crazy,* pp. 220–227.

page 322: she dropped the bomb . . .: LC, diary, Oct. 6, 1934.

page 323: scuffed upstairs . . .: *Christian Science Monitor,* Jan. 9, 1935.

page 323: So final . . .: Manhattan telephone directory, 1934–36.

page 324: "only for communication . . .": *NYT,* Nov. 22, 1934.

page 324: "not contemplating any long flight.": *NYT,* Nov. 22, 1934.

page 324: Amelia had her picture . . .: Doris Rich, *Amelia Earhart,* p. 187.

page 324: The coast guard cutter *Itasca* . . .: Don Dwiggins, *Hollywood Pilot,* p. 90.

page 324: She "may" . . .: *NYT,* Dec. 19, 1934.

page 324: "I thought I would . . .": GPP, *SW,* p. 256.

page 325: Major Halstead Dorey, . . .: JM, notes, SLRC.

page 325: "There is nothing intelligent . . .": quoted in the *NYT,* Nov. 30, 1934.

page 325: To disprove it . . . GPP, *SW,* p. 258.

page 325: "Gentleman, there is an aroma of . . .": John Burke, *Winged Legend,* p. 147.

page 326: a trailing wire antenna jutted out . . .: Richard S. Allen, diagram, NASM.

page 326: "a large black box, . . .": AE, *LF,* p. 23.

page 327: two and a half feet long . . .: GPP, *SW,* p. 212.

page 327: "A.E., the noise . . .": AE, *LF,* p. 27.

page 327: "It was a night of stars," . . .: Ibid.

page 327: "I am getting tired . . .": Ibid., p. 31.

page 327: "Not while there's life . . .: *NYT,* Jan. 13, 1935.

page 328: "I thought there might be . . .": Ibid.

page 328: The Nation, acting a bit prim, . . .: *Nation,* Jan. 30, 1935.

page 328: She extended Amelia . . .: Eleanor Roosevelt, telegram to AE, Jan. 16, 1935, FDRL.

page 328: "you need not always . . .": Eleanor Roosevelt, letter to AE, Mar. 12, 1935, FDRL.

page 329: "Would you like GP . . .": AE, letter to Eleanor Roosevelt, Mar. 9, 1935, FDRL.

page 329: "GP has left . . .": Jean Backus, *Letters From Amelia,* p. 171.

page 329: "touching on matters . . .": GPP, letter to Eleanor Roosevelt, Mar. 14, 1935, FDRL.

page 329: Eleanor shot this down. . . .: Eleanor Roosevelt, to GPP, Mar. 15, 1935, FDRL.

page 329: "No discussion . . .": GPP, letter to Eleanor Roosevelt, Mar. 19, 1935, FDRL.

page 329: "if Amelia is free.": Eleanor Roosevelt, letter to GPP, Mar. 22, 1935, FDRL.

page 329: "Definitely a plane . . .": GPP, letter to Eleanor Roosevelt, Mar. 25, 1935, FDRL.

page 329: Tugwell felt . . .: Rexford Tugwell, letter to Eleanor Roosevelt, Apr. 15, 1935, FDRL.

page 330: he thought her decision "admirable,": GPP, letter to Eleanor Roosevelt, May 24, 1935.

page 330: Within a short time . . .: Maurine Beasley, *Eleanor Roosevelt and the Media,* p. 82.

page 330: he was "highly irritated . . .": Mexico Press Agency, National Archives.

page 331: Their sale, some reputedly . . .: *Newsweek,* May 11, 1935.

page 331: She pulled out her chart . . .: AE, *LF,* p. 36.

page 331: At the Mexico City . . .: *NYT,* Apr. 21, 1935.

page 332: "Nature does as thorough . . .": *NYT,* May 3, 1935.

page 333: "Slowly I climbed . . .": AE, *LF,* p. 42.

page 333: "Did Wiley Post, . . .": Ibid., pp. 34–35.

page 333: shot out over the Gulf.: . . .: *Newsweek,* May 18, 1935.

page 334: As her green and red navigation lights . . .: *NYT,* May 9, 1935.

page 334: Reporters noted that he . . .: *Newsweek,* May 18, 1935.

page 334: "her face was tanned . . .": *NYT,* May 9, 1935.

page 334: "That's a *flier!*": GPP, *SW,* p. 270.

page 334: "No one should . . .": AE, *LF,* p. 31.

page 335: The newspaper coverage . . .: *NYT,* May 9, 1935.

New Frontiers

page 336: After all, . . .: William Manchester, *The Glory and the Dream,* p. 149.

page 336: "Flying with me . . ." *New York World Telegram,* May 9, 1935.

page 336: "I received an invitation . . .": Ibid.

page 336: All the famous fliers, . . .: Carl B. Allen article, NASM.

page 337: "During the menstrual period . . .": Malcolm C. Grow and Henry G. Armstrong, *Fit to Fly.*

page 337: In 1943 the Air Transport Command . . .: Sally Keil, *Those Wonderful Women in Their Flying Machines,* p. 129.

page 337: The order only became moot, . . .: Ibid, p. 169.

page 338: Amelia was assembling evidence.: GPP, *SW,* p. 163.

page 338: "We never think about it . . .": Ibid.

page 339: she spoke 136 times . . .: Don Dwiggins, *Hollywood Pilot,* p. 95.

page 339: a time when the average stenographer . . .: *Fortune,* Aug. 1935.

page 339: He had watched . . .: Biographical information from Dwiggins, *Hollywood Pilot.*

page 340: But in September 1934 he buzzed . . .: Ibid., p. 79.

page 340: While testing Amelia's Vega . . .: Ibid., p. 144.

page 340: "Damn near . . .": GPP, *SW,* p. 235.

page 340: "warmed their paws . . .": Ibid.

page 340: She had stayed with the Mantzes . . .: Dwiggins, *Hollywood Pilot,* p. 78.

page 340: There was never evidence . . .: Ibid.

page 341: each got twenty thousand dollars.: James Haggerty, *Aviation's Mr. Sam,* p. 38; JM, *LITHW,* SLRC.

page 341: "all hep about this too.": AE, letter to AOE, Jul. 28, 1935, Backus, *Letters,* p. 178.

page 341: "constant hammering": Dwiggins, *Hollywood Pilot,* p. 86.

page 342: "the old family bus,": Paul owned an equally old and slow Vega; according to Don Dwiggins, they couldn't decide which would be faster and finally flipped to see which one to use—but the story lacks credibility. Possibly this is what Paul told his biographer to save face, but it would not have been Amelia's style to race across the country in a plane with *The Honeymoon Express* emblazoned on its fuselage.

page 343: It was just one more flight . . .: *NYHT,* Aug. 31, 1935.

page 343: Then Amelia went off . . .: AE itinerary, Sept. 30 to Nov. 3, SLRC.

page 343: "I'd like to find the tree . . .": *St. Paul Pioneer Press,* Oct. 6, 1935.

page 344: "Wiley, you'd better . . .": Clarence L. Johnson with Maggie Smith, *More Than My Share of It All,* p. 41.

page 345: There were four Electra 10 models, . . .: Ibid., p. 50.

page 346: "My boss called me . . .": John A. Diehl, letter to author.

page 346: She was one of two . . .: *PA,* Oct. 1937.

page 346: "sensible, very studious, . . .": Johnson, *More Than My Share,* p. 46.

page 346: "I could write poetry . . .": *NYT,* Aug. 30, 1935.

page 347: Later they had to deal . . .: Glenn Kerfoot, *Propeller Annie,* p. 65.

page 347: Their problems paled, . . .: Louise Thaden, *High, Wide, and Frightened,* p. 184.

page 347: "I'm afraid you won . . .": Blanche Noyes, Columbia OH, p. 22.

page 348: "I don't think there was a jealous . . .": Ibid., p. 35.

page 348: "I don't know . . .": *NYT,* Sept. 6, 1936.

page 348: she was obviously nervous": *Washington Post,* May 1, 1936.

page 349: "Amelia has consented . . .": Paul Mantz, letter to Gene Vidal, June 26, 1936, Vidal collection, American Heritage Center, University of Wyoming.

page 349: "Still can't leave here.": Gene Vidal, letter to AE, June 30, 1936, Vidal collection.

page 349: What did Amelia think?: Gene Vidal, letter to AE, June 16, 1936, Vidal collection.

page 349: "After your note . . .": Gene Vidal to AE, June 30, 1936, Vidal Collection.

page 349: "it is the quietest period . . .": Gene Vidal, letter to AE, Aug. 14, 1936, Vidal collection.

page 349: even though FDR . . .: White House Ushers Diary.

page 350: I AM WIRING . . .: FDRL.

page 350: burst out laughing. . . .: JM, *LITHW,* XVI p. 11, SLRC.

page 350: The next day he had lunch . . .: *NYT,* Sept. 17, 1936.

page 351: THANK YOU SINCERELY . . .: AE, cable to Eleanor Roosevelt, FDRL.

page 351: "I am aligned . . .": *NYT,* Sept. 20, 1936.

page 351: she, not George, was at the wheel . . .: *NYT,* Sept. 27, 1936.

page 352: "she plans to include . . .": Gene Vidal, letter to Mary Dewson, Dewson file, FDRL.

page 352: "We really are very grateful . . .": Mary Dewson, letter to Gene Vidal, Oct. 1, 1936. Dewson file, FDRL.

page 352: "What *color* is . . .": JM, *LITHW,* XVI p. 5, SLRC.

page 352: "as her fans peered . . ." Gore Vidal, *Armageddon,* p. 25.

page 352: The first person to race . . .: Carroll V. Glines, *Round-the-World Flights,* p. ix. This account of the first round-the-world travelers is based on Glines' excellent book.

page 353: By 1913, . . .: Ibid., p. x.

page 353: "Would you do it . . .": Ibid., p. 1.

page 353: Major Jimmy Doolittle . . .: *Air Pilot* magazine, Apr. 1933.

page 353: Wiley Post and Harold Gatty, . . .: Glines, *Round-the-World Flights,* p. 63.

page 354: Amy Mollison . . .: International Women's Air and Space Museum, Quarterly, vol. I no. 3 (1987).

page 354: Here was shining adventure . . .: AE, *LF,* p. 55.

The Plan

page 356: "She was caught up in the hero racket . . .": Railey, *Touch'd with Madness,* p. 110.

page 356: "it is the only major flight . . .": Louise Thaden, *High, Wide, and Frightened,* p. 260.

page 357: The Purdue Research Foundation statement . . .: Report of the director of the Purdue Research Foundation, G. Stanley Meikle, in *Campus Copy* (former Purdue publication), Oct. 1962.

page 357: "become associated in the . . .": Ibid.

page 357: Purdue had already been involved . . .: *PA,* July 1936.

page 357: The most important subject today . . .: *St. Louis Post-Dispatch,* Apr. 7, 1936.

page 358: He arranged for a leading . . .: Carl Allen, unpublished manuscript, NASM.

page 358: The furnishings . . .: JM, *The Christian Herald* magazine, Jan. 1936.

page 358: "a Roman dream of elegance, . . .": GPP to AOE, Nov. 16, 1937.

page 358: "I am deeply sorry . . .": AE, letter to MEM, Jan. 31, 1937, SLRC.

page 359: "Please tell Pidge . . .": AE, letter to MEM, Nov. 23, 1935, Jean Backus, *Letters from Amelia,* p. 183.

page 359: "was just completely covered . . .": MEM, Columbia OH.

page 359: The Department of Agriculture . . .: Capt. E.C. Edelmann. *America's First Lady of Flight,* Fraternal Order of Air Mail Pilots, June 1, 1962.

page 360: Would Gene find out . . .: GPP, letter to Gene Vidal, Aug. 3, 1936, State Department records, National Archives.

page 360: The original proposed route . . .: GPP, letter to Gene Vidal, Oct. 15, 1936, State Department records, National Archives.

page 361: superbly manipulative letter . . .: Malvina Schneider, letter to Southgate, June 29, 1936, FDRL.

page 361: Every single country . . .: Numerous letters from the State Department to foreign governments, National Archives. Only France thought to query the department as to the intrinsic safety of the so-configured Electra.

page 361: "considers the plane to be satisfactory . . .": State Department files, National Archives.

page 361: "There is no hope of permission . . .": Day letter from Southgate, Mar. 8, 1937, National Archives.

page 361: "Dear Mrs. Earhart," . . .: GPP, letter to AOE, Jan. 16, 1937, SLRC.

page 362: The navy, according to internal memos, . . .: Records of the office of the Chief of Naval Operations, National Archives.

page 362: "Dear Mr. President; . . .: AE, letter to FDR, Nov. 10, 1936, FDRL.

page 363: "The ability of the pilot of the receiving plane . . .": Commander Aircraft, Base Force, letter to Commander in Chief, U.S. Fleet, Nov. 29, 1936, National Archives.

page 363: Moreover, Pan American . . .: *NYT,* Mar. 14, 1935. Pan Am immediately began loading a supply ship at Seattle with machinery and equipment for its air bases.

page 364: The first China Clipper . . .: William Grooch, *Skyway to Asia,* p. 129.

page 364: "whoever first moved . . .": C. B. Allen, *NYHT,* Feb. 28, 1937.

page 365: "there is gallantry even in . . .": Ibid.

page 365: "During the late part of 1936," . . .: Richard Black, Columbia OH.

page 365: Gene sent Robert L. Campbell, . . .: Ibid.

page 365: She wrote about her . . .: Acting budget director, memo to FDR, Jan. 8, 1937, FDRL.

page 366: "competent aviation mechanics . . .": GPP to secretary of war, Jan. 30, 1937, National Archives.

page 366: Brad received a phone call . . .: Washburn interview. At least one other biographer, Paul Briand, Jr., interviewed Washburn. Washburn, a scrupulously honest man, must have told Briand that Amelia never asked him to be navigator, and in the interests of telling a good story, Briand left it out of his book.

page 367: He, too, remembered spreading . . .: Paul Collins, *Tales of an Old Air-Faring Man,* p. 147.

page 367: The navy was notified . . .: Telegram, naval files, National Archives.

page 368: He would be visiting . . .: *NYT,* Mar. 5, 1937.

page 368: "I can say this much, . . .": *NYT,* Mar. 21, 1937.

page 368: Gene's orders to William Miller . . .: Secretary of the navy, cable of instructions, Feb. 15, 1937, National Archives.

page 369: The countdown . . .: Amelia planned to put the maps into one suitcase; that and another suitcase, containing an extra pair of slacks, a few shirts, a mechanic's garb, a change of linen, and a toothbrush, were all she would take with her. Four half-pound Nestlé chocolate bars, six cans of malted milk tablets, three one-pound packages of raisins, one package of dried apricots, one package of prunes, two cans of ripe bananas, and three cans of tomato juice would end up stored in a waterproof zipper bag.

page 369: (Amelia posed with the loop . . .: *NYHT,* Mar. 7, 1937.

page 369: "unless the weather . . .": *San Francisco Chronicle,* Mar. 11, 1937.

page 369: the lowest barometric reading . . .: *San Francisco Chronicle,* Mar. 13, 1937.

page 369: Amelia was handling . . .: Ibid.

page 369: "Well, between 185 pounds . . .": *San Francisco Chronicle,* Mar. 11, 1937.

page 370: The Pan Am plan . . .: This account, and subsequent accounts, are based on information from William Grooch, *Skyway to Asia.*

page 370: "Scared?" she repeated. . . .: *NYT,* Mar. 13, 1937.

page 370: black, orange, and red stripes . . .: *NYHT,* Mar. 7, 1937.

page 370: he enlisted the aid . . .: Don Dwiggins, *Hollywood Pilot,* p. 96.

page 371: "She was very sensible, . . .": Johnson, *More Than My Share of It All,* p. 53.

page 371: She didn't drive him crazy . . .: Ibid., p. 46.

page 371: four feet eight inches . . .: AE, *LF,* p. 183.

page 371: Amelia planned to broadcast . . .: C. B. Allen, *NYHT,* Mar. 16, 1937.

page 372: When the China Clipper . . .: *PA,* July 1936.

page 372: "She and Putnam exchanged . . .": C. B. Allen, draft of a review of *The True Amelia Earhart Story,* NASM.

page 372: "as she writes . . .": C. B. Allen, *NYHT,* Mar. 15, 1937.

page 372: "she hardly ever refuses . . .": Ibid.

Years later, when Allen was searching for a scapegoat for Amelia's disappearance, he hit upon George, and in his mind's eye he was sure that the stay at the Oakland airport had lasted weeks, not days, and that Amelia had felt that she had to escape from her husband. Allen wrote, "Toward the end of the first week I spent with the couple at Oakland Airport, Amelia told me she would be leaving Friday afternoon 'to get away from things here and relax in the desert until Monday at Palm Springs.' I gave her a searching look but said nothing." Only one trouble—it wasn't true. Amelia was observed flying or talking at the Oakland airport every day.

page 373: Manning was "perturbed" . . .: *NYHT,* Mar. 13, 1937.

page 373: "All were in high spirits . . .": *NYHT,* Mar. 14, 1937.

page 374: "The two of us, . . .": Johnson, *More Than My Share,* p. 44.

page 374: As she told Carl Allen, . . .: *NYHT,* Mar. 14, 1937.

page 375: According to Page Smith, . . .: Page Smith, interview with author.

page 375: "didn't think he was a great risk" . . .: Clara Livingston, interview with author.

page 375: She then asked Gene . . .: Gore Vidal, *New York Review of Books,* Jan. 17, 1985.

page 375: "might have missed a trip . . .": Smith interview.

page 375: "Amelia Earhart urgently requests . . .": Mar. 16, 1937, SLRC.

page 375: "to assume complete responsibility . . .": *NYHT,* Mar. 14, 1937.

page 376: The Oakland airport switchboard . . .: *NYHT,* Mar. 17, 1937.

page 377: "Her husband was . . .: *NYHT,* Mar. 18, 1937.

page 378: Bill Miller sent off the cable . . .: Naval message, National Archives.

page 378: He smiled . . .: UPI, Mar. 17, 1937, unidentified newspaper, SLRC.

The Beginning

page 379: Paul circled . . .: *NYHT,* Mar. 18, 1937.

page 379: "in a steep bank": Don Dwiggins, *Hollywood Pilot,* p. 102.

page 379: The landing was terrible . . .: JM, *LITHW,* XIII, SLRC.

page 379: "very fatigued . . .": Ibid.

page 380: "Mr. Mantz departed . . .": Records of the U.S. Army Overseas Operations and Commands, This information is contained in the report of the Hawaiian Air Force Headquarters investigation "upon the crash of Miss Amelia Earhart's airplane NR 16020 at Luke Field, Oahu . . . and circumstances relating to her arrival and stay at Wheeler and Luke Fields, March 18 to 20, 1937," hereinafter referred to as Hawaiian Investigation, National Archives.

page 380: He also told them, "insisted" . . .: Hawaiian Investigation.

page 380: "And speaking of breakfast, . . .": AE, *LF,* p. 67.

page 381: "if it became necessary.": GPP, *SW,* p. 281.

page 382: "The airplane spun . . .": Hawaiian Investigation.

page 382: "that I thought the take-off . . .": AE, *LF,* p. 72.

page 382: Paul's hard landing. . . .: Only to Janet Mabie did she lay the blame at Paul's feet. JM, *LITHW,* SLRC.

page 382: "It is amazing," . . .: GPP, *SW,* p. 281.

page 382: "based on the written . . .": Hawaiian Investigation.

page 383: Lockheed's bill . . .: Lockheed records.

page 383: "because she thought . . .": Harry Bruno, Columbia OH.

page 383: "On the prosaic . . .": AE, *LF,* p. 78.

page 384: "To you Carl. . . .": Carl M. Dunrud, "amelia earhart in wyoming," *In Wyoming,* Jan.–Feb. 1974.

page 384: "Africa," she had answered. . . .: Gore Vidal, *Armageddon,* p. 25.

page 385: I hope your guess . . .: Carl Allen, unpublished manuscript, NASM.

page 385: "No-o-o I don't . . .": JM, *LITHW,* XV p. 6, SLRC.

page 385: "sneak departure.": Dwiggins, *Hollywood Pilot,* p. 105.

page 386: "streaked out of the setting sun, . . .": Reporters, as often happened, suddenly materialized from nowhere as word passed that she was coming down. *New Orleans Times Picayune,* May 23, 1937.

page 386: "I've never been on the ground . . .": Ibid.

page 386: "I thought it would give . . .": AE, *LF,* p. 135.

page 387: "they were willing . . .": Ibid., pp. 88–89.

page 387: "Oh," she said, "that . . .": Allen, manuscript, NASM.

page 388: He ventured a brusque . . .: Helen Day Bible, interview with author.

page 389: "He said," Helen recalled . . .: Ibid.

page 389: "Are you going to drink . . .": Ibid.

page 389: a crowd estimated at five hundred . . .: Doris Rich, *Amelia Earhart*, p. 257.

page 389: Fred called her back . . .: Bible interview.

The Flight

page 392: "besieged" with invitations . . .: Fred Noonan, letter to Helen Day, June 5, 1937, from Fortaleza.

page 392: "little by little . . .": AE, *LF,* p. 113.

page 392: Those routes . . .: FN to Helen Day, June 5, 1937.

page 392: "change to 36 degrees" . . .: AE, *LF,* p. 136.

page 393: "where Frenchmen are . . .": Ibid., p. 142.

page 393: They slept . . .: Fred Noonan, letter to Helen Day, June 22, 1937, from Java.

page 393: Amelia's thoughts strayed back . . .: AE, *LF,* p. 145.

page 393: "as hollow . . .": Ibid., p. 169.

page 394: "We had a glorious . . .": Fred Noonan, letter to Helen Day, June 22, 1937.

page 394: "whole attitude . . .": JM, *LITHW,* XIV, SLRC.

page 394: "Better wear . . .": AE, *LF,* p. 181.

page 394: "robust healthfulness . . .": Ibid., p. 177.

page 395: "You betja! . . .": Ibid., p. 178.

page 395: "a grand person . . .": letter from FM, reprinted in *NYHT,* July 8, 1937.

page 395: notes penciled on pages . . .: Mary Lovell, *The Sound of Wings,* p. 266.

page 395: "I wish you were. . . .": GPP, *WM,* p. 292.

page 395: "giving its pilot . . .": AE, *LF,* p. 191.

page 396: "I'm starting to have . . .": Paul Collins, *Tales of an Old Air-Faring Man,* p. 147.

page 396: "We hoped to squeeze . . .": AE, *LF,* p. 194.

page 396: "after two hours . . .": Ibid., p. 197.

page 396: The hooded clouds . . .: Ibid., p. 199.

page 397: "There were details . . .": *NYHT,* June 22, 1937.

page 397: "filled with flowers.": AE, *LF,* p. 210.

page 397: three-hour car trip . . .: Fred Noonan, letter to Helen Day, June 22, 1937, from Bandung.

page 398: "licked a small trouble . . .": *NYHT,* June 22, 1937.

page 399: "the last conversation" . . .: AE, *LF,* p. 178.

page 399: "I hear the dinner gong . . .:" Fred Noonan, letter to Helen Day, from Kupang, June 27, 1937.

page 399: Amelia, it was noted, . . .": Report by Ang Poen King, KPVM representative, Seaver Center.

page 399: "Once aboard . . .": AE, *LF,* p. 216.

page 400: They replaced it . . .: Enclosure no. 2 to Dispatch no. 507 from the American Consulate-General, Sydney, Australia, August 21, 1937, in file entitled "Round-the-World Flight of Miss Earhart," National Archives.

page 400: "radio phone being used . . .": Ibid.

Lost

page 402: upon which Fred Noonan also relied.: Fred Noonan, letter to Commander P. V. H. Weems, quoted in Mary Lovell, *The Sound of Wings,* p. 396.

page 403: "had some drinks . . .": Ann Pellegreno, *World Flight,* p. 143. Pellegreno, a pilot, replicated Amelia's flight years later and questioned people in Lae.

page 403: "Everyone has been . . .": "By Amelia Earhart By Telephone to the Herald Tribune," *NYHT,* June 30, 1937, datelined Lae, New Guinea.

page 403: "my navigator, has been unable . . .": *NYHT,* July 1, 1937.

page 403: RADIO MISUNDERSTANDING . . .: The telegram, dated June 30, was sent at 5:53 P.M., according to Helen Schreuer (Curator, Earhart Collection, Purdue University).

page 403: The coast guard . . .: Records of the U.S. Army Overseas Operations and Commands, National Archives.

page 403: Gene Vidal told . . .: Gore Vidal, *New York Review of Books,* Jan. 17, 1985.

page 403: Since Amelia's views . . .: JM, *Christian Herald* magazine, Feb. 1938.

page 403: "Amelia stated that she was still . . .": Paul Collins, *Tales of an Old Air-Faring Man,* p. 148.

page 404: "Denmark's a prison.": AE, *LF,* p. 223.

page 404: "We commandeered . . .": Ibid., p. 224.

page 404: There was no partying . . .: Pellegreno, *World Flight,* p. 194.

page 404: Several junior flight officers . . .: William Grooch, *Skyway to Asia,* p. 177.

page 404: "The crew maintained . . .": Ibid., p. 89.

page 404: he was dead on course . . .: Ibid., p. 194.

page 405: "Making the landfall . . .": AE, *LF,* p. 66.

page 405: For Earhart, Lae . . .: Copy of weather report, sent to William Miller at the Bureau of Air Commerce in response to his query; dated July 22, 1937, from Richard Black.

page 406: Southeast trade winds . . .: *NYHT,* June 4, 1937.

page 407: According to navy records, . . .: "The following weather forecast was received by the navigator prior departure Lae; Lae to 165 degrees E: winds ESE 12–15; 165 degrees to 175 degrees: ENE 18; 175 degrees E to Howland; ENE 15 and squalls to be detoured."

page 407: As the plane reached . . .: Pellegreno, *World Flight,* p. 144; Bertie Heath, interview with Pellegreno.

page 407: Not much more . . .: AE, *LF,* p. 226.

page 408: The chart of the area . . .: Number 1198, published by the Hydrographic Office for the navy in 1919.

page 408: the coordinates to the day beacon . . .: Position of Howland Island, NOAA, Office of Coast Survey; James Dailey, interview with author.

page 408: emulating Amelia's world flight, . . .: Pellegreno, *World Flight,* p. 191.

page 409: the sky was clear to the south . . .: Report of the *Itasca* to the *Colorado* in explanation of why they first started searching to the northwest.

page 409: "Cloudy weather cloudy.": *Itasca,* cable to Commander, San Francisco Division, July 6, 1937. There were later, edited versions, as the coast guard cleaned up its report, but all versions are similar, with very slight variations.

page 410: "This was a trick . . .": Richard Black, Columbia OH.

Later

page 412: "a craft of that type . . .": AE in *National Geographic,* May 1935.

page 413: The sharks . . .: Report of Lt. Daniel Cooper, Army Air Corps observer in charge of repairing the runways on Howland, navy records, National Archives.

page 413: "if the plane . . .": *Report of the Earhart Search,* navy records, National Archives.

page 413: "The pilots received three dashes," . . .: interview with Page Smith.

page 414: George's first thought . . .: cable to *Itasca;* the *Colorado* also checked out Winslow Banks, a long reef formation 175 miles east of Howland.

page 414: "have an eye . . .": J. J. Clark, Columbia OH. In 1937 Admiral Clark, later commander of the Seventh Fleet, was the air officer on the *Lexington.*

page 415: "made complete sense . . .": C. B. Allen, draft of a review of *The True Amelia Earhart Story,* NASM.

page 415: although there was also a report . . .: *San Francisco Chronicle,* July 1, 1937.

page 416: "a thorough surface search" . . .: Department of State telegram, National Archives.

page 417: "I am satisfied" . . .: Charles Edison, letter to J. Gordon Vaeth, Oct. 7, 1964, provided to author by Vaeth.

page 417: In 1981 the Japanese writer . . .: Fukiko Aoki, interview with author.

page 418: "but says she doesn't know . . .": Fukiko Aoki, "Was Amelia Earhart Executed?" *Bungei Shunju,* April 1983.

page 418: "she was really young . . .": Ibid.

page 418: "About once a year . . .": Ibid.

page 419: The day after the attack on Pearl Harbor, . . .: Richard Black, Columbia OH.

page 419: "raise our flag . . .": Ibid.

page 420: "She was great; . . .": JM, *LITHW,* IX p. 13, SLRC.

page 420: never left it, . . .: JM, unidentified fragment, SLRC.

page 420: "It's worth it, . . .": quoted by Antoine Saint-Exupery, *Wind, Sand and Stars,* in *Airman's Odyssey,* p. 117.

page 421: So close was he . . .: GPP, *SW,* p. 237.

Sources

Published Sources

Addams, Jane. *Twenty Years at Hull House.* New York: Macmillan, 1910.

Allen, Richard Sanders. *Revolution in the Sky: Those Fabulous Lockheeds. The Pilots Who Flew Them.* Brattleboro, Vt.: Stephen Greene Press, 1967.

Amory, Cleveland. *The Proper Bostonians.* New York: E.P. Dutton & Co., 1947.

Amory, Cleveland, and Frederic Bradlee. *Vanity Fair: A Cavalcade of the 1920s and 1930s.* New York: Viking Press, 1960.

Backus, Jean L. *Letters From Amelia.* Boston: Beacon Press, 1982.

Balchen, Bernt. *Come North With Me.* New York: E.P. Dutton & Co., 1958.

———. *The Next Fifty Years of Flight.* New York: Harper and Brothers, 1954.

Beasley, Maurine H. *Eleanor Roosevelt and the Media: A Public Quest for Self-Fulfillment.* Chicago: University of Illinois Press, 1987.

Benson, C.B. *Map Reading for Aviators.* New York: Edwin N. Appleton, 1918.

Bergin, Edward J. *A Star to Steer Her By.* Centreville, Md.: Cornell Maritime Press, 1983.

Bijur, George, ed. *Choosing a Career: Speeches Delivered at the First Conference for College Men and Women.* New York: Farrar & Rinehart, 1934.

Biles, Roger, *A New Deal for the American People.* De Kalb: Northern Illinois University Press, 1991.

Blackman, Frank W. *Kansas: A Cyclopedia of State History.* Chicago: Standard Publishing Co., 1912.

Blixen, Bror. *The Africa Letters.* New York: St. Martin's Press, 1988.

Boegner, Peggie Phipps, and Richard Gachot. *Halcyon Days: An American Family Through Three Generations.* New York: Old Westbury Gardens and Abrams, 1986.

Briand, Paul L., Jr. *Daughter of the Sky.* New York: Duell, Sloan & Pearce, 1960.

Brink, Randall. *Lost Star: The Search for Amelia Earhart*. New York: W.W. Norton & Co., 1994.

Brooks, Peter W. *Cierva Autogiros*. Washington, D.C.: Smithsonian Institution Press, 1988.

Brooks-Pazmany, Kathleen. *United States Women in Aviation 1919–1929*. Washington, D.C.: Smithsonian Institution Press, 1991.

Bryan, C. D. *The National Air and Space Museum*. New York: Harry N. Abrams, 1979.

Burke, John. *Winged Legend*. New York: G.P. Putnam's Sons, 1970.

Burrell, John Angus. *A History of Adult Education at Columbia University*. New York: Columbia University Press, 1954.

Byrd, Richard Evelyn. *Alone*. New York: Jeremy Tarcher, 1986.

———. *Skyward*. New York: G.P. Putnam's Sons, 1928.

Caidin, Martin. *Barnstorming*. New York: Duell, Sloan & Pearce, 1965.

Carrington, G. *Amelia Earhart: What Really Happened at Howland*. Canada: Britnav Services, 1977.

Challiss, Mrs. W. L. *The Story of the First Baptist Church of Atchison, Kansas: 1857–1897*. Atchison, Kans.: Home Printing Co.

Chamberlin, Clarence. *Record Flights*. New York: Beechwood Press, 1942.

Coburn, Carol. *Life at Four Corners: Religion, Gender, and Education in the German-Lutheran Community, 1868–1945*. Lawrence: University Press of Kansas, 1992.

Cochran, Jacqueline. *The Stars at Noon*. Boston: Little, Brown & Co., 1954.

Cochran, Jacqueline, and Maryann Bucknum Brinley. *Jackie Cochran*. New York: Bantam Books, 1987.

Collins, Paul F. *Tales of an Old Air-Faring Man: A Half Century of Incidents, Accidents and Providence*. Stevens Point, Wis.: University of Wisconsin–Stevens Point Foundation Press, 1983.

Conway, Jill Ker. *True North*. New York: Alfred A. Knopf, 1994.

Corn, Joseph J. *The Winged Gospel*. New York: Oxford University Press, 1983.

Curtiss Aeroplane and Motor Corporation. *The Curtiss Standard JN4-D Military Tractor Handbook*. Buffalo, N.Y.: Curtiss Aeroplane and Motor Corporation, 1918.

Davies, R. E. G. *Airlines of the United States Since 1914*. Washington, D.C.: Smithsonian Institution Press, 1972.

de Saint-Exupéry, Antoine. *Airman's Odyssey*. New York: First Harvest/Harcourt Brace Jovanovch, 1984.

———. *Wind, Sand and Stars*. Cornwall, N.Y.: Cornwall Press, 1939.

de Sibour, Violette. *Flying Gypsies*. New York: G.P. Putnam's Sons, 1930.

Dewson, Mary W. *An Aid to the End*, 2 vol. Unpublished manuscript, FDR Library.

Dwiggins, Don. *Hollywood Pilot*. New York: Doubleday & Co., 1967.

———. *They Flew the Bendix Race*. New York: J.B. Lippincott Co., 1965.

Earhart, Amelia. *20 Hrs., 40 Min*. New York: Arno Press, 1980.

———. *Last Flight*. New York: Harcourt, Brace and Company, 1937.

———. *The Fun of It*. New York: Harcourt, Brace and Company, 1932.

Earhart, David. *A Brief History of the Ancestors and Near Kindred of the Author*. Unpublished ms., Jan. 1, 1898.

Edel, Leon. *Writing Lives.* New York: W.W. Norton Co., 1959.

Elliott, Edward C. *Where They Go and What They Do.* West Lafayette, Ind.: Purdue University Press, 1936.

Faber, Doris. *The Life of Lorena Hickok.* New York: William Morrow & Co., 1980.

Ferris, Helen. *Five Girls Who Dared.* New York: Macmillan, 1936.

Fokker, Anthony, and Bruce Gould. *Flying Dutchman.* New York: Henry Holt & Co., 1931.

French, Joseph Lewis. *The Big Aviation Book for Boys.* Springfield, Mass.: McCloughlin Brothers, 1929.

Garst, Shannon. *Amelia Earhart: Heroine of the Skies.* New York: Julian Messner, 1947.

Gilroy, Shirley Dobson. *Amelia: Pilot in Pearls.* McLean, Va.: Link Press, 1985.

Glassman, Donald. *Jump! Tales of the Caterpillar Club.* New York: The Junior Literary Guild, 1935.

Glines, Carroll V. *Round-the-World Flights.* Blue Ridge Summit, Pa.: Aero/Tab Books, 1990.

Goerner, Fred. *The Search for Amelia Earhart.* New York: Doubleday & Co., 1966.

Goodwin, Doris Kearns. *No Ordinary Time.* New York: Simon & Schuster, 1995.

Gosnell, Mariana. *Zero 3 Bravo.* New York: Alfred A. Knopf, 1993

Grooch, William Stephen. *Skyway to Asia.* New York: Longman's Green & Co., 1936.

Grow, Malcolm C., and Henry G. Armstrong. *Fit to Fly.* New York: D. Appleton-Century, 1941.

Guggenheim, Harry F. *The Seven Skies.* New York: G.P. Putnam's Sons, 1930.

Haggerty, James. *Aviation's Mr. Sam.* Fallbrook, Calif.: Aero Publishers, 1974.

Harbold, Major General Norris B. *The Log of Air Navigation.* San Antonio, Tex.: Naylor, 1970.

Hatfield, D. D. *Los Angeles Aeronautics.* Northrop Institute of Technology, 1973.

Hawks, Frank. *Once to Every Pilot.* New York: Stackpole Sons, 1936.

———. *Speed.* New York: Brewer, Warren & Putnam, 1931.

Howe, E. W. *Country Town Sayings.* Topeka, Kans.: Crane & Co., 1911.

———. *Plain People.* New York: Dodd, Mead & Co., 1929.

Jablonski, Edward. *Atlantic Fever.* New York: Macmillan, 1972.

Johnson, Clarence L. with Maggie Smith Kelly. *More Than My Share of It All.* Washington, D.C.: Smithsonian Institution Press, 1985.

Johnson, Roy. *The History of Thiel College: 1866–1974.* Philadelphia: Dorrance & Co., 1974.

Jones, Bradley. *Avigation.* New York: John Wiley & Sons, 1931.

Jordanoff, Assen. *Jordanoff's Illustrated Aviation Dictionary.* New York: Harper & Brothers, 1942.

Josephy, Alvin M., Jr. *The Civil War in the American West.* New York: Alfred A. Knopf, 1991.

Keil, Sally Van Wagenen. *Those Wonderful Women in Their Flying Machines.* New York: Four Directions Press, 1990.

Kerfoot, Glenn. *Propeller Annie.* Lexington Ky.: Kentucky Aviation History Round-table, 1988.

Klaas, Joe. *Amelia Earhart Lives.* New York: McGraw Hill, 1970.

Knight, Clayton, and Robert C. Curham. *Hitch Your Wagon: The Story of Bernt Balchen.* Drexel Hill, Pa.: Bell Publishing Co., 1950.

Komons, Nick A. *Bonfires to Beacons.* Washington, D.C: Smithsonian Institution Press, 1989.

Lindbergh, Anne Morrow. *Hours of Gold, Hour of Lead.* New York: Harcourt Brace Jovanovich, 1973.

———. *Gift from the Sea.* New York: Pantheon Books, 1955.

———. *North to the Orient.* New York: Harcourt, Brace & Co., 1935.

———. *The Steep Ascent.* New York: Harcourt, Brace & Co., 1944.

Lindbergh, Charles A. *The Spirit of St. Louis.* New York: Charles Scribner's Sons, 1953.

———. *We.* New York: G.P. Putnam's Sons, 1927.

Lomax, Judy. *Women of the Air.* London: John Murray, 1986.

Loomis, Vincent, with Jeffrey Ethell. *Amelia Earhart: The Final Story.* New York: Random House, 1985.

Lovell, Mary S. *The Sound of Wings.* New York: St. Martin's Press, 1989.

Mabie, Janet. *Lady in the High Winds.* Unpublished biography of Amelia Earhart.

Maloney, Elbert S. *Chapman Piloting.* New York: Hearst Marine Books, 1989.

Manchester, William. *The Glory and the Dream.* New York: Bantam Books, 1980.

Martin, Ruth Mellenbruch. *Family Tree: Challiss, Harres, Martin, Tonsing, Otis.* Paul Tonsing, 1979.

McCullough, David. *Truman.* New York: Simon and Schuster, 1992.

Menninger, Flo. *Days of My Life: Memories of a Kansas Mother and Teacher.* New York: R.R. Smith, 1939.

Mitchell, General William. *Skyways.* Philadelphia: J.B. Lippincott Co., 1930.

Monaghan, James. *Civil War on the Western Border.* Boston: Little, Brown, 1955.

Morrissey, Muriel Earhart. *Courage Is the Price.* Wichita, Kans.: McCormick Armstrong Publishing Division, 1963.

Morrissey, Muriel Earhart, and Carol L. Osborne. *Amelia, My Courageous Sister.* Santa Clara, Calif.: Osborne Publisher, 1987.

Nichols, Ruth. *Wings for Life.* Philadelphia: J. B. Lippincott Co., 1957.

Nunes, Sue. *Tree Top Baby.* Baltimore: Gateway Press, 1984.

Oakes, Claudia M. *United States Women in Aviation 1930–1939.* Washington, D.C.: Smithsonian Institution Press, 1991.

O'Neill, William. *Feminism in American History.* New Brunswick, N.J.: Transaction Publishers, 1969.

Otis, William A. *A Geneological and Historical Memoir of the Otis Family in America.* Chicago: 1924.

Palmer, Henry R., Jr. *This Was Air Travel.* New York: Bonanza Books, 1962.

Parsons, Bill. *The Challenge of the Atlantic.* Newfoundland: Robinson-Blackmore Book Publishers, 1983.

Peckham, Betty. *Women in Aviation.* Norwood, Mass.: Thomas Nelson & Sons, 1945.

Pellegreno, Ann. *World Flight*. Ames, Ia.: Iowa State University Press, 1971.

Pettigrew, Eileen. *The Silent Enemy: Canada and the Deadly Flu of 1918*. Saskatoon, Saskatchewan: Western Producer Prairie Books.

Post, Wiley, and Harold Gatty. *Around the World in Eight Days: The Flight of the Winnie Mae*. Garden City, N.Y.: Garden City Publishing Co., 1931.

Putnam, George Palmer. *Soaring Wings*. New York: Harcourt, Brace & Co., 1939.

——. *Wide Margins*. New York: Harcourt, Brace & Co., 1942.

Railey, Hilton Howell. *Touch'd with Madness*. New York: Carrick & Evans, 1938.

Rich, Doris L. *Amelia Earhart*. Washington, D.C.: Smithsonian Institution Press, 1989.

Serling, Robert. *From the Captain to the Colonel: An Informal History of Eastern Airlines*. New York: Dial Press, 1980.

Simkhovitch, Mary W. *Neighborhood: My Story of Greenwich House*. New York: W. W. Norton & Co., 1938.

Sims, C. A. *British Aircraft*. London: A and C Black, 1931.

Smallwood, J. R., ed. *The Book of Newfoundland*. St. John's: Newfoundland Book Publishers, 1968.

Smith, Constance Babington. *Amy Johnson*. London: Collins, 1967.

Smith, Corinna Lindon. *Interesting People: Eighty Years with the Great and Near-Great*. Norman, Okla.: University of Oklahoma Press, 1962.

Smith, Elinor. *Aviatrix*. Thorndike, Me.: Thorndike Press, 1981.

Smith, Frank Kingston. *Legacy of Wings*. Lafayette Hill, Pa.: T-D Associates, 1981.

Smith, Richard K. *First Across*. Annapolis, Md.: Naval Institute Press, 1973.

Sobel, Dava. *Longitude*. New York: Walker & Co., 1995.

Southern, Neta Snook. *I Taught Amelia to Fly*. New York: Vantage Press, 1974.

Spring, Leverett. *Kansas: The Prelude to the War for the Union*. Boston: Houghton, Mifflin & Co., 1885.

Strachey, Lytton. *Eminent Victorians*. Garden City, N.Y.: Garden City Publishing Co.

Streeter, Floyd B. *The Kaw*. New York: J. J. Little & Ives Co., 1941.

Sullivan, Mark. *Our Times: The United States 1900–1925. Pre-War America*. New York: Charles Scribner's Sons, 1930.

——. *Our Times: The United States 1900–1925. The Twenties*. New York: Charles Scribner's Sons, 1935

Sutherland, Abby A. *100 Years of Ogontz*. Ogontz Center, Pa., 1958.

Tate, Grover. *The Lady Who Tamed Pegasus*. United States: Maverick, 1984.

Taylor, John W. R., ed. *Aircraft Seventy One*. New York: Arco Publishing Co., 1971.

Taylor, Michael J. H., and David Mondey. *Milestones of Flight*. United Kingdom: Jane's Publishing Co., 1983.

Thaden, Louise. *High, Wide, and Frightened*. New York: Stackpole Sons, 1938.

Thayer, Eli. *A History of the Kansas Crusade*. New York: Harper & Brothers, 1889.

Topping, Robert W. *A Century and Beyond, The History of Purdue University*. West Lafayette, Ind.: Purdue University Press, 1988.

Treadway, William Eugene. *Cyrus K. Holliday*. Topeka, Kans.: Kansas State Historical Society, 1979.

Trollope, Frances. *Domestic Manners of the Americans*. New York: Alfred A. Knopf, 1949.

Tuchman, Barbara. *The March of Folly.* New York: Alfred A. Knopf, 1984.

Underwood, John. *Madcaps, Millionaires and "Mose."* Glendale, Calif.: Heritage Press, 1984.

Veca, Donna, and Skip Mazzio. *Just Plane Crazy: Biography of Bobbi Trout.* Santa Clara, Calif.: Osborne Publisher, 1987.

Vecsey, George and George C. Dade. *Getting Off the Ground.* New York: E.P. Dutton, 1979.

Vidal, Gore. *Armageddon?.* London: A. Deutch, 1987.

———. *Palimpsest: A Memoir.* New York: Random House, 1995.

Ware, Susan. *Still Missing: Amelia Earhart and the Search for Modern Feminism.* New York: W.W. Norton & Co., 1993.

White, The Rev. Francis. *The Story of a Kansas Parish.* Atchison, Kansas: Burbank Printshop.

Whyte, Edna Gardner. *Rising Above It.* New York: Orion Books, 1991.

Williams, Brad. *The Anatomy of an Airline.* Garden City, N.Y.: Doubleday & Co., 1970.

Williams, Burton J. *Senator John James Ingalls, Kansas' Iridescent Republican.* Lawrence, Kans.: University Press of Kansas, 1972.

Wise, Sydney F. *The Official History of the Royal Canadian Air Force.* Toronto: University of Toronto Press, 1980.

Wright, Monte Duane. *Most Probable Position.* Lawrence, Kans.: University Press of Kansas, 1972.

Unpublished Sources

Manuscript Collections and Personal Papers

The Franklin D. Roosevelt Library

Dewson, Mary
Roosevelt, Eleanor
Roosevelt, Franklin Delano
White House Ushers Diaries

The Schlesinger Library, Radcliffe College

American Woman's Association
Earhart, Amelia
Earhart, Amy Otis
Mabie, Janet
Women's Educational and Industrial Union
Denison House

The National Air and Space Museum

Allen, Carl B.
Earhart, Amelia
Studer, Clara

The International Women's Air and Space Museum

Earhart, Amelia
The First Women's Air Derby

The Natural History Museum of Los Angeles County; Seaver Center for Western History Research
Amelia Earhart Collection

National Archives
General Records of the Department of the Navy
Records of the Hydrographic Office
Records of the Bureau of Naval Personnel
Records of the Office of the Chief of Naval Operations
Records of Naval Districts and Shore Establishments
Records of U.S. Army Overseas Operations and Commands
Records of the War Department General and Special Staffs
Records of the Department of State

Eisenhower Library
Collection of Jacqueline Cochran, containing the files of the Ninety-Nines, since transferred to the Ninety-Nines Archives

University of Wyoming; American Heritage Center
Collection of Eugene Luther Vidal

Manuscript Collections at Purdue University
Amelia Earhart Collection in the Archives and Special Collections of the Library
Records of the Purdue Research Foundation

Manuscript Collections at the Atchison Public Library
Collection of Amelia Earhart
History of Atchison, Kansas

Luther Library at Midland Lutheran College
Collection of papers on the history of Midland Lutheran College

Federal Aviation Administration
Aircraft records of the Department of Commerce, Aeronautics Branch

Columbia University Oral History Collection
Black, Richard Blackburn (1962)
Bruno, Harry A. (1960)
Clark, James Joseph (1962)
Noyes, Blanche (1960)
Morrissey, Muriel Earhart (1960)
Nichols, Ruth (1960)

Interviews

Antich, Patricia Pollock
Aoki, Fukiko
Baker, Frank
Bible, Helen Day
Darrow, Louise de Schweinitz
Guest, Mrs. Pope
Lindbergh, Anne
Livingston, Clara
Manning, Diana Guest
Morrissey, Muriel Earhart
Morse, Nancy Balis
Park, Ann
Parsons, Bill
Pollock, Kathryn (Katch) Challiss
Smith, Page
Smith, Katharine Vidal
Southern, Neta Snook
Stabler, Marian
Tier, Nancy Hopkins
Trout, Bobbi
Vidal, Gore
Washburn, Bradford
Wells, Fay Gillis

Acknowledgments

This book mostly relies on primary materials: interviews, diaries, letters, newspapers, and manuscript collections, as well as the books written by Amelia Earhart and her husband George Palmer Putnam.

For access to this material the help of Amelia's relatives was crucial. Pointing the way, especially in the beginning, was Amelia's sister, Muriel Earhart Morrissey. Her daughter, Amy Morrissey Kleppner, and Amy's son, Adam, were also a great help. Kathryn Challis Pollock, who grew up with Amelia, gave me a particularly insightful interview. I wish as well to thank Patricia Antich, Kathryn's daughter, who found and gave to me after her mother's death her mother's childhood diaries and the diaries of Kathryn's sister, Lucy Van Hoesen Challiss, who lived with Amelia and George in Rye. I also want particularly to thank Nancy Balis Morse, who gave me many insights into her relatives and shared with me the personal letters of the Otis family; and Robert Tonsing, who sent me *Family Tree,* the anecdotal history of Amelia's mother's family, and John David Martin, who gave me permission to quote from his mother's work. Other relatives of Amelia who generously gave of their time were Beatrice Challiss Laws, James Otis, and Ruth M. Martin.

I want to thank Helen Day Bible, and her family. The letters from Fred Noonan to Helen were donated by her as her small contribution to the history of aviation. Kenneth Clapp gave me some wonderful photos from the collection of his mother, Janet Mabie and permitted me to be the first biographer to quote from her unpublished biography of Amelia Earhart. I am also grateful to the Columbia University Oral History Collection for permission to quote from the oral histories of Muriel Earhart Morrissey, Blanche Noyes, Richard Blackburn Black, Harry A. Bruno, Ruth Nichols, and James Joseph Clark.

I want to thank Schlesinger Library, Radcliffe College, for permission to quote from the Denison House records, the Amy Otis Earhart papers, the Janet Mabie papers, and the records of the Women's Educational and Industrial Union. At the Franklin D. Roosevelt Library Robert Parks initiated me into the intricacies of the various collections. Claudia Spencer, of the Atchison Public Library, was unstintingly generous of her time and the library's resources. Joan Hrubek opened the files of the International Women's Air and Space Museum to me. Loretta Gregg, president of the Ninety Nines, patiently responded to all my inquiries. Doris Pearson, secretary of the Board of Trustees at Purdue University; Bill Griegs of the Purdue Research Foundation; and Katherine M. Markee, Purdue Special Collections & Archives supplied much information, as did Louise Foudray, director of the Amelia Earhart Birthplace Museum in Atchison; Paul Palmer at Columbia University; and Anne M. Gefell, who presides over the Oral History Research Office at Columbia University. At the National Air and Space Museum Larry Wilson helped me find the files I needed; Nora Walkup aided me at the Federal Aviation Administration. At the Hyde Park High School Tom Staniszewski provided all the information the school possessed, as well as Amelia's yearbook photo. Peter Filardo guided me in the Tamiment Library at New York University, Paul Vesiopi supplied information about Greenwich House. At the Provincial Archives of Newfoundland and Labrador Howard Brown, archivist, helped me. The New York Public Library with its excellent staff (particularly Philip Yockey) and extraordinary holdings was a great resource.

For an understanding of latitude and longitude I want to thank Richard Newick; for help on medical matters, Joel A. Danisi. For keeping my nose to the grindstone I must thank Pat Beard.

At Addison-Wesley I owe thanks to Liz Maguire, Lynne Reed and to Albert De Petrillo. I was very fortunate to have Albert De Petrillo as my editor; his enthusiasm, editing skills, and focus on the many details involved in pulling the book together were crucial. I also owe thanks to my agent, Julian Bach and his very able assistant, Carolyn Krupp.

And I couldn't have done it without the support and encouragement of my husband, Allan Churchill Butler. The book took years and he was always behind me.

Index